Christianity and Modern European Literature

By the same author

Imagination and Religion in Anglo-Irish Literature, 1930–1980
Martin Buber's Philosophy of Education
Tolstoy and Education
Comenius: A Critical Reassessment of His Life and Work

Christianity and Modern European Literature

Daniel Murphy
Fellow of Trinity College, Dublin

FOUR COURTS PRESS

This book was set in
10.5 on 12.5 Ehrhardt
by Verbatim Typesetting & Design for
FOUR COURTS PRESS
E-mail: fcp@indigo.ie
55 Prusia Street, Dublin 7
and in North America for
FOUR COURTS PRESS
c/o ISBS, 5804 N.E. Hassalo Street, Portland, OR 97213.

© Daniel Murphy 1997

ISBN 1-85182-295-x

A catalogue record for this title
is available from the British Library

This book is printed on acid-free and wood free paper.

ACKNOWLEDGMENT

The publishers wish to acknowledge the financial assistance
of the Arts Council/An Chomhairle Ealaíon, Dublin.

Printed in Ireland by ColourBooks Ltd, Dublin

Contents

To my father
Timothy Murphy, 1908–52
and my mother
Josephine Murphy, 1914–94
with grateful remembrance and love

Preface

In the years in which this book has been in preparation I have incurred debts of gratitude to a large number of people which I now wish to acknowledge, however inadequately. In doing so I feel obliged to say that the views expressed in the book are entirely my own and should not be seen as reflecting those of any of the individuals whose names I propose to mention.

As the book deals with writers of a great variety of cultural backgrounds, I found it necessary to undertake extensive travel down through the years in pursuit both of documentation and of interviews with individuals in a position to provide me with specialist knowledge and information. My purpose on many occasions was simply to enhance my appreciation of the cultural and environmental conditions in which the writings discussed in the book were originally produced. My most frequent visits were to Eastern Europe – ten trips in all since the mid 1970s – and I was able, in the course of these visits, to meet with scholars well-versed in the writings I was examining and to obtain numerous publications unavailable in the West. I thank them sincerely for their help. I was fortunate on many of these trips to have had the congenial company of colleagues and M.Ed. Degree students from Trinity College, Dublin. I particularly recall a memorable visit on a cold, bright Sunday in March of 1996 to the Tolstoy Estate at Yasnaya Polyana where we had the unforgettable experience of walking for many hours in the snow covered landscape and were given access to family photographs, manuscripts and various Tolstoy memorabilia. I am deeply grateful to the Intourist authorities for this experience and for their hospitality on numerous other occasions in the past.

My appreciation of Russian literature has been greatly enriched by analysis of my earlier work in this field by a number of notable Slavic scholars. I have been greatly encouraged by this and my confidence to persevere with the present study owes much to their helpful comments on my work. I particularly want to thank Professor R.F. Christian of the University of St Andrews, Professor Elliott Mossman of the University of Pennsylvania, Professor John Dunstan of the University of Birmingham, Dr James Muckle of the University of Nottingham and Dr Sarah Smyth of Trinity College, Dublin. I want to express my gratitude to the Polish scholar, Dr Petr Sadowski, for reading a draft of my chapter on Milosz and for providing me with some new insights on the poet.

In the early 1980s I undertook a tour of the Basque country of Northern Spain and visited various locations associated with Unamuno's life and writ-

9

ings. This work was greatly assisted by translations provided by my daughter, Fidelma, a long-time resident of Spain who is thoroughly fluent in the language and exceptionally well-versed in the whole world of Spanish culture. I want to thank her sincerely for her assistance. I have also undertaken a similar tour of the Bordeaux region and the Landes in South West France where again I was given access to various places associated with Mauriac's life and work – in Bordeaux, Verdelais, Langon, Malagar, Arcachon, St Symphorien and Bazas. In this regard I have another family debt to acknowledge. My daughter, Nuala, a naturalised Parisienne, provided me with translations of work by, and about, Mauriac, for which I am deeply grateful.

My colleague from Trinity College, Michael Curran, travelled with me to various locations in England associated with T.S. Eliot's poetry, in the summer of 1986, when we planned to produce a video documentary on the poet. We were received very hospitably by the Head of the Community at Little Gidding, by the owners of Burnt Norton near Chipping Campden, by the Rector of St Michael's Church in East Coker, by the Vicar of Finstock Church in the Cotswolds, and by the Pastor of St Stephen's Church, Gloucester Road, London. I found all this an immeasurably moving experience and I thank my hosts sincerely for their welcoming assistance and, in some instances, for providing some very useful documentation as well. I have spent much time in libraries at Oxford, Cambridge and London examining documents relating to Eliot, Auden and White and here again I have yet another family obligation to acknowledge. My daughter, Deirdre, an Oxford resident, traced and secured documentation for me on many occasions when I could not travel to Oxford personally to obtain it and I am very happy to thank her for this.

I thank my colleagues at the School of Education in Trinity College, particularly the Director of the School, Professor Valentine Rice, for many years of friendship and support. I want to thank my immediate academic neighbours, Patrick Wall, for reading some of my drafts, and Dr John Follent, a visiting scholar from Australia, for some fruitful discussions on Patrick White. I am very grateful to my friend and colleague, Professor Brendan Kennelly, for many conversations, all of them deeply illuminating, on the theme of religion and literature through the years.

I wish to thank the Director of the Arts Council and particularly its Literature Officer, Ms Sinead Mac Aodha, for a generous grant-in-aid for the publication of the present study.

I also want to record my thanks to the library staffs of the Bodleian Library, University of Oxford, the Library of Cambridge University and the Library of the University of London. My main debt, however, is to the library staff of my own university, particularly the Keeper of Readers' Services,

Mrs Eileen McGlade, whom I want to thank once again, together with her colleagues, for their friendly and efficient service.

I want to say 'thank you' to the staff of Four Courts Press, particularly Michael Adams and Martin Fanning, for taking their customary care to produce the kind of book of which an author can justifiably feel proud.

Most of all, I want to thank my wife, Margaret, for consistent support and encouragement in all the years that I have worked on the book.

Introduction

This book examines the writings of twelve modern European authors, each of whom has drawn inspiration primarily from the ethico-religious, cultural and intellectual traditions of scriptural Christianity. It aims to elucidate the significance of Christian themes and motifs in the various works selected and seeks thereby to evaluate their meaningfulness and relevance to the needs and concerns of the present time. The work is the product of two decades of research and reflection by the author on the whole relationship of religion and literature and particularly on the contemporary significance of the traditions of New Testament Christianity as seen from the standpoint of the literary artist. The work challenges the widely held assumption that Christianity is a diminishing force in European life and culture and affirms its continuing and enduring importance as evidenced by the works of some of the most eminent figures in the literature of the present age.

The work is focussed on European literature of the late nineteenth and twentieth centuries. Its starting point is the publication of the first volume of Dostoevsky's great fictional tetralogy – which it sees as initiating some of the most significant developments in the evolution of modern literature – and it proceeds from an analysis of this to a consideration of the place of Christianity in the works of contemporary writers such as Auden, White, Milosz and Brodsky. The method of the work is primarily that of literary-critical analysis. Attention is focussed on the writings of particular authors, critical interpretations being based on close investigation of the primary texts and of a wide range of relevant secondary sources. It is in no sense a work of theological, or quasi-theological, exegesis, its methodology being that of the critical traditions of literary scholarship extending in modern times from Coleridge to Leavis, but traceable ultimately to the traditions of classical aesthetics. This method is seen to be compatible, i.e., logically and imaginatively consistent with, the subject-matter examined, interpretations of image, metaphor and symbol being its basic rationale.

The relationship of religion and art is itself one of the foremost themes in the writings discussed in this book. It was felt that the complexities of that relationship could best be comprehended by examining it in the context of the work of individual writers instead of attempting to offer a generalised explanation of all the issues involved. The latter approach would sacrifice the highly individualised character of the standpoints taken by different writers on this issue for the sake of generalised statements that could not possibly do justice to the diversity of perceptions involved. Each chapter of the book includes a section, therefore, treating the whole question of the relationship of art and faith and of the implications of this for the individual writer's understanding of his/her artistic aims and purposes.

The range of viewpoints comprehended in this is extraordinarily rich and diverse. It includes Dostoevsky's conception of art as multi-voiced or polyphonic utterance, Tolstoy's vision of the creative process as inspired revelation, analogous to, and continuous with, the method of the scriptures; it includes the sacramentalism of Acmeist poetics as exemplified by Akhmatova and Mandelstam, the non-didactic concept of narrative realism exemplified by Mauriac, Pasternak and Unamuno, the 'negative way' of Eliot and White, Auden's poetic dialogics, Milosz's anti-modernist, anti-aestheticist realism, and the transcendental lyricism of Brodsky. All are examined in detail in the appropriate chapters.

Between them the twelve writers selected represent both denominational and non-denominational perspectives on Christianity. Some represent positions, for example, that are distinctively Catholic, Protestant or Eastern Orthodox; others stand for a strictly non-institutional Christianity, indeed suggest that the universality of Christian truth can only be maintained by transcending its historic inheritance of denominational divisiveness. All, however, can be said to give direct testimony in their work to the central and continuing relevance of the Judaeo-Christian ethical and religious heritage to the culture of the modern age. They see their role as essentially one of spiritual restoration (to use the terminology favoured by Milosz and Brodsky): restoration to modern culture of the religious heritage from which it has consistently been cut off by the inexorable progress of scientific rationalism since the Renaissance.

Curiously, the spirit of secularist rationalism, while being so powerfully challenged in much of contemporary literature, is quite strongly in evidence in contemporary critical scholarship. Literary criticism, it would appear, has almost universally adopted the methods of the sciences, has itself become a quasi-scientific mode of intellectual enquiry. Its currently fashionable methodologies – structuralism, semiotics, deconstructionism, critical strategy etc. – all derive in some degree from the traditions of rationalism, in some instances are directly drawn from the methods of positivistic science. A tension, perhaps even a mismatch, exists between these methodologies and much of the literature they purport to interpret and explain. Thus, one finds that explicitly religious themes in contemporary works of literature are frequently ignored or misrepresented in critical scholarship, their religious significance apparently being deliberately played down. There appears a strange and perverse reluctance by large numbers of modern scholars to accept the preponderance of

Christian concerns in modern literature, even in the works of authors who have explicitly acknowledged the centrality of Christian influences in their work. Patrick White has offered a possible explanation for this. 'I believe,' he wrote, 'that most people have a religious factor but are afraid that by admitting it they will forfeit their right to be called intellectuals.'[1] Is it this kind of anxiety that prevents so many modern scholars from honestly acknowledging the all-pervasive presence of Christian tradition in the literature of the modern period and from endeavouring seriously to determine its meaningfulness in their critical writings?

The present work, as has been said, aims to determine the *contemporary* meaningfulness of Christianity as evidenced by the works of the various writers selected. But, as Marina Tsvetaeva has remarked, 'the genuinely contemporary is what is eternal in time.'[2] The essential affirmation of all these works is the *permanence* of Christian truth, the timeless character of the teachings enunciated in the Judaeo-Christian scriptures. The values and truths that are affirmed are seen to transcend culture and history, being indicative ultimately of what Eliot described as the spirit of 'orthodoxy' – 'the sense of the timeless as well as of the temporal and of the timeless and the temporal together'.[3] This is the theme that Christianity ultimately comprehends; its central affirmation is the mystery of God's immanent presence in the temporal and the finite, the mystery of the Incarnation. It will be shown presently that the contemporary significance of the Incarnation is the recurring theme in all these works, this being seen as the heart of the Christian message and the source of its eternal relevance and truth. That truth is conveyed non-didactically in the various writings that are discussed; together they attest the inherent presence of Christian tradition in our culture – its endemic rootedness in the languages we speak, in our aesthetic and intellectual heritage. 'Our civilisation,' Czeslaw Milosz has said, is 'shaped by the Bible and, for that reason, eschatological to the core.'[4]

Some comment may be appropriate on reasoning behind the selection of the authors included in the study. All the writers discussed are figures of undoubted European stature and influence. Seven are East European and Slavic, the remaining five are West European. Between them they embrace a variety of national traditions – Russian, Russo-Ukrainian, Polish, French, Spanish, English, Anglo-American and Anglo-Australian. The slight imbalance favouring East European writers can be explained by the greater evidence of Christian influences, and the more explicit treatment of Christian themes, in the literatures of the Slavic peoples than is the case with West European writers. Czeslaw Milosz has given two reasons for this. He points firstly to the much greater impact of scientific rationalism on West European culture, with its attendant secularising influences, than is the case in the East. He attributes this to a number of factors, the main one being the powerful impact of Renaissance humanism on Western culture and its relatively slight impact on the dominant Russo-Byzantine culture of the East. Secondly, he suggests that Eastern writers, faced with the horrors of Marxist totalitarianism, were made more acutely aware of the dangers of secularist humanism than their counterparts in the West, and, as a consequence, far more vigorously asserted the ethical and religious traditions of the Judaeo-Christian heritage in the face of the humanist challenge.[5] This is certainly evident in the work of writers who have lived and suffered under the tyranny of Soviet rule – Akhmatova, Pasternak, Mandelstam, Milosz himself and Brodsky – as will hopefully become apparent in later chapters of this book.

Some comment is needed finally on the inclusion of the work of Patrick White. White's work embraces two traditions. The offspring of an immigrant family who came to Australia from Somerset in the nineteenth century, White himself was born in London and spent some of his most formative years in England, receiving his secondary education at Cheltenham College and completing three years of university studies at King's College, Cambridge. Thereafter he spent several years in England and various parts of Europe before finally returning to settle in Australia in 1946 at the age of thirty-four. The colonial world of Australian culture was to provide the setting and atmosphere of some of his most significant works of fiction, particularly *The Tree of Man* and *Voss*. 'Australia is in my blood – my fate – which is why I have to put up with the hateful place, when at heart I am a Londoner,' he wrote, pointing to the mixed nature of his cultural identity.[6] Though profoundly aware of his roots in the immigrant culture of Australia, he has acknowledged that the most significant literary and intellectual influences on his life and work had been European. Those he identified include: Dostoevsky, Pasternak, Buber, Maritain, Eliot, Marcel and Weil.[7] His writings consistently exemplify his deep affinities with contemporary European writers such as Beckett, Auden, Milosz and Brodsky, as is evident especially in his treatment of religious themes. The worlds of European and Australian culture are so closely intertwined in his work that he can legitimately be regarded as a writer belonging to either or both traditions.

'A Child of Unbelief and Doubt': Self-conflict, Scepticism and Faith in Dostoevsky's Fiction

'If someone were to prove to me that Christ is outside the truth, then I would prefer to remain with Christ than with the truth.'[1] So wrote Dostoevsky to Natalya Fonvizina on 20 February 1854. The wife of a Decembrist prisoner who went to Siberia to be with her husband, Madame Fonvizina befriended Dostoevsky shortly after his arrival there to serve his prison sentence for political conspiracy. She presented him with a copy of the New Testament, a gift he treasured for the rest of his life. He kept it constantly on his desk and had his wife, Anna, read to him from it on the day of his death. 'I believe,' he wrote, in the letter to Fonvizina, 'that there is nothing more beautiful, profounder, more sympathetic, more reasonable, more courageous and more perfect than Christ and not only is there nothing, but I tell myself with jealous love that never could there be.' Wide-ranging and somewhat enigmatic in their implications, his words in the letter vividly illustrate the radically Christian character of his religious beliefs and point to their central significance in his life and work. Equally, they indicate his deep suspicion of abstract formulations of truth, especially those of the rationalistic variety he saw as dominating European culture since the Renaissance.

There is substantial support – autobiographical, biographical and critical – for Dostoevsky's impassioned affirmation of the depth of his Christian faith in this letter to Fonvizina. Nikolai Strakhov, one of his closest friends, spoke of the 'Christian tendency' as the 'distinguishing characteristic of his spirit'.[2] Dostoevsky himself told a young literary novice who had sought his advice that 'a Russian writer must be a believer, for Christ alone is the true way'.[3] Commenting in his Diary on an article he had written extolling the faith of the peasantry, he explained: 'I merely wished to show that one cannot live without Christianity.'[4] Konstantin Mochulsky, one of his biographers, described him as preeminently a Christian artist. 'For Dostoevsky, at the centre of the world stands Christ, the meaning and goal of mankind's history,' he wrote. 'To Dostoevsky,' he continued, 'belongs a place beside the great Christian writers of world literature: Dante, Cervantes, Milton, Pascal.' Referring to the troubled nature of his faith, he said: 'Like Dante, he passed through all the circles of human hell, one more terrible than the mediaeval hell of the *Divine Comedy*, and was not consumed in hell's flame: his *duca e maestro* was not Virgil, but the "radiant image" of the Christ, love for whom was the greatest love of his whole life.'[5]

Mochulsky emphasised the transcendental nature of Dostoevsky's Christianity, refuting the subtle and insidious label of 'Christian humanist' attached to him by socialist critics of the Soviet period. 'His historical mission,' Mochulsky wrote, 'consisted in asserting the failure of humanism and exposing its religious lie. All his great novels are devoted to struggling against the seductions of atheistic love for mankind. Love for men can be only in Christ and man's brotherhood is possible only on a Christian foundation.'[6] Powerful support for this view can be found in an entry from Dostoevsky's Diary for December 1876 where he insists that Christian love springs from a source higher than nature, i.e. from the transforming power of man's faith in the immortality of his soul:

> Neither a person nor a nation can exist without some higher idea. And there is only one 'higher' idea on earth, and it is the idea of the immortality of the human soul, for all other higher ideas of life by which humans might live derive from that idea alone … Moreover, I maintain that the awareness of one's own utter inability to assist or bring any aid or relief at all to suffering humanity, coupled with one's complete conviction of the existence of that suffering, can even *transform the love for humanity in your heart to hatred for humanity*. Those gentlemen of cast-iron convictions will not believe this, of course, and won't even understand it: for them, love for humanity and its happiness are such cheap things; everything has been so conveniently arranged, and has been given and set down for so long, that it is not worth even thinking about. But I intend to give them a good laugh: I declare (again, without substantiation, at least *for the moment*) that love for humanity is even entirely unthinkable, incomprehensible, and *utterly impossible without faith in the immortality of the human soul to go along with it* … I even affirm and venture to declare that love for humanity in general is, *as an idea*, one of the most difficult ideas for the human mind to comprehend. Precisely as an idea. Feeling alone can justify it. But such a feeling is possible only with the conviction of the immortality of the human soul to accompany it … In short, the idea of immortality is life itself, life in the full sense; it is its final formula and humanity's principal source of truth and understanding.[7]

The passage identifies – clearly and incontrovertibly – the transcendent, i.e. non-humanist, character of his Christian faith, a position for which there is massive support in his fiction, as will be shown in some detail later in this chapter. Lev Shestov, the Russian existentialist philosopher, admirably conveyed Dostoevsky's sense of the time-transcending character of Christian love in the following passage from his *Speculation and Revelation*: 'This is not that feeble impotent love which can only shed floods of tears over the little boy who is hunted down by the dogs and the little girl, tormented by her own parents, who beats her breast with her little fist, or for the unfortunate Ippolit who is condemned to death although innocent, and so on; rather, it is the love of Him who created the world and to whose will all are subject.'[8] The Russian Orthodox theologian, Vladimir Soloviev, described Dostoevsky's Christianity in similar terms in a graveside eulogy delivered at his funeral in St Petersburg on 1 February 1881:

> Above all he loved the living human soul in everything, and he believed that we are all God's servants. He believed in the infinite strength of the human soul, the strength that triumphs over all outer force and all inner defects ... The reality of God and Christ revealed itself to him in the inner strength of love and forgiveness, and it was this forgiving and blessed strength which he preached as a basis for the union of all men in one common brotherhood, in order to realise the kingdom of truth upon earth, the kingdom for which all his life he thirsted and strove.[9]

Dostoevsky's Diary, his letters, the memoirs of family and friends and the evidence of biographical research all testify to the lifelong character of his Christian faith as well as to the self-conflict and torment of soul in which it was rooted. They indicate how deeply troubled he was by his beliefs and how sceptical he remained throughout his life about all the truths in which he believed. By birth and upbringing an Orthodox believer, he himself recalled the devout Christian household in which he grew up. 'I came from a pious Russian family,' he wrote. 'In our family we knew the Gospels almost from the cradle.'[10] Both his grandfather and greatgrandfather had been priests and his father had been a seminarian in the Uniat Church in the Podolia district of the Ukraine where the family originated. The family were regular attenders of Church services; prayers were recited on a daily basis in the home and parents and children frequently went on pilgrimages to the Kremlin churches and to the monastic settlement at Zagorsk. All the children were taught to read the scriptures and the lives of the saints. In later years Dostoevsky recalled his particular attachment to a book of Bible stories, *One Hundred and Four Sacred Stories from the Old and New Testaments Selected for Children* – the same work that Zossima identified as the source in which he too encountered the Book of Job. Shortly before his death Dostoevsky spoke of this work in a letter to his wife: 'I am reading Job and it has moved me to a painful ecstasy. I put the book down and wander about the room for hours. I can barely restrain myself from weeping … It is so strange, dear Anya, this book was one of the first that affected me deeply, and then I was only a little child.'[11]

Dostoevsky's lifelong attachment to Orthodoxy was briefly interrupted by his involvement with the Petrashevsky circle in the mid 1840s and particularly by his friendship with Vissarion Belinsky (the prototype of Ivan Karamazov) and with Nikolai Speshnev, probably the model for Stavrogin. Through them he encountered and briefly espoused the doctrines of revolutionary socialism. He recalled that Belinsky 'immediately set himself to convert me to his creed'. 'He was a passionate socialist when I met him and he started me off with atheism straight away,' he recalled, confessing that he 'passionately accepted his [i.e. Belinsky's] entire doctrine at the time'.[12] Deeply shocked at the social conditions existing in Russia under the repressive regime of Nicholas I (his feelings on this issue found expression particularly in the pages of *Poor Folk*), Dostoevsky was filled with a desire to rectify the rampant injustices in evidence all around him and threw himself enthusiastically into the work of the socialist movement. That he had definite reservations on the question of atheism, despite the depth of his fascination with Belinsky, is apparent, however, from this Diary entry in which he reviews the latter's impact on his youthful radical propensities:

> I found him to be a passionate socialist, and in speaking to me he began directly with atheism. That was very significant, I thought, and revealed his amazing intuition and his unusual capacity to become totally inspired by an idea … While cherishing reason, science, and realism above all, he also understood better than anyone that reason, science and realism alone could only create an antheap and not the social 'harmony' in which man could create a life for himself. He knew that moral principles are the basis of everything. He believed in the new moral principles of socialism to the point of folly and with no reflection at all; here there was only enthusiasm. But as a socialist he had first to dethrone Christianity. He knew that the revolution must necessarily begin with atheism. He had to dethrone the religion that provided the moral foundation of the society he was rejecting …
>
> There remained, however, the radiant personality of Christ himself, which was most difficult to contend with. Belinsky, as a socialist, was absolutely bound to destroy Christ's teachings; to label them false and uninformed philanthropy, proscribed by contemporary science and by economic principles. Still there remained the most radiant image of the God-man, its moral unattainability, its marvellous and miraculous

beauty. But Belinsky, in his continuous unflagging enthusiasm, did not pause even before this insurmountable enthusiasm, as did Renan when he proclaimed in his *Vie de Jésus*, a book filled with unbelief, that Christ is still the ideal of human beauty, an unattainable type, never to be repeated in the future.[13]

Belinsky's influence on Dostoevsky, though profound for a time, remained a significant force in his thought for little more than two or three years. Looking back on his involvement with the Petrashevsky group in later years, he spoke of having been 'heavily polluted by mangy Russian liberalism as propagated by that dung-beetle Belinsky'.[14] He parodied the language of socialist humanism in *The Insulted and the Injured* in the episode where Alyosha joins a group of young radicals strongly reminiscent of the Petrashevsky group. 'They're all fresh young people filled with ardent love for all humanity,' Alyosha says. 'We all talked of our present, of our future, of science and literature, and talked so well, so frankly and simply ... I am enthusiastic over lofty ideas. They may be mistaken, but what they rest upon is holy.' Dostoevsky fulminated against the socialists who gathered in Geneva in 1867 for an international conference. 'The lies they told from the platform to an audience of five thousand: fantastic, they beggar description,' he wrote. 'Absurdity, feebleness, muddleheadedness, contradictions, inconsistencies! It's grotesque. And this is the filth that tries to stir up the wretched workers! How sad! Their premiss was that to achieve peace on earth it was first necessary to destroy the Christian faith.'[15] These sentiments found their most powerful expression in the pages of *The Devils*, a work in which Dostoevsky's distaste for all the doctrines of atheistic socialism was conveyed dramatically through the mouths of its fictional ideologists.

The impact on Dostoevsky of the more moderate form of socialism associated with the anarchist movement is more difficult to assess. Following his break with the Petrashevsky group, he found a new outlet for his radical sympathies – and one more compatible with his Christian convictions – in the activities of a group of utopian socialists, led by Aleksei Beketov and Valerian Maikov, both disciples of the French anarchists Proudhon, Fourier, Saint-Simon and Lamennais. In his testimony to the Commission of Inquiry that investigated the activities of subversive political organisations, Dostoevsky insisted that he had rejected socialism but not his social ideals. 'All of my liberalism has consisted,' he said, 'of a desire for the best for my Fatherland, of a desire that everything should move forward to perfection.' 'Socialism,' he declared, 'is chaos – alchemy before chemistry, astrology before astronomy – and yet I believe that the present chaos can develop into something harmonious, sensible, and beneficial, just as chemistry has developed from alchemy and astronomy from astrology.'[16] The ideal of creating God's kingdom on earth through the brotherhood of man was one that found expression consistently in his writings from *Poor Folk* to *The Dream of a Ridiculous Man* and there are strong elements of it in the pages of *The Brothers Karamazov*. It was a belief to which he fervently adhered throughout his life but, as will be shown in some detail later, it was one that was firmly subordinated to his primary Christian beliefs, especially his belief that the reform of mankind could only be genuinely effected through penitence, prayer, humility and grace.

Whatever the attractions of utopian socialism for Dostoevsky, and whatever the ultimate nature of its impact on his thought, he clearly underwent a profound process of spiritual rediscovery during his years of imprisonment and exile in Siberia and this was to lead eventually to his resumption of the faith of his childhood and his formal return to the Orthodox Church. In Siberia he grew to appreciate the simple faith of the masses, contrasting it with the spurious wisdom of the intelligentsia. He recognised the fatal flaw of intellectual elitism as lying in the assumption by groups, such as the members of the Petrashevsky Circle, that they held a responsibility to educate the masses, and concluded, like Tolstoy, that the reverse was the truth: that they in turn should learn from the masses the wisdom that comes from faith. 'At the time fate came to my rescue,' he wrote of his years in Siberia. 'Prison saved me ... I became a completely new person ... Yes, Siberia and imprisonment became a great joy for me ... Only there was I able to lead a pure and happy life. It was there that I came to see myself clearly and there that I learned to understand Christ.'[17] To a lady who asked about the suffering he had to endure, he responded: 'You are mistaken. I have no complaint at all. It was a good school. It strengthened my faith and awakened my love for those who bear all their suffering with patience. It also strengthened my love for Russia and opened my eyes to the great qualities of the Russian people.'[18] Shortly after his return from Siberia he conveyed the depth of his Christian faith in a notebook entry written on the occasion of his first wife's death. As he contemplated the body of his recently deceased wife, he reflected on the absolute selflessness of Christ, seeing this as indicative of his divine-human character and the transcendent nature of his message to mankind:

> Masha is lying on the table. Will I see Masha again? To love a person as one's own self, as Christ commanded, is impossible. On earth the law of personality binds us; the 'I' stands in the way ... Christ was able, but Christ was eternal ... After Christ's appearance, it became clear that the highest development of personality must attain to that point where man annihilates his own 'I', surrenders it completely to all and everyone without division or reserve ... And this is the greatest happiness ...

> This is Christ's paradise ... And so, on earth man strives towards an ideal contrary to his nature. When man has not fulfilled the law of striving toward the ideal, i.e., has not *by love* offered his 'I' in sacrifice to people or to another being (Masha and I), he experiences suffering and has called this condition sin.[19]

Dostoevsky scholars generally suggest that his re-espousal of Orthodoxy was greatly strengthened by the influence of his second wife, Anna Grigoryevna, a devout Orthodox believer. At the time of their marriage Dostoevsky was engaged in extensive research into scriptural and theological studies of Christianity as he prepared drafts of *The Idiot*, his proposed fictional exploration of the theme of 'the perfect man'.[20] His friendship with the philosopher-theologian, Vladimir Soloviev, some years later (Soloviev probably inspired the character of Alyosha in *The Brothers Karamazov*) was also a potent factor in his reacceptance of Orthodox teachings. A biographer of Soloviev has spoken of the latter's reverence for Dostoevsky, particularly for his Orthodox beliefs. 'Soloviev viewed the great novelist almost as a prophet,' he writes, 'and the fact that this prophet was with body and soul devoted to the Orthodox Church, not only in theory but also in his deepest beliefs, was to bring Soloviev even closer to the positive Church.'[21] Soloviev's lectures, which Dostoevsky attended in 1877, strengthened his belief in the immortality of the soul, in the doctrine of divine grace and, above all, in the Christian ideal of *sobornost*, proclaimed in *The Brothers Karamazov* in the words, 'Each is responsible for all.'

Following the death of his young son in June 1878, Dostoevsky went, together with Soloviev, to the monastery of Optina Pustyn to seek consolation from Starets Amvrosy. Later he wrote to a friend, Apollon Maikov: 'The whole vocation of Russia is contained in Orthodoxy, in *the light from the East*, which will stream to mankind who is blinded in the West, having lost Christ.'[22] And in his Diary he wrote in 1877: 'During the ages the lost image of Christ has been preserved in all the light of its purity in Orthodoxy.'[23] The confident faith expressed in entries such as these was constantly at war however with a deep-lying scepticism which, as he himself had predicted many years earlier, would be his constant condition. In the correspondence with Fonvizina he had described himself as 'a child of unbelief and doubt' and asserted it would remain so 'till the day I die'. He continued:

> What terrible sufferings it has cost me and still does cost me – the craving to believe, becoming the stronger in my soul, the more there is in me of contrary reasonings. And yet sometimes God sends me moments in which I am utterly at peace; in those moments I love and find that I

am loved by others and in such moments I have constructed for myself a symbol of faith in which everything is clear and holy for me.[24]

He spoke in a similar vein in 1869 of 'the problem by which I have been consciously or unconsciously tormented all my life: the existence of God'.[25] Some years later, responding to a young theology student who sought his advice about his loss of faith, Dostoevsky described the torment of his own unbelief but counselled his correspondent on the consolation that comes ultimately with faith: 'In the most difficult hours of my life, when I felt abandoned by everyone and everything, I always found a support in God. From my own experience I know that there is nothing worse than unbelief. Let all who wish to be convinced of the truth of this make a visit to the ostrog. If they do not commit suicide they will return believers.'[26] All the great novels provide abundant testimony of the tragic, but ultimately fruitful tension that existed between faith and unbelief in Dostoevsky's mind. Czeslaw Milosz in his essay, 'Dostoevsky and the Religious Imagination of the West', sees the tensions of faith and unbelief in Dostoevsky as a reflection of the whole faith-reason dichotomy that has dominated European culture since Descartes. In *The Land of Ulro* he writes:

> In 1875 Dostoevsky noted: 'Science in our century refutes everything formerly held in high regard. Your every sin has been brought about by your unsatisfied needs, which are completely natural and therefore must be satisfied. A radical refutation of Christianity and its morality. Christ was not acquainted with science, they say.' Earlier in his famous letter of 1854 to Fonvizina, Dostoevsky says: 'Had I to choose between Christ and the truth I would choose Christ.' A desperate statement, of far-reaching implications. I would advance the thesis that Dostoevsky's religious thought distils the leading Western controversy of the seventeenth and eighteenth centuries. At that time the assault on religion in the name of so-called objective truth entailed a threefold negation: the denial of Original Sin, the rejection of the Incarnation, and the secularisation of Christian eschatology ... Dostoevsky was, so to speak, deprived of God the Father. And his only hope was to cling to Christ ... Yet he was never able to resolve the contradiction contained in his statement on the choice between Christ and truth.[27]

It was, as Milosz argues in this passage, because he could not resolve the conflict of faith and rational doubt that Dostoevsky chose to present it as it was, both sides of the dichotomy being given equal representation in his fiction. This, in turn, dictated the artistic method of his work. Of all the voluminous studies of Dostoevsky's artistic methods that have appeared, those in the dialogicist tradition have, in the view of the present writer, most adequately explained this process and have most successfully clarified the links between Dostoevsky's artistic purposes and the communication of his religious beliefs. As Paul de Man has shown in his essay, 'Dialogue and Dialogicism', the metaphysical and religious insights of dialogic thought take it far beyond the realms of the aesthetic and the literary and render it especially appropriate therefore to a consideration of the issues under discussion here.[28] Drawing on influences as diverse as Plato's Dialogues and Gadamer's hermeneutics, the chief exponents of dialogicist thought – Buber, Bakhtin, Bialostovsky, Morson, Thomson, Todorov[29] – have provided vital critical insights for an understanding of the complexities of Dostoevsky's fiction, particularly illuminating its insistent dramatisation of the coexistent tensions of faith and unbelief, the overarching religious theme in his work. What follows is not an attempt to deal comprehensively with these issues but a brief consideration of the relevance of dialogicist thought for an understanding of the ways in which religious themes are treated in Dostoevsky's fiction. Drawing especially on Buber and Bakhtin, it seeks to identify the methodological framework within which those themes are developed and explored.

Vladimir Seduro has documented the extraordinary sequence of events that resulted in the reissuing of Bakhtin's *Problems of Dostoevsky's Poetics* in the USSR in the 1960s, leading eventually to its translation into English and its subsequent dissemination in the West where it generated a whole new movement in critical thought.[30] Initially published in 1929, the work was praised for its originality by the then Commissar for Education and the Arts, Anatoli Lunacharsky, and acclaimed by the Soviet literary establishment. Some time later, however, Bakhtin was arrested, largely on the basis of suspicions arising from his close links with the Orthodox Church, and was sentenced to exile in Kazakhstan, where he lived in obscurity for more than thirty years. He came to prominence again with the republication of the work, by then greatly revised and expanded by himself, in the Soviet Union in 1963. The work was enthusiastically welcomed both by Marxist scholars and by those interested in the metaphysical and religious aspects of Dostoevsky's writings, its distinctive appeal in both cases being its strong anti-formalist orientation. Two Soviet critics, writing in 1964, declared: 'To formalism Bakhtin opposes not impotent incantations and curses but an objective scholarly analysis. And for that reason Bakhtin's book is anti-formalistic.'[31]

The American scholar, Wayne C. Booth, writing from a very different ideological standpoint, has similarly endorsed the anti-formalist merit of Bakhtin's study, seeing its great strength as consisting in its sensitive balancing of meaning and form in his conception of the nature of art. 'In our century,' he writes,

'an astonishing number of critics have equated art with the purgation of meaning ... In our time we are told that even Pater's terms were not severe enough:
art is not a question of beautiful intertwining, for there should be no "content" to intertwine ... Form is all, or, as the newest version has it, language is
all.'[32] Writers of prose-fiction, he argues, have been especially resistant to the
fashions of formalism, their art being explicitly 'made of human events', clearly endowed with the meaning and significance of lived experience. Bakhtin, he
suggests, closely follows the traditions of classical aesthetics in his conception
of the work of art as an organic whole 'with a kind of soul or essential informing principle, by reference to which one could explain, ideally, every choice
the author had made'.[33] He identifies closely with Bakhtin's concept of authorial discourse, seeing his ideal of polyphonic utterance or multi-voiced dialogue
as being particularly sensitive to the complexities of the Dostoevskeyan narrative mode.

Bakhtin speaks of Dostoevsky as one of the great innovators in the realm of
artistic form. He sees him as the creator of a completely new type of artistic
genre which he identifies as the polyphonic novel. What Dostoevsky created,
he says, was ultimately a new artistic model of the world, a radical restructuring of its basic sense and meaningfulness. Insisting that Dostoevsky remained
first and foremost an artist, the key to the meaning of his work lies, he argues,
in an understanding of its structural or formal elements. All the novels, he
suggests, are characterised by techniques of multi-voiced utterance, the method
of polyphonic dialogue. In each of the novels one hears many voices, each the
autonomous carrier of his own individual message, yet each existing in a profound dialogic tension or harmony with the voice of the author himself. This
passage conveys the essence of the polyphonic idea:

> Dostoevsky, like Goethe's Prometheus, creates not voiceless slaves (as
> does Zeus), but free people, capable of standing alongside their creator,
> capable of not agreeing with him and even of rebelling against him. A
> plurality of independent and unmerged voices and consciousnesses, a
> genuine polyphony of fully valid voices is in fact the chief characteristic
> of Dostoevsky's novels. What unfolds in his works is not a multitude of
> characters and fates in a single objective world, illuminated by a single
> authorial consciousness; rather a plurality of consciousnesses, with equal
> rights and each with its own world, combine but are not merged in the
> unity of the event. Dostoevsky's major heroes are, by the very nature of
> his creative design, not only objects of authorial discourse but also sub-
> jects of their own directly signifying discourse. In no way, then, can a
> character's discourse be exhausted by the usual functions of characteri-
> sation and plot development, nor does it serve as a vehicle for the

author's own ideological position (as with Byron for instance). The consciousness of a character is given as someone else's consciousness, another consciousness, yet at the same time it is not turned into an object, is not closed, does not become a simple object of the author's consciousness. In this sense the image of a character in Dostoevsky is not the usual objectified image of a hero in the traditional novel.[34]

Previous scholars,[35] Bakhtin suggests, offered perspectives on Dostoevsky which, he says, were based on a monologic view of the novels, treating them as being reducible to a single message, that supposedly intended by the author himself. They attempted, he says, to reduce the views of his characters to a 'systemically monologic whole', failing to appreciate the 'fundamental plurality of unmerged consciousnesses which was part and parcel of the artist's design'.[36] Dostoevsky's work was treated as belonging in the tradition of the socio-psychological European novel, reducible to philosophical monologue, its message corresponding to a 'single unified authorial consciousness'. It is essential, he insists, to penetrate both the plurality and the cohesion of 'personalised consciousnesses' of a Dostoevsky novel if the complexity of its message is to be grasped:

> Both dialectics and antinomy are in fact present in Dostoevsky's world. The thinking of his characters is indeed sometimes dialectic or antinomic. But all *logical* links remain within the limits of individual consciousness, and do not govern the event-interrelationships among them. Dostoevsky's world is profoundly personalised. He perceives and represents every thought as the position of a personality. Therefore even within the limits of individual consciousnesses, a dialectic or antinomic series can be no more than an abstract element, indissolubly interwoven with other elements of an integral and concrete consciousness. Through this concrete consciousness, embodied in the *living voice of an integral person*, the logical relation becomes part of the unity of a represented event. Thought, drawn into an event, becomes itself part of the event and takes on that special quality of an 'idea-feeling', an 'idea-force', which is responsible for the unique peculiarity of the 'idea' in Dostoevsky's creative world. Extracted from this interrelationship of consciousnesses in the event, forced into a systemically monologic context (even the most dialectic) the idea inevitably loses its uniqueness and is transformed into a philosophical assertion.[37]

While stressing the distinctive cohesion and integrity of elements that constitutes individual character in the Dostoevskeyan novel, Bakhtin emphasises the dialogic nature of the interrelation that exists *between* its characters as well. 'To affirm someone else's "I" not as an object but as another subject: this is the principle governing Dostoevsky's world-view,' he writes – strongly echoing Buber's 'I-Thou' dialogics. Every novel, he insists, 'presents an opposition which is never cancelled out dialectically, of many consciousnesses, and they do not merge in the unity of an evolving spirit, just as souls and spirits do not merge in the formally polyphonic world of Dante.'[38] 'Multileveledness' and 'contradictoriness', he concludes, are the hallmarks of the polyphonic novel. In a most significant passage he asserts the *metaphysical* primacy of dialogue in Dostoevsky. 'Here,' he says, 'we are dealing with an 'ultimate dialogicality, that is, a dialogicality of the ultimate whole ...'

> In Dostoevsky's polyphonic novel we are dealing not with ordinary dia-
> logic form, that is, with an unfolding of material within the framework
> of its own monologic understanding and against the firm background of
> a unified world of objects. No, here we are dealing with an ultimate dia-
> logicality, that is, a dialogicality of the ultimate whole. The dramatic
> whole is, as we have pointed out, in this respect monologic;
> Dostoevsky's world is dialogic. It is constructed not as the whole of a
> single consciousness, absorbing other consciousnesses as objects into
> itself, but as a whole formed by the interaction of several consciousness-
> es, none of which entirely becomes an object for the other; this interac-
> tion provides no support for the viewer who would objectify an entire
> event according to some ordinary monologic category (thematically, lyri-
> cally or cognitively) – and this consequently makes the viewer also a
> participant. Not only does the novel give no firm support outside the
> rupture-prone world of dialogue for a third, monologically all-encom-
> passing consciousness – but, on the contrary, everything in the novel is
> structured to make dialogic opposition inescapable. Not a single element
> of the work is structured from the point of view of a non-participating
> 'third person.' In the novel itself non-participating 'third persons' are
> not represented in any way. There is no place for them, compositionally
> or in the larger meaning of the work. And this is not a weakness of the
> author but his greatest strength. By this means a new authorial position
> is won and conquered, one above the monologic position.[39]

It is at this point one can detect a significant convergence between Buber and Bakhtin. Buber in essays such as 'Man and His Image Work'[40] defined the ontical primacy of art as consisting in its disclosure of the absoluteness of dia-logue, its intimation of the ultimacy of the interpersonal. Its accommodation of opposing tendencies – of self and other, of distance and relation, of faith and unbelief, of the temporal and intemporal, of the finite and the infinite – exemplifies, he says, the all-inclusive character of dialogue as the definitive fact of human existence. This is affirmed explicitly in the words of *I and Thou*: 'In the beginning is the relation ... All actual life is encounter . . .' That text further emphasises the striving for the perfection of relation by which all dialogic encounter is characterised. The third part of *I and Thou* opens with the following affirmations: 'Extended the lines of relationships intersect in the eternal You. Every single You is a glimpse of that. Through every single You the basic word addresses the eternal You.'[41] And this striving for the perfection of relation – a fulfilment unrealisable in the antinomic conditions of mortal existence – further intensifies the dialogic opposition by which that existence is defined. Together with the potencies of loving, knowing and believing, Buber saw the creative activity of the artist as a striving for this fulfilment in its unconditioned, non-finite, intemporal forms. Like Bakhtin he saw the complex relationships of the spiritual and the sensible, of content and form, in the work of art as an especially intense manifestation of the conflicts embraced in the process. In *I and Thou* he defined art as a radically relational potency, embracing the antinomies of sense and spirit, of self and other, of distance and relation, of soul and form. Like Bakhtin, he emphasised its metaphysical ultimacy:

> This is the eternal origin of art that a human being confronts a form that wants to become a work through him. Not a figment of his soul but something that appears to the soul and demands the soul's creative power. What is required is a deed that man does with his whole being: if he commits it and speaks with his being the basic word to the form that appears, then the creative power is released and the work comes into being.
>
> The form that confronts me I cannot experience or describe; I can only actualise it. And yet I see it, radiant in the splendour of the confrontation, far more clearly than all clarity of the experienced world. Not as a thing among the 'internal' things, not as a figment of the 'imagination', but as what is present. Tested for its objectivity, the form is not 'there' at all; but what can equal its presence? And it is an actual relation: it acts on me as I act on it. Such work is creation, inventing is finding. Forming is discovery.[42]

Truth, therefore, for Bakhtin and Buber, lies in betweenness, dialogue, subjective-objective oppositions, the dichotomies of faith and doubt, the temporal and the timeless, the finite and the infinite – all of which they saw as being resolved only in the realm of the infinite. In this fact lies the special relevance of their thought to the work of Dostoevsky in whose writings those same dialogic principles are profoundly exemplified. The voice of the sceptic and the voice of the believer are given equal prominence in Dostoevsky's fiction – being facilitated in this through the resources of polyphonic dialogue – simply because he believed that faith always co-exists with doubt, that self-conflict is its abiding characteristic in mortal life. Throughout his own life he fluctuated between unbelief and faith – 'craving to believe', yet tormented by the everpresent spectre of scepticism, self-delusion, unbelief and despair. All this he saw as signifying the radical freedom in which faith is rooted, its attendant conflicts being the existential manifestations of that freedom. The theme finds expression both in the highly asserted faith of characters such as Alyosha, Zossima, Shatov, Myshkin and Sonia, and just as emphatically in the (highly qualified) atheism of Ivan Karamazov, Kirillov and Stavrogin. (The ambivalent nature of Stavrogin's atheism is the subject of a masterly analysis by Buber in his essay, 'Guilt and Guilt Feelings'.)[43]

Christianity is Dostoevsky's all-embracing theme, his concern quite obviously being to demonstrate the conditions in which faith must exist, and the conflicts with which it must contend, in the circumstances of everyday life. What he asserts repeatedly in the novels is a fundamental truth of the 'human condition': that is, that the seeds of unbelief are present in all men, however fervent and impassioned their faith, and paradoxically, that faith is sustained and vitalised by the challenge of scepticism, doubt and unbelief to which it must endlessly respond. Like his great contemporary, Kierkegaard, he might be described as a 'Christian in process', his faith being manifested as the pursuit of 'an objective uncertainty with the passion of the infinite'. 'I contemplate the order of nature in the hope of finding God,' Kierkegaard wrote in the *Postscript*, 'and I see omnipotence and wisdom; but I also see much else that disturbs my mind and excites anxiety. The sum of all this is an objective uncertainty.'[44] Dostoevsky saw the role of the Christian novelist as the representation of the existential conditions in which faith must exist – the conditions of 'objective uncertainty'. He sought through his writings to exemplify its coexistence with evil, sinfulness, unbelief and despair. Christianity he saw ultimately as the religion of fallen mankind, the faith of the sinner, humbled by his consciousness of his sinfulness and the huge propensity towards evil that is present in his nature. The polyphonic method so superbly defined by Bakhtin and Buber was the means by which all this found expression in his fiction.

'A FAITH GIVEN FREELY'

The technique of 'doubling' is one of the fundamental applications of the polyphonic method in Dostoevsky's fiction. It vividly conveys the dialectical interdependence of unbelief and faith which he saw as a manifestation of the freedom inherent in the nature of man and an intrinsic feature of all religious awareness and experience. In a letter to Yekatarina Yunge, written towards the end of his life, he asked: 'What do you mean by complaining of your doubleness? I too suffer from the same kind of doubleness and I have done so all my life. It is a great torment but a great delight too.' And he continued: 'If you had been more limited you would have been less conscientious and would not have suffered from that doubleness. On the contrary you would have suffered from great conceit.'[45] In *The Raw Youth* Versilov states: 'I am capable of experiencing in complete comfort two contradictory feelings at one and the same time – independently of course of my own will.' Both comments illustrate the central importance of ambiguity in Dostoevsky's work and the extremes of thought and feeling which it usually comprehends. The polarisation of personalities in the novels – Stavrogin versus Shatov, Rogozhin versus Myshkin, Ivan versus Alyosha – is an obvious employment of the technique of 'doubling,' as is his persistent contrasting of different beliefs and ideologies, in some instances within the experience of a single personality, as in his early novel, *The Double*.

This fondness for paradox and doubleness indicates a fundamental principle about the nature of Dostoevsky's own religious beliefs as well as about the manner in which they are conveyed in his fiction. As the letter to Yunge suggests, his own experience of faith was characterised by ambiguity, that is, by the persistent interpenetration of belief and unbelief, of certainty and doubt, which he came to recognise as being inherent in the whole process of faith itself. The dialectical method of his fiction, therefore, directly reflects a dialectic at the heart of his religious beliefs and points to a deep consistency between his own personal experience and the form in which it is projected in his art. 'Only a believer constantly wresting with his unbelief could speak with both voices with the same strength and conviction,' the author of one study of Dostoevsky declared. 'And his predicament was an extreme case of the Christian predicament in general. It is not Christians,' he continues, 'but their detractors who expect them to step into the world readymade.'[46]

The theme of freedom is powerfully explored in Dostoevsky's fiction through the voices of those characters who articulate the claims of reason and will to challenge the traditions and conventions of religious faith. The theme is represented with particular vividness in the monologue of the Underground Man, in the debate between Kirillov and the narrator of *The Devils* on the nature and existence of God, in Stavrogin's articulation of the philosophy of self-will and his defence of atheistic freedom, and in the dialogue on the conflict of authority and freedom between the Grand Inquisitor and Christ, as described by Ivan in *The Brothers Karamazov*. The theme is introduced in a passage from the *Notes from Underground* where the protagonist points to the limitations of rationality and asserts the preeminence of volitional freedom in the individual's growth towards self-consciousness and wholeness of being:

> You see gentlemen, reason is a good thing, that can't be disputed, but reason is only reason and satisfies only man's intellectual faculties, while volition is a manifestation of the whole of life, I mean of the whole of human life including both reason and speculation. And although in this manifestation life frequently turns out to be rubbishy, all the same it is life and merely the extraction of a square root. After all, I, for example, quite naturally want to live so as to fulfil my whole capacity for living, and not so as to satisfy simply and solely my intellectual capacity, which is only one-twentieth of my whole capacity for living. What does reason know? Reason knows only what it has succeeded in finding out (and perhaps there are some things which it will never find out; there may be no consolation in this idea, but why not express it?), but man's nature acts as one whole, with everything that is in it, conscious or unconscious, and although it is nonsensical, yet it lives.

While affirming the preeminence of will as the source and foundation of individual freedom, the Underground Man simultaneously points to the tensions and oppositions that arise from this. The novel is generally considered to be a satire on Chernyshevsky's polemical 'textbook of life', *What Is to Be Done*,[47] which appeared the year before Dostoevsky's work was published, and which advocated 'rational egoism' or enlightened self-interest as the goal of all human endeavour. This whole philosophy is rejected by the Underground Man; he sees freedom as problematic i.e. as embracing the essential dichotomy of self-directed or other-directed choices which lies at the heart of all human experience and is the root-cause of the personal tragedy and self-conflict which his monologue evokes. In every choice he makes, man is poised between self and otherness, he says: these are the polarised goals between which he is endlessly torn. While being bound up in the demands of his own self-will, he recognises that an existence directed towards self-fulfilment would ultimately be deterministic and unfree. 'Why was I made with such desires,' he cries. 'Can I have been made for only one thing, to come at last to the conclusion that my whole make-up is nothing but a cheat? Is that the whole aim? I don't believe it.' The moral dialectic in which he is caught up, as Edward Wasiolek says, is ultimately the choice between self and God. 'These two poles,' Wasiolek writes, 'are absolute and unqualified and man makes his nature by choosing his acts to serve one or the other. The values his acts have are born with the choices he makes. Love, sacrifice and other "good" acts are not good in themselves; for Dostoevsky,' he adds, 'they are, like all acts, without value until that value is chosen. Man in Dostoevsky's world does not choose what is already determined but determines what he chooses.'[48]

The Underground Man, though coming close to some notion of a transcendence attained through an other-affirming faith, does not explicitly express his dilemma in religious terms, but he points to the stark nature of the choices which it involves. Those choices are further explored by Kirillov in *The Devils*. A self-proclaimed atheist, Kirillov believes in the absolute freedom conferred on man by the power of his own self-will, a freedom he sees manifested in man's ability to free himself from suffering through the act of self-destruction. 'Full freedom,' he asserts, 'will come only when it makes no difference whether to live or not to live. That's the goal for everybody.' Ironically, it is Stavrogin, himself an atheist also, who points up the absurdity of this position. To the query whether he loves children, Kirillov replies, 'I do,' and to the question, 'In that case you must love life, too, mustn't you?' he replies, 'Yes, I love life.' To the further question why then he wants to shoot himself, he responds meaninglessly, 'What about it? Why put the two together? Life's one thing and that's another. Life exists but death doesn't exist at all.' He proclaims a subjectivist and circular morality: 'All's good – all. It's good for all those who know that all's good. If they knew that it was good for them, then it would be good for them, and as long as they don't know that it is good for them, it will not be good for them.' Stavrogin exposes the contradictions inherent in this: 'If you found out that you believed in God you would believe in Him, but as you don't know that you believe in God you don't believe in Him.' To Kirillov's insistent declaration, 'He who teaches that all are good will bring about the end of the world,' Stavrogin replies, 'He who taught it was crucified,' pointing to the irony of Kirillov's inverted Christianity. His substitution of the 'man-God' for the 'God-man' is an absurdity. The fallacy on which it is based is the pursuit of a happiness conceived negatively as the absence of suffering and pain. 'Life is pain, life is fear, and man is unhappy,' Kirillov tells the narrator. 'Now all is pain and fear. Now man loves life. And that's how they've done it. You're given life now for pain and fear, and that's where the whole deception lies. Now man is not yet what he will be. A new man will come, happy and proud. To whom it won't matter whether he lives or not. He'll be the new man! He who conquers pain and fear will himself be a god. And that other God will not be.' The vision of happiness he describes is a nihilistic absurdity, the product of a directionless freedom leading ultimately to the meaningless void of inexistence. This is the logical outcome of his philosophy of independence attained through the power of self-will.

Self-love leads man back to himself and is ultimately meaningless: this is the conclusion implicit in Kirillov's philosophy. It is reaffirmed in the life of

Stavrogin, a character Edward Wasiolek described as Dostoevsky's 'most complete and consistent embodiment of the principle of freedom without God'. 'Stavrogin,' he wrote, 'is Satan in heroic defiance against God, proud unto damnation. He represents the totally free will which in Dostoevsky's logic becomes the despotic will.'[49] To maintain his freedom Stavrogin believes he must cut himself off from all human attachment and humanitarian feeling; his only lapse from total self-control is the night he spends with Liza and this he dismisses later as an 'impossible sincerity.' Like his supposed real life model, the Marxist revolutionary, Nikolai Speshev (Dostoevsky described the latter as 'my Mephistopheles'[50]) Stavrogin's glory is the power of his own self-will and the strength and independence of mind that it provides. He recognises, however, that the inevitable outcome of his beliefs must be his own self-destruction and in his final letter before his suicide acknowledges the sterility of a life dedicated to the pursuit of self-fulfilment. 'From me,' he writes, 'nothing has come but negation, with no magnanimity and no force. Even negation has not come from me. Everything has always been petty and lifeless.'

In assessing the full significance of the character of Stavrogin, however, a good deal depends on how one views the disputed chapter entitled 'Stavrogin's Confession', which was omitted from the first published version of the novel. Dostoevsky withdrew the chapter on the advice of his publisher, who feared criminal proceedings on the grounds of obscenity, because of Stavrogin's reference to the rape of a young girl. It is significant that Dostoevsky pleaded with his publisher to include it and went so far as to produce a revised chapter which the latter still refused to include in the novel. Recently, the practice has been to append this chapter at the end of the novel, giving the reader the option of determining its significance for himself. Mochulsky, described it as 'Dostoevsky's loftiest artistic creation',[51] and another critic has argued that without it 'the whole construction and meaning of the novel is destroyed'.[52] Yet another has said: 'Without it the novel loses its one effective confrontation of light and darkness; with the removal of Tikhon there is no religious character remaining to exhibit the religious stance to which Stavrogin testifies only negatively by his failure.'[53] Generally, the chapter is considered to provide an essential balance in Stavrogin's character, affording the dialectical symmetry that was typical of Dostoevsky's artistic method.

In 'The Confession' Stavrogin comes unexpectedly close to faith and to the final surrender of self to the omnipotent will of God. 'The struggle of faith with disbelief which grows through the duration of the whole novel here attains its most extreme tension,' Mochulsky writes. 'The opposition of the two ideas is embodied in the encounter of two personalities – the atheist Stavrogin and the mystic Tikhon.'[54] Through his dedication to an absolute selfness, Stavrogin has closed himself off from God, yet he comes to see that freedom of the self is an empty and purposeless freedom. It has placed him beyond the categories of evil and good: 'I don't know and don't feel evil and good and not only have I lost the sensation but I know that there is no evil and good,' he declares. Wracked by internal pain and guilt, he goes to Tikhon in the hope that he can stifle his self-conflict through 'boundless' cathartic suffering. They find a surprising affinity in their responses to the words from Revelations, 'Because thou art lukewarm, and neither cold nor hot, I will spue thee out of my mouth.' Tikhon tells Stavrogin he will overcome the darkness of nihilistic pride through self-humiliation and repentance: 'If you believe that you can forgive yourself and obtain that forgiveness for yourself in this world through suffering, if you set that purpose before you with faith then you believe in everything already,' he says. Tikhon fails, however, and Stavrogin remains defiant and unrepentant, determined to pursue his belief in self-will and the powers of reason to the point of self-destruction. But the whole episode dramatically affirms a principle which Dostoevsky explored in depth in his other novels, that is, the principle that faith is rooted in the conquest of pride, in the subordination of individual self-will to the will of God – in a relinquishing of the faith in man and in the power of human will which have led Kirillov and Stavrogin to nihilism and self-destruction.

It is most significant that it is through the mouth of yet another unbeliever, Ivan Karamazov, that Dostoevsky provides his most powerful affirmation of the radical freedom of the experience of faith. Ivan, through his narration of the story of Christ's meeting with the Grand Inquisitor, dramatically articulates the Christian concept of faith as an assertion of the freedom of the individual person and demonstrates how this principle has been corrupted historically by the institutional Church. Returning to fifteenth-century Seville, Christ does not recognise the Church that has been founded in his name, the tyranny of its hierarchical structures being in direct violation of the freedom of conscience that he preached. 'Instead of taking men's freedom from them, Thou didst make it greater than ever,' the Inquisitor declares. 'The freedom of their faith was dearer to Thee than anything in those days fifteen hundred years ago,' he reminds Christ. Man, however, he suggests, is willing, even eager, to sacrifice that freedom for the prospect of material well-being or the apparent security of temporal authority and power:

> Thou wouldst go into the world, and art going with empty hands, with some promise of freedom which men in their simplicity and natural unruliness cannot even understand, which they fear and dread – for nothing has ever been more insupportable for a man and a human society than freedom. But seest Thou these stones in this parched and barren wilderness? Turn them into bread, and mankind will run after

Thee like a flock of sheep, grateful and obedient, though forever trembling lest Thou withdraw Thy hand and deny them thy bread. But
Thou wouldst not deprive man of freedom and didst reject the offer,
thinking what is that freedom worth, if obedience is bought with bread?
Thou didst reply that man lives not by bread alone. But dost thou
know that for the sake of that earthly bread the spirit of the earth will
rise up against Thee and will strive with Thee and overcome Thee, and
all will follow him crying, 'Who can compare with this beast? He has
given us fire from heaven!' Dost Thou know that the ages will pass, and
humanity will proclaim by the lips of their sages that there is no crime,
and therefore no sin; there is only hunger ... In the end they will lay
their freedom at our feet, and say to us, 'Make us your slaves but feed
us'. They will understand themselves, at last, that freedom and bread
enough for all are inconceivable together, for never, never, will they be
able to share between them! They will be convinced, too, that they can
never be free, for they are weak vicious, worthless and rebellious.

The Inquisitor attributes the emergence of an authoritarian Church to
man's inherent need for certainty and collectivist security. 'Nothing is more
seductive for man than his freedom of conscience, but nothing is a greater
cause of suffering,' he says. 'Man is tormented by no greater anxiety than to
find someone quickly to whom he can hand over that gift of freedom.' He
cannot endure the responsibility that his freedom entails. 'Didst Thou forget,'
he asks Christ, 'that man prefers peace, and even death, to freedom of choice
in the knowledge of good and evil.' Man craves the comfort of community, the
Inquisitor declares, and in the process surrenders personal conscience and
responsibility for the security that authoritarian power provides:

The craving for community of worship is the chief misery of every man
individually and of all humanity from the beginning of time. For the
sake of common worship they've slain each other with the sword. They
have set up gods and challenged one another, "Put away your gods and
come and worship ours, or we will kill you and your gods." And so it
will be to the end of the world, even when gods disappear from the
earth; they will fall down before idols just the same. Thou didst know,
Thou couldst not but have known, this fundamental secret of human
nature, but Thou didst reject the one infallible banner which was
offered Thee to make all men bow down to Thee alone – the banner of
earthly bread; and Thou hast rejected it for the sake of freedom and the
bread of Heaven. Behold what Thou didst further. And all again in the
name of freedom! I tell Thee that man is tormented by no greater anxi-

ety than to find someone quickly to whom he can hand over that gift of freedom with which the ill-fated creature is born ... We have corrected thy work and have founded it upon miracle, mystery and authority. And men rejoiced that they were again led like sheep, and that the terrible gift that had brought them such suffering was, at last, lifted from their hearts.

The faith that Christ had preached was one that was founded not on authority, mystery or miraculous proof, but solely on the freedom of individual conscience and choice. 'Thou didst crave faith given freely, not based on miracle, Thou didst crave for free love and not the base raptures of the slave before the might that has overawed him forever,' the Inquisitor concludes. The freedom of which he speaks finds expression in the self-destructive pride and self-will of characters such as the Underground Man, Kirillov, Stavrogin and Ivan Karamazov, as has been shown. But it is manifested in a different way in characters such as Prince Myshkin, Father Zossima, Alyosha and Sonya. What they exemplify is the freedom that finds fulfilment not in the self-destructive resources of pride and self-will but in the more enduring power of humility, selflessness and altruistic love, the ultimate sources of faith.

'LOVING HUMILITY IS MARVELLOUSLY STRONG'

'Loving humility is marvellously strong, the strongest of all things and there is nothing else like it.' Father Zossima's words in *The Brothers Karamazov* point to a paradox that is central to the Christian faith: that power belongs ultimately with the meek and the humble – those whom Christ promised would 'inherit the earth' – and not with the proud and the mighty whose belief in a purely humanist fulfilment is shown by life itself to be groundless and illusory. In contrast to the characters just described – the Stavrogins and Kirillovs who exemplify the forces of pride and independence of the spirit – Dostoevsky's novels are peopled with characters whose every action and utterance is indicative of the simplicity and self-effacement with which they conduct their daily lives. They include Makar Devushkin, Stepan Trofimovich, the Bible-reading convict in *The House of the Dead*, Ivan Petrovich, Vasya Shumkov, Makar Dolgoruky, the Marmeladovs, Lebedev, Prince Myshkin, Elizaveta, Father Zossima and Alyosha – humble, self-denying, inoffensive beings, poorly endowed by nature, yet exemplifying the qualities on which Dostoevsky would base his ideal of *sobornost*, the potential for brotherhood and fellowship in which he believed an authentic religious fulfilment is finally achieved.

In the meditation he wrote on the death of his first wife, Maria, Dostoevsky said that the central problem for a Christian is the conquest of pride: the 'main business of the I is always to annihilate the I', he wrote.[55] The theme dominates *The Idiot*, his extended fictional exploration of the complexities of human failure and its paradoxical triumph over worldly success. 'The chief idea of the novel is to depict the positively good man,' he wrote. 'There is nothing on earth more difficult than that, especially nowadays ... The good is an ideal and both our ideal and that of civilised Europe is far from having been worked out. There is only one positively good figure on earth and that is Christ.'[56] Prince Myshkin embodies the humility Dostoevsky considered an essential characteristic of the 'positively good man.' His name, as Richard Peace has shown, itself points to the paradoxical nature of humility. His Christian name, 'Lev', derives from the Russian word for 'lion', while his surname derives from the word 'mysh' meaning 'mouse' – the conjuncture of both words conveying the paradox of power and meekness that humility represents. His motto is 'Let us be servants in order to be leaders'.[57] His strength is his refusal to be humiliated; he endures insult in the knowledge that he thereby breaks the cycle of offence and retaliation which intensifies and perpetuates conflict.

Rogozhin sees him as the *yurodivy*, the 'holy fool' of Russian religious tradition. 'You are a regular holy fool, Prince, and such as you God loves', he tells him. The Prince identifies with the humble ass, the animal chosen by Christ to bear him on his triumphant entry to Jerusalem before the Crucifixion. He recalls an occasion in Basle when he was awakened by the cry of an ass which 'impressed him terribly'. 'From that time on I have been terribly fond of asses,' he says. 'They strike a sort of sympathetic chord with me.' Like the 'poor knight' of Pushkin's poetry, he believes mankind will be saved by the contemplation of beauty, an ideal within the grasp of the humblest being. 'How many beautiful things there are at every step, things even the most wretched man cannot but find beautiful,' he cries. 'Look at a child, look at God's sunset, look at the grass, how it grows, look at the eyes that gaze at you and love you.'

Myshkin's ideal of Christian humility is rejected by Ippolit who questions the whole concept of a holiness attained through service of mankind and resignation to the will of God: 'What moral obligation,' he asks himself rhetorically, 'demands not only your life, but the last gasp with which you give up your last atom of life, listening to words of comfort from the prince, whose Christian arguments are bound to bring him to the happy thought that it is really for the best that you should die.' 'Christians like him always come to that idea,' he adds. 'It's their favourite obsession.' Ippolit's contempt for the lowly and the downtrodden is evident in his treatment of Surikov, the pauper

who lives in the apartment above him. In Ippolit's eyes, Surikov is responsible
for his own misfortunes, as he tells him when the latter shows him the body of
his child who has died from cold and malnutrition. Ironically, however, it is
Ippolit who most forcibly demonstrates the tensions inherent in the Christian
ideal of humility and resigned acceptance of the will of God. Those tensions
derive from the conflicts of divine omnipotence and justice which are manifest
in the whole order of existential being – conflicts which, he concedes, are
inexplicable in human terms ultimately:

> Religion! Eternal life I can admit, and perhaps I always have admitted
> it. Let consciousness, kindled by the will of a higher Power, have
> looked round upon the world and have said – 'I am!' and let it suddenly
> be doomed by that Power to annihilation, because it's somehow neces-
> sary for some purpose – so be it, I admit it all but again the eternal
> question: what need is there of my humility? Can't I simply be
> devoured without being expected to praise what devours me? Can there
> really be Somebody up aloft who will be aggrieved by my not going on
> for a fortnight longer? I don't believe it; and it's a much more likely
> supposition that all that's needed is my worthless life, the life of an
> atom, to complete some universal harmony; for some sort of plus and
> minus, for the sake of some sort of contrast, and so on, just as the life
> of millions of creatures is needed every day as a sacrifice, as, without
> their death, the rest of the world couldn't go on (though that's not a
> very grand idea in itself, I must observe). But so be it!
> ... And yet, in spite of all my desire to do it, I could never conceive
> of there being no future life, no Providence. It seems most likely that
> they do exist, but that we don't understand anything about the future
> or its laws. But if this is so difficult and even impossible to understand,
> surely I shan't be held responsible for not being able to comprehend the
> inconceivable. It's true, they tell me, and the prince of course is with
> them there, that submissive faith is needed, that one must obey without
> reasoning, simply from piety, and that I shall certainly be rewarded in
> the next world for my humility. We degrade God too much, ascribing
> to Him our ideas, in vexation at being unable to understand Him.

Ippolit points to one of the most fundamental dilemmas of the experience of
Christian humility and faith: while asserting the seemingly uncontrollable and
self-determining forces of nature, he simultaneously affirms his own faith in a
future governed, not by the order of nature, but by a providence that inexplica-
bly comprehends the principles of necessity and freedom. That mystery, he
suggests, is epitomised in the person of Christ. He who 'vanquished Nature in

his lifetime' was himself, apparently, subject to its inexorable determinism in death. What sustained his disciples was their humble, irrational faith that the power to surmount nature he had demonstrated in his life would again be manifested in his resurrection from the dead. 'They must have parted in the most awful terror, though each one bore within him a mighty thought which could never be wrested from him.' This is the conclusion Ippolit proclaims in one of the most eloquent passages in the novel, as he recalls his reflections on the painting of Christ's Crucifixion he had seen in Rogozhin's room:

I know that the Christian Church laid it down, even in the early ages, that Christ's suffering was not symbolical but actual, and that His body was therefore fully and completely subject to the laws of nature on the cross. In the picture the face is fearfully crushed by blows, swollen, covered with fearful, swollen and blood-stained bruises, the eyes are open and squinting: the great wide-open whites of the eyes glitter with a look of deathly, glassy light. But, strange to say, as one looks at this corpse of a tortured man a peculiar and curious question arises: if just such a corpse (and it must have been just like that) was seen by all His disciples, by those who were to become His chief apostles, by the women that followed Him and stood by the cross, by all who believed Him and worshipped Him, how could they believe that that martyr would rise again? The question instinctively arises: if death is so awful and the laws of nature so mighty, how can they be overcome? How can they be overcome when even He could not conquer them, He who vanquished nature in His lifetime, who exclaimed, 'Maiden, arise!' and the maiden arose – 'Lazarus, come forth!' and the dead man came forth? Looking at such a picture, one conceives of nature in the shape of an immense, merciless, dumb beast, or more correctly, much more correctly, speaking, though it sounds strange, in the form of a huge machine of the most modern construction which, dull and insensible, has aimlessly clutched, crushed and swallowed up a great priceless Being, a Being worth all nature and its laws, worth the whole earth, which was created perhaps solely for the sake of the advent of that Being. The picture expresses and unconsciously suggests to one the conception of such a dark, insolent, unreasoning and eternal Power to which everything is in subjection. The people surrounding the dead man, not one of whom is shown in the picture, must have experienced the most terrible anguish and consternation on that evening, which had crushed all their hopes, and almost their convictions. They must have parted in the most awful terror, though each one bore within him a mighty thought which could never be wrested from him.

Like the apostles, Prince Myshkin is also guided by a simple faith in Providence, to which he submits with self-effacing humility and trust. In purely human terms, or in terms of the laws of nature, he would be adjudged a failure. 'I'm indignant,' Radomsky says, 'when someone … calls you an idiot. You're too clever to be called that … I have made up my mind that what's at the bottom of all that's happened is your innate inexperience … and your extraordinary simple-heartedness, and then the phenomenal lack of all feeling for proportion in you … and finally, the huge mass of intellectual convictions, which you, with your extraordinary honesty, have hitherto taken for real, innate, intuitive convictions.' It is the Prince's apparently limitless tolerance which finally fails him, his extraordinary forbearance and his refusal to respond to ill-treatment by others being, as Radomsky says, the eventual cause of the misfortunes which befall both himself and all who come in contact with him.

Implicit, however, in Radomsky's assessment of the Prince is the suggestion that it was not so much his humility as his *passivity* that has brought so much suffering and misfortune to himself and others. Charging the Prince with humiliating the woman to whom he had proposed marriage, he accuses him of merely passively acknowledging his guilt and failing both to desist from, and to make reparation for, his sin in a spirit of genuine Christian penitence: 'Is it enough to cry out: "Ach I'm to blame!" You are to blame and yet you persist. And where was your heart then, your "Christian" heart?' he cries. The Prince's practice of Christian humility is flawed, being demonstrated by his willingness to endure endless humiliation from others, but lacking the commitment to active love that is implied in the words of Father Zossima on the nature of Christian humility, which were quoted at the beginning of this section. '*Loving* humility is marvellously strong,' Zossima declared, 'the strongest of all things and there is nothing else like it.'

The suggestion in Zossima's words is that the truly humble Christian does not merely endure the presence of evil but grapples with it actively, seeking endlessly by his words and deeds to promote love amongst men. Myshkin is passively humble; submerged in the stream of events, he is helpless and inactive as those events proceed inexorably towards tragedy. He fails to confront Nastasya with the cruelties she inflicts on others, believing naively that her innate goodness will ultimately triumph over her 'intolerable, diabolical pride, her arrogant, rapacious egoism'. 'How could you, out of compassion, for the sake of her pleasure, put to shame another, a pure and lofty girl, humiliate her in those haughty, those hated eyes. What will compassion lead you to next?' Radomsky screams at the Prince. In his compassion the latter has failed to kindle the love in others that he undoubtedly feels for them; he is helpless in the face of evil, forced to contemplate passively its destructive impact on the

lives of those he loves. It is significant, in this respect, that he has been portrayed so negatively in much recent criticism, especially in the works of Soviet
writers. Maxim Gorky called him 'a fatalist';[58] another Soviet critic spoke of
him as 'powerless and even ludicrous in the face of real life with its human
passions';[59] yet another described him as 'feeble, lifeless and reactionary'.[60]

In Zossima and Alyosha Dostoevsky portrayed a more fulfilled form of
Christian humility, showing how the intertwined ideals of self-effacement and
active love find expression in their dedication to fostering the spirit of community and brotherhood amongst themselves and all whom they encounter in
their daily lives. Earlier, through the voice of Vassin in *The Raw Youth*,
Dostoevsky had pointed to the dangers of a humility insufficiently informed
by love when he wrote the following: '... many very proud people like to
believe in God, especially those who despise other people ... They turn to
God to avoid doing homage to men, of course without recognising how it
comes about in them; to do homage to God is not so humiliating.' Father
Zossima similarly warns his followers that humility without love may be a
form of spiritual pride. 'Always decide to use humble love', he warns them,
while emphasising the effort required to achieve it:

> At some thoughts one stands perplexed, especially at the sight of men's
> sin, and wonders whether one should use force or humble love. Always
> decide to use humble love. If you resolve on that once for all, you may
> subdue the whole world. Loving humility is marvellously strong, the
> strongest of all things and there is nothing else like it.
>
> Every day and every hour, every minute, walk round yourself and
> watch yourself, and see that your image is a seemly one. You pass by a
> little child, you pass by, spiteful, with ugly words, with wrathful heart;
> you may not have noticed the child, but he has seen you, and your
> image, unseemly and ignoble, may remain in his defenceless heart. You
> don't know it, but you may have sown an evil seed in him, and it may
> grow, and all because you were not careful before the child, because you
> did not foster in yourself a careful actively benevolent love. Brothers,
> love is a teacher; but one must know how to acquire it, for it is hard to
> acquire, it is dearly bought, it is won slowly by hard labour. For we
> must love not only occasionally, for a moment, but for ever. Everyone
> can love occasionally, even the wicked can.

And, significantly, he echoes Ippolit in suggesting that it is ultimately pride
that causes man to seek rational explanations for the impenetrable mysteries
and contradictions of life. 'We cannot,' Zossima says, 'comprehend the reality
of things on earth.' Faith demands humble acceptance of the inexplicable mys-

teriousness of our being, an acceptance that is manifested in a resigned submission to God's will:

> Of the pride of Satan what I think is this: it is hard for us on earth to comprehend it, and therefore it is so easy to fall into error and to share it, even imagining that we are doing something grand and fine. Indeed many of the strongest feelings and movements of our nature we cannot comprehend on earth. Let not that be a stumbling-block, and think not that it may serve as a justification to you for anything. For the Eternal Judge asks of you what you can comprehend and not what you cannot. You will know that yourself hereafter, for you will behold all things truly then and will not dispute them. On earth, indeed, we are, as it were, astray, and if it were not for the precious image of Christ before us, we should be undone and altogether lost, as was the human race before the Flood. Much on earth is hidden from us, but to make up for that we have been given a precious mystic sense of our living bond with the other world, with the higher heavenly world, and the roots of our thoughts and feelings are not here but in other worlds. That is why the philosophers say that we cannot apprehend the reality of things on earth.

Alyosha resembles Myshkin in certain respects. His meekness too is manifested in a trusting and accepting attitude towards everyone he meets, though it evokes a different response in his case than it does in the Prince. 'He seemed throughout his life to put implicit trust in people, yet no one ever looked on him as a simpleton or naive person,' the narrator says at the beginning of *The Brothers Karamazov*. He further resembles Myshkin in his unwillingness to pass judgment on others: 'There was something about him which made one feel at once (and it was so all his life afterwards) that he did not care to be a judge of others – that he would never take it upon himself to criticise and would never condemn anyone for anything. He seemed, indeed, to accept everything without the least condemnation though often grieving bitterly: and this was so much so that one could surprise or frighten him even in his earliest youth.' Where he differs from Myshkin is in his assumption of responsibility for others – for his father, for his brothers, for Grushenka, for his brother monks – and in his discharge of that responsibility in the spirit of active love. This, in turn, is rooted in his awareness of his own sinfulness. Together with his sense of being 'responsible to all men for all and everything', this is one of the central principles of the monastic creed that he has espoused. The basic precepts of that creed were stated eloquently by Zossima in the following words:

'Love one another, Fathers,' said Father Zossima, as far as Alyosha could remember afterwards. 'Love God's people. Because we have come here and shut ourselves within these walls, we are no holier than those that are outside, but, on the contrary, from the very fact of coming here each of us has confessed to himself that he is worse than others, than all men on earth ... And the longer the monk lives in his seclusion, the more keenly he must recognise that. Else he would have had no reason to come here. When he realises that he is not only worse than others but that he is responsible to all men for all and everything, for all human sins, national and individual, only then the aim of our seclusion is attained. For know, dear ones, that every one of us is undoubtedly responsible for all men and everything on earth, not merely through the general sinfulness of creation, but each one personally for all mankind and every individual man. This knowledge is the crown of life for the monk and for every man. For monks are not a special sort of men, but only what all men ought to be. Only through that knowledge, our heart grows soft with infinite, inexhaustible love. Then every one of you will have the power to win over the whole world by love and to wash away the sins of the world with your tears ... Each of you keep watch over your heart and confess your sins to yourself unceasingly. Be not afraid of your sins, even when perceiving them, if only there be penitence, but make no conditions with God. Again I say, be not proud. Be proud neither to the little nor to the great. Hate not those who reject you, who insult you, who abuse and slander you. Hate not the atheists, the teachers of evil, the materialists – and I mean not only the good ones – for there are many good ones among them, especially in our day – hate not even the wicked ones. Remember them in your prayers thus: Save, O Lord, all those who have none to pray for them, save too all those who will not pray. And add: it is not in pride that I make this prayer, O Lord, for I am lower than all men ... Love God's people, let not strangers draw away thy flock, for if you slumber in your slothfulness and disdainful pride, or, worse still, in covetousness, they will come from all sides and draw away your flock.'

Significantly, Zossima warns that loving humility is achieved only through a constant struggle with nature – 'it is hard to acquire', he says, 'it is dearly bought, it is won slowly by long labour'. Penitence, man's consciousness of his own sinfulness and his struggle ceaselessly to surmount it is, he says, the source of authentic Christian humility and of the responsibilities it enjoins on the believer. This whole process is explored by Dostoevsky in his dramatic evocation of Raskolnikov's progression from guilt to penitence in *Crime and*

Punishment, the first major novel he published after his return from his five year incarceration in a prison camp in Siberia.

THE RAISING OF LAZARUS: REPENTANCE AND REBIRTH

In an essay, 'Guilt and Guilt Feelings', where he examines the treatment of the theme of repentance in Dostoevsky's and in Kafka's fiction, Martin Buber suggests that self-illumination is the first condition for the authentic expiation of guilt.[61] In the life and death of Stavrogin, he says, Dostoevsky portrayed an individual successfully resisting the urge to self-illumination that he himself had willingly set in motion by his visit to Tikhon to make atonement for his sins. 'Listen, Father Tikhon,' Stavrogin cries, 'I want to forgive myself. That is my chief purpose, my only purpose ... that is why I seek boundless suffering.' Stavrogin fails to sustain the process he has himself initiated. 'Without this powerful wave of light which illuminates self-being,' Buber writes, 'the confession of guilt remains without substance in the life of the guilty man and the religious confession is only a guilty prattle that no one hears.' Stavrogin had hoped for a sudden release from the torment of his guilt, while the priest advises him that such a release will come only from the painful process of self-illumination and repentance to which he is unwilling to subject himself. These are the main conclusions of Buber's essay:

> The decisive moment, excised in the usual version of the novel as abridged by the author, is precisely the failure of the confession: Stavrogin has wanted the holy man to believe in its existential character and thereby help him, Stavrogin, to existence. But existential confession is possible only as a breaking-through to the great action of the high conscience in self-illumination, persevering self-identification, and a reconciling relationship to the world. This possibility, however, is in Stavrogin's eyes one of two things: either essentially not accorded to him or destroyed by him through his life-game. In Dostoevsky's own eyes, however, man is redeemable when he wills redemption as such and thereby also his share in it – the great act of the high conscience ... Stavrogin makes a confession in words. He describes therein in horrible detail the course of his crime, but both in remembering it and in recording it he remains incapable of self-illumination. He lacks the small light of humility that alone can illuminate the abyss of the guilty self in broad waves. He seeks for some kind of foothold, no matter how meagre; then he gives up and kills himself ... Both Stavrogin and Joseph K have not taken the crucial hour of man upon themselves, and now have lost it. It is the crucial hour of man of which we speak. For,

to use Pascal's language, the greatness of man is bound up with his misery. Man is the being who is capable of becoming guilty and is capable of illuminating his guilt.[62]

In keeping with the dialectical method generally employed in his fiction, Dostoevsky portrayed the process of resistance to self-illumination in the character of Stavrogin, while in the same novel he portrayed all the agony and self-torment which a genuine experience of self-illumination entails in the character of Stepan Trofimovich Verkhovensky. Before this is discussed, it may be useful to mention some pointers to the whole process of moral self-illumination that occur in *Notes from Underground* where the protagonist, while falling short of the experience of repentance and faith, displays strong signs of the deepening self-consciousness which Dostoevsky considered to be an essential prelude to both. 'The whole meaning of human life,' the Underground Man declares, 'can be summed up in the one statement that man only exists for the purpose of proving to himself every minute that he is a man and not an organstop.' The deepened self-awareness which is the supreme value of human existence is also its 'supreme misfortune', he declares. Consciousness, he says, is deepened by suffering ... 'Suffering is doubt, negation ... Suffering ... is the sole cause of consciousness ...'

> As for my own personal opinion, I find it somehow unseemly to love only well-being. Whether it's a good thing or a bad thing, smashing things is also sometimes very pleasant. I am not here standing up for suffering, or for well-being either. I am standing out for my own caprices and for having them guaranteed when necessary. There is no place for suffering in farces, for example, I know that. It is quite inconceivable in a millennium: suffering is doubt, negation, and what sorts of millennium would it be of which one could have any doubts? All the same, I am certain that man will never deny himself destruction and chaos. Suffering – after all, that is the sole cause of consciousness. Although I declared to begin with that in my opinion consciousness is man's supreme misfortune, I know that man loves it and would not change it for any gratification. Consciousness is infinitely greater than, for example, two and two make four. After twice two is achieved there will of course be nothing left to do, much less to learn. All that will then be possible will be to shut off one's five senses and immerse oneself in meditation. But with consciousness, even if it has the same result, I mean that there will be nothing to do, at least one could sometimes resort to self-flagellation, and that stimulates at any rate. It may be retrograde, but all the same it's better than nothing.

'Humiliation is purification, it is the acutest and most vivid consciousness', he says later, as he reflects on the suffering he has caused Liza. 'Her humiliation will elevate and purify her ... through hate and ... h'm perhaps ... forgiveness also,' he concludes. But for all the wisdom of his insights, the Underground Man fails to reach the awareness of his own sinfulness that would enable him to expiate his guilt. Though he comes quite close to faith – 'surely', he says, 'I have not been created merely to come to the conclusion that I have been created' – the focus of his self-consciousness remains his own selfishness and pride. His failure, like Stavrogin's, is a failure to love – to elect to love – and thereby induce the genuine spirit of self-humiliation which would lead him to self-forgiveness and faith.

This latter process is vividly exemplified in the character of Stepan Trofimovich whose progress from self-atonement to faith stands in dramatic contrast to the self-deception that leads the Underground Man and Stavrogin to their doom. Stepan's penitential conversion begins when he humbles himself before Lisa: 'In bidding a last farewell to the world I'd like to take a leave of all my past, too, in your person,' he tells her as he kneels before her, weeping. 'I kneel to everything that was beautiful in my life. I kiss and offer up thanks. Now I've torn myself in half: there is the madman who dreamed of soaring to the clouds, *vingt-deux ans*! Here is a broken and shivering old man – a tutor – *chez ce marchand, s'il existe pourtant ce marchand* ...' His pilgrimage, in contrast to Stavrogin's, leads to self-forgiveness; he discovers he must repent to himself before he can repent before God. Meeting the humble bible-seller, Sofia Ulitina, he discovers the healing power of penitence. 'O let us forgive, let us forgive, first of all let us forgive all and always,' he cries. 'Let us hope that we too shall be forgiven. Yes, because all, every one of us, have wronged one another. We are all guilty.' Repenting of his sins, he recognises the scale of his self-deception:

> My friend, I've been telling lies all my life. Even when I told the truth. I never spoke for the sake of the truth, but always for my own sake. I knew it before, but I only see it now ... Oh, where are those friends whom I have insulted with my friendship all my life? And all, all! Savez-vous, perhaps I'm telling lies now. The worst of it is that I believe myself when I am lying. The hardest thing in life is to live without telling lies ... and – and without believing in one's lies.

Sofia reads him the same passage from *Revelations* that Tikhon had read to Stavrogin: 'Because thou art lukewarm, and neither cold nor hot, I will spue thee out of my mouth.' She also reads the story of Christ healing the man possessed by a demon to signify Stepan's renunciation of the false ideology he had previously espoused. On his death-bed he recognises that his need for God is his need for the eternal and the infinite: 'God is necessary to me if only because he is the only being whom one can love eternally,' he cries.

> My immortality is necessary if only because God will not be guilty of injustice and extinguish altogether the flame of love for Him once kindled in my heart. And what is more precious than love? Love is higher than existence, love is the crown of existence; and how is it possible that existence should not be under its dominance? If I have once loved Him and rejoiced in my love, is it possible that He should extinguish me and my joy and bring me to nothingness again? If there is a God, then I am immortal. Voilà ma profession de foi ...
>
> The mere fact of the ever present idea that there exists something infinitely more just and more happy than I am fills me through and through with tender ecstasy – and glorifies me – oh, whoever I may be, whatever I have done! What is far more essential for man than personal happiness is to know and to believe at every instant that there is somewhere a perfect and serene happiness for all men and for everything ... The one essential condition of human existence is that man should always be able to bow down before something infinitely great. If men are deprived of the infinitely great they will not go on living and will die of despair. The Infinite and the Eternal are as essential for man as the little planet on which he dwells.

The polarities of rationalistic pride and humble self-repentance which Dostoevsky dramatised through the contrasting attitudes of Stavrogin and Stepan Trofimovich are embraced within the personality of a single character in *Crime and Punishment*. Raskolnikov, Edward Wasiolek writes, embodies 'two kinds of logic that are basic to the human condition'. 'They correspond,' he says, 'to the two poles of Dostoevsky's moral dialectic. There is God and there is the self. Each has roots in the real impulses of men. There is no bridge between these two natures and man is poised in fearful anxiety with every choice between them.'[63] Throughout the novel Raskolnikov is poised between the self-oriented urge towards a purely individualistic fulfilment and the altruistic urge towards compassion and care for his fellowman. The former tendency is manifested in his brutal murder of Alyona and Elizaveta, the latter in his concern for the Marmeladovs and his love for their daughter, Sonia.

The complexities of the whole process of spiritual transformation through repentance are demonstrated by Dostoevsky as he shows how both of these tendencies interpenetrate in the life of Raskolnikov. Like Stavrogin, he too feels the urge to unburden himself of his guilt and turns to Sonia in the hope that he will alleviate his torment by confessing his sins. Earlier he had been surprised by the feeling of spiritual release he had experienced when he came to the aid of the Marmeladovs. 'The sensation might be compared to that of a man condemned to death who has quite unexpectedly been pardoned,' he said. But shortly afterwards he recommitted himself to the pursuit of self-will and power: 'Now begins the reign of reason and light and of will and strength,' he declares. When he comes to Sonia and they read the New Testament story of the raising of Lazarus, he tortures her with questions about the injustice perpetrated on mankind by an omniscient and supposedly benevolent God. Her faith, he says, will not prevent the death of her mother or provide for her family in their destitution. Yet, as he bows before her – 'bowing down to all suffering humanity' – he begins to realise that the force that sustains her faith is the self-sacrificing and limitless power of love:

> He grasped her by the shoulders with both his hands and gazed into her weeping face. His eyes were dry, feverish, piercing; his lips trembled violently. Suddenly he bent down quickly, and falling on his knees kissed her foot. Sonia shrank back from him as from a madman. And, indeed, he did look like a madman
>
> 'What are you doing? What are you doing? Before me?' she murmured, turning pale, and her heart suddenly contracted with pain.
>
> He got up at once.
>
> 'I did not bow down to you, I bowed down to all suffering humanity,' he said wildly, and walked off to the window. 'Listen,' he added, coming back to her in a minute. 'I told some bully an hour or so ago that he was not worth your little finger and – and that I did my sister an honour to-day when I made her sit beside you.'
>
> 'Oh, you shouldn't have said that to them! And was she there too?' Sonia cried, frightened. 'Sit beside me? An honour? Why, I'm a dishonourable creature! I'm a great sinner! Oh, what did you say that for?'
>
> 'I did not say it because of your dishonour and your sin but because of your great suffering ... Because you have betrayed and ruined yourself for nothing ... Tell me, at least,' he went on almost in a frenzy, 'how can such shame and such disgrace live in you side by side with your other quite different and holy feelings? Would it not have been a thousand times more just and more sensible to throw yourself into the river and finish it all at one blow?
>
> 'But what will happen to them?' she asked faintly, gazing at him with tortured eyes, but seemingly not at all surprised at his suggestion.
>
> Raskolnikov looked strangely at her. He read everything in that look ... What he thought, what could so far have checked her firm resolve to

put an end to it all at one blow? And it was only now that he realised
what those poor little orphan children and that wretched half-crazy Mrs
Marmeladov, with her consumption and knocking her head against the
wall meant to her.

When she reads the story of the raising of Lazarus, Sonia hopes that
Raskolnikov will, in a similarly miraculous fashion, find the grace of faith and
turn to God for forgiveness: 'At the last verse, "could not this man who
opened the eyes of the blind", she lowered her voice, conveying, fervently and
passionately, the doubts, reproaches, and censure of the blind, unbelieving
Jews, who would in another minute fall down as though struck by lightning
and weep and believe. And he, he, too, blinded and unbelieving as he is, he,
too, will hear it now, and he, too, will believe – yes, yes, now, this minute, she
hoped, and she trembled with joyous anticipation.' Raskolnikov continues to
assert his belief in 'freedom and power ... power above all else ... power over
all the tumbling vermin and over all the ant-hill.' He tells her, however, that
he will come to her and confess his guilt. 'I shall not come to ask you for forgiveness. I shall tell you frankly,' he says.

It is when he contemplates the visible projection of the two sides of his
own nature in the personalities of Svidrigaylov and Sonia – the one characterising the impulse towards pride and self-will, the other towards compassion
and love – that the process of repentance begins in Raskolnikov. Svidrigaylov's
dream of the girl he has violated and her subsequent death by suicide parallels
Raskolnikov's dream of the murders of Alyona and Elizaveta. At the same time
as Svidrigaylov kills himself in his squalid guest-room, Raskolnikov is also
contemplating suicide, but is driven by his horror of isolation and his need for
human companionship to go and confess his crime. He recalls Sonia's words,
'Go to the cross-roads, bow down to the people, kiss the earth, for you have
sinned against it, and proclaim in a loud voice to the whole world: I am a
murderer.' His decision to confess is accompanied by a recognition of the
infinity of love that is manifested in Sonia's devotion to him:

> And so utterly crushed was he by his feeling of hopelessness and deso-
> lation and by the great anxiety of all those days, but especially of the
> last few hours, that he simply plunged head over heels into this new
> and overwhelming sensation. It seemed to come upon him as though it
> were some nervous fit: it glimmered like a spark in his soul, and then,
> suddenly, spread like a conflagration through him. Everything within
> him grew soft all at once, and tears gushed from his eyes. He fell to the
> ground just where he stood.
> He knelt down in the middle of the square, bowed down to the

earth, and kissed the filthy earth with joy and rapture. Then he got up and bowed down once more ...

The second time he had bowed down to the ground in the Haymarket he saw, as he turned to the left, Sonia, standing about fifty feet away. She was hiding from him behind one of the wooden huts in the square. So she had accompanied him all along his sorrowful way! Raskolnikov at that moment knew once for all that Sonia was with him for ever, and that she would follow him to the ends of the earth, wherever fate might lead him. He felt deeply moved, but now he had reached his destination.

It is widely suggested that Raskolnikov does not fully repent of his actions, at least not in the fully Christian sense of humbling himself and surrendering totally to the will of God. In the prison-camp he longs for the suffering and self-torment he associates with a truly penitential experience: 'And if fate had only sent him repentance – burning repentance that would have rent his heart and deprived him of sleep, the sort of repentance that is accompanied by terrible agony which makes one long for the noose or the river! Oh, how happy he would have been if he could have felt such repentance!' He tortures himself with questions on the nature of his guilt: 'What does "crime" mean? My conscience is clear. No doubt I have committed a criminal offence, no doubt I have violated the letter of the law and blood was shed. All right execute me for the letter of the law and have done with it.' The urge to repentance is still in conflict with the claims of his own pride and self-will: the tension between them persists to the end. But he does finally elect for love and foresees the prospect of a genuine spiritual fulfilment and rebirth in the life he shares with Sonia:

> How it happened he did not know, but suddenly something seemed to seize him and throw him at her feet. He embraced her knees and wept. At first she was terribly frightened, and her face was covered by a deathly pallor. She jumped to her feet and, trembling all over, looked at him. But at once and at the same moment she understood everything. Her eyes shone with intense happiness; she understood, and she had no doubts at all about it, that he loved her, loved her infinitely, and that the moment she had waited for so long had come at last.
>
> They wanted to speak, but could not; tears stood in their eyes They were both pale and thin; but in those sick and pale faces the dawn of a new future, of a full resurrection to a new life, was already shining. It was love that brought them back to life: the heart of one held inexhaustible sources for the life of the other.

> They decided to wait and be patient. They still had to wait for another seven years, and what great suffering and what infinite joy till then! And he had come back to life, and he knew it with every fibre of his renewed being, and she – why, she lived only for him.

The significance of the novel's epilogue lies in its revelation of a principle which is crucial to Dostoevsky's treatment of the nature of repentance: that is, that it originates not in the kind of psychological leap that Porfiry described at an earlier stage in the work, but in the growth towards the selflessness of love that is exemplified in Raskolnikov's relationship with Sonia. Raskolnikov discovers that the pain of guilt is healed not through the contemplation of his sinfulness but through the pursuit of active love. (Dostoevsky's treatment of the theme recalls the words of the sixteenth chapter of *The Cloud of Unknowing* on the repentance of Mary, the sister of Lazarus: 'Did she descend from the heights of love's desire to examine closely her base, foul, sinful life, turning the filth over to brood and weep over each sin as she individually recalled it? Certainly not. God had let her know by his grace within her soul that she could never come close to him this way. Much more likely she would have fallen into sin again through it.') The essential message of the Epilogue is that Raskolnikov cannot reach the point of repentance until he overcomes his own selfishness and pride, and this he does through his love for Sonia. By demonstrating the persistence of the conflict in Raskolnikov between the urge to repentance and the urge to pride and self-will almost to the end of the novel, Dostoevsky points to the obstacles that lie in the way of the whole process of self-illumination and penitence, but clearly indicates the dependence of the latter on the conquest of pride through selfless love. Through his love for Sonia Raskolnikov discovers the conditions in which self-penitence becomes possible and in the process experiences a spiritual rebirth. The torment of guilt he had hitherto experienced seems insignificant from the standpoint of his transformed condition:

> And what did all, all the torments of the past amount to now? Everything, even his crime, even his sentence and punishment appeared to him now, in the first transport of feeling, a strange extraneous event that did not seem even to have happened to him. But he could not think of anything long and continuously that evening or concentrate on anything. Besides, now he would hardly have been able to solve any of his problems consciously; he could only feel. Life had taken the place of dialectics, and something quite different had to work itself out in his mind.

Under his pillow lay the New Testament. He picked it up mechanically. The book belonged to her; it was the same book from which she had been reading the raising of Lazarus to him. At the beginning of his prison life he had feared that she would drive him frantic with her religion, that she would talk constantly about the Gospels, and would force her books on him. But, to his amazement, she had never spoken to him about it, and had not even once offered him the New Testament. He had asked her for it himself shortly before his illness. He had never opened it till now.

He did not open it now either, but one thought flashed through his mind: 'Is it possible that her convictions can be mine, too, now?

Her feelings, her yearnings, at least ...

'WE CAN TRULY LOVE ONLY WITH SUFFERING'

'Man is not born for happiness; he has to earn his happiness, and always by suffering,' Dostoevsky wrote in his notes for *Crime and Punishment*.[64] His words have been cited by several of his critics, most notably those writing in Soviet journals, to suggest a seemingly endless preoccupation with the misery and gloom of human existence throughout his writings. One of the authors of *Tvorschestvo Dostoevskogo* spoke of his 'religion of suffering' as 'reactionary' and 'degrading to humanity'.[65] He cited the example of Mikolka confessing to a crime he did not commit, in order 'to find suffering', and of Father Zossima advising Alyoshsa that he 'will see great sorrow and in that sorrow will be happy'. Many have referred to some comments in Dostoevsky's Diary that would lend strong support to such interpretations. 'I believe the main and most fundamental spiritual quest of the Russian people is their craving for suffering – perpetual and unquenchable suffering – everywhere and in everything,' he writes in an entry for 1873. 'Even in happiness,' he continues, 'there is in the Russian people an element of suffering; otherwise, felicity to them is incomplete.' 'The Russian people,' he concludes, 'delight in their afflictions. The suffering stream flows through their whole history – not merely because of external calamities and misfortunes: it gushes from the people's very heart.'[66]

Dostoevsky's preoccupation with suffering, however, requires more complex explanations than those suggested by some of his critics. Much of it is bound up with a sense of the irrationality and mysteriousness of suffering, a feeling which is powerfully articulated by Ivan Karamazov. 'With my pitiful, earthly, Euclidean understanding, all I know,' he says, 'is that there is suffering and that there are none guilty; that cause follows effect simply and direct-

ly: that everything flows and finds its level – but that's only Euclidean nonsense.' It is significant that Ivan links his sense of the injustice of suffering
with the problem of faith. The horrific examples of human cruelty that he
cites – the Turks who slaughter babies with their bayonets, the General who
sets his hounds on a child to tear him to pieces, the parents who smear their
child with excrement – suggest a world so evil and depraved as to exclude the
possibility of its being the creation of a just, omnipotent and merciful God.
The suffering he witnesses is senseless, Ivan declares; if such suffering is
inevitable, he asks, how then is life to be made meaningful:

> Oh, Alyosha, I am not blaspheming! I understand, of course, what an
> upheaval of the universe it will be, when everything in heaven and earth
> blends in one hymn of praise and everything that lives and has lived
> cries aloud: 'Thou art just, O Lord, for Thy ways are revealed.' When
> the mother embraces the fiend who threw her child to the dogs, and all
> three cry aloud with tears: 'Thou art just, O Lord!' then, of course, the
> crown of knowledge will be reached and all will be made clear. But
> what pulls me up here is that I can't accept that harmony. And while I
> am on earth I make haste to take my own measures. You see, Alyosha,
> perhaps it really may happen that if I live to that moment, or rise again
> to see it, I, too, perhaps, may cry aloud with the rest, looking at the
> mother embracing the child's torturer: 'Thou art just, O Lord!' but I
> don't want to cry aloud then. While there is still time I hasten to pro-
> tect myself and so I renounce the higher harmony altogether. 'It's not
> worth the tears of that one tortured child who beat itself on the breast
> with its little fist and prayed in its stinking outhouse, with its unexpiat-
> ed tears to 'dear, kind God!' It's not worth it because those tears are
> unatoned for. They must be atoned for or there can be no harmony.
> But how? How are you going to atone for them? Is it possible? By their
> being avenged? But what do I care for avenging them? What do I care
> for a hell for oppressors? What good can hell do, since those children
> have already been tortured? And what becomes of harmony, if there is
> hell? I want to forgive. I want to embrace. I don't want more suffering.
> And if the sufferings of children go to swell the sum of sufferings
> which was necessary to pay for truth, then I protest that the truth is
> not worth such a price. I don't want the mother to embrace the oppres-
> sor who threw her son to the dogs! She dare not forgive him! Let her
> forgive him for herself, if she will, let her forgive the torturer for the
> immeasurable suffering of her mother's heart. But the sufferings of her
> tortured child she has no right to forgive; she dare not forgive the tor-
> turer, even if the child were to forgive him! And if that is so, if they

dare not forgive, what becomes of harmony? Is there in the whole world a being who would have the right to forgive and could forgive? I don't want harmony. From love for humanity I don't want it. I would rather be left with the unavenged suffering. I would rather remain with my unavenged suffering and unsatisfied indignation, even if I were wrong. Besides, too high a price is asked for harmony; it's beyond our means to pay so much to enter on it. And so I hasten to give back my entrance ticket, and if I am an honest man I am bound to give it back as soon as possible. And that I am doing. It's not God that I don't accept, Alyosha, only I most respectfully return Him the ticket.

For all his eloquence, there is a contradiction implicit in Ivan's argument, one that becomes clearer in his subsequent conversation with Alyosha and in his narration of the Legend of the Grand Inquisitor. Accompanying his questioning of divine justice is an assertion of the fundamental freedom of man's nature – and the radical character of that freedom is repeatedly emphasised in the Legend – yet by attributing the cruelties he has described to God he is denying man responsibility for his actions and ultimately denying him his freedom. While insisting on the absolute character of human freedom, he denies the evidence of that freedom, seeing it as negating the possibility of a higher, divinely ordained harmony. Unwittingly, he points to one of the central dilemmas of the experience of faith: the conflict between man's need for certitude – such as would be guaranteed in a benign and divinely ordered universe – and the torment and anxiety of a free and conditionless faith. That, as has been shown in an earlier section, is the conflict which is explored in the Legend, its torment being evoked particularly in the Inquisitor's words: 'Nothing has ever been more insupportable for a man and a human society than freedom ... Nothing is more seductive for man than his freedom of conscience, and nothing is a greater cause of suffering.'

If suffering is endemic in human existence, as Ivan suggests, it is also as transient and fleeting as the conditions in which it occurs. It is Zossima who shows that the impermanence of mortal suffering is also the key to man's power ultimately to transcend it. In this he draws powerful support from the Old Testament and especially the Book of Job. Since childhood, he tells the monks who are gathered round his death-bed, he has drawn comfort from the story of Job. 'What a book the Bible is,' he exclaims, 'what a miracle, what strength is given with it to man. It is like a mould cast of the world and man and human nature, everything is there, and a law for everything for all the ages ...' Recalling the impact on him of the story of Job when he first heard it read in a church as an eight year old child, he tells the monks: 'Ever since then ... I've never been able to read that sacred tale without tears. And how

much that is great, mysterious and unfathomable there is in it ... the greatness
of it lies just in the fact that it is a mystery – that the passing earthly show
and the eternal verity are brought together in it.' 'How', he asks, 'could God
give up the most loved of his saints for the diversion of the devil, take from
him his children, smite him with sore boils so that he cleansed the corruption
from his sores with a potsherd ...' In his misery, he says, Job learns to recognise both the transience of suffering and his capacity to transcend it. He continues to trust in God, despite the inexplicable character of his suffering, and
its apparent meaninglessness when judged from a purely human standpoint.
He continues to see the hand of God in the midst of the darkness that overwhelms him. 'I know that my Redeemer liveth,' is his constant cry of hope. It
is the unsuppressible optimism of Job, and the example of his unshakeable
faith, that is the source of the joyous hopefulness with which Zossima himself
faces the imminent prospect of death:

> And what mysteries are solved and revealed; God raises Job again, gives
> him wealth again. Many years pass by, and he has other children and
> loves them. But how could he love those new ones when those first
> ones are no more, when he has lost them? Remembering them, how
> could he be fully happy with those new ones, however dear the new
> ones might be? But he could, he could. It's the great mystery of human
> life that old grief passes gradually into quiet tender joy. The mild
> serenity of age takes the place of the riotous blood of youth. I bless the
> rising sun each day, and, as before, my heart sings to meet it, but now I
> love even more its setting, its long slanting rays and the soft tender
> gentle memories that come with them, the dear images from the whole
> of my long happy life – and over all the Divine Truth, softening, recon-
> ciling, forgiving! My life is ending, I knew that well, but every day that
> is left me I feel how my earthly life is in touch with a new infinite,
> unknown, but approaching life, the nearness of which sets my soul
> quivering with rapture, my mind glowing and my heart weeping with
> joy.

Zossima's words recall a moving passage in Kierkegaard's *Christian Discourses*
on the temporality of suffering: 'We suffer only once but we triumph eternally
... the "once" of suffering is the instant, that of triumph eternity; the "once"
of suffering therefore when it is past is no time, the once of triumph is,
in another sense, no time, for it is never past; the "once" of suffering is a
transition or a thing we pass through, that of triumph, an eternally enduring
triumph.'[67]
The transience of suffering, and the hopefulness that comes from contem-

plation of its 'onceness', is further conveyed by Dostoevsky in the various images of the resurrection of the innocent that occur throughout his work. Two of the most moving of these occur in works that were inspired by personal tragedy. When his three-month-old daughter, Sonya, died in 1868 Dostoevsky described the depth of his grief in a letter to his friend, the poet Appollon Maykov: 'People try to comfort me by saying I'll have other children. But where is Sonya? Where is the tiny creature? To restore her to life I'd accept the torments of crucifixion.'[68] Some time later he wrote the story, 'A Little Boy at Christ's Christmas Tree,' in which this beautiful image occurs of children playing amongst the angels in Paradise:

> 'Who are you, little boys?' Who are you, little girls?' – he asks them, smilingly, and he feels that he loves them all.
> 'This is Christ's Christmas Tree,' – they tell him. 'On this day of the year Christ always had a Christmas Tree for those little children who have no Christmas tree of their own.'
> And then he learned that these little boys and girls were all once children like himself, but some of them have frozen to death in those baskets in which they had been left at the doors of Petersburg officials; others had perished in miserable hospital wards; still others had died at the dried-up breasts of their famine-stricken mothers (during the Samara famine); these, again, had choked to death from stench in third-class railroad carts. Now they are all here, all like little angels, and they are all with Christ, and He is in their midst, holding out His hands to them and to their sinful mothers ... And the mothers of these babes, they all stand there, a short distance off, and weep: each one recognises her darling – her little boy or her little girl – and they fly over to their mothers and kiss them and brush away their tears with their little hands, begging them not to cry, for they feel so happy here ...

A few years after he wrote this story Dostoevsky had to face the repeated tragedy of the death of another of his children. His two-year-old son, Alyosha, died in May 1878, of a fatal epileptic seizure – a condition he probably inherited from his father. Stricken with grief, Dostoevsky went to the monastery of Optina Pustyn, to seek consolation from the starets, Father Amvrosy (probably the real life model for Father Zossima). In *The Brothers Karamazov* – which was largely inspired by what he had observed of monastic life at Optina Pustyn – there is another image of a young child's death. At Ilyusha's funeral Alyosha Karamazov rejoices with his young companions, sharing their faith that 'all shall rise again from the dead'. 'You are all dear to me, boys, Alyosha says ...

'... from this day forth I have a place in my heart for you all, and I beg you to keep a place in your hearts for me! Well, and who has united us in this kind, good feeling which we shall remember and intend to remember all our lives? Who, if not Ilyusha, the good boy, the dear boy, precious to us for ever! Let us never forget him. May his memory live for ever in our hearts from this time forth!'

'Yes, yes, for ever, for ever!' the boys cried in their ringing voices, with softened faces.

'Let us remember his face and his clothes and his poor little boots, his coffin and his unhappy sinful father, and how boldly he stood up for him alone against the whole school.'

'We will remember, we will remember,' cried the boys. 'He was brave, he was good!'

'Ah, how I loved him!' exclaimed Kolya.

'Ah, children, ah, dear friends, don't be afraid of life! How good life is when one does something good and just!'

'Yes, yes,' the boys repeated enthusiastically.

'Karamazov, we love you!' a voice, probably Kartashov's, cried impulsively.

'We love you, we love you!' they all caught it up. There were tears in the eyes of many of them.

'Hurrah for Karamazov!' Kolya shouted ecstatically.

'And may the dead boy's memory live for ever!' Alyosha added again with feeling.

'For ever!' the boys chimed in again.

'Karamazov,' cried Kolya, 'can it be true what's taught us in religion, that we shall all rise again from the dead and shall live and see each other, all, Ilyusha, too?'

'Certainly we shall all rise again, certainly we shall see each other and shall tell each other with joy and gladness all that has happened!' Alyosha answered, half laughing, half enthusiastic.

It is this belief in the resurrection of the soul that underlies the insistent emphasis on the gladness, gaiety and the non-puritanical character of Christianity in Dostoevsky's writings. 'My friends, pray to God for gladness,' Zossima tells the monks. 'Be glad as children, as the birds of heaven. And let not the sin of men confound you in your doings ... Do not say: "Sin is mighty, wickedness is mighty, evil environment is mighty, and we are lonely and helpless, and evil environment is wearing us away and hindering our good work from being done." Fly from that dejection, children!' The most dramatic assertion of this Christian joyousness comes in Alyosha's dream of the miracle at Cana. (It is significant that in his letters Dostoevsky described this as the most essential scene in the novel.)[69] Following Zossima's death the monks had expected that his body would remain miraculously incorruptible; when this does not occur Alyosha is tempted to despair of his faith. As he rests in his cell, listening to Father Paissy intone the words of the Psalter over the body of Zossima, he dreams of Christ's miraculous changing of the water into wine at the marriage feast in Cana. His thoughts turn to the significance of this, the first miracle performed by Christ. 'It was not men's grief but their joy Christ visited,' he muses. 'He worked his first miracle to help men's gladness ... He who loves men loves their gladness too ... His Mother knew that he had come not only to make his great terrible sacrifice. She knew that his heart was open even to the simple, artless merry-making of some obscure and unlearned people, who had warmly bidden him to their poor wedding.' In his dream the dead Zossima comes to Alyosha to release him from his dejection, inviting him to share the joy which is the essence of the Christian vision of life:

> The elder raised Alyosha by the hand and he rose from his knees.
> 'We are rejoicing,' the little, thin old man went on. We are drinking the new wine, the wine of new, great gladness; do you see how many guests? Here are the bride and bridegroom, here is the wise governor of the feast, he is tasting the new wine. Why do you wonder at me? I gave an onion to a beggar, so I too, am here. And many here have given only an onion each – only one little onion ... What are all our deeds? And you, my gentle one, you, my kind boy, you too have known how to give a famished woman an onion to-day. Begin your work, dear one, begin it, gentle one! ... Do you see our Sun, do you see Him?'
> 'I am afraid ... I dare not look,' whispered Alyosha.
> 'Do not fear Him. He is terrible in his greatness, awful in His sublimity, but infinitely merciful. He has made Himself like unto us from love and rejoices with us. He is changing the water into wine that the gladness of the guests may not be cut short. He is expecting new guests. He is calling new ones unceasingly for ever and ever ... There they are bringing new wine. Do you see they are bringing the vessels? ...'
> Something glowed in Alyosha's heart, something filled it till it ached, tears of rapture rose from his soul ...He stretched out his hands, uttered a cry and waked up.

Faith, therefore, is the source of the hopefulness which enables man to transcend the sufferings of temporal existence. Self-illumination, humility and penitence are, in turn, the essential prerequisites for faith, as has been shown in earlier sections. The ultimate source of faith, however, and the foundation

of the whole Dostoevskeyan vision of Christian fulfilment, is the all-encompassing spirit of brotherhood and love which is repeatedly affirmed throughout his novels, especially *The Brothers Karamazov*. This is what is finally
disclosed to Alyosha in his dream as he comes to realise that Christian belief
is sustained, not by the wonders of miracle, but by service and love of his fellowman. This is the thought which overwhelms him as he prepares to leave
the monastery, to 'sojourn in the world', as Zossima had bidden him in his
dream:

> In his rapture he was weeping even over those stars, which were shining
> to him from the abyss of space, and 'he was not ashamed of that
> ecstasy'. There seemed to be threads from all those innumerable worlds
> of God, linking his soul to them, and it was trembling all over 'in
> contact with other worlds'. He longed to forgive everyone and for
> everything, and to beg forgiveness. Oh, not for himself but for all men,
> for all and for everything. 'And others are praying for me too', echoed
> again in his soul. But with every instant he felt clearly and, as it were,
> tangibly that something firm and unshakable as that vault of heaven
> had entered into his soul. It was as though some idea had seized the
> sovereignty of his mind – and it was for all his life and for ever and ever.
> He had fallen on the earth a weak boy, but he rose up a resolute champi-
> on, and he knew and felt it suddenly at the very moment of his ecstasy.
> And never, never, all his life long, could Alyosha forget that minute.
>
> 'Someone visited my soul in that hour', he used to say afterwards,
> with implicit faith in his words.
>
> Within three days he left the monastery in accordance with the
> words of his elder, who had bidden him 'sojourn in the world'.

'EACH IS RESPONSIBLE FOR ALL'

The significance of Alyosha's dream lies in its disclosure that faith is rooted in
the authentic power of love. Three aspects of this theme are explored in *The
Brothers Karamazov*: one, the idea of love as an active expression of altruistic
fellowship, requiring a constant struggle against the tendencies in nature that
prevent its fulfilment; two, the idea of *sobornost* or universal brotherhood as its
communal fulfilment; and three, the idea of love as a celebration of God's
immanent presence in the natural universe and the means to individual self-
transcendence by virtue of its disclosure of the presence of the infinite, the
intemporal and the unconditioned in the circumstances of everyday life.

The first of these themes is introduced in the scene between Father

Zossima and Madame Hohlakov which occurs at an early point in the novel. Father Zossima has cured her daughter of a serious malady and she returns to ask how she can recover her lost faith. 'If everyone has faith, where did it come from,' she asks. 'How can I prove that God exists?' 'There's no proving it,' the elder replies, 'though you can be convinced of it.' 'You can be convinced,' he says, 'by the experience of active love ... Strive to love your neighbour actively and indefatigably. In as far as you advance in love you will grow surer of the reality of God and of the immortality of your soul.' When she replies that she loves humanity and dreams of forsaking all her wealth to work with the sick and the destitute, Father Zossima makes a crucial distinction between the abstract love of humanity – which he sees as a subtle form of self-love – and the genuinely selfless altruism which begins in the immediacy of the interpersonal and extends therefrom into the wider sphere of the community and of humanity as a whole. He illustrates his distinction through an anecdote about the doctor who loved mankind but could not endure those who were closest to him:

> 'It's just the same story as a doctor once told me,' observed the elder. 'He was a man getting on in years, and undoubtedly clever. He spoke as frankly as you, though in jest, in bitter jest.' 'I love humanity,' he said, 'but I wonder at myself. The more I love humanity in general, the less I love man in particular. In my dreams,' he said, 'I have often come to making enthusiastic schemes for the service of humanity, and perhaps I might actually have faced crucifixion if it had been suddenly necessary; and yet I am incapable of living in the same room with anyone for two days together, as I know by experience. As soon as anyone is near me, his personality disturbs my self-complacency and restricts my freedom. In twenty-four hours I begin to hate the best of men: one because he's too long over his dinner; another because he has a cold and keeps on blowing his nose. I become hostile to people the moment they come close to me. But it has always happened that the more I detest men individually the more ardent becomes my love for humanity.'

Ivan Karamazov points in similar fashion to the difficulty of 'loving one's neighbour'. 'I could never understand how one could love one's neighbour,' he exclaims to Alyosha. 'It's just one's neighbours to my mind that one can't love, though one might love those at a distance ... To my thinking Christlike love for men is a miracle impossible on earth.' Zossima, while similarly recognising the difficulty of loving one's neighbour, insists that it is possible always, but emphasises the struggle that is necessary to achieve it. 'Brothers, love is a teacher,' he tells the monks assembled around his death-bed, 'but one must know how to acquire it, for it is hard to acquire, it is dearly bought, it is won slowly by long labour.' 'Love in action is a harsh and dreadful thing compared with love in dreams,' he tells Madame Hohlakov. He describes the great effort of will and perseverance that is necessary for its attainment:

> Above all avoid falsehood, every kind of falsehood, especially falsehood to yourself. Watch over your own deceitfulness and look into it every hour, every minute. Avoid being scornful, both to others and to yourself. What seems to you bad within you will grow purer from the very fact of observing it in yourself. Avoid fear, too, though fear is only the consequence of every sort of falsehood. Never be frightened at your own faint-heartedness in attaining love. Don't be frightened overmuch even at your evil actions. I am sorry I can say nothing more consoling to you, for love in action is a harsh and dreadful thing compared with love in dreams. Love in dreams is greedy for immediate action, rapidly performed and in the sight of all. Men will even give their lives if only the ordeal does not last long but is soon over, with all looking on and applauding as though on the stage. But active love is labour and fortitude, and for some people too, perhaps, a complete science. But I predict that just when you see with horror that in spite of all your efforts you are getting further from your goal instead of nearer to it — at that very moment I predict that you will reach it and behold clearly the miraculous power of the Lord who has been all the time loving and mysteriously guiding you.

The practice of active love, focussed initially on the immediate circle of relationships in which every individual person exists, extends naturally, Zossima says, into a responsibility and concern for the welfare of humanity as a whole. 'Every one of us is responsible for all men and everything on earth,' he declares as he unfolds his vision of a society united in the spirit of brotherhood. The idea of *sobornost* – a concept that has deep roots in the traditions of Russian Orthodoxy – is based on the combined principles of individual and communal responsibility, i.e. the responsibility of each individual for the good of the entire community in which he exists and of the community in turn for each of its members and by extension for all of mankind. 'There is only one means of salvation,' Zossima says, 'then take yourself and make yourself responsible for all men's sins, that is the truth, you know, friends, for as soon as you sincerely make yourself responsible for everything and for all men, you will see at once that it is really so, and that you are to blame for everyone and for all things.' In pursuit of the ideal of *sobornost* man must seek to conquer his selfishness and pride, exercising his freedom in the practice of active love.

The ideal society of which he dreams is one founded on the exercise of personal freedom and responsibility — not on the precepts of an abstract ideology:

> I dream of seeing, and seem to see clearly our future. It will come to pass, that even the most corrupt of our rich will end by being ashamed of his riches before the poor, and the poor, seeing his humility, will understand and give way before him, will respond joyfully and kindly to his honourable shame. Believe me that it will end in that; things are moving to that. Equality is to be found only in the spiritual dignity of man, and that will only be understood among us.

It is the practice of active love that gives meaning to existence, Zossima says. 'If you love everything you will perceive the divine mystery in things,' he tells his monks. 'Once you perceive it you will begin to comprehend it better every day.' That meaning derives from his belief that God is immanently present in his creation and that love, being actively focussed on this, discloses the intentional presence of God in the whole of phenomenal reality. 'Look around you at the gifts of God, the clear sky, the pure air, the tender grass, the birds,' he urges his monks. 'Nature is beautiful and sinless,' he says, 'and we, only we, are sinful and foolish, and we don't understand that life is heaven, for we have only to understand that and it will at once be fulfilled in all its beauty, we shall embrace each other and weep.' In a beautiful lyrical sequence he symbolically links the dynamism of nature with the miracle of Genesis, i.e. with the act of creation that brought the universe into being and to which it endlessly testifies by its order and its beauty:

> It was a bright, warm, still July night, a cool mist rose from the broad river, we could hear the splash of a fish, the birds were still, all was hushed and beautiful, everything praying to God. Only we too were not sleeping, the lad and I, and we talked of the beauty of this world of God's and of the great mystery of it. Every blade of grass, every insect, ant, and golden bee, all so marvellously know their path, though they have not intelligence, they bear witness to the mystery of God and continually accomplish it themselves. I saw the dear lad's heart was moved. He told me that he loved the forest and the forest birds. He was a birdcatcher, knew the note of each of them, could call each bird. 'I know nothing better than to be in the forest,' said he, 'though all things are good.'
> 'Truly,' I answered him, 'all things are good and fair, because all is truth. Look,' said I, 'at the horse, that great beast that is so near to man; or the lowly, pensive ox, which feeds him and works for him; look

at their faces, what meekness, what devotion to man, who often beats them mercilessly. What gentleness, what confidence and what beauty! It's touching to know that there's no sin in them, for all, all except man, is sinless, and Christ has been with them before us.'

'Why,' asked the boy, 'is Christ with them too?'

'It cannot be so,' said I, 'since the Word is for all. All creation and all creatures, every leaf is striving to the Word, singing glory to God, weeping to Christ, unconsciously accomplishing this by the mystery of their sinless life.'

Love, therefore, he suggests, is the basis of all faith, by virtue of its disclosure of the presence of the infinite in the finite, the timeless in the temporal. Before his death, Stepan Trofimovich proclaims his belief in the immortality disclosed through love. 'Love is higher than existence ... love is the crown of existence,' he declares. 'My immortality is necessary if only because God would not do anything unjust to extinguish completely the flame of love for him once kindled in my heart.' 'God is necessary to me,' he says, 'if only because he is the only being we can love eternally.' Without the sense of the infinite afforded by faith, existence becomes meaningless, he concludes: 'The whole law of human existence consists merely of making it possible for every man to bow down before what is infinitely great. If man were deprived of the infinitely great, he would refuse to go on living and die of despair. The infinite and immeasurable,' he says, 'is as necessary to man as the little planet which he inhabits.' The force that gives meaning to life, Shatov declares, is the quest for the infinite – a quest which is empowered and sustained not by reason, logic or science, but by the faith which derives from love:

> Reason and science have always, to-day and from the very beginning of time, played a secondary and a subordinate part; and so they will to the end of time. People are formed and moved by quite a different force, a force that dominates and exercises its authority over them, the origin of which, however, is unknown and inexplicable. That force is the force of an unquenchable desire to go on to the end and, at the same time, to deny the existence of an end. It is the force of an incessant and persistent affirmation of its existence and a denial of death. It is the spirit of life, as the Scripture says, 'rivers of living water', the running dry of which is threatened in Revelation. It is the aesthetic principle, as the philosophers call it, an ethical principle, with which they identify it, the 'seeking of God', as I call it much more simply.

Ironically, Ivan Karamazov by defining the basis of his own scepticism, unwittingly identifies the essential links between love and the infinite. Miusov quotes his words: 'If you were to destroy in mankind the belief in immortality, not only love but every living force maintaining the life of the world would at once be dried up.' By asserting the interdependence of faith and love, he simultaneously asserts the self-transcendence that each affords. Conversely, Zossima, in his reflections on 'hell and hell fire', defines eternal damnation as an existence without love. He illustrates his theme with an anecdote inspired by the parable of Dives and Lazarus:

> Once in infinite existence, immeasurable in time and space, a spiritual creature was given, on his coming to earth, the power of saying: 'I am and I love.' Once, only once, there was given him a moment of active, living love and for that was earthly life given him, and with it times and seasons. And that happy creature rejected the priceless gift, prized it and loved it not, scorned it and remained callous. Such a one, having left the earth, sees Abraham's bosom and talks with Abraham as we are told in the parable of the rich man and Lazarus, and beholds heaven and can go up to the Lord. But that is just his torment, to rise up to the Lord without ever having loved, to be brought close to those who have loved when he has despised their love. For he sees clearly and says to himself: 'Now I have understanding and though I now thirst to love, there will be nothing great, no sacrifice in my love, for my earthly life is over, and Abraham will not come even with a drop of living water (that is the gift of earthly, active life) to cool the fiery thirst of spiritual love which burns in me now, though I despised it on earth; there is no more life for me and there will be no more time! Even though I would gladly give my life for others, it can never be, for that life is passed which can be sacrificed for love, and now there is a gulf between that life and this existence.'

In mortal life, Zossima says, man is poised between the loving and unloving tendencies in his nature, the tension between the two being indicative of the radical character of his freedom. The suffering engendered by this is inescapable, he says, but is endlessly surmountable through the will or election to love. This is vividly asserted in his words on the conquest of despair: 'If all men abandon you and even drive you away by force, then when you are left alone, fall on the earth and kiss it, water it with your tears and it will bring forth fruit even though no one has seen or heard you in your solitude.' The will to love is nurtured by prayer, he says, by the spirit's election for love, its intentional seeking after God:

Young man, be not forgetful of prayer. Every time you pray, if your prayer is sincere there will be new feeling and new meaning in it, which will give you fresh courage, and you will understand that prayer is an education. Remember too, every day, and whenever you can, repeat to yourself: 'Lord, have mercy on all who appear before Thee to-day.' For every hour and every moment thousands of men leave life on this earth, and their souls appear before God. And how many of them depart in solitude, unknown, sad, dejected, that no one mourns for them or even knows whether they have lived or not. And behold, from the other end of the earth perhaps, your prayer for their rest will rise up to God though you knew them not nor they you. How touching it must be to a soul standing in dread before the Lord to feel at that instant that, for him too, there is one to pray, that there is a fellow creature left on earth to love him too. And God will look on you both more graciously, for if you have had so much pity on him, how much more will He have pity Who is infinitely more loving and merciful than you. And He will forgive him for your sake.

'It was his genuine conviction that evil could not be eradicated by violence, that brute force could only be fought not with brute force but with the infinite strength of love.'[70] So declared Vladimir Soloviev in his graveside eulogy for Dostoevsky. The ideal of brotherhood, of 'each being responsible for all', as advocated by Zossima, together with his consistent emphasis on the virtues of meekness and humility, would seem to preclude the use of violence in any circumstances, including those traditionally recognised by Christian theologians as constituting legitimate grounds for its employment, such as the need for self-defence or the execution of criminals. 'To kill for murder is an immeasurably greater evil than the crime itself,' Prince Myshkin says. 'Murder by legal process is immeasurably more dreadful than murder by a brigand.' There are many passages in Dostoevsky's Diary, however, which explicitly justify violence and warfare, and which seem starkly in conflict with the spirit of his fictional writings, particularly with the emphasis on meekness and humility in *The Idiot* and *The Brothers Karamazov*. In an essay, for example, entitled, 'Not Always Is War A Scourge, Sometimes it is a Salvation', we find the following: 'Believe me that in certain, if not in all cases (save in the case of civil wars) war is a process by means of which specifically international peace is achieved with a minimum loss of blood, with minimum sorrow and effort, and at least more or less normal relations between the nations are evolved.'[71](sic) It is significant, however, that he is careful not to endorse the morality of war as a general principle, but recognises it as an historical necessity, inevitable in the relations that generally exist between nations. 'Thus,' he writes, ' it appears that war, too, is needed for some purpose, that it is salutary and that it alleviates mankind. This is abominable, if conceived abstractly, but in practice this seems to be so,' he concludes.[72]

The Brothers Karamazov, however, leans decidedly towards an endorsement of the pacifist position. Two episodes in the novel are highly indicative of this. The first is the episode where Alyosha is viciously attacked by a young hooligan, but refrains from attacking him, even in his own defence. The following exchange occurs at the final stage in the encounter:

> The boy waited in silent defiance, certain that now Alyosha would attack him. Seeing that even now he would not, his rage was like a little wild beast's; he flew at Alyosha himself, and before Alyosha had time to move, the spiteful child had seized his left hand with both of his and bit his middle finger. He fixed his teeth in it and it was ten seconds before he let go. Alyosha cried out with pain and pulled his finger away with all his might. The child let go at last and retreated to his former distance. Alyosha's finger had been badly bitten to the bone, close to the nail; it began to bleed. Alyosha took out his handkerchief and bound it tightly round his injured hand. He was a full minute bandaging it. The boy stood waiting all the time. At last Alyosha raised his gentle eyes and looked at him.
>
> 'Very well,' he said, 'you see how badly you have bitten me. That's enough isn't it? Now tell me what have I done to you?'
>
> The boy stared in amazement.
>
> 'Though I don't know how and it's the first time I've seen you,' Alyosha went on with the same serenity, 'yet I must have done something to you – you wouldn't have hurt me like this for nothing. So what have I done? How have I wronged you, tell me?'
>
> Instead of answering, the boy broke into a loud tearful wail and ran away.

This episode, a practical illustration of the application of Christ's injunction 'not to resist one who is evil', is followed by a similar one later in the novel – Zossima's story of the duel, which he recalls in the course of his disquisition on brotherhood. He recalls how he sought reconciliation with his opponent at the moment when they faced one another with their pistols poised for a bloody encounter. 'Forgive me, young fool that I am, sir,' I said, 'for my unprovoked insult to you and for forcing you to fire at me. I am ten times worse than you and more maybe.' To the question from his visitor, how precisely he felt at the moment he sought reconciliation with his enemy, Zossima spoke of the trust which is created through the act of non-resistance, and this, he suggests, is a crucial step in the attainment of *sobornost*: 'All the while he was speaking I was looking at him straight in the face,' he says, 'and I felt all at once a complete trust in him and great curiosity on my side also, for I felt there was some strange secret in his soul.' His opponent treats him as a coward, but violence is averted nonetheless. Subsequently, Zossima, closely echoing Christ's words in the Sermon on the Mount, counsels his monks never to avenge wrong-doing, to turn the other cheek – responding to evil with forgiveness, trusting in God to reach the soul of the evil-doer. That spirit of forgiveness, which is manifested in the ideal of non-resistance to evil, is rooted, he says, in the humility and faith on which the practice of *sobornost* is ultimately based:

> If the evil of men moves you to indignation and overwhelming distress, even to a desire for vengeance on the evil-doers, shun above all things that feeling. Go at once and seek suffering for yourself, as though you were guilty of that wrong. Accept that suffering and bear it and your heart will find comfort, and you will understand that you too are guilty, for you might have been a light to the evil-doers, even as one man sinless, and you were not a light to them. If you had been a light, you would have lightened the path for others too, and the evil-doer might perhaps have been saved by your light from his sin. And even though your light was shining, yet you see men were not saved by it, hold firm and doubt not the power of the heavenly light. Believe that if they were not saved, they will be saved hereafter. And if they are not saved hereafter, then their sons will be saved, for your light will not die even when you are dead. The righteous man departs but his light remains. Men are always saved after the death of the deliverer. Men reject their prophets and slay them, but they love their martyrs and honour those whom they have slain. You are working for the whole, you are acting for the future. Seek no reward, for great is your reward even on this earth: the spiritual joy which is only vouchsafed to the righteous man. Fear not the great nor the mighty, but be wise and ever serene. Know the measure, know the times, study that. When you are left alone, pray. Love to throw yourself on the earth and kiss it. Kiss the earth and love it with an unceasing, consuming love. Love all men, love everything. Seek that rapture and ecstasy. Water the earth with the tears of your joy and love those tears. Don't be ashamed of that ecstasy, prize it, for it is a gift of God and a great one; it is not given to many but only to the elect.

It is important, by way of conclusion, to emphasise the intrinsically religious character of the ideal of *sobornost* and to distinguish it clearly from the humanistic social ideologies with which it has sometimes been linked. There is abundant evidence, some of which was cited at the beginning of this chapter, of Dostoevsky's rejection of Christian humanism and his insistence on the transcendental character of Christian truth. It is in this context that his social ideals must be defined. As was intimated earlier, a clear distinction is maintained in Dostoevsky's writings (as in Tolstoy's) between the 'abstract' or utopian ideal of social equality and the authentic spirit of communal responsibility that springs from the practice of love in the immediate realm of interpersonal mutuality. The contradictions of an abstract love of humanity are emphasised in the words from Father Zossima to Madame Hohlakov which were cited earlier; they are emphasised again in the satiric comparisons made by the Ridiculous Man between the utopian dream of universal harmony and the ideal of earthly brotherhood which is realisable only through humility, penitence and faith. Brotherhood will not be achieved through ideological theory, Zossima says – 'no sort of scientific teaching, no kind of common interest will ever teach men to share property and privileges with equal consideration for all.' He emphasises the dependence of his vision of social transformation on the process of individual self-reform: 'To transform the world, to recreate it afresh, men must turn into another path psychologically. Until you have become really, in actual fact, a brother to everyone, brotherhood will not come to pass.'

It is in the light of such distinctions that several of Dostoevsky's protagonists so vehemently condemn the systematised, rationalistic socialism of the ideologists, many of whose ideals Dostoevsky had himself supported in his youth, before abandoning them eventually during his sojourn in the Siberian prison-camp. Shatov describes socialism as 'a half-science', based entirely on the tenets of reason and therefore essentially humanistic. 'Socialism is by its very nature bound to be atheistic because it has proclaimed from the very first that it is an atheistic institution and that it intends to organise itself exclusively on the principles of science and reason.' This position is reiterated by Alyosha Karamazov who, for all his youthful idealism, declares he cannot be a socialist, because of his belief in immortality: 'For socialism is not merely the labour question,' he says, 'it is before all things the atheistic question, the question of the form taken by atheism to-day, the question of the tower of Babel built without God, not to mount to Heaven from earth but to set up Heaven on earth.' The naivete of the materialist theory of consciousness, and its implicit denial of individual freedom, is exposed in a brilliantly satiric analysis by Razumikhin in *Crime and Punishment*:

'Nothing is admitted!' Razumikhin interrupted heatedly. 'I'm not wrong! I can show you their books: they reduce everything to one common cause – environment. Environment is the root of all evil – and nothing else! A favourite phrase. And the direct consequence of it is that if society is organised on normal lines, all crimes will vanish at once, for there will be nothing to protest against, and all men will become righteous in the twinkling of an eye. Human nature isn't taken into account at all. Human nature is banished. Human nature isn't supposed to exist. They deny that mankind, following the lines of historical development to the very end in a living way, will at last be transformed into a normal society. On the contrary, they maintain that a social system, emerging out of someone's mathematical brain, will at once organise mankind and transform it in an instant into a sinless and righteous society, and that much quicker than any living process and without any normal historical development ... Human nature wants life. It has not completed the living process. It is too soon for it to be relegated to the graveyard. You can't jump over human nature by logic alone! Logic can only foresee three possibilities, but there is a whole million of them! Disregard the million and reduce it all to a question of comfort? What an easy solution of the problem! So temptingly clear and no need to think at all!.

Shatov's and Razumikhin's views, however, represent one side only of a very complex dialectic, the rationalistic and atheistic character of socialism being merely one aspect of its appeal for those committed to realising the age-old dream of a more just and egalitarian society. In a typically Dostoevskeyan paradox, socialism is shown to be ultimately both rational and irrational, its appeal to young radicals consisting essentially in the contradictory manner in which it combines both tendencies. The irrational aspect, for instance, is implicit in the Ridiculous Man's presentation of the utopian vision of an earthly Paradise as essentially a *dream* – one to be contrasted with the reality of life on earth and with the struggle necessary to achieve justice in the conditions that actually exist. In *The Possessed* Stepan Verkhovensky similarly argues that the appeal of socialism lies precisely in its dream-like irrationality, in what he sees as a spurious, essentially sentimental religiosity. 'What fascinates them,' he says, describing a group of young radicals, 'is not realism but the sentimental and idealist side of socialism; its religious aspect as it were; its poetry – all of it second-hand, of course.' Shigalov comes to a similar conclusion, tracing the origins of social utopianism back to Plato and the early classical philosophers: 'Having devoted all my energies to the study of the social organisation of the society of the future which is to replace our present one, I have come to the conclusion that all the inventors of social systems, from the ancient times to our present year, have been dreamers, story-tellers, fools who contradicted themselves and had no idea of natural science or that strange animal called man. Plato, Rousseau, Fourier, aluminium pillars, all that is only good for sparrows, and not for human society.' Ultimately, it would appear, for Dostoevsky, socialism embodied a very profound and complex paradox: being simultaneously the product of reason and unreason, its appeal lay in the very potent, but spurious and contradictory, fashion in which it could unite the attractions both of reason and faith.

For all his condemnations of socialism, there is abundant evidence, however, both in his fictional and non-fictional writings, that Dostoevsky himself shared the revulsion of contemporary socialists for the injustices of capitalism and the horrors of materialist exploitation in contemporary European society. His comparison of the capitalist, Luzhin, with the socialist Lebezyatnikov in *Crime and Punishment* clearly favours the latter and exposes the greed and all-consuming self-interest that underlies the capitalist philosophy. In his *Winter Notes on Summer Impressions*, a series of travel sketches that was written in 1863, he roundly condemned the materialist affluence he had witnessed in European cities, showing particular contempt for the French bourgeoisie and considerable sympathy for the newly emerging utopian movement. Even Zossima, while condemning doctrinaire socialists, concedes that 'there are many good ones among them'. Dostoevsky's fellow-countryman, Nikolai Berdyaev – a reformed revolutionary like himself – described him as 'a Christian Orthodox socialist of an original kind' who is 'oriented towards the coming Kingdom of God', and contrasts him with the revolutionaries who 'wanted to build a tower of Babel on this earth'.[73]

What was singularly original in Dostoevsky's writings was the sharpness and depth of their analysis of the inadequacies of ideological socialism several decades before the Bolshevik Revolution: an analysis that now seems extraordinarily prophetic in the aftermath of the collapse of governments dedicated to its propagation for a period of more than seventy years. What was traditionalist, and specifically Christian, about his vision of social transformation was his insistence that such a vision is realisable: but only through the practice of humility, penitence, self-sacrificing love and faith – most of all through the moral and spiritual precepts implicit in the injunction that 'every one of us is responsible for all men and everything on earth'. That was the essence of the doctrine of *sobornost* and the basis of its conception of social transformation as simultaneously a process of individual and community reform.

'Where Love Is, There God Is Also': The Novels and Stories of Leo Tolstoy

ELEMENTS OF A CHRISTIAN AESTHETIC

In view of the persistent controversy that has been focussed on the status of Christianity in Tolstoy's writings, it seems appropriate at the outset to clarify the precise sense in which the term 'Christian' can be used in relation to his work. Tolstoy himself wrote the following note in his diary on 24 August 1906, four years before his death: 'I am counted among the anarchists, but I am not an anarchist, but a Christian. My anarchism is only the application of Christianity to human relationships.'[1] Despite the emphatic nature of statements such as this, several notable scholars have disputed the validity of his claim to be described as a Christian. R.F. Christian, for example, the editor of Tolstoy's *Diaries* and *Letters*, has written: 'Was Tolstoy a Christian? I would say not. He did not observe the ritual of the Orthodox Church or subscribe to its dogmas. He did not recognise Christ as the only-begotten Son of God or believe in His physical resurrection. He had no strong faith in a life after death, although his views on the subject were not rigid. At times he seemed more of a Hindu or a Buddhist than a Christian. He was excommunicated by the Orthodox Church and buried without any rites on his estate at his own request.'[2] Tolstoy indeed rejected the conventions of institutionalised religion and could not, as this passage suggests, be called a Christian in any orthodox sense of the term. To say this, however, is merely to identify the informal character of his Christian beliefs, their independence of the traditions and dogmas of the Churches. His Christianity, like that of his contemporary, Kierkegaard, lies outside the confines of institutionalised faith, indeed was deliberately chosen to be so, as this chapter will attempt to show in some detail presently. Insisting on the radical freedom of the experience of faith, he argued that Christian belief and morality must be guided by the dictates of conscience alone and by the authority of the Christian scriptures by which these should be informed.

Father Georges Florovsky, a well-known Orthodox theologian, has questioned the authenticity of Tolstoy's Christianity on grounds similar to those of Christian. In his essay, 'Three Masters: The Quest for Religion in Nineteenth Century Russian Literature', he argued that Tolstoy was a 'child of the Enlightenment', deeply influenced by the writings of Rousseau and Kant, naively confident of the infallibility of reason and the author of a rationalised

Christianity deeply imbued with the spirit of idealist philosophy.[3] He endorsed the view of the Russian historian, Kulikovsky, that Tolstoy's was 'not a religion of the soul, but a religion of syllogisms' and pointed to the 'total absence of transcensus' in his interpretations of the scriptures. Tolstoy, he said, was pre-Christian in his mentality, was deeply sympathetic to stoicism and was determined to cleanse religion of mysticism and sentimentality. The extent to which these claims are explicitly contradicted by the evidence of Tolstoy's writings – both fictional and non-fictional – is something that will hopefully be made clear in the course of this chapter. It should suffice for the moment to point to the difficulty of reconciling the image of the rationalist thinker constructed by Florovsky with that of a writer who based all his beliefs on Christ's teachings in the Sermon on the Mount, especially on the absolute authority of the law of love, as is repeatedly attested by his novels and stories, particularly his last great work of religious fiction, the novel *Resurrection*.

Similar charges of creating a rationalised Christianity have been levelled at Tolstoy by the Russian-Jewish existentialist philosopher, Lev Shestov. In an early work, *Dostoevsky, Tolstoy and Nietzsche*, Shestov argued that while Tolstoy drew extensively on the scriptures, he ultimately based all his teachings on a rationalistic and abstract ideal of the Good. 'Such a faith,' he said, 'does not really exclude absolute atheism, complete unbelief, and it leads inevitably to the desire to destroy ... to crush others in the name of a principle.'[4] 'Even though he always refers to the Gospel there is very little that is Christian in his doctrine,' Shestov continued. 'If we wanted to compare his works with Scripture, we could only think of the Old Testament, of the prophets, whom he resembles in the character of his preaching and the strictness of his demands. He does not wish to persuade men but to intimidate them.' Here again an obvious contradiction is apparent. If Tolstoy drew as extensively from the scriptures as Shestov allows – he did in fact produce several volumes of exegetic writings, most of which are focussed on the New Testament, not on the Old – it seems absurd to suggest that his ethical convictions were not based on the moral injunctions of scripture but on an abstract notion of the Good constructed purely from rationalist deduction. Indeed there are numerous instances – as in the lengthy disquisition on nonresistance to evil in *My Religion* – where Tolstoy explicitly justified his ethical teachings on the basis of the authority of scripture alone. It should be said that Shestov's position on these issues was considerably modified in a late essay, 'The Gift of Prophecy', and in a related work, *In Job's Balances*,[5] which he published towards the end of his life, but the charge of rationalist reductionism levelled by others against Tolstoy was given strong support in his writings and has endured in subsequent interpretations of Tolstoy's work, both by eastern and by western scholars.

The charge of rationalising or humanising Christianity has recently been made also by George Steiner in *Tolstoy or Dostoevsky*, where the Legend of the Grand Inquisitor is seen as an allegorical expression of the differences in outlook between the two writers, Tolstoy being identified with the Inquisitor and Dostoevsky with Christ. Pointing to Tolstoy's supposed denial of the doctrine of immortality (he did in fact affirm his belief in a spiritual but not a physical immortality in *My Religion* and in his 'Reply to the Synod's Edict of Excommunication'), Steiner charges Tolstoy with reducing Christianity to a humanised creed and suggests he shared with utopian socialists a belief in the prospect of an earthly paradise attained through the ideal of brotherly love. 'Both the Grand Inquisitor and the later Tolstoy stood in mysterious rivalry to their images of God,' he writes, 'Both were intent upon establishing utopian kingdoms in which God would be a rare or unwelcome guest. In their different ways, they exemplified one of Dostoevsky's essential theses: that humanitarian socialism is, fatally, a prelude to atheism.'[6] It will be shown later that far from espousing the cause of socialism Tolstoy argued that social reform must always be founded on spiritual self-reform – a position profoundly consistent with Christian teaching – and that he explicitly disassociated himself from ideological socialism in works such as the *Essays From Tula* and *The Kingdom of God is Within You*. (Neither of these works is mentioned in Steiner's study.) Indeed one of the sharpest refutations of Tolstoy's supposed socialist leanings can be found in some words by Lenin to his followers in an essay of 1911:

> In our days any attempt to idealise Tolstoy's teaching, to justify or tone down his doctrine of 'non-resistance', his appeals to the 'Spirit', his call for 'moral self-improvement', his teaching about 'conscience' and about 'universal love', his preaching of asceticism and quietism etc., would result in most direct and far-reaching harm.[7]

As for the outrageous linking of Tolstoy with the Grand Inquisitor, one brief quotation from *The Kingdom of God is Within You* should suffice to demonstrate its absurdity. 'A Christian,' Tolstoy wrote, 'is free from every human authority by the fact that he regards the divine law of love implanted in the soul of every man, and of which Christ has made us conscious, as the sole guide of his life and of the lives of others.'[8]

Behind all these views is a general overestimation of the place of reason in the evolution of Tolstoy's religious and ethical beliefs. Rousseau and Kant indeed were potent influences on his intellectual formation, especially in his early years. Rousseau's belief in the natural goodness and innocence of man greatly strengthened Tolstoy's admiration for the values and lifestyle of the simple peasant people, but the doctrine of natural goodness was itself greatly modified in his growing awareness of the human capacity for evil, as is evident from his later writings, especially *Resurrection*, his great fictional exploration of the themes of guilt, penitence and expiation. And while he clearly applied his own formidable reasoning powers to the definition of his ethical and religious beliefs, those beliefs were ultimately justified from sources explicitly seen to transcend the spheres of the rational and the empirical. Commenting on the charge that he had rationalised or even secularised Christian teaching, E.B. Greenwood has written: 'It seems to me that nothing is further from the truth than such a view ... Tolstoy's religious quest is a noble endeavour, and one which arguably brought him nearer to exercising the charismatic function of the prophet than any other "Western" man in modern times. His rationalism is not that of a dry legalist. On the contrary, it is inspired by a fervent turning from the dogma and fetishism of priests and the egoism of mystics to the old prophetic message of the centrality of doing justice and loving mercy and walking humbly with God.'[9] There can certainly be no doubting the ultimate subordination of reason to faith that is attested personally by Tolstoy in these words from *A Confession*: 'Rational knowledge, as presented by the learned and the wise, negates the meaning of life, yet the vast masses – humanity as a whole – recognise that this meaning lies in irrational knowledge.'[10] That higher irrational knowledge he defines as the 'faith which affords the possibility of living'. The essential convictions informing this faith were stated explicitly and unambiguously by Tolstoy in his 'Reply to the Synod's Edict of Excommunication':

> What I believe is this: I believe in God whom I understand as spirit, and in Love as the beginning of everything. I believe that the will of God is most clearly and understandably expressed in the teachings of the man called Christ, but I consider it the greatest of blasphemies to look on this man as God and to pray to him. I believe that man's true good lies in following the will of God, and that God's will is for men to love one another and so do unto others as they wish others to do unto them; according to the gospels, this is the whole of the law and the prophets. I believe that the meaning of every man's life lies only in increasing the store of love within him; that this increase of love leads a man to greater and greater blessings in this life, and to blessings after his death that are in proportion to the amount of love within him; and I believe that it contributes more than anything else towards the establishment of the Kingdom of God on earth, that is, towards the establishment of an order under which the discord, deception and violence that now hold sway will be replaced by free agreement, truthfulness and brotherly love between all people. I believe that there is only one way to

progress in love and that that is prayer: not the public prayer in churches that Christ expressly forbade (Matthew 6:5-13), but the solitary prayer of which Christ gave us an example and whose essence lies in the renewal and affirmation in our own consciousness of the meaning of our life and of our dependence on God alone.[11]

Some years before he wrote his Response to the Edict of Excommunication these convictions had been given forceful expression in Tolstoy's *A Confession*, a work of the early 1870s which dramatically describes his 'conversion' to the Christian faith. There are intimations, however, that the growth of his distinctive and highly unconventional Christian faith was a gradual process that matured slowly through the years, beginning as early as the period when he was a student at the University of Kazan. 'I was baptised in the Orthodox Christian faith', he recalled in *A Confession*. 'I was taught it in childhood and all through my boyhood and youth. But when I left the university in my second year at the age of eighteen I no longer believed anything I had been taught.'[12] His rejection of Orthodox, and indeed institutional, Christianity was based on a deep intellectual questioning of the ways in which he believed the Churches had distorted the teachings of Christ – especially on matters such as violence, property and wealth. But while abandoning his observance of the rituals of Orthodox Christianity in the years at Kazan he continued to read the scriptures – especially the Gospel of St Matthew – and maintained the practice of regular meditation and prayer. We find the following Diary entry, for example, for July 1854. (He was then twenty-six years old):

My prayer: 'I believe in one, almighty and good God, in the immortality of the soul, and in eternal retribution for our deeds; I wish to believe in the religion of my fathers and I respect it.'

'Our Father,' etc. 'For the repose and salvation of my parents.' 'I thank Thee, O Lord, for Thy mercies, for this and for that' (here recall all the happiness that has been my lot). 'I pray Thee, inspire me to good undertakings and thoughts, and grant me happiness and success in them. Help me to correct my faults, save me from sickness, suffering, quarrels, debts and humiliations.'

'Grant me to live and die in firm faith and hope in Thee, in love for others and from others, with a clear conscience, and with profit to my neighbour. Grant me to do good and shun evil; but whether good or evil befall me, may Thy holy will be done!'[13]

He did, in fact, briefly resume the practice of church-going as he was completing *Anna Karenina* in 1873 but this renewed enthusiasm for the rituals of

Orthodoxy was short-lived. A short time later he wrote in his Diary: 'If Churchmen are Christians then I'm not a Christian and vice versa.'[14] Long before this he had been giving fictional expression to his belief in the transcendent power of altruistic love, his foremost Christian theme. 'Happiness lies in living for others,' says Dmitri Olenin in *The Cossacks*, Tolstoy's first novel, published in 1863 and probably begun while he served as a soldier in the Caucasus in the early 1850s. 'The desire for happiness,' Olenin says, 'is innate in every man; therefore it is legitimate. When trying to satisfy it selfishly – that is, by seeking for oneself riches, fame, comforts or love – it may happen that circumstances arise which make it impossible to satisfy these desires. It follows that it is these desires that are illegitimate, but not the need for happiness. But what desires can always be satisfied despite external circumstances? What are they? Love, self-sacrifice.' Later he adds: 'The one way to be happy is to love self-denyingly, to love everybody and everything; to spread a web of love on all sides and to take all who come unto it.' The famous declaration on love by Prince Andrei and Pierre's disquisition on God's immanent presence in creation in *War and Peace* are anticipated in a passage occurring towards the end of *The Cossacks*. From a religious standpoint the passage is enormously significant by virtue of its emphasis on the interrelation of human and divine love, its disclosure of the potentiality for *transcensus* Tolstoy saw as being inherent in all love. Olenin is reflecting on his love for the Cossack girl, Maryanka:

> Perhaps in her I love nature: the personification of all that is beautiful in nature; but yet I am not acting by my own will, but some elemental force loves through me; the whole of God's world, all nature, presses this love into my soul and says, love her. I love her not with my mind or my imagination, but with my whole being. Loving her I feel myself to be an integral part of all God's joyous world ... I do not live my own life, there is something stronger than me which directs me. I suffer; but formerly I was dead and only now do I live.

The seeds of Tolstoy's Christian pacifism – his most radical application of the Christian law of love – can similarly be traced to his earliest writings. 'The Raid', a story he wrote in 1852 when he was twenty-four years old, shows his detestation of violence and war and his longing for peace and brotherhood amongst all men. 'Could it be,' the narrator asks, 'that there was not room for all men to live in this wonderful world, under this fathomless starry sky? Was it really possible that in the midst of such natural splendour, feelings of hatred or vengeance, or the passion to destroy one's fellows could reside in the hearts of men?' Three years later in the Sebastopol Sketches he condemned war-making in a similar spirit. The first of the sketches has strong satiric passages pointing to the bestiality of war; the second contrasts its savagery with the beauty and serenity of the natural world and the third implicitly links the practice of the Christian faith with the active pursuit of peace. 'It might be supposed,' the narrator remarks rhetorically, 'that when these men — Christians, recognising the same great law of love — see what they have done, they will instantly fall to their knees in order to repent before Him who, when He gave them life, placed in the soul of each, together with the fear of death, a love of the good and the beautiful, and that they will embrace one another with tears of joy and happiness, like brothers. Not a bit of it!'

All of Tolstoy's religious beliefs, therefore — his belief in God, in the infinity of His love, in the mystery of His immanent presence in creation, in the immortality of the soul, in the power of faith, humility and prayer — all were present in his work from his early years and reached maturity in works such as *A Confession* and *My Religion* as well as in his great works of narrative fiction from *War and Peace* to *Resurrection*. He did not believe that Christ was God, seeing the whole idea as a theological fabrication unsupported by the words of the scripture text. But he did believe in Christ as the Son of God and as Mediator of His divinely inspired message to mankind. Whether he can be described as a Christian or not, on the basis of such beliefs, is an issue beyond the scope of the present study. What can be asserted is that he maintained a deep and lifelong interest in the teachings of Christ and that his own beliefs were profoundly influenced by this. Three positions seem relevant for the purposes of the present study:

1. All his religious beliefs were authenticated and supported from the words of the Christian scriptures. He sought tirelessly to interpret the words of scripture as fully as he could, acquiring competence in the Greek and Hebrew languages to ensure he did so with the most scrupulous attention to its pure and authentic meaning. He meticulously explained his interpretations of the Christian scriptures in several volumes of exegetic prose and conveyed their message of love with all the brilliance of his artistic powers in his novels and stories.

2. All his ethical beliefs were drawn also from the Christian scriptures — especially from The Sermon on the Mount — and his moral teachings were consistently supported from these sources. This applied particularly to the most radical of his moral teachings — those on non-resistance and social reform — where he challenged conventional ethical orthodoxy on the basis of its departure from the authentic message of Christ in the Gospels.

3   His aesthetic beliefs were founded on a conception of the artist's role that was rooted in his religious and ethical beliefs. As a writer he conceived his mission as the communication of Christian truth through the non-didactic, parable-like style of narrative fiction. In works such as *What Is Art?* he explicitly defined his understanding of the role of the artist in these terms and scrupulously adhered to these convictions in his fictional and non-fictional writings.

All of Tolstoy's religious and ethical beliefs will be examined in detail presently. Initially, however, it is necessary to clarify the nature of his artistic purposes as expressed particularly in *What Is Art?* Tolstoy scholars point to the extraordinary degree of integrity that existed between his life and his art. 'In few writers,' wrote T.G. Cain, 'is the greatness of the art so closely related to what may reasonably be called the greatness of the life, the intense spiritual struggles, the doubts, desires and vicissitudes of the man himself'.[15] John Bayley in *Tolstoy and the Novel* spoke of the remarkable degree of self-sufficiency' that is evident in his work. 'The sense of Tolstoy *being* the great world he writes about, must have struck every reader of his work,' he says. For Tolstoy, he adds, 'the creation of character was not a controlled shaping of abstract material' but a 'process of recognition', a recognition of his own self and his beliefs in the world of image and symbol, in the wholeness and harmony of artistic form.[16] All the major characters – Pierre, Prince Andrei, Natasha, Levin, Maslova and Nekhlyudov – embody not only the major themes of the novels they inhabit, but closely reflect the personal quest for truth and spiritual self-fulfilment in which Tolstoy himself was engaged. All these characters are 'I-heroes', wrote Kate Hamburger in her essay 'Tolstoy's Art';[17] all are in some degree autobiographical self-projections of Tolstoy himself, particularly giving expression to the moral and religious truths he intended his novels to convey. As Renato Poggioli has written: 'Tolstoy had always been, even before his conversion, a writer with a message.' Speaking of the 'unique fusion of literary intelligence and ethical insight' that exists in his work, he wrote: 'The world of Tolstoy the creator and the world of Tolstoy the prophet may not fully coincide, but they are closely related to each other.' In works such as 'The Death of Ivan Illych' and the 'Master and Man' stories, he adds, 'Tolstoy was able to convey an allegorical vision the like of which the western world had hardly seen since the waning of mediaeval culture and the decline of religious art.'[18] These interpretations are confirmed in an entry in Tolstoy's Diary for April 1885 in which he declared: 'The whole business of my life is the awareness of and expression of truth.' Significantly, he adds: 'Art is only true art when the inner striving coincides with the awareness of fulfilling the work of God.'[19]

Tolstoy's conception of the relationship between art and faith remains complex, however, despite the apparent simplicity of the sentiments expressed in this Diary entry. Isaiah Berlin has argued that a creative tension existed between Tolstoy's moral and artistic purposes, between his radical pursuit of realism and his determination to communicate the ethico-religious message of the scriptures. He suggests that the narrative brilliance of his novels and stories is to be attributable largely to the conflicts generated by this.[20] For a fuller understanding of this issue we can turn to *What is Art*, the product of fifteen years of reflection by Tolstoy on the nature of art and the most sustained, if somewhat eccentric, statement of his aims and purposes as an artist. At the time of its publication the work was recognised as a powerful diatribe against the fashionable aestheticism of the period, the doctrine of 'art for art's sake'. Tolstoy traced the separation of art from morality and faith back to the Renaissance and saw the whole process as reaching its lowest point of decadence and depravity in the literature of his own time. Insisting that true art must necessarily embody some degree of moral and religious awareness – this being universally present in the experience of man and therefore requiring expression in art – he wrote the following in a preface preceding the work:

> Truth will be known not by him who knows only what has been, and really happens, but by him who recognises what should be according to the will of God. He does not write the truth who describes only what has happened and what this or that man has done, but he who shows what people do that is right – that is, in accord with God's will; and what people do wrong – that is contrary to God's will.
>
> Truth is a path. Christ said, ' I am the way, the truth and the life.'
>
> And he who looks down at his feet will not know the truth, but he who discerns by the sun which way to go.
>
> Verbal compositions are good and necessary, not when they describe what has happened, but when they show what ought to be; not when they tell what people have done, but when they set a value on good and evil – when they show men the narrow path of God's will, which leads to life.[21]

Taken too literally, these words might suggest a didactic, almost evangelical function for art, though the most cursory reading of Tolstoy's fiction would make nonsense of such an assumption. (The complex narrative techniques and devices employed by Tolstoy to give expression to his beliefs are explained by Renato Poggioli in his essay, 'Tolstoy As Man and Artist' and by Kate Hamburger in 'Tolstoy's Art'.) What the passage suggests is that an awareness of the presence of God in the universe is necessary for a full sense of its existential reality. A complete image of reality would have to include a sense of the religious and moral truths which make it wholly meaningful. Art therefore is seen as necessarily involved in the revelation of truths which belong ultimately in the realms of the moral, the spiritual, the religious. Echoing the words of Aquinas, Tolstoy sees it as combining the three classic elements of scholastic aesthetics – the good (*bonum*), the beautiful (*pulchrum*) and the true (*verum*):

> A perfect work of art will be one in which the content is important and significant to all men, and therefore it will be *moral*. The expression will be quite clear, intelligible to all, and therefore *beautiful*; the author's relation to his work will be altogether sincere and heartfelt, and therefore *true*. Imperfect works, but still works of art, will be such productions as satisfy all three conditions though it be but in unequal degree. That alone will be no work of art, in which either the content is quite insignificant and unnecessary to man, or the expression quite unintelligible, or the relation of the author to the work quite insincere. In the degree of perfection attained in each of these respects lies the difference in quality between all true works of art. Sometimes the first predominates, sometimes the second, sometimes the third.[22]

Further defining his understanding of the moral and religious truths that art should convey, Tolstoy sees them as being reducible ultimately to the all-embracing Christian ideal of love. 'The purpose of human life is the brotherly union of man,' he writes in the opening sentence of the eighteenth chapter of *What Is Art?* He stresses the artist's responsibility to reaffirm the Christian ideals of brotherhood and love. Reiterating his complaint that the Christian Churches through the centuries had distorted the message of the Gospels, he stresses the responsibility of writers to reinvoke this message in its pure and uncorrupted form. Amongst his contemporaries he singles out Dickens, Hugo and Dostoevsky in literature, and Millet, Bastien Lepage, Breton and Lhermitte in painting, as authentically fulfilling this role:

> During the present century works of the higher kind of religious art, permeated by a truly Christian spirit, have appeared more and more frequently both in literature and in painting, as also works of the universal art of common life accessible to all. So that even art knows the true ideal of our times and tends towards it. On the one hand the best works of art of our time transmit religious feelings urging towards the union and brotherhood of man (such are the works of Dickens, Hugo, Dostoevsky; and in painting, Millet, Bastien Lepage, Jules Breton, Lhermitte, and others); on the other hand they strive towards the trans-

mission, not of feelings which are natural to people of the upper classes
only, but of feelings that may unite everyone without exception. There
are as yet few such works, but the need of them is already acknowledged. In recent times we also meet more and more frequently with
attempts at publications, pictures, concerts, and theatres, for the people.
All of this is still very far from accomplishing what should be done, but
the direction in which good art instinctively presses forward to regain
the path natural to it, can already be discerned.

The religious perception of our time – which consists in acknowledging that the aim of life (both collective and individual) is the union
of mankind – is already so sufficiently distinct that people have now
only to reject the false theory of beauty – according to which enjoyment
is considered to be the purpose of art – and religious perception will
naturally take its place as the guide of the art of our time.[23]

Elaborating further on this theme, he argues that the religious writer not
only brings new perspectives to bear on the words of the scriptures but that
life itself is made endlessly meaningful by virtue of being viewed from the
standpoint of scriptural truth. 'The feelings flowing from the religious perceptions of our times, Christian feelings, are infinitely new and varied,' he writes,
'not only because they repeat in new forms the Christian truths of unity,
brotherhood, equality and love, but because all the oldest, commonest and
most hackneyed phenomena of life evoke the newest, most unexpected and
poignant emotions as soon as a man regards them from a Christian point of
view.'[24] Crucially, he insists that the perceptions of the religious artist be universally intelligible, that the truths he conveys be rendered meaningful to all.
An art which proclaims the union and brotherhood of all men, must, he
argues, by definition be comprehensible and accessible to all. 'As soon as the
religious perception, which already unconsciously directs the life of man, is
consciously acknowledged, then,' he writes, 'immediately and naturally the
division of art for the lower and art for the upper classes will disappear.'
'There will,' he declares, 'be one common, brotherly universal art.'[25] A severe
critic of modernism as well as aestheticism, Tolstoy was deeply critical of the
obscurities of contemporary art and of its remoteness from the lives of ordinary people; he predicted that the whole future of art would lie in its potential
to reveal the universally held beliefs and aspirations of the masses:

Art of the future, that is to say, such part of art as will be chosen from
among all the art diffused among mankind, will consist not in transmitting feelings accessible only to members of the rich classes, as is the
case to-day, but in transmitting feelings embodying the highest religious

perceptions of our time. Only those productions will be esteemed art which transmit feelings drawing men together in brotherly union, or such universal feelings as can unite all men. Only such art will be chosen, tolerated, approved and diffused. But art transmitting feelings flowing from antiquated, outworn religious teaching; ecclesiastical art, patriotic art, voluptuous art; transmitting feelings of superstitious fear, of pride, of vanity, of ecstatic admiration of national heroes; art exciting exclusive love of one's own people, or sensuality, will be considered bad, harmful art, and will be censured and despised by public opinion. All the rest of art, transmitting feelings accessible only to a section of the people, will be considered unimportant, and will be neither blamed nor praised. And the appraisement of art in general will devolve not as is now the case on a separate class of rich people, but on the whole people; so that for a work to be thought good and to be approved and diffused, it will have to satisfy not the demands of a few people living under similar and often unnatural conditions, but of all those great masses of people who undergo the natural conditions of laborious life.[26]

In this passage he sees a vital conjuncture between aesthetic excellence and popular accessibility. 'The ideal of excellence in the future will not,' he continues, 'be exclusiveness of feeling, accessible only to some, but, on the contrary, its universality; and not bulkiness, obscurity and complexity of form, which are now valued, but on the contrary, brevity, clearness and simplicity of expression.' He points to the contradiction inherent in the view that art can attain excellence and yet remain impenetrable to the masses: 'The assertion that art may be good art and at the same time incomprehensible to a great number of people is extremely unjust and ruinous to art itself,' he writes. The Bible, he suggests, is the perfect model of an art that combines aesthetic excellence with universal intelligibility. 'The majority,' he declares, 'have always understood and still understand what we recognise as being the very best art: the epic of Genesis, the Gospel parables, folk legends, fairy-tales, and folk-songs are understood by all.'[27] Numerous Tolstoy scholars – Bayley, Hamburger, Poggioli, Berlin, Greenwood, Spence and Christian, to mention only some of the most influential – have testified to the success with which Tolstoy achieved his ideals of artistic excellence and popular accessibility. (A book by the present author has explored the educational implications of this issue.)[28] The concern of the present study is the nature of the message Tolstoy sought to convey in his novels and stories, a message profoundly religious and moral, embracing the nature of faith, the law of love, the problem of evil, and the moral and social reform of mankind. These are the issues that will be addressed in detail in the forthcoming sections of this chapter.

'CAN THIS BE FAITH?'

At first I began experiencing moments of bewilderment; my life would come to a standstill, as if I did not know how to live or what to do, and I felt lost and fell into despair. But they passed and I continued to live as before. Then these moments of bewilderment started to recur more frequently, always taking the same form. On these occasions, when life came to a standstill, the same question always arose: 'Why? What comes next?'

At first I thought the questions pointless and irrelevant. I felt the answers were well known and that should I wish to resolve them it would not cost me much effort; that for the time being I did not have the time to work it all out, but that when I put my mind to it I would find all the answers. However, the questions repeated themselves over and again, demanding answers with more and more urgency. They fell like full stops, always on the same spot, uniting in one large black spot.

And then, what happens to everyone stricken with a fatal inner disease happened to me. At first minor signs of indisposition appear, which the sick person ignores; then these symptoms appear more and more frequently, merging into one interrupted period of suffering. The suffering increases and before the sick man realises what is happening he discovers that the one thing he had taken for an indisposition is in fact the thing that is more important to him than anything in the world: it is death.

So wrote Tolstoy in Chapter 3 of *A Confession* where he describes the crisis in his life that precipitated his discovery of the power of faith. Tormented by the apparent meaninglessness of life, he came, by way of painful self-discovery, to the realisation that the purpose of life cannot be disclosed by reason alone and must be sought from sources transcending the rational, the empirical, the conditioned and the finite. His quest for faith is movingly described in the pages of his Diary as well as *A Confession* and is paralleled in the search for truth pursued by his fictional protagonists – Pierre, Prince Andrei, Levin, Nekhlyudov, Ivan Illych and others. Each seeks a fulfilment that transcends the suffering of mortal existence. Each endures emotional and spiritual conflict, at times verging on despair, as he proceeds towards the transformed consciousness of faith which discloses the prospect of transcending the mortal and the earthly through the power of love.

In all cases – in the case of Tolstoy himself and his fictional heroes – the experience which focusses the mind on the need for faith is the consciousness of death and mortality. This is the whole point of the passage quoted above from *A Confession*. It is reiterated in the fourth chapter of the work. 'The truth was that life is meaningless,' he writes. 'It was as if I had carried on living and walking until I reached a precipice from which I could see clearly that there was nothing ahead of me other than destruction. But it was impossible to stop, and impossible to turn back or close my eyes in order not to see that there was nothing ahead other than deception of life and of happiness, and the reality of suffering and death: of complete annihilation.' It is significant that faith comes to Prince Andrei on his deathbed, as it does to Ivan Illych and to the protagonist of the 'Diary of a Madman'. The latter work was directly inspired by a personal experience of Tolstoy's which occurred when he stayed overnight at an inn in Penza in 1869 and was overwhelmed during the night by his apprehension of approaching death. 'Everything was hidden by the terrible consciousness that my life was ebbing away,' his fictional alter ego recalls. 'Life and death somehow merged into one another. Something was tearing my soul apart and could not complete the severance.' 'There is nothing in life,' he exclaims. 'Death is the only real thing, and death ought not to exist.' In 'Master and Man' Vassili Brekhunoff similarly finds faith on the brink of death. As he stands shivering in the freezing cold, with death staring him in the face, all his existence is suddenly made meaningful by the faith in God he attains at the end. The climactic passage of the story – one of the most significant in Tolstoy's fiction – is worth citing for its disclosure of the dramatic transformation in consciousness that comes with the awareness of death, with the stripping away of the illusions that nurture self-sufficiency and pride, and with the realisation that only faith in God enables man to surmount the despair of his mortal state:

> Then he began to think about his money, his store, his house, his sales and purchases, and Mironoff's millions. He could not understand how that man whom men called Vassili Brekunoff could bear to interest himself in such things as he did. 'That man can never have known what is the greatest thing of all,' he thought of this Vassili Brekunoff. 'He can never have known what I know. Yes, I know it for certain now. At last – I KNOW.'
>
> Once again he heard the Man calling him who had called to him before, and his whole being seemed to respond in joy and loving-kindness as he replied: 'I am coming, I am coming!' For he felt that he was free at last, and that nothing could hold him further.
>
> And, indeed, nothing further than that did Vassili Andreitch see or hear or feel in this world.
>
> Around him the tempest still kept on. The same swirls of snow kept circling in eddies and covering the coats of the dead Vassili Andreitch

and the trembling Brownie, the sledge (now almost invisible) and, stretched out upon its floor, the now reviving Nikita as he lay prone beneath the body of his dead master.

By definition, that which enables man to transcend the mortal and the earthly must be a force greater than reason, which is rooted in the world of finitude and temporality. As early as 1853 Tolstoy was asserting the necessity for faith by virtue of the impossibility of 'proving the existence of God'. In a Diary entry for July 1853 he wrote: 'I can't prove to myself the existence of God; I can't find a single sensible piece of evidence, and I find the concept unnecessary. It's easier and simpler to understand the eternal existence of the whole world with its incomprehensibly beautiful order than a being who creat-ed it ... I don't understand the necessity for God's existence, but I believe in Him and ask Him to help me understand him.'[29] Repeatedly in *A Confession* he points to the failure of rational knowledge to provide him with a solution to the meaning of existence, the preoccupation with which brought him to the brink of suicide. 'After all, our wisdom, however comfortable it may be, has provided us with no understanding of the meaning of life,' he tells himself. Reflecting on the fact that rational knowledge is the province of small learned elites, he ponders the question, by what kind of knowledge are the masses of mankind sustained? 'It seems to me strange now,' he writes, 'so utterly incom-prehensible, that in my reasoning of life I could have overlooked the life of humanity that surrounded me on all sides and that I could have been so ridiculously mistaken as to think that my life, and the life of Solomon and Schopenhauer, was the true, normal life, while the lives of millions was not worthy of attention.'[30] He contrasts the spontaneous, intuitional, faith-affirm-ing wisdom of the masses with the abstract, rationally directed knowledge of learned minorities:

> I lived in this state of madness for a long time. It is a state which if not in deed then in words is very characteristic of more liberated and learned people. But whether it was thanks to my somewhat strange and instinctive love of the true working people that I was forced to under-stand them and to realise that they are not as stupid as we thought; or whether it was thanks to the sincerity of my conviction that I knew of nothing better to do than hang myself, I sensed anyway that if I wanted to live and to understand the meaning of life I must not seek it among those who have lost it and wish to kill themselves, but among the mil-lions of people living and dead who have created life, and who carry the weight of our lives together with their own. And I looked around at the enormous masses of simple, uneducated people without wealth, who

have lived and who still live, and I saw something quite different. I saw that with a few exceptions all those millions do not fit into my divisions, and that I could not categorise them as people who did not understand the question because they themselves posed, and answered, the question with unusual clarity. Neither could I categorise them as epicureans, since their lives rest far more on deprivation and suffering than on pleasure. I could still less regard them as living out their meaningless lives irrationally, since they could explain every act of their lives, including death. They considered suicide the greatest evil. It appeared that mankind as a whole had some kind of comprehension of the meaning of life that I did not acknowledge and derided. It followed that rational knowledge does not provide the meaning of life, but excludes it; while the meaning given to life by the millions of people, by humanity as a whole, is founded on some sort of knowledge that is despised and considered false.[31]

The inadequacies of reason are stressed by the Freemason visited by Pierre in *War and Peace*. 'The infinite God in His omnipotence is not to be apprehended by reason but by life,' the Freemason says. 'The highest wisdom is not founded on reason alone,' he adds. 'The highest wisdom is one attained through the light of conscience that God has implanted in our souls.' Levin, seeking to unravel the mysteries of life, had 'read and reread thoroughly Plato, Spinoza, Kant, Schelling, Hegel, and Schopenhauer' but finds their answers fruitless in his quest for ultimate solutions. He too contrasts the intellectual escapism of abstract learning with the simple, life-affirming faith of the masses:

What puzzled and distracted him above everything was that the majority of men of his age and circle had, like him, exchanged their old beliefs for the same new convictions, and yet saw nothing to lament in this, and were perfectly satisfied and serene. So that, apart from the principal question, Levin was tortured by other questions too. Were these people sincere? he asked himself, or were they playing a part? or was it that they understood the answers science gave to these problems in some different, clearer sense than he did? And he assiduously studied these men's opinions and the books which treated of these scientific explanations.

One fact he had found out since these questions had engrossed his mind, was that he had been quite wrong in supposing from the recollections of the circle of his young days at college, that religion had outlived its day, and that it was now practically non-existent. All the people nearest to him who were good in their lives were believers. The old prince, and Lvov, whom he liked so much, and Sergei Ivanovitch, and all the women believed, and his wife believed as simply as he had believed in his earliest childhood, and ninety-nine hundredths of the Russian people, all the working-people for whose life he felt the deepest respect, believed.

Another fact of which he became convinced, after reading many scientific books, was that the men who shared his views had no other construction to put on them, and that they gave no explanation of the questions which he felt he could not live without answering, but simply ignored their existence and attempted to explain other questions of no possible interest to him, such as the evolution of organisms, the materialistic theory of consciousness, etc.

The question that reason cannot penetrate, as Levin realises, is the relationship of the temporal to the timeless, of the finite to the infinite. This is the question, he says, that scientists are content merely to ignore. Tolstoy himself identified this as representing the main limitation on reason in *A Confession*. 'Having understood this,' he recalls, 'I realised that it was impossible to search for an answer to my questions in rational knowledge; that the answer given by rational knowledge simply suggests that the answer can only be obtained by stating the question in another way, by introducing the question of the relation of the finite to the infinite.' He continues: 'I realised that no matter how irrational and distorted the answers given by faith might be, they had the advantage of introducing to every answer a relationship between the finite and the infinite, without which there can be no solution.'[32]

And yet the dichotomy between reason and faith was not so severely drawn by Tolstoy as all this might suggest. Valentin Bulgakov recalled a remark made by Tolstoy in the last year of his life. 'Reason,' he said. 'is not the basis of belief but there can be no unreasonable belief.'[33] The notion of 'reasonable consciousness' put forward in *On Life* by Tolstoy comprehends both the tensions and harmony of the whole relationship. While he insists that the truth of the infinite can be perceived only through faith, he also suggests that this truth should be communicable in rational terms.[34] He suggests that it is reason that demands a solution to the meaning of existence while not being able itself to provide it. In *A Confession* he pointed to the kind of dilemma that this creates: 'According to faith it follows that in order to comprehend the meaning of life I must renounce my reason, the very thing for which meaning was necessary.'[35] The meaning disclosed by faith would have to satisfy the demands of reason, i.e. it would have to be rationally communicable. Revelation alone, he realised, could provide this meaning but it would have to be defined and made intelligible through the resources of reason and be wholly consistent with its requirements. This he himself sought to achieve in his ethical writings and in several volumes of meticulously researched exegetic commentary on the scriptures. This passage from his Introduction to *A Union and Translation of the Four Gospels* succinctly defines the nature of the relationship:

> By revelation I understand that which discovers to the human reason something transcending its highest capacity, the will of God, a truth beyond the unaided attainment of reason. I call that revelation which gives an answer to the question, what meaning has life? – a question reason cannot solve, and the inability to answer which brought me to despair, and tempted me to commit suicide. The answer given by revelation must be intelligible and not contrary to the laws of reason, as would be, for example, the assertion that an infinite number is an equal, or an unequal, number. The answer must not be in conflict with reason, because I can have no faith in such an answer; and it must therefore be neither unintelligible nor arbitrary, but an answer as necessarily acceptable to the human understanding as the conception of infinity is recognised and acknowledged by every man who is able to count.
>
> The answer must solve my question, What meaning has my life? If it does not answer that qu'stion, I have no need of it at all. The answer must be such that, though in its essential nature unattainable, even as God is unattainable, none the less all the logical deductions drawn from it respond to my reasonable demand that the meaning given to my life solve all the problems of my life. The answer must be not only rational and clear, but also true; that is, an answer in which I believe with all my soul, and in the truth of which I am compelled to believe, even as I am obliged to believe in the existence of infinity.[36]

In *On Life* he sees reason as embodying the 'law of existence', as the voice of its intelligible logic: 'Reason for man is the law by which his life is accomplished, just such a law as that for the animal by which it feeds itself and multiplies; as the law for the plant by which grass and trees blossom and bear fruit; as the law of the heavenly bodies by which the earth and planets move.'[37] It is the laws of reason, he suggests, that provide the key to our understanding of the functioning of God's will in the universe. This principle, we shall see presently, is particularly in evidence in Tolstoy's ethical writings where the powers of analytic reason are employed most effectively to identify the moral laws by which a life lived in accordance with Christian faith are to be defined. While emphasising the reasonableness of faith, however, he continues to insist on its essential simplicity. Pierre Bezukhov declares 'there is no greatness there where simplicity, goodness and truth are absent.' Levin, in his frustration at the failure of science and philosophy to provide the solutions he needs, discovers the simplicity of faith as he contemplates the mysteriousness of the infinite as attested in natural phenomena:

> Lying on his back, he gazed up now into the high cloudless sky. 'Do I not know that that is infinite space, and that it is not a round arch? But, however, I screw up my eyes and strain my sight, I cannot see it not round and not bounded, and in spite of my knowing about infinite space, I am incontestably right when I see a solid blue dome, and more right than when I strain my eyes to see beyond it.'
>
> Levin ceased thinking, and only, as it were, listened to mysterious voices that seemed talking joyfully and earnestly within him.
>
> 'Can this be faith?' he thought, afraid to believe in his happiness. 'My God, I thank Thee!' he said, gulping down his sobs, and with both hands brushing away the tears that filled his eyes.'

The simple faith that Levin finds is sustained by prayer, the means by which the soul finds union with God. Tolstoy's Diary records numerous instances of his own heartfelt pleas to God for the grace to live in accordance with his beliefs. An entry for 24 March 1852 reads: 'Grant me, O Lord, that I may live without sin and suffering and die without fear and despair – with faith, hope and love I surrender myself to Thy will.'[38] An entry for July of the same year reads: 'This is how I pray; O God deliver me from evil, i.e., deliver me from the temptation to evil, and grant me good, the possibility of doing good. Am I to experience evil or good? – Thy will be done.'[39] His favourite prayer was the Pater Noster – 'Any requests I can make to God are expressed more loftily and in a way more worthy of Him by the words, "Thy will be done on earth as it is in heaven".' 'Prayer fortifies and purifies me and it makes me glad,' he writes in an entry for November 1890.[40] Valentin Bulgakov has described Tolstoy's habit of praying in solitude during his morning walk, which he refused to share even with his closest friends.[41] This practice he saw as being in keeping with the ideal of prayer advocated by Christ himself in the Sermon on the Mount – 'And when you pray, you must not be like the hypocrites; for they love to stand and pray in the synagogues and at the street corners, that they may be seen by men. Truly, I say to you, they have received their reward. But when you pray, go into your room and shut the door and pray to your Father who is in secret; and your Father who sees in secret will reward you.'[42] This is the ideal of prayer he proclaimed in his Reply to the Synod's Edict of Excommunication:

I believe there is only one way to progress in love and that that is prayer: not the public prayer in churches that Christ expressly forbade (Matthew 6:5-13), but the solitary prayer of which Christ gave us an example and whose essence lies in the renewal and affirmation in our own consciousness of the meaning of our life and of our dependence on God alone.[43]

Tolstoy insisted on the essential freedom of the experience of faith, seeing it as being authenticated only by the voice of conscience and by the words of the scriptures. His faith was definitively a Christian faith by virtue of its roots in the scriptures, yet it was strictly non-institutional in character because he saw the dogmatism and didactic theology propagated by the churches as threatening the freedom of conscience which, like Dostoevsky, he considered to be an essential condition of genuine faith. In 'The Law of Violence and the Law of Love' he spoke of conscience as 'the essence of Christianity.' Of those who chose only to follow the dictates of its 'inner voice' he wrote: 'These kind of people are, and always have been, Christians because instead of setting themselves an external goal which needs the cooperation of others to be achieved, they set themselves an inner goal, which requires cooperation from no one else and which is the essence of Christianity in its true meaning.'[44] *A Confession* repeatedly praises the heretics of all ages for challenging the dogmatism of the Church and preserving the true meaning of Christianity by reaffirming its scriptural authenticity. 'Despite the efforts made by the Church to conceal from the people the essence of the teaching revealed in the Gospels, neither the prohibition of their translation into languages more accessible to the people, nor the false interpretation of them, could extinguish the light filtering through the deceit of the Church and illuminating men's souls as they grasped the enormous truth of the teaching with ever-increasing clarity,' he declares.[45]

For all his disenchantment with the institutions of Christianity Tolstoy fervently believed therefore in the traditions of the Christian faith as revealed in the words of the scripture text. Repeatedly, he asserted his belief that the scriptures were the only authoritative source of Christian truth. In *My Religion* he attributed his reconversion to Christianity entirely to his reading of the Gospels. 'For thirty years of my life,' he wrote, 'I was, in the proper acceptance of the word, a nihilist, a man who believed in nothing. Five years ago my faith came to me; I believed in the doctrine of Jesus and my whole life underwent a sudden transformation.'[46] What he rediscovered was his childhood fervour for the scriptures. 'From my childhood,' he continues, 'from the time I first began to read the New Testament, I was touched most of all by that portion of the doctrine of Jesus which inculcates love, humility, self-denial and the duty of returning good for evil. This to me has always been the substance of Christianity; my heart recognised its truth in spite of scepticism and despair.'[47] In *My Religion* he describes how he decided to set aside all external sources for an understanding of Christ's teaching in favour of a close personal response to the words of the Gospel text. Christ's words in the Sermon on the Mount, he suggests, contained the essentials of his message to mankind:

> Of all the other portions of the Gospels, the Sermon on the Mount always has had for me an exceptional importance. I now read it more frequently than ever. Nowhere does Jesus speak with greater solemnity, nowhere does he propound moral rules more definitely and practically, nor do these rules in any other form awaken more readily an echo in the human heart; nowhere else does he address himself to a large multitude of the common people. If there are any clear and precise Christian principles, one ought to find them here ... These chapters I read very often, each time with the same exceptional ardour as I came to the verses which exhort the hearer to turn the other cheek, to give up his cloak, to be at peace with all the world, to love his enemies ...[48]

The essence of Christ's message in the Sermon on the Mount was contained in his teaching on love, a teaching in which Tolstoy saw radical implications for the spiritual and moral reform of mankind. The nature of this teaching can now be more fully explored.

'LOVE HINDERS DEATH'

> I believe that the meaning of every man's life lies only in increasing the store of love within him; that this increase of love leads a man to greater and greater blessings in this life, and to blessings after his death that are in proportion to the amount of love within him.[49]

Thus wrote Tolstoy in his 'Reply to the Synod's Edict of Excommunication' on 4 April 1901. His words simultaneously affirm the metaphysical primacy of love as the originating and all-embracing force in the spiritual development of man and its infinity as manifested in its power to transcend the temporal conditions of mortal life. 'The longer I live the more I am convinced that love is the most important thing, that it should fill our entire life, and is what we should strive for. It determines everything and gives happiness,' he told Valentin Bulgakov in the last year of his life.[50] To an atheist with whom he corresponded at that same time he wrote: 'Love is one of the

manifestations of God ... We apprehend God by means of love and understanding, but the essence of God is not revealed to us in all its fullness. It is
beyond human understanding and it is through love that we strive to apprehend the divine essence.'[51] In *A Confession* he spoke of faith as 'giving an infinite meaning to the finite existence of man, a meaning that is not destroyed by
suffering, deprivation or death'. That meaning, he suggests, originates in the
infinitude of love, in its disclosure of God's presence in His creation. Alone
among world religions, he declared, Christianity has recognised the law of love
as 'the highest law of human life', applying equally to the whole of
humankind:

> It is becoming more and more evident in our age that the true signifi-
> cance of the Christian doctrine is that the essence of human life is the
> ever-growing manifestation of the source of everything, indicated in us
> through love; and, therefore, that the essence of human life and the
> highest law governing it is love. The fact that love is a necessary and
> happy aspect of human life was recognised by all the ancient religious
> beliefs. In all the teachings of the Egyptian sages, the Brahmins, the
> Stoics, the Buddhists, Taoists and others, amicability, pity, mercy, char-
> ity and love in general are considered the chief virtues. In the most
> superior of these teachings this recognition reached the point where love
> towards every living thing was advocated, and even recompense of good
> for evil, as is taught by the Taoist and Buddhist religions in particular.
> But not one of these doctrines made this virtue the basis of life, a
> supreme law that should be not only the chief, but the only, guiding
> principle in people's conduct, as did the most recent religion:
> Christianity. In all the pre-Christian doctrines love was regarded as one
> of the virtues, but not as that which the Christian teaching acknowl-
> edges it to be: metaphysically the origin of everything, practically the
> highest law of human life, i.e. that which under no circumstances
> admits of exception ... And thus the Christian teaching on love is not,
> as in former doctrines, merely a teaching about a certain virtue, but it is
> a definition of the supreme law of human life and the guidance for con-
> duct that inevitably follows from it.[52]

Seldom in the history of religious thought has the distinctive character of
Christian teaching been so eloquently expressed or the central message of the
Christian faith been so succinctly defined. In an earlier chapter of *A Confession*
Tolstoy spoke of the 'metaphysical essence of religion' as lying in the fact that
'the spirit of God is in man', from which he deduces the 'practical law' that
man must 'behave towards others as he would wish others to behave towards

him'. He cites support for his exposition of this issue from these words in the Gospel of St John: 'Beloved let us love one another: for love is of God; and everyone that loveth is born of God and knoweth God ... No man hath seen God at any time. If we love one another God dwelleth in us, and His love is perfected in us ... God is love; and he that dwelleth in love dwelleth in God and God in him.'[53] Like Dostoevsky, he insists that love is a practical ideal, whose truth is manifested in action and deed. 'One of the first principles of a Christian life is love, not in words, but in deed,' he writes in *The Kingdom of God is Within You.* 'I want to live for love always and everywhere,' he wrote in his Diary in February 1891.'[54]

In *A Confession* he further cites the words of St John celebrating love as the power which enables man to triumph over death: 'We know that we have passed from death into life, because we love the brethren. He that loveth not his brother abideth in death. (Con. 173)' 'The essence of any faith consists,' he says, 'in giving a meaning to life that will not perish with death.'[55] This theme is explored imaginatively in a number of his novels and stories, most notably 'The Death of Ivan Illych' and *War and Peace.* Both emphasise the power which love gives man to overcome the most universal and fundamental of all fears: the fear of death. Reviewing his life on his death-bed, Ivan Illych rails against God's injustice – 'Why hast Thou done all this?' he cries, 'Why dost Thou torment me so terribly?' He recognises the vanity of all earthly ambition and sees his life as a pursuit of futile hopes and aspirations. 'Incredible,' he cries, 'that my life should have been so disgusting and meaningless.' 'Death,' E.B. Greenwood wrote in a commentary on this story 'is most terrible to those who have never really learned how to live.'[56] Ivan Illych fears death because he has never realised the true meaning of life. He attains spiritual insight on his death-bed, however, and sees that life's true meaning is manifested in the self-less love shown him by his wife and children. It is when he reciprocates this love that he finally overcomes his fear of death:

> 'I am torturing them,' he thought. 'They feel sorry for me, but things will be better for them when I am gone.' He wanted to tell them this, but lacked the strength. 'But what is the use of speaking? I must do something,' he thought. He turned to his wife and indicated his son with his eyes.
>
> 'Take him away,' he said. 'Poor boy ... And you ...' He wanted to add, 'Forgive', and it came out, 'Forget', but he had not the strength to correct himself; he merely gave a little wave of his hand, knowing that the one who was to understand would understand.
>
> And presently it became clear to him that all he had been tortured by and been unable to throw off, was now falling away of itself, falling

away on two sides, ten sides, all sides at once. He felt sorry for them, he must do something to ease their pain. He must relieve them and himself of this suffering. 'How good and how simple!' he thought. 'And the pain? he asked himself. 'How am I to dispose of it? Here, where are you, pain?'

He felt for the pain.

'Ah, here it is. What of it? Let it be.'

'And death? Where is death?'

He searched for his accustomed terror of death and could not find it. Where was death? What was death? There was no fear because there was no death.

There was light instead of death.

Prince Andrei similarly attains spiritual illumination in his contemplation of the impending prospect of death. The horrifying sight of bleeding bodies on the battle-field at Borodino, his memories of Natasha's infidelity, his own pain and suffering – all recede into insignificance when measured against the transforming power of love. 'Sympathy, love for our brothers, for those who love us, love for those who hate us, love for our enemies; yes the love that God preached upon earth ... that is why I am sorry to part with life, that is what was left me if I had lived,' he cries. Love, he says, discloses the reality of the eternal, transcends the boundaries of mortality. Echoing the words of St John, he exclaims: 'Love hinders death. Love is life. All, all that I understand I understand only because I love. All is, all exists only because I love. All is bound up in love alone. Love is God, and dying means for me a particle of love, to go back to the universal and eternal source of love.' What he discovers at the end of his life is the self-denying, endlessly and unconditionally forgiving love which is radically distinct from the egotistic, self-pitying feeling he had earlier experienced and finally learned to overcome. Reflecting on his reconciliation with Natasha, he recognises the divine power that is present in selfless love and is especially manifested in the act of forgiveness:

'Yes love (he thought again with perfect distinctness), but not that love that loves for something, to gain something, or because of something, but that love that I felt for the first time, when dying, I saw my enemy and yet loved him. I knew that feeling of love which is the very essence of the soul, for which no object is needed. And I know that blissful feeling now too. To love one's neighbours; to love one's enemies. To love everything – to love God in all His manifestations. Some one dear to one can be loved with human love; but an enemy can only be loved with divine love. And that was why I felt such joy when I felt that I loved that man. What happened to him? Is he alive? ... Loving with human love, one may pass from love to hatred; but divine love cannot change. Nothing, not even death, nothing can shatter it. It is the very nature of the soul. And how many people I have hated in my life. And of all people none have I loved and hated more than her.'

It is important in this context to clarify Tolstoy's understanding of the idea of immortality in view of the controversy the issue has evoked in recent scholarship. In *My Religion* he rejects the notion of a bodily resurrection as a crude pagan superstition with no basis in the Jewish or Christian scriptures. 'We are obliged to believe,' he writes, 'that belief in a future life is a primitive and crude conception based upon a confused idea of the resemblance between death and sleep – an idea common to all savage races.'[57] He argues that the word 'resurrection', as used in the New Testament, was a mistranslation of Greek and Hebrew originals, none of which suggested a bodily resurrection but simply a reawakening of the spirit after death. Christ, he insists, never promised a bodily resurrection, and in fact explicitly rejected it in the debate with the Sadducees as recounted by Mark (XII, 21-4). What he affirmed, Tolstoy suggests, is the Jewish teaching that all who follow the will of God will be reunited with Him in eternal life. In *My Religion* he explains how Jesus extended the Jewish concept of 'eternal life' to include the whole of humankind:

> Whenever he made use of the phrase in speaking to the Jews, he employed it in exactly the same sense in which it was expressed in their own law – the accomplishment of the will of God. In contrast with the life that is temporary, isolated, and personal, Jesus taught of the eternal life promised by God to Israel – with this difference, that while the Jews believed the eternal life was to be perpetuated solely by their chosen people, and that whoever wished to possess his life must follow the exceptional laws given by God to Israel – the doctrine of Jesus holds that the eternal life is perpetuated in the Son of Man, and that to obtain it we must practise the commandments of Jesus, who summed up the will of God for all humanity.[58]

The eternal, Tolstoy suggests, is disclosed to man in the conditions of mortal life through the immanence of divine love, i.e., through God's informing presence in all creation. It is this which enables man to transcend the limitations and constrictions of his finite existence. The theme is vividly affirmed in the exchanges between Pierre and Platon Karataev at the end of *War and Peace*. Pierre's faith in humanity has been virtually destroyed by the spectacle of the execution of prisoners by the French soldiers and by the brutality he witnesses amongst them as they retreat from Moscow. He finds faith when he meets the peasant, Karataev, to whose innocence, simplicity and unaffected gaiety he is instantly drawn. 'He loved and lived on affectionate terms with every creature with whom he was thrown in life, and especially so with man – not with any particular man, but with the men who happened to be before his eyes,' the narrator says. Karataev saw the universe as a spiritual and physical whole, believing its order and harmony derived from God's presence within it. It is his fervent affirmation of this truth that restores faith to Pierre. 'Life is everything. Life is God,' the latter exclaims ...

> All is changing and moving, and that motion is God. And while there is life, there is the joy of the consciousness of the Godhead. To love life is to love God. The hardest and the most blessed thing is to love this life in one's sufferings, in undeserved suffering.
>
> 'Karataev!' flashed into Pierre's mind. And all at once there rose up, as vivid as though alive, the image, long forgotten, of the gentle old teacher, who had given Pierre geography lessons in Switzerland. 'Wait a minute,' the old man was saying. And he was showing Pierre a globe. This globe was a living, quivering ball, with no definite limits. Its whole surface consisted of drops, closely cohering together. And those drops were all in motion, and changing, several passing into one, and then one splitting up again into many. Every drop seemed striving to spread, to take up more space, but the others, pressing upon it, sometimes absorbed it, sometimes melted into it.
>
> 'This is life,' the old teacher was saying.
>
> 'How simple it is and how clear,' thought Pierre. 'How was it I did not know that before? God is in the midst, and each drop strives to expand, to reflect Him on the largest scale possible. And it grows, and is absorbed and crowded out, and on the surface it disappears, goes back into the depths, and falls not to the surface again. That is how it is with him, with Karataev; he is absorbed and has disappeared.'

Some scholars have seen this passage as indicating Tolstoy's belief in a pantheistic Deity in which the idea of a personal God is replaced by a concept of the world as itself manifesting and reflecting the divine essence. This is incompatible, in the first instance, with repeated assertions by Tolstoy himself of his belief in a personal God, directly in his Diaries and Letters and indirectly in his fictional prose. And, as G.W. Spence points out, a pantheistic view of God would not have provided an adequate foundation for his ethical teachings. 'The pantheistic world-view cannot in itself supply such a foundation – *sub specie aeternitatis* everything is permitted,' he writes. 'Therefore in order to establish an ethic, Tolstoy was compelled after all to acknowledge a personal God, Creator, Lawgiver and Appointer of aims ... God is immanent and the truth is at our feet.'[59] This is certainly the import of Pierre's declaration of faith at the end of *War and Peace*. He has learnt from Karataev that faith is not to be found in 'any sort of principles, or words, or ideas' but in the living witness to an 'everliving God' whose presence is 'everywhere manifest' – a clear affirmation of his belief in a personal God and in His immanent presence in the universe:

> He could seek no object in life now, because now he had faith – not faith in any sort of principles, or words, or ideas, but faith in a living, ever palpable God. In old days he had sought Him in the aims he set before himself. That search for an object in life had been only a seeking after God; and all at once in his captivity he had come to know, not through words or arguments, but by his own immediate feeling, what his old nurse had told him long before; that God is here, and everywhere. In his captivity he had come to see that the God in Karataev was grander, more infinite, and more unfathomable than the Architect of the Universe recognised by the masons. He felt like a man who finds what he has sought at his feet, when he has been straining his eyes to seek it in the distance. All his life he had been looking far away over the heads of all around him, while he need not have strained his eyes, but had only to look in front of him ...
>
> Now he had learned to see the great, the eternal, and the infinite in everything; and naturally therefore, in order to see it, to revel in its contemplation, he flung aside the telescope through which he had hitherto been gazing over men's heads, and looked joyfully at the ever-changing, ever grand, unfathomable, and infinite life around him. And the closer he looked at it, the calmer and happier he was. The terrible question that had shattered all his intellectual edifices in old days, the question: What for? had no existence for him now. To that question, What for? he had now always ready in his soul the simple answer: Because there is a God, that God without whom not one hair of a man's head falls.

Underlying Tolstoy's affirmation of the infinity of God's love and its accessibility to mankind through His immanent presence in the world, there is also a deep sense of the tensions deriving from the conflict of human and divine love. Throughout his writings he reveals a profound sense of the imperfection of all human love, while simultaneously pointing to its complex relationship to the divine and the infinite. The relationships of Natasha and Andrei, of Maslova and Nekhlyudov, are highly suggestive of this; each is flawed and corruptible but is ultimately transformed by virtue of the higher altruistic love inherent in the relationship from the outset. Each exemplifies the dualism of human and divine love that lies at the heart of all human relationships. Tolstoy's sense of the dangers inherent in this conflict is particularly manifested in his treatment of romantic and sexual love. 'The Kreutzer Sonata' exhibits an especially negative view of human sexuality, indicating the deep sense of fear and suspicion with which it was regarded by Tolstoy. Written at a time of great marital conflict and stress for himself, the story not only sees sexuality as potentially evil and destructive but represents woman as a temptress and agent of sexual bondage. The attitudes expressed by Pozdnyshev to the story's narrator in the following sequence typify the debased view of romantic passion which is conveyed throughout the story:

> Women, especially those who get their knowledge from men, know only too well that talk on elevated themes is mere talk, and that what a man really wants is the body, and whatever adds to the seductiveness of the body, and so this is what they offer him. If we could view the life of the upper classes in its true light, not through the prism of a habitual attitude that has become second nature to us, we would see that it is a veritable brothel. You disagee? Here, I shall prove it to you,' he said, not giving me a chance to speak. 'You say the women of our class have other interests than the women in a brothel, but I say you are wrong and will prove you are wrong. If people have different aims in life, if their inner lives are different, the outer forms of their lives will be different too. But look at the unfortunate women whom we despise and then at young ladies from the very highest society: the same toilettes, the same fashions, the same perfumes, the same bare arms, shoulders and bosoms, the same exaggerated behinds, the same passion for precious stones and expensive, glittering ornaments, the same amusements – dancing, music and singing. All the same means of enticing men are used by one as by the other. No difference at all. To make a very strict distinction between them we can only say that short-term prostitutes are usually despised whereas long-term prostitutes are esteemed.'

Tolstoy gave strong support to the widely held view that this reflected his own beliefs about human sexuality by declaring in the Afterword to the story that 'sexual love is, from a Christian point of view, a fall, a sin'. He had put forward the view in *My Religion* that lust is potentially an evil and destructive force in life and advised that 'men and women, knowing indulgence in sexual relations to lead to strife, should avoid all that evokes sexual desire'.[60] Writing to his son, Misha, in October 1885, he warned him repeatedly of the dangers of sexual temptation. 'Your situation – and there are many people like yourself – is a very frightening one,' he wrote. 'You recognise no rules or ideals and so are hurtling, as though on rails, down the steep slope of lust. Inevitably you end up in the swamp which remains always the same, and which is almost impossible to escape from – the swamp of wine and women.'[61] Valentin Bulgakov spoke of Tolstoy's spiritual monism, seeing it as being rooted in a deep distaste for the body and its functions. He quotes his words as follows: 'As I have always said, and I say it again, the chief aim of human life, its incentive, is a striving for good. And this is not achieved through the life of the body; the life of the body causes suffering. Happiness is achieved through the life of the spirit.'[62] That same view is given powerful expression in *Resurrection* through Nekhlyudov's feelings of disgust at his own recollected experiences of sexual love:

> 'The animalism of the brute nature in man is disgusting,' he thought, 'but as long as it remains in its native form we observe it from the height of our spiritual life and despise it; and – whether one has fallen or resisted – one remains what one was before. But when that same animalism hides under a cloak of poetry and aesthetic feeling and demands our worship – then we are swallowed up by it completely and worship animalism, no longer distinguishing good from evil. Then it is awful!'

Maria Pavlovna and Katyusha share his revulsion for the sexual. 'They were united,' the narrator says, 'by the repulsion both felt for sexual love. The one loathed that love, having experienced all its horrors; the other, never having experienced it, looked on it as something incomprehensible, and at the same time as something repugnant and offensive to human dignity.'

But all this is merely the other side of the dualism of human and divine love – which in turn is a manifestation of the metaphysical dualism of the finite and the infinite, the temporal and eternal – that informs all of Tolstoy's thinking on the nature and purpose of human existence. The sordid and corrupted images of human passion and love that find expression in works such as 'The Kreutzer Sonata' and parts of *Resurrection* must be balanced against the idyllic and transcendent love that transforms the lives of Natasha, Prince Andrei, Pierre, Maslova and Nekhlyudov. Implicit in the negative portrayal of sexuality by Tolstoy is a profound belief in the need for ethical direction to release the selflessness that is potentially present in all human love and that is the key to its transformative potentiality. What is implicitly, and sometimes explicitly, asserted in his writings is the need for the guiding force of morality to ensure that the baser and more selfish forms of love are transformed into that higher love he saw as being epitomised ultimately in the life of Christ, in the absolute selflessness exemplified in his Passion and Crucifixion. This theme will be explored in detail in the next section.

'IF YE LOVE ME KEEP MY COMMANDMENTS'

And I and millions of men, men who lived ages ago and men living now – peasants, the poor in spirit and the learned, who have thought and written about it, in their obscure words saying the same thing – we are all agreed about this one thing: what we must live for and what is good. I and all the men have only one firm, incontestable clear knowledge, and that knowledge cannot be explained by the reason – it is outside it, and has no causes and can have no effects.

'If goodness has causes, it is not goodness; if it has effects, a reward, it is not goodness either. So goodness is outside the chain of cause and effect.'

'And yet I know it, and we all know it.'

'What could be a greater miracle than that?'

'Can I have found the solution of it all? Can my sufferings be over?' thought Levin, striding along the dusty road, not noticing the heat nor his weariness, and experiencing a sense of relief from prolonged suffering. This feeling was so delicious that it seemed to him incredible.

Levin, in this self-reflective passage from the end of *Anna Karenina*, touches on the central principle of Christian ethics: the autonomous status of the Good, its independence of cause and effect, of reward and punishment. 'If goodness has causes it is not goodness,' he says; 'if it has effects, a reward, it is not goodness either. So goodness is outside the chain of cause and effect.' The absoluteness of the Good, i.e. its independence of cause and effect, derives, Tolstoy suggests, from the transcendent nature of its source in the infinity of divine love. The pursuit of the Good, he suggests, is a matter of individual choice; its attainment is dependent on the assistance of God's grace. In practical terms, he saw the pursuit of the Good as the everyday enactment of the Christian injunction, 'Thou shalt love thy neighbour as thyself.' The ideal of active love is the foundation of all his moral teaching, its guiding principles being the commandments of Christ as enunciated in the scriptures. First and foremost a Christian moralist, he repeatedly asserted the importance of ethical behaviour as the hallmark of the Christian way of life, its scriptural authentication being the incontrovertible imperative of Christ himself as conveyed in the words of St John's Gospel, 'If Ye Love Me Keep My Commandments.'

In the words cited earlier from *The Law of Violence and the Law of Love* Tolstoy asserted the essentially ethical character of the act of love. He spoke of it as 'practically the highest law of human life ... and the guidance for conduct that must follow from it'. 'The Christian dogma,' he said, 'states very clearly that since it is the supreme law its fulfilment cannot admit any exceptions, as former teachings did, and that the love which defines these laws is only love when ... it is applied equally to foreigners, to all sectarians, and likewise to the enemies who hate us and wrong us.'[63] Deeply aware, unlike his childhood mentor, Rousseau, of the fallenness and corruptibility of man (affirmed explicitly, for instance, in *On Life* and *Resurrection*), he saw morality as requiring the control by man of his own animal nature, the conquest of his selfishness and pride, and the release in himself of the selfless love that leads to the attainment of the Good. It is morality, he suggests, which transforms self-oriented human love into the selflessness of divine love. The 'Christian relationship to the world consists', he says, 'in man's recognising himself as an instrument for fulfilling the aims of a higher will', i.e., in subordinating himself humbly to the law of love as the earthly manifestation of God's will. The great flaw in post-Renaissance thought, he says, has been its rationalisation of a philosophy of life that elevated reason and the pursuit of individual self-fulfilment above the Christian ideal of service to God:

> The Christian ethic – that which we acknowledge as a consequence of our worldly outlook – demands not just the sacrifice of the individual to the individuality of the group, but demands the renunciation of both personal and group individuality for service to God. Pagan philosophy only explores the means of acquiring the greatest well-being for the individual, or for a group of individuals, and the contradiction is inevitable. The only method of concealing this contradiction is to accumulate abstract conditional concepts, one on top of the other, and to avoid departing from the nebulous sphere of metaphysics. This is what the majority of philosophers have done since the time of the Renaissance, and it is to this circumstance – the impossibility of reconciling the previously accepted demands of Christian philosophy with a moral philosophy based on paganism – that one must attribute the peculiar abstraction, lack of clarity, unintelligibility, and irrelevance to life of modern philosophy.[64]

The passage comes from an essay called 'Religion and Morality,' the main theme of which is the interdependence of ethics and faith. In modern times, he argues, the Christian ethic of love has been replaced by a humanist ethic whose foundation is reason and which, by virtue of its separation from the absolutes of faith, has issued in a relativist, secular morality. The latter, he says, finds expression either as a striving for individual well-being – a morality he describes as 'primitive, savage and personal' – or a striving towards social well-being, i.e. the welfare of the group, the community or the state. The latter he denounces as a directionless, contradictory pseudo-morality:

> The unfortunate Nietzsche who has lately become so famous, made a valuable exposition of this contradiction. He cannot be refuted when he says that from the point of view of existing non-Christian philosophies all laws and morality are mere lies and hypocrisy, and that it is far more pleasant and reasonable for a man to create his own fellowship of super-men and to be one of them, than to be one of the crowd that serves as the stage for these supermen. None of the philosophical arguments stemming from a religious view of life that is pagan can prove to a person that it is more advantageous and reasonable not to live for his own well-being, which he desires, understands, finds possible, or for the well-being of his family, or society, but for the well-being that is unknown, undesired, incomprehensible, and unattainable by human means. A philosophy founded on an understanding of human life and confined to the welfare of man will never be in a position to prove to a rational person, who knows that he might die at any moment, that it is good for him and that he must deny himself his own desired, appreciat-ed and undoubted well-being, and do so not for the good of others (because he will never know the results of his sacrifices) but simply because it is necessary and worthy, and a categorical imperative.[65]

It is this humanist ethic, based on the illusion that reason can solve all of life's mysteries, that Levin rejects, seeing it as leading to the cul-de-sac of a meaningless subjectivity. 'By reason could I have arrived at knowing that I must love my neighbour and not oppress him?' he asks. 'I was told that in my childhood and I believed it gladly, for they told me what was already in my soul.' Pierre and Prince Andrei reach similar conclusions, as do Nekhlyudov and Maslova, each of them seeing the ideal of active love as the ethical mani-festation of their newly discovered faith. One of the most dramatic instances of an individual's discovery of the ethic of active love occurs in the story, 'Father Sergius'. Sergius has resolved on a life of austerity and self-abnegation, mainly to avenge a wrong done to him by the Tzar. In the words of his sister, he became a monk 'in order to stand above those who wanted to show him that they stood above him'. 'By becoming a monk,' she says, 'he showed that he despised all that seemed important to others ... and he now ascended a height from which he could look down from above on those people he had formerly envied.' The story shows that his ascetic pursuit of holiness is motivated largely by hurt pride and vanity – a truth he himself comes to realise following a humiliating seduction in his cell. He decides to abandon his ascetic way of life and rediscovers faith through the service of others. His new model of holiness in his cousin, Pashenka, through whose example of unselfconscious goodness he finds a more Christ-like fulfilment than that which he had sought in the isolation of his hermitage. In this passage he commits himself to the ideal of active service and love which he sees epitomised in the life of Pashenka:

'Pashenka is precisely what I ought to have been. I lived for man, pretending to live for God; but she lives for God, imagining that she lives for man. Yes, one good deed, a cup of water offered without thought of reward, is dearer than all those I have helped for the sake of man's approval.' 'But,' he asked himself, 'was there not some particle of the true wish to serve God?' And he had no answer. 'Yes, but all that was defiled, overgrown by the wish for glory among men. No, there is no God for one who has lived, like me, for glory among men. But I shall go, then, and search for Him.'

And he went, as he had come to Pashenka, wandering from village to village, now joining, now parting with other pilgrims, men and women; asking food and shelter in Christ's name. At times some ill-tempered housewife might scold at him, or some peasant in his cups abuse him: but far more often he would be given food and drink, and even provision for his way. His appearance, betraying his aristocratic origin, inclined some people in his favour. Others, on the contrary, seemed well pleased to see one of the gentry reduced to beggary. But his gentle ways conquered all with whom he came in contact.

Often, finding the Gospel in some home, he would read aloud from it; and always, everywhere, people would listen, touched and amazed, as to something ever new, though long familiar.

If he had an opportunity to help people, by advice, or by writing letters or documents for the illiterate, or by conciliating wranglers, he never heard their gratitude, for he would leave before it could be tendered. And, little by little, he began to find his God.

The ideal of active love is beautifully exemplified in three of Tolstoy's parables – 'Where Love Is, There God Is Also', 'The Two Old Men' and 'That Whereby Men Live'. The first describes how the shoemaker, Martin Avdeitch, overcomes his sorrows and misfortunes by resolving to help those in greater need than himself: the old man, Stepanitch, the poor soldier's wife and the pedlar-woman. The moral of the tale is affirmed at the end: 'Inasmuch as ye have done it unto one of the least of these my brethren ye have done it unto Me.' The second story describes a pilgrimage to Jerusalem by two old men, one of whom fails to reach the Holy Land because of a decision to help a family in need that he meets on the way. Unlike his companion who enjoys the excitement of seeing the holy places, the narrator suggests the other sees Christ more truly in the faces of the poor than he would have at a shrine in Jerusalem. The theme of the third story is the Gospel text, 'He that loveth not knoweth not God: for God is love.' Simon the cobbler, the story's hero, discovers, through a series of bizarre experiences, that Christ's message of love offers the only genuine fulfilment of God's plan for mankind. These are his concluding reflections:

> 'I had known before that God gave life to men, and that He would have them live; but now I understood another thing.'
>
> 'I understood that God would not have men live apart from one another – wherefore He had not revealed to them what was needful for each one: but that He would have them live in unity – wherefore He had revealed to them only what was needful both for themselves and for their fellows *together*.'
>
> 'Yes, at last I understood that men only *appear* to live by taking thought for themselves, but that in reality they live by Love alone. He that dwelleth in Love dwelleth in God, and God in him: for God is love.'

'Some one dear to one can be loved with human love; but an enemy can only be loved with divine love,' Prince Andrei declares as he lies wounded on the battlefield at Borodino. The theme of reconciliation is central to Tolstoy's treatment of the ideal of active love. The forgiveness of wrong-doing is presented in the three main novels as that which makes possible the progress towards loving faith in which the major characters are engaged. The transforming power of penitential love is shown with a special vividness in the reconciliation scene between the dying Prince Andrei and Natasha. With forgiveness comes understanding and a love purified of guilt and remorse. 'Yet how many people have I hated in my life,' he exclaims, 'and of them all I loved and hated none as I did her.' The narrative continues: 'And he vividly pictured to himself Natasha, not as he had done in the past with nothing but charms which gave him delight, but for the first time picturing to himself her soul. And he understood her feelings, her suffering, shame and remorse. He now understood for the first time all the cruelty of his rejection of her, the cruelty of his rupture with her.' There follows one of the tenderest love scenes in Tolstoy's fiction as each forgives the other the offences they have suffered and they are reconciled in a union profoundly enriched by the purifying power of repentance.

A more complex treatment of the theme is evident in *Anna Karenina*. Karenin, feeling deeply betrayed by his wife, cannot bring himself to forgive the wrong she has done him. 'Forgive her I cannot and do not wish to. I regard it as wrong,' he says. 'I have done everything for this woman and she has trodden it all in the mud to which she is akin. I am not a spiteful man. I have never hated anyone, but I hate her with my whole soul and I cannot ever forgive her because I hate her too much for all the wrong she has done me.' Yet he too finds the strength to forgive as he kneels by the bedside of his ailing wife:

> The nervous agitation of Alexei Alexandrovich kept increasing, and had by now reached such a point that he ceased to struggle with it. He sud-denly felt that what he had regarded as nervous agitation was on the contrary a blissful spiritual condition that gave him all at once a new happiness he had never known. He did not think that the Christian law he had been all his life trying to follow enjoined on him to forgive and love his enemies; but a glad feeling of love and forgiveness for his ene-mies filled his heart. He knelt down, and laying his head on the curve of her arm, which burned him as with fire through the sleeve, he sobbed like a little child. She put her arm around his head, moved towards him, and with defiant pride lifted up her eyes.

The reconciliation is short-lived and does not survive Anna's recovery from her illness. But it is presented nonetheless as a momentary response by Karenin to the action of divine grace, a brief if only sub–conscious awareness of its transformative potential: 'He knew that when, without the slightest idea that his forgiveness was the action of a higher power, he had surrendered directly to the feeling of forgiveness, he had felt more happiness than now when he was thinking every instant that Christ was in his heart, and that in signing official papers he was doing His will.'

Three of Tolstoy's parables are devoted to the theme of forgiveness and the active reparation of guilt. A story called 'Neglect a Fire and 'Twill Not Be Quenched' describes a feud between neighbours that seems unresolvable until one of the participants undertakes to humiliate himself and seek reconciliation with the other. 'The Penitent Sinner' is a dialogue between an old man and St Peter at the gates of Paradise, the main point of which is the limitlessness of divine forgiveness. In the third story, 'God Sees the Light Though He Be

Slow to Declare It', the main character, Aksenoff, has been framed for a murder he did not commit and meets the real murderer in a Siberian prison camp. He forgives the latter who, as a result, is overcome with remorse for his crime and seeks reconciliation with the man he has wronged.

Dilemmas arising from remorse and guilt are a significant feature of the gradual progress of Nekhlyudov towards repentance. Deeply aware of the depth of his sinfulness, he nevertheless is reluctant to unburden himself of his guilt. In his weakness he listens to the voice of the tempter who exploits his weakening self-confidence – 'Have you not turned before to perfect yourself and become better, and nothing has come of it' – but he resolves nonetheless to repent of his sin. 'At any cost,' he declares, 'I will break the lie that binds me; will tell everybody the truth and act the truth.' A beautiful sequence of lyrical imagery conveys the joy of his unburdening:

> He prayed, asking God to help him, to enter into him and cleanse him; and what he was praying for had happened already; the God within him had awakened in his consciousness. He felt himself one with Him, and therefore felt not only the freedom, fullness and joy of life, but all the power of righteousness. All, all the best that a man can do, he felt capable of doing.
>
> His eyes filled with tears as he was saying all this to himself; good and bad tears; good because they were tears of joy at the awakening of the spiritual being within him, the being that had been asleep all these years, and bad tears because they were also tears of tenderness towards himself at his own goodness.
>
> He felt hot, and went to the window and opened it. The window faced the garden. It was a moonlit, fresh, quiet night; something rattled past, and then all was still. The shadow of a tall poplar fell on the ground just opposite the window, and all the intricate pattern of its bare branches was clearly defined on the clean-swept gravel. To the left the roof of a coach-house shone white in the moonlight – in front the black shadow of the garden wall was visible through the tangled branches of the trees. Nekhlyudov gazed at the roof, the moonlit garden, and the shadows of the poplar, and drank in the fresh invigorating air.

Nekhlyudov is at ease with the voice of his conscience – in Tolstoy's view the final arbiter in all matters of ethical behaviour and morality. 'Conscience is our best and surest guide,' he wrote in his Diary for June 1852, shortly after he abandoned the practice of Orthodoxy. 'But where are the signs that distinguish this voice from other voices?' he asked. 'The voice of vanity speaks with equal force.' 'I believe in goodness and love but I don't know what can show me the way to it,' he wrote. 'Conscience reproaches me for actions with good intentions which have bad consequences.'[66] Only the relentless scrutinising of conscience, illuminated in all cases by the words of the scriptures, enables us, he concludes, to identify its authentic call to goodness. Valentin Bulgakov has described Tolstoy's daily habit of examining his conscience at every possible moment. 'He ascribed tremendous importance,' he says, 'to "work on oneself" mentally, which is to say that a man should keep watch on his thoughts and catch himself in any feeling of ill-will toward another, or evil thoughts in general, and strive to check and suppress them instantly.'[67]

In the episode of the dinner party at the governor's mansion Nekhlyudov appears to lapse into a temporary state of self-complacency, ignoring the promptings of his conscience on the extent of his guilt and his obligations towards the woman he has wronged. He falls 'into a state of complete satisfaction with himself such as he had not known for a long time as if he had only now found out what a good man he was'. As he overcomes the temptations of spiritual pride, Nekhlyudov realises his moral responsibility not only to acknowledge his guilt towards Maslova but to make active reparation for the wrong he has caused her. As he pleads with her to forgive him, he finds that there are great emotional barriers to be overcome before they can be finally reconciled. 'He felt that there was in her soul one who was hostile to him, and who was supporting her, as she now was, preventing him from getting at her heart.' 'Strange to say,' the narrator says, 'this did not repel him but drew him nearer to her by some fresh peculiar power.' As she finally responds to his pleas for forgiveness, he concludes that the solution to the problem of evil lies in the unreserved willingness to forgive – 'not until seven times, but until seventy times seven'. The cycle of evil is broken only, he says, by those who, in their humble awareness of their own guilt, are prepared endlessly to forgive the evil in those around them. This, he concludes, is the central message of the Sermon on the Mount:

> And it happened to Nekhlyudov as it often happens to men who are living a spiritual life. The thought that at first seemed strange, paradoxical, or even only a jest, being confirmed more and more often by life's experience, suddenly appeared as the simplest, truest certainty. In this way the idea that the only certain means of salvation from the terrible evil from which men are suffering is, that they should always acknowledge themselves to be guilty before God, and therefore unable to punish or reform others, became clear to him. It became clear to him that all the dreadful evil he had been witnessing in prisons and jails, and the quiet self-assurance of the perpetrators of this evil, resulted from men attempting what was impossible: to correct evil while themselves evil.

Vicious men were trying to reform other vicious men, and thought they could do it by using mechanical means. And the result of all this was that needy and covetous men, having made a profession of this pretended punishment, and reformation of others, themselves became utterly corrupt, and unceasingly corrupt also those whom they torment. Now he saw clearly whence came all the horrors he had seen, and what ought to be done to put an end to them. The answer he had been unable to find was the same that Christ gave to Peter. It was to forgive always, everyone, to forgive an infinite number of times, because there are none who are not themselves guilty, and therefore none who can punish or reform. Hoping to find a confirmation of this thought in the Gospel Nekhlyudov began reading it from the beginning. When he had read the Sermon on the Mount, which had always touched him, he saw in it to-day for the first time not beautiful abstract thought, setting forth for the most part exaggerated and impossible demands, but simple, clear practical laws which if carried out in practice (and this is quite possible) would establish perfectly new and surprising conditions of social life.

Of the moral principles revealed in the Sermon on the Mount, none, in Tolstoy's view, had more fundamental validity and more challenging implications than that conveyed in the words: 'Ye have heard that it hath been said, An eye for an eye and a tooth for a tooth. But I say to you, That ye resist not evil; but whosoever shall smite thee on thy right cheek, turn to him the other also. And if anyone will sue thee at the law, and take away thy coat, let him have thy cloak also.' The implications of this will now be explored.

'RESIST NOT EVIL'

The doctrine of non-resistance to evil is at once the most comprehensive and the most controversial of Tolstoy's religious teachings. He saw it as the key to the whole message of love revealed by Christ in the Gospels. 'I had only to grasp the simple and exact meaning of these words, just as they were spoken, when the whole doctrine of Jesus, not only as set forth in the Sermon on the Mount, but in the entire Gospels, became clear to me,' he writes in the opening pages of *My Religion*. 'In the Sermon on the Mount, as well as in the whole Gospel,' he adds, 'I found everywhere affirmation of the same doctrine, "Resist not evil".' He insisted that Christ's words be interpreted exactly as he spoke them – 'I understood that Jesus meant neither more nor less than what he said'[68] – and that they should be applied without exception to all the circumstances of life, all situations where evil is encountered. He saw Christ's words as constituting a sacred command that had been diluted and distorted by the Churches through the centuries to such a degree that it was no longer held by Christians in the sense in which it had been stated in the scriptures. In *A Confession* he charged the Churches with betraying the teachings of Christ through the specious logic of their 'just war' theology. It was the Orthodox Church's teaching on war, he recalled, that first shocked him into recognition of the inauthenticity of its interpretations of the scriptures:

> At the time Russia was at war. And, in the name of Christian love, Russians were killing their fellowmen. It was impossible not to think about this. It was impossible to avoid the fact that killing is evil and contrary to the most basic principles of any faith. And yet prayers were said in the churches for the success of our armies, and our religious teachers acknowledged this killing as an outcome of faith. And this was not only applied to murder in time of war, but, during the troubled times that followed the war, I witnessed members of the Church, her teachers, monks, and ascetics, condoning the killing of helpless, lost youths. As I turned my attention to all that is done by people who profess Christianity, I was horrified.[69]

Looking back at the history of institutional Christianity he particularly blames theologians for providing rationalistic justifications for their distortion of Christ's message on non-resistance. Insisting that Christ's words do not admit of any exceptions, that they incorporate the essential precepts of the law of love, he argues that a theology of war 'presents an inner contradiction resembling cold fire or hot ice'. 'It seems evident,' he continues, 'that if some people, despite recognising the virtue of love, can admit the necessity of tormenting or murdering certain people for the sake of some future good, then others, by just the same right, and also acknowledging the virtue of love, can claim the same necessity in the name of some future good.' Allowing for any exception to Christ's teaching 'diminishes its entire significance', he writes, as he cites an impressive body of authority from early Christian writers in support of his interpretations of the scripture text:

> The Christian community of the first to the fifth centuries AD categorically declared, through its leaders, that Christianity forbids any murder, including murder in war.
>
> In the second century, the philosopher Tatian, a convert to Christianity, declared that killing in war was inadmissible for Christians, as was any kind of murder, and he regarded the honoured military wreath as an obscenity for a Christian. In the same century Athinagoras

of Athens stated that not only must Christians themselves not kill, but they must not be present at any scene of murder.

In the third century Clement of Alexandria contrasted the warrior-like pagans with the peaceful race of Christians. But it was the renowned Origen who most clearly expressed the Christians' dislike of war. Applying to the Christians the words of Isaiah, who said that a time would come when people would beat their swords into ploughshares and their spears into pruning-hooks, Origen said firmly: 'We will not raise arms against any other nation, we will not practise the art of war, because through Jesus Christ we have become the children of peace ...'

Tertullian, a contemporary of Origen, expressed himself equally decisively on the impossibility of Christians becoming soldiers. He said of military service: 'It is not fitting to serve the emblem of Christ and the emblem of the devil, the fortress of light and the fortress of darkness. One soul cannot serve two masters ...'

The celebrated Cyprian said: 'The world is going mad in mutual bloodshed. And murder, which is considered a crime when people commit it singly, is transformed into a virtue when they do it en masse. The offenders acquire impunity by increasing their ravaging.'

In the fourth century Lactancius said the same thing: 'There must not be any exception to God's commandment that it is always a sin to kill a person. It is not permitted to bear arms, for our only weapon is the truth.'[70]

From the time that Christians joined the armies of Constantine, Tolstoy writes, 'the simple, indubitable and evident truth that the profession of Christianity is incompatible with the readiness to admit any kind of violence' was consistently suppressed by the Churches. For fifteen centuries, he argues, they propagated a false and contradictory interpretation of Christ's teachings. Those who remained loyal to the doctrine of non-violence – he mentions the Manicheans, Montanists, Cathars, Molokans, Quakers, Jehovists, Klisti, Skoptsi, Dukhobors and Moravians – were despised by the Churches and their followers. In *The Law of Violence and the Law of Love* he urges Christian believers to rediscover the simplicity of the scriptural injunction on love and to abide by Christ's command never to inflict violence on a fellow human being. In *My Religion* he recalls his own personal rediscovery of this truth:

When I understood that the words 'Resist not evil' did indeed mean 'Resist not evil', my whole understanding of Christ's teaching was suddenly changed; I was appalled at the peculiar way in which I had understood it until then. I knew – we all know – that the meaning of the Christian teaching lies in love for other people. To say 'Turn your cheek, love your enemies,' is to express the very essence of Christianity. I had known all this since childhood, but why had I not understood these straightforward words in a straightforward manner? Why had I searched instead for some allegorical meaning in them? 'Do not resist evil' means 'Do not ever resist him that is evil, do not commit acts of violence, acts that are contrary to the spirit of love'. And if you are insulted, then suffer the insult and still do not commit acts of violence. It is impossible to say any of this more clearly and straightforwardly than Christ did.[71]

He argues therefore that the only possible solution to interhuman conflict lies in the refusal by every individual to respond to force with more force, a stance, he concedes, which requires exceptional humility on the part of the respondent. In this regard he cites the words of the Stoic philosopher, Epictetus, on the need for total submission to God's will for the attainment of true freedom: 'When you can say in all truth with your whole heart: "My Lord, my God, do with me as you will", only then will you free yourself from slavery and be completely free.' Epictetus, he said, had seen dominance as a subtle form of self-enslavement. 'If you see a person wishing to control not himself, but others,' he wrote, 'you know that he is not free, he has become a slave to his own desire to dominate people.'[72] The urge to dominate – in Tolstoy's view, the root-cause of violence – will be overcome, he says, only when each individual is awakened to the voice of conscience urging him to refuse to confront evil with more evil, force with more force. 'The salvation of men will only be achieved,' he writes, 'by every person who is called upon to participate in violence over his fellowman and his own self recognising the true spiritual I within himself and asking in amazement, "Well why should I do that?".' The true Christian will refuse to engage in violent conflict on the grounds that violence is itself intrinsically evil and cannot therefore be employed for the suppression of evil. In *The Law of Violence and the Law of Love* he writes:

> The question of what I should do to counteract acts of violence committed before my eyes is always based on the same primitive superstition that it is possible for man not only to know, but to organise, the future in the way he likes. For a man free of this superstition the question does not and cannot exist. A rogue has raised his knife over his victim. I have a pistol in my hand and kill him. But I do not know, and cannot possibly know, whether the purpose of the raised knife would have been implemented. The rogue may not have carried out his evil

intention, whereas I certainly commit my evil deed. Therefore the only thing that a person can and must do in this and similar instances is what he must always do in all possible circumstances: he must do what he believes he ought to do before God and before his own conscience. A man's conscience may demand that he sacrifice his own life but not that of another person. The same principle can be applied to the method of counteracting social evil.

Thus, to the question of what a person should do in the face of the evil committed by one, or a number of persons, the answer given by a man free of the superstition that it is possible to foresee, and to employ violence to organise, the conditions of the future, is always the same: do unto others as you would have them do unto you.[73]

These issues are explored imaginatively in Tolstoy's fiction, especially in the parables. The previously mentioned story, 'Neglect A Fire and 'Twill Be Quenched' describes how a long-standing feud between neighbours is resolved only when one of the neighbours ignores provocation from the other side, thereby releasing the feelings of self-guilt and remorse in the others that lead eventually to reconciliation of their differences. 'The Godson', a fairytale legend, again affirms the principle that it is humility, not power, that enables us to exercise moral influence over the actions of others and to withstand the offences they inflict on us. In 'The Candle', a pre-Emancipation story about serfdom, the narrator describes how a cruel overseer tyrannises the peasantry, provoking them into a conspiracy in which they plan to murder him. They are admonished by a peacemaker, Peter Michieff, to restrain their desire for vengeance. Peter confronts the overseer with evidence of his cruelties. Conscience-stricken, the latter sinks into an alcoholic depression from which he dies. In his words to the peasants Peter emphasises the futility as well as the immorality of resisting evil through evil means:

> If God had intended that we should remove evil by evil, He would have given us a law to that effect and have pointed us to it as the way. No. If you remove evil by evil it will come back to you again. It is folly to kill a man, for blood sticks to the soul. Take a man's soul and you plunge your own in blood. Even though you may think that the man whom you have killed was evil, and that thus you have removed evil from the world – look you, you yourselves will have done a more wicked deed than any of his. Submit yourselves rather to misfortune, and misfortune will submit itself to you.

The theme of non-violence is implicit in the novels, especially *War and Peace* where the horrific descriptions of the suffering caused by war point to

its savagery and inhumanity. *Hadji Murad* – the work which Wittgenstein considered 'the most disclosive of Tolstoy's Christian philosophy'[74] – has been
seen by many critics as essentially a parable of non-violence, its graphic
descriptions of the slaughter of war-making underlining the horror and degradation of all violence and pointing, by implication, to the necessity for brotherhood and love among men. *Resurrection*, the work Tolstoy wrote specifically to
raise money for the pacifist Dukhobors, has many passages condemning acts of
institutional violence – the incarceration of prisoners in inhuman conditions,
the sanctioning of official executions, the forcible conscription of young soldiers, all on the spurious grounds that they are necessary for the defence of
the state. The following passage suggests that criminal behaviour amongst the
masses is largely a reaction to the violence practised by the state, and is justified in the minds of criminals by the same criteria as those that state institutions employ to give moral sanction to their activities:

> They were dealt with as in war, and they naturally employed the same
> means as were used against them. And just as military men live in an
> atmosphere of public opinion that not only conceals from them the guilt
> of their actions but represents these actions as feats of heroism, so these
> political offenders lived among people of their own persuasion who cre-
> ated an atmosphere which made the cruel actions they committed in the
> face of danger and at the risk of liberty and life and all that is dear to
> men, seem not wicked but glorious. Nekhlyudov found in this the
> explanation of the surprising phenomenon that men of the mildest char-
> acter who seemed incapable of witnessing the suffering of any living
> creature, much more of inflicting pain, should be quietly prepared to
> murder men; almost all of them considering murder lawful and just on
> certain occasions: as a means of self-defence, and for the attainment of
> their high purpose, which was the general welfare. The importance the
> revolutionists attributed to their cause, and consequently to themselves,
> flowed naturally from the importance the government attached to their
> actions, and the cruelty of the punishments it inflicted on them. They
> had to have a high opinion of themselves to be able to bear what they
> were made to suffer.

These words are echoed in 'I Cannot Be Silent', an essay where Tolstoy
condemns various violent practices – such as the interrogation, torture and
execution of prisoners – commonly practised by state institutions in the name
of law enforcement. Insisting that violence simply breeds more violence, he castigates state authorities for exemplifying the antithesis of the values they purport to serve, and thereby creating a climate in which violence is legitimised:

That is how the crimes committed by the government act on the worst, the least moral, of the people, and these terrible deeds must also have an influence on the majority of men of average morality. Continually hearing and reading about the most terrible, inhuman brutality committed by the authorities, that is, by persons whom the people are accustomed to honour as the best of men, the majority of average people, especially the young, preoccupied with their own affairs, instead of realising that those who do such horrid deeds are unworthy of honour, involuntarily come to the opposite conclusion, and argue that if men generally honoured do things that seem to us horrible, probably these things are not as horrible as we suppose.[75]

Ever since he served as an officer in the Crimean War and witnessed the atrocities perpetrated in the name of patriotism and freedom, Tolstoy had been loud in his condemnation of war-making in all its forms. All this reached a climax with 'Bethink Yourselves!' a manifesto issued after the outbreak of the Russo-Japanese War in 1904. Denouncing those responsible for this 'universal stupefaction and brutalisation', he declared: 'Men who are separated from each other by thousands of miles, hundreds and thousands of such men (on the one hand Buddhists whose law forbids the killing, not only of men, but of animals, on the other hand, Christians professing the law of brotherhood and love) like wild beasts, on land and sea, are seeking out one another in order to kill, torture and mutilate each other in the most cruel way possible.'[76] Brought by the 'deceit of centuries' to recognise the greatest crime on earth – the murder of one's fellow man – as a 'virtuous act', they are the victims, he says, of a huge fraud perpetrated by churchmen and statesmen, seeking, by spurious means, to convince them of the morality of their deeds. There is pathos as well as anger in his description of the deluded masses leaving their homes to risk their lives in pursuit of utterly false and misguided ideals:

Stupefied by prayers, sermons, exhortations, by processions, pictures and newspapers, the cannon-fodder – hundreds of thousands of men, uniformly dressed, carrying divers deadly weapons, leaving their parents, wives, children, with hearts of agony but with artificial bravado – go where they, risking their own lives, will commit the most dreadful acts of killing men whom they do not know and who have done them no harm. And they are followed by doctors and nurses who somehow imagine that at home they cannot serve simple peaceful suffering people but can only serve those who are engaged in slaughtering each other. Those who remain at home are gladdened by news of the murder of men, and when they learn that many Japanese have been killed they thank someone whom they call God.

All this is not only regarded as the manifestation of elevated feeling, but those who refrain from such manifestations, if they endeavour to disabuse men, are deemed traitors and betrayers, and are in danger of being abused and beaten by a brutalised crowd, which in its defence of its insanity and cruelty can possess no other weapon than brute force.[77]

Tolstoy insisted therefore that the refusal to engage in war-making was the only legitimate stance for a Christian and he advised his followers that they must always follow this course of action, regardless of the consequences of doing so. He warned they could expect personal vilification for their beliefs and would be accused of cowardice, treason against their country, betrayal of their fellowman, or worse. Even in the instance of self-defence – the most fundamental dilemma for all pacifists – he still insisted violence could not be employed. His position on this matter was the same as that of earlier advocates of non-violence, such as Erasmus and Comenius, which is, that total trust in God and submission to His will, even should this require the sacrifice of life itself, is the only defensible option for a Christian in such conditions. The impact of these teachings was manifested in the communities of Tolstoyan Christians that sprang up all over the world in the 1890s, all of them dedicated to the radical ideals he had promoted, particularly the ideal of non-resistance which they too saw as the heart of the Christian message. Outside the Christian fold his most notable disciple was Mohandas Gandhi. Gandhi, then a young lawyer in Johannesburg, wrote to Tolstoy the year before the latter's death: 'I, as well as some of my friends, have for some time firmly believed in the teaching of non-resistance to evil by force, and we still believe it. Besides it has fallen to my good luck to study your writings which have profoundly affected my outlook on life.'[78]

To many, however, the ideal of non-resistance seems unrealisable in practice; to some the very concept seems simplistic and naive. A final judgement on Tolstoy's position on the whole issue would need, however, to take account of three main considerations. The first is prompted by a distinction to be found in correspondence from Tolstoy to Adin Ballou, the nineteenth-century American pacifist and author of *Christian Non-Resistance*. In a letter to Ballou Tolstoy spoke of 'compromise as being inevitable in practice', but insisted 'it cannot be admitted in theory'. 'The great sin,' he said, is compromise in theory, the plan to lower the ideal of Christ in order to make it attainable.'[79] While recognising the inevitability that Christian ideals – especially one so challenging as non-resistance to evil – will be constantly violated in practice, he would not countenance any dilution of the ideals themselves. Like Kierkegaard he insisted on the absolute truth of Christ's injunction, 'Be ye perfect as your heavenly Father is perfect',[80] however remote the likelihood of its realisation, and saw Christian morality as being essentially aspirational, i.e.

constantly driven by the aspiration to perfection. Secondly in an essay, 'Thou shalt Kill No One', he interprets Christ's words as prohibiting 'resistance to evil *by evil*',[81] clearly allowing for the morality of non-violent opposition and protest. He himself relentlessly opposed the authorities of Church and State in Russia for the last thirty years of his life, denouncing the injustices he witnessed all around him – draconian laws and punishments, inhuman conditions in industry, inequalities in the distribution of material resources, the exploitation of women, cruelty to animals, and many other issues. And his opposition extended to urging young people to refuse to accept state employment or to serve in the armed forces so long as those injustices continued. Thirdly, as Nikolai Berdyaev has shown, Tolstoy was profoundly influenced by the traditions of ethical maximalism associated with certain strands in Russian religious philosophy and this goes a long way towards explaining his uncompromising stance on non-resistance. In his Introduction to Tolstoy's *Essays From Tula* Berdyaev explains the issue in the following terms:

> Tolstoy used to say that the only thing in which he had unshakeable faith was the Good. The Good for him was God. This shows his greatness, but also his limitations. Unlike Dostoevsky he remained unaware of the mysterious, mystical aspect of Christianity: and it is not easy to acquit him on the charge of stuffy moralism, though this applies perhaps more to the 'Tolstoyans' than to Tolstoy himself. But, however much he may have put a moral straightjacket on himself and upon those to whom he preached, his very moralism was a sign of his clear and utterly truthful conscience and of his love for unadulterated truth. Like a true Russian he was a maximalist, and we may reiterate how important it is that the testimony of maximal moral truth should sound in our age when truth is dimmed or falsified or lost. In the great conflict between Tolstoy's artistic genius and his moral convictions, in which the former was, in the end, sacrificed for the latter, there was revealed something eternally human as well as morally significant. His ethical maximalism was itself bound up with his belief in true, undivided, integral humanity, and with his awareness that life is doomed to unrelieved isolation and atomisation unless men recover their original, uncorrupted manhood.[82]

In this, as in all other issues of moral or ethical concern, the final explanation for Tolstoy's position lies in the absolutist character of his Christian beliefs, a truth abundantly testified not merely in his purely religious writings, but in those he devoted to philosophical and social issues as well. It is vividly attested in his writings on the nature of history and the whole process of social reform as will be shown in the forthcoming section.

'SEEK YE FIRST THE KINGDOM OF GOD'

The nature and meaning of the historical process is one of Tolstoy's major preoccupations – it is the overarching theme of *War and Peace* – and is deeply bound up with his most fundamental religious beliefs. Its importance can only be fully understood in the context of his faith. Dismissed by some commentators on *War and Peace* as an irrelevant digression in that work, it is recognised by others as the focus of Tolstoy's understanding of the events which the novel describes. The theme has been seriously misinterpreted by George Steiner in his work, *Tolstoy or Dostoevsky*, but has been the subject of enlightened critical attention from scholars such as Berlin, Spence, Hengel, Sampson and Seeley.[83] As Berlin has said, Tolstoy's eminence as a novelist has overshadowed his importance as a philosopher and critical thinker, and a full and thorough appreciation of his work demands that all its elements be properly integrated in a single comprehensible whole. Though stopping short of tracing his philosophy of history to its origins in his religious beliefs, Berlin's comments in *The Hedgehog and the Fox* clearly suggest that Tolstoy's interest in the historical process was essentially an interest in 'first causes', in the ultimate laws governing the existence of mankind. Tolstoy, he writes, 'was tormented by the ultimate problems which face young men in every generation – about good and evil, the origin and purpose of the universe and its inhabitants, the causes of all that happens; but the answers provided by theologians and metaphysicians struck him as absurd, if only because of the words in which they were formulated – words which bore no apparent reference to the everyday world of ordinary common sense to which he clung obstinately, even before he became aware of what he was doing, as being alone real'.[84]

Tolstoy rejected the rationalist historicism of nineteenth century philosophy, particularly condemning the Hegelian version of the nature of historical progress and all others that derived authority and support from it. He also rejected the closely linked historicist interpretations of the scriptures by writers such as Renan, Strauss and Bauer – each of whom he studied closely in the 1870s – seeing their attempts to integrate the Gospel narrative into the evolutionary process of history as falsifying its essential character and significance. 'The Christian truth,' he wrote in a letter to a friend in 1878, 'that is to say the expression of the Absolute good, the highest good that can be, is an expression that has regard to the essence, consequently, is outside the forms of time.' He continued: 'However, Renan makes its absolute expression and its historical expression coincide, thus reducing it to temporary appearance. If the Christian truth is deep and great, it is uniquely because it is an absolute subjectivity. But if you must study Christianity in its objective manifestation then it is put on the same level as the Napoleonic Code.'[85] Christian truth, he insisted – like Pasternak almost a century later—transcends history and all temporal issues and events must be understood ultimately in their relation to its trans-historical reality. All ideologies, all social and philosophical theories must be judged, he said, in the context of the spiritual message conveyed by Christ. His quarrel with the historicists derived from what he saw as their failure to identify the dualism at the heart of the entire historical process – the dualism of the temporal and the eternal. This was a conclusion that was reached by Tolstoy, however, only after a slow process of soul-searching, of which we see some early intimations in *War and Peace*.

At an early point in the novel we find a strong emphasis on the dualistic character of history. At the opening of Part IX Tolstoy, as narrator, is reflecting on the apparently deterministic course of historical events. 'If Napoleon had not taken offence at the request to withdraw beyond the Vistula, and had not commanded his troops to advance, there would have been no war,' he writes. 'But if all the sergeants had been unwilling to serve on another campaign, there could have been no war either.' These, he suggests, are the seemingly contingent happenings which lead in turn to the major events that determine the fate of thousands, possibly millions, of individuals. Where, he asks, does the concept of individual responsibility and freedom fit into all this:

> We are forced to fall back upon fatalism in history to explain irrational events (that is those of which we cannot comprehend the reason). The more we try to explain those events in history rationally, the more irrational and incomprehensible they seem to us. Every man lives for himself, making use of his free-will for attainment of his own objects, and feels in his whole being that he can do or not do any action. But as soon as he does anything, that act, committed at a certain moment in time, becomes irrevocable and is the property of history, in which it has a significance, predestined and not subject to free choice.
>
> There are two aspects to the life of every man: the personal life, which is free in proportion as its interests are abstract, and the elemental life of the swarm, in which a man must inevitably follow the laws laid down for him.
>
> Consciously a man lives on his own account in freedom of will, but he serves as an unconscious instrument in bringing about the historical ends of humanity. An act he has once committed is irrevocable, and that act of his, coinciding in time with millions of acts of others, has an historical value. The higher a man's place in the social scale, the more connections he has with others, and the more power he has over them, the more conspicuous is the inevitability and predestination of every act he commits. 'The hearts of kings are in the hands of God.' The king is the slave of history.

> History – that is the unconscious life of humanity in the swarm, in
> the community – makes every minute of the life of kings its own, as an
> instrument for attaining its ends.

He sees the consciousness of freely elected choice as an essential feature of
human existence yet perceives a greater necessity determining the final course
of events which lies beyond the control of man's will. Individual actions and
choices seem mere entities in a grand mosaic that is ultimately governed by
Necessity. Throughout the novel, however, he repeatedly questions the fatalis-
tic implications of this view. Does free will have any meaning at all? Is there a
freedom outside space and time unconditioned by its finite causality? Is moral
freedom one great illusion? Is everything subject to one vast inexorable
Necessity? These are the tortured questions that run through *War and Peace*,
and Tolstoy's concluding position seems a depressing affirmation of the naturalistic determinism of the historical process itself. Isaiah Berlin gives this
paraphrase of his position at the end of the novel: 'History, only history, only
the sum of the concrete events in time and space – the sum of the actual experience of actual men and women in their relation to one another and to an
actual three-dimensional, empirically experienced, physical environment – this
alone contained the truth, the material out of which genuine answers –
answers needing for their apprehension no special senses or faculties which
normal human beings did not possess – might be constructed.'

But even in *War and Peace* there are intimations of a more complex dualism than all of this would suggest. If causal determinism is all pervasive in
human existence, the novel suggests its workings are enormously complex and
mysterious, there being a multiplicity, perhaps an infinity, of possible causes
for any event. This points to the possibility of an order of freedom beyond the
realm of rationalistic explanation. To quote G.W. Spence: 'He was driven into
believing in the co-existence of two distinct realms: the realm of events subject
to time and space and in dependence on cause, and an obscure realm of metaphysical freedom.'[86] There are hints in the novel that human consciousness
inhabits a realm of metaphysical freedom that transcends the laws of Necessity
to which human *behaviour* is nevertheless subordinate. In Chapter 8 of the
Second part of the Epilogue this passage occurs:

> If history had to deal with external phenomena, the establishment of
> this simple and obvious law would be sufficient, and our argument
> would be at an end. But the law of history relates to man. A particle of
> matter cannot tell us that it does not feel the inevitability of attraction
> and repulsion, and that the law is not true. Man, who is the subject of
> history, bluntly says: I am free, and so I am not subject to law.

The presence of the question of the freedom of the will, if not openly expressed, is felt at every step in history.

All seriously thinking historians are involuntarily led to this question. All the inconsistencies, and the obscurity of history, and the false path that science has followed, is due to that unsolved question.

If the will of every man were free, that is, if every man could act as he chose, the whole of history would be a tissue of disconnected accidents.

If one man only out of millions once in a thousand years had the power of acting freely, that is, as he chose, it is obvious that a single free act of that man in opposition to the laws governing human action would destroy the possibility of any laws whatever governing all humanity.

If there is but one law controlling the actions of men, there can be no free will, since men's will must be subject to that law.

In this contradiction lies the question of the freedom of the will, which from the most ancient times has occupied the best intellects of mankind, and has from the most ancient times been regarded as of immense importance.

Looking at man as a subject of observation from any point of view – theological, historical, ethical, philosophical – we find a general law of necessity to which he is subject like everything existing. Looking at him from within ourselves, as what we are conscious of, we feel ourselves free.

This consciousness is a source of self-knowledge utterly apart and independent of reason. Through reason man observes himself; but he knows himself only through consciousness.

These words strongly anticipate a passage from *On Life* (written almost twenty years later) which addresses the question of man's relation to time and space: 'When a man asks himself about his place in time and space it seems to him at first that he stands in the midst of infinite time extending in both directions, and that he is the centre of a sphere whose surface is everywhere and nowhere. And it is just this self outside of time and space that a man really knows.'[87] Both passages point to a higher freedom of consciousness coexisting ambiguously with the concept of life as being governed by causal Necessity. G.W. Spence has explained this paradox through the idea of 'will as a thing-in-itself', manifested as a free consciousness, in tension with the causality of finite existence. 'Tolstoy,' he writes, 'seems to be saying: "I am free because I am alive, for my manifestation in time and space is a manifestation of the essence of life, which is free. But I am not free to decide how my existence shall be arranged, or even what I shall do".'[88] *A Confession*, which was also written several years after *War and Peace*, links consciousness with faith, with man's awareness of the infinite, that which exists beyond space and time. And *The Kingdom of God Is Within You* (a later work again) sees consciousness as the trans-causal force that brings the soul into contact with God, which it finds within its own spiritual interiority. By that stage Tolstoy saw the meaning of history as being determined, not by the historical process itself, but by a force outside time and space, the infinite, or God, which is reachable through faith.

Berlin distinguishes between two kinds of understanding in Tolstoy's writings: the rationalist/scientific view which is the method of inquiry by which historical issues are normally addressed, and the intuitional understanding of believers, poets and mystics which seeks to penetrate beyond the realms of the empirical and the phenomenal. The latter, he says, is exemplified in *War and Peace* in the spiritual vision attained by Prince Andrei and Pierre. He finds their newly discovered vision vague and unspecified but focussed nonetheless on suprarational truths. 'Something is perceived,' he writes, 'there is a vision, or at least a glimpse, a moment of revelation which in some sense explains and reconciles, a theodicy, a justification of what exists and happens, as well as its elucidation. What does it consist in? Tolstoy does not tell us in so many words.'[89] One must question the accuracy of the latter statement, even in relation to *War and Peace*. Is the answer to the question posed by Berlin not given by Prince Andrei as he lies on his deathbed, ('Love hinders death ... All, everything that I understand, I understand only because I love ... Love is God' etc.) and by Pierre in his dialogue with Karataev ('Now he had learned to see the great, the eternal and the infinite in everything' etc.) This vision of God and the power of loving consciousness or faith may only be briefly disclosed in passages such as these but it is fully explained by Tolstoy in subsequent writings, both didactic and fictional. All affirm his belief that the meaning of the historical or the temporal must be sought beyond both, in a sphere not reachable by reason, only by faith. It is faith, he insists, again and again, which enables man to penetrate the infinite; the freedom it confers derives from its power to transcend the finite, the materio-temporal, the historical. The dualism of freedom and necessity must be comprehended therefore in the context of the higher dualism of the eternal and the temporal, the finite and infinite. Man's freedom, he concludes, consists ultimately in the power afforded him by faith to transcend the dualities of the historical and the temporal, to see both from the higher vantage point of the infinite and eternal.

That vision becomes fully apparent in Tolstoy's writings from the time he wrote *A Confession*. It remained profoundly in conflict with the claims of reason, as is evident from several passages in that work, and it remained a tortured vision to the end. It provided him with the moral and spiritual perspectives, however, against which all temporal and material issues could be appraised. This is evident particularly in his writings on social reform. Though passionately committed to changing the inhuman conditions in contemporary Russian society, as well as the myriad instances of exploitation and injustice existing throughout European society in general, he nonetheless insisted that such reforms would have to be effected through the individual pursuit of moral self-perfection rather than the revolutionary praxis of social or political ideology. The extent of his commitment to social reform is evident from essays such as 'The Slavery of Our Times, 'An Appeal to Social Reformers', 'The End of the Age' and 'I Cannot Be Silent' – in all of which he denounced the capitalistic exploitation of workers, the inequitable distribution of wealth, coercive policies on taxation, and the evils of private property. He urged his readers to exercise their Christian responsibility to oppose all such injustices actively and relentlessly. But underlying all these essays is a questioning both of the whole idea of the evolutionary progress of mankind and of the social utopias founded on this. In works such as 'Progress and Education' he attacked the whole notion of human progress, seeing it as an outcome of Hegelian rationalism, a historicist concept whose most horrific outcome he eventually came to recognise as the ideology of Marxism. In the second chapter of *A Confession* he admits that he himself was once an adherent of 'the religion of progress', the myth of the progressive development of mankind, effected through the process of cultural evolution. But he reasserted the position he had earlier affirmed in 'Progress and Education' that what matters are the eternal laws that are 'written in the soul of each man', against which all temporal progress becomes insignificant and inconsequential.

In *Anna Karenina* these questions are closely explored by Levin who insists, like Tolstoy himself in his socio-philosophical writings, that genuine social reform must be founded on personal morality, to which social morality must always be subordinated. His portrait of his brother Sergei, a socialist, points satirically to the ambivalent character of his humanitarianism, founded as it is on an abstract, generalised love of mankind, lacking the humility and selflessness of a genuinely altruistic love. For Sergei, his brother says, this commitment to an abstract ideal merely gratified a selfish pride by affording him an image of himself as a great benefactor of mankind:

> Konstantin Levin regarded his brother as a man of immense intellect and culture, as generous in the highest sense of the word, and possessed of a special faculty for working for the public good. But in the depths of his heart, the older he became, and the more intimately he knew his brother, the more and more frequently the thought struck him that this faculty of working for the public good, of which he felt himself utterly

devoid, was possibly not so much a quality as a lack of something – not a lack of good, honest, noble desires and tastes, but a lack of vital force, of what is called heart, of that impulse which drives a man to choose someone out of the innumerable paths of life, and to care only for that one. The better he knew his brother, the more he noticed that Sergei Ivanovich, and many other people who worked for the public welfare, were not led by an impulse of the heart to care for the public good, but reasoned from intellectual considerations that it was a right thing to take interest in public affairs, and consequently took interest in them. Levin was confirmed in this generalisation by observing that his brother did not take questions affecting the public welfare or the question of the immortality of the soul a bit more to heart than he did chess problems, or the ingenious construction of a new machine.

Persistently Tolstoy warns that the pursuit of purely social ideals is endlessly open to the corrupting force of self-interest masquerading as an altruistic devotion to the welfare of mankind. 'I imagine the mainspring of all our actions is after all self-interest,' Levin tells his brother as they debate the need to improve the conditions of the poverty-stricken masses. 'No sort of activity is likely to be lasting unless it is founded on self-interest … that's a universal principle, a philosophical principle,' he says. Later he abandons all such solutions to the problems of life, i.e. those founded on abstract, philosophical principles, in favour of those founded on the Christian ideal of self-perfection attained through humility, faith and love. Nekhlyudov undergoes a similar transformation. Initially drawn to the socialist theories of Henry George, he grows disenchanted with all solutions to the ills of society that are based on purely socio-economic principles. This occurs mainly as a result of his meeting with the Marxist revolutionary, Markel Kondratyev. A cold-blooded fanatic, single-minded in his pursuit of social objectives Kondratyev is ultimately driven by a venomous and indiscriminate hatred of all those he blames for the corruption and disorder of society. Tolstoy' portrayal of Kondratyev's fanaticism is unalleviated by his suggestion that the latter was capable of some limited compassion for one of his comrades and for Maslova:

> His religious views were of the same negative nature as his views of existing economic conditions. Having seen the absurdity of the religion in which he was brought up, and having freed himself from it with great effort – at first with fear but later with rapture – he, as if wishing to revenge himself for the deception that had been practised on him and on his ancestors, was never tired of venomously and angrily ridiculing priests and religious dogmas.

He was ascetic by habit, contenting himself with very little, and like all who have been used to work from childhood and whose muscles have been developed, he could work much and easily and was quick at any manual labour; but what he valued most was the leisure in prisons and at the halting-stations, which enabled him to continue his studies. He was now studying the first volume of Karl Marx, and carefully hid the book in his sack, as if it were a great treasure ... He behaved with reserve and indifference to all his comrades, except Novodvorov, to whom he was greatly attached, and whose arguments on all subjects he accepted as irrefutable truths.

He had an infinite contempt for women, whom he looked upon as a hindrance in all useful activity. But he pitied Maslova and was gentle with her, for he considered her an example of the way in which the lower are exploited by the upper classes. The same reason made him dislike Nekhlyudov, so that he talked little with him and never pressed his hand, but when greeting him only held out his own to be pressed.

Tolstoy portrays a similarly misguided fanaticism in Kondratyev's comrade, Novodvorov. Equally dogmatic and resolute – 'Having once chosen a direction, he never doubted or hesitated, and was therefore certain that he never made a mistake' – he too was driven both by his belief in an abstract creed and by unrestrained hatred for most of those with whom he came in contact: 'He did not love anyone, and looked upon all men of note as rivals, and could he have done it would willingly have treated them as old male monkeys treat young ones. He would have torn all mental power, all capacity, from other men, so that they should not interfere with the display of his talents.' Like Levin, Nekhlyudov finds fulfilment, not primarily in the pursuit of social ideals, but in the spiritual self-renewal that comes from repentance of his sins and reconciliation with those he has wronged. The message that is conveyed by both novels is that the spiritual fulfilment that is attained through the individual quest for moral self-perfection, together with the selfless love of one's neighbour, is the only true basis for the social reform of mankind.

This message is reaffirmed by Tolstoy in the more explicit language of his non-fictional prose. In *The Law of Violence and the Law of Love* he condemns revolutionary movements for their assumption of responsibility to act on behalf of the masses with the object of changing the conditions of their lives. 'The belief that some people can arrange the lives of the majority in the name of which the greatest crimes are committed is the greatest hindrance to achieving the true well-being of humanity,' he warned. 'Rivers of blood have been shed in the name of this, inestimable suffering has been caused by such movements and these form the greatest obstacle to society's successful creation of those particular improvements in life appropriate to our time.' The reason such movements cannot succeed in their objective to transform society, he says, is because they neglect to begin the process of social reform with the moral perfection of their own members: 'Under the pretext of altering and improving social conditions, they put all their energy into influencing other people, thus neglecting their own inner self-perfection which alone can enhance a change in the structure of society as a whole.' 'Human life in its totality,' he declares, 'advances and cannot help moving forward towards the eternal ideals of perfection, only if each individual person advances towards his own personal and unrestricted perfection.' The reform of humanity will be achieved, he declares, in one of the most eloquent passages in *The Law of Violence and the Law of Love*, when each individual confronts the root causes of the ills of society in the corruption of his own soul:

> All you suffering men of the Christian world, both rulers and rich and poor and oppressed, need only free yourselves from the deception of false Christianity and government (concealing what Christ revealed to you and what is demanded by your reason and your heart) and it will become clear to you that it is in yourselves and only in yourselves that you will find the cause of all the bodily suffering (want), and spiritual suffering (awareness of injustice, envy and annoyance) that torments you—the oppressed and poor. And that it is also in yourselves, the rich and powerful, that you will find the cause of those fears, pangs of conscience and awareness of the sinfulness of our lives, all of which disturbs you in varying degrees according to your moral sensitivity ...
>
> 'Come to me, all ye that labour and are heavily laden, and I will give you rest. Take my yoke upon you and learn of me; for I am meek and lowly in heart; and ye shall find rest unto your souls. For my yoke is easy and my burden is light.' (Matt. 1, 28-31) You will be saved and delivered from the evil you endure and receive the true well-being you so clumsily strive after, not through personal desire nor envy, nor through adherence to a party programme; nor through hatred, indignation, or the pursuit of fame, nor even through a sense of justice, and above all not through troubling yourselves about the organisation of other people's lives. However strange it may seem, it is only through an activity within your own soul, involving no external aim and no consideration of what might come of it.[90]

3

'Knight-Errantry of the Spirit': Unamuno's Poetry and Prose

HERMENEUTICS OF CHRISTIAN ART

In most of the histories of philosophy that I know, philosophic systems are presented to us as if growing out of one another spontaneously, and their authors, the philosophers, appear only as mere pretexts. The inner biography of the philosophers, of the men who philosophised, occupies a secondary place. And yet it is precisely this inner biography that explains for us most things.[1]

So wrote Miguel de Unamuno in the opening pages of his philosophical auto-biography, *Tragic Sense of Life*. It is indeed to the inner biography of his life that we must turn for an understanding of the place that Christianity occupies in his life and work. Significant events and experiences in his life provide the key both to the highly unconventional nature of his Christian faith and to its place in the evolution and development of his art. A lifelong dissenter – he repeatedly challenged Church and State authorities on matters of politics and faith – his independence of spirit goes a long way towards explaining the indi-vidualistic character of his religious beliefs. He was denounced as a heretic by Bishop Plá y Deniel of Salamanca in 1942 and was charged with attempting to undermine the teachings of the Catholic Church. The same prelate, by then the Cardinal-Primate of Spain, asked the Minister for Education in 1953 to prohibit the study of Unamuno's work in schools and universities. Four years later the Vatican assigned two of his books, *Tragic Sense of Life* and *The Agony of Christianity*, to the Index of Forbidden Books, clearly designating them as undesirable reading for Catholics. Though he was long since dead by the time these events occurred, it is unlikely that Unamuno would have been disturbed by them. In an essay, 'The Faith of Pascal', he declared that all 'orthodoxies began by being heresies';[2] in another essay called 'Faith' he pointed to the original meaning of the Greek word *heresias* as 'election' or 'choice',[3] i.e. elect-ing for faith in accordance with personal convictions and beliefs. Despite his disagreements with the Church, he consistently proclaimed his belief in the traditions of the Christian faith and those beliefs found impassioned expression in the prolific output of novels, poems, plays, philosophic and exegetic texts that he maintained from the 1890s to his death in 1936.

In *Recuerdos de niñez y de mocedad* ('Memories of Childhood and Youth')
Unamuno described the strict and orthodox Catholic upbringing he received
both in his childhood home in Bilbao and at the local schools where he was
sent for his primary and secondary education. He recalled the long periods of
silent prayer, the readings in Catholic apologetics, the processions on Church
holidays and the various pious practices that were observed by the Catholics of
the Basque region of Northern Spain. He described how he began to grow disillusioned with Catholic dogmatics when he encountered German idealism as a
student of philosophy and literature at the University of Madrid. Describing
this in a letter to a friend, Federico Urales, he spoke of his loss of faith as a
'conversion' to a more rationalised form of Christian belief than the dogmatic
religion in which he had been raised:

> I carried out my determination to rationalise my faith, and clearly,
> dogma disappeared from my consciousness. By this I mean that my reli-
> gious conversion (such was its name) was slow and gradual. Having
> been a fervent and practising Catholic, I stopped being one, little by
> little, because I tried to make my faith intimate and rational. And one
> Carnival day, I remember well, I suddenly stopped hearing Mass. I then
> hurled myself down the dizzy highway of philosophy. I learned German
> in Hegel, in the stupendous Hegel, who has been one of the thinkers
> who has left the greatest imprint on me. Even today, I believe that the
> root (*fondo*) of my thought is Hegelian. Then I fell in love with
> Spencer; but always interpreting him after the fashion of Hegel. And I
> always returned to my preoccupations and readings concerning the reli-
> gious problem, which is what has always bothered me most. Later I
> read Schopenhauer, who came to enchant me, and who, with Hegel, has
> been among those who have left the greatest imprint on me.[4]

Unamuno's interest in socialism coincided with, and was probably reinforced by, his short-lived 'conversion' to rationalistic Christianity. He joined
the Socialist Party of Bilbao (Agrupacion Socialista) in 1894 and contributed
several articles to its journal, *La Lucha de Clases* ('The Class Struggle').
Within a few years, however, he was expressing reservations about the secularist and socially reductionist ideology of the socialist movement. 'I dream that
socialism may become a true religious reform when Marxist dogmatism fades
away, that it may become something more than purely economic,' he wrote in
a letter to a friend in 1895.[5] Socialism, he wrote, 'sets itself up as one single
doctrine and forgets that after the problem of life comes the problem of
death'. 'From the very bosom of the resolved social question,' he predicted,
'will surge the religious question: is life worth living?'[6] He continued to

denounce injustice, greed and social exploitation and called repeatedly on the state to initiate a range of social reforms. However, he eventually rejected the concept of a 'political Christianity'. 'The Fatherland of a Christian is not of this world,' he wrote in *The Agony of Christianity*.[7] In an article, 'So-Called Social Christianity', he condemned politically radical Christians, arguing that Christianity is essentially concerned with grace and self-sacrifice, that its essence consists in its transcendence of history and all temporal realities. Christ, he said, summoned all, rich and poor alike, to participate in the process of redemption and salvation. Significantly, however, he acknowledged that while the pursuit of justice is not one of the primary concerns of religious faith, it is always a matter of moral concern, and therefore of relevance to the practical expression of that faith. His mature position on the issue is conveyed clearly and unambiguously in this passage from *The Agony of Christianity*:

> It is not the mission of Christianity to resolve socio-economic problems, to solve the problem of poverty amidst wealth, to redistribute earthly goods, the world's goods. And such is the case even if we accept that to redeem the poor from their poverty also means to redeem the rich from their riches, just as to redeem the slave is to redeem the tyrant; so that we must abolish the death sentence not so much to save the condemned as to save the executioner. And yet all this is not the mission of Christianity. Christ summons the rich and the poor, slaves and tyrants, the condemned and the executioners. In the face of doom, of the end of the world and of death, what do poverty and riches amount to, what difference slavery or tyranny, to be executed or to be the executioner?[8]

Unamuno's rejection of ideological socialism coincided with a second religious 'conversion' that was precipitated by a family crisis in 1897. (The whole story of his progression from conventional Catholicism to rationalism and thence to a highly individualised form of Christian belief is portrayed imaginatively in the life of his fictional alter ego, Pachico, in his first novel, *Peace in War*, which was published in 1897; see especially pp. 66-71.) There were already some signs of a growing disenchantment with idealist philosophy in a work he published in 1896, entitled *Filosofía Lógica*. In this work there are indications of a newly emerging logico-existentialist mode of philosophical enquiry which was eventually to mature in his work under the influence of Kierkegaard and Dostoevsky. (There were some intimations of this also in a collection of essays, *en torno al casticismo*, 'On Authentic Tradition', published in 1895.) In 1897 however he underwent a deep personal crisis following the birth of his child, Raimondo. The child was born with a fatal hydrocephalic condition from which he died a few years later. The whole experience brought great spiritual and emotional turmoil to Unamuno. Witnessing the tragedy of a young child's suffering, and finding himself face to face with the terrible reality of death, he once again questioned his most fundamental beliefs. In a letter of 30 October 1897, he wrote:

> I have passed through such internal anguish! It has revealed to me the very depths of the eternal problems, above all of the problem of one's own salvation. I have felt myself at the boundary of unending Nothingness, and I have ended by feeling that there are more ways of entering relation with reality than just reason, that there is grace and there is faith, the faith which is in the last analysis a matter of wanting to believe. Do I in reality believe, or is it just that I want to believe? I do not know. I walk disoriented, but with greater inward peace.[9]

Some months later he told a friend, Jimenez Ilundain: 'When the image of death surprises us we should think without ceasing on it even to the point of seeing everything through it as one sees through a pair of dark glasses.'[10] And in a highly self-revealing comment he wrote: 'And today I find myself to a great extent in a state of disorientation, but a Christian, and asking of God the strength and light to feel that the joy is true. What I long for above all and before everything else is freedom, freedom, real freedom. Freedom to be master, not the slave of myself. Freedom which consists in being what I am, and not what others would make me be.'[11] In these passages we can recognise the basic principles of the philosophy eventually unfolded in *Tragic Sense of Life*: the insistence on the radical freedom of the experience of faith, the concept of faith as transcending reason, the idea of faith as the 'will to faith'.

All three principles are comprehended in the all-embracing conviction that faith is ultimately disclosed through love. If the death of his young son brought him face to face with the question of immortality, Unamuno, by his own admission, discovered the power of love, its potential to disclose the infinite, through his profoundly loving relationship with his wife, Concepción Lizárraga (Concha), whom he married in 1891 and with whom he lived until her death two years before his own, in 1934. 'We knew each other almost as children, in Bilbao,' he wrote to Juan Maragall. 'At twelve years of age she returned to her village, Guernica, and there I went as often as I could, to walk with her beneath the shade of the old and symbolic oak. And there I married. The joy of the heart overflows from the eyes of my wife, and before her I am ashamed to be sad.'[12] He described the faith-giving power of their love in a passage from *Como se hace una novela* ('How A Novel Is Made') which recalls an episode from the period when they were both plunged into despair at the condition of their young son:

> In a moment of supreme and abysmatic anguish, seeing me weeping with superhuman sobs, in the clutches of the Angel of Nothingness, she rushed into my arms and cried out from the depths of her maternal heart, "My son!" Then it was that I discovered all that God has done for me in this woman, the mother of my children, my virgin mother, who has made my story her own, my mirror of eternity.[13]

In these years Unamuno briefly resumed the practice of traditional Catholicism but again became disillusioned with institutionalised religion, opting instead for the unconventional, radically scripture-based Christianity that became his lifelong faith. He now saw his role as that of rediscovering the wellsprings of the Christian faith that lay hidden beneath the layers of rationalistic philosophy. In a letter of 1898 he wrote: 'The past generation was able to live in intellectual positivism, because educated in Christian faith, it carried this faith beneath its positivism, as its unconscious support. But a generation educated in positivism must return by force to seek the hidden spring which its parents closed for it.'[14]

The most eloquent statement of his new position was given in an essay-drama, 'Nicodemus the Pharisee', one of a series of meditations on scripture he wrote in 1898 and eventually published in *The Agony of Christianity*. In this work he reenacts the visit to Christ by Nicodemus who comes for spiritual counsel under the cover of darkness, fearing the disapproval of society, especially of his fellow Pharisees. In Christ's words Nicodemus finds a faith that transcends the sterile and elitist intellectualism of the Pharisaic movement. The deadening spirit of that intellectualism is condemned by the narrator in the following terms: 'This intellectualism is a terrible illness which undermines the strength of the most distinguished, of those who consider themselves the flower of the human stock, of those who feign to believe that the millions of simple beings who keep quiet, and pray, and work, are merely there to produce a handful of geniuses and sub-geniuses. In short, these intellectualists are Pharisees in the strict definition of that word.'[15] He speaks of intellectual elitism as an infirmity 'similar in the spiritual order to what in the material order constitutes autophagia: as in an ulcerated stomach, for example, where the epithelium having been destroyed, the organ begins to devour itself'. By comparison he sees faith as a universal potentiality, accessible to all. Faith is confidence and trust in God, a 'heartfelt handing-over of the will, a serene confidence in which nature and spirit concur in a final end' ...

> Faith! How little we meditate with our hearts, rather than with our heads alone, concerning the nature and importance of faith! It can not be a mere intellectual adherence to an abstract principle, to a formula

almost without content; nor can it be the affirmation of metaphysical or theological principles. No, it must be an act of abandonment and a heart-felt handing-over of the will, a serene confidence in which nature and the spirit concur in a final end, in which by naturalising the spirit we render it more intensely spiritual, and in which by spiritualising nature we render it more intensely natural; faith is a firm confidence that truth dwells within us, that we are its vase and receptacle, and that truth is consolation, a firm confidence that if we act with a pure and simple intention we serve a supreme design, whatever it may be.[16]

The implications of this important statement on the nature of faith will be explored in some detail later. Meanwhile it is necessary to identify some significant influences in the development of Unamuno's religious beliefs and in the manner in which they find expression in his art. Three stand out as being especially fruitful: Kierkegaard, the Spanish mystics and Cervantes. In 1899, the same year as he wrote his essay, 'Faith', with its crucial emphasis on faith as *pistis* rather than *gnosis*, he encountered Kierkegaard's name in a study of Ibsen by Georg Brandes. In the course of his philological studies as a student at the University of Madrid, Unamuno had taught himself Dano-Norwegian to read the works of Ibsen and this led to his discovery of the work of Kierkegaard which he also read in the vernacular. Immediately he found powerful affinities with Kierkegaard – with his criticism of institutional religion, his rejection of dogmatism, his irrationalist view of faith, his sense of the infinite and unconditional, above all, his concept of an aesthetico-religious totality. *Tragic Sense of Life* has numerous references to Kierkegaard. 'What a man!' he exclaims in the opening pages; 'let us hear what our brother Kierkegaard has to say',[17] he prefaces his comments on the inadequacies of abstract thought. He quotes the words from the *Concluding Unscientific Postscript* on the relationship of art to faith: 'Poetry is illusion before knowledge; religion illusion after knowledge. Between poetry and religion the worldly wisdom of living plays its comedy. Every individual who does not live either poetically or religiously is a fool.'[18] He closely follows Kierkegaard in defining imagination as the creative potentiality that integrates reason and faith, sensibility, feeling and thought. This passage is critical for an understanding of his own literary-philosophic method:

> For reason annihilates and imagination completes, integrates or totalises; reason by itself alone kills, and it is imagination that gives life. If it is true that imagination by itself alone, in giving us life without limit, leads us to lose our identity in the All and also kills us as individuals, it kills us by excess of life. Reason, the head, speaks to us the word

Nothing! imagination, the heart, the word All! and between all and nothing, by the fusion of the all and the nothing within us, we live in God, who is All, and God lives in us who, without Him are nothing. Reason reiterates, Vanity of vanities! all is vanity! And imagination answers, Plenitude of plenitudes! all is plenitude! And thus we live the vanity of plenitude or the plenitude of vanity.[19]

Kierkegaard's philosophy blended easily with the purely Spanish influences on Unamuno's work. Convinced from the early 1890s that the authentic spirit of the Spanish philosophic tradition was represented by its mystics rather than its rationalist thinkers, he immersed himself in the work of writers such as St Teresa of Avila and St John of the Cross, each of whom had close associations with the Salamanca region where he had held a university appointment since 1891. Phrases from mystical literature occur frequently in his essays and letters from the 1890s onwards, indicating a preference for its metaphoric language over what he saw as the imaginatively sterile terminology of rationalist thought. 'I became more and more convinced,' he writes in 'The Religion of Quixotism', 'that our philosophy, the Spanish philosophy, is liquescent and diffused in our literature, in our life, in our action, above all, in our mysticism, and not in philosophical systems'.[20] He writes approvingly of 'the philosophy latent in the abstract but passionate thought of the mystics' and asks: 'What is the mysticism of St John of the Cross but a knight-errantry of the heart in the divine warfare.'[21]

The term 'knight-errantry' immediately points to his interest in Cervantes who provided him with the concept of faith as Quixotism, i.e. 'knight-errantry of the spirit.' In 1905, the 300th anniversary of the publication of Cervantes's masterpiece, Unamuno published his *Life of Don Quixote and Sancho*. 'I wrote that book,' he recalled, 'in order to rethink Don Quixote in opposition to the Cervantists and erudite persons, in order to make a living work of what was and still is for the majority a dead letter.' 'We must look for the hero of Spanish thought,' he says, 'not in any actual flesh-and-bone philosopher but in a creation of fiction – a man of action, who is more real than all the philosophers – Don Quixote'[22] Cervantes's hero, he felt, embodied in himself the irrationalism, irrepressible optimism and limitless *joie de vivre* of the genuine Christian spirit – all of which he saw as being comprehended in the ideal of knight-errantry, in the recklessness and incorrigible hopefulness of the spirit of faith. Unamuno gives the essence of the Quixotic philosophy in this passage from *Tragic Sense of Life*:

And the philosophy of Don Quixote cannot strictly be called idealism; he did not fight for ideas. It was of the spiritual order; he fought for

the spirit. Imagine Don Quixote turning his heart to religious speculation – as he himself once dreamed of doing when he met those images
in bas-relief which certain peasants were carrying to set up in the
retablo of their village church – imagine Don Quixote given up to meditation upon eternal truths, and see him ascending Mount Carmel in the
middle of the dark night of the soul, to watch from that summit the
rising of that sun which never sets, and, like the eagle that was St
John's companion on the isle of Patmos, to gaze upon it face to face and
scrutinise its spots ...

And the speculative or meditative Quixotism is, like the practical
Quixotism, madness, a daughter-madness to the madness of the Cross.
And therefore it is despised by the reason. At bottom, philosophy
abhors Christianity, and well did the gentle Marcus Aurelius prove it.
The tragedy of Christ, the divine tragedy, is the tragedy of the Cross.
Pilate, the sceptic, the man of culture, by making a mockery of it,
sought to convert it into a comedy; he conceived the farcical idea of the
king with the reed sceptre and the crown of thorns, and cried 'Behold
the man!' But the people, more human than he, the people that thirsts
for tragedy, shouted, 'Crucify him, crucify him!' And the human, the
intra-human, tragedy is the tragedy of Don Quixote, whose face was
daubed with soap in order that he might make sport for the servants of
the dukes and for the dukes themselves, as servile as their servants.
'Behold the madman!' they would have said ... And the comic, the irrational, tragedy is the tragedy of suffering caused by ridicule and contempt. The greatest height of heroism to which an individual, like a
people, can attain is to know how to face ridicule; better still, to know
how to make oneself ridiculous and not to shrink from the ridicule.[23]

The theme of Quixotism has a dual function in Unamuno's writings: it
points not only to the irrationalist character of the experience of faith but
embodies in itself the method he considered most appropriate for the revelation of that faith. Reference has been made already to his emphasis on the unifying power of the imagination, its integration of spirituality, faith, feeling and
thought in a meaningful and comprehensible whole. 'Imagination,' he declared,
'is the faculty of intuition or inward vision.' 'Our feeling of the world, upon
which is based our understanding of it, is necessarily anthropomorphic and
mythopoeic,' he adds. 'The longing for faith and hope,' he writes, 'is more
than anything else an aesthetic feeling ... We seek in art an image of eternalisation. If for a brief moment our spirit finds peace and rest and assuagement
in the contemplation of the beautiful, even though it finds therein no real cure
for the distress, it is because the beautiful is the revelation of the eternal, of

the divine in things, and beauty but the perpetuation of momentaneity.'[24] In a critical passage he explains that the wholeness of meaning that art conveys is inherent in the language we speak – in its metaphoric structures, its radical imagery and symbolism:

> And it avails us nothing to seek to repress this mythopoeic or anthropo-morphic process and to rationalise our thought, as if we thought only for the sake of thinking and knowing, and not for the sake of living. The very language with which we think prevents us from so doing. Language, the substance of thought, is a system of metaphors with a mythic and anthropomorphic base. And to construct a purely rational philosophy it would be necessary to construct it by means of algebraic formulas or to create a new language for it, an inhuman language – that is to say, one inapt for the needs of life – as indeed Dr Richard Avenarius, Professor of Philosophy at Zürich, attempted to do in his *Critique of Pure Experience (Kritik der reinen Erfahrung)*, in order to avoid preconceptions. And this rigorous attempt of Avenarius, the chief of the critics of experience, ends strictly in pure scepticism.[25]

Repeatedly, he insists on the ontical primacy of the word, seeing all human experience as being structured and shaped by language. 'The child is born unconscious and he makes his consciousness in the breast of his people which is, as it were its spiritual womb,' he declared in an address to his colleagues at Salamanca in 1934. 'It [the child] receives the maternal speech, which is the blood of its spirit, and with it all the vision and all of the conception of the word which it includes,'[26] he said. In *Tragic Sense of Life* he defines thought as 'inward language', and adds that 'the inward language originates in the outward'.[27] Language, he writes in an essay on Dostoevsky, 'is not form, body or wrapping of thought, but thought itself. One does not think *with* words – or other signs, such as pictorial or plastic images – one *thinks* words!'[28] Love itself, he says, is defined, given form, made meaningful, by language: 'Love does not discover that it is love until it speaks, until it says, I love you.'[29]

Further emphasising the originative function of language he speaks of the act of speech as primarily a 'naming' of reality. Naming, he says, using the imagery of Genesis, is the original act of creation: 'To give names to things, as did Adam, is to know them and to make them one's own. Naming is an act of spiritual possession ... To give a name to something is to create it spiritually.' By his naming of the world man 'feels that he lives in a continual creation ... that everything under the sun is new ... and that each moment he goes from one vision to a new vision'.[30] The naming process, he says, defines the person-

hood of all reality: 'The person, the substantial and essential man, is the name
... "My name is" means "I want to be". The man who is made a name
becomes a person.'[31] The act of naming is essentially a symbolic act, an image-
giving gesture, a product of the unified consciousness that Unamuno identified
with the creative power of the imagination. The power of imagination, in turn,
he says, derives its dynamism and force from man's relation to the world – a
relation which, in its highest form, is charged with the power of love. That
relation finds expression in the word, the *logos*, which, by virtue of its symbolic character, is essentially aesthetic, empowered by the unifying force of the
imagination:

> Language is that which gives us reality, and not as a mere vehicle of
> reality, but as its true flesh, of which all the rest, dumb or inarticulate
> representation, is merely the skeleton. *And thus logic operates upon aes-*
> *thetics*, the concept upon the expression, upon the word, and not upon
> the brute perception ... *All things were made by the word, and the word*
> *was in the beginning*. Thought, reason – that is, living language – is an
> inheritance, and the solitary thinker of Aben Tofail, the Arab philoso-
> pher of Guadix, is as absurd as the ego of Descartes. The real and con-
> crete truth, not the methodical and ideal, is: *homo sum, ergo cogito*. To
> feel oneself a man is more immediate than to think.[32]

'I have never been anything but a poet, that is nothing less than a poet,'[33]
Unamuno wrote in a letter to his friend and editor, Federico de Onís. He
wrote to the Catalan poet, Juan Maragall, that 'there is a world of poetry in
which everything is harmonised'.[34] He saw poetic language as the highest fulfilment of the naming, narrating process characterising the creative and loving
dialogue of man with all reality – with his fellowman, with the world and with
God. Thus, while his writings are a compendium of lyrical, autobiographical,
fictional, expositional and philosophic statements, they transcend the boundaries of disciplined discourse to effect a synthesis that is, in essence, aesthetic
and literary. The method of all his work is based on narrative or symbolic evocation, manifested both in the styles of lyrical, fictional and dramatic statement
adopted in his novels, poems and plays and in the process of literary-philosophic self-revelation exemplified in works such as *The Agony of Christianity*
and *Tragic Sense of Life*. Though concerned profoundly with philosophical –
especially metaphysical, ethical and religious – questions, he believed these
could not be resolved though purely rational agencies and needed the unifying
vision of the aesthetic to disclose and clarify their total meaningfulness and
significance. 'Everything and especially philosophy is strictly speaking novel or
legend,' he wrote in the Preface to *Love and Pedagogy*.[35]

All his works – his novels, poems, plays, essays, letters and various prose treatises – testify to his belief in the unifying power of the poetic logos and the truths inherent within it. In an essay, 'What is Truth?' he expressed this principle in specifically Christian terms, seeing Christ as embodying in His person the absolute truth inherent in the Logos or the Word. Echoing the words of St John, 'In the beginning was the Word and the Word was with God and the Word was God,' he writes: 'The word, when it is the true word, the word of truth – and the word of Jesus was the word of absolute truth, so that He was the incarnation of His word – is the creative force that raises man above brute, inhuman nature. Man is what he is because of the word.'[36] That same conviction is expressed in a beautiful lyric from *The Christ of Velázquez*. The poem proceeds from its homage to the work of Velazquez to affirm the mysterious truth of the Incarnation, i.e. the Word as embodied in the Person of the Crucified Christ:

> 'Yet a little while, and the world seeth me
> no more; but ye see me; because I live
> ye shall live also'—Thou didst say; and see,
> the eyes of faith grasp Thee in the most secret
> recesses of the soul and we create,
> through art, thy visible form. By the brush
> of Don Diego, the great master Velazquez—
> his the magic wand. And through it we see
> Thee in flesh today. Thee, the Man eternal
> that makes of us new men. Thy death is travail.
> Thou didst rise to heaven, and thence didst send
> the Comforter to us, the Holy Spirit,
> inspirer of thy faithful flock, that works
> in art and brings us our vision of Thee.
> Incarnate here in this white, silent word
> that speaks with lines and with colours, my tragic
> people tell their faith. It is the supreme
> sacramental drama, for it sets us
> high above death and face to face with God.

DILEMMAS OF A SCEPTICAL FAITH

Unamuno's novel *Amor y pedagogia* ('Love and Pedagogy') is his most forceful condemnation of the spirit of rationalist abstraction, something he sees as having contaminated the traditions of Christianity almost from its inception.

Through the medium of fictional satire he exposes the deficiencies of abstract reason, pointing to its separation of the rational from the irrational elements in human experience as the fundamental weakness in post-Renaissance European culture. He describes the novel's protagonist, Don Avito, as the living embodiment of the spirit of scientific rationalism: 'He appears on the scene for our tale as a young man enthusiastic about all progress and in love with sociology ... He has secretly carried out a Herculean task, that of submitting all his instincts to the power of reason and of making everything about himself purely scientific. He moves by mechanics, digests by chemistry and has his suits cut by projective geometry. But his forte is sociological pedagogy ...' Don Avito entrusts the education of his son, Apolodoro, to his equally science-obsessed companion, Don Fulgencio, who seeks to inculcate in him the positivist values in which they both believe. Their plans are frustrated when Apolodoro falls in love with Clarita, who eventually rejects him. In his despair Apolodoro hangs himself. Don Avito, in his grief, turns for consolation to his wife, Marina, and in his disillusionment with the values of positivistic thought learns the lesson that it is love, not science, that ultimately gives meaning to life and is therefore the only ideal that is truly worthy of our endeavours.

Artistically a very imperfect work, *Love and Pedagogy* nonetheless powerfully underlines the inadequacies of rationalistic thought, a theme that runs through all of Unamuno's writings. In *Tragic Sense of Life* he repeatedly denounces the evils of intellectual abstraction, particularly in the realm of religion and matters of faith. In one impassioned sequence he writes: 'The logical, rational God, the *ens summum*, the *primum movens*, the God who is reached by the three famous ways of negation, eminence and causality, *viae negationis, eminentiae, causalitatis*, is nothing but an idea of God, a dead thing. The traditional and much debated proofs of his existence are, at bottom, merely a vain attempt to determine his essence.'[37] He condemns the scholastic theologians with whose work he had grown disillusioned in his university years at Madrid. In 'What Is Truth' he speaks of the 'vulgarity, imbecility and dotage into which the doctrine we call Thomism has fallen'.[38] His greater criticism is directed, however, at the science-dominated culture that emerged in the wake of mediaeval scholasticism. To the Renaissance and Reformation, he says, we 'owe a new Inquisition, that of science and culture which turns against those who refuse to submit to its orthodoxy the weapons of ridicule and contempt'. 'The end of man,' he writes, parodying the values of the new culture, 'is to create science, to catalogue the universe so that it may be handed back to God in order.'[39] In his essay 'The Vertical of Le Dantec' he deplores the contempt for eternal truths that is manifested in scientific rationalism. He insists, however, that it is not reason itself, but the separation of rational from non-rational modes of knowing and feeling, particularly from the experience of faith, that is the root-cause of the rot that has corrupted European culture. Faith, he insists, is ultimately enriched by reason, albeit through a process of dialectical tension by which it is intellectually vitalised:

> Faith in immortality is irrational. And, notwithstanding, faith, life and reason have mutual need of one another. This vital longing is not properly a problem, cannot assume a logical status, cannot be formulated in propositions susceptible of rational discussion; but it announces itself in us as hunger announces itself. Neither can the wolf that throws itself with the fury of hunger upon its prey or with the fury of instinct upon the she-wolf, enunciate its impulse rationally and as a logical problem. Reason and faith are two enemies, neither of which can maintain itself without the other. The irrational demands to be rationalised and reason only can operate on the irrational. They are compelled to seek mutual support and association. But association in struggle, for struggle is a mode of association.[40]

He insists that faith transcends reason and clearly lies in the realm of the irrational. In a beautiful parable, 'Spin From Your Entrails', which is strongly reminiscent of mystical literature, he describes the irrationalist quest for truth as a descent into darkness, the darkness of the unapprehended and the unknown, which is illuminated only by the inner light of the soul's trust in God. 'It behooves us,' he writes, 'to act like the female glow-worm, which generates light from within, from its own entrails produces the small light which serves, more than to illuminate its way, to illuminate itself, so that its male companion may see it.'[41] Such a faith, he says, was that of Pascal, the 'thinking reed' who 'sought an availing belief to save him from his reason'. Pascal sought it 'in submission and in habit', insisting ''tis the heart, not reason, that feels God.' This irrationalist trust in God, as exemplified by Pascal in the *Pensées*, is seen by Unamuno as the source of all faith:

> The faith which St Paul defined, *pistis* in Greek, is better translated as trust, confidence. The word *pistis* is derived from the verb *peiqw*, which in its active voice means to persuade and in its middle voice to trust in someone, to esteem him as worthy of trust, to place confidence in him, to obey. And *fidare se*, to trust, is derived from the root *fid* – whence *fides*, faith, and also confidence. The Greek root *piq* and the Latin *fid* are twin brothers. In the root of the word 'faith' itself, therefore, there is implicit the idea of confidence, of surrender to the will of another, to a person. Confidence is placed only in persons. We trust in Providence, which we conceive as something personal and conscious, not in Fate,

which is something impersonal. And thus it is in the person who tells us the truth, in the person who gives us hope, that we believe, not directly and immediately in truth or in hope itself.[42]

The role that reason plays in the growth of faith is adversative, therefore, and dialectical; it vitalises faith by subjecting it to endless challenge and scrutiny, occasioning thereby a dialectical tension at the heart of the whole experience. 'There is no certainty in faith,' he declares. 'Absolute certainty and absolute doubt are both alike forbidden to us.' But total scepticism, he argues, is as foreign to nature as total certainty. Complete scepticism, he says, would be 'the extinction of the intelligence and the total death of man', something from which nature recoils. 'It is not given to man to annihilate himself; there is in him something which invincibly resists destruction, I know not what vital faith, indomitable even by his will. Man is simply unable, by virtue of his own nature, to resort to total unbelief: whether he likes it or not, he must believe, because he must act, because he must preserve himself.'[43] Disbelief is not therefore a negative state; Unamuno sees the challenge of scepticism and doubt as a creative tension, enlivening the experience of faith, however dormant, tentative or residual it might be. He distinguishes, however, between two kinds of doubt: Cartesian or philosophic doubt which he sees as cold and analytic – 'of little vitalising force, rather artificial, especially since Descartes degraded it to the function of a method' – and impassioned doubt which is based on 'the eternal conflict between reason and feeling, science and life.' It is the uncertainty generated principally by this latter conflict which characterises the dialectic of faith. This is described in a moving passage from *Tragic Sense of Life*:

> In the ninth chapter of the Gospel according to Mark it is related how a man brought unto Jesus his son who was possessed by a dumb spirit, and wheresoever the spirit took him it tore him, causing him to foam and gnash his teeth and pine away, wherefore he sought to bring him to Jesus that he might cure him. And the Master, impatient of those who sought only for signs and wonders, exclaimed: 'O faithless generation, how long shall I be with you? how long shall I suffer you? bring him to me', and they brought him unto him. And when the master saw him wallowing on the ground, he asked his father how long it was ago since this had come unto him and the father replied that it was since he was a child. And Jesus said unto him: 'If thou canst believe, all things are possible to him that believeth.' And then the father of the epileptic or demoniac uttered these pregnant and immortal words: 'Lord, I believe; help thou mine unbelief.' ... A contradiction seemingly, for if he

believes, if he trusts, how is it that he beseeches the Lord to help his lack of trust? Nevertheless, it is this contradiction that gives to the heart's cry of the father of the demoniac its most profound human value. His faith is a faith that is based on incertitude. Because he believes – that is to say, because he wishes to believe, because he has need that his son should be cured – he beseeches the Lord to help his unbelief, his doubt that such a cure could be effected. Of such is human faith.[44]

Faith therefore involves a lifelong, relentless, 'agonic' struggle. Doubt (*dubitare*), Unamuno points out in his essay, 'Agony', has the same root as *duellum*, meaning struggle or self-conflict. Pascal, he writes, epitomised the tragic and painful struggle with doubt and despair which is the mark of genuine faith: 'Pascal did not resign himself, did not succumb to doubt, submit to negation or *scepsis* ... He did not seek a synthesis of thesis and antithesis, he abided by contradiction ... He avoided victory and feared it, for it might after all be that of his reason over his faith ...'[45] The tragedy of life, he says, lies in the never-ending struggle it involves to create faith from scepticism and doubt. Unamuno illustrates the significance of all this in a highly self-revealing passage from his essay, 'My Religion', on the nature of his own faith:

In religion there is but little that is capable of rational resolution, and as I do not possess that little I cannot communicate it logically, for only the logical is rational and transmissible. I have, it is true, as far as my affections, my heart and my feelings are concerned, a strong bent towards Christianity, but without adhering to the special dogmas of this or that Christian confession. I count every man a Christian who invokes the name of Christ with respect and love, and I am repelled by the orthodox, whether Catholic or Protestant – the latter being usually as intransigent as the former – who deny the Christianity of those who interpret the Gospel differently from themselves ...

I frankly confess that the supposed rational proofs – ontological, cosmological, ethical etc. – of the existence of God, prove to me nothing; that all the reasons adduced to show that a God exists appear to me to be based on sophistry and begging of the question. In this I am with Kant. And in discussions of this kind, I feel that I am unable to talk to cobblers in the terms of their craft. Nobody has succeeded in convincing me rationally of the existence of God, nor yet of His non-existence; the arguments of atheists appear to me even more superficial and futile than those of their opponents. And if I believe in God, or at least believe that I believe in Him, it is, first of all, because I wish that God may exist, and then, because He is revealed to me, through the channel of the heart, in the Gospel and in Christ and in history.[46]

Faith, therefore, he argues, is essentially the 'will to faith'. Commenting further on the words of the father of the demoniac – 'Lord I believe, help thou my belief' – he adds: 'I believe' here means 'I want to believe. A truly living faith, a faith living on doubt and never carrying the believer beyond doubt ... is a will to know transformed into a will to love, a will to comprehend becomes a comprehension of will ...'[47] Again in *Tragic Sense of Life* he writes: 'Faith is in its essence simply a matter of will ... To believe is to wish to believe and to believe in God is, before all and above all, to wish that there may be a God.'[48] (The influence of Schopenhauer's *The World As Will and Idea* is strongly in evidence in these writings; his name is cited explicitly both in *Tragic Sense of Life* and in *The Agony of Christianity*.) This passage from *Tragic Sense of Life* conveys the essential meaning of the concept of faith as will:

> Faith is the creative power in man. But since it has a more intimate relation with the will than with any other of his faculties, we conceive it under the form of volition. It should be borne in mind, however, that wishing to believe – that is to say, wishing to create – is not precisely the same as believing or creating, although it is its starting-point. Faith, therefore, if not a creative force, is the fruit of the will, and its function is to create. Faith, in a certain sense, creates its object. And faith in God consists in creating God; and since it is God who gives us faith in Himself, it is God who is continually creating Himself in us. Therefore St Augustine said: 'I will seek Thee, Lord, by calling upon Thee, and I will call upon Thee by believing in Thee. My faith calls upon Thee, Lord, the faith which Thou hast given me, with which Thou hast inspired me through the Humanity of Thy Son, through the ministry of Thy preacher.' (*Confessions*, Book I, Chapter I.) The power of creating God in our own image and likeness, of personalising the Universe, simply means that we carry God within us, as the substance of what we hope for, and that God is continually creating us in His own image and likeness.[49]

The will to faith is nourished by hope, is endlessly revitalised by man's yearning for personal immortality. Unamuno quotes the words of St Paul to the effect that 'faith is the substance of things hoped for, the evidence of things not seen'. 'We do not hope because we believe,' he adds, 'but rather we believe because we hope. It is hope in God, it is the ardent longing that there may be a God who guarantees the eternity of consciousness, that leads us to believe in Him.'[50] Thus, he urges the reader: 'Wish for it with all your heart and all your might and hope – for hope is already faith.'[51] It is its reaching towards the impossible, the unattainable that characterises this hope-impelled faith: 'Faith feeds on the ideal, and on the ideal alone, on a concrete, real, live, incarnate and at the same time unattainable ideal. Faith seeks the impossible, the absolute, the infinite, and the eternal: life at the full.'[52] Faith, he asserts even more fundamentally, is the intentional *creation* of that for which we hope. 'Only faith can create,' he writes in 'Nicodemus the Pharisee'. 'For faith does not so much consist in creating what we have not seen but in creating what we do not see.'[53] Faith, he explains, 'creates' God, to save the universe from nothingness, to save consciousness itself from nothingness. 'He in whom you believe,' he concludes, 'he is your God':

> We have created God in order to save the Universe from nothingness, for all that is not consciousness and eternal consciousness, conscious of its eternity and eternally conscious, is nothing more than appearance. Here is nothing truly real save that which feels, suffers, pities, loves, and desires, save consciousness; here is nothing substantial but consciousness. And we need God in order to save consciousness; not in order to think existence, but in order to live it; not in order to know the why and how of it, but in order to feel the wherefore of it. Love is a contradiction if there is no God …
>
> The God whom we hunger after is the God to whom we pray, the God of the *Pater Noster*, of the Lord's Prayer; the God whom we beseech, before all and above all, and whether we are aware of it or not, to instil faith into us, to make us believe in Him, to make Himself in us, the God to whom we pray that His name may be hallowed and that His will may be done – His will, not His reason – on earth as it is in heaven; but feeling that His will cannot be other than the essence of our will, the desire to persist eternally.[54]

There are two vivid metaphoric images in Unamuno's writings illustrating this irrationalist, volitional, hope-affirmed faith. The first is that of Don Quixote whom he describes as 'the prototype of the vitalist whose faith is based on uncertainty'. 'What is Quixotism?' he asks. 'It is a whole method, a whole epistemology, a whole aesthetic, a whole logic, a whole ethic – above all, a whole religion – that is to say, a whole economy of things eternal and things divine, a whole hope in what is rationally absurd.'[55] What Don Quixote embodied in himself was the irrepressible humour and optimism of a truly life-affirming faith, together with the humility that empowers that faith. 'The greatest thing about him,' Unamuno writes, 'was his having been mocked and vanquished, for it was in being overcome that he overcame; he overcame the world by giving the world cause to laugh at him.' Don Quixote's optimism and gaiety derived from his belief in the soul's immortality, from his humility, his trust in God's providence, his sense of the transience and worthlessness of earthly realities:

> And Don Quixote does not surrender, because he is not a pessimist, and he fights on. He is not a pessimist, because pessimism is begotten by vanity, it is a matter of fashion, pure intellectual snobbism, and Don Quixote is neither vain nor modern with any sort of modernity (still less is he a modernist), and he does not understand the meaning of the word 'snob' unless it be explained to him in old Christian Spanish. Don Quixote is not a pessimist, for since he does not understand what is meant by the *joie de vivre* he does not understand its opposite. Neither does he understand futurist fooleries ...
>
> But Don Quixote hears his own laughter, he hears the divine laughter, and since he is not a pessimist, since he believes in life eternal, he has to fight, attacking the modern, scientific, inquisitorial orthodoxy in order to bring in a new and impossible Middle Age, dualistic, contradictory, passionate. Like a new Savonarola, an Italian Quixote of the end of the fifteenth century, he fights against this Modern Age that began with Machiavelli and that will end comically. He fights against the rationalism inherited from the eighteenth century. Peace of mind, reconciliation between reason and faith – this, thanks to the providence of God is no longer possible. The world must be as Don Quixote wishes it to be, and inns must be castles, and he will fight with it, and will, to all appearances, be vanquished, but he will triumph by making himself ridiculous. And he will triumph by laughing at himself and making himself the object of his own laughter.[56]

Quixotism therefore represents the 'foolishness' of Christianity, its disregard for the things of this world, its contempt for mortality. Like Christ who was mocked by his tormentors, like Dostoevsky's Prince Myshkin, Don Quixote has the humility to endure the derision of the crowd, knowing in his heart that his future lies in God in whose protection he has absolute faith. 'For an individual, as for a people,' Unamuno writes (in words that echo Kierkegaard's essay, 'It Is Blessed to Suffer Derision In A Good Cause'), 'the highest heroism is being willing to face ridicule – still more, being willing to make oneself ridiculous and not flinching at the ridicule.' Quixote's mission is to proclaim the 'madness' of Christianity – the madness of a faith that is oriented wholly towards the eternal and that sees earthly life as ridiculous and absurd:

> Don Quixote does not believe that his doctrines will triumph in this world, because they are not of it. And it is better that they should not triumph. And if the world wished to make Don Quixote king, he would retire to the mountain, fleeing from the king-making and king-killing crowds, as Christ retired alone to the mountain when, after the miracle of the loaves and fishes, they sought to proclaim Him king. He left the title of king to be written upon the cross.
>
> What, then, is the new mission of Don Quixote in the world of to-day? To cry aloud, to cry aloud in the wilderness. But the wilderness hears, though men do not hear, and one day it will be transformed into a sounding forest, and this solitary voice that falls upon the wilderness like seed, will yield a gigantic cedar, which with its hundred thousand tongues will sing an eternal hosanna to the Lord of life and of death.[57]

Don Manuel, the central figure in the novel, *San Manuel Bueno, Mártir*, also stands for the foolishness and madness of Christianity and, even more so than Don Quixote, embodies the uncertainty and doubt on which faith is founded. Generally considered Unamuno's finest artistic achievement, the novel was published in 1931, a few years before his death. By then Spain was plunging headlong towards a conflict that was shortly to engulf its entire populace in a bloody and catastrophic civil war. Don Manuel cannot believe in the immortality of the soul, yet he devotes himself tirelessly to the welfare of his parishioners, so much so that after his death he is considered a suitable candidate for beatification by the Church. The novel's narrator, Angela Carballino, recalls how lovingly he tended to the spiritual and pastoral needs of the people of his mountain parish, having willingly chosen to forego the prospect of high office in the Church to live the simple life of a country priest. 'We all loved him, especially the children,' Angela recalls. 'How he loved his flock! His life consisted of reconciling married couples in discord, of making unruly children submit to their parents, or the parents to their children, and especially of comforting the embittered and the wearied, and helping everyone to make a happy death.' Full of charity and goodness, he longs to believe in eternal life but cannot do so. As his life draws to a close he confesses his secret to Angela and her brother, Lázaro. Faith in immortality has eluded him, despite the scrupulous care with which he has discharged his duties to his people. He is a Christian who cannot believe. This is how she recalls the experience:

The whole village observed that Don Manuel's strength was waning, that he was tiring. Even his voice, that voice which was a miracle, took on a certain inner tremor. Tears started to his eyes for no particular reason. Especially when he talked to the people about the other world, the other life, he had to stop at times and shut his eyes. 'He can see it,' they said. At such moments it was daft Blasillo who wept most broken-heartedly, because now Blasillo cried more than he laughed, and even his laughter sounded like weeping.

When Passion Week came round – the last that Don Manuel kept with us, in our world, in our village – everyone had a presentiment of the end of the tragedy. And how it rang out then, that 'My God, my God, why hast Thou forsaken Me?', the last time that Don Manuel sobbed it in public! And when he repeated the Divine Master's words to the good thief – 'All thieves are good', our Don Manuel used to say – the words: 'This day shalt thou be with me in Paradise.' And the last general communion which our saint administered! When he came to give it to my brother, this time with a surer hand, after the liturgical '... *in vitam aeternam*' he bent over and said in his ear: 'There is no eternal life other than this one ... let them dream that it is eternal ... eternal for a few years ...' And when he gave it to me, he said: 'Pray, my daughter, pray for us.' And then something so extraordinary that I carry it in my heart as the greatest of mysteries, and it was that he said to me in a voice that seemed to belong to another world: '...and pray too for Our Lord Jesus Christ'.

One is reminded here of the moving words of Unamuno's sonnet, 'The Atheist's Prayer': 'Hear my plea Thou God who does not exist/ and receive these my plaints into Thy nothingness,/ Thou who never leavest sorrying man/ Without the solace of deception.' In *Tragic Sense of Life* he had written that 'it is monstrous to teach that salvation depends on subscribing to a partic-ular faith, such as Catholicism'.[58] Don Manuel is an unbelieving priest who has never departed from the spirit of the Christian faith. He recognises the people's need to believe in eternal life and out of his love for them reinforces their faith. His own loss of faith only strengthens his love for the people and his resolve to serve them. He shows that holiness can co-exist with doubt, even unbelief. One thinks of these words from *The Agony of Christianity*: 'A truly living faith, a faith living on doubt and never carrying the believer beyond doubt ... is a will to know transformed into a will to love.'[59] In Don Manuel unbelief and personal despair are transcended by love. At the end of the novel one is left wondering whether the will to love – which he manifests so abundantly and so selflessly – is not a disguised will to faith, a faith not felt in the heart but given expression nonetheless in a relentless determination to serve. This is the paradox on which Angela reflects in the closing pages of the work. Don Manuel and her brother Lázaro died, she says, 'believing that they did not believe what concerns us most, but without believing that they believed it, they did believe it in an active and resigned desolation'. Moreover, she concludes it was God's will that this should be so:

> But why – I have often asked myself – did Don Manuel not try to convert my brother too with a deception, with a lie, pretending to be a believer without being one? I have realised that it was because he realised he would not deceive him, that deceit was of no use in his case, that only with the truth, his truth, would he convert him; that he would have achieved nothing if he had attempted to act a play – or rather a tragedy – the one he acted to save the village. And so he won him over, in short, for his pious fraud; won him over with the truth of death to the reason for living. And so he won me, and I never let others have the faintest notion of his divine, his most holy game. It is that I believed and do believe that God our Lord, for I know not what sacred and inscrutable designs, made them believe themselves to be incredulous. And that perhaps at the end of their passing over the bandage fell from their eyes. And I, do I believe?

LOVE AND THE INFINITE

'Each of us exists for others'
Mist

Love, therefore, is the source of faith, whether that faith is 'felt in the heart' or is simply willed or desired by its subject. The will to love is transformed by grace into the will to faith, even in those such as Don Manuel and Lázaro Caraballino whose belief does not exist at the level of intellectual conviction. This is one of the most insistent affirmations of Unamuno's writings and one of his most original insights into the nature of religious faith. It is through love, through his tireless attention to the needs of his fellowmen, that Don Manuel is able to live the life of faith, despite the anguished and persistent self-conflict generated by his disbelief in the mysteries of that faith, especially the mystery of personal immortality. Through loving alone he maintains his faith. It is this that attracts the atheist Lázaro to the priest as he too undergoes an experience of religious conversion. In his case, as in Don Manuel's, conversion is not based on an intellectual acceptance of the truths of Christianity but

on his recognition that atheistic despair can be transcended through love. He
has learned this from the example given him by the priest.

Paradoxically, love is the source of infinite freedom but also has a con-
straining impact on that freedom, as Unamuno suggests in one of the poems
from his *Rosary of Lyrical Sonnets*. 'For man does not enjoy/ liberty if he is
not in bondage to the ties/ of love, his companion on the road of life,' he
writes in Sonnet XXI. 'In love it is the same thing to conquer and be conquered,' Augusto declares in similar vein in *Mist*. 'All the great works of faith
have been daughters of true, that is, painful love,' Román says in 'The Portico
of the Temple'. Like Dostoevsky's Father Zossima, Unamuno repeatedly
emphasises the pain and self-conflict that are necessary to attain a truly selfless
love, the kind that is exemplified by Don Manuel. 'The most tragic thing in
the world and in life, readers and brothers of mine, is love,' he writes in
Chapter VII of *Tragic Sense of Life*. 'Love,' he says, 'is the child of illusion
and the parent of disillusion; love is consolation in desolation; it is the sole
medicine against death, for it is death's brother.' Later in the same chapter he
identifies wisdom with the suffering that accompanies love. 'We can know
nothing well save what we love,' he declares.[60] Wisdom comes to Alejandro
Gomez in 'Nothing Less Than A Man' when he begins to conquer his selfishness and pride and gradually discovers the power of a genuinely self-sacrificing
love. Rich and powerful, he dominates his wife, Julia, driving her first to infidelity and thence into a physical and psychological decline. As she slips from
his power, he offers to sacrifice all his wealth if this will enable the doctors to
save her life. In his frantic attempts at prayer Julia at last recognises the truth
of his love for her:

> Then to Julia, his wife, who was pale but more beautiful than ever –
> beautiful with the beauty of approaching death – he would say:
> 'Julia, where is God?' She, looking upwards with her large blank
> eyes would say in a low voice:
> 'He is there ...'
> Alejandro looked at the crucifix that hung at the head of his wife's
> bed, he took it down and crushing it in his fist he would exclaim: 'Save
> her for me, save her for me and ask me anything, anything, my entire
> fortune, all my blood, all myself ...' Julia would look at him and smile.
> Her husband's blind fury filled her soul with a very sweet light. At last
> she was really happy! How had she ever doubted that this man loved
> her?

Tragically, Alejandro's conversion comes too late to save Julia's life. But he
has attained the wisdom that comes from selfless love. Throughout his writ-

ings Unamuno insists repeatedly that it is love primarily that leads man to God. 'Only by the way of love and suffering do we come to the living God, the human God,' he writes in *Tragic Sense of Life*. 'We cannot first know Him in order that afterwards we may love Him; we must begin by loving Him, longing for Him, hungering after Him before knowing Him.'[61] In the following passage from *Mist* Augusto reflects on the special nature of the understanding that love provides: 'Love comes before knowledge, and knowledge kills love. *Nihil volitum quia praecognitum*, as Padre Zaramillo used to say; nothing is willed which has not first been known. But I have reached the opposite conclusion, namely, that nothing is known which has not first been willed: *nihil cognitum quia praevolitum*. To understand is to forgive, they say. No, to forgive is to understand. First comes love and then understanding.' In one of the final lyrics from *The Christ of Velazquez* the poet prays for the gift of love that alone will enable him to know God:

> Give to us, oh Lord, a passionate longing
> to love Thee; a yearning to love amidst
> battles with the Enemy, who lays siege
> to us tirelessly. The man who loves
> is too trusting, he falls asleep, but there
> is no room for sleep in ardent desire
> to love ...
> > Be Thou the bread
> that incites to hunger; be Thou the wine
> that kindles the thirst of our mouths. As long
> as our life on earth doth last, may desire
> to love Thee be our life; with love attained
> we do sleep, and sleep is not life but death.

Significantly, in the same poem the poet prays to God to transform the natural world by the grace of His presence in its base materiality. He points to the mystery of God's immanent presence in all creation which is the basis of his claim that love leads man to discover the reality of God. In *Tragic Sense of Life* he emphasises the same theme: 'To believe in God is to love Him and in our love to fear Him; and we begin by loving Him even before knowing Him, and by loving Him we come at last to see and discover Him in all things.'[62] God's presence, he suggests in this passage from the same work, is particularly attested in the beauty of the phenomenal universe:

> And how is this individual essence in each several thing – that which makes it itself and not another – revealed to us save as beauty? What is

the beauty of anything save its eternal essence, that which unites its past with its future, that element of it that rests and abides in the womb of eternity? or, rather, what is it but the revelation of its divinity?

And this beauty, which is the root of eternity, is revealed to us by love; it is the supreme revelation of the love of God and the token of our ultimate victory over time. It is love that reveals to us the eternal in us and in our neighbours.

Is it the beautiful, the eternal in things, that awakens and kindles our love for them, or is it our love for things that reveals to us the beautiful, the eternal, in them? Is not beauty perhaps a creation of love, in the same way and in the same sense that the sensible world is a creation of the instinct of preservation and the supersensible world of that of perpetuation. Is not beauty, and together with beauty eternity, a creation of love?[63]

It is love, he says, which discloses the eternal reality that manifests itself in the beauty of creation. It does so by virtue of the personal character of the relationship it creates. 'For everything that it loves, everything that it pities, love personalises,' he writes. Thus he advises: 'In order to love everything, in order to pity everything, human and extra-human, living and non-living, you must feel everything within yourself, you must personalise everything.'[64] Love is the gateway to the infinite consciousness in which individual consciousness participates. It is the means by which we participate in the infinity of consciousness which is God. This truth is powerfully exemplified in a passage from *Peace and War* where Pachico – generally seen as a self-projection of Unamuno himself – feels the spirit of God as he contemplates the immensity and beauty of the sea:

In his wanderings he liked to stop for a while at a promontory overlooking the sea. There he filled his eyes with the sight of the immense deep waters and the sky which embraced them. The sea and sky – each one giving life to the other in solemn communion! The waves followed on one another in their noise, while cloud followed cloud in silence. When he lowered his gaze toward the vast and turbulent surface of the sea, he felt a dark intuition about life, the intuition that life is simply what it is, with no meaning beyond itself. Then he felt a strange sense that the fugitive moment of the present had come to a stop, that it had become immobile. From that promontory, the vast waves moving endlessly before him suggested the breathing of Nature, as it slept its deep and dreamless sleep. But at other times, moments when he watched the wind stirring up the waves and seeping away the clouds, he thought about the Spirit of God moving upon the waters and imagined that at any second the august spirit of the Omnipotent and Ancient of Days would appear before him, exactly as He was pictured on altars – resting on clouds, His full, wide-pleated garments floating out behind Him as He makes new worlds surge into being out of the submissive waters.

Love therefore reveals the presence of God, the ultimate consciousness, in all reality by personalising that reality through the inclusive and all-embracing intimacy that it creates 'The work of charity, of the love of God, is to endeavour to liberate God from brute matter, to endeavour to give consciousness to everything, to spiritualise or universalise everything,' he writes in *Tragic Sense of Life*. 'It is to dream that the very rocks may find a voice and work in accordance with the spirit of this dream; it is to dream that everything that exists may become conscious, that the Word may become life.'[65] The miracle of the Incarnation, of God Made Man, is the ultimate expression of this truth. It is this truth that Christianity celebrates, he says, in the sacrament of the Eucharist: 'The Word has been imprisoned in a piece of material bread and it has been imprisoned therein that we may eat it ... It has been imprisoned in this bread in order that, after being buried in our body, it may come to life again in our spirit.'[66] The significance of the Eucharist is powerfully conveyed in these lines from *The Christ of Velázquez*:

> The love of Thee consumes us, oh white body;
> love that is hunger, the love of the bowels;
> hunger for the creating Word made flesh;
> fierce love for life, love that cannot be satisfied
> with embraces or kisses or with any
> of the joys of wedded love.
>   Our desire
> is appeased only by feeding on Thee,
> bread of immortality, flesh divine.
> The love of our innermost depths, love made
> hunger, oh Lamb of God, desires Thee
> for food, and would know the taste of thy caul,
> would feed on thy heart ...
> And with arms outspreading as if in sign
> of loving surrender, Thou dost repeat:
> 'Come thou, eat and drink, for this is my body!'
> Flesh of God, oh incarnated Word, penetrate
> our divine and carnal hunger for Thee!

What the Eucharist signifies most clearly is the interdependence of human and divine love. It signifies the cointentionality of the relationship of man to God, a cointentionality, Unamuno suggests, which is attainable through the love that exists in us all: 'And this God, the living God, your God, our God, is in me, is in you, lives in us, and we live and move and have our being in Him. And He is in us by virtue of the hunger, the longing we have for Him … And God is in each one of us in the measure in which each one feels Him and loves Him.'[67] God is the infinity of consciousness which is manifested in the infinity of love, as is suggested in the above quoted passage from *Peace and War*. That infinity is comprehended, in turn, in the absolute selflessness of Christ as manifested in his sacrificing of himself on the cross. Christ incarnated was the perfection of love, the living attestation of its absoluteness and infinity. Another of the poems from *The Christ of Velázquez* celebrates this truth, drawing on the imagery of Ezekiel, Joshua, Mark, John and the Book of Revelations to convey the dramatic character of Christ's sacrifice:

'It is finished!' Thou didst cry like the roar
of a thousand cataracts, voice of thunder,
like the thunder of an army in combat
– Thou, fighting death to the death –; and thine outcry
overthrew the walls of the new proud Jericho
of the pagans, city of the palm trees,
of Greek wisdom, the spiritual Alexandria,
and flung wide to Thee the portals of Rome.
There followed a silence, measureless, mystical,
as if the air with Thee had died, and then
new music surged forth of unearthly sound,
made stormy in the recesses of heaven
by the grief of thy passion. With the tendons
and muscles stretched taut, like strings on the harp
of the sad wood of thy cross, in their torture,
thy limbs emitted at the touch of love
– boundless love –, the triumphant song of life.
It is finished! At last, Death has died!

But love, however infinite its potentiality, is corruptible in its human forms, reflecting the flawed nature of man, its endemic propensity towards selfishness and pride. This is especially manifested, Unamuno suggests, in the conflicts of interhuman love, particularly in romantic and sexual love. 'Without doubt,' he writes, 'there is something tragically destructive in the essence of love … in the unconquerable instinct which impels the male and female to mix their being in a fury of conjunction. The same impulse that joins their bodies, separates, in a certain sense, their souls; they hate one another while they embrace, no less than they love ...' 'Love is a mutual selfishness,' he declares; those who love are 'tyrants and slaves, each one at once the tyrant and slave of the other.'[68] And this holds true, he says, for all forms of interhuman love, not only the carnal and the sexual. The love-hatred dialectic lies at the heart of all human loving, has been part of the nature of man from his origin.

This latter truth is explored by Unamuno through his treatment of the Cain-Abel theme in his novel, *Abel Sanchez*. The Biblical theme is given a modern reformulation in the conflict between the novel's two main characters, Joaquin Monegro and his childhood friend, Abel Sanchez. Envy and hatred of Abel is the driving force in all of Joaquin's activities. He resents Abel's success as an artist, together with his success in securing the love of Helena whose portrait he paints, winning himself instant fame in the process. Joaquin fails to find similar fulfilment in his career as a doctor and despises his pious, self-sacrificing wife, Antonia. Hatred is his passion and his torment. 'I began to hate Abel with all my soul,' he recalls, 'and at the same time I resolved to hide that hatred, to fertilise it, to nurse it, to foster it in the darkest places of the depths of my soul ... Hatred? I was not yet willing to give it its true name, I didn't want to admit that I was born, predestined, with the bulk of it and the seed of it inside me.' When he reads Byron's *Cain* Joaquin recognises a mirror-image of himself in the portrait of the Biblical character whose hatred of his brother Abel is the consuming passion of his life. He recognises the fact that hatred consumes the one who hates, not the one at whom it is directed. What terrifies him most of all is the transformation in himself that hatred has brought about, its destruction of his capacity for love: 'I felt worse than a monster,' he reflects. 'I felt as if I did not exist, as if I were nothing but a piece of ice, as if I would be one forever. I even touched my skin, pinched myself, and took my pulse. I said to myself, "But am I alive? Is this really I?"'

Joaquin ponders the possibility that he might have conquered his hatred had he learned to love his wife, Antonia: 'Ah, if I had been capable of loving her, I would have been saved. For me she was another instrument of vengeance. I wanted her as the mother of a son or daughter who would avenge me ... Did I not perhaps marry to create other hateful beings like myself to transmit my hate, to immortalise it?' He is torn between his passion for hatred and his desire to be free from it. He asks himself if hatred has so taken possession of his consciousness that it will survive even after his death: 'I wondered if hatred survives the haters, if it is something substantial and can be transmitted, whether it is the soul, the very essence of the soul ... And I shuddered with terror at the thought of living forever in order to hate forever. That would indeed be Hell.' Facing death he sees that the root of his hatefulness lies in his hatred of himself. As he prays to God he sees that self-hatred has been his downfall: 'Lord, Lord! You told me: love thy neighbour as thyself! And I don't love my neighbour, I can't love him because I don't love myself. I don't know how, I can't love myself. What have You done to me Lord?' He concludes: 'Here below we all live hating ourselves.' The novel ends on a question of universal relevance: is all hatred a form of self-hatred, and is this in turn rooted in man's hatred of his own fallenness, his corruptibility, his finitude, his mortality? Even more fundamentally, is it possible that hatred is merely the corrupted love of mortal man – corrupted and distorted by the conditions of mortal life. Is this the root-cause of Joaquin's despair? And if, as Unamuno repeatedly asserts, faith springs from despair, is it possible that faith may spring also from the corrupted passions of man's envy and his hatred. This passage from *Tragic Sense of Life* suggests that it might:

> Those who say that they believe in God and yet neither love nor fear Him, do not in fact believe in Him but in those who have taught them that God exists, and these in their turn often enough do not believe in Him either. Those who believe that they believe in God, but without any passion in their heart, without anguish of mind, without uncertainty, without doubt, without an element of despair even in their consolation, believe only in the God-Idea, not in God Himself. And just as belief in God is born of love, so also it may be born of fear, and even of hate, and of such kind was the belief of Vanni Fucci, the thief, whom Dante depicts insulting God with obscene gestures in Hell. (Inf., xxv., 1-3) For the devils also believe in God, and not a few atheists.[69]

In his essay, 'Abishag the Shunammite', Unamuno asks: 'Which is the more terrible for a soul: not to be able to love, or not to be loved?' 'The truth,' he responds, 'is that hatred, and even more so envy, are forms of love. True atheists are madly enamoured of God.'[70] He points to the dialectical interdependence of love and hate, hope and despair, scepticism and faith which characterises the conditions in which human existence must be conducted. It is these oppositions which lie at the root of the suffering which is endemic in mortal life. In his transcendence of suffering – through his conquest of pride, his humility, his love and his faith – man, however, can disclose for himself the ultimate prospect that gives hope to all existence, the prospect of personal immortality and eternal union with God.

QUEST FOR IMMORTALITY

Love, being flawed and corruptible in mortal life, being simultaneously ego-centred and other-centred, being rooted in the self while reaching towards the selfless, is necessarily a cause for lifelong suffering and despair. 'There is no true love save in suffering,' Unamuno writes, echoing the words of Dostoevsky, 'and in this world we have to choose either love, which is suffer-ing, or happiness. And love leads us to no other happiness than that of love itself and its tragic consolation of uncertain hope.' Love, he declares, is 'resigned despair'; love and suffering 'mutually engender one another and love is charity and compassion, and the love that is not charitable and compassion-ate is not love.'[71] It is the finitude of love, its inherent mortality, side by side with its potentiality for disclosing the infinite, that lies at the root of the suf-fering it entails: 'Love is at once the brother, son and father of death ... And thus it is that in the depth of love there is a depth of eternal despair.' 'The most tragic thing in the world is love,' he declares.[72] A beautiful lyric from *The Christ of Velázquez* associates the image of Christ as Man with the arche-typal symbol of love and suffering – the rose – to signify the perfection of goodness and beauty which they share, together with the sorrows endemic in mortal life:

> Thy body, like the wild rose of the bramble
> with five white petals, is the perfect flower
> of creation; thy full heart, where Thou dost
> distil the essence of the cream of life,
> is its blood-stained chalice. Sorrow filled it
> to the very brim, vessel of the fathomless
> anguish that the mortal breast cannot hold ...
> Thou art like the wild rose of the bramble
> with its five petals – a bramble thy cross,
> thy bed of thorns – thy body is as white
> as the rose of the bush that burned with fire
> on the mount of God and was not consumed,
> a taper of flame in the midst of briars
> is the white fire of thine eternal love.

The theme of diseased consciousness is closely linked in Unamuno's writ-ings with his explorations of the nature of love. If love is tragically flawed, torn between temporality and the infinite, so is the consciousness which it empowers. If consciousness is 'co-feeling' or cointentionality, if it is enabled by love to personalise all that it addresses, then it too must be charged with the tragedy of opposing tendencies. 'Man by the very fact of being man, of possessing consciousness, is a diseased animal.' he writes in *Tragic Sense of Life*. Man, he says, has been subject to disease 'since the Sin of Adam', a disease manifested in the endemic presence of suffering in his existence. But suffering has a positive function; it is the 'path of consciousness', he writes, the means by which we come into the possession of self-consciousness. It deepens the awareness of the finitude of existence which is necessary for the growth of self-consciousness: 'For to possess consciousness of oneself, to possess personality, is to know oneself and to feel oneself distinct from other beings, and this feeling of distinction is only reached through an act of collision, through suffering more or less severe, through the sense of one's limits.'[73]

Tragically, therefore, suffering creates the need for more suffering: 'The cure for suffering … is not to be submerged in unconsciousness, but to be raised to consciousness and to suffer more. The evil of suffering is cured by more suffering, by higher suffering.'[74] 'There are two men in each of us, the temporal and the eternal,'[75] Christ tells Nicodemus in Unamuno's version of the Gospel parable. From the conflict of the two comes our diseased consciousness, our despair, the darkness of soul in which our existence must be lived. The image of the dark night of the soul, clearly drawn from mystical literature, occurs many times in the poems of *The Christ of Velázquez*. The work entitled 'God – Darkness' suggests, like Eliot's 'East Coker,' that while darkness of the spirit is dominant in mortal life, light inheres in the darkness, the light of hope in eternal life which it ultimately discloses:

> Through the night the round moon proclaims to us
> that the sun is breathing beneath the earth:
> and so also thy light: since Thou alone
> dost bear witness to God, in this night only
> by Thee do we reach the Father eternal:
> it is thy moonlight alone in our night
> that tells us the sun lives …
> Thou dost draw
> from impenetrable night the hidden thing
> of the Divinity, its wasted white
> blood light; because Thou, the Man, didst take body
> where the unembodied light, which is darkness
> for the bodily human eye of flesh,
> in love was embodied.

Life, however, remains a struggle with suffering and despair, as Unamuno repeatedly insists in the essays of *The Agony of Christianity*. Struggle, he says, defines the character of the Christian way of life. 'And Christ came to bring us agony, struggle and not peace,' he writes. 'The Christ worshipped on the cross is the agonising Christ, the one who cries out: *consummatum est*. And it is this Christ, the Christ of "My God, my God, why hast thou forsaken me?" that agonic believers worship.'[76] A poem from *The Christ of Velázquez* has an image of Christ as the wounded deer whose death agony symbolises the sorrow and despair inevitable in mortal existence:

> Wounded by us as the deer that when dying
> runs to its native copse, even so Thou,
> to the summit of Mount Calvary dying
> with thirst because of thy free-flowing blood
> didst escape, crossing the pathway of bitterness,
> to the heavenly drinking place of thy love,
> and didst cry out, 'I thirst!' And we, thy brothers
> and cruel hunters, we too make our way
> through the bloody trails of this life of bitterness,
> dying with thirst, seeking the well of thy wine.

In *San Manuel, Mártir*, the priest's dark night of despair and unbelief gives way to an illumination of the spirit that is attained through the power of love. This is also the message Christ gives to Nicodemus: 'All those seers who achieved the peace and wisdom you so desire, Nicodemus, made their way along the path of suffering, of sacrifice and humility, amid biting serpents and oppressive crosses, with their eyes fixed upon the cross of the Saviour. They gained their knowledge of love through the school of sorrow.'[77] Such wisdom, he insists, cannot be attained through 'intellectual lucubrations': 'True wisdom is a vision of love, it is an active wisdom, a faculty one achieves through abnegation and sorrow, through humility, above all with incessant contemplation of the cross raised on the desert so that those who gaze on it will be able to live under the weight of the cross they bear.'[78] The theme of illumination through suffering runs through the poems of *The Christ of Velázquez*. In 'Ecce Homo' Unamuno speaks of 'the pain that exalts'; in another poem he describes Christ's crown of thorns as 'irradiating light'. In 'From Sinai to Calvary' Christ's death-agony on the cross is seen as the force that releases the light of faith and the grace that brings salvation and redemption to all of mankind:

> But Thou humble on the crest of Mount Calvary,
> gentle hill of sorrow and blood, the womb
> of thy native land, that pregnant with grief
> unfathomable, to the cross gave birth;

naked, in the sun without clouds, in silence
giving to us the grace that is redemption,
Thou dost say, 'I am the vine, and ye are
the branches!'
Death and love teaching, with sacred
humanity watering, like a river
of milk sweet peace is entering the depths
of our soul. Now we have not God, thy Father,
but like the sun, the Calvary of love
stains the clouds of Mount Sinai and shows
us the smile of heaven, which is the abode
where at last our hope will find its rest

The wisdom that man attains through suffering is his sense of the eternal, his belief in personal immortality. This is the all-embracing theme of Unamuno's work. All his writings – philosophic, fictional, poetic and dramatic – are finally focussed on this. Life, he insists repeatedly, is meaningless without the prospect of immortality. 'If I die then nothing has any meaning for me,' he writes in the chapter from *Tragic Sense of Life* called 'The Starting Point'. 'There is no point in living if death is the end,' he writes.[79] The desire for immortality, he insists, is the force that motivates our love, all the love in our being: 'The thirst for eternity is what is called love among men and whosoever loves another wishes to eternalise himself in him.' The transcendent power of love derives, in turn, from its potentiality to disclose the eternal: 'The feeling of the vanity of the passing world kindles love in us, the only thing that triumphs over the vain and transitory, the only thing that fills life again and eternalises it.'[80]

He speaks of the critical role of feeling and will in fostering man's faith in immortality. He cites Kant who replaced the God of reason, the abstract God, deduced from rational proof, with the God of conscience, the God of feeling and volition. 'Kant,' he says, 'reconstructed with the heart that which with the head he had overthrown.' It was his preoccupation with immortality in his final years, he writes, that convinced Kant of the existence of God, not the rational deductions of his philosophy. 'The question of the immortality of the soul, of the persistence of individual consciousness, is not rational, it falls outside reason,' Unamuno concludes.[81] Repeatedly, he identifies the reality of the immortal with the 'will-to-immortality', a will that is nurtured by hope and love. To the charge that this is a 'slippery foundation' on which to base such a crucial tenet of Christian belief he responds: 'I believe in the immortal origin of this yearning for immortality, which is the very substance of my soul.' He continues: 'There is nothing truly real save that which feels, suffers, pities, loves and desires, save consciousness.'[82] It is consciousness, he adds, which has created God and immortality: 'It is ourselves, it is our eternity we seek in God ... It is hope in God, it is the ardent longing that there may be a God who guarantees the eternity of consciousness that leads us to believe in Him.'[83] That unquenchable hope for immortality springs from the infinite potentiality of the love that exists universally in all of mankind:

> Love hopes, hopes ever and never wearies of hoping; and love of God, our faith in God, is, above all, hope in Him. For God dies not, and he who hopes in God shall live for ever. And our fundamental hope, the root and stem of all our hopes, is the hope of eternal life.
>
> And if faith is the substance of hope, hope in its turn is the form of faith. Until it gives us hope, our faith is a formless faith, vague, chaotic potential; it is but the possibility of believing, the longing to believe. But we must needs believe in something, and we believe in what we hope for, we believe in hope. We remember the past, we know the present, we only believe in the future. To believe what we have not seen is to believe what we shall see. Faith, then, I repeat once again, is faith in hope; we believe what we hope for.[84]

He speaks of love as the force that *compels* us to believe. Love is the driving-force that generates the will-to-faith: 'Love makes us believe in God, in whom we hope and from whom we hope to receive life to come; love makes us believe in that which the dream of hope creates for us.' Faith, empowered by love, is a triumph of will over reason; this applies especially to our faith in immortality: 'To believe in the immortality of the soul is to wish that the soul may be immortal but to wish it with such force that this volition shall trample reason under foot and pass beyond it.' Faith in eternal life, therefore, is ultimately dependent on hope. 'Is not eternal happiness,' he asks, 'an eternal hope, with its eternal nucleus of sorrow in order that happiness shall not be swallowed up in nothingness?'[85] It is the serenity of his hope, a hope nurtured by love and will and oriented towards the eternal, that brings comfort to Pedro Antonio in *Peace and War* as he recalls the tragedy of his young son's death. As he dwells on his memories of his son, he feels a deep inward freedom and peace, a peace of the soul inspired by his hope-affirming faith in eternal life:

> The memory of his son tints everything with calm, giving nourishment to his resignation. Without the worries and alarms Ignacio sometimes gave him when he was alive, he enjoys his son now, in the secret recesses of his soul, when he is by himself, there where he has him in pure and serene memory. He remembers with grateful pleasure the moments

when he would approach the child's cradle to make certain that he was still alive and breathing. Pedro Antonio's inward peace is reflected in his external world, the world of lines, colours and sounds; and from its external reflection new currents of sweet calm flow back to him as from a living fountain. It is a reflection reflected, as if mirrors mirrored each other to give each other life. He is living in the depth of life's true reality, free of all transcendent intent and above time. Like a bare sky, his serene consciousness reflects the slow invasion of the gentle dream of final rest, the great calm of eternal things and of the infinity that sleeps within its closeness. He lives in the true peace of life, letting himself be rocked in indifference to daily events and cares, grown easier now as he grows more detached from those things which pass. In eternity: he lives the day in eternity. He hopes that this profound life will last beyond death, so that he may enjoy, on a day without night, perpetual light, infinite clarity, sure rest, steady peace – imperturbable, permanent peace, inside and out. Such hope is the reality which makes his life peaceful in the midst of his cares, and eternal within its short and perishable course. He is already free, truly free, not with the illusory freedom sought in action, but with the true freedom of being everything. Out of pure simplicity he had made himself free

That same spirit of inner serenity and peace – 'the peace that passeth understanding' – is invoked on a number of occasions in Unamuno's fiction, especially when he treats of the subject of death. In *The Agony of Christianity* he spoke of death as the absoluteness of solitude. 'For as human beings we live together but each one dies alone and death is the supreme solitude,' he wrote.[86] But the utter loneliness of death is relieved, he suggests, by the soul's expectation of immortality and union with God. This is conveyed vividly in the moving description of Josefa Ignacia's death in *Peace and War*. As her husband prays at her bedside and the priest administers the Sacrament of the Dying, she drifts towards the infinite peace of death, secure in her faith in the prospect of eternal life:

When they brought the Viaticum, Pedro Antonio was left to pray, on his knees before the Eucharist, beside the bed, glancing from time to time at the flames from the large tapers which danced about the darkness of the enclosed room during the slow, drawn-out *ora pro nobis* of the litany. The sick woman let the prayers lull her halfway to sleep, as a child is rocked to sleep by a lullaby. When she opened her mouth to receive the Host, her eyes met those of her life's companion and she felt pity for him, who was to be left alone. Her gaze rested on him, her gentle eyes sparkling with a smiling serenity, eyes which reflected, too, the long habit of living together with him.

A similar hope-affirming acceptance of death is evident in the description of the death of Julia Yañez in *Nothing Less Than a Man*. As he gazes on the body of his dead wife, Alejandro reflects on the beauty of her lifeless form: 'Soon Alejandro felt that his strong arms were holding only a lifeless form. The deathly cold of the great final night seemed to settle on his soul. He got up and looked at the now rigid and lifeless beauty. He had never seen her look more beautiful. She seemed to be bathed in the radiance of that light filtering down from the eternal dawn which follows after the final night.' One of Unamuno's most beautiful lyrics, 'She Will Come By Night' also deals with the theme of death. Written in exile at Hendaye in 1928, the poem represents death as a healing spirit that brings solace to the troubled soul:

> She will come by night, when all is sleeping;
> she will come by night, when the ailing soul
> is muffled in life;
> she will come by night, with her quiet footstep;
> she will come by night, and lay her finger
> upon the wound ...
> She will come by night when time is waiting,
> when the daylight lingers among the shadows
> and waits for dawn.
> She will come by night, on a night of pureness,
> a night when the blood is purged from the heat
> of noonday sun.
> A night must be when she comes and enters,
> when the worn-out heart will give itself to her,
> a night of calm.
> She must come by night ... she, he or it?
> By night she must stamp her dusty seal,
> night without care.
> And night will come, the night that gives us life,
> in which the soul forgets all night at last,
> and bring the cure; the night will come, the night that covers all,
> and reflects the heavens in the shining mire
> that purges it.

The imagery of night, silence, sleep, motherhood and light symbolises the peace and beauty of the infinite to which death gives access. In *Tragic Sense of*

Life Unamuno spoke of beauty as the visible manifestation of the eternal: 'We seek in art an image of eternalisation. If for a brief moment our spirit finds peace and rest and assuagement in the contemplation of the beautiful ... it is because the beautiful is the revelation of the eternal, of the divine in things ...'[87] Such an image is that which the poet, Rafael, contemplates in the poem, 'Teresa'. Recalling his memory of his lover who died from consumption, he dwells on his recollected image of her youthful beauty. As he waits for his own impending death, he contemplates the transcendence of time that death will bring. The mortal love that was cut short by death will be transcended by the immortal love they both will share in the sphere of the eternal. In Stanza 75 he addresses the spirit of his dead lover:

> Man cannot see God's face and live;
> together you and I have seen God's face;
> now you are dead
> and I, in the desert,
> can only walk behind your saintly steps.
> But I died too;
> I died, and dream now of our mother Death;
> I died in you,
> that is the greatest love.
> I saw God in your eyes and with them,
> our mingled eyes saw God together;
> our sight was common,
> and then our two lives died together
> in one embrace.
> Since you and I saw living God together
> by God's grace death has given me life.

Like the love that Rafael finds in the sphere of the eternal, true peace, Unamuno suggests, is to be found only beyond the conditions of mortal life. This is the conclusion reached by Pachico at the end of *Peace and War*. Like Tolstoy he sees true peace as lying in the realm of the infinite but asserts that the infinite lies within all of us, is attainable by each individual 'in the silence beyond silence,' the silence of his own soul where he can enjoy 'true peace as if in the life of death'. 'What time is to eternity, war is to peace, its fleeting form,' Pachico declares. Though the infinity of peace belongs ultimately in the sphere of the eternal we can find it within ourselves through our faith, our hope, above all, through our love. This is the substance of Pachico's reflections at the end of the novel:

In him a communion wakes up between the world around him and the
world inside him: the two worlds fuse. Free from the consciousness of
time and space, he contemplates them in their fusion. There in that
silence beyond silence and in the aroma of the diffuse light, all desire
extinguished and in tune with the song of the soul of the world, he
enjoys true peace, as if in the life of death. How much there is that he
will never express! ... Rose-hued clouds in a golden sky which will
never be painted! ... There is an immensity of peace. The sea chants
peace, the earth mutely speaks peace, the sky rains down peace. In a
surpassing harmony of dissonance, peace wells up out of the struggle
for life. There is peace within war and underlying it; peace sustains war
and crowns it. What time is to eternity, war is to peace: its fleeting
form. In peace, death and life seem to join as one.

For Unamuno the image of the Resurrected Christ embodied the perfection
of the eternal and the consummation of man's hope for personal immortality.
Just as he gives the theme of suffering a specifically Christian justification
through his poetic and fictional explorations of the image of the Crucified
Christ, so he sees the image of Christ's Resurrection as the supreme evocation
of the truth of immortality. He cites St Paul to the effect that the authenticity
of the Christian faith depends on the truth of the Resurrection. In *Tragic
Sense of Life* he writes: 'The important thing for him [St Paul] was that Christ
had been made man and had died and had risen again, and not what he did in
his life – not his ethical work as a teacher, but his religious work as a giver of
immortality. and it was he who wrote those immortal words: "Now if Christ
be preached that He rose from the dead, how say some among you that there
is no resurrection from the dead? But if there be no resurrection of the dead,
then is Christ not risen; and if Christ be not risen, then is our preaching vain,
and your faith is also vain."'[88] This is the wholly irrational truth on which
Christianity is ultimately founded. Christ's resurrection is seen by the
Christian believer as the guarantee of his own immortality: 'For the Christian
to believe in the resurrection of Christ – that is to say, in tradition and in the
Gospel, which assure him that Christ has risen, both of them personal forces –
is to believe that he himself will one day rise again by the grace of Christ.'[89]
The poem, 'Dawn', from *The Christ of Velázquez* celebrates the mystery of
Christ's Resurrection, seeing it as signifying the dawn of eternal fulfilment for
which all Christians hope and pray:

Thou art white as the heavens in the east
are white at dawn before the sun begins
to appear from the limbo of the earth

at night: for Thou gav'st the whiteness of dawn
to our life, become the dawn of death, portal
of eternal day: as white as the pillar
of cloud that led the people of the Lord
through the wilderness by day. Like the snow
of the hermit summits girdled by sky,
where the sun without hindrance is reflected,
from thy body, that is summit of life,
descend pure crystalline waters that form
a limpid mirror of celestial light,
to sprinkle the subterranean caverns
of the darkness that surrounds the abyss.

4

'Misère de L'Homme Sans Dieu': The Novels of François Mauriac

This is the secret of Grace: it is never too late. Time does not exist, and all the love of all the saints may be contained in a sigh.

François Mauriac: *Mémoires Intérieurs*

DILEMMAS OF THE CHRISTIAN NOVELIST

In the south-western region of France where François Mauriac grew up in the last two decades of the nineteenth century the repressive, life-denying morality of Jansenism was the dominant and all-pervasive faith, particularly amongst the bourgeois class to which the Mauriac family belonged. Piety, austerity and a rigorously enforced code of personal ethics were its distinguishing characteristics. Reverence for property was its social hallmark. 'Capital,' Mauriac recalled later, 'appeared to us holy and venerable and agreeable to God.'[1] Greed wore the halo of virtue, he wrote, and the Church saw no contradiction in the great social inequalities that its vigorous defence of the rights of the propertied classes had ensured. (In *The Desert of Love* he spoke of the 'desert that separates the classes as much as it separates individuals.') The sense of sin was omnipresent, the fear of damnation being the primary motivation towards virtue. 'Our upbringing was pefectly designed,' he wrote, 'to arouse the monster which in every human being seeks a way of escape.'[2]

In *Souffrances et bonheur du chrétien* Mauriac described his disillusionment with this childhood faith – with its negativity and dogmatism, its virtual denial of the spirit of love on which he believed the authentic religious spirit is founded. When he left the Bordeaux region in his early twenties he took with him, he said, 'a religious sensibility fortified by an inhuman inhibition, the favour of the Muses, and the gift of writing'.[3] The faith which ultimately sustained him, and which informs every facet of his writing, is that which he eventually discovered through his personal exploration of the scriptures, and to this he gave full expression in *Vie de Jesus*, the exegetic commentary on New Testament Christianity which he completed in 1933. The spiritual and emotional dilemmas underlying the Jansenist creed remained a potent presence in his fiction, nonetheless, and were consistently juxtaposed with the traditions of scriptural Christianity, which he felt they had corrupted and denied.

One of the most fundamental of Mauriac's objections to Jansenism concerned its claim to offer the sole and exclusive means to redemption and salvation. The teaching that 'outside the Church there is no salvation' shocked him for its contradiction of the scriptural teaching on the universal redemption of humankind through the sacrifice of Christ. Indeed, he argued that the atheistic challenge to conventional religion was frequently inspired by the urge to reassert the spirit of love that is implicitly denied by this exclusivity. 'I have always had a predilection for these eager and noble souls who, in their search for God, come up against the false God of their bourgeois milieu,' he wrote in *D'autres et moi*. 'The idols of a conformist religion intervene between them and the Trinity, and their atheism is the unconscious homage they pay to the infinite Being.'[4]

This desire for a more tolerant and universally oriented Christianity was immensely strengthened by his early discovery of the writings of Pascal, the greatest single influence on his life and work. As his biographer, Robert Speaight, wrote: 'Pascal had walked at his side ever since he had sat at the feet of Fortunat Strowski in Bordeaux.'[5] 'I am never parted from him,' Mauriac himself wrote in *Mémoires Intérieurs*, 'especially not from the Pascal of the *Provinciales*, who has been my master ever since I began crossing swords in *l'Express*.'[6] Recalling how 'abandoned spiritually' he had felt as a child, Mauriac described how he came to read Pascal and how profoundly attracted he was by the critical spirit that informed his faith. Above all, he was attracted by Pascal's insistence on the infinite mercy of God, the denial of which he saw as the basic distortion of the Jansenist creed. 'If certain casuists are ridiculous when they cheat with God and oppose an imbecile and cunning procedure to His justice, the Jansenists are even more repellent when they assign limits to the infinite mercy and decree its laws,' he wrote in *Blaise Pascal et sa soeur Jacqueline*. 'One only has to live in the provinces,' he adds, 'to realise the ravages of Jansenism in this respect. How many frightened hearts have been severed from what should have been their strength and their joy,' he exclaims.[7] Of Pascal he said:

> It was not from Jansenius that he learned his knowledge of the human heart ... Pascal throws a light on the valleys and mountain tops of the same heart and the same nature that had attracted the observation of Montaigne. His lightning tears open the brassy sky, and bathes the human landscape where the author of the *Essais* walked without fear. What was only a hollow becomes an abyss, and what was only a mountain touches the sky.[8]

The influence of Pascal is further in evidence in Mauriac's dislike for theological rationalism, and especially for the writings of Aquinas, whom he saw as

the most eminent and influential of the religious rationalists. When he attended religious retreats at Meudon in the late 1920s, he complained of the excessive attention given there to Aquinas's theology, and spoke of his preference
for the works of the Spanish mystics, particularly the writings of St John of
the Cross. St John's words 'We shall be judged according to our love' – which
he cited at the end of *A Woman of the Pharisees* – seemed to him to epitomise
the essence of the Christian faith. (In *Trois Grands Hommes devant Dieu* he
contrasted these words with Rousseau's 'All I shall need to be happy is
myself'[9] to indicate the essentially other-directed character of the Christian
faith.) The writings of Pascal and St John of the Cross proved to be wholly
compatible with his essentially literary, rather than philosophical, assimilation
of the traditions of Christianity, and they blended easily with all the major figures who influenced his development as a writer – Racine, Balzac, Dickens,
Emily Bronte, Baudelaire and, above all, Dostoevsky, whom he cites repeatedly
on the dilemmas that must be faced by the Christian novelist.

The central dilemma for the religious novelist – as Mauriac realised at an
early stage in his career as a writer – was how to communicate religious
themes without lapsing into moralism or didacticism. This, he recognised, was
rooted in a deeper dilemma: how to reconcile the demands of individual freedom with the novelist's faith in an all-seeing and omnipotent Godhead. He
wondered, for instance, how he could treat a theme such as the universal availability of divine grace without excessively emphasising the extent of divine
intervention in the individual quest for salvation and thereby implicitly
restricting the scope of individual freedom. The progress of an individual soul
towards salvation, he felt, would have to be represented in his fiction as an
entirely free and spontaneous process, emerging naturally and authentically
from the complexities of personal experience, yet his faith demanded that he
emphasise the efficacy of divine grace in the actual attainment of the goal of
personal salvation. The problems arising from all this were the subject of a
heated correspondence with André Gide in 1928 and with Jean-Paul Sartre in
1935. Gide suggested that Mauriac had compromised his religious beliefs in
the interests of his art. In this particular letter he contrasts Mauriac's treatment of religious themes in his book on Racine with the ambivalent attitudes
to matters of faith disclosed in his novel, *Lines of Life* (*Destins*):

> You show a greater advance here in your knowledge of mankind, per-
> haps, than in any of your novels; and I think I prefer the author of
> Racine to the disturbing author of *Destins*. But for all the involutions of
> your specious thought, the Catholic point of view of the ageing Racine
> and your own point of view as a Catholic novelist differ to such an
> extent as to be positively opposed. Racine thanks God for His clemency

in accepting him as His own in spite of his tragedies which he wished he had not written and which he talked of burning ... You, on the other hand, congratulate yourself that before Racine died, God spared him the time to write his plays, and to write them in spite of his conversion. In fact, what you are searching for is the permission to write *Destins* – the permission to be a Catholic without having to burn your books; and it is this that makes you write them in such a way that you will not have to disown them on account of your Catholicism. This reassuring compromise, which allows you to love God without losing sight of Mammon, causes you anguish of conscience and at the same time gives a great appeal to your face and a great savour to your writings; and it ought to delight those who, while abhorring sin, would hate not to be able to give a lot of thought to it. You know, moreover, what the effect would be on literature and especially on your own; and you are not sufficiently Christian to cease to be a writer. Your particular art is to make accomplices of your readers ... Doubtless if I were more Christian I should be less of your disciple.[10]

In his responnse to Gide Mauriac insisted that he had 'inherited Christianity', he 'had not chosen it'. 'I shake the bars all the more violently because I know they are indestructible,' he declared. To the suggestion in Gide's letter that a conflict existed between his beliefs as a man and as an artist, he replied trenchantly: 'I am 43 years old, and I can no longer be torn in half ... The question is to know whether the process of growing old should not be a process of sanctification. Shall this flesh of ours, which nobody can love, turn us away any longer from the Spirit which is not bound by time and which is also – supremely and uniquely – made for love – the Spirit which is love itself?'[11] He argued that his whole life had been enriched intellectually by his faith: 'My intellectual life is far richer since I have been living in a more Christian way; my curiosity is greater; and I am much more interested in ideas.'[12] He restated his belief – articulated earlier in *Le Roman* and in *Souffrances et bonheur du chretién* – that the novelist must avoid moralising at all costs, as he must avoid the manipulation of character to express a particular point of view. 'The ambition of the modern novelist,' he writes, 'is to comprehend man in his entirety, with all his conflicts and resolutions (of conflict).' 'Good souls in pure states of grace do not really exist,' he claimed. 'One finds them only in novels – bad novels, I would say.'[13] Addressing the central problem of representing the action of divine grace in the lives of his characters, he identified the dilemmas that would have to be confronted if this were to be achieved successfully, without loss of artistic credibility:

> Every time one of us tries to represent the pathways of Grace, her con-
> flicts and triumphs, in romantic fiction, we have always a feeling of
> arbitrariness and contrivance. Nothing is less tangible than the finger of
> God in the course of human destiny. Not that He is invisible but that
> His touches are so delicate that they dispel what the novelist seeks to
> pin down. No, God is inimitable, He escapes the hold of the novelist.
> The failure of the majority of novelists whose desire it is to give life to
> saints, comes perhaps from being exhausted from portraying those who
> are sublimely and angelically inhuman, when their unique opportunity
> ought to be to encompass and illuminate the ways in which saintliness is
> nurtured and survives in so miserable a fashion in every human crea-
> ture.[14]

One of the solutions that Mauriac found to this problem, as will be demonstrated in some detail presently, was to represent the workings of divine grace
obliquely through the use of a lyrical imagery which symbolically links the
beauty of nature – the pines, the rains, the song of the nightingale – with the
presence of God in the world of material creation. In this way he could suggest a transformation in the lives of his characters that was brought about, not
through a direct process of divine intervention, but through their proximity to
the spiritual presence of God in the world of material being. This has been
mistakenly interpreted by one scholar as indicating a fusion of pagan and
Christian influences in Mauriac's fiction;[15] it would seem far more appropriate
to interpret it as a poetic attestation to the Christian truth of the Incarnation,
as is clearly suggested in these words from *Souffrances et bonheur du chrétien*:
'At the flight of a bird the Host is no further away from me than He would be
in a cathedral. Cybele is purified by Him I do not see. She closes upon Him
under leaves and stones; she contains Him; the rays of the monstrance are
vines and forests.'[16]

In 'M. François Mauriac et la Liberté', a lengthy review of *The End of the
Night* that was published in *la Nouvelle Revue Française*, Jean Paul Sartre
expressed criticisms of Mauriac's fiction similar to those articulated by Gide.
He too suggested that Mauriac had failed to reconcile the conflicting demands
of his religious and artistic beliefs. In the preface to the novel Mauriac had
declared that he had not sought to determine the progress of the narrative in
accordance with a preconceived plan of action. 'Before ever this book was written I had decided to call it *The End of the Night*, though I had no idea how
this particular night might end,' he wrote.[17] Sartre argued that Mauriac had
failed to fulfil this objective in the novel. The business of the novelist, he said,
is not to explain action, but 'to present actions and passions that are unpredictable'. Characters come alive in a novel, he said, by fashioning their own

future. 'The future is yet to make,' he declared. 'Do you want your characters to come alive?' he asked Mauriac. 'Then see that they are free.'[18] The issues raised by Sartre are most comprehensively addressed by Mauriac in *Mémoires Intérieurs* and in the Postscript to *The Loved and the Unloved. (Galigai)*. In the *Mémoires* he argues that his Catholicism, far from inhibiting his artistic creativity, had in fact rendered it more fruitful. 'The religious life does not curb, rather does it satisfy the poetic craving,' he writes. It does so, he adds, 'not like a fairy-tale which might be true, but like a coherent vision of existence, while, at the same time, leaving a sufficient margin of uncertainty, mystery and darkness to maintain that element of disquiet without which there could be no art.'[19] In the Postscript to *The Loved and the Unloved* he expresses his concern that some of his readers might ask, as a priest-correspondent did on an earlier occasion, how he could reconcile the essential hopefulness of his Catholic faith, and the ideal of service to humanity which it enjoins on all believers, with the overwhelming image of human depravity that he projected in his fiction. 'My priestly correspondent,' he writes, 'will find here fresh reason to wonder what the results of my labours amount to, what good they will do, spiritually to those who read them, and how I can reconcile so distorted a view of the human animal with the faith I claim to have in his vocation of sanctity.'[20] His response involves a repeated emphasis on the non-didactic character of the act of artistic creativity and on the radically imaginative nature of the world the artist creates:

> It would be easy for me to get out of the difficulty, by arguing as I have done on more than one occasion, during the last forty years. I might point out that evil is a reality in this world of ours, that the people I set out to paint are fallen creatures, tainted from birth ... This is all perfectly true, but it does not really answer the objections put forward by the priest ... But, as I myself have often pleaded, the work of art is of service to mankind simply because it does not seek deliberately to 'serve'. Do I really believe that? Let me confess at once that the work of art tends much more frequently to distort than to instruct. For the creative writer to pretend that he helps us to an understanding of mankind by painting a picture in dark and extravagant colours, is sheer hypocrisy. Living persons are never like the characters of fiction. The people presented in novels or on the stage are a race apart. They in no way instruct us about ourselves, or, at least, not usefully; in the first place because these invented creatures are conditioned and circumstanced by the author; in the second, because, no matter how complex they may be, they inevitably express some tendency, some passion, or some vice, and are, to that extent, detached from the human context ...

And even when the artist goes out of his way to avoid the introduction
of 'types' and 'characters', the colourless and insubstantial world into
which he introduces us has little in common with our own. Admittedly,
the elements which go to build it up are borrowed from reality. That is
true of all novels of no matter what kind. The best as well as the worst
are composed from details provided by recollection, fixed by memory,
but retouched and rehashed for the purpose of presenting a 'picture'.
There is no such thing as a novel which genuinely portrays the *indetermination* of human life as we know it.[21]

The methodological implications of all this are explored in detail by
Mauriac in *Le Roman*, his commentary on the nature of the novelist's art.
Here he describes literary creativity as analogous to divine creativity, by virtue
of the autonomy and freedom that both God and the artist must allow their
own creations. 'Of all men the novelist most resembles God,' he writes. 'He
apes after God. He creates living beings, invents destinies, weaves them with
events, tragedies, intertwines them and brings them to their end.'[22] He points,
however, to a fundamental distinction between the two. Divine creation is '*cre-
atio ex nihilo*' he writes, but the novelist creates from what he sees; he does
not originate reality but transposes it, informs it with his own subjectivity.
The novelist, he argues, will always have a predictive sense of the course of
the narrative he creates, but this need not detract from the freedom of his
characters to choose their own destiny:

> When one of my heroes proceeds obediently in the direction assigned to
> him, when he reaches the stages decided by me and makes all of the
> moves which I expect of him, he disturbs me. This submission to my
> design proves that he does not have a real life, that he is not separate
> from me, that he remains still an entity, an abstraction. I am not con-
> tent with my work until my creation (the character I have created)
> resists me, when she rebels against the deeds which I have resolved will
> be committed. I am never confident of the value of my work until such
> time as my characters force me to change the direction of the plot, and
> lead me towards horizons until then I had hardly envisaged.[23]

Having said all this, Mauriac suggested that a tension would always exist
for the novelist between the freedom he had to allow his characters to develop
authentically, and the temptation to influence the course that his narrative
would take, in accordance with his own personal beliefs. This tension was
likely to be particularly acute in novels treating of matters of religious faith, as
he acknowledged in a lecture on Paul Claudel. Here he described the Christian

novelist as conducting 'an uncertain struggle between two antagonistic vocations'. There is, on the one hand, he wrote, 'the call to every Christian, who has received the gift of speech and the gift of writing, to propagate the fire which the Son of Man has come to spread over the earth; and on the other hand the necessity he is under to probe the sounds of human nature until, from one circle to another, he touches the abyss'.[24]

The key to the whole issue may lie, however, in the example of Dostoevsky, by whose writings Mauriac was profoundly influenced, and whose words are cited many times in *Le Roman* and in other works dealing with the nature of the novelist's art. Referring in *Le Roman* to the difficulties that Dostoevsky faced in reconciling the conflicting claims of art and faith, he made a comment which proves highly significant for an understanding of his own position on the same issue. 'The individual as explored by the novelist is an invention,' he writes. The novelist 'can only isolate from his teeming thoughts and ideas a passion, a virtue or vice, which he amplifies disproportionately ... In the individual the novelist isolates and fixes a passion, and in the group he isolates and fixes the individual.'[25] His comments are strongly reminscent of Bakhtin's analysis of Dostoevsky's fictional style which was discussed in an earlier chapter. The dialectical method of characterisation described by Bakhtin in relation to Dostoevsky was basically the method that was employed also by Mauriac. This is confirmed by Robert Speight in his study of Mauriac. In his commentary on *Le Roman* he spoke of the extent of Dostoevsky's influence on Mauriac. 'In this work,' he said, 'Mauriac invoked the influence of Dostoevsky, not only because Dostoevsky believed that man had a soul, but because he shattered the idea that man was all of a piece. He had shown that, more often than not, contradiction was the clue to character.'[26] Like Dostoevsky, Mauriac expressed a vision of life in his fiction which is deeply and profoundly Christian, but that vision embraced many conflicting and sometimes contradictory elements. These he explored through the lives of his characters, both in terms of the isolation of their individual experiences and in terms of their complex and frequently tragic relationships.

On the one hand, therefore, Mauriac fully acknowledged the personal nature of the vision that is conveyed in his fiction. 'The characters in our books,' he wrote, 'do not always belong to our past, they are often an image of ourselves that we project on to the screen of the future. In our novels we are, to some extent, our own prophet.' Of his most celebrated creation he said: 'Thérèse Desqueyroux – c'est moi ... She was made up of everything that in myself I have been obliged to overcome, or circumvent, or ignore.'[27] Equally, he stressed the need for the novelist to allow his characters to function autonomously, in accordance with the spontaneous and largely unpredictable tendencies of the personalities with which they have been endowed. 'We must leave to our heroes the illogical, indeterminate and complex characteristics which are proper to living creatures,' he said. It had been the practice of novelists like Balzac and Stendhal, he wrote, to provide characters with a '*passion dominante*' or a '*passion maitresse*', but with Dostoevsky, he argued, this fashion had changed and novelists began to depict character entirely in terms of its disorder and illogicality.[28] The modern novel, he argued, is characterised by a movement towards 'l'illogisme, l'indetermination, le complexite des etres vivants'.[29] That movement towards illogicality was expressed by Dostoevsky, he said, through ambiguity and contradiction, through the complex and apparently irresolvable conflicts that occurred both within the minds of individual characters and in the relationships that existed *between* them. This is largely what Mauriac himself sought to achieve in his own fiction. It is what he attempted to achieve through the character of Gradère, for example, in *The Dark Angels* – significantly described by one of his critics as his most Dostoevskeyan creation[30] – and through the contrasting behaviour of Gradère and Alain Forcas, on which much of the action of the novel is focussed. This is how he described these two characters in his Preface to the novel:

> The cycle of Alain Forcas is the novel of the reversibility of merits, and it is also the novel of vocation. Alain, chosen and called from the midst of a world doomed to damnation, suffers and pays for all my wretched protagonists. But *Les Anges Noirs* illustrates another idea which obsessed me at that time; that in the worst criminal there subsists certain elements of the saint that he might have become, and that in the purest human being hideous possibilities lie concealed. Gradère, perverted from childhood, sacrilegious, a pimp, procurer, thief, blackmailer and assassin, belongs none the less to the world of the spirit. He is no stranger to the pious Alain, for he is a citizen of the same invisible city. Burdened with every sin, he communicates with the supernatural from below. Beside him, Alain Forcas, brother of a debauched and incestuous sister, only escapes from the sin for which he seems to have been born by cutting himself off from the world, putting on the dress which makes him an object of ridicule, and throwing himself into the arms of God. If *Les Anges Noirs* has a merit in my eyes, it is because the metaphysical system which the book expresses nowhere appears in an abstract form; I see it as the most carnal of my novels, the most deeply rooted in the mire of human experience.

Like Dostoevsky, Mauriac developed the themes of his works principally through the lives of the characters he created. This will be demonstrated in some detail in the remaining parts of this chaper. The novels are dominated by three major themes, each of which will be explored in the three forthcoming sections. They are: firstly, the theme of evil which he identifies with lovelessness, with the failure or rejection of love, or the tragedy of its loss; secondly, the all-encompassing theme of the universal availability of divine grace and the potential for redemption that exists in all of humankind and is realised through its limitless potentiality for love; and finally, the complementary theme of spiritual self-fulfilment which, again like Dostoevsky, he believed could be achieved only through the active pursuit of love in all its forms.

THE DESERT OF LOVE

Critical studies of Mauriac frequently cite Pascal's phrase, 'misère de l'homme sans Dieu', as aptly describing the central concerns of his fiction. Since he ultimately conceived of God as manifesting the infinity and absoluteness of all love, the phrase might be rendered more meaningfully perhaps as 'misère de l'homme sans amour'. He saw the loss or failure of love as the commonest existential manifestation of the fallenness of mankind. 'Nature itself is fallen and everything natural is not therefore in conformity with God', he declared once in the course of a debate on the treatment of the theme of love in the modern novel.[31] His persistent emphasis on human fallenness has led to charges of an excessive concern with evil and with the ugliness of life in his fiction, a concern which is frequently attributed to residual traces of Jansenism from his childhood years in Bordeaux and the Landes. He, in turn, charged certain modern thinkers with projecting a Rousseauistic faith in nature in their work, a position he saw as dangerously underestimating the human potentiality for evil. 'Nothing,' he writes, 'is stranger to the moderns, nothing more distasteful to them when they come across it in its last, Christian possessors, than the metaphysical knowledge of evil.'[32] Anticipating sentiments articulated many years later by Milosz, he declares that 'the religion of humanity has been responsible for as many victims as has authoritarian government'.[33] In *A Woman of the Pharisees* he announced he would deal with subjects that most people find repellent and insisted he would not shirk his responsibility as a novelist to reveal the potential for evil in man in all its grossness and depravity. In a passage from the novel which is addressed directly to the reader he wrote:

> I hope that the reader will realise how very repugnant it is to me to put all this down in words. But it does, at least, prove that what I am relating is true and in no wise invented. Subjects of this kind are, as a rule, instinctively avoided by the professional novelist, because he knows that

most people find them repellent. But those who turn their backs on fiction, and set out to follow up the destinies of persons with whom they have actually been connected, are forever coming on the traces of these miseries and aberrations of the flesh. And even worse than the aberrations are the insufficiencies. For those are just the things about which we do not wish to hear, because so many of us may have been, to some extent, their victims. Renan once said that the truth may well be depressing. He was thinking in terms of metaphysics. On the level of human affairs it may be not only depressing but ridiculous and embarrassing – so much so that decency forbids us to put it into words. Hence the silence in which such things are usually shrouded.

That Mauriac viewed the problem of evil in a way that is entirely non-Jansenist is made equally clear in the same work. The inherent flaw in Jansenism, he suggests, was its implicit denial of the limitlessness and infinitude of divine mercy and love. 'Forty years ago,' he writes at the end of the novel, 'a spirit of fear and trembling still ruled the minds of certain persons in their relations with the Incarnate Love, who, so they had been taught by Jansenism to believe, was implacable.' In the novel he sees love as the primary existential manifestation of human freedom and by inference sees the will to love as the basis of all faith. Equally, he sees the failure of love, or the unwillingness to love, as the universal manifestation of the potentiality for evil present in all mankind. He rejects the Jansenist (and Calvinist) doctrine of Predestination as a denial of the radical freedom of man, by virtue of its implicit rejection of the infinitude of God's love and of man's capacity to draw on this through the power of his own love. 'All through the centuries,' Monsieur Calou says, 'Christians have believed that the humble crosses to which they were nailed on the right and left hand of Our Lord meant something for their own redemption and for the redemption of those they loved. And then Calvin came and took away that hope.'

Mauriac's fiction seems dominated, nonetheless, by the evidence of man's failure to attain the fulfilment made possible through love, and the novels seem filled with characters whose lives have been blighted by its loss. All need love whatever they believe, all aspire to its absoluteness, the Abbé Calou says: 'However little of a Christian a man may be, he wants to be loved in and for God alone – even though he does not believe in God.' Lovelessness, whether the denial of love, its failure, its rejection or distortion, is the root of all evil, the basis of self-corruption: this is the recurring theme of the novels and the source of their persistent concern with the fallenness of mankind. This can be illustrated by way of reference to four of Mauriac's characters whose lives variously depict the different manifestations of lovelessness and its potential for self-corruption. They are: Thérèse Desqueyroux, the central character of four works grouped together under the collective title, *Thérèse*; Paul Courrèges from *The Desert of Love*; the lawyer, Louis, from *The Knot of Vipers*; and Brigitte Pian from *A Woman of the Pharisees*.

The lovelessness in the life of Thérèse results directly from her marriage to Bernard, a man apparently incapable of altruistic feeling of any kind. 'Nothing is ever wholly serious for those who are incapable of love,' the narrator says, as he describes Bernard's thoughts in the hospital where he lies recovering from his wife's attempt on his life. 'Because he was without love Bernard felt only that flicker of joy which comes to a man when some great danger has been safely surmounted.' Correspondingly, the novel emphasises his wife's great need for love. 'The love of which, more than any other living creature, she had been deprived, penetrated her utterly,' the narrator says. As she lies on her bed, plunged into a terrible loneliness of the spirit, she takes refuge in dreams and fantasies of the loving intimacy which she has been denied:

> Thérèse's mind drifted away from the unknown body of flesh and blood which she had conjured up for her delight. She grew weary of her happiness, felt the satiety of her imagined pleasures – and invented new methods of escape. People (she pretended) were kneeling round her ruckle bed. A child from Argelouse (one of those who commonly fled at her approach) was brought dying to her room. She touched it with her hand – all yellowed with nicotine – and it got up, cured. Other, humbler, dreams she improvised – seeing in imagination, a house at the sea's edge, a garden and a terrace. She set about arranging the rooms, choosing the furniture piece by piece, deciding where to put what she had brought from St Clair, involving herself in long arguments about covers and materials. Then the scene would fade, losing its clearness of outline, until nothing remained but a beech-hedge and a bench overlooking the sea. Seated there, she rested her head on her companion's shoulder, rose at the sound of the dinner-gong, entered the gloom of the long pleached alley. Someone walking at her side put sudden arms about her, held her close. A kiss, she thought, can stay the wheel of time. The seconds of love can draw out to infinity. Or so she imagined, for she would never know. She saw the house, still gleaming white, the well. Somewhere a pump creaked. Freshly watered heliotrope scented the air. Dinner would be an interval of rest before the evening's happiness, before that night of which she could not think, so far did it exceed the power of human heart to contemplate. Thus did the love of which, more than any living creature, she had been deprived, possess and penetrate her utterly.

The suffering resulting from the denial of love dominates her life: 'Almost without willing it her pain had become her sole preoccupation, the sole reason – why not? – of her existence.' In her need for intimacy she seeks to indulge a purely predatory, self-gratifying passion, of the nature of which she herself is fully aware: 'What you call love is nothing but a prowling demon who roams the waste places of the earth, seeking whom he may devour. And when she has been duly made away with he starts again on the old weary round. Such love, for all it glories in its sense of freedom, must ever be obedient to the law of its being – which is to seek out someone else whom it may kill for food.' Her deterioration is horrific, a seemingly relentless descent into depravity, and the love to which she cannot give expression is transmuted into self-hatred and the darkness of despair.

Despite her misfortunes, however, Thérèse never succumbs to despair, and in this lies her potential for redemption and salvation. In the Preface to *The End of the Night* Mauriac had said: 'She took form in my mind as an example of that power, granted to all human beings – no matter how much they may seem to be the slaves of a hostile fate – of saying "No" to the law which beats them down ... She belongs to that class of human beings (and it is a huge family!) for whom night can end only when life itself ends. All that is asked of them is that they should not resign themselves to night's darkness.' Her salvation lies in her will to endure, which is essentially the will to love, and ultimately, the will to faith. What she seeks in her reckless quest for love is the spiritual self-fulfilment to which it leads: 'No matter how guilty our passion, it always sees through to the spirit's mystery,' the narrator says. 'A life may have been dragged in the filth of the gutter, but not for a single moment can that fact lessen the splendour which is seen by the eyes of love.' These words alone would indicate the extent of Mauriac's rejection of the Jansenist faith in which he had been reared.

The agony of unrequited love is the theme again of *The Desert of Love*. Dr Paul Courrèges and his son, Raymond, develop an obsessive passion for Maria Cross which in each case is unreciprocated, Maria treating them both with scarcely disguised contempt. So enfeebled is the father by his passion for Maria that he finds relief even in the mere mention of her name by his son: 'Raymond had only to say "I saw Maria Cross" for the passion he had thought dead to stir again. Alas! it was merely a state of torpor ... a single word could bring it back to life, provide it with the food it craved. It was already stretching its limbs, yawning and getting to its feet. If it couldn't embrace in flesh and blood reality the woman of its choice, it would find relief in speech. No matter what the cost, he must talk about Maria Cross.' His failure to attain intimacy with her epitomises the failure of his entire life, his failure either to love or to be loved:

The doctor loved Maria, but he could see her with detachment. He loved her as the dead must love the living. She made one with all the other loves of his life, from boyhood on ... Feeling his way along the pathway of this thought, he now saw that one and the same sentiment had always held him in thrall down the years. It had always been like the one that had caused him the torment from which he had only just been released. He could feel his way back along the dreary sameness of that eternal pilgrimage, could have put a name to each one of all the passionate adventures most of which, like this one, had ended only in frustration. Yet, in those days he had been young. It wasn't, then, age alone that stood between him and Maria Cross. No more successfully at twenty-five than now could he have crossed the desert separating this woman and himself. He remembered how, just after he left college, when he was the same age as Raymond, he had loved, yet never known a woman's hope ... It was the law of his nature that he could never make contact with those he loved ... Other men – his father had been one such, Raymond would be another – can follow the law of their being into old age, obedient to the demands of their vocation of love. But he, even in his youth, had been obedient only to the call of his pre-destined solitude.

'It was the law of his nature that he could never make contact with those he loved.' The loneliness of Paul Courrèges typifies the tragedy of all the unloved, those involuntarily consigned to a life of solitude by virtue of their failure to find love. 'How importunate are those who do not touch our hearts, those whom we have not chosen,' Maria reflects, pointing to the contingent and inequitable character of earthly love. 'They are wholly external to ourselves,' she says. 'There is nothing about them that we want to know. Should they die, their death would mean no more to us than their lives ... yet it is they who fill our whole existence.' Equally, she points to the moral complexity of earthly love. Recalling her own attitude to Raymond on the train, she reflects on the ambivalent character of sexual seduction: 'The desire that had come to birth in her heart had been pure and limpid, yet her every action had the appearance of a monstrous depravity.' (It is significant, in this respect, that the narrator describes the stereotypic image of the 'fallen woman' as 'theological in character', intimating the moral simplification that underlies conventional ethical judgments of sexual love.) The tragedy of sexual passion lies in the all-consuming force that it generates. In the case of Paul Courrèges, this becomes a cancer, consuming the life blood of his existence. His son describes the suffering that his passion for Maria has brought him:

The young man began silently to calculate 'He must be sixty-nine or seventy. Is it possible to go on suffering at that age, and after all these years?' He became suddenly aware of his own hurt, and the consciousness of it frightened him. It wouldn't last ... very soon it would pass into forgetfulness. He remembered something that one of his mistresses had said: 'When I'm in love and going through hell, I just curl up and wait. I know that in a very short while the particular man in question will mean absolutely nothing to me, though at the moment I may be ready to die for him, that I shan't so much as spare a passing glance for the cause of so much suffering. It's terrible to love, and humiliating to stop loving ...' All the same, this old man has been bleeding from a mortal wound for seventeen long years. In lives like his, hedged about with routine, dominated by a sense of duty, passion becomes concentrated, is put away, as it were, in cold storage. There is no way of using it up, no breath of warm air can reach it and start the process of evaporation. It grows and grows, stagnates, corrupts, poisons and corrodes the living flesh that it holds prisoner.

On the other hand, the novel clearly affirms the positive potential of earthly love. 'Only by physical contact, by the embraces of the flesh, by, in short, the sexual act, can two persons ever really communicate,' Maria says. Furthermore, Paul Courrèges himself emphasises the power of the will to control passion: 'The essential thing is that you should believe in the power of your own will,' he tells Maria. 'You must believe that it is in your power to control all those wild beasts in yourself that are not the real you at all.' It is left to Raymond to underline the novel's main conclusion on sexual love: the tragedy of unrequited love is resolved by death but, since all earthly love is mortal, the fate of the unloved is no worse ultimately than that of all those who have enjoyed its transient self-fulfilment. Looking back on his own fruitless passion for Maria, he concludes: 'If he decided that, at no matter what cost, he must fight his way out of the dense blackness, must escape from this murderous law of gravity, what choices were there open to him but the alternatives of stupor or sleep? – unless this star in the firmament of his heart should go suddenly dead, as all love goes dead.'

'Time which always spells defeat for love, treats hatred more slowly – but the end in either case is the same', Mauriac wrote in the closing pages of *The End of the Night*. The theme of love transmuted into hatred is developed further in *The Knot of Vipers* where Louis, the lawyer from Bordeaux, looks back on a life dominated by his resentment of his own family, particularly of his wife, to whom he has hardly spoken for over forty years. In the Preface to the novel Mauriac wrote: 'The man here depicted was the enemy of his own flesh and blood. His heart was eaten up by hatred and avarice.' Tormented by sexual jealousy, Louis broods endlessly on the image of his wife's former lover, Rodolphe, stifling all communication between his wife and himself in the process. The bed on which they slept had been 'the silent witness of their bitter wordlessness'. Louis realises that hatred is a wholly self-corrupting emotion, endlessly destructive of all the love within him, blinding him to the true feelings of those around him:

> The setting sun pierced through with difficulty to light that buried world. I could feel, I could see, I could touch my guilt. It was not only that my heart had become a nest of vipers, that it had been filled with hatred for my children, with a lust for vengeance and a grasping love of money. What was worse than that was that I had refused to look beyond the tangle of vile snakes. I had treasured their knotted hideousness as though I had been the central reality of my being – as though the bleating of the life-blood in my veins had been the pulse of all those swarming reptiles. Not content with knowing, through half a century, only of myself what was not truly me at all, I had carried the same ignorance into my dealing with others. The expression of squalid greed on the faces of my children had held me fascinated. Confronted by Robert, I had been able to see only his stupidity, because it was all I had wanted to see. I had never once realised that the superficial appearance of others was something I must break through, a barrier that I must cross, if I was ever to make contact with the real man, the real woman beyond and behind it. That was the discovery I ought to have made when I was thirty or forty.
>
> But now I am an old man. The movement of my heart is too sluggish. I am watching the last autumn of my life as it puts the vines to sleep and stupefies them with its fumes and sunlight. Those whom I should have loved are dead, and dead, too, those whom I could have loved. I have neither the time now, nor the strength, to embark upon a voyage of exploration with the object of finding the reality of others. Everything in me, even my voice, even my gestures, belongs to the monster whom I reared against the world, the monster to whom I gave my name.

Hatred, he realises, feeds on itself, perpetuates and recycles itself through its own intensity. 'All my life,' he reflects, 'I have made sacrifices and the memory of them has poisoned my mind, nourishing and fattening the kind of rancorous resentment which grows worse with the passage of years.' At the root of his failure to love lies, not malice or evil intent, but a deficient self-awareness, together with continuous misjudgment of those with whom he lives. He recognises his own tendency to 'simplify others', to misinterpret their thoughts and feelings towards him. This is particularly the case in his relations with his wife. 'Is it possible,' he asks, 'that a man can live for nearly half a century noticing one side only of the person who shares his life.' 'Can it be,' he asks, 'that, from long habit, he picks and chooses from among her gestures and her words, keeping for use only those that feed his grievances and perpetuate his resentments.' 'There is a fatal tendency in all of us to simplify others, to eliminate in them everything that might soften the indictment, give some human lineaments to the caricature which our hatred craves in order to justify itself,' he concludes.

Tragically, it is not until shortly before her death that Louis realises how much his wife had loved him. He is stunned by her confession that for years she had lain alone in her bed, longing for him to join her. This is the moment of self-illumination for Louis: he discovers the existence of a love to which he had denied himself access by his own self-deception. 'All through his dreary life squalid passions stood between him and that radiance which was so close that an occasional ray could still break through to touch and burn him,' the narrator writes. Instead of the love which he might have enjoyed, he had taken refuge in self-pity, jealousy, vindictiveness – the enemies of love – because of a distorted understanding of himself and others. Delusion, he realises, breeds further delusion, entangling its victim in a knot of vipers, from which love offers the only prospect of release. He finally recognises the extent of his self-delusion and, at the age of sixty-eight, bequeaths his property to his children, seeks their forgiveness and repents of his wrong-doings.

At the end of *The Knot of Vipers* one sees the point of the words quoted from St Teresa of Avila on its opening page: 'Consider, O God, that we are without understanding of ourselves; that we do not know what we would have, and set ourselves at an infinite distance from our desires.' The lovelessness that comes from diminished self-awareness is again the theme of *A Woman of the Pharisees*, in this instance finding expression in the idea of religion without love. (Mauriac described this novel as having an especially strong appeal for Protestants and was told that it particularly impressed the Swedish authorities assessing his work for the award of the Nobel Prize.)[34] The theme of religion without love had been briefly intimated in the portrait of Isa in *The Knot of Vipers*. Her faith is a matter merely of formal observance. 'I did all I could, no matter how trivial the circumstances, to show how ill your practice squared with your faith,' her husband says. 'You must admit, my poor Isa, that, good Christian though you were, I had an easy task! You had forgotten, if, indeed, you had ever known, that charity is synonymous with love.' This disparity between faith and religious practice is demonstrated on a much larger scale in the portrait of Brigitte Pian, the 'Woman of the Pharisees'. A figure of impeccable rectitude, she strives relentlessly to realise what she conceives to be the goal of spiritual perfection. 'She measured her progress in the spiritual life very much as she would have done in the study of a foreign language,' the narrator says. Seeing it as her duty to enforce the highest standards of morality amongst all those around her, she is harsh and judgmental in her attitudes towards them, is deeply intolerant of their weaknesses and rigorous in her insistence on the inflexibility of the Jansenist ethic. The failure at the heart of her creed is spiritual arrogance; a self-indulgent pride lies at the root of her intolerance and readiness to judge. Her faith is self-contradictory; it lacks the essential and all-encompassing dynamic of love:

> Was she a saint? She was making great efforts to be one, and at each step forward, fought hard to hold the ground that she had gained. No one had ever told her that the closer a man gets to sanctity the more conscious does he become of his own worthlessness, his own nothingness, and gives to God, not from a sense of duty, but because the evidence is overwhelming, all credit for the few good activities with which Grace has endowed him. Brigitte Pian pursued an opposite course, finding each day ever stronger reasons for thanking her Creator that He had made of her so admirable a person. There had been a time when she was worried by the spiritual aridity which marked her relations with her God: but since then she had read somewhere that it is as a rule the beginners on whom the tangible marks of Grace are showered, since it is only in that way that they can be extricated from the slough of this world and set upon the right path. The kind of insensitiveness which afflicted her was, she gathered, a sign that she had long ago emerged from those lower regions of the spiritual life where fervour is usually suspect. In this way her rigid soul was led on to glory in its own lack of warmth. It did not occur to her that never, for a single moment, even in the earliest stages of her search for perfection, had she felt any emotion which could be said to have borne the faintest resemblance to love: that she had never approached her Master save with the object of calling His attention to her own remarkably rapid progress along the Way, and suggesting that He give special heed to her singular merits.

Lacking self-awareness, her conscience remains unilluminated by the kind of understanding described in the words of St Teresa that were cited at the beginning of *The Knot of Vipers*. It was this deficient self-knowledge that enabled her to convince herself she was following the path to genuine sanctity. Her self-confidence is nurtured by self-delusion. All her actions were well-

intentioned, however painful their consequences for others. 'In every circum-
stance of her life Brigitte Pian was sincerely anxious to do good. Or that at
least was what she believed,' the author says. Her mind being untroubled by
anxiety or guilt, she remained convinced of the morality of all her actions:
'She was a logically minded woman who kept a straight road marked out by
clearly labelled principles. She never took a step that she could not immediately justify.' She is repeatedly contrasted with the Abbé Calou whose faith is
founded on the humility, love and depth of conscience vision that she lacks.
Her progress towards self-illumination is slow and painful. 'Many were to be
her victims,' the narrator says, ' before the true vision dawned on her of that
love in whose service she thought herself enrolled, but of which, in fact, she
was wholly ignorant.'

'NOT OUR MERITS THAT MATTER ... BUT OUR LOVE'

> It had been revealed to her that our Father does not ask us to give a
> scrupulous account of what merits we can claim. She understood at last
> that it is not our merits that matter but our love.

The last two sentences from *A Woman of the Pharisees* might be said to encapsulate the theme that underlies the whole of Mauriac's work. That theme finds
expression in two fundamental affirmations. The first is the universal need for
love: all, he says, yearn for love, whether consciously or unconsciously, by
virtue of the nature of their being. Secondly, what they long for is the
absoluteness of love, its potential for transcendence of the mortal and the
finite. Of this, he suggests, they are assured through the power of divine
grace, i.e. through the presence of the infinite in the realm of the material and
the finite. The universal availability of divine grace, i.e., its availability through
love, is the all-encompassing message of his fiction.

Repeatedly, Mauriac affirms the potential for sanctity that is always present
in love, even in its most earthly and most sensual forms. In *The Enemy* (*Le
Mal*) while he warned of the potential dangers of sexual passion – 'Once let
human beings set their feet upon that slippery slope and there was no stopping
their headlong descent' – he also insisted that 'the body too can be sanctified.'
At one point in the novel its hero, Fabien, recalls how 'the pleasures of the
flesh, that blunt so many hearts, had restored to him a mystic sensibility'. In
Flesh and Blood (*La Chair et Le Sang*) sexual love is seen as a source of God's
grace. The novel's central character, May, describes the physical consummation of her love for her newly married husband as a sacramental communion
comparable to the Eucharist. Her diary recording of the event ends with the

following words: 'Obsessed by tormenting desires, subdued by the urgencies of flesh and blood, he believed that he could communicate something of his flame to me, and, all unknowing, gave me God. Grace spread from the mere fact of his being there, as light spreads from a lamp. It welled from his body's craving, and I received it.'

In his last novel, *Young Man in Chains* (*L'Enfant chargé de chaines*), Mauriac spoke of 'the human love that is the prefiguration of the love that created us'. 'However sinful it may be,' he wrote, 'it resembles the love of the creator for his creature, and of the creature for the creator.' Earthly love, while imperfect in itself, is the means, he suggests, to the absoluteness of love in its infinite forms. But, crucially, he insists that love is truly love only when it is selfless. And it is through the gift of grace that the inherent selflessness and the potentiality for the infinite that is present in all love is ultimately realised. All nature is redeemable, he declares – redeemable through love and the infinite workings of God's grace. If, as has been suggested, his novels seem unduly preoccupied with the ugliness and murkiness of life, their purpose is to disclose the universal presence of grace in all the conditions of human existence, and to underline the ultimate redeemability of nature, now matter how hopeless that prospect might appear. This can now be illustrated by returning to the four characters just described whose lives tragically exemplify the lovelessness and sinfulness that distances man from God. Out of their misery and suffering comes their eventual discovery of their own potential for redemption and salvation through love.

'No matter how guilty our passion it always sees through to the spirit's mystery,' the narrator says in *Thérèse*. 'A life may have been dragged in the filth of the gutter, but not for a single moment can that fact lessen the splendour which is seen by the eyes of love.' The influence of Kierkegaard, particularly his theme of faith as the product of despair, is strongly in evidence in this work. Mauriac spoke of Kierkegaard's *Journal* as 'telling what is, in effect, the story of my own life', clearly indicating the extent of the latter's influence on the evolution of his personal and artistic beliefs.[35] The imagery of darkness is used frequently by Mauriac, as it was by Kierkegaard and St John of the Cross, to intimate the spiritual desolation that leads ultimately to a hope-giving faith 'The night has never had another heart than mine, nor other passions,' he wrote in a beautiful lyrical passage in *Mémoires Intérieurs*. 'It speaks of God only to those whose hearts already brim with God, but they no longer need to make that détour of the stars to bring them to their Love. If I pray before the darkened distance, it is not on Cassiopeia that my eyes are fixed ... I look not at the sky, but at the plain, where the vessel of a village church lies anchored in the mist.'[36] 'For the Christian,' he wrote in the same work, 'a certain type of despair is not necessarily at odds with hope: it is the rending indictment of

Saint Teresa who wept "because love is not loved"; it is Pascal gazing upon Christ "in agony until the end of the world"'.[37]

Significantly, the fourth of the Thérèse novels is entitled *The End of the Night*. Thérèse is sustained by her will to live, by her refusal to succumb to despair, which in essence is the will to faith. Her faith finds expression in a persistent quest for love which, however unconscious and aimless its course, is fundamentally a search for God. Her faith is rewarded with the grace that finally ensures her salvation. Recognising the unconventional nature of her quest, Mauriac represents her final reconciliation with God as something attained entirely through her own will to faith, and without the sanction of religious ritual. 'I could not see the priest who would have possessed the qualifications necessary if he was to hear her confession with understanding,' he writes. She enters the 'eternal radiance of death', confident of the grace that will enable her to attain the light and the peace that marks the ending of the night:

> Marie opened the door and called to him that the five minutes were up. Leaning against the frame, she could see Georges standing there, bent slightly forward above Thérèse's chair, which, for her, was out of sight. He seemed not to have heard her voice, and repeated the question he had put:
>
> 'Do you want to go to sleep?'
>
> The sick woman shook her head. She scarcely ever slept now, because of the difficulty she found in breathing. The nights seemed endless.
>
> 'Would you like a book?'
>
> No, she could not read now. 'I just do nothing. I hear the clocks strike, I wait for the end ...'
>
> 'The end of the night, you mean?'
>
> Suddenly she seized his hands. Only for a few seconds could he bear upon his face the fire of desperate tenderness that flamed in her eyes.
>
> 'Yes, my dear: the end of life, the end of the night.'

'It is the novelist's task,' Mauriac wrote in *God and Mammon*, 'to show the element which holds out against God in the highest and noblest characters – the innermost evils and dissimulations – and also to light up the secret source of sanctity in creatures which seem to us to have failed.'[38] Like Thérèse, Paul and Raymond Courrèges have given their lives to an apparently fruitless passion, having dissipated their love on a woman who is indifferent to them both. In this instance again, Mauriac reaffirms the power of love, even when it is despised and rejected, to disclose its own absoluteness and its access to the infinite. But that prospect, he asserts, is realised finally only in death. 'It is not death that tears us from those we love,' Paul Courrèges says; 'rather it keeps them safe, preserving them in all the adorable ambience of youth. Death is the salt of love; it is life that brings corruption.' All love is created by God, Raymond concludes. Some lives it fulfils, others it destroys. In all its earthly forms it dies, its final fulfilment occurring only when the soul attains union with its Creator:

> For how many living creatures had not his mere proximity meant death and destruction? Even now he did not know to what lives he had given purpose and direction, what lives he had cut adrift from their moorings; did not know that because of him some woman had killed the young life just stirring in her womb; that, because of him a young girl had died, a friend had gone into a seminary; and that each of these single dramas had given birth to others in an endless succession. On the brink of this appalling emptiness, of this day without Maria, which was to be but the first of many other days without her, he was made aware, at one and the same moment, of his dependence and his solitude. He felt himself forced into the closest possible communion with a woman with whom he would never make contact. It was enough that her eyes should see the light for Raymond to live forever in the darkness. For how long? If he decided that, at no matter what cost, he must fight his way out of the dense blackness, must escape from this murderous law of gravity, what choices were there open to him but the alternatives of stupor or of sleep? – unless this star in the firmament of his heart should go suddenly dead, as all love goes dead. He carried within him a tearing, frantic capability of passion, inherited from his father – of a passion that was all-powerful, that would breed, until he died, still other planetary worlds, other Maria Crosses, of which, in succession, he would become the miserable satellite. There could be no hope for either of them, for father or for son, unless, before they died, He should reveal Himself Who, unknown to them, had drawn and summoned from the depths of their beings this burning, bitter tide.

Looking back on a lifetime consumed by envy, resentment and greed, Louis, the criminal lawyer from *The Knot of Vipers*, realises that the prospect of redemption lies only in his release from his own hatred. That release can be effected only through love. 'Isn't there, Isa, in my very vileness, something which, more than all their virtues, resembles the Sign of your adoration?' he asks his wife – in the scene where he condemns so-called religious believers for their intolerance and hypocrisy. Recognising his own potential for self-reform, he asks rhetorically: 'What power is leading me on? Is it blind – or is it love? Perhaps it may be love ...' He affirms the infinite character of the love that still remains in his soul, seeing it as the fruit of God's grace, made accessible to the repentant soul through the potency of prayer. 'Even the genuinely good cannot, unaided, learn to love,' he declares ...

> To penetrate beyond the absurdities, the vices, and, above all, the stupidities of human creatures, one must possess the secret of a love which the world has now forgotten. Until that secret shall have been rediscovered, all betterment in conditions of life will be in vain. I used to think that it was selfishness which kept me uninterested in questions of sociology and economics, and to some extent that was true, for I have been a monster of solitude and indifference. Still, I had a feeling, an obscure certainty, that it was no use merely to revolutionise the face of the world, that what was needed was the power to reach the world through the medium of the heart. Him whom I seek can alone achieve that victory, and he must needs be the heart of all hearts, the burning centre of all love. The desire I felt may well have been a prayer. On that night I was within an ace of falling on my knees with my arms on the back of a chair, as Isa used to do, long summers ago, with the three children pressing round her. In those days I would come back from the terrace towards the lighted window. I would muffle my footsteps and, invisible in the darkness of the garden, look on the group at prayer within. *'Prostrate at Thy feet, O God'* – Isa would say – *'I thank thee that Thou hast given me a heart to know and love Thee ...'*.

Louis's last words reassert his faith in the redemptive power of love: 'Something, as I sit to-night writing these lines, is stifling me, something is making my heart feel as though it would burst – it is the Love whose name at last I know, whose ador ...'

It is her discovery of the same truth that gives Brigitte Pian the self-awareness that releases her from the delusions of spiritual arrogance and pride. Full of remorse for her denunciation of the Abbé Calou, she begins to doubt her conventional faith, her conscience no longer finding contentment in the simplistic morality which she had previously practised. She doubts the sincerity of her own self-repentance: 'Which do you think is worse,' she asks Louis, 'to disobey the Church by not communicating at Easter, or, by obeying, to expose oneself to the risk of receiving the Eucharist in an improper state of mind?' When she goes to the Abbé Calou to confess her sins, he advises her to 'dwell on her own insignificance' and to submit herself wholly to God in a spirit of resigned humility. Subdued by her recognition of her guilt, she discovers the potency of the grace that comes from the active pursuit of love. Even after her husband's death, it is her memory of their love that leads her back to 'the ways of God' on the few occasions when she lapses into her former hypocrisy. 'You see,' she tells Louis, 'the real, secret truth is that I have not lost him ... but there is no one I can tell ...

> Dear Monsieur Gellis was never so close to me as he is now, not even when he was alive. He had already embarked on his mission to me while he was in this world, but we are all of us poor mortal flesh, and our bodies were a barrier. But there is nothing between us now.'
>
> She spoke much on this theme, and at first I suspected a trick of sorrow seeking to cheat death of the dear doctor. But at the end of a few days I realised that the sun of human love had not risen too late on the arid destiny of this woman of the Pharisees, that the 'whited sepulchre' had been unsealed and stood open at last. Perhaps it still contained a few dried bones, a trace of corruption. Occasionally the formidable eyebrows met in a frown above the smouldering eyes. Some grievance, long chewed over, brought, now and then, a bitter word to her lips. But 'dear Monsieur Gellis' was never far away, was always there at the critical moment to lead Brigitte Pian into the calm ways of God.

Inherent in the theme of grace is one of the most intractable problems in the entire tradition of Christian thought. It is a problem vividly evoked in the Book of Job and given particular attention by Dostoevsky in *The Brothers Karamazov* and by Beckett in *Waiting for Godot*. The problem centres on the apparent arbitrariness of divine justice, by virtue of which the innocent seem to suffer and the wicked to prosper and the prospect of salvation appears to bear little relation to the nature of the life that is lived. It is this mystery that Alain Forcas of *The Dark Angels* contemplates when, in a moment of weakened faith, he questions the justice of a Creator who can grant salvation indiscriminately both to those who have lived in sin and to those, like himself, who have sought to live virtuously in accordance with the teachings of the scriptures. He is temporarily overcome with a 'savage uprush of emotion' at the injustice which allows Gradère to be saved, despite a life devoted to wrong-doing, while he, in a moment's despair, runs the risk of losing his soul. His agony is described in one of the most moving sequences in the novel. Like Job, his solution is to entrust himself wholly and unquestioningly to the mercy of God:

> The Abbé shook his head without replying. He was clenching his teeth. He muttered something about needing air, and, while Andrés took his place beside the bed, went back to the window. The nightingales were

now asleep, the poplars had ceased their rustling. 'Did I yield to my impulse of hatred?' – he asked himself in an access of mental torment: 'Am I still in a state of grace?' Would he be able, in a few hours' time, to say his Mass? 'Well,' murmured the same voice of the tempter, 'why not refrain from going to the altar to-morrow evening? Where there is the slightest doubt ...' But what reason for his defection could he give young Lassus? No longer seeing his way plain before him, Alain clung to a rule that he had made his own: to surrender to a very lunacy of trust: to be trusting even to the brink of lunacy. But what of sacrilege? The memory that he could never silence brought to his mind a fragment of the Gospel: *Friend, how camest thou in hither not having a wedding garment? And the servants took him and cast him into darkness ...*

But now the sick man had awakened, and was speaking in a low voice to Andrés. The Abbé, from the depths of his temptation, lost not a word of what they were saying. 'I am dying in peace, dear Andrés' – Gradère repeated more than once – 'in a peace beyond imagining'. Then, in Alain's heart the old grievance rose again. He had been cheated, robbed! What mockery, what derision! This criminal would be saved, but he ... he was lost ... And yet, in spite of the stormy surface of his spirit, another voice, muted by distance, made itself heard within his heart across a great chasm of misery: 'I am there, fear not. I am there for ever.'

What Forcas affirms, in a spirit of total trust in God, is his faith in the ultimate mystery of Christianity: the mystery of the Incarnation – God's indwelling presence in the sphere of finite being. 'The world is a place full of suffering, to which Christ alone can give meaning and value,' Mauriac wrote in *The Enemy*. It is the mystery of the Incarnation that ultimately gives meaning to suffering. That mystery finds expression, existentially, in the miracle of grace, i.e. the universal availability of God's love to mankind through his presence in created being. In his repeated assertion of this doctrine, Mauriac most emphatically rejected the Jansenist creed of his childhood, with its insistence on the intrinsically evil character of the material world. All nature is fallen, he declares, but is redeemed through grace, through God's presence in its finite materiality. Nature is holy by virtue of its material attestation of the presence of divine grace. The power of evil is great and all-pervasive, but the power of God's grace is greater still and is available to all through love. Love is both its source and its manifestation. Man is saved, he suggests, through his freely chosen *election* to love. (By emphasising the freedom of the decision of faith – the election to love – he was rejecting the idea of grace as an act of direct intervention by God, the notion on which Sartre had based his claim that

Mauriac's characters were not free to work out their own destiny.)

The whole theme of grace is beautifully evoked in Mauriac's fiction through his employment of symbolic patterns of nature imagery designed to evoke the sanctity of all creation, i.e. its embodiment of the presence of divine grace in its material reality. This can be illustrated through three of the major image-motifs in the novels: the imagery of water, of trees, and of birdsong. The final transformation of Louis from a greedy, resentful, envious husband and father to a repentant sinner, convinced of the extent of his wrong-doing and of the potency of the love he had suppressed within himself, is conveyed through images of cleansing rain which symbolically evoke the purification of spirit that he has attained in the final months of his life. For Thérèse water symbolises the infinity of being that separates the soul from God, but which is finally transcended through faith. Approaching her death, the narrator says, she 'was the only one who could walk on that watery surface, and so draw near to the last mortal on the farther shore'. Following the death of Jean Péloueyre, his wife Noémie lies on a grassy bank, contemplating the wonders of nature, and yearns for the repose her husband has attained. 'What more natural,' the narrator asks, 'than that a poor woman dying of thirst in this world of smouldering ash, in this life of utter solitude, should raise her eyes and stretch her hands to the cool waters of Eternal Life?'

The great pine-trees of the Landes, in their seeming endlessness, also symbolise the infinity of God's presence in nature and the limitless availability of divine grace. As Jean Péloueyre lies dying, 'drenched with sweat, nauseated by the smell of his own sick-bed', he is renewed in spirit by the spectacle of the pines which he can see through the open window of his room: 'Oh, those shooting mornings!' he exclaims. 'Blest magic of the pines with their tufted tops of faded grey against the blue of the sky, with their look of humble folk caught up in glory!' The smoke that comes from the fire in his room seems 'the very life-breath of the blazing pines which, so often, on torrid summer days, had been blown into his face from off his native heaths'. As Georges contemplates the future without Thérèse, the pines seem to unite with him in his grief: 'The moaning of the pines around the abandoned farmstead filled the air with the sound of an infinite lamentation.' (After Mauriac's mother died, he was told her last words were: 'It is the light that I am sad to be leaving, and these trees.')[39] In one of the finest lyrical sequences from *The Lamb*, Xavier, who is gazing on the landscape from his open window, recovers his capacity to pray as he looks towards the pines. They signify the mystery of the Incarnation, by virtue of their symbolic attestation both to the redemptive miracle of the Cross and to the infinity of all natural being:

As soon as Xavier was ready, he left his room, began to go downstairs, thought he heard a sigh, leaned over the bannisters, and saw Mirbel sitting on the bottom step, waiting for him. Had it been a man armed with a cudgel his heart could not have beat more violently. He returned to his room and went to the window. There was still a trace of mist hanging about the branches of the trees. The virginia creeper, which had grown almost up to the shutters, was as wet as though it had been raining. The misty sun was not yet strong enough to have any effect upon the dew. He could hear the rumble of country carts, cocks crowing, the noise of the hammer on the anvil at the forge, dogs barking, the scream of the sawmill – all the sounds of the life he loved so well. He had omitted to say his Morning Prayers, not from forgetfulness, but because he did not want to pray, was afraid of praying. He had put off the moment when he would have to. And now here he was dragged back to the full contemplation of Heaven, looking up at the sky, seeing the black crucified limbs of the pine-trees. No need for him even to say 'Dear God ...' He knelt down and rested his forehead on the window ledge.

The imagery of birdsong similarly attests to the miracle of God's grace and to the presence of the infinite in the finiteness of natural being. In his use of this image Mauriac has strong affinities with his fellow-countryman, Olivier Messiaen, whose music similarly employs the sounds of birdsong to evoke the presence of God in the natural world. A particularly striking instance of the image occurs in the final pages of *The Dark Angels*. In the sequence describing Gradère's reconciliation with God there are images of cleansing rain, the 'silence of living snow' and the light breeze that blows from 'a thousand murmuring pines' to signify God's redemptive presence in nature. These images are accompanied by a sustained evocation of the love-song of two nightingales. As Gradère lies dying in Tota's arms, he hears the nightingales singing in the Frontenac woods – 'so far away that their call seemed to come from some unknown world'. Tota's prayer is enhanced by the sounds of the nearby stream and by the beauty of the nightingales' song: 'She prayed, conscious of nothing but the wheezing of asthmatic lungs, and, far away, in spite of the closed windows, from beyond the meadows, the sound of the stream punctuated by the song of the two nightingales. It ceased, perhaps because the two birds had found one another at last, and nothing broke the silence but the gurgling of swift water flowing beneath the alders.' The union of the two nightingales signifies the permanence of love in the world of the infinite, the world of the spirit. It is their song that the Abbé Forcas hears also as he gazes from the window of the dying man's room, reflecting on the transformation he had brought about in the repentant sinner through the infinite resources of his faith, his hope and his love:

> Then and then only, had Alain, quite worn-out, gone over to the window. He had poured out on this man all his faith, all his hope, all his love. He felt empty, as though his treasure had been taken from him. The Balion, a bare stone's–throw away, eddied above the deep hole into which Gradère had dropped his spade on the night of the crime. Now and again the breeze set the poplars on the river bank quivering, and when the rustle of the leaves died down, the Abbé could hear far off the singing of two hidden nightingales. The darkness was like a human presence. Its quiet breath of sleep touched his hair and dropped in silence. It brought to him the smell of wild mint from the river bank, the scent of syringas in the gardens of the town, now in flower, of the last of the lilac. From the room on his right came an insistent murmur (broken at times by a cough, by the sound of a spitoon being moved on the bed-table) from which emerged occasionally the words, 'Pray for us miserable sinners'. This enemy of men's souls, this murderer, was going in peace to Heaven, was leaving this world with a heart that overflowed with joy.

'NOT YOURS TO UNDERSTAND, BUT TO RESEMBLE ME'

The conquest of pride is the key to self-fulfilment through love and the means by which the soul ultimately finds redemption and salvation. This is the truth that finally becomes clear to Louis, Thérèse and Brigitte, as they realise the destructive character of the forces that have dominated their lives. In several other characters, however, Mauriac depicted the living practice of goodness and love in a manner that convincingly demonstrates their potentiality to realise this in all the circumstances of their daily lives. Four of his characters vividly exemplify this whole process: the Abbé Calou from *A Woman of the Pharisees*, Alain Forcas from *The Dark Angels*, Noémie d'Artiailh from *A Kiss for the Leper*, and Xavier Dartigelongue from *The Lamb*. If Pascal was the decisive influence in Mauriac's conception of faith as being rooted in individual freedom, the influence of Dostoevsky is all pervasive in his further insistence that it is rooted in the humble practice of active love.

Mauriac closely followed Dostoevsky in his repeated affirmation of the Christian paradox that from humility comes strength, i.e. that the power of the humble and the meek springs from their invulnerability to malice and offence. Like Dostoevsky also, he saw the authentic spirit of Christian humility as being manifested, not in self-effacing passivity – such as the former had portrayed in the character of Prince Myshkin – but in the humble and active pursuit of love, such as he exemplified in the lives of Father Zossima and Alyosha Karamazov. That same sense of humble and loving responsibility is evident in the life of the Abbé Calou from *A Woman of the Pharisees*. His faith is dramatically contrasted with the arrogant and self-righteous sanctity of Brigitte Pian, whose self-complacent humility is based ultimately on self-love. 'What is important', the Abbé says, is 'to love in one's heart'. Unlike Brigitte's, his is a tolerant and strictly non-judgmental faith. 'It's no use trying to force one's way into other people's lives,' he tells Jean. 'Never push open the door of another person's life, for it can be known only to God. Never turn your eyes upon that secret city, that place of damnation, which is the soul of another, unless you wish to be turned into a pillar of salt ...' All his relations with people are inspired by Christ's injunction, 'Love your enemies and pray for those who persecute you.' Pointing to the complexity of this message, he tells Jean that sometimes loving one's enemies may even be easier that truly loving those who love us. 'Our Lord told us to love our enemies,' he says. 'It is often easier to do that than not to hate those we love.' 'Yes,' Jean replies, 'because they can hurt us so frightfully.' On his arrival at Baluzac, the Abbé soon discovers the need for love to be actively pursued. Believing, initially, that he should await the working of God's grace to revitalise his people's indifferent faith, he is dramatically made aware of the necessity of actively fostering the love of Christ amongst them, following an incident that occurs after he delivers his first sermon in the church:

> On the very first Sunday after his installation he spoke as simply as he could – and such was always his habit – to about forty faithful parishioners, but without any deliberate attempt to put himself on their level. The subject with which his sermon dealt was the priest's mission. What he really did was to meditate out loud, speaking to himself rather than to them. The next day he found, slipped beneath his door, an anonymous letter of eight pages. A woman had heard him and had understood. She must be someone of education. She had come to church, she said, out of curiosity, and because she had nothing else to do. She had gone away completely overwhelmed. But she complained that priests had fallen into the error of waiting until the lost sheep came to them. They should imitate their Master who sought them out and carried them home upon His shoulders. She alluded to something shameful that could not be put into words, to a state of despair from which the human soul could not free itself unless God took the first steps towards achieving its release. That morning, the Abbé Calou believed that a sign had been vouchsafed to him. He was, by temperament, inclined (like Pascal) to expect from God sensible marks of His intentions, the provi-

sion of material evidence. This cry which, on the very first day of his new life, had reached him from the wastes of a forgotten countryside, he interpreted as an answer to his prayer for comfort, it is true, as a reply to his questing heart, but also as a gentle reproach.

Following his denunciation by Brigitte, the Abbé humbles himself before God in his disgrace. 'These activities of mine have, to some extent, served the purposes of Grace,' he reflects, 'because such is the Love of God that it turns all things to the greater good of those on whom it is lavished.' Forgiving Brigitte, he accepts his fate, seeing self-humiliation as a condition of the self-lessness essential for the genuine pursuit of love. He even suggests that it may be a necessary state for those who are entrusted with the discharge of a spiritual ministry:

> There is no form of calumny that has not been heaped upon me. People believe of me what they will, both in the Archbishop's palace and out of it. I can say without fear of contradiction that now, in my old age, I have lost every scrap of that honourable reputation I once enjoyed in men's eyes, that, in my own person, I have allowed outrage to be done upon that Jesus who has marked me as His own. My family is humiliated and fretted as a result of the shame which I have brought upon it, to say nothing of the material embarrassment which my constant presence in this house has caused to its inmates. My youngest nephew has had to give up his room to me, and share with his brother. I need hardly say that they are all very kind to me. But my sister-in-law is just a little too insistent with her questions. What am I going to do with myself? she asks, and I can answer only that I do not know, for, truth to tell, I am good for nothing, and can be of use to none ... It would be foolish to deceive myself further. I stand now in the presence of my God, as naked, as much stripped of all merit, as utterly defenceless as a man well can be. Perhaps that is the state in which those of us should be whose profession it is – if I may so express myself – to be virtuous. It is almost inevitable that the professionally virtuous should hold exaggerated ideas of the importance of their actions, that they should constitute themselves the judges of their own progress in excellence, that, measuring themselves by the standards of those around them, they should at times be made slightly giddy by the spectacle of their own merits.

The image of the priest as a child in the Prologue to *The Dark Angels* once again emphasises the interdependence of humility and love. Ironically, it is the renegade seminarian, Gabriel Gradère, who first uses this image to describe the simple faith of the Curé, Alain Forcas. 'You have the eyes of a child,' he says, 'of a completely innocent child, though God has given you the power to know precisely to what depths a man's depravity can sink.' It is this quality of child-like innocence and simplicity of faith that sustains Alain in the humiliations he has to endure. Despised by his flock, especially by the young, he takes comfort in the Gospel image of Christ, mocked and reviled by his executioners. 'Did I fear scandal,' he asks, 'when I was stripped of my garments, bound naked to a pillar, nailed naked to a cross? ... Not yours to understand but to resemble Me.' Gradère describes his degradation in words that echo both the suffering servant sequence from the Book of Isaiah and the New Testament account of Christ's Passion and Crucifixion[40]: 'He's the laughing stock of the place, bent double under a load of ridicule and shame. He's a coward: they spit at him and he says nothing. They could lead him to the slaughter-house and not a bleat would he utter! They lay upon him all the filthy acts of their own secret lives, and he consents to carry the load. Even if he is tempted to answer back that he's not the one who is guilty, he, a mere rag of a man, a poor butt at whom everyone laughs, he doesn't yield, but prefers to say nothing. Alone in his church he mutters his prayers – and his good parishioners, you among them, flee from him and despise him.' The childlike character of his faith is stressed repeatedly. As he prayed, the narrator says, 'he was once more like a little child burying its face in a shoulder. He closed his eyes because his mother was holding him tight.' In worldly terms, he is a failure; like the yurodivy, or 'holy fools' of Dostoevsky's fiction, his sole purpose in life is his absolute devotion to his mission to serve God through his love of mankind:

> He knew the nature of his mission: never to turn aside his head, never to make the gesture of refusal. In all other ways he had been a failure. Neither with the children nor with the old people would he find a welcome. Here, in this little town, it was not a question of apathy or ignorance, but of active hatred, which, in some, was virulent. He was looked on with a mistrust which had become deep-rooted during the ten years in which two lukewarm priests had held this cure of souls. The inexperience due to his youth had been exploited; his every fault of tactlessness had been exposed to the full light of day; any feeling of affection he might have for one or other of his parishioners had been mocked, or attributed to base motives, until, with the arrival of his sister, the attitude of his neighbours had become one of definite persecution. 'You have failed in whatever you have turned your hand to ... you are incapable of doing anything except endure ... Endure, then!'

Paradoxically, his humility becomes his strength. 'He would try to visit all the sick of the parish. He fully expected to be welcomed no better than a dog, but he felt sufficiently strong now to bear the mistrust which would be his portion.' His tolerance and willingness to help seem limitless. 'Of him she could demand anything, because he was a priest,' Mathilde says, 'and when a man is a priest we may soil his spirit with any abomination, no matter how gross, may darken his heart with any secret, no matter how foul.' The power that sustains him is a power beyond nature – a power to which he gains access through prayer. The following passage is from the scene where Mathilde comes upon him praying in his sacristy, after he has celebrated Mass. His physical surroundings seem transformed by the fervour of his prayer:

> There was nothing very strange about what she saw, nothing but a young priest on his knees after Mass. His head was inclined slightly towards the left, his eyes were closed, his hands resting on one of those backless stools designed to keep choirboys from lolling. The room was untidy because young Lassus had not been able to put back in their places the cruets, the alb and the chasuble. No, the scene was nothing at all out of the ordinary. Nevertheless, Mathilde had a feeling that she ought to go away, that she was prying into a secret. The humblest objects in this little country Sacristy – the cruets, the metal platter, the old wash-basin and tap fixed to the wall – seemed to stand out in a light that was not of this world, a light of which this rigid, motionless man was the source. It was as though a dog's distant barking, the drone of the sawmill waxing and waning with the breeze, reached her from another planet.

The themes of innocence and humility are explored further in *A Kiss for the Leper*, in this instance in the context of a relationship blighted by the frustration of sexual love. In *A Woman of the Pharisees* Mauriac, through the voice of Octavia Tronche, declared that 'all flesh, imperfect and corrupt though it may be, is holy'. Fate, however, has decreed that carnal love is impossible for Noémie d'Artiailh and Jean Péloueyre. The victims of an arranged union, their marriage seems doomed by sexual incompatibility. The description of their wedding night is one of the most sordid in Mauriac's fiction. Each lives in dread of their nightly encounters in bed – he, tortured by his impotent physicality, she, by her physical disgust at the idea of sexual union. She prays to God for the love that will enable them both to endure their torment:

> When the meal was over, and Monsieur Jérome sat dozing with his feet on the fire-dogs, husband and wife would find themselves at last irremediably alone. Jean Péloueyre settled down as far as possible from the

lamp, scarcely breathed, and did his best to fade into the surrounding darkness. But nothing could alter the fact that he was there, and at ten o'clock Cadette brought in the candles. The journey up the stairs was terrible! The autumn rain whispered on the roof, a shutter banged, a farm wagon rumbled into the distance. Noémie, kneeling beside the dreaded bed, repeated in a low voice the words of her evening prayer: 'O God, here on my knees, I thank thee that thou hast given me a heart capable of knowing and of loving thee ...' In the darkness Jean Péloueyre could feel the adored body shrink away from him. He put as much space between them as he possibly could. Now and again Noémie, stretching a hand to touch the face which now, because she could not see it, seemed less odious, would find it warm and moist with tears. At such times, filled with remorse and pity, she would strain the unhappy creature to her, as, in the Roman amphitheatre, a Christian virgin might, with closed eyes and teeth fast clenched, have leapt forward to throw herself before the waiting beast.

For all the physical horror of their relationship, Noémie and Jean care deeply for each other, both manifesting their love in caring gestures and in mutual recognition of the suffering that each has to endure. 'They never had any of those quarrels that usually flare up between lovers,' the author says. 'They knew themselves to be so deeply wounded that they dared not strike at one another. The tiniest cause of offence would have carried mortal poison, would have been beyond all hope of cure ... Their every gesture was calculated to spare unnecessary pain.' Of necessity, their union becomes deeply and intensely spiritual: 'The eyes of each implored the other's pardon. They decided to say their prayers side by side. Enemies in the flesh, they found union in their nightly supplications. Their voices at last could mingle. Kneeling there together, each in a world apart, they met in the infinite.' The novel has strong anti-Nietzschean undertones, which reinforce its affirmation of the self-denying character of altruistic love. Rejecting Nietzsche's version of the master-slave dialectic, Jean asserts the necessity of a slave-like denial of self for the authentic expression of love. He cites Pascal approvingly on this: 'There are no Masters. We are all of us born slaves and we grow with the freedom of the Lord.' He plans to write an anti-Nietzschean essay, 'The Will to Power and the Will to Holiness', extolling the potentiality of will to transcend suffering through love. It is the will to love, manifested in their active concern for each other and in their determination not to hurt or inflict pain, that enables Noémie and Jean to find fulfilment, despite the non-carnal character of their union. On his death-bed Jean feels like a man reborn – reborn through the infinite potency of a truly selfless love, a love rendered absolute by its transcendence of its carnal mortality:

> Jean Péloueyre would not let her kiss him, but liked to feel her cool
> hand on his forehead. Did he believe now that she loved him?
> Assuredly he did, for he was heard to murmur: 'Be thy Name for ever
> blessed, O Lord, for that thou hast let me know the love of a woman
> before I die ...' And, as once on his lonely walks, so now, he pondered
> endlessly one single line of poetry, and, weary of saying his Rosary,
> while Noémie was feeling his pulse, would mutter over and over again,
> in a low voice, Pauline's outburst: Mon Polyeucte touche à son heure
> derniére – and smile. Not that he thought of himself as a martyr.
> People had always said of him that he was a 'poor creature', nor had he
> ever doubted that they were right. Looking back over the grey waters of
> his life, he felt strengthened in his self-contempt. What stagnation! But
> under that sleeping surface had stirred a life-giving freshet, and now,
> having passed through life like a corpse, he was, on his death-bed, as a
> man reborn.

The same themes of innocence, humility and selflessness are sustained in
one of Mauriac's last and most controversial novels, *The Lamb*. Much of the
controversy surrounded its underlying theme of homosexual love and the mysterious circumstances of the hero's death. He described the novel's protagonist,
Xavier Dartigelongue, as 'the young saint, my hero, who is burning at the
heart of the furnace'. Xavier's life is consumed by his boundless desire to be
of service to others. He reconsiders his plans to become a priest when he
meets Jean de Mirbel on the Bordeaux-Paris train, and recognises that he has a
duty to help him. He feels he may be able to serve God more effectively
through love of his fellow man than he could through years of theological
study, and postpones his plans to enter the seminary, following his meeting
with Jean. 'As soon as a book began to talk about God, he at once ceased to
recognise that Being to whom he was accustomed to address himself,' the narrator says. He begins to see God's presence in the faces of the needy and the
afflicted, and, like Alyosha Karamazov, resolves to dedicate himself directly to
the service of his fellowman: 'This God of his had no face save that of those
whom he had cherished all his life long, those millions of Christs with tender
brooding eyes ...where had he read that? ... He heard within himself the
ardent words – "Inasmuch as ye have done it unto the least of these my
brethren, ye have done it unto me ..." which meant that each of them was
Christ, was one with Christ.'

As he joins Jean and Michelle, together with Dominique, Roland and
Brigitte, at their home in Larjuzon, he discovers, however, that human love is

complex and perverse and is endlessly confused by the conflicts which it generates by virtue of its earthly imperfection. 'What a terrible ordeal it must
have been for him to find that his mere presence at Larjuzon had loosed a
storm, to realise that he had achieved the utter destruction of the very people
he had set out to save,' Jean says. And he adds: 'Unless he knew, for he knew
everything before it happened, that each of us must follow that road, in order
to reach our present peace; that road and no other.' Love and suffering are
inextricably related in mortal life. 'I know now that love does exist in the
world,' Michelle says. 'And it is crucified in the world and we with it.'
Xavier's conversation with the Curé points to the mystery at the heart of all
suffering: the inexplicable and irresolvable conflict of human freedom and the
omnipotence of the divine will to which man must ultimately submit. The tensions and mysteries of that conflict are tragically manifested in the suffering
attendant on the experience of love. This is vividly conveyed in this last enigmatic exchange between Xavier and the Curé:

> A shadow seemed to pass away from Xavier's face:
> 'Then you have got faith!' he said.
> The priest nodded: 'In the widest sense of that word, of course, I
> have ... I believe in hidden forces with which it is dangerous to have
> anything to do. ...'
> Xavier said again: 'You have got faith!'
> 'I believe in a Power which, perhaps, is not what you think it is.
> Don't let it force an entry into your life!'
> 'It is in my life already,' said Xavier in a low voice: 'since you are in
> it. I cannot root you out of my life. Nobody has the power to leave
> another ...'
> The priest murmured: 'That is true enough ...' He added, with
> some hesitation, 'One of my fellow-priests is closely bound to a woman
> ... He knows quite certainly that if he ever left her, she would, all the
> same, be part of his destiny for ever!'
> 'So much to answer for!' sighed Xavier: 'All these personal relation-
> ships between men and women, between man and man, for which each
> one of us will, separately, have to answer. The question – "What has
> thou done with thy brother" will be asked of us as often as in the
> course of our existence we have influenced anybody, have exercised
> power over another's heart or body, have used, and abused, a body ...'
> 'Go! go!' said the priest: 'Leave me alone!'
> He had opened the door. Setting his hands on Xavier's shoulders, he
> pushed him from the house.
> 'This is the secret of Grace: it is never too late. Time does not exist, and

all the love of all the saints may be contained in a sigh,' Mauriac wrote in one of the most eloquent and significant passages of *Mémoires Interieurs*.[41] This is the theme that is finally affirmed in *The Lamb*. (It had been explored earlier in a similar context both in *The Little Misery* and in *Flesh and Blood*.) Mauriac said it had been his intention that *The Lamb* should 'show the doubtful struggle that goes on, right up to the end, in a human being, no matter how saintly they may be'. 'Even more than in my other novels, *L'Agneau* brings it to light,' he wrote. 'The Christian life,' he added, 'is indeed this struggle, where the victor is only sure of his victory at the last second, because he assumes not his own destiny alone but, like his Master, that of the souls committed to his charge.'[42] In Xavier's case, that struggle continued to the end, and may even have determined the circumstances of his death. Whether he died accidentally, or killed himself in a moment of despair, we do not know. What is clearly intimated, however, is that he has finally found peace with God. 'Why should we cry, Michelle?' Jean asks. 'Now, at least, he has entered into the possession of Him whom he loved.' Is it possible that Mauriac may have gone so far in his rejection of Jansenist Catholicism as to suggest that the mercy of God extends even to those traditionally thought to have placed themselves beyond it by the act of self-destruction? That is the enigmatic question on which this, the most intriguing of his novels, concludes.

5

'Darkness of God':
T.S. Eliot's Quest for Faith

FAITH AND METHOD IN ELIOT'S POETRY

T.S.Eliot's baptism and his reception into the Anglo-Catholic communion at Finstock Church in the Cotswolds on 29 June 1927 marked the culmination of a long search for faith that grew out of his rejection of the Unitarian beliefs of his childhood some twenty years previously when he was a young student at Harvard University. 'I was brought up outside the Christian fold, in Unitarianism', he wrote in a *Criterion* article in 1931, 'and had become dissatisfied with its intellectual and puritanical rationalism.'[1] Rejecting the humanist and quasi-materialist ethos of Unitarian Christianity, he turned initially to idealist philosophy, particularly to the writings of F.H. Bradley, to Bergsonian metaphysics, and significantly, to Buddhism – the latter largely through the influence of an inspirational teacher at Harvard, Irving Babbit. All three remained important influences on his subsequent formation – Bradley's theory of reality, Bergson's theory of time, and the negative mysticism of the Buddhists being particularly significant – though he clearly and emphatically rejected the humanist strain he found both in Bradleyan idealism and in some of the philosophical writings of Babbit. This passage from 'Religion Without Humanism' provides definite pointers to the path he would follow in subsequent years:

> Humanism has much to say of Discipline and Order and Control; and I have parroted these terms myself. I found no discipline in humanism; only a little intellectual discipline from a little study of philosophy. But the difficult discipline is the discipline and training of emotion; this the modern world has great need of; so great that it hardly understands what the word means; and this I have found is only attainable through dogmatic religion ... It takes perhaps a lifetime merely to realise that men like the forest sages, and the desert sages, and finally the Victorines and John of the Cross (and in his fashion, Ignatius) really mean what they say. Only those have the right to talk about discipline who have looked into the Abyss.[2]

Here he clearly identifies himself with the sages and the mystics, finding in them a strong sense of the limitations of cognitive thought as well as intima-

201

tions of a reality transcending the empirical, the rational and the phenomenal. While a student at Harvard he had also encountered the works of St Augustine, St Thomas Aquinas and, most significantly, St John of the Cross. In these he found mystical affirmation of the truth of a non-empirical, transcendent reality, a realisation that was to guide him decisively towards his eventual adoption of the Anglo-Catholic faith. Additionally, he found the non-rationalist formulations of religious truth in the works of the mystical writers highly compatible with his needs as an emerging artist: specifically, as an artist whose poetry was even then preeminently an exploration of the truths of his faith. Together with Dante, Shakespeare, Pascal, the Metaphysical Poets, Blake, Valéry and Baudelaire, the mystical writers decisively shaped the direction that his poetry was to follow over a period of almost forty years.

Before considering the manner of Eliot's progress towards faith, the issue that first needs to be clarified is the precise character of the relationship between his artistic and religious beliefs. Fortunately, there is substantial guidance on this from his own critical writings. In his essay, 'Religion and Literature', he charted out some of the fundamental features of what he understood to be the relationship between literature and faith.[3] Initially, he differentiated between three main types of religious literature. There is firstly, he said, the kind of literature that can be called 'religious', by virtue of the explicitly religious or theological character of its content. The Bible, he writes, is a work of 'religious literature' in this sense; it can be described as 'religious', he says, in the same way that Gibbon's *Decline and Fall of the Roman Empire* could be designated 'historical', or Bradley's *Logic* could be called 'philosophical'. Though each might have certain literary merits and attractions, their significance, he insists, consists primarily in the religious, historical or philosophical nature of their content. The second type of religious literature is what he describes as 'devotional': that is, literature exemplifying a 'special religious awareness'– an awareness he adds, rather significantly, which is usually divorced from 'what men consider their major passions', and which lacks the 'general awareness which we expect of the major poet'. The third type of religious literature is that, he says, which seeks directly to advocate and promote the cause of religion, a type he designates merely 'propagandist', though he includes certain works of light fiction – such as the Father Brown novels of Chesterton – in this category.

What is especially significant about this classification is Eliot's exclusion of several of his favourite 'religious' poets, such as Dante, Corneille, Racine, Baudelaire and Villon, from each of his three categories. Their work, he suggests, would not be described as primarily religious, in the sense that the Bible would, nor could it be described as 'devotional' or 'propagandist' either. Yet he described them as 'great Christian religious poets', even in respect of 'works which do not touch upon religious themes'.[4] The key to the distinction underlying these comments can be found in a lecture on Dante which he delivered in 1950 – a work which illuminates not only Dante's but to a great extent his own position as well. He spoke, firstly, of Dante's mastery of the craft of verse, his reverence for language and poetic form, and his sense of responsibility to the traditions of his own culture; he spoke, secondly, of 'the width of his emotional range' – a quality he saw as being particularly indicative of Dante's greatness as a Christian religious poet. This passage has a particular bearing on the latter issue:

> We have for instance in English literature great religious poets, but they are, by comparison with Dante, specialists. That is all they can do. And Dante, because he could do everything else, is for that reason the greatest 'religious' poet, though to call him a 'religious poet' would be to abate his universality. The *Divine Comedy* expresses everything in the way of emotion, between depravity's despair and the beatific vision, that man is capable of experiencing. It is therefore a constant reminder to the poet of the obligation to explore, to find words for the inarticulate, to capture those feelings which people can hardly even feel, because they have no words for them; and at the same time, a reminder that the explorer beyond the frontiers of ordinary consciousness will only be able to return and report to his fellow-citizens, if he has all the time a firm grasp upon the realities with which they are already acquainted.[5]

Unlike the devotional poet, whose work deliberately excludes 'what men consider their major passions', Dante, he writes, had integrated religion within the whole range of his emotional experience. He had demonstrated the eclectic character of the religious imagination and its comprehension of the truths of faith in the context of all the passions and conflicts of his life. It is significant that Eliot wrote in a similar fashion of his own experience as a Christian poet. When an associate accused him of using religion as a means of escape from conflict and suffering, he responded that, on the contrary, it had 'forced him to face the full dangers of the human predicament, not just in this life but for eternity, and it had burdened his soul with a terrible and hitherto unrealised weight of moral responsibility'.[6] The more complex question, however – which is also addressed in the lecture on Dante – is the nature of the transmutation that occurs when belief is turned into poetry. While he argues in the essay that Dante's beliefs were always central to his poetry, he qualifies this by insisting that the reader is not 'called upon to believe them himself'. Differentiating between 'philosophical belief and poetic assent', he argues that it is possible to identify fully with the spirit of Dante's poetry, without necessarily affirming its theological or philosophic truth. 'If you can read poetry as poetry,' he writes, 'you will believe in the "physical" reality of his journey: that is, you suspend both belief and disbelief.' Distinguishing between 'what Dante believed as a poet and what he believed as a man', he argues that 'private belief becomes a different thing in becoming poetry'; it elicits a response different from that which is evoked by theological or philosophic formulations of the same truths.[7]

The conception of poetic response as a suspension of both belief and disbelief in the Dante essay points to a deeper paradox embracing the whole relationship of religion and literature in Eliot's writings. The suspension of belief and disbelief, and the depth of poetic assent which religious literature invites, are both rooted in a dialectic at the heart of the experience which it conveys. In an essay on Valéry, he made the following comment: 'In *La Pythie* I find, not a philosophy but a poetic statement of a definite and unique state of the soul dispossessed ... There is only one higher state possible for civilised man: that is, to unite the profoundest scepticism with the deepest faith.'[8] And in an Introduction to Pascal's *Pensées* he declared that it was primarily the depth of his (Pascal's) explorations of religious doubt, and not the intensity of his beliefs, that attracted him to this work:

> Pascal is a man of the world among ascetics, and an ascetic among men of the world; he had the knowledge of worldliness and the passion of asceticism, and in him the two are fused into an individual whole. The majority of mankind is lazy-minded, incurious, absorbed in vanities, and tepid in emotion, and is therefore incapable of either much doubt or much faith; and when the ordinary man calls himself a sceptic or an unbeliever, that is ordinarily a simple pose, cloaking a disinclination to think anything out to a conclusion. Pascal's disillusioned analysis of human bondage is sometimes interpreted to mean that Pascal was really and finally an unbeliever, who, in his despair, was incapable of enduring reality and enjoying the heroic satisfaction of the free man's worship of nothing. His despair, his disillusion, are, however, no illustration of personal weakness; they are perfectly objective, because they are essential moments in the progress of the intellectual soul; and for the type of Pascal they are the analogue of the drought, the dark night, which is an essential stage in the progress of the Christian mystic. A similar despair, when it is arrived at by a diseased character or an impure soul, may issue in the most disastrous consequences though with the most superb manifestations; and thus we get *Gulliver's Travels*; but in Pascal we find no such distortion; his despair is in itself more terrible than Swift's, because our heart tells us that it corresponds exactly to the facts and

cannot be dismissed as mental disease; but it was also a despair which was a necessary prelude to, and element in, the joy of faith ...[9]

Pascal's 'despair', Eliot suggests in this passage, was an essential feature of his progress towards faith; it was comparable in its intensity and pain to the 'dark night of the soul' described by St John of the Cross in *Ascent of Mount Carmel*, one of the profoundest influences on his own poetry. The negativity of the dark night might find expression even in blasphemy, Eliot wrote in an essay on Baudelaire, whom he also describes as an 'essentially Christian poet'. 'Genuine blasphemy, genuine in spirit and not purely verbal, is the product of partial belief,' he writes ... 'It is a way of affirming belief and is as impossible to the complete atheist as to the perfect Christian.[10] This kind of 'partial belief' is vividly exemplified, he says, in Baudelaire's *Journaux Intimes*. Here, he writes, Baudelaire is 'discovering Christianity for himself ... He is beginning in a way at the beginning and, being a discoverer, is not altogether certain what he is exploring and to what it leads; he might almost be said to be making again, as one man, the effort of scores of generations.' (Interestingly, François Mauriac gives a similar interpretation of Baudelaire's use of blasphemy in *Mémoires Intérieurs*. 'No matter how often Baudelaire denies,' he writes, 'his denial turns always to blasphemy, in other words, to the act of faith.')[11] Eliot's comments on the religious dimension of Tennyson's poetry similarly emphasise the predominant evidence of religious doubt that is apparent throughout his work. He describes Tennyson as a man 'desperately anxious to hold the faith of the believer', as someone 'capable of illumination which he was incapable of understanding' and as a person 'teased by the hope of immortality and reunion beyond death'. '*In Memoriam* can justly be called a religious poem', he concludes, not because of 'the quality of its faith but because of the quality of its doubt ... Its faith is a poor thing', he writes, 'but its doubt is a very intense experience'. 'It is a poem of despair,' he adds, 'but despair of a religious kind.'[12]

It is this dialectical conception of belief and disbelief as interdependent facets of the search for faith which, together with the emotionally complex nature of the whole experience as described in his writings on Dante, that particularly defines the religious character of Eliot's poetry. 'My beliefs,' he said, 'are held with a scepticism which I hope never to be rid of.'[13] And he added in *After Strange Gods*: 'It is in fact in moments of moral and spiritual struggle depending upon spiritual sanctions, rather than in those bewildering minutes in which we are all very much alike, that men and women come nearest to being real.'[14] It was by exploring such moments of moral and spiritual struggle – the struggle between reason and faith, between belief and doubt, despair and hope, the spiritual and the sensual – that he defined the nature of his personal quest for faith. The dark night of the soul, as will be shown in the forthcoming section, became his favourite analogue for the negativity, suffering and pain of the whole process ...

These conflicts, he suggests, were intensified for him by the all-prevailing secularism of modern society, a condition, he says, which is universally in evidence in its literature. 'My complaint against modern literature,' he writes, 'is that it repudiates or is wholly ignorant of, our most fundamental and important beliefs, and that in consequence its tendency is to encourage its readers to get what they can out of life while it lasts.'[15] 'The whole of modern literature is corrupted by what I call secularism,' he declares. 'It is simply not aware of, and simply cannot understand the meaning of, the primacy of the supernatural over the natural life.'[16] This, he suggests, imposes certain responsibilities on authors like himself who write from a definite Christian standpoint. He insisted on the permanence of ethical and religious potentialities, seeing them as inherent in the very nature of humankind and, though gravely threatened by the secularist-humanist forces of the modern age, as profoundly rooted nonetheless in the depths of individual consciousness. Thus he referred almost contemptuously to the idea that religion should be 'revived'; 'religion', he declared, 'can hardly revive, because it cannot decay'. And he clearly saw the artist as having a crucial role in communicating both the ultimacies of ethico-religious truth and the aspiration towards a religious self-transcendence that are inherent in very nature of humankind. 'For it is ultimately the function of art,' he wrote, 'in imposing a credible order on ordinary reality, and thereby eliciting some perception of an order *in* reality, to bring us to a condition of serenity, stillness and reconciliation – and then leave us, as Virgil left Dante, to proceed towards a region where that guide can lead us no farther.'[17] (The term 'stillness' has particularly strong religious connotations in Eliot's writings, as will be shown in forthcoming sections of this chapter.)

But while asserting his belief in his responsibility as a religious writer to convey his sense of the ultimacy of an ethico-religious order, Eliot simultaneously insisted on his intention to do so through the complex modes and procedures of his art. He would communicate his vision of ethico-religious order, not through the formal or didactic processes of philosophic or theological statement, but through the medium of the poetic image and symbol. He would communicate it in terms of the tensions of belief and doubt, of reason and feeling, of the temporal and the eternal in which it is ordinarily perceived – or, to use the words that he himself employed in the essay on Dante, by 'expressing everything in the way of emotion between depravity and despair and the beatific vision that man is capable of experiencing'.[18] Thus, in a letter to William Force Stead, a young American poet who followed a path to the Anglican faith, similar to that of Eliot himself, he wrote: 'Between the usual subjects of poetry and "devotional verse" there is a very important field still very unexplored by modern poets – the experience of man in search of God, and trying to explain to himself his intense human feelings in terms of the divine goal.' 'The poet's aim,' he wrote, 'is not so much to persuade others of his truth or of his dogma, but to explain first to himself, and then, perhaps, afterwards to others, his intenser human feelings in terms of the divine goal.'[19] The manner in which this objective was realised in Eliot's poetry will be the concern of the remaining sections of this chapter.

'LET THE DARK COME UPON YOU': ELIOT'S VIA NEGATIVA

Critical studies of Eliot's life and writings over the past twenty years have consistently emphasised the importance of negative mysticism in the evolution of his religious beliefs and in his treatment of religious themes in his poetry. A number of scholars have seen the *via negativa* as a comprehensive analogue for all the main developments in his life and work, both before and after his conversion to the Anglo-Catholic faith. Eloise Hay[20] spoke of his conversion as a progress from the negativity of philosophic scepticism to the more spiritually rewarding negativity of Christian mysticism, and Edward Lobb[21] saw the whole process as indicating his rejection of the traditions of western epistemology for the deeper and more far-reaching spiritual insights of writers such as St Augustine, St John of the Cross and the anonymous author of *The Cloud of Unknowing*. Helen Gardner, writing in 1949, traced the roots of this tradition to the neo-Platonists. 'The tradition Mr Eliot is here writing in is a tradition that goes back beyond Christianity to the neo-Platonists who turned what had been a method of knowing – the dialectical method of arriving at truth by successive negations of the false – into a method of arriving at experience of the One.' 'This doctrine of ascent or descent into union with reality ... found a natural metaphor in darkness and night', she writes. 'It was a double-edged metaphor,' she adds, 'since night expressed both the obliteration of self and all created things, and also the uncharacterised Reality which was the object of contemplation.'[22] Negative mysticism embodied what Eliot himself described in his essay on Valéry as 'a definite and unique state of the soul dispossessed', that higher state in which 'the profoundest scepticism is united with the deepest faith'.[23]

Of the various explorations of the *via negativa* in mystical literature, two works were particularly well-known to Eliot from his Harvard years: *The Spiritual Canticle* and *The Ascent of Mount Carmel* of St John of the Cross. His notebooks show that he was studying both of these works in the years 1912-14.[24] His interest in the subject was strengthened by the influence of his teacher and friend, Paul Elmer More, from whose versions of the writings of St John of the Cross he drew extensively in subsequent years. He cited the words of St John at the beginning of 'Sweeney Agonistes' in the early 1920s and the writings of the saint appear thereafter as a strong and clearly discernible influence throughout most of his work. 'I cannot think of any mystic who was also a fine poet except St John of the Cross', he wrote in 1961, the convergence of spiritual and poetic originality emphasised in these words probably explaining the depth of his interest in St John over a period of more than fifty years.[25] From the works of the Spanish mystic he took the conception of Christian spirituality as a three-stage process, beginning with purgation, leading to illumination of the spirit and ultimately to union with God. The first stage of the process, the stage of purgation, was described by St John as a dark night of sense and spirit in which the soul acutely experiences the pain of separation from God. This he saw as a necessary prelude to the illuminating knowledge of the reality and presence of God and ultimately to the soul's union with God, a fulfilment, he said, which is attained only through self-renunciation, penitence and prayerful submission to the divine will. This process is evoked in several of Eliot's poems, particularly in *Four Quartets*, his most expansive statement of the *via negativa* and of its place in the soul's quest for faith.

Eliot's interest in the negative mysticism of St John of the Cross was significantly strengthened by his studies in the Buddhist mystical tradition which he began also in his years as a student at Harvard. 'It becomes increasingly clear,' Eloise Hay writes, 'that if Eliot had not steeped himself in the negative way of Buddhism, he would not have found his bearings towards the negative way of Christianity.'[26] 'Buddhism remained a lifelong influence on his work,' Stephen Spender wrote, adding that 'at the time he wrote *The Wasteland* he almost became a Buddhist, or so I once heard him tell the Chilean poet, Gabriele Mistral, who was herself a Buddhist.'[27] He had been introduced to Oriental religion and philosophy at Harvard by Irving Babbit and attributed his lifelong interest in the subject to Babbit's influence. Babbit had translated the *Dhammapada* and had published a long essay, 'Buddha and the Occident', both of which Eliot had studied while a student on Babbit's literature course at Harvard. The year after he took Babbit's course on literature he enrolled in a three year programme in philosophy, in the course of which he studied all the major Hindu and Buddhist texts, acquiring a considerable mastery of various Oriental languages so that he could read these texts in their original form. In the final year of this programme he took a full course in Buddhism from a leading Buddhist philosopher, Masaharu Anesaki.

Certainly, for Eliot, the Buddhist doctrine of the attainment of Nirvana, or union with the Unknowable, through the extinction of desire, and through freedom from worldly attachments, powerfully reinforced the teachings on self-renunciation of St John of the Cross and earlier Christian mystics. Equally, its doctrine of the Unknowable Absolute, reached through self-perfection, proved a welcome alternative to the philosophic scepticism of his Harvard years. There are indications from an early stage of how closely the two traditions were to be intertwined in his writings. 'The Fire Sermon' in 'The Wasteland', for instance, suggests a strong collocation of Buddhist and Augustinian teaching on the ideal of moral regeneration attained through the renunciation of bodily passion and lust – the 'burning of desire' being the first stage in the progress towards the Absolute in both traditions. The 'stair' symbolism of 'Ash Wednesday' has also been linked with the Buddhist way of purification; the steps of devotion, self-discipline and earthly suffering are seen as stages in the soul's progress towards the Absolute in the Buddhist *Visuddhimagga* ('The Way of Purification') by Buddhaghosa, which Eliot had studied at Harvard.

The *via negativa*, with its Christian and Buddhist origins, provides an analogue both for Eliot's progress towards faith in the years leading to his conversion and for the way to salvation that he followed in the years when he had formally adopted the Anglo-Catholic faith. It serves as an image both for the darkness of unbelief and the self-conflict attendant on the struggle for faith. His early poetry is full of the negativity of unbelief. Poems such as 'Mr Eliot's Sunday Morning Service', 'The Hippopotamus', 'The Death of St Narcissus' and 'The Love Song of St Sebastian' ridicule the very idea of religion, lampooning the institutions of Christianity, and satirising its rituals and traditions. The first of these poems shows the poet looking contemptuously at a religious service – 'The sable presbyters approach/ The avenue of penitence; The young are red and pustular/ Clutching piaculative pence'. It implicitly denounces the clergy as materialistic exploiters of their followers: 'Along the garden-wall the bees/ With hairy bellies pass between/ The staminate and pistillate,/ Blest office of the epicene'. 'The Hippopotamus', which begins with an epigraph from St Paul pointing to the lukewarmness of the clergy, ironically contrasts the 'broad-backed hippopotamus', a creature of flesh and blood whose feet are sunk in mud, with the True Church which Christ predicted would 'never fail', being founded upon rock. The poem shows that the destinies of both are closely intertwined, the Church possessing the same flesh and blood as the hippopotamus and being similarly susceptible to its frailties.

'The Death of St Narcissus', a work inspired by Valéry's 'Narcisse' and by Gide's 'Traite de Narcisse', portrays the saint as a young aesthete crazed by the beauty of his own body and confusing his sexual obsessions with a longing for God. Withdrawing to the desert, he dies in an ecstasy of sexual intoxication. In 'The Love Song of St Sebastian' spiritual neurosis is again represented as a crazed eroticism, the saint flagellating himself before the lady in white, until finally he dies with his head between her breasts. Reading these poems, one thinks inevitably of Eliot's comment in his essay on Baudelaire that blasphemy may be a 'sign of faith', an evocation of partial belief ... as impossible to the complete atheist as to the perfect Christian'. In *After Strange Gods* he spoke of it as 'one of the rarest things in literature', requiring 'both literary genius and profound faith joined in the mind in a peculiar and unusual state of spiritual sickness'. In the same work he lamented the state of the modern world as 'one where blasphemy is impossible', seeing the tendency to ridicule religion as 'a symptom that the soul is still alive'.[28]

The sense of spiritual sickness described in *After Strange Gods* is profoundly reinvoked in 'The Wasteland', a work of the most radical and persistent negation, in which Eliot represented the disease of the modern age in terms of a deadening isolation of mankind from all the sources of faith. The work evokes a world where God seems totally concealed from humankind – a wasteland characterised by vacuity, incoherence, silence, emptiness and desolation, its sterility mirrored in the barrenness of the whole of nature. Eliot echoed both the words of St Augustine – 'I wandered O my God too much away from thee, far from your steady strength, in the days of my youth. Of myself I made a wasteland'[29] – and those of Isaiah, Ecclesiastes and Luke in their respective images of a land deprived of vitality and life.[30]

It is significant, however, that Eliot rejected suggestions that the poem evoked either total disillusion or total unbelief. In *Thoughts After Lambeth* he responded to critics who took the view that the poem expressed the 'disillusionment of a generation'. 'I have expressed for them their own illusion of being disillusioned but that did not form part of my intention,' he wrote.[31] And he also responded angrily to a review by I.A Richards which suggested that the theme of the poem was the total denial of faith. 'I cannot for the life of me see the complete separation from all belief in the poem,' he wrote. 'It is not a separation from belief, it is nothing so pleasant. In fact, doubt, uncertainty, futility would seem to me to prove anything except this agreeable partition; for doubt and uncertainty are merely varieties of belief.'[32] His words point to the fundamental dilemma of the experience of faith: its comprehension both of belief and disbelief, a condition succinctly described in the words of Eliot's friend and fellow dramatist, Charles Williams – 'We are, I know not how, double in ourselves, so that what we believe we disbelieve, and cannot rid ourselves of what we condemn.'[33] Implicit in his words is the view that the negation of faith is itself a source of faith, that its anguish and desolation can be spiritually enriching and affirming in the manner described by the mystics.

This same sense of an ultimately fruitful negativity underlies the dark atmosphere of 'The Hollow Men', where the images of scarecrows inhabiting a hollow valley darkened by dying stars again suggest the desolation of unbelief, while echoes of the Lord's Prayer, of Dante and the exilic writers of the Old Testament, simultaneously suggest a residual if scarcely perceptible faith. The work may have been inspired by Dowson's poem, 'Non sum qualis eram bonae sub regno Cynarae' where the theme is also the paradoxical relationship of belief and unbelief.[34] In 'Ash Wednesday', which he published five years after 'The Hollow Men', the theme of the *via negativa* is embraced much more consciously, the influence of St John of the Cross being directly in evidence in the confessional mode adopted in this poem. In an essay about Pascal which Eliot published within a year of 'Ash Wednesday' he wrote: 'His (Pascal's) despair, his disillusion ... are no illustration of personal weakness; they are essential moments in the progress of the intellectual soul, and for the type of Pascal they are the analogue of the drought, the dark night which is an essential stage in the progress of the Christian mystic.'[35] He declares that the despair and disillusion are 'essential' for the attainment of faith because, in common with St Augustine, Aquinas and St John of the Cross, he believed that God cannot be reached through affirmation, since He is 'wholly other than being'. 'God,' wrote St Augustine, 'is better known by knowing what he is not.'[36] Aquinas similarly emphasised the paradoxical negativity of faith in the *Summa Theologica*: 'The created mind only knows what is already there to be known ... God, however, is not there: he is beyond what is there ... hence he is not intelligible, he is beyond understanding ... God is said to be "not there" not in the sense that he does not exist at all, but because being his own existence he transcends all that is there.'[37] And in *The Ascent of Mount Carmel* we find the following: 'For all things of earth and heaven, compared with God are nothing ... even as darkness is not only nothing, but less than nothing, since it is privation of light ... Wherefore, upon this road, to enter upon the road is to leave the road ... to enter on that which is no way, which is God.'[38]

That imagery of darkness is used with particular effect by Eliot in *Four Quartets* to convey the paradox of a faith attained through negation. In 'Burnt Norton', the presence of God is invoked firstly through the paradoxical imagery of silence (non-speech) and stillness (non-time), both pointing to the incomprehensible being-ness of God. It is through its contemplation of nothing-ness (to adopt the terminology of Brodsky) or negation, he suggests, that the soul encounters God – which is a painful and anguished process involving negation of the light of sense, of temporality, of all worldly knowledge and experience. It may even involve a negation or 'inoperancy' of the spirit itself:

> Here is a place of disaffection
> Time before and time after
> In a dim light: neither daylight

Investing form with lucid stillness
Turning shadow into transient beauty
With slow rotation suggesting permanence
Nor darkness to purify the soul
Emptying the sensual with deprivation
Cleansing affection from the temporal ...

Descend lower, descend only
Into the world of perpetual solitude,
World not world, but that which is not world,
Internal darkness, deprivation
And destitution of all property,
Dessication of the world of sense,
Evacuation of the world of fancy,
Inoperancy of the world of spirit;
This is the one way, and the other
Is the same, not in movement
But abstention from movement; while the world moves
In appetency, on its metalled ways
Of time past and time future.

The lines echo both the words of St John and of the *Bhagavad-Gita*. 'The point from which the soul goes forth ... is deprivation and denial', St John wrote in *The Ascent of Mount Carmel*. 'The road along which the soul must travel ... is faith, which is likewise as dark as night to the understanding ... The point to which it travels is God who equally is dark night to the soul in this life.'[39] This image is paralleled in the *Bhagavad-Gítá*: 'What is night for all beings is the time of awakening for the self-controlled.'[40] The darkness is the darkness of negation, of descent, which paradoxically, is ultimately an ascent to God. In his use of this image Eliot echoes the words of Aquinas who, in the *Summa Contra Gentiles*, wrote: 'Man begins from the lowest things and rising by degrees advances to the knowledge of God; thus, too, in corporeal movements, the way down is the same as the way up, and they differ only as regards their beginning and end.'[41]

The downward way, the way of darkness, Eliot declares, therefore, in one of the finest passages in 'East Coker', is ultimately the way of light. The sequence begins with echoes of Samson Agonistes – 'O dark, dark, dark ...' – and offers a processional image of bankers, merchants, industrialists, statesmen and bureaucrats, men of worldly success and power, all of whom are shown proceeding towards extinction. 'We all go with them into the silent funeral', the poem says as the poet welcomes the onset of darkness, now a hope-giving darkness – the darkness of 'waiting for God'. In *The Ascent of Mount Carmel* St John differentiated between two kinds of darkness. The first was the dark night of sense, such as Eliot described in the lines quoted from 'Burnt Norton'. The second was the dark night of the spirit, which, St John says, can be active or passive; it may be an active seeking for illumination through a conscious activity of the will, or a passive suffering of the deprivation of sense and spirit which also leads finally to union with God.[42] It is this latter 'waiting' for darkness that Eliot evokes in the beautiful lyrical imagery of 'East Coker':

> I said to my soul, be still, and let the dark come upon you
> Which shall be the darkness of God ...
>
> I said to my soul, be still, and wait without hope
> For hope would be hope for the wrong thing; wait without love
> For love would be love of the wrong thing; there is yet faith
> But the faith and the love and the hope are all in the waiting.
> Wait without thought, for you are not ready for thought:
> So the darkness shall be the light, and the stillness the dancing.
> Whisper of running streams, and winter lightning.
> The wild thyme unseen, and the wild strawberry,
> The laughter in the garden, echoed ecstasy
> Not lost, but requiring, pointing to the agony
> Of death and birth.

Like his great forebears, Augustine, Aquinas, St John and the Buddhist mystics, Eliot saw the life of darkness and negation as all-pervasive in temporal life, and therefore as an occasion for endemic suffering and desolation. But he also saw it as affording the ultimate illumination of the spirit and the prospect of final union with God. It was this paradox, he believed, which made suffering meaningful, and it therefore remained a central preoccupation in his poetry. It found expression in three main themes: the problem of temporality and the mystery of the timeless, the necessity for self-illumination, penitence and humility before God, and the resolution of all temporal conflicts in the mystery of the Incarnation. Each will be explored in the forthcoming sections of this chapter.

'ONLY THROUGH TIME TIME IS CONQUERED'

Like St Augustine, whose vision of spiritual self-reform as a progression from darkness to faith so profoundly influenced his own conception of Christian

redemption, Eliot recognised the significance of the temporal-timeless polarity
as an essential and problematic feature of this whole process and repeatedly
demonstrated its centrality in the evolution of his religious beliefs. His treatment of the whole question of temporality has been widely interpreted as a
rejection of the Heraclitean and Bergsonian view of time as ultimately pure
process, duration or flux, in favour of a conception of a time-timelessness tension which draws on Christian/Neo-Platonist influences, being particularly
indebted to the writings of Plotinus and St Augustine. Eliot rejected the
Heraclitean conception of time for its circularity and relativity and defined the
reality of the temporal as something inextricably related to the ultimate reality
of the intemporal. In common with Christian and specifically neo-Platonist
philosophers, he conceived of the temporal as a reality immanently manifesting
the presence of the timeless: a reality ultimately explicable and made meaningful only in terms of this truth. Thus, in 'Tradition and Individual Talent' he
spoke of the 'historical sense' as a 'sense of the timeless as well as of the temporal and of the timeless and of the temporal together', and declared that
every moment in time invokes the simultaneous order of history, the continuum of past, present and future which is made meaningful in terms of the
timelessness immanently present within it.[43] Temporality, divorced from the
immanence of the timeless, he suggests, is devoid of ultimate meaning, is total
endness, nothingness and void.

Insofar as Eliot's poetry can be said to have an underlying philosophy, it is
based primarily on this concept of the immanence of the timeless: a concept
which is deeply rooted in Christian tradition and which is consistently in evidence in his work from 'Ash Wednesday' to the Four Quartets. His most vivid
and most consistently used analogy for the paradoxical time-timelessness polarity is the sea and river imagery which appears in his work at an early stage and
recurs thereafter in various poems dealing with the theme of time. Both
images were rooted in childhood memories: memories of the Mississippi river
which flowed through St Louis, his birthplace – 'I feel,' he wrote in later life,
'that there is something in having passed one's childhood beside the big river
which is incommunicable to those who have not'[44] – and memories of the
seascape at Cape Ann in Massachusetts where the Eliots spent their summer
vacations. In 'The Dry Salvages' the sea symbolises the eternal and the timeless – witnessing to 'an earlier and other creation' – while the 'great brown
river' symbolises human or earthly time and the processes of flux, temporality
and change:

> The river is within us, the sea is all about us;
> The sea is the land's edge also, the granite
> Into which it reaches, the beaches where it tosses

Its hints of earlier and other creation:
The starfish, the horseshoe crab, the whale's backbone;
The pools where it offers to our curiosity
The more delicate algae and the sea anemone.
It tosses up our losses, the torn seine,
The shattered lobster-pot, the broken oar
And the gear of foreign dead men. The sea has many voices,
Many gods and many voices ...

The tolling bell
Measures time, not our time, rung by the unhurried
Ground swell, a time
Older than the time of chronometers, older
Than time counted by anxious worried women
Lying awake, calculating the future,
Trying to unweave, unwind, unravel
And piece together the past and the future,
Between midnight and dawn, when the past is all deception,
The future futureless, before the morning watch
When time stops and time is never ending;
And the ground swell, that is and was from the beginning,
Clangs
The bell.

The lines encapsulate the essential features of the time-timelessness polarity: the order of 'God's time' as contrasted with the disorder of human time, the bondage of the temporal, its pain and its suffering contrasting with the freedom afforded by death and the spirit's entry into the timeless. The simultaneity of past, present and future time, the burden of memory, the possibility of the 'might have been', all point to a profound responsibility that has to be confronted in the present moment, in the immediacy of the here and now:

Time present and time past
Are both perhaps present in time future
And time future contained in time past.
If all time is eternally present
All time is unredeemable.
What might have been is an abstraction
Remaining a perpetual possibility
Only in a world of speculation.

What might have been and what has been
Point to one end, which is always present

As he walks in the rose-garden pondering on the 'might-have-been', which is symbolised by the images of those who have not yet been born, as he reflects on the memories of a past age, as he looks at the bustle of modern life, the poet affirms his belief that all the modes of temporality which he contemplates 'point to one end' – to a reality which is outside time but which, paradoxically, is always present in time. The still point on the cycle of time, i.e., the eternal or intemporal, is contrasted with the images of time-bound life – 'garlic and sapphires in the mud', the world of the hunters and the hunted – but the poem affirms that this stillness of the eternal is known to man only in terms of the nowness of immediate, present temporality. We transcend time, he declares, only through time itself, through the tragedy and suffering of experience lived, imagined or recalled in the immediacy of present time:

At the still point of the turning world. Neither flesh nor fleshless;
Neither from nor towards; at the still point, there the dance is,
But neither arrest nor movement. And do not call it fixity,
Where past and future are gathered. Neither movement from nor
    towards,
Neither ascent nor decline. Except for the point, the still point,
There would be no dance, and there is only the dance ...
Time past and time future
Allow but a little consciousness.
To be conscious is not to be in time
But only in time can the moment in the rose-garden,
The moment in the arbour where the rain beat,
The moment in the draughty church at smokefall
Be remembered; involved with past and future.
Only through time time is conquered.

The theme of transcendence in time is further explored as Eliot contemplates the role of memory and the impingements of historical time on immediate, present experience. In 'East Coker' he explores the potentialities of remembered experience as a guide to future conduct, but dismisses it as ultimately inadequate for this purpose. In 'The Dry Salvages' the flow of time is seen initially as an evolutionary process, but this also is rejected on the grounds that it relegates the past into insignificance. Time, the poet insists, is a 'destroyer and a preserver'; the past becomes meaningful through reinterpretation, is informed with a new significance in moments of sudden illumination, is reappraised in the here and now, in its constant motion towards the future. The pattern of time is constantly renewed as present moments are relegated to memory, but is recreated in newly emerging moments of present time, which themselves are in constant motion towards future moments and events. Every moment, therefore, is crucial and unique, charged with new meaning and potentiality, as is suggested in a sequence from 'The Dry Salvages' where the mortal process is symbolised as a journey through time. 'The time of death is every moment', the poem says; its significance lies in the stillness or absolute momentness of the final reality in which it exists, the reality of non-time:

> Fare forward, travellers! not escaping from the past
> Into different lives, or into any future;
> You are not the same people who left that station
> Or who will arrive at any terminus,
> While the narrowing rails slide together behind you;
> And on the deck of the drumming liner
> Watching the furrow that widens behind you,
> You shall not think, 'the past is finished'
> Or 'the future is before us' ...
> At the moment which is not of action or inaction
> You can receive this: 'on whatever sphere of being
> The mind of a man may be intent
> At the time of death' – that is the one action
> (And the time of death is every moment)
> Which shall fructify in the lives of others:
> And do not think of the fruit of action.
> Fare forward.

The reality of the timeless, he suggests, is perceived by man, not ultimately through the powers of intellect and reason, but through the darkness and negation of faith. This is the theme of the beautiful fourth and fifth movements of 'Burnt Norton'. As evening approaches and the sunlight fails, the poet wonders if in future time the sunflower will still turn towards him, if the clematis will still caress him, if the fingers of the yew tree will still curl downward towards him, and he sees the lingering light caught momentarily on a kingfisher's wing – the light of God's stillness which remains gleaming in the twilight. 'The light is still/ At the still point of the turning world.' It is a stillness which is ultimately joyous and life-giving, its laughter suggesting the innocence of childhood – the archetypal symbol of Paradise, timelessness and the infinity of 'unmoving love':

The detail of the pattern is movement,
As in the figure of the ten stairs.
Desire itself is movement
Not in itself desirable;
Love is itself unmoving,
Only the cause and end of movement,
Timeless, and undesiring
Except in the aspect of time
Caught in the form of limitation
Between un-being and being.
Sudden in a shaft of sunlight
Even while the dust moves
There rises the hidden laughter
Of children in the foliage
Quick, now, here, now, always –
Ridiculous the waste sad time
Stretching before and after.

The theme of time-transcendence is reemphasised in the sea-imagery of 'The Dry Salvages'. As the mariners sail out into the ocean, into its pre-human timelessness, they have a final glimpse of the great 'ragged rock in the restless waters', which symbolises their faith. On 'halcyon days' the rock is merely a monument, in navigable weather it is a 'sea-mark to lay a course by', but in 'the sombre season/or the sudden fury' it is 'what it always was' – their final refuge in despair. Also visible is the shrine of the Virgin Mary, the patroness of mariners, standing on a promontory. As the mother of Christ, she mediates between two worlds, the world of time and the world of eternity. The mystery of time is resolved in the person of Christ her Son, in the miracle of his Incarnation – the 'impossible union of spheres' – in the reality of God Become Man. This is the truth which the poem finally affirms:

The hint half guessed, the gift half understood, is Incarnation.
Here the impossible union
Of spheres of existence is actual,
Here the past and future
Are conquered, and reconciled,
Where action were otherwise movement
Of that which is only moved
And has in it no source of movement –
Driven by daemonic, chthonic
Powers. And right action is freedom

From past and future also.
For most of us, this is the aim
Never here to be realised;
Who are only undefeated
Because we have gone on trying;
We, content at the last
If our temporal reversion nourish
(Not too far from the yew-tree)
The life of significant soil.

'TORMENT OF LOVE UNSATISFIED'

For Eliot the significance of the Incarnation lay, firstly, in its comprehension of the spheres of the temporal and the timeless in the person of Christ, and secondly, in its exemplification of the necessity of the *via negativa* in the sacrificial events of Christ's Passion and Crucifixion. The life and death of Christ vividly demonstrated the central principle of his teaching, i.e., that the way to God is the way of suffering, penitence and purgation. Christ's final cry of despair, 'My God, my God why hast thou forsaken me?' dramatically voiced the sense of isolation, of spiritual dispossession and darkness, that Eliot, following St Augustine, Aquinas, and St John of the Cross, believed the soul must endure in its quest for union with God. 'Time is no healer', Eliot warns in 'The Dry Salvages'; 'the time of death is every moment'. Endurance of the temporal, the daily confrontation of the reality of death and of the prospect it unfolds of a final release from the bondage of time, is the way of life signified by Christ in his life and teaching and fully comprehended in the miracle of his Incarnation.

The death of Eliot's mother in September 1929, and the agony of marital conflict he had endured for some years previously, both found expression in 'Ash Wednesday', his most powerful evocation of the torment of temporal suffering and its significance in the context of Christian belief. He had explored the theme of the Incarnation in a number of poems from the Ariel cycle some years before. Two of them, 'The Journey of the Magi' and 'A Song for Simeon', both symbolically link Christ's birth with his crucifixion to intimate the inevitability of suffering and its place in the way to salvation. 'They shall praise Thee and suffer in every generation/ With glory and derision', Simeon says, indicating the significance of Christ's Nativity as initiating the process that would culminate in his sacrificial death on the cross. 'What faith in life may be I know not,' Eliot himself wrote in a *Criterion* article in 1933.[45] 'For the Christian,' he said, 'faith in death is what matters.' In 'Ash Wednesday'

the everpresent reality of death is invoked in images of the agony and transience of earthly love, side by side with an image of the penitent-poet turning
to God for forgiveness. The mood of the poem is one of humility, resignation
and penitential prayer:

> And I pray to God to have mercy upon us
> And I pray that I may forget
> These matters that with myself I too much discuss
> Too much explain
> Because I do not hope to turn again
> Let these words answer
> For what is done, not to be done again
> May the judgment not be too heavy upon us
>
> Because these wings are no longer wings to fly
> But merely vans to beat the air
> The air which is now thoroughly small and dry
> Smaller and dryer than the will
> Teach us to care and not to care
> Teach us to sit still.
>
> Pray for us sinners now and at the hour of our death
> Pray for us now and at the hour of our death.

In one of the most vivid sequences from 'Ash Wednesday' a series of
Biblical images emphasises the pain and transience of earthly love and its
potential for transformation into a higher love transcending the mortal state.
The sequence opens with an Old Testament image from Ezekiel of three leop-
ards lying under a juniper tree, having fed to satiety on the flesh of a man.
The organs of desire have all been consumed and only the bones remain;
relieved of their sensual burden, these bones are cleansed, transformed in their
whiteness into the transcendent purity of unearthly love. The transcendence of
temporality is further symbolised by the rose-garden (an image from *The
Spiritual Canticle* of St John of the Cross), the place 'where all loves end' and
all earthly conflicts are resolved. In words heavily charged with the tones of
the Anglo-Catholic liturgy, the poet prays for relief from the torment of the
mortal state:

> Lady of silences
> Calm and distressed
> Torn and most whole

Rose of memory
Rose of forgetfulness
Exhausted and life-giving
Worried reposeful
The single Rose
Is now the Garden
Where all loves end
Terminate torment
Of love unsatisfied
The greater torment
Of love satisfied
End of the endless
Journey to no end
Conclusion of all that
Is inconclusible
Speech without word and
Word of no speech
Grace to the Mother
For the garden
Where all love ends.

In these lines he prays to the Virgin Mary, the mediator between the worlds of time and eternity, to terminate the torment of earthly love and to lead him to the Garden of Paradise where all earthly conflicts are resolved. She leads him towards the summit of the stair – a Dantesque image for the ascent to self-perfection and to final union with God – though he remains troubled by carnal passion and desire and is still plagued by the ever present 'demon of doubt' and the 'deceitful face of hope and despair'. He finds release in an act of humble submission to the will of God – 'Lord I am not worthy ... but speak the word only' ('and I shall be saved'). In the image of Mary he sees a symbolic manifestation of the ambiguity and conflict of the whole human condition. As the woman of sorrows, *the mater dolorosa*, she embodies the suffering and pain of the mortal state; as the lady transmuted into light she symbolises the self-perfection of the soul redeemed through suffering. He petitions her to reveal to him 'the blessed fruit of thy womb,' i.e., the Incarnate mystery in which his hope for redemption lies:

... Redeem
The time. Redeem
The unread vision in the higher dream
While jewelled unicorns draw by the gilded hearse.

The silent sister veiled in white and blue
Between the yews, behind the garden god,
Whose flute is breathless, bent her head and signed but spoke no word
But the fountain sprang up and the bird sang down
Redeem the time, redeem the dream
The token of the word unheard, unspoken

Till the wind shake a thousand whispers from the yew

And after this our exile.

Mary, the mother of Christ, is his guide to the 'higher dream', to the mystery of the 'word unheard, unspoken', to the profound and unintelligible paradox which is God. God is at once Word and Not-Word, He is simultaneously sound and silence, darkness and light. In the absolute silence is heard His voice, in itself the negation of all sound. 'Where shall the word be found,' the poem asks. 'There is not enough silence ... for those who walk in darkness ... for those who avoid the face ...' ... 'no time for those who walk among noise and deny the voice'. They are exiles from the Word and the Voice, denied access to its sound by time and sense, caught in a dream-crossed twilight, the 'time of tension between dying and birth'. In this condition the poet reaffirms the need for repentance and humble submission to God – 'Lord, hear my prayer and let my cry come unto Thee.' Entering on the way of penance, dying into new life, he hopes to find 'peace in His will'. In the final sequence of the poem the cry of a lost child mingles with the tones of the liturgy to convey an image of the sinner as outcast, submitting himself in a spirit of humility wholly to the will of God:

Blessèd sister, holy mother, spirit of the fountain, spirit of the garden,
Suffer us not to mock ourselves with falsehood
Teach us to care and not to care
Teach us to sit still
Even among these rocks,
Our peace in His will
And even among these rocks
Sister, mother
And spirit of the river, spirit of the sea,
Suffer me not to be separated

And let my cry come unto Thee.

The theme of redemption through suffering recurs throughout Eliot's poetry and lies at the heart of his exploration of the nature of Christian faith. Two of its most vivid representations occur in 'East Coker' and 'Murder in the Cathedral'. In the first Christ is depicted as a 'wounded surgeon' who heals the sickness and alleviates the sufferings of humankind. The image has been traced to St Augustine's *Confessions*, to 'The Songs Between the Soul and the Spouse' of St John of the Cross, and to Andrew Marvell's poem, 'A Dialogue between the Soul and the Body'. In Eliot's poem the world is compared to a hospital, endowed by 'a ruined millionaire' (generally interpreted as Adam, the father of mankind). The patients are tended by a 'dying nurse', representing the Church, while a wounded surgeon with bleeding hands examines their diseased bodies to find the cause of their sickness. Their sickness, he suggests, is the universal condition of fallen man, the curse of original sin. To be restored, the poem says, 'their sickness must grow worse'; spiritual healing and salvation will come only through further suffering. The patients 'quake in frigid purgatorial fires'; they are tortured by 'briars of smoke', but are enflamed by roses, symbolising the infinite love of God, and its earthly manifestation in the miracle of Christ's Incarnation, on which their hope for redemption and for a final release from their suffering rests. The poem concludes with an image of the transubstantiation of bread and wine into the body and blood of Christ in the Eucharist, the liturgical commemoration of the sacrificial event of the Crucifixion:

> The chill ascends from feet to knees,
> The fever sings in mental wires.
> If to be warmed, then I must freeze
> And quake in frigid purgatorial fires
> Of which the flame is roses, and the smoke is briars.
>
> The dripping blood our only drink,
> The bloody flesh our only food:
> In spite of which we like to think
> That we are sound, substantial flesh and blood –
> Again, in spite of that, we call this Friday good.

The concept of life as a continuous martyrdom is again the theme of *Murder in the Cathedral* where Eliot, appropriately taking the metrical structures of Isaiah and Ezekiel as his models for dramatic verse, reenacted the last days in the life of Thomas a Becket, seeing his suffering as an analogue for the universal condition of mankind. The essential message of the play is intoned in the Christmas Sermon where Thomas sees the events of Christ's birth and his crucifixion as continuous happenings, signifying the ultimate meaning of the Incarnation as a sacrificial event. In his sermon Thomas links the joyful tidings of the Nativity with the pain and sorrow of Christ's martyrdom, an association that had already been intimated in 'A Song for Simeon', 'The Journey of the Magi' and 'Ash Wednesday'. Christ, Becket says, entered the world to sacrifice his mortal life; in his death, he declares, lies the ultimate hope of mankind. 'It was in this same night,' he tells his Christmas congregation, 'that a multitude of the heavenly host appeared before the shepherds at Bethlehem saying,"Glory to God in the highest and peace on earth to men of good will"; at the same time of all the year that we celebrate at once the Birth of the Lord and His Passion and Death Upon the Cross.' He sees martyrdom as part of God's design for mankind, as a continuous reenactment in temporal life of the suffering epitomised in the life and death of Christ:

> Beloved we do not think of a martyr simply as a good Christian who has been killed because he is a Christian: for that would be solely to mourn. We do not think of him simply as a good Christian who has been elevated to the company of the Saints: for that would be simply to rejoice: and neither our mourning nor our rejoicing is as the world's is. A Christian martyrdom is never an accident, for Saints are not made by accident. Still less is a Christian martyrdom the effect of a man's will to become a Saint, as a man by willing and contriving may become a ruler of men. A martyrdom is always the design of God, for His love of men, to warn them and to lead them, to bring them back to His ways. It is never the design of man; for the true martyr is he who has become the instrument of God, who has lost his will in the will of God, and who no longer desires anything for himself, not even the glory of being a martyr. So thus as on earth the Church mourns and rejoices at once, in a fashion that the world cannot understand; so in Heaven the Saints are most high, having made themselves most low, and are seen, not as we see them, but in the light of the Godhead from which they draw their being.

The fundamental point of Thomas's sermon is that the true martyr is the one who allows himself to become an instrument of God, freely subordinating his own will to that of God, thereby acknowledging the place of individual freedom in the divine pattern of being. 'To act is to suffer', he says; 'action is suffering and suffering is action'; both are 'fixed in an eternal action, an eternal patience'. The words 'patience' and 'suffering', as Nevill Coghill has observed, both derive from the Latin verb, *pati*, to suffer. 'As well as the sense of suffering (enduring) there is the sense of stillness and waitingness in patience ...' he writes. 'We must neither act nor suffer for our own advantage, but, divested of the love of created beings, unite a will made perfect with the will of God, to sustain the design and pattern of perfection, to which we are called.'[46] In his death Becket gave witness to the belief that the daily martyrdom of temporal suffering, and the dramatic finality of martyrdom in death, are not explicable in human terms and can only be made meaningful through free submission to the will of God, through the recognition that 'the Law of God' and not the 'Law of man' is the way to the stillness and peace beyond the suffering of mortal life. The theme is summed up in his words about the women of Canterbury and their prophecies of doom:

> They know and do not know, what it is to act or suffer.
> They know and do not know, that action is suffering
> And suffering is action. Neither does the agent suffer
> Nor the patient act. But both are fixed
> In an eternal action, an eternal patience
> To which all must consent that it may be willed
> And which all must suffer that they may will it,
> That the pattern may subsist, for the pattern is the action
> And the suffering, that the wheel may turn and still
> Be forever still.

'THE GROUND OF OUR BESEECHING'

The themes of negation, temporality and suffering dominate Eliot's poetry, yet they all point consistently towards a transcendence of the conditions of mortal life. That transcendence, he declares, becomes known to man through faith, which is itself attained through penitence, prayer and humble submission to the will of God. Self-transcendence through faith is the theme of 'Little Gidding', the last of the *Four Quartets*. In this work Eliot consciously sought to unite the themes of all his poetry in a final religious resolution. Faith, the poem suggests, is the means by which the final and absolute order in existence is revealed; it points to the pattern of the intemporal in which all temporal and finite realities become finally meaningful. The first of the epigraphs cited at the beginning of the *Quartets* was taken from Heraclitus. It reads: 'Although the Logos is common to all, the majority of people live as though they had an understanding of their own.' That understanding, Eliot suggests, is one which comes, not primarily from reason, but from a higher source of wisdom and truth. Heraclitus had also said: 'Much learning does not teach one to have understanding; else it would have taught Hesiod and Pythagoras and again

Xenophanes and Hekataios.'[47] That sentiment underlies the sense of the transcendent potentiality of faith which recurs throughout the poem.

The presence of St John of the Cross is all-pervasive in 'Little Gidding', as it is in the three preceding poems of the Quartets. Its opening sequence has a series of metaphors recalling St John's description of the disciplines of the *via negativa*. The poet comes, in his quest for the light and the stillness of God, to the oratory at Little Gidding, a place of prayer sanctified by generations of pilgrims who had come there to find spiritual solace and self-renewal. To attain illumination, the poet reflects, he must 'put off sense and notion'; he must follow the way of the mystic who strives to attain union with God through self-negation. The illumination he seeks will be attained, he says, through prayer, his means of communing with the dead – with those who are blessed with the wisdom to be attained only in an existence beyond time:

> ... You are not here to verify,
> Instruct yourself, or inform curiosity,
> Or carry report. You are here to kneel
> Where prayer has been valid. And prayer is more
> Than an order of words, the conscious occupation
> Of the praying mind, or the sound of the voice praying.
> And what the dead had no speech for, when living,
> They can tell you, being dead: the communication
> Of the dead is tongued with fire beyond the language of the living.

The poem stresses the vanity of human ambition, representing it through an intricate pattern of elemental symbolism, all of which is drawn from Heraclitus. Fire, said Heraclitus, survives the death of air, while, paradoxically, air lives in the death of fire. Water, he said, lives in dead soil, while soil survives the death of water. Extending the analogy to its human context, Eliot symbolises the inevitable decline of human passion and feeling, intimating its inexorable descent towards self-destruction, until it is finally consumed by its own fire. The image of passion in decline is intertwined with that of an old man burning mementos of youthful love in the ruins of his burnt-out mansion:

> Ash on an old man's sleeve
> Is all the ash the burnt roses leave.
> Dust in the air suspended
> Marks the place where a story ended.
> Dust inbreathed was a house –
> The wall, the wainscot and the mouse.
> The death of hope and despair,
> This is the death of air.

The theme of destruction and regeneration by fire is reinforced by images of a landscape blighted by drought – the 'parched eviscerate soil/ Gapes at the vanity of human toil' – followed by images of ruined cities and temples, the deserted abbey at Little Gidding, and the ruins of the monasteries dissolved at the Reformation – all of them monuments to the inexorable processes of temporal decay.

> There are flood and drouth
> Over the eyes and in the mouth,
> Dead water and dead sand
> Contending for the upper hand.
> The parched, eviscerate soil
> Gapes at the vanity of toil,
> Laughs without mirth.
> This is the death of earth.
>
> Water and fire succeed
> The town, the pasture and the weed.
> Water and fire deride
> The sacrifice that we denied.
> Water and fire shall rot
> The marred foundations we forgot,
> Of sanctuary and choir.
> This is the death of water and fire.

These images are followed by a description of London during the blitz, the spectacle of mass destruction evoking the nightmare horror of 'interminable night'. In the darkened and deserted streets the poet meets a visitor from Purgatory temporarily at large in the world of time, possibly a reembodied figure from the past or simply a ghost-like double of the poet himself. This meeting leads him to contemplate the events of his past, his transgressions, his self-deceit, his pursuit of worldly glory, all of which seem inconsequential and futile, though still painful and distressing, when seen from the vantage-point of present time. He finds release from his disillusionment in the hope that all temporal experience is purged by repentance and by suffering, 'restored by the refining fire' of God's love which transforms existence and elevates it to its ultimate transcendence, its triumph over time:

> Let me disclose the gifts reserved for age
> To set a crown upon your lifetime's effort.
> First, the cold friction of expiring sense

Without enchantment, offering no promise
But bitter tastelessness of shadow fruit
As body and soul begin to fall asunder.
Second, the conscious impotence of rage
At human folly, and the laceration
Of laughter at what ceases to amuse.
And last, the rending pain of reenactment
Of all that you have done, and been; the shame
Of motives late revealed, and the awareness
Of things ill done and done to others' harm
Which once you took for exercise of virtue.
Then fools' approval stings, and honour stains.
From wrong to wrong the exasperated spirit
Proceeds, unless restored by that refining fire
Where you must move in measure, like a dancer.

Contemplating the ruined chapel at Little Gidding, the poet ponders on the fluctuating modes of attachment and detachment occasioned by the passage of time. The soldiers who took refuge in Little Gidding during the Cromwellian Civil War represent a passionate attachment to a cause; with the passage of time, their cause is relegated to the sphere of memory – the collective memory of recorded history – where it is liberated from the emotional attachments to which it was bound in its own time. In individual existence, he suggests, memory can similarly liberate from the bondage of egotistical passion and this can lead, in turn, to a further liberation from the pressing demands of the future. Seen in the total pattern of past, present and future time, temporarily rooted experience declines in emotional significance and acquires a more detached meaningfulness in terms of the total pattern of flux and change. And while sin and suffering are inevitable in mortal life – being essentially manifestations both of human weakness and freedom – they also, he says, will be seen eventually in terms of the final pattern or design. In the words of the mediaeval mystic, Dame Julian of Norwich, 'all manner of thing shall be well'. All that occurs, in past, present and future time, attains its final significance in the intersection of the worlds of the time-bound and the timeless. That mysterious order, involving the immanent presence of the eternal in the temporal, is embodied in the mystery of the Incarnation, in the person of Christ as God Become Man. He is 'the ground of our beseeching':

Sin is Behovely, but
All shall be well, and

All manner of thing shall be well ...
Whatever we inherit from the fortunate
We have taken from the defeated
What they had to leave us – a symbol:
A symbol perfected in death.
And all shall be well and
All manner of thing shall be well
By the purification of the motive
In the ground of our beseeching.

Yet the suffering which is endemic in mortal life has to be endured and must be seen as the means to salvation and the self-liberation of the individual soul. This is the meaning conveyed by God's messenger, the pentecostal dove, who is represented in the poem as a harbinger of fire who brings suffering and destruction to mankind, but simultaneously brings the fire of God's love. The message of the dove is the paradoxical truth that we are 'redeemed from fire by fire'. There is no escape from suffering; it is the condition of our temporality and finitude. Like Hercules who could free himself from the blood-stained shirt that burned into his flesh only by throwing himself on to the flaming pyre, so we find redemption from time only by our endurance of the conditions of temporal life:

The dove descending breaks the air
With flame of incandescent terror
Of which the tongues declare
The one discharge from sin and error.
The only hope, or else despair
Lies in the choice of pyre or pyre –
To be redeemed from fire by fire

Who then devised the torment? Love.
Love is the unfamiliar Name
Behind the hands that wove
The intolerable shirt of flame
Which human power cannot remove.
We only live, only suspire
Consumed by either fire or fire.

Several scholars have commented on Eliot's imitation of certain musical structures in the composition of *Four Quartets*.[48] Each of the poems, for example, follows the convention of symphonic composition by concluding with a coda-like movement in which all the themes of the work are finally synthe-sised. The concluding sequence of 'Little Gidding' not only restates the main themes of the poem itself, but is generally seen as reaffirming the major themes of all of Eliot's poetry. 'This section of the poem,' Eliot himself wrote in 1950, 'cost me far more time and trouble and vexation than any passage of the same length that I have ever written.'[49] Admirable in its condensation of all his themes, the sequence is above all a testament to, and reaffirmation of, the primary principles of Eliot's religious faith. Returning to the theme of tempo-rality and the timeless – the major preoccupation of each of the four poems of the Quartets – he reaffirms his belief that death marks the beginning of life; it signifies the soul's release from the bondage of the temporal, and its entry into the stillness of the eternal. 'The end is where we start from', he declares as he emphasises the continuity of all time and its place in the eternal pattern. The rose-tree that lasts for a day, and the yew-tree that lasts for centuries, are both, he says, 'of equal duration' when seen from the standpoint of the final pattern. Every moment, he suggests, has a significance beyond its immediate temporality; detached from time, its significance consists in its relation to the timeless Absolute in which it ultimately becomes meaningful:

> What we call the beginning is often the end
> And to make an end is to make a beginning.
> The end is where we start from ...
> We die with the dying:
> See, they depart, and we go with them.
> We are born with the dead:
> See, they return, and bring us with them.
> The moment of the rose and the moment of the yew-tree
> Are of equal duration. A people without history
> Is not redeemed from time, for history is a pattern
> Of timeless moments. So, while the light fails
> On a winter's afternoon, in a secluded chapel
> History is now and England.

'Little Gidding' ends, appropriately, with sea and river symbolism, both highly evocative of Eliot's childhood. They are the symbols by which he most consistently conveyed his sense of the mysterious intersections of the temporal and the timeless. He reaffirms the coexistence of all time – 'the end of all our exploring/Will be to arrive where we started'; the 'gateway' by which we enter into temporal life is the same, he says, as that by which we re-enter the time-less. He recalls the image of the rose-garden from St John, the place where the soul attains final illumination. He reiterates the words of Julian of Norwich –

'all manner of thing shall be well',[50] and ends with an image of the rose, simultaneously the symbol of suffering and the symbol of the fire of God's love. 'The fire and the rose are one', he concludes; the two are inextricably linked in the conditions of temporal life;

> We shall not cease from exploration
> And the end of all our exploring
> Will be to arrive where we started
> And know the place for the first time.
> Through the unknown, remembered gate
> When the last of earth left to discover
> Is that which was the beginning;
> At the source of the longest river
> The voice of the hidden waterfall
> And the children in the apple-tree
> Not known, because not looked for
> But heard, half-heard, in the stillness
> Between two waves of the sea.
> Quick, now, here, now, always –
> A condition of complete simplicity
> (Costing not less than everything)
> And all shall be well and
> All manner of thing shall be well
> When the tongues of flame are in-folded
> Into the crowned knot of fire
> And the fire and the rose are one.

6

'An Atheist Who Has Lost His Faith': The Prose and Verse of Boris Pasternak

'A SEEKER AFTER FAITH'

In *Safe Conduct*, the first of his two volumes of autobiography, Pasternak describes his early discovery of the Judaeo-Christian scriptures and the nature of their impact on his life and work. 'I came,' he writes, 'to understand that the Bible is not so much a book with a hard and fast text as the notebook of humanity and the key to everything that is eternal.'[1] He speaks of the importance of tradition for the writer and sees the scriptures as embodying the essence of the spiritual and cultural traditions that shaped his own development as a poet. 'I understood,' he says, 'that the history of culture is a chain of equations in images, binding two by two the unknown with the known, and this known makes its appearance as legend, folded into the rudiments of tradition.'[2] Recalling his baptism and initiation into Christianity – which occurred when he was five years old – he told a French correspondent, Jacqueline de Proyart: 'I believe this is at the root of my distinctiveness. Most intensively of all my mind was occupied with Christianity in the years 1910-12 when the main foundations of this distinctiveness – my way of seeing things, the world, life – were taking shape.'[3]

There are many similar comments that might be cited to indicate the centrality of the Judaeo-Christian scriptural traditions in Pasternak's life and work. What is less clear, however, is the extent to which his interest in the scriptures developed into the full commitment of the religious believer. He described himself once as 'a seeker after religious faith'. In an interview recorded in 1959, the year before his death, he said: 'I was born a Jew. My family was interested in music and art and paid little attention to religious practice. Because I felt an urgent need to find a channel of communication to the Creator I was converted to Russian Orthodox Christianity. But try as I might I could not achieve a complete spiritual experience. Thus I am still a seeker.'[4] Olga Ivinskaya, a close friend for fifteen years, described his Christianity as 'unconventional' and saw him as having strong affinities with Tolstoy by virtue of their shared suspicion of religious dogmatism. In *A Captive of Time* she cites a conversation between Pasternak and the Slavic scholar, Nils Ake Nilsson, in which he (Pasternak) argued that each individual must define his own 'relationship to existence'. He added, rather significantly:

'This means a revival of our inner world, a revival of religion – not religion in the sense of church dogma, but as a feeling about life.'[5]

Many questions have been raised about the orthodoxy of Pasternak's interpretations of Christianity. An Italian Jesuit found that they lacked the supernatural element essential to religion. 'The abundance of religious elements in this latest work of Pasternak's,' he wrote in a review of *Doctor Zhivago*, 'does not in itself justify our proclaiming his faith in God and the supernatural. His Christ is emphatically human.'[6] A Russian Orthodox theologian, however, distinguished between two concepts of immortality in Pasternak's writings: the idea of personal immortality as a prolongation of individual existence – which he evidently did not accept – and the notion of the soul's survival through its participation in the infinity of love – for which there is significant support throughout his work.[7] The most prominent instance of the latter occurs in the scene from *Doctor Zhivago* where Yury comforts the dying Anna Gromeko with these words: 'You in others are yourself, your soul ... This is what you are. This is what your consciousness has breathed and lived on and enjoyed throughout your life – your soul, your immortality, your life in others ... You have always been in others and you will remain in others.'

This whole question is central to Pasternak's Christianity and will be discussed in some detail presently. At this point, however, it may be appropriate to point to Pasternak's Jewish origins and to the impact of the traditions of Judaism on his writings, particularly in his treatment of the theme of immortality. The child of Jewish parents, he was descended on his father's side from Don Isaac ben-Yehuda Abravarel, the fifteenth century philosopher and political leader, who claimed ancestry in turn from the royal house of David. And though he seems to have encountered little of the Jewish heritage in his home – it is clear from his recollections that his family were not conventional observers of Jewish rituals and prayer customs – he gained a deep understanding of its spiritual traditions in the years he was a student of philosophy under Herman Cohen at Marburg University. Though he became disillusioned with philosophy as an abstract discipline – 'a little philosophy', Yury Zhivago says, 'should be added to life and art by way of spice, but to make it one's speciality seems to me as strange as feeding on nothing but pickles' – it is evident from various sources that Pasternak was deeply influenced by Cohen's Jewish spirituality and this remained a significant factor in his subsequent interpretations of the scriptures. A Slavic scholar, Rimvydas Silbajoris, describes him as 'a devout Christian thinker with roots in the Hebraic tradition',[8] and a Jewish writer, Judith Stora,[9] points to specific Jewish elements in his predominantly Christian sensibility: the prophetic idea of universal happiness, the hallowing of the everyday; the notion of faith as *praxis* (stressed, for example, in Yury's words to Anna Gromeko), and the idea of immortality as paradoxically attained in the conditions of time. This latter principle is repeatedly attested in his poetry, as will be illustrated shortly.

However one interprets the religious influences on Pasternak's work, it is clear from various sources – both the internal evidence of his writings and the recorded testimony of close friends and associates – that his quest for faith was deep and sincere and that it profoundly influenced all his work from the lyrics of the early 1900s to the prose and verse of the last decade of his life. His lengthy correspondence with Olga Freidenberg provides numerous instances of this. On one occasion he writes to her about a series of misfortunes that had recently afflicted him. (They included news of his father's impending death and numerous personal ailments.) 'Through all this grief and suffering,' he writes, 'I experience an upsurge of inexplicable good humour, indestructible faith, irrepressible vitality.'[10] 'You emanate great faith,' she tells him on another occasion when he had sent her some of his poems, inviting her to comment on them.[11] Two of his poems from the 1950s describe his faith in terms that are specifically Christian. The first is 'Daybreak', one of the Zhivago poems which several scholars have interpreted as a personal affirmation by Pasternak of his rediscovery of the Christian faith in the years he was writing *Doctor Zhivago*. De Mallac speaks of the poem's 'Augustinian or Pascalian atmosphere'[12] and Gifford, in his biography, says 'it tells of Christ's rediscovered significance for the poet after many years of neglect'.[13] Katkov, in his commentary on the links between the poem and the prose text of the novel, writes: 'It refers to the peculiar conversion to which, it is reported, he alluded when he described his religious convictions as "those of an atheist who has lost his faith". ... For him acceptance of the New Testament, which was like an awakening or coming to life after a swoon, was the acceptance of the story and legend of Christianity as a system of symbols, which, when applied to everyday life, changes it beyond recognition.'[14] The poem begins:

> You meant everything in my destiny.
> Then came the war, the disaster.
> For a long, long time,
> No trace, no news of you.
>
> After all these years,
> Again your voice has disturbed me.
> All night I read your testament.
> It was like reviving from a faint.

The second poem, 'In Hospital', was written in 1953 when Pasternak was recovering from a heart attack. In these four quatrains he praises God for the

wonders of his creation and looks to his comforting presence as he faces the
imminent prospect of death:

> 'O Lord', he was thinking, 'how perfect
> Thy works are, how perfect and right;
> The walls and the beds and the people,
> This death-night, the city at night!
>
> I drink up a sedative potion,
> And weeping, my handkerchief trace.
> O Father, the tears of emotion
> Prevent me from seeing thy face.
>
> Dim light scarcely touches my bedstead.
> It gives me such comfort to drift
> And feel that my life and my lot are
> Thy priceless and wonderful gift.
>
> While dying in fading surroundings
> I feel how thy hands are ablaze,
> The hands that have made me and hold me
> And hide like a ring in a case.'

Music provided Pasternak with one of his favourite metaphors for the inner
perfection and harmony of religious faith. His early passion for music is made
evident in both volumes of his autobiography, especially in his recollections of
the influence of Scriabin on his childhood. In *Doctor Zhivago* the imagery of
music is used frequently to signify an inner peace and spiritual fulfilment.
'What has for centuries raised man above the beast is not the cudgel but an
inward music,' Uncle Nikolai declares. Zhivago, in the midst of his labours,
longs for 'the wordlessness of sound sleep ... of true music, of a human
understanding rendered speechless by emotion'. This inward music of the
spirit is linked explicitly with religious faith – though not with religious conventions and rituals – in a passage from the novel describing Lara's occasional
visits to church: 'Lara was not religious. She did not believe in ritual. But
sometimes to enable her to bear her life she needed the accompaniment of an
inward music and she could not always compose it for herself. That music was
God's word of life and it was to weep over it that she went to church.'

One of the most positive and enthusiastic assessments of the religious
dimensions of Pasternak's work occurs in an essay entitled 'The Pasternak
Affair' by the contemplative priest and writer, Thomas Merton. Merton had

corresponded with Pasternak and had sent him the text of some commentaries on his work; it appears from letters appended to his *Literary Essays* that Pasternak fully approved of Merton's interpretations.[15] Merton writes euphorically of Pasternak's 'spontaneous and rudimentary Christianity'. 'His witness,' he says, 'is essentially Christian ...' 'Its problematical quality lies,' he writes, 'in the fact that it is reduced to its barest and most elementary essentials: intense awareness of all cosmic and human reality as "life in Christ", and the consequent plunge into love as the only dynamic and creative force which really honours this "Life" by creating itself anew in Life's – Christ's image.' Pointing to Pasternak's extensive use of scriptural imagery – 'he reads the scriptures with the avidity and the spiritual imagination of Origen' – Merton found in his work the same kind of parable-like simplicity as Pasternak's own fictional character, Nikolai Vedniapin, identified as the defining characteristic of the Gospel texts. 'Pasternak's Christianity, Merton says, 'is something very simple, very rudimentary, deeply sincere, utterly personal and yet for all its questionable expressions, obviously impregnated with the true spirit of the Gospels and the liturgy.'[16]

Underlying the question of Pasternak's personal interest in religion, however, is the more complex matter of its place in his conception of his role as artist. 'My oldest passion is art,' he wrote to his friend, Nina Tabidze. 'I and the circumstances of my life are ruled by it as unambiguously and firmly and with as much clarity as people were once upon a time ruled by religious convictions.'[17] The two passions – that for religion and for art – were closely intertwined in all his activities and the implications of this must be addressed before his treatment of religious, and specifically Christian, themes can be more fully explored. In his aesthetic writings he defined the act of artistic creation as the revelation of mystery, as inspiration, as a sacrificial act, and as a process of radical realism. All four conceptions are deeply bound up with his understanding of the relation between religious and artistic truth.

The question in particular of the relation of art to reality is central to the whole matter of the religious significance of his work. In one of his last letters he spoke of art as a transposition into image of the dynamism of reality and especially of its processes of self-renewal and change. 'I loved movement in its most diverse manifestations,' he writes. 'I loved to seize the whirling world as it was rushing headlong and to reproduce it.'[18] Guy de Mallac points to similarities between this and both Bergson's notion of art as 'recorded movement' and Klee's idea that 'a work of art is born in movement and is itself a fixed movement.'[19] Like Bergson and Klee, Pasternak sees the process of artistic creation originating in the motion of reality. 'Art,' he says, 'is concerned not with man but with the image of man. The image of man ... is greater than man. It can come into being only in the act of transition ... In art the man is silent and the image speaks. And it becomes apparent that only the image can keep pace with the successes of nature.'[20]

The dynamism which art records is further defined by Pasternak as a dynamism of *form,* i.e., of the form which is already inherent in reality itself. In his essay, 'Some Tenets,' he defines beauty as 'delight in form'; that form, he says, 'is the key to organic life since no living thing can exist without it'.[21] The notion strongly recalls Coleridge's concept of organic form as 'something that shapes itself as it develops itself from within', something 'whose fullness of development is one and the same with the perfection of its outward form'.[22] These sentiments are echoed by Yury Zhivago as he reflects on the nature of poetic composition: 'As he scribbled his odds and ends he made a note reaffirming his belief that art always serves beauty and beauty is the joy of possessing form and form is the key to organic life since no living thing can exist without it so that every work of art, including tragedy, witnesses to the joy of existence.'

Repeatedly, Pasternak stresses the fidelity to the naturally real that the process of artistic revelation involves. 'It is as realistic an activity and as symbolic as fact,' he writes in *Safe Conduct.* 'It is realistic since it has not itself invented metaphor but discovered it in nature and reproduced it faithfully.'[23] The artist, he says, 'copies from nature'; when its 'features are transferred on to paper ... the characteristics of life become the characteristics of creation'. The realism of art consists, he adds, in 'clarity of form', requiring 'an unusual vein of precision', and 'close fidelity to nature'.[24] In an article on Chopin he speaks of a 'depth of biographical impression' which acts as 'the main impulse on the artist's life and pushes him into innovation and originality'. Chopin's work, he says, was 'thoroughly original' because 'it was similar to nature'. It was intentionally biographical, 'not because of egocentricity' but because Chopin 'looked on his life as a means of knowing every kind of life on earth'.[25] Thus, he insists on fidelity to the real and the existential as the mark of genuine artistic realism. 'For me,' he declares, 'art is a possession and the artist is a man attacked and stricken, possessed by reality.'[26]

This is the kind of possession which Yury Zhivago describes when he decides he should cease imitating the classical masters and let the 'world of concrete things' enter spontaneously into his poetry: 'It's as if the air, the light, the noise of life, of real substantial things burst into his poetry from the street as through an open window. Concrete things – things in the outside world, things in current use, names of things, common nouns – burst in and take possession of his verse, driving out the vaguer parts of speech.' What he liked best of all in the whole world of Russian literature, he says later, was 'the childlike Russian quality of Pushkin and Chekhov, their shy unconcern with such matters as the ultimate purpose of mankind or their own salvation'. Their work, he says, 'has ripened like apples picked green from the trees and has increasingly matured in sense and sweetness'. It is most significant, as has already been intimated, that it is this same quality of existential simplicity that Nikolai Vedniapin considers to be the essential characteristic of the parable style of the new Testament. 'It has always been assumed,' he says, 'that the most important things in the Gospels are the ethical teaching and commandments. But for me the most important thing is the fact that Christ speaks in parables taken from daily life, that he explains the truth in terms of everyday reality. The idea that underlies this is that communion between mortals is immortal and that the whole of life is symbolic because the whole of it has meaning.' The implications of this comment will be considered in detail later since it provides an important key to the relationship between the aesthetic and religious dimensions of Pasternak's work.

It is necessary, first, however, to clarify some further issues arising from the theory of artistic realism just outlined. The first of these issues is the immense complexity and mysteriousness of the reality the artist describes, despite the clarity and the simplicity of the formal imagery employed in his art. In a letter to Stephen Spender Pasternak wrote: 'From my earliest years I have been struck by the observation that existence was more original and extraordinary and inexplicable than any of its separate astonishing incidents and facts. I was attracted by the unusualness of the usual.' Reality lies, he said, in a letter to another correspondent, 'in the multiplicity of the universe, in the large number of possibilities ... in a coincidence of impulses and inspirations'. 'I would claim,' he wrote, 'to have seen nature and universe themselves not as a picture made or fastened on an immovable wall, but as a sort of painted canvas roof or curtain in the air, incessantly pulled and blown and flapped by a something of an immaterial unknown and unknowable wind.'[27] The artist's concern, he suggests, is to unravel this radical mysteriousness at the heart of reality. His art, therefore, becomes an activity of *revelation*, a naming of the not-yet known.

A key passage in *Safe Conduct* expresses it like this: 'We come to recognise reality. It appears in some new form. This form appears to be a quality inherent in it, and not in us. Apart from this quality everything in the world has its name. It alone is new and without name. We try to give it a name. The result is art.'[28] The images by which the artist 'names' reality are already, therefore, inherent in that reality itself. The spontaneous energy at work in artistic creation, in its radical activity of revelation and meaning-making, has its origins in the autonomous reality of the imagery the artist employs. The form inherent in what he discloses is an organic principle and law of its unfolding. Thus, Yury Zhivago sees the process of artistic composition not only as an activity of revelation but one of *inspired* revelation. He speaks of the essential autonomy of language itself, of its power to enter the creative consciousness of the artist, and to assume a perfect synthesis of the subjective and objective, the personal and the universal:

> After two or three stanzas and several images by which he was himself astonished, his work took possession of him and he experienced the approach of what he called inspiration. At such moments the correlation of the forces controlling the artist is, as it were, stood on its head. The ascendancy is no longer with the artist or the state of mind which he is trying to express, but with language, his instrument of expression. Language, the home and dwelling of beauty and meaning, itself begins to think and speak for man and turns wholly into music, not in the sense of outward, audible sounds but by virtue of the power and momentum of its inward flow. Then, like the current of a mighty river polishing stones and turning wheels by its very movement, the flow of speech creates in passing, by the force of its own laws, rhyme and rhythm and countless other forms and formations, still more important and until now undiscovered, unconsidered and unnamed.
>
> At such moments Yury felt that the main part of his work was not being done by him but by something which was above him and controlling him: the thought and poetry of the world as it was at that moment and as it would be in the future. He was controlled by the next step it was to take in the order of its historical development; and he felt himself to be only the pretext and the pivot setting it in motion.

Thomas Merton described this as a process of *religious* revelation: 'When in the moment of inspiration the poet's creative intelligence is married with the unborn wisdom of human language (the Word of God and Human Nature) then in the very flow of new and individual intuitions the poet utters the voice of that wonderful and mysterious world of God-manhood – it is the transfigured, spiritualised and divinised cosmos that speaks through him and through him utters its praise of the Creator.'[29] Pasternak himself, on several occasions, used the Biblical image of miracle-working for the process of poetic revelation. In an article dating from the 1920s he had used the word 'chudo' or 'miracle' to designate the poet's power to transform reality.[30] In his poem, 'August', the Transfiguration of Christ becomes an image for the miraculous transformation of reality occurring in the work of art, and in another of the Zhivago poems, 'Winter', the candle symbolism simultaneously suggests religious, mystical and poetic illumination.

Sima Tuntseva, the seamstress of Yuriatin, directly links the miracle of Christ's Incarnation with the phenomenon of poetic inspiration (the incarnation of the *logos*). She sees the birth of Christ as an event which is comparable to the generative activity of the creative imagination, the activity in which man most closely approaches the creativeness of God. In this we find the significance of Uncle Nikolai's comment that the most radical fact about the Gospels is that Christ employed the simplicity of the parable form to convey his meaning – that he 'explains the truth in terms of everyday reality'. Art, he suggests, is a process of poetic incarnation comparable to the prototypical miracle of the Incarnation, the birth of Christ. To quote Martin Green's words from his study of Pasternak: 'Christ has redeemed man by redeeming common (and above all private) experience – by showing that such experience can be a means of communication ...' Referring to the notes on poetic composition found amongst Yury's papers after his death, he writes: 'There we see the artist finding the material for his parables – "following Christ" in the sense this version of Christianity makes central.'[31]

The artist's bridging of self and otherness, through his receptivity to the inspiration of image and word, is expressed yet again by Pasternak in his image of the poet as actor, i.e., one who assumes an identity from a reality outside himself. The theme is most dramatically expressed in his poem, 'Hamlet', but is anticipated in some earlier stories which elaborate in various ways on the idea of art as inspiration and a sacrificial act, i.e., as the sacrificing of the self to the inspiration of external reality. 'Il Tratto di Apelle' is an allegorical tale in which the poet, Heine, is described arriving at a hotel in Pisa where he finds a card addressed in his name and bearing the imprint of a bloody thumb. He recognises the mark as that of the poet, Emilio Relinquimini, who had earlier asked him for an equally simple image to signify his understanding of the nature of love. Heine goes to Ferrara to find the lady who had inspired Relinquimini's love poems, and seduces her. Cynically, he acts out the role of lover, but the force of the love he simulates enters into and transforms the entire relationship between himself and the lady. When she reproaches him with behaving like an actor, he responds: 'We spend our whole lives on the stage and it is only with the greatest difficulty that some of us are capable of the naturalness which, like a role, is assigned to us at the moment of birth.'

The story allegorises the poet's capacity to let reality enter into his art in the same way that Heine has allowed the force of genuine love to enter into his soul. Michel Acouturier writes: 'One can see that this paradox of the actor is nothing else but the paradox of art, the synthesis of two apparently contradictory components: that of craft and that of inspiration, of technique and creation, of artifice and spontaneity, of labour and gift, words and grace.'[32] In an essay on Shakespeare Pasternak declared that 'art can do nothing higher than lend its ear to the voice of love itself, that voice forever new and unprecedented'.³³ This is the truth that Heine discovers, but he finds it ultimately not in his own thoughts but in the reality of the role he incarnates. The artist similarly finds truth in the sacrificing of the self to the force of that absolute and primordial reality he contemplates.

The theme of the actor-poet as sacrificial hero is developed again in 'Letters From Tula' and 'The Last Summer', two stories Pasternak wrote some years before *Doctor Zhivago*. The first is the story of a young poet who writes to his lover of a chance meeting he has had with some travelling players at the railway station at Tula. He describes them as 'the worst species of bohemian'; their 'posturings' and 'vapourings' disgust him, but he gradually realises that the qualities he despises in them are the same qualities which he also loathes in himself. 'How frightful,' he moans, 'to recognise one's traits in others.' He realises that 'everything would begin when he ceased listening to himself and when an absolutely physical silence would fill his soul'. In 'The Last Summer' Sergei, also a young poet, meets a widow, Arild, who tells him of the humiliations she endures from her employers. He falls in love with her and proposes to marry her. He then meets a young prostitute, Sasha, and is deeply distressed by *her* misfortunes as well. He prepares a sketch for a play which he plans to submit to a theatre director in order to raise money to alleviate their miseries. In the play he imagines himself as a young artist who offers himself for sale at an auction and when eventually he is purchased by a rich patron is able to donate the proceeds to the young widow and the prostitute.

Both stories allegorically suggest that the poet is the servant of his destiny: he fulfils himself through the sacrifice of his own self-identity to the role to which his destiny calls him. This whole theme is given a religious, and specifically Christian, definition in the poem, 'Hamlet'. Here Pasternak combines the image of the actor who fulfils his destiny by subordinating himself wholly to the demands of his art with the images of Hamlet and Christ fulfilling their destinies by subordinating themselves wholly to the will of a father. Their missions are similar: they consist essentially in the sacrifice of self in fulfilment of their appointed roles. In an article in *Literaturnaya Moskva* Pasternak drew parallels between the 'To be or not to be' soliloquy and Christ's pleas to his Father in Gethsemane, 'My God, my God, why hast Thou forsaken me?'. 'These,' he wrote, 'are the most heartfelt and frenzied lines ever written on the anguish of the unknown at the gates of death.'³⁴ Hamlet, fearful of executing the duty imposed on him by his father is compared to Christ beseeching his father to save him from death on the cross. Both proceed, inexorably, towards the martyrdom of cathartic, sacrificial death:

> The noise is stilled. I come out on the stage.
> Leaning against the door-post

I try to guess from the distant echo
What is to happen in my lifetime.

The darkness of night is aimed at me
Along the sights of a thousand opera-glasses.
Abba, Father, if it be possible,
Let this cup pass from me.

I love your stubborn purpose,
I consent to play my part.
But now a different drama is being acted;
For this once let me be.

Yet the order of the acts is planned
And the end of the way inescapable.
I am alone; all drowns in the Pharisees' hypocrisy.
To live your life is not as simple as to cross a field.

The archetypal image of the suffering Christ in Gethsemane is one of many such images from the scriptures which are used throughout Pasternak's work. They are the most significant pointers to the religious vision which informs the whole of his work but which is particularly evident in the prose and verse of *Doctor Zhivago*. It is a vision which is rooted in two main principles. The first derives from his view of history as the record of man's free collaboration with the forces of motion and change in nature and reality. He saw the artistic process as a special enactment of that collaboration. 'The poetry that I understand,' he wrote in *Safe Conduct*, 'proceeds after all in history and in collaboration with real life.'[35] Art, he declared, embodies man's historical collaboration with nature at its highest level: that of inspired meaning-making. He further suggested that the radical freedom which is the essential condition of man's collaboration with the forces of change received its strongest historical and cultural impetus from Christ's teaching on the primacy of individual personality. The second principle is closely related to this. The life-renewing dynamism which he defined as the regenerating force in all nature is seen ultimately as God's immanent presence in the world he created. The artist both evokes, and collaborates with, these immanent, self-renewing forces in nature. They enter his work through the inspirational sources of the language and imagery he employs. The whole process is especially discernible in the nature lyricism and the romantic imagery of *Doctor Zhivago*. This is the second sense in which his work can be seen as disclosing a religious and predominantly Christian vision of life. Both themes – the theme of Christianity as an affirmation of individual freedom and the theme of art as a celebration of immanence – can now be considered in some detail. It can then be shown that the religious vision they disclose is simultaneously life-affirming, tragic and profoundly hopeful.

CHRISTIANITY, HISTORY AND FREEDOM

The themes of historical progress and freedom are explored by Pasternak in the context of the greatest social and political upheaval of the twentieth century: the Russian Revolution of 1917. The themes are explored at two levels: firstly, in terms of the actual events of the Revolution; and secondly, in terms of its impact on the life of Yury Zhivago. 'The epoch contributed the main element to the novel,' he said. 'I wrote it with great ease. The circumstances were so definite, so fabulously terrible. All that I had to do was listen to their prompting with my whole soul and follow obediently their suggestions.'[36] In the novel he examines the ideals which inspired the Revolution as well as its consequences for the Russian people and its symbolic importance for the whole of mankind. The same themes are explored at the level of individual experience through the life of the novel's hero, Yury Zhivago. Zhivago, whose sympathies for the Revolution bring him material hardship and disgrace, renews his spiritual integrity through his poetry and his love for Lara Antipova. He sees his artistic creativity as enacting the kind of sacrificial identification with the sufferings of the people that Pasternak had described through the image of Christ in his poem, 'Hamlet'. 'If there is suffering anywhere,' he writes, 'why should not my art suffer and myself with it. I am speaking of the most artistic in the artist, of the sacrifice without which art becomes unnecessary, and without which works of art are covered outside with a sprinkling of superficial talent, but inside stick to the ideas which mankind has known well and even outgrown since it emerged from savagery.'

Through Zhivago's experiences Pasternak evaluates the Revolution and defines its significance in the continuum of history. While affirming its inevitability in the conditions that existed in Tsarist Russia, and while enthusiastically approving the social advances that it achieves for his people, he questions the validity of purely political, social or economic solutions to the complexities of human existence and defends the fundamental value of individual freedom – a freedom he believes is ultimately attained through love. There are several points in the novel where the Revolution is shown to have a transforming impact on the lives of the Russian people. Samdevyatov, for instance, recalls the horrors of imperialist exploitation. 'Gluttons and parasites sat on the backs of the starving workers and drove them to death and you imagine things could stay like that,' he cries. 'Don't you understand the rightness of the people's anger, of their desire to live in justice, of their search for truth?' he asks Zhivago.

Zhivago endorses this view of the conditions existing in pre-Revolutionary Russia: '... people with means could indulge their follies and eccentricities at the expense of the poor. The fooling, the right to idleness enjoyed by the few while the majority suffered, could itself create an illusion of genuine character and originality.' At various stages the Revolution is identified metaphorically with the life-renewing forces in nature. 'Mother Russia is on the move,' Zhivago tells Lara. 'She can't stand still, she's restless and she can't find rest, she's talking and she can't stop. And it isn't as if only people were talking. Stars and trees meet and converse, flowers talk philosophy at night, stone houses hold meetings.' The Revolution, he says, is the life-force regenerating the energies of the people; it is the 'sea of life': 'The Revolution broke out willy nilly, like a breath that's been held in too long. Everyone was revived, reborn changed, transformed ... Socialism is the sea, and all these separate streams, these private individual revolutions are flowing into it – the sea of life, of life in its own right.' He compares the change to the transformation in Christ's disciples after his resurrection: 'It's like something out of the Gospels ... like in the days of the apostles. Like in St Paul – do you remember? "You will speak with tongues and prophecy. Pray for the gift of understanding."'

While recognising the need for the Revolution and its inevitability, and while celebrating its life-renewing impact on the lives of the Russian people, the novel warns nonetheless of the danger of expecting too much from a Revolution conceived purely in terms of social and political advancement. 'The idea of social betterment, as it is understood since the October Revolution, doesn't fill me with enthusiasm.' Yury tells Liberius Mikulitsin ... 'And when I hear people speak of reshaping life it makes me lose my self-control and I fall into despair.' The ideals of the Revolution proved to be inadequate in the face of the social realities confronting the Russian people, because ultimately they were *humanist* ideals only. 'They were unattracted,' Lara says, 'to the modern fashion of coddling man, exalting him above the rest of nature and worshipping him. A sociology built on this false premise and served up as a politics struck them as pathetically home-made and amateurish beyond their comprehension.'

It is in terms of its socio-political and humanist reductionism, therefore, that Marxism is rejected as a solution to the needs of the people. To Samdevyatov's claim that Marxism is a 'positive science, a doctrine of reality, a philosophy of history', Yury responds: 'Marxism is not sufficiently master of itself to be a science. Science is more balanced. You talk about Marxism and objectivity. I don't know of any teaching more self-centred and further from the facts than Marxism.' The purely materialistic explanation of history stands in conflict with the idea of man as essentially and radically free. It is both reductive and determinist: reductive because it focusses all on the material, the economic and the social; and determinist because it denies the freedom of individual man to effect his own destiny. Describing how her husband, Pasha, was changed by the Revolution, Lara speaks of the loss of faith in the individual personality that resulted from the indoctrination of the masses in the principles of Marxism: 'The great misfortune, the root of all the evil to come, was the loss of faith in the value of personal opinions. People imagined that it was out of date to follow their own moral sense, that they must all sing the same tune in chorus, and live by other people's notions, the notions that were being crammed down everybody's throat.' (It is not surprising, in view of all this, that the supposedly liberal Khrushchev regime, which had only recently denounced the horrors of Stalinism, should have taken such exception to *Doctor Zhivago*. As Lazar Fleishman wrote: 'It called into question the theoretical basis for the existence of a socialist state – the doctrines of Marxism – and advanced an alternative set of values.')[37]

Marxism is represented in the novel, therefore, as a philosophy grounded in a materialist concept of nature, proceeding in accordance with the determinist modes of its own organic forces. Against this Pasternak puts forward both his view of man as one who relates freely to the world and to his destiny and his view of history as a record of the free action of man in furthering that destiny. History, as he sees it – he sees it through the eyes of Zhivago, Nikolai Vedniapin and Sima Tuntseva – records the freedom which is inherent in *individual* man and is manifested in his collaboration with nature and its changing processes. It is enacted in the lives of ordinary individuals – in the profundity of their inner lives, in their thoughts, actions and feelings, in their sufferings and their hopes – in all these they enact the motion and dynamics of historical being. 'Seeing a deep connection between the microcosm and the macrocosm, Pasternak ascribes to the individual personality an absolute meaning, yet not separately from life nor against it, but in union and harmony with it,' Andrei Sinyavsky writes. He cites a letter of Pasternak's in which the image of a child's mind evokes the wisdom which is attainable through individual consciousness. 'The amazing thing,' Pasternak writes, 'is that an innate talent is a child's model of the universe which has been placed in the heart in infancy, a teaching aid for understanding the world from within, in its best and most amazing aspect.'[38]

Czeslaw Milosz similarly saw Pasternak as defending the virtues of individual freedom in the face of the menacing forces of the totalitarian state. 'Pasternak,' he writes in his essay, 'On Pasternak Soberly', 'stood for the individual against whom the huge state apparatus turns in hatred with all its police, armies and rockets'.[39] He sees Yury's chosen vocation as poet as an act of protest against the collectivist character of the communist ideology: 'The only act left to Yury,' Milosz writes, 'is a poetic act, equated with the defence of the language menaced by the totalitarian double-talk or, in other words, with the defence of authenticity.'[40] Yet he detects a certain ambivalence in Yury's recognition of the historical necessity of the Revolution, despite its destruction of the very freedoms it sought to create. This Milosz attributes in some degree to the influence on Pasternak of the writings of Teilhard de Chardin, an influence Pasternak himself acknowledged in a letter to Jacqueline de Proyart.[41] 'No wonder Pasternak liked the writings of Teilhard de Chardin so much,' he writes. 'The French Jesuit also believed in the Christological character of lay history, and curiously combined Christianity with the Bergsonian "creative evolution" as well as with the Hegelian ascending movement.' This, Milosz suggests, underlies Yury's resigned acceptance of the Revolution as an inevitable, if tragic, outcome of the inexorable progress of history:

> The latent 'Teilhardism' of *Doctor Zhivago* makes it a Soviet novel in the sense that one might read into it an esoteric interpretation of the Revolution as opposed to the exoteric interpretation offered by official pronouncements. The historical tragedy is endowed with all the trappings of necessity working towards the ultimate good. Perhaps the novel is a tale about the individual versus Caesar, but with a difference: the new Caesar's might has its source not only in his legions. What could poor Yury do in the face of a system blessed by history and yet repugnant to his notions of good and evil? Intellectually, he was paralysed. He could only rely on his subliminal self, descend deeper than state-monopolised thought. Being a poet, he clutches at his belief in communion with ever reborn life. Life will take care of itself. Persephone always comes back from the underground, winter's ice is dissolved, dark eras are necessary as stages of preparation, life and history have a hidden Christian meaning. And suffering purifies.[42]

Nicola Chiaromonte, editor of *Tempo Presente* with Ignazio Silone, speaks of a tension in the novel between the theme of historical necessity and the emphasis on individual consciousness and freedom. It is, in substance, he says, 'a meditation on the infinite distance which separates the human conscience from the violence of history and permits a man to remain a man, to rediscover the track of truth that the whirlwind of events continually cancels and confuses'. 'One might say,' he writes, 'that all of *Doctor Zhivago* is dedicated to a description of this distance and to the insistent representation of the truth manifested in it.' He sees Pasternak as belonging in the Tolstoyan tradition of evoking the constancy of the individual's survival in history: 'At every point the novel draws its life from the will to oppose the true story of individuals to history as it is made by force and chance on the world's stage.' The novel, he says, 'proclaims that no matter who is entrusted with the material power, the power over consciences belongs to him who knows how to make himself its instrument and voice'.[43]

Like Tolstoy, or for that matter Dostoevsky as well, Pasternak sees progressive social and historical change as being rooted in the freedom of individual man and in the expression of that freedom through the practice of interhuman and communal love. Despite his temporary enthusiasm for the Bolsheviks, Nikolai Vedniapin condemns their emphasis on collectivism: 'The fashion nowadays is all for groups and societies of every sort.' 'It is always,' he says, 'a sign of mediocrity in people when they herd together, whether their group loyalty is to Soloviev or to Kant or Marx. The truth is sought only by individuals and they break with those who do not love it enough.' (Much of Uncle Nikolai's philosophy is, in fact, drawn from the writings of Soloviev and, as Martin Green has shown in his study of Pasternak, there are sufficiently strong parallels between the two to suggest that Nikolai was created as a fictional *alter ego* of the famous philosopher.)[44] Nikolai explicitly links the celebration of the free personality with the coming of Christ. 'History as we know it began with Christ,' he says. 'It was founded by him on the Gospels.' The two concepts he considers essential to the makeup of modern man – 'the ideas of free personality and of life regarded as sacrifice' – he attributes directly to the teaching of Christ: 'There was no history in this sense in the classical world. There you had blood and beastliness and cruelty and pock-marked Caligulas untouched by the suspicion that any man who enslaves others is inevitably second-rate ... It was not until after the coming of Christ that time and man could breathe freely.' Later as he discusses the natural cosmogonies of the ancient world, Nikolai again describes the coming of Christ as inaugurating the age of freedom when the destiny of individual man superseded that of the collective:

> Rome was a flea market of borrowed gods and conquered peoples, a bargain basement on two tiers – earth and heaven – slaves on one, gods on the other. Dacians, Herulians, Scythians, Sarmatians, Hyperboreans. Heavy, spokeless wheels, eyes sunk in fat, bestialism, double chins, illiterate emperors, fish fed on the flesh of learned slaves. Beastliness convoluted in a triple knot like guts. There were more people in the world than there have ever been since, all crammed into the passages of the Coliseum and all wretched.

And then into this tasteless heap of gold and marble He came, light-footed and clothed in light, with his marked humanity, his deliberate Galilean provincialism, and from that moment there were neither gods nor peoples, there was only man – man the carpenter, man the plough-man, man the shepherd with his flock of sheep at sunset, man whose name does not sound in the least proud but who is sung in lullabies and portrayed in picture galleries the world over.'

This theme is taken up in several of the Zhivago poems – especially those celebrating the birth of Christ – where the prophetic role of the artist and the phenomenon of creative individuality are both linked with the emergence of the Christian era in history. In the tenth stanza of 'Christmas Star', for example, the birth of Christ is seen as inaugurating a renaissance of intellectual and artistic freedom: 'In a strange vision all time to come/ Arose in the distance:/ All the thoughts, hopes, worlds of the centuries,/ The future of art galleries and of museums.' In the novel Sima Tuntseva compares the different conceptions of man in the Old and New Testaments and sees a fundamental difference between the emphasis on nations and peoples in the old dispensation and the emphasis on individual freedom in the new. In this passage she explores the significance of two Biblical events, the story of the return of the Israelites from their exile in Egypt from the Old Testament and the story of Christ's nativity from the New:

'In one case you have a national leader, the patriarch Moses, ordering the sea to withdraw, and at the stroke of his magic staff it parts and allows a whole nation – countless numbers, hundreds of thousands of people – to go through, and when the last man is across, it closes up again and submerges and drowns the pursuing Egyptians. The whole picture is in the ancient style – the elements obeying the magician, great jostling multitudes like Roman armies on the march, a people and a leader. Everything is visible, audible, deafening, tremendous.

In the other case you have a girl – a very commonplace figure who would have gone unnoticed in the ancient world – quietly, secretly, bringing forth a child, bringing forth life, bringing forth the miracle of life, the 'life of all' as he was afterwards called. The birth of her child is not only illegitimate from the standpoint of the scribes, it is also against the laws of nature. She gives birth not of necessity but by a miracle, by an inspiration. And from now on, the basis of life is no longer to be compulsion, it is to be the very same inspiration – that is what the New Testament offers – the unusual instead of the commonplace, the festive instead of the workaday, inspiration instead of compulsion.'

Like Tolstoy and Dostoevsky, Pasternak saw individual freedom as being rooted in the universal potentiality for love and this he saw, in turn, as constituting the essential message of the Christian faith. 'We have all become people only to the measure in which we have loved people and had the opportunity to love,' Pasternak wrote in *Safe Conduct*, his first autobiography. 'To love selflessly and unreservedly with a strength equal to the square of the distance – this,' he says, 'is the task of our hearts while we are children.'[45] Nikolai Vedniapin speaks of 'the love of one's neighbour' as 'the supreme form of living energy'. 'Once it fills the heart of man it has to overflow and spend itself,' he declares. That spirit of love, seen as the universal manifestation of individual freedom, is celebrated in Pasternak's poetry and prose as a continuous attestation of the presence of God in all existent being. It is the whole basis of the faith that is affirmed in his writings and ultimately the source of the triumph over suffering and death which they repeatedly proclaim.

'HOW PERFECT THY WORKS ARE!'

Pasternak's poetry and prose vividly evoke his sense of the presence of God in all existent being. Like Dostoevsky, he sees nature as visibly and tangibly manifesting the presence of the spiritual in the material – and by implication attesting to the Christian mystery of the Incarnation. He gives expression also to the older Jewish conception of life as a process of continuous creation, seeing all that exists as being continuously renewed through the benign influence of its Creator. His images evoke the continuity of both traditions. 'All the time,' Zhivago says, 'life, one, immense, identical throughout all its identifications and transformations, fills the universe and is continually reborn.' 'Life is never a material substance to be moulded,' he tells Liberius Mikulitsin. 'If you want to know, life is the principle of self-renewal, it is constantly renewing and remaking and changing and transfiguring itself, it is infinitely beyond your or my theories about it.' The theme of continuous renewal is further conveyed in the beautiful image of the motherhood of nature in Chapter 12: 'There seemed to be a close living connection between the birds and the tree, as if the rowan had watched them for a long time, refusing to do anything, but had in the end had pity on them, as though, like a foster mother, she had unbuttoned herself and offered them her breast.' It is conveyed also through the image in which Yury Zhivago sees himself as participating in the continuous activity of creation through his cultivation of the soil:

What happiness it is to work from dawn to dusk for your family and yourself, to build a roof over their heads, to till the soil to feed them, to create your own world, like Robinson Crusoe, in the imitation of the Creator of the universe, and to bring forth your life, as if you were your own mother, again and again.

Thomas Merton speaks of Pasternak's nature imagery as 'sacramental', as comparable to liturgical ritual in its symbolic revelation of the mysterious presence of the spiritual in the world of finite being. 'Pasternak,' he writes, 'is a prophet of the original cosmic revelation, one who sees symbols and figures of the inward spiritual world working themselves out in the mystery of the universe around him.' It is this 'inextricable union of symbolism and communion', he says, 'that gives Pasternak's vision of the world its liturgical and sacramental character (always remembering that his liturgy is entirely non-hieratic and that in him sacrament implies not so much established ritual form as living mystery)'.[46] 'In Holy Week', one of the Zhivago poems, illustrates this synthesis of sacramental and non-hieratic liturgical imagery. The poem combines the themes of seasonal change and religious renewal. Its images focus on the despair of the winter season, evoked through its metaphors of darkness, nakedness and cold, and its transformation through the life-renewing processes of springtime. It associates the theme of Spring's victory over winter with Christ's victory over death and shows all nature as participating in the liturgical rituals which commemorate Christ's Passion and Resurrection:

> It is still the dark of night
> And still so early in the world
> That the stars in the sky are without number
> And each is bright as day,
> And if it could, the earth
> Would sleep through Easter
> To the chanting of the Psalms.
>
> It is still the dark of night
> And still so early in the world
> That the square lies like an eternity
> Between the corner and the crossroads
> And dawn and warmth
> Are a thousand years away.
>
> The earth is still quite naked,
> Has nothing to wear at night
> While it rings the bells
> In response to the choir inside.

> And from Maundy Thursday
> Till Holy Saturday
> The water burrows into the river banks
> And spins the whirlpools.

The same theme pervades *When Skies Clear*, a collection of nature lyrics written in the same period as *Doctor Zhivago*, where once again images from nature directly evoke the immanence of God's presence in the universe. The poems are structured round a dialogue conducted between the poet and the world of nature. They embrace the familiar landscape of Peredelkino, his country home outside Moscow – Lake Ismalkovo, the river Setun, and the forests and hills of the region. Nature speaks through the poems, attesting in Hopkins-like fashion, to the wonder of God's creation and the transforming power of God's presence in the whole world of created being. Andrei Sinyavsky saw these poems as being deeply expressive of the poet's religious convictions, being far more than merely lyrical evocations of the beauty of the regional landscape. 'When Pasternak writes of springs and winters, rains and dawns,' he says, 'he is telling us about the nature of life itself, about the very existence of the world. He is confessing his faith in life – and this, I think, is the most important thing in his poetry generally, this is its moral foundation. Life to him is something unconditional, eternal, absolute; it is an all-pervasive element of the greatest miracle.'[47] Asserting the all-triumphant vitality of nature, the poems ultimately affirm the immortality of life itself. The following verses are from a poem entitled 'When It Clears Up', translated by the poet's younger sister, Lydia Pasternak Slater:

> When, after days of rainy weather,
> The heavy curtain is withdrawn,
> How festive is the sky, burst open!
> How full of triumph is the lawn!

> The wind dies down, the distance lightens,
> And sunshine spreads upon the grass;
> The steaming foliage is translucent,
> Like figures in stained window-glass.

> Thus from the church's narrow windows
> In glimmering crowns, on spreading wings
> Gaze into time in sleepless vigil
> Saints, hermits, prophets, angels, kings.

The whole wide world is a cathedral;
I stand inside, the air is calm,
And from afar at times there reaches
My ear the echo of a psalm.

World, Nature, Universe's Essence,
With secret trembling, to the end,
I will thy long and moving service
In tears of happiness attend.

Czeslaw Milosz has also demonstrated the manner in which Pasternak obliquely revealed his faith in the Christian doctrine of the Incarnation through the employment of nature imagery. Reiterating Yury Zhivago's conception of art as inspired utterance, Milosz sees this as being manifested as poetic receptivity to the wonders of creation. 'Pasternak's poetry,' he writes, 'is antispeculative, anti-intellectual. It is poetry of sensory perception. His worship of life meant a fascination with what can be called nature's moods – air, rain, clouds, snow in the streets, a detail changing thanks to the time of the day or night, to the season.'[48] He argues that Pasternak is a Christian writer whose beliefs are disclosed not through intellectual affirmation – but through 'atheological' celebrations of God's ordering presence in creation – a presence manifested in the perfection of its everyday reality:

> *Doctor Zhivago* is a Christian book, yet there is no trace in it of that polemic with the anti-Christian concept of man which makes the strength of Dostoevsky. Pasternak's Christianity is atheological. It is very difficult to analyse a Weltanschauung at all, but simply 'closeness to life', while in fact it blends contradictory ideas borrowed from extensive readings. Perhaps we should not analyse. Pasternak was a man spellbound by reality, which was for him miraculous. He accepted suffering because the very essence of life is suffering, death, and rebirth. And he treated art as a gift of the Holy Spirit.[49]

This celebration of the presence of God in nature leads to frequent metaphoric identifications of the poet himself with the objective world of natural being. 'In Pasternak's poetry one cannot distinguish between man and his surroundings or between living feeling and dead matter,' Andrei Sinyavsky writes. 'By means of the shorthand of metaphor, reality is depicted in the merging of heterogeneous parts, the intersections of facets and contours, as a single indivisible whole.' Contrasting him with Mayakovsky and Tsvetaeva, whose work he sees as predominantly an expression of the subjective voices of the poets themselves, Sinyavsky suggests that Pasternak's work is essentially an evocation of the poet's sense of oneness with the whole of objective being. 'While Mayakovsky and Tsvetaeva want to speak for the whole world in their person, ' he writes, 'Pasternak prefers that the world should speak for him and in his stead ... The poet's oneness with nature is his first and fundamental credo.'[50] It is essential, Nicola Chiaromonte says, that Pasternak's Christianity should be interpreted in the light of this subjective-objective fusion of the world of the individual spirit and the externality of objectified being. 'Tolstoyan and Dostoevskeyan motifs, and also not a little of Shestov and Berdyaev, come together in Pasternak's Christianity,' she writes. 'In the overall equilibrium of the work it is the Tolstoyan inspiration that predominates, particularly in the expression of religious emotion of the individual's dependence on the life of the cosmos and the noble pride that comes from this dependence.'[51] One of the most vivid instances of this unity of self and nature occurs in the chapter of *Doctor Zhivago* entitled 'Forest Brotherhood':

> Ever since his childhood Yury had been fond of woods seen at evening against the setting sun. At such moments he felt as if he too were being pierced by blades of light. As if the gift of the living spirit were streaming into his breast, piercing his being and coming out by his shoulders like a pair of wings. The archetype, which is informed in every child for life and seems for ever after to be the inward image of his personality, arose in him in its full primordial strength and compelled nature, the forest, the afterglow and everything else visible to be transfigured into a similarly primordial and all-embracing likeness of a girl. 'Lara.' Closing his eyes, he whispered and thought, addressing the whole of life, all God's earth, all the sunlit space spread out before him.

This whole theme finds powerful expression in Pasternak's treatment of the emotional and spiritual complexities of romantic love, as is intimated in the closing sentences of this passage from the novel. Yury's love for Lara Antipova dramatically exemplifies the yearning of the individual spirit to achieve oneness with the reality of external being. In *Safe Conduct* Pasternak spoke of love as the primordial life-force informing the whole of creation with the dynamism of its spirituality and infinitude. 'Love is as simple and absolute as consciousness and death,' he wrote. 'It is not a state of soul, but the first foundation of the universe. The fundamental and primordial principle, love is thus the equivalent of creation.' 'Art,' he declared, 'can conceive nothing higher than to lend its ear to the voice of love itself, that voice forever new and unprecedented.'[52] Love, he suggests, is the most potent attestation by man of the reality of the Creator's presence in creation. Thus Yury's love for Lara is described in images suggesting a paradise-like existence on earth: 'He had complained that

Heaven had cast him off but now the whole breadth of heaven leaned low over his bed holding out two strong white, woman's arms to him.' Lara seemed to him to embody in herself the perfection of God's creation: 'She was lovely by virtue of the matchlessly simple and swift line which the Creator at a single stroke had drawn round her and in this divine outline she had been handed over, like a child, tightly wound up in a sheet after its bath, into the keeping of his soul.' 'You could not communicate with life,' he reflects, 'but she was its representative, its expression, the gift of speech and hearing granted to inarticulate being.' Their love, Lara herself recalls at the end of the novel, was willed by the whole of nature:

> 'Oh what a love it was, how free, how new, like nothing else on earth!'
> They really thought what other people sing in songs.
> It was not out of necessity that they loved each other, 'enslaved by passion', as lovers are described. They loved each other because everything around them willed it, the trees and clouds and the sky over their heads and the earth under their feet. Perhaps their surrounding world, the strangers they met in the street, the landscapes drawn up for them to see on their walks, the rooms in which they lived or met, were even more pleased with their love than they were themselves.
> Well, of course, it had been just this that had united them and had made them so akin! Never, never, not even in their moments of richest and wildest happiness, had they lost the sense of what is highest and most ravishing – joy in the whole universe, its form, its beauty, the feeling of their own belonging to it, being part of it.

There are two fundamental affirmations in Pasternak's treatment of this theme, each of which derives from the essentially Christian context in which it is conceived. The first is his emphasis on the understanding and wisdom that comes from love, by virtue of its attestation of the presence of God in material being and its disclosure of the universal meaningfulness that springs from this. In his love for Lara, Zhivago finds the key to life's mysteries: 'The moments when passion visited their doomed human existence like a breath of timelessness were moments of revelation, of even greater understanding of life and of themselves.' His words recall those of Father Zossima to his monks ... 'If you love everything you will perceive the divine mystery in things. Once you perceive it you will begin to comprehend it better every day.' 'I have often tried,' Yury tells Lara, 'to define the enchantment of which you sowed the seeds in me – that gradually fading light and dying sound which have spread throughout the whole of my being and have become to me the means of understanding everything else in the world through you.' Secondly, he suggests, love has within it the potential to surmount the tragedy and suffering that are inherent in the nature of temporal life. Both aspects – the tragedy and the triumph – are conveyed simultaneously in the magnificent lyrical imagery of Yury's monologue after Lara's departure with Komarovsky:

> Grief had sharpened Yury's vision and quickened his perception a hundredfold. The very air surrounding him seemed unique. The evening breathed compassion like a friendly witness of all that had befallen him. As if there had never been such a dusk before and evening were falling now for the first time in order to console him in his loneliness and bereavement. As if the valley were not always girded by woods growing on the surrounding hills and facing away from the horizon, but the trees had only taken up their places now, rising out of the ground on purpose to offer their condolences ...
>
> He went into the house. A double monologue was going on in his mind, two different kinds of monologue, the one dry and business-like, the other, addressed to Lara, like a river in flood.
>
> 'Now I'll go to Moscow,' ran his thoughts. 'The first job is to survive. Not let insomnia get the better of me. Not go to bed at all. Work all through the night till I drop. Yes, and another thing, light the stove in the bedroom at once, not to freeze to-night.'
>
> But there was also another inward conversation. 'I'll stay with you a little, my unforgettable delight, for as long as my arms and my hands and my lips remember you. I'll weep for you so that my lament will be lasting and worthy of you. I'll write your memory into an image of infinite pain and grief. I'll stay here till this is done, then I too will go. This is how I'll trace your image. I'll trace it on paper as the sea, after a fearful storm has churned it up to its foundations, leaves the traces of the strongest, furthest reaching wave on the shore. Seaweed, shells, pumice, all the lightest debris, all those things of least weight which it could lift from its bed, are cast up in a broken line on the sand. This line endlessly stretching into the distance is the tide's high-watermark. This is how you were cast up in my life, my love, my pride, this is how I'll write of you.'

'THERE WILL BE NO DEATH!'

Love conquers suffering: ultimately it conquers death. This is the truth discovered by Tolstoy's Prince Andrei as he lies wounded on the battlefield. 'Love hinders death,' he declares. 'Love is life. All, all that I understand, I

understand only because I love. All is, all exists, only because I love. All is
bound up in love alone. Love is God and dying means for me, a particle of
love, to go back to the eternal and universal source of love.' That same truth is
reiterated by Yury Zhivago as he comforts the dying Anna Gromeko with an
assurance of her immortality: 'You in others are yourself, your soul. This is
what you are. This is what your consciousness has breathed and lived on and
enjoyed throughout life, – Your soul, your immortality, your life in others.'
This is the central message of Christianity, as the novel repeatedly affirms.
Christ, Nikolai Vedniapin declares, has freed man by teaching him to transform his life through love. Love, which is epitomised in the person of Christ,
is the source of man's immortality. 'How many things in the world deserve
our loyalty?' he asks. 'Very few indeed.' 'I think,' he says, 'one should be loyal
to immortality which is another word for life, a stronger word for it. One must
be true to immortality, true to Christ.' It is this conviction that enables Yury
to assure Anna Gromeko that death is not the end but the beginning of life –
eternal life: 'There will be no death, says St John, and just look at the simplicity of his argument. There will be no death because the past is over; that's
almost like saying there will be no death because death is already done with,
it's old and we are tired of it. What we need is something new and that new
thing is life eternal.' In his delirium later he composes a poem in which he
contrasts the darkness and corruption of death with the spring-like renewal of
life which is achieved through love:

> The subject of his poem was neither the entombment nor the resurrec-
> tion but the days between; the title was 'Turmoil'.
> He had always wanted to describe how for three days the black, raging,
> worm-filled earth had assailed the deathless incarnation of love, storm-
> ing it with rocks and rubble – as waves fly and leap at a sea coast, cover
> and submerge it – how for three days the black hurricane of earth
> raged, advancing and retreating.
> Two lines kept coming into his head:
> 'We are glad to be near you.'
> and
> 'Time to wake up.'
> Near him, touching him, were hell, corruption, dissolution, death;
> yet equally near him were the spring and Mary Magdalene and life. –
> And it was time to awake. Time to awake and get up. Time to arise,
> time for the resurrection.

Images of suffering and death alternate with images of love, hope and
immortality throughout the Zhivago poems. The very name of their author is

suggestive of immortal life. In his essay, 'Dr Life and His Guardian Angel' Edmund Wilson pointed out that the word *zhivago* means 'living' in Old Church Slavonic and is used in the sense of 'life everlasting' in the Orthodox liturgy. (In the same essay he spoke of the publication of *Doctor Zhivago* as 'one of the great events in man's literary and moral history'.)[53] The essential affirmation of the poems is that love – 'our life in others' – is the source of faith and the foundation of all hope. That hope, the poems suggest, is epitomised in the miracle of Christ's Resurrection, just as the torment of mortal suffering is epitomised in his Passion and Crucifixion. Gospel imagery is constantly intertwined in the poems with images from nature suggestive both of the death of life and its persistent potential for resurgence and renewal. The poem 'Earth', for example, was written in 1943, on the occasion of Pasternak's mother's last illness and death. At that time he wrote to his cousin, Olga Freidenberg: 'Only in a state of well-being can people grieve, despair, feel dejected. In moments of stunning misfortune life is flipped over like a coin to reveal its true meaning.'[54] His grief is poignantly conveyed in these lines from the poem: 'April knows a thousand stories/ Of human sorrow,/ And along the fence the twilight grows chill/ Spinning out the tale.' His suffering is relieved by his expectation of the comfort and reassurance that comes from human love and companionship. This is beautifully expressed in the poem through an image which recalls Christ in the company of his disciples shortly before his last agony and crucifixion. This image is intertwined with images of the reawakening of nature in springtime:

> Then why does the horizon weep in mist
> And the dung smell bitter?
> Surely it is my calling
> To see that the distances should not lose heart,
> And that beyond the limits of the town
> The earth should not feel lonely?
>
> That is why in early spring
> My friends and I gather together
> And our evenings are farewells
> And our parties are testaments,
> So that the secret stream of suffering
> May warm the cold of life.

A similar spirit of hopefulness pervades the two Magdalene poems where the theme is the love that springs from repentance and the forgiveness of sin. In a passage from the novel which closely complements the theme of these poems, Sima Tuntseva condemns the Church for its excessive concentration on the corruptions of sexual immorality, and she speaks of a tolerance and charity in Christ's love for the Magdalene she feels is insufficiently emphasised in Christian ethics. She describes the depth of love that is manifested in Mary's repentance of her sin: 'She begs Christ to accept her tears of repentance and be moved by the sincerity of her sighs, so that she may dry His most pure feet with her hair ... "Let me kiss Thy most pure feet and water them with the hair of my head, which covered Eve and sheltered her when, her ears filled with sound, she was afraid in the cool of the day in Paradise."' The poem reenacts the scene where Mary begs Christ's forgiveness; it emphasises the infinite mercy and the prospect of salvation that endlessly await the penitent soul:

> And I will fall at its feet,
> Silent and dazed, biting my lips.
> Your arms will spread out to the ends of the cross
> To embrace too many.
>
> For whom in all the world
> Is your embrace so wide,
> For whom so much torment,
> So much power?
>
> In all the world
> Are there so many souls?
> So many lives?
> So many villages, rivers and woods?
>
> Those three days will pass
> But they will push me down into such emptiness
> That in the frightening interval
> I shall grow up to the Resurrection.

It is significant, in the same context, that Pasternak uses the familiar symbolism of life-renewal in nature to intimate the prospect of immortality that lies beyond the grave. The image of the Magdalene is recalled in the scene where Yury is laid out in death, his body surrounded by flowers. The scene prompts the reflection by the narrator that the green life of the earth holds the solution to life's mysteries and in this, he suggests, may lie the significance of the Gospel image of Mary Magdalene mistaking the newly risen Christ for a gardener:

In these hours when the silence, unfilled by any ceremony, was made almost tangibly oppressive by a sense of absence, only the flowers took the place of the singing and the psalms.

They did more than blossom and smell sweet. In unison, like a choir, perhaps hastening decomposition, they unstintingly poured out their fragrance and, imparting something of their scented strength to everyone, seemed to be accomplishing a ritual.

The kingdom of plants can easily be thought of as the nearest neighbour of the kingdom of death. Perhaps the mysteries of transformation and the enigmas of life which so torment us are concentrated in the green of the earth, among the trees in graveyards and the flowering shoots springing from their beds. Mary Magdalene, not at once recognising Jesus risen from the grave, took Him for the gardener.

The ultimate significance of Christianity, Pasternak concludes, is that it has unravelled the riddle of history by solving its greatest mystery: the mystery of death. 'Now what is history?' asks Nikolai Vedniapin. 'Its beginning is that of the centuries of systematic work devoted to the solution of the enigma of death, so that death itself may eventually be overcome. This is why people write symphonies, and why they discover mathematical infinity and electromagnetic waves.' 'Now you can't advance in this direction without a certain upsurge of spirit,' he declares. 'You can't make such discoveries without spiritual equipment, and for this, everything necessary has been given us in the Gospels.' The 'spiritual equipment' of which he speaks consists in the two principles that were cited previously and are worth reiterating in the present context. The first, he says, is 'the love of one's neighbour – the supreme form of living energy'; the second the idea of life regarded as sacrifice, the freely chosen subordination of the self to the will of God. Both constitute the essential elements in the Christian vision of life. Both principles are evoked in 'Gethsemane' the last of the Zhivago poems. The poem emphasises Christ's humanness, his weakness and susceptibility to despair, but its main theme is his ultimate triumph over suffering and death – a victory, it suggests, which is achieved through the infinite potentialities of the spirit that are released through the free exercise of self-sacrifice and love. By his death he has solved the mystery of history ... 'the passage of centuries is like a parable/ ... the centuries will float to me out of the darkness/ And I shall judge them.':

The night was a kingdom of annihilation,
Of non-being,
The whole world seemed uninhabited,
And only this garden was a place for the living.

He gazed into the black abyss,
Empty, without beginning or end.
Sweating blood, he prayed to His Father
That this cup of death should pass him by.

Having tamed his agony with prayer
He went out through the garden gate.
There, overcome by drowsiness,
The disciples lay slumped in the grass.

He woke them: 'God has granted you to live in my time,
And you loll about like this …
The hour of the Son of Man has struck,
He will deliver himself into the hands of sinners. …

You see, the passage of the centuries is like a parable
And catches fire on its way.
In the name of its terrible majesty
I shall go freely, through torment, down to the grave.

And on the third day I shall rise again.
Like rafts down a river, like a convoy of barges,
The centuries will float to me out of the darkness.
And I shall judge them.'

7
'Imitation of Christ':
The Poetry of Osip Mandelstam

There: the Eucharist, a gold sun,
hung in the air – an instant of splendour.
Here nothing should be heard but the Greek syllables –
the whole world held in the hands like a plain apple.

The solemn height of the holy office; the light
of July in the rotunda under the cupola;
so that we may sigh from full hearts, outside time,
for that little meadow where time does not flow.

And the Eucharist spreads like an eternal noon;
all partake of it, everyone plays and sings,
and in each one's eyes the sacred vessel
brims over with inexhaustible joy.

These lines from Mandelstam's poem, 'The Eucharist', celebrate the theme which, directly or indirectly, informs all of his poetry: the miracle of the Incarnation – the mystery of the Word Made Flesh. Described by Sidney Monas in the Introduction to the first collected edition of his poems in English[1] as 'the most Christian of modern poets', Mandelstam in fact was, born a Jew but converted to Orthodox Christianity sometime in his early twenties, largely under the influence of his friend, the priest-theologian, Pavel Florinsky, and his fellow-poets, Viktor Khlebnikov and Marina Tsvetaeva. Thenceforward, his poetry reflects the combined influences of both the Jewish and Christian traditions, together with the traditions of Hellenist culture for which he had also formed a deep attachment since early childhood.

His poem, 'The Eucharist', reinvokes the rituals of the Orthodox liturgy, each of its three stanzas being built around three key stages in the celebration of the Mass. The first is the consecration of the bread and wine, following which the priest raises the chalice and host before the worshipping congregation. The moment of the elevation is symbolically linked by Mandelstam with the presence of eternity in time, the Eucharist being compared to the golden sun that never sets – a common image in icon painting for the material presence of the infinite and the eternal. The second stanza is focused on the epiclesis, the moment in the ceremony when the priest, with arms uplifted, prays for the coming of the Holy Spirit and the fulfilment of the Eucharistic miracle. The congregation, feeling transported beyond the boundaries of their temporal existence by this momentary glimpse of the presence of the timeless, join with the celebrant in affirming its wonder and its mystery. The third stanza reenacts the Communion of the Faithful, the stage when all participate in the feast of the Eucharist and, through prayer and song, give testimony to its 'inexhaustible joy'. The poem establishes the centrality of the theme of the Incarnation in Mandelstam's poetry. It issues in three sub-themes which will be addressed in the present section of this chapter: firstly, the idea of the poetic *logos* as a phenomenon which simultaneously embodies and discloses the meaning of the Incarnation; secondly, the universal manifestation of the Incarnation as the immanent presence of God in all material reality; and thirdly, the mysterious interpenetration of the timeless and the temporal which it signifies.

'I find it difficult to name what precisely had shaped M's personality because his basic ideas cannot be put into simple words,' Nadezhda Mandelstam wrote in her Memoirs. 'It was really a question of his view of poetry as a gift from above.'[2] She spoke of the sense of the integrity of all being as a fundamental principle of the Acmeist movement, of which Mandelstam was a prominent member, together with Akhmatova and Gumilev. This integrity, she suggests, is especially evidenced in the process of artistic creativity. 'The poet's mode of thought,' she writes, 'is the product of all sides of his personality: the intellectual, physiological, spiritual and emotional, a synthesis of what he perceives through the senses, his instincts and desires, and the higher aspirations of his spirit.'[3] In the case of the Acmeists, she says, this whole process was reinforced by the all-informing presence of faith in their poetry – an impassioned faith in the holiness of all living things, in their disclosure of God's immanent presence in the material world. 'I believe,' she writes, 'that the cleansing power of lyric verse flows from the poet's acceptance of life with its sorrows and misfortunes, from his certainty that through ordinary everyday existence one achieves awareness of another life, thus coming to know the Creator through what He has created.'[4] Contrasting the Acmeist outlook with the mystical – the one, she suggests, seeks God in the concretion of earthly reality, the other seeks God beyond the realm of the material and the empirical – she writes of Mandelstam's sense of the spirituality inherent in all objectified being:

> To M. as a self-styled Acmeist, three-dimensional space and life on earth were essential because he wanted to do his duty by his 'host' – he

felt that he was here to build, which can only be done in three dimensions. This explains his attitude towards the world of things. In his
view this world was not hostile to the poet or – as he put it – the
builder, because things are there to be built from ... Berdyaev often
speaks of man's higher destiny and his creative powers – but he does
not define the nature of this creativity. This is probably because he
lacked the artist's sense of things and words as inert matter to be used
in building. Berdyaev's experience was that of the mystic and it took
him to the limit of the world of things. The artist's intuition is similar
to the mystic's, but it reveals the Creator through his creation, God
through man.[5]

This process of identifying through the concrete was described by
Mandelstam himself in his essay, 'Pushkin and Scriabin', as the artist's 'imitation of Christ', his reenactment through language of the miracle of the
Incarnation.[6] Language, he suggests, by virtue of its radical materiality, has
inherent within it the spirituality and informing presence of God. The disclosure of truth through the poetic *logos* is, therefore, a sacred activity, an 'eternal
return to the single creative act that began our historical era', i.e., the
Incarnation. This principle, which is the fundamental conviction behind his
entire poetic creed, is elaborated in this notable passage from the essay:

> Christian art is always based on the great idea of redemption. It is an
> 'imitation of Christ' infinitely varied in all its manifestations, an eternal
> return to the single creative act that began our historical era. Christian
> art is free. It is 'art for art's sake' in its fullest meaning. No necessity of
> any kind, not even the highest, darkens its bright inner freedom, for its
> prototype, that which it imitates, is the very redemption of the world by
> Christ. Thus, neither sacrifice, nor redemption in art, but rather the
> free and joyous imitation of Christ is the keystone of Christian aesthet-
> ics. Art cannot be sacrifice, because a sacrifice has already been made; it
> cannot be redemption because the world, along with the artist, has
> already been redeemed. What remains? Joyous communion with God,
> like some game played by the Father and his children, some blind-
> man's-bluff or hide-and-seek of the spirit! The divine illusion of
> redemption in Christian art is explained precisely by the game in which
> the Divinity plays with us, allowing us to wander the pathways of mys-
> tery so that we might happen upon salvation on our own, as it were,
> having experienced catharsis, redemption in art. Christian artists are like
> men free of the idea of redemption, neither its slaves nor preachers.
> Our entire two-thousand year old culture, thanks to the marvellous

charity of Christianity, is the world's release into freedom for the sake
of play, for spiritual joy, for the free 'imitation of Christ'.

Christianity adopted a completely free relationship to art which no
human religion either before or since has been able to do.[7]

Commenting on this essay, the Polish scholar, Ryszard Przybylski wrote:
'The poet (i.e. Mandelstam) always remembered that simplest of truths, which
is frequently forgotten even by Christian philosophers: man is a "thinking
body". Because he remembered this he never lost sight of the holiest mystery
of Christianity – the Incarnation of the Logos and the consequent commandment to imitate Christ, the God who started communicating with people man-
to-man, as it were, by means of speech.'[8] A poem which Mandelstam wrote
during his exile in Voronezh beautifully conveys the notion of poetic creativity
as an artistic 'imitation of Christ' and a reenactment of the Incarnation. Again
employing the imagery of the Eucharist, the poem unites two concepts; the
bread of the Eucharist and the poetic logos are combined in the compound
expression 'loaf-word.' Domestic and liturgical imagery together suggest a
process of spiritual revitalisation and self-renewal which is common both to
the experience of faith and to the act of poetic creativity:

> As the bread sponge rises,
> Fine at first.
> And the domestic soul
> Grows mad from the heat –
>
> So, flooded with encircling heat,
> The cupolas rise
> From the cherubs' table
> Like Sophias of bread.
>
> In order to coax a miraculous yield from the dough
> By force or by caress,
> Time – the imperial shepherd boy –
> Catches the round loaf-word.
>
> And the stale stepson of the ages
> Finds his place –
> The shrivelling extra chunk
> Of breads already taken out.

In his essay, 'The Word and Culture', Mandelstam had similarly spoken of
the word as 'flesh and bread' and had prophesied: 'Whoever shall raise the
word on high and confront time with it, as the priest displays the Eucharist,

shall be a second Joshua of Nun.'⁹ The full implications of this will be
addressed presently; for the moment it is important to point to two further
analogies used by Mandelstam to represent poetic creativity as an incarnational
process by which material reality is penetrated by the spiritual. In a number of
poems images of matter transformed by light are used to communicate this
theme. In the poem, for example, which begins 'How I wish I could fly' a
whispered word (Mandelstam frequently suggested that his poems originated
as whispered sound) becomes a ray of starlight which transfigures the earthly
reality that it penetrates. The poet seeks to be one with the starlight, with the
source of all truth and wisdom, with the Creator of life:

> How I wish I could fly
> where no one could see me,
> behind the ray of light
> leaving no trace.
>
> But you – let light encircle you.
> That's the one happiness.
> Learn from a star the meaning
> of light.
>
> If it's a ray, if it's light,
> that's only because
> the whisper and chatter of lovers
> strengthen and warm it.
>
> And I want to tell you
> that I'm whispering,
> I'm giving you to the ray,
> little one, in whispers.

The paradox of matter informed by spirit, and of the temporal informed by
the timeless, is similarly conveyed through the use of musical imagery in a
number of poems. Images of silence generally signify the chaos and disorder of
primordial being or the preconscious existence of the disembodied soul in
Mandelstam's poetry. Correspondingly, the image of silence transformed into
sound generally signifies the creative process by which the formless acquires
form and the disembodied spirit takes shape as material reality. In his essay,
'Pushkin and Scriabin' he differentiates between the classical and Christian
conceptions of this process, pointing in both instances to the employment of
musical analogies to communicate its complexities. He suggests the pure
melody of Hellenism, which signified the pure spirituality of the 'I', became

the harmony of Christianity, representing the concept of embodied spirit, of eternity in time as comprehended in its central myth, the mystery of the Incarnation. Scriabin's music, he suggests, epitomised the spirit of Christian harmony:

> Scriabin's art is directly connected with the historical task of Christianity that I call the Hellenisation of death, and through that task it acquires its profound meaning ... there is music which contains in itself the atoms of our being. Just as pure melody (*melos*) corresponds to the unique feeling of individuality as it was known in Hellas, so harmony characterises the complex post-Christian sense of the 'I'. For the world not implicated in the Fall, harmony was a kind of forbidden fruit. The metaphysical essence of harmony was most closely linked with the Christian concept of time. Harmony as eternity crystallised, harmony contained in a cross-section of time, in that cross-section of time which knows only Christianity ... the mystics energetically reject the idea of eternity in time, assuming that this cross-section is perceptible only to the righteous, affirming that eternity is the Kantian category cloven by the Seraph's sword. The centre of gravity of Scriabin's music lies in harmony: harmonic architectonics.[10]

This whole theme is explored in the poem 'Silentium' where the musical analogies of both the classical and Christian traditions are used to underline the fundamental precept that all creativity is ultimately the product of love. The central image in the poem is that of the Goddess of Love, Aphrodite, whose birth symbolises the unity of being, the harmony and order, that comes from love. That harmony, the poem suggests, is epitomised in the transformation of word into music, of the poetic *logos* into the perfection of sound to which it aspires. The first stanza describes the emergence of word and music from the silence of formless being. The second celebrates the birth of the Goddess from this primal chaos of formlessness, which is symbolised by the ocean foam, an image from Botticelli's painting of the birth of Aphrodite. The third stanza expresses the spirit's nostalgia for the silence from which it emerged. The poem concludes with an assertion that form, speech and music are rooted in the chaos and formlessness in which they originate – not in an otherworldly realm of being remote from its disordered reality. For the poet, as for the religious believer, the inference to be drawn is the necessary interpenetration of spirit and matter, of order and chaos, of speech and silence, of the real and the ideal:

> It still has not been born,
> it is both music and the word,

and therefore of all living things
the indestructible connection.

The breasts of the sea breathe peacefully,
but like a madman day is bright,
and the pale lilac of the foam
lies in its dark and azure vessel.

And my lips will attain
their original dumbness,
like a crystalline tone
that is pure from birth.

Remain as foam, Aphrodite,
and turn words into music,
make heart ashamed of heart,
fused with primordial life.

The more fundamental inference for the poet, however, is that poetry has its genesis in love and that what it communicates primarily is the poet's loving attention to the reality of existential being. 'That conviction,' Przybylski writes, 'is the foundation of Mandelstam's poetics; he believed that the poet, imitating God, creates poetry out of love, for it was from love that He created the world. A poem is a witness to love of life, a great paean to the three-dimensional cage, but if that love is to last through the generations it must be named, which is to say, it must pass from the abyss of indefiniteness into the human world.'[11] Nadezhda Mandelstam spoke of a 'sacramental' quality in Mandelstam's poetry, indicating its embodied attestation of the sanctity of all that exists. Recalling the years she devoted to preserving his work and preparing it for eventual publication, she writes: 'In the years when we preserved M's verse we scarcely dared hope, but we never ceased to believe in its rebirth. It was only this faith that kept us going. And what was it but faith in the abiding value of poetry and its sacramental nature.'[12] Mandelstam himself, in 'Morning of Acmeism', spoke of the reverence and piety with which the poet addresses the world of objective, material being:

Genuine piety before the three dimensions of space is the first condition of successful building: to regard the world neither as a burden nor as an unfortunate accident, but as a God-given place. Indeed, what can you say about an ungrateful guest who lives off his host, taking advantage of his hospitality, all the while despising him to the depths of his soul, thinking only of how to deceive him? Building is possible only in the name of the 'three dimensions', for they are the conditions of all architecture. That is why the architect must be a good stay-at-home, and the Symbolists were poor architects. To build means to conquer emptiness, to hypnotise space. The handsome arrow of the Gothic belltower rages because its function is to stab the sky, to reproach it for its emptiness.[13]

Joseph Brodsky spoke of a particularly intensive lyrical quality in Mandelstam's poetry, and saw this as having a profound moral and ethical significance. 'It was the immense intensity of lyricism in Mandelstam's poetry which set him apart from his contemporaries,' he writes. 'For lyricism is the ethics of language,' he says, 'and the superiority of this lyricism to anything that could be achieved within human interplay, of whatever denomination, is what makes for a work of art and lets it survive.'[14] The whole Acmeist movement was based on this radical concept of poetic lyricism. The Acmeist poets sought their inspiration in the dynamism of the phenomenal world, as opposed to the relative stasis of the noumenal or the divine that was celebrated in Symbolist poetry. They opposed the abstract, otherworldly mysticism of the Symbolists, concentrating on the lyrical celebration of objective, concrete, tangible and visible reality. In Mandelstam's case such convictions were greatly reinforced by the Polish/Hasidic culture he inherited from his Jewish parents, with its persistent emphasis on the worship of the Creator through his revealed presence in the created universe. (This is a quality he shares with his fellow-countryman, Boris Pasternak, as already indicated, and with the Australian novelist, Patrick White, as will be shown in a later chapter.) For Mandelstam this merged easily with his adopted Christian faith, the Hasidic principle of the immanence or indwelling of the spirit in material creation being wholly compatible with the Christian doctrine of the Incarnation. Thus, in 'Morning of Acmeism' he speaks of poetic creativity as being governed by the 'law of identity', i.e, by the poet's identification of his own subjective consciousness with the objectivity of God's creation:

> $A=A$: what a magnificent theme for poetry! Symbolism languished and yearned for the law of identity. Acmeism made it its slogan and proposed its adoption instead of the ambiguous *a realibus ad realiora*.
>
> The capacity for astonishment is the poet's greatest virtue. Yet how can we not be astonished by the law of identity, the most fruitful of all poetic laws? Whoever has experienced reverence and astonishment before this law is a true poet. Hence, having recognised the sovereignty of the law of identity poetry receives, absolutely and unconditionally, lifelong feudal claims over all existence. Logic is the kingdom of the unexpected. To think logically is to be perpetually astonished. We have

come to love the music of proof. Logical connection for us is not some popular song about a finch, but a choral symphony, so difficult and so inspired that the conductor must exert all his energy to keep the performers under his control.

How convincing the music of Bach! What power of proof! The artist must prove and prove endlessly. The artist worthy of his calling cannot accept anything on faith alone, that is too easy, too dull ... We cannot fly, we can ascend only those towers which we build ourselves.[15]

This, as Ryszard Przybylski has commented, is essentially a religious, and specifically a Christian, conception of the artistic process. '*Principium identitatis*,' he writes, 'does not exclude but, on the contrary, implies a religious understanding of the world ... For Mandelstam Christ was not a symbol, but a person, a thinking body, the God-man whose life allowed us to resolve the problem of symbolism: God became man because, after the tragic conflicts with men in the era of the Old Testament, with Job in particular, He was forced to seek a common language with man.'[16] The key to this whole issue, as Nadezhda Mandelstam has shown, lies in the complexities and paradoxes of the temporal, or more specifically, the antinomies of the temporal and the timeless. In *Hope Abandoned*, she writes:

For M., dwelling on the passage of time was not an end in itself but rather, perhaps, an aspect of his quest for the Spirit, of his thirst for grace ... Sometimes it was by way of trying to get a sense of eternity, with the Eucharist seen as the only moment that lasts eternally ... 'The passing moment,' he writes, 'has all the pressures of the ages bearing down on it and yet remains precisely where it is.' In a sense this applied to eternity as well, since he understood it as the everlasting 'present moment', like the Eucharist, or as harmony ('harmony is crystallised eternity'). He did not share the view of the mystics who believe that eternity is outside time; for him the eternal passing moment existed in time. It must be as a result of M.'s influence that I believe such harmony as one may create on earth is a manifestation of the spirit living in eternity.[17]

Joseph Brodsky has commented on the two images of the infinite most commonly employed in Mandelstam's poetry: the poetic *logos* and the sea. 'The common parent of these two elements, it must be remembered, is time,' he writes.[18] What he points to is the paradox comprehended both in the idea of the Incarnation and in the *logos*; each embodies the mysterious disclosure of the eternal in the temporal, the Eternal Now of the Eucharist being complemented by similar intimations of the timeless in the poetic image. This yearning for the timeless is the subject of a beautiful short lyric written by Mandelstam at Koktebel in the Crimea in 1920. The poem opens with an image of beauty as 'heaviness' transformed into 'tenderness'. The 'rose of time' – a Dantesque image – is burdensome, like the heaviness of time and space. Just as a bee draws honey from the flower, the poet draws out the tenderness that transforms the heaviness of time and space into the lightness of spirit. Both images – the heaviness of materiality and the lightness, tenderness and spirituality of the infinite – are juxtaposed throughout the poem to emphasise their interpenetration both in the conditions of time and in the conditions of art. These conditions are changed only by death, symbolised in the poem as a sunset marking the end of existence in time. The poem culminates with a confession of faith: the poet yearns to be freed from the heaviness of his earthly existence, but simultaneously recognises that the timelessness for which he longs is already disclosed in the stillness of the temporal – a stillness crystallised in the heaviness and tenderness of the rose. Like all material phenomena, the rose embodies the immanence of the eternal in the temporal, God's presence in creation. As Sergei Gorodetsky wrote: 'For the Acmeists the rose has once more become beautiful in and of itself. Its petals are beautiful, its fragrance and colour, and not the thoughts, correspondences, mystical love and other things of that sort that are evoked by it.'[19] The poem celebrates the beauty of the rose, seeing in that beauty the evidence both of the stillness and mutability that its immanent materiality represents:

> Heaviness and tenderness – sisters: the same features.
> Bees and wasps suck the heavy rose,
> Man dies, heat leaves the sand, the sun
> of yesterday is borne on a black stretcher.
>
> Of the heavy honeycomb, the tender webs – easier
> to hoist a stone than to say your name!
> Only one purpose is left me, but it is golden:
> to free myself of the burden, time.
>
> I drink the roiled air like a dark water.
> Time has been plowed; the rose was earth. In a slow
> whirlpool the heavy tender roses,
> rose heaviness, rose tenderness, are plaited in double wreaths.

It will be shown presently how this affirmation of the temporal as a material disclosure of the timeless manifests itself as a celebration of the essential joyousness of Christianity in Mandelstam's poetry. That quality is particularly conveyed in the Armenian cycle of poems and in some associated works that he completed in the last, tragic decade of his life. These will be examined in the third section of this chapter. But, firstly, it is necessary to examine the impact on his poetry of the cataclysmic social and political upheaval that followed the Revolution of 1917 and that radically changed his own life and the lives of his people for decades to come. In this whole process he recognised a fundamental rejection of the values inherent in the heritage of Russian culture and a denial of the synthesis of material and spiritual (i.e. incarnational) principles at the heart of the Christian traditions that were central to that culture.

'THE DARKENED SUN'

Poets greeted the Russian Revolution with wild shouts, hysterical tears, laments, enthusiastic frenzy, curses. But Mandelstam alone understood the pathos of events, the scale of what was occurring.

Ilya Ehrenberg.[20]

In 'The Young Levite', a poem he wrote in 1917, shortly after the Revolution, Mandelstam gave full expression to his fears for the future of his country under the dominance of the new materialist ideology of communism. Through the voice of the young Levite, he foretells the destruction of the city (Jerusalem/St Petersburg), seeing ominous signs in the yellow sky above it of the encroaching shadows of the dark sun by which its light will shortly be eclipsed. The yellow sky is generally interpreted as signifying the Incarnation, the 'joy of Judaea', while the black sun, an apocalyptic image from scripture,[21] signifies the materialist ideology which seeks to suppress the spiritual traditions of the people. The image of the dead Christ, swathed in his burial clothes, together with the nihilistic gloom conveyed by the 'murk of non-being', intimate the universal devastation shortly to descend on Russia. Significantly, however, the imagery of candlelight provides a brief foretokening of the Resurrection and the people's eventual release from their suffering:

Amongst the priests a young Levite,
On morning watch he delayed long,
The Jewish night thickened above him,
And the ruined temple created gloom.

He said: 'The sky is a worried yellow,
Surely over the Euphrates night, you may run about!'
And the old thought: 'That is not our guilt,
Lo! the black and yellow light. Lo, the joy of Judaea.'

He was with us when on the bank of a stream,
We swathed the Sabbath in precious linen,
And with heavy seven-sided candles
Illumined the Jerusalem night and the murk of non-being.

The debasements of Bolshevism must be traced, Mandelstam wrote in his essay, 'Humanism and the Present', to the secularist ideology which regarded the spiritual as ultimately a product of material reality. 'There are epochs,' he writes, 'which maintain that man is insignificant, that man is to be used like bricks and mortar, that man should be used for building things, not vice-versa – that things can be built for man. Social architecture is measured against the scale of man. Sometimes it may turn against man to enhance its own grandeur by feeding on his humiliation and insignificance.'[22] His poem, 'The Twilight of Freedom' dwells on this theme of the degradation of the individual under communism and evokes the social turmoil already evident in the Soviet Union in the immediate aftermath of the Revolution. Allusions to the New Testament in the poem form a highly intricate symbolic pattern to give expression to the poet's disillusionment with the Revolution. The title image of twilight is deliberately ambiguous, suggesting both the semi-darkness that precedes the dawn or the half-light that signifies the onset of darkness. The poem can be interpreted through its four main structural images: the judging populace, the ship and the fishing nets, the ensnared swallows, and the darkened sun. The people are seen as the judges of the power exercised on their behalf by their leader. The leader in whom all power is vested is Lenin; the ship which he commands, and which is slowly sinking, is the Russian state heading for disaster under Bolshevism:

Let us praise the twilight of freedom, brothers,
the great year of twilight!
A thick forest of nets has been let down
into the seething waters of the night.
O sun, judge, people, desolate
are the years into which you are rising.

Let us praise the momentous burden
that the people's leader assumes, in tears.
Let us praise the twilight burden of power,
its weight too great to be borne.
Time, whoever has a heart
will hear your ship going down.

There are echoes of the Acts of the Apostles in the image of the ship sailing directionlessly without the guiding presence of the sun. The following passage from the twenty-seventh chapter has been mentioned as a possible source: 'And when much time was spent and when sailing now was dangerous, because the fast was now past, Paul comforted them, saying to them: "Ye men, I see that the voyage beginneth to be with injury and much damage, not only of the cargo and the ship, but also of our lives ... And when neither sun nor stars appeared for many days and no storm lay on us, all hope of our being saved was now taken away."'[23] The darkened sun also has several possible sources in scripture, such as the following words from the Book of Revelations – 'And I saw when he had opened the sixth seal, and behold, there was a great earthquake and the sun became black as sackcloth of hair' – or these from the Gospel of St Matthew: 'And immediately after the tribulation of those days the sun shall be darkened and the moon shall not give her light.'[24] The image of the ship, lowering its nets into the seething waters in the night, again has obvious New Testament sources, though in this instance it is not fish but swallows – symbolising the souls of the Russian people – which are now enmeshed in its nets. Trapped in the nets, their freedom denied them, the swallows threaten to obscure the sun:

> We have roped swallows together
> into legions.
> Now we can't see the sun.
> everywhere nature twitters as it moves.
> In the deepening twilight the earth swims into the nets
> and the sun can't be seen.

The darkened sun of 'The Twilight of Freedom' becomes the buried sun of 'We Shall Meet Again in Petersburg', the most accomplished of the religious lyrics that Mandelstam wrote in the immediate aftermath of the Revolution. This work is constructed around two metaphors – the sun and the blessed women – each of which has a complex spiritual significance. The scene of the poem is a cold winter's night in Petersburg where an opera is being performed in one of the city's great theatres. Horrendous images of the terror – the blackness of the night, the wild cat poised for attack, the cars of interrogators speeding through the streets – suggest a city whose people are paralysed by fear:

> The capital is arched like a wild cat,
> on a bridge the sentry stands,
> only an angry motor darts by in the gloom
> calling like a cuckoo.

I need no night pass here,
watchmen do not frighten me:
for that blessed senseless word
I shall pray in the Soviet night.

The sun, as in the earlier poem inspired by the Orthodox liturgy, is here again the eternal stillness of the Eucharist. The image also has a particular cultural significance, the key to which may be found in this passage from Mandelstam's essay, 'Pushkin and Scriabin': 'Pushkin and Scriabin are two transformations of the same sun, two transformations of the same heart. Twice the death of an artist has united the Russian people and lighted a sun above them. They served as an example of a collective Russian death, they died a full death, as some people live full lives, for in dying, their individuality expanded to the dimensions of a national symbol, and the sun-heart of the dying man remained forever at the zenith of suffering and glory.'[25] The sun which now seems buried in Petersburg represents, therefore, both the religious and artistic heritage of the Russian people:

We shall meet again in Petersburg
as though we had interred the sun in it
and shall pronounce for the first time
that blessed, senseless word.
In the black velvet of the Soviet night,
in the velvet of the universal void
the familiar eyes of blessed women sing
and still the deathless flowers bloom.

With the sun buried, the city is dark and cold. But in the cold, cosmic void there exist blessed women who are willing to suffer for the survival of their culture and their Christian faith. Their culture is symbolised by the bouquet of 'deathless roses' which one of them, an actress, receives as her performance draws to a close. Their faith is manifested in the blessedness of sacred song. They are entrusted with a sacred duty: the 'light ash' they are asked to gather and preserve is the remaining trace of a spirituality that has only been temporarily suppressed:

I hear a light theatrical rustle
and a girlish 'oh!' –
and the enormous heaps of deathless roses
piled high in Aphrodite's arms,
By the fire we warm ourselves from boredom,
perhaps whole centuries will pass,

and the familiar arms of blessed women
will gather the light ash.

For Mandelstam, Petersburg in the throes of its death-agony symbolised
the condition afflicting all the Russian people. But, for all their pessimism,
there was also an underlying hopefulness in the works he wrote in the years
following the Revolution. His essay, 'The Word and Culture', for example,
which was published in 1921, has an image of green grass struggling to grow
upwards through the pavements of Petersburg, suggesting a dormant spirituality striving desperately for survival in a culture dominated by a materialist ideology: 'Grass on the streets of Petersburg – the first sprouts of a virgin forest
that will cover the site of modern cities. This bright, tender verdure, astonishing in its freshness, belongs to a new, inspired nature. Petersburg is truly the
most advanced city in the world. Speed, the pace of the present, cannot be
measured by subways or skyscrapers, but only by the cheerful grass thrusting
itself forth from under city stones.'[26] There is the same guarded optimism in
his concluding image of the city in the poem. With the candles extinguished,
all is in darkness, but the blessed women continue to sing, and it appears that
the burial of the sun may be a temporary phenomenon:

The red flower-beds of the theatre-pit,
the fluffed-out wardrobes of the boxes;
an officer's wind-up doll;
not for black souls or cowardly hypocrites.
Extinguish then our candles if you will
in the black velvet of the universal void.
Still the steep shoulders of blessed women sing
and you will not notice the nocturnal sun.

The pessimism of Mandelstam's Revolution lyrics springs partly from his
disillusionment at the apathy of the masses and their indifference to the suppression of their religious and cultural traditions, but it is more deeply rooted
in his abhorrence of the humanist ideology which has caused this to occur.
The feeling given expression in his poems, and reemphasised in his prose, is
that the break with the past, though partly attributable to political accidence
and change, is ultimately to be traced to the essentially humanist and secular
character of the ideology which inspired the Revolution. Reflecting on this in a
section from *Hope Abandoned* where she describes the growing sense of isolation experienced by writers in Soviet society in the 1920s, Nadezhda
Mandelstam writes: 'The really important and tragic stages of secularisation
were not the separation of church from state, or theology from science, since

these were only a consequence of the more crucial moment when humanism was divorced from the Christianity which gave it birth. As a result of this process, which was completed in the first half of the twentieth century, we have witnessed an unparalleled dehumanisation of people – individuals as well as whole societies and nations.'[27]

The poems that Mandelstam wrote in the last decade of his life provide further evidence of the brutalising impact on everyday life of a purely humanist ideology, as will be shown in a later section. There is recognition, however, in all these poems of the providential presence of God amidst all the horrors that are described, and there is repeated affirmation of the hopefulness that springs from this. Thus, a work such as the following, which again is filled with images of blackness and doom, envisions a future when all such horrors will have passed, and confirms through its scriptural metaphors that the prospect of such an occurrence lies entirely within the power of the Creator of the universe, the 'Lord God' of the Apocalypse, to whom these lines are directly addressed:

> Like a cap of alpine cold,
> From year to year,
> In summer's heat,
> On the lofty brow of mankind,
> Are war's cold palms.
> And you, deep and sated,
> Pregnant with the azure,
> Many-eyed like scales,
> Both the alpha and omega
> Of the storm; for you,
> Foreign, eyebrowless,
> From generation to generation,
> Always a new and lofty wonder is transmitted.

CHRISTIAN FREEDOM AND JOY

'Neither sacrifice nor redemption in art, but rather *the free and joyous imitation of Christ* is the keystone of Christian aesthetics,' Mandelstam declares in his essay, 'Pushkin and Scriabin'. It is remarkable how insistently he emphasises the link between freedom, gaiety and the joyous affirmation of faith throughout this essay. 'Christian art is free,' he writes. 'No necessity of any kind, not even the highest, darkens its *bright inner freedom*, for its prototype, that which it imitates, is the very redemption of the world by Christ.' 'Art cannot be sacrifice,' he continues, 'because a sacrifice has already been made; it cannot be redemption, because the world, along with the artist, has already been redeemed. 'What remains? he asks. '*Joyous communion with God*, like some game played by the Father with his children, some blind-man's bluff or hide-and-seek of the spirit!' (my italics).[28]

That spirit of Christian freedom and joy is vividly exemplified in the cycle of poems that he wrote during a tour of Armenia in 1930. The poems are in stark contrast to those he wrote in the immediate aftermath of the Revolution, by virtue of their celebration of the spirit of inner freedom that he described in the Revolution poems as being suppressed by the materialist doctrines of Bolshevism. With assistance from an influential friend in the Kremlin, Nikolai Bukharin, he had gained a temporary respite from the state-sanctioned ostracism to which he had been subjected throughout the 1920s and set out on a tour of Armenia, together with his wife, Nadezhda, in April of 1930. The place held profound attractions for them both, by virtue of its great physical beauty and its deep roots in the traditions of Judaeo-Christian culture. The thirteen lyrics that make up the Armenian cycle record Mandelstam's affection for the place and provide a composite imagery of its landscape, people, culture and history. Its spiritual traditions are singled out for particular attention. Here, for instance, in the second of the lyrics, the unique church architecture of Armenia is seen as providing visible testimony of its tenacious adherence throughout history to its heritage of Christian faith:

> You sway the rose of Hafiz,
> you suckle children like little foxes,
> you breathe with the octagonal shoulders
> of peasant bull churches.
>
> Dyed with raucous ochre
> you are always behind the hill.
> To the air here you stuck a mere transfer
> out of a saucer of water.

Mandelstam's interest in Armenia owed a good deal also to its associations with Jewish culture. He referred to it on one occasion as 'the younger sister of the Jewish homeland' though, as Nadezhda points out in her memoirs, this is probably indicative of his recognition of the Jewish roots of Christian culture rather than a nostalgic yearning for his ancestral Jewishness. The attraction of Armenia for him lay, she says, in its steadfast defence of its Christian tradition against the threat of Islam from the East. 'There was a live curiosity in a little country, a Christian outpost in the East, remaining steadfast in its tradition against the Mohammedan,' she writes. 'Perhaps in this crisis of Christian consciousness we have the attraction of Armenia for Mandelstam.'[29] The images of the 'wayside shrine at Ararat' and of 'the library of earthenware authors' are suggestive of the primeval continuity of its religious and cultural traditions:

> I will never see you,
> nearsighted Armenian sky,
> and will never look with screwed-up eyes
> at the wayside shrine of Ararat,
> and will never open
> in the library of earthenware authors
> the hollow book of the beautiful earth
> from which the first men learned.

Mandelstam was further drawn to the continuity with Hellenist culture which he saw as an especially vitalising and joyous feature of Armenian Christianity. Together with its Jewish and Christian elements, he saw the Hellenist influence as defining the specifically western character of Armenian culture, and he contrasted its liveliness, gaiety and energy of spirit with the lethargy and inertness he generally attributed to eastern cultures. The term 'Buddhist', for example, frequently has strong negative connotations in his writing. 'Time can go backward', he complains in 'Pushkin and Scriabin'. 'Witness the entire course of recent history which, with a frightening force, has turned away from Christianity towards Buddhism and theosophy.'[30] What had been rejected, he says, was the spirit of Christian joy, the inner freedom which comes from 'joyous communion with God'. Nadezhda Mandelstam spoke of his own essentially cheerful and grateful acceptance of the world: 'There was nothing of the ascetic about M. and no end to the things he was fond of, or would like to have. He was always hankering after the south; he loved large rooms with plenty of light, a bottle of dry wine for dinner.' 'I believe,' she writes, 'he was able to live out his life fully because he was blessed with the gift of play and joy. I have never known his equal in this.'[31] Armenia epitomised this joyous, non-ascetical Christianity; it had 'turned away in shame and sorrow/ from the bearded cities of the East.' Its capital, Erevan, was a model of exuberant gaiety:

> O I see nothing, and my poor ear has grown deaf.
> Of all those colours remain to me minium and raucous
> ochre alone.
>
> And somehow I began to dream of the Armenian morning.
> I thought of how the tom-tit lives in Erevan,

how the baker stoops, playing blind man's buff with his bread
as he takes from the oven the moist hides ...

O Erevan, Erevan! Did a bird draw you,
or was it a lion, like a child, who coloured you, with a
coloured crayon-box ?

O Erevan, Erevan! Not a city – a roasted nut,
I love the crooked Babylons of your wide-mouthed streets.

I fingered my incoherent life like a mullah his Koran,
I froze my time, did not pour my hot blood.

O Erevan, Erevan, I need nothing more,
I do not want your frozen clusters of grapes.

The principle that faith is the basis of individual freedom finds expression, he says, in the spirit of simple joyfulness through which Christian culture has traditionally been expressed. 'Our entire two-thousand-year-old culture, thanks to the marvellous charity of Christianity, is the world's release into freedom for the sake of play, for spiritual joy, for the "free imitation of Christ",' he writes in 'Pushkin and Scriabin'.[32] A magnificent sequence of imagery from the ninth poem in the Armenian cycle reinforces this Christian ideal of joyous freedom. It evokes the gladness, simplicity and limitless *joie de vivre* which the Armenian landscape signifies:

The rose is cold in the snow:
on Lake Sevan the snow lies three arshins deep ...
The mountain fisherman has dragged out his
painted blue sledge,
the whiskered snub-mouths of fat trout
carry out policy duty
on the limy bottom.

But in Erevan and Echmiadzin
the enormous mountain has drunk in all the air,
if only one could entice it with an ocarina
or tame it with bagpipes
so that the snow might melt in its mouth.

Snow, snow, snow on rice paper,
the mountain floats to my lips.
I am cold. I am glad.

Reading these verses, one recalls the sequence in *The Brothers Karamazov* where the dying Zossima reminds his monks of the 'gladness' of Christianity, and Alyosha, in his dream about the miracle at Cana, sees Christ's changing of the water into wine as confirming his wish that his followers should be joyful. 'My friends, pray to God for gladness,' Zossima tells the monks. 'Be glad as children, as the birds of heaven. And let not the sin of men confound you in your doings ... Do not say: "Sin is mighty, wickedness is mighty, evil environment is mighty, and we are lonely and helpless, and evil environment is wearing us away and hindering our good work from being done." Fly from that dejection, children!' Neither Mandelstam nor Dostoevsky identified Christian gladness and joy with the absence of suffering; on the contrary, both of them saw it as being rooted in the inner freedom and integrity that comes from faith and the willingness to suffer for the freedom which it confers. Nadezhda Mandelstam, dismissing the notion of human fulfilment through happiness as a purely humanist concept, spoke of the capacity to surmount suffering that comes from faith and spoke of 'the mysterious joy which sometimes comes over us at moments of silence and sadness.'[33] That spirit of joyous sadness is much in evidence in the poems Mandelstam wrote after his return from Armenia when he was still shunned by his colleagues, apart from exceptions such as Pasternak, Akhmatova and Bely. The theme of the poet-as-outsider becomes increasingly prominent in his work, as does the supreme value of poetic conscience – the ultimate source of the inner freedom and of the 'joyous imitation of Christ', of which he speaks in 'Pushkin and Scriabin'. These are the themes of the poem, 'Keep My Words Forever', which he addressed to Anna Akhmatova, an 'outsider' like himself. He feels obliged in conscience to speak what he believes, while realising the inevitable proscription that will follow. He compares the fate of the poet to that of the victims of the cruelty of the Tartars. He hopes that his poetry will survive him and prays desperately that it will be saved:

> Keep my words forever for their aftertaste of misfortune and smoke,
> their tar of mutual tolerance, honest tar of work.
> Sweet and black should be the water of Novgorod wells
> to reflect the seven fins of the Christmas star.
>
> And in return, father, friend, rough helper, I
> the unrecognised brother, outlawed from the people's family,
> promise to fit the beam-cages tight to the wells
> so the Tartars can lower the princes in tubs, for torture.
>
> O ancient headsman's blocks, keep on loving me!
> Players in the garden seem to aim at death, and hit nine-pins.

I walk through my life aiming like that, in my iron shirt
(why not?) and I'll find an old beheading axe in the woods.

Again, in 'Pushkin and Scriabin', he speaks of the transcendence of the
temporal, and the potentiality to triumph over all mortal suffering, which is
made possible through the Christian faith, by virtue of the inner freedom and
joyousness afforded by its celebration of the infinity of the human spirit. 'The
danger of inner impoverishment poses no threat to Christian culture,' he
writes. 'It is inexhaustible, infinite, for in triumphing over time, it repeatedly
condenses grace into magnificent clouds from which it pours forth in life-
giving rain.'[34] In 'Canzone', the transcendence of time is expressed both as the
poet's sense of the continuity of all culture and wisdom and as the prophetic
voice of his art. Against the background of the Armenian landscape, he evokes
both the visionary gifts of the Epyptologists and numismatists, whose attention
was focused on the wisdom of the past, and the visionary powers of the
psalmist whose gift is prophetic insight into the future. Together they signify
the all-encompassing insight of the poet:

To-morrow, heart pounding, praise flowing,
I'll see you – can it be ? –
you bankers of mountain ranges,
holders of prodigious shares in gneiss,

with the eagle eye of professors,
Egyptologists and numismatists,
or of sombre-crested birds
lean in flesh, wide-breasted,

and, like Zeus, with the golden fingers
of a cabinet-maker, expertly adjust
those astounding onion-lenses
the Psalmist's legacy to a seer,

then peer through exquisite Zeiss
binoculars, King David's precious gift,
spying out wrinkles in the gneiss,
a pine, or tiny village-nit.

The theme of time transcended through historical recall and prophetic
vision is complemented in the poem by another, the theme of cultural rootedness and integrity signified by the image of the poet returning to the Promised
Land of his Judaeo-Christian forebears. This is conveyed through the scriptur-

al image of the Prodigal Son returning to the bosom of his Father. Mandelstam, his wife recalled, was deeply impressed by Rembrandt's picture of the story of the Prodigal Son at the Hermitage Museum in Leningrad where he had spent much of the winter of 1930-1.[35] In the picture the father's hands and cloak are painted a bright warm red and the red glow floods the entire picture with light. The prodigal is represented in the poem, therefore, as the son who yearns to return to the 'crimson caress' of his father's welcoming hand:

> Thus I'll quit these Hyperborean parts
> to steep in vision destiny's finale
> and say 'selah' to the Chief of the Jews
> for his crimson caress.
>
> The land of unshaven peaks still looms unclear,
> Stubble of low forest pricks the eyes
> and, fresh as a laundered fable,
> a green valley sets the teeth on edge.
>
> Military binoculars rejoice my heart
> with their usurer's power of vision;
> the world has only two unfaded colours left:
> bilious yellow and impetuous red.

In *Hope Abandoned* Nadezhda Mandelstam explained the relevance of the image of the Return of the Prodigal to Russian society in the 1930s: 'Given the concrete way in which M's mind worked, both the national and the religious themes are here united in the same image: return to your own people from a world which has lost its guiding light is the same as returning to the God of the fathers who sent his Son into the world.' Such a return was made urgent, she said, by the rapid decline of Russian society under the new materialist ideology. Reversal of its impact would be possible only by a process of Christian renewal such as that symbolised in the reconciliation of the prodigal with his father. 'The ideas at the basis of European culture and the Christian world are a priceless inheritance, like the vocabulary and language we speak,' she writes. 'There are always attempts to limit us to a basic word-stock and tawdry notions strained through the sieve of ideology. These notions were formed out of the detritus of humanism in the second half of the nineteenth century.'[36]

'UNDER PURGATORY'S TEMPORARY SKY'

The events that followed Mandelstam's return to Moscow from Erevan in 1930 – his arrest in 1934, his exile subsequently in Voronezh and his death at a transit camp in Vladivostok in 1938 – have all been described in detail by his wife in *Hope against Hope*. The poems he wrote throughout the 1930s are filled with an awareness of doom, an awareness deepened by his fears for his own and his family's safety, his concern for the future of his people, and his apprehensions about the fate of his poetry. Equally, they manifest his belief in the limitless endurance of the human spirit and its ultimate triumph over suffering and adversity. That belief finds expression in the Christian symbolism of the Resurrection which is increasingly a feature of the poems he wrote in the last tragic years before his death. Many years earlier in 'Pushkin and Scriabin' he had described Christ's Resurrection as signifying the promise of immortality which is the heart of the Christian faith. 'Christianity Hellenizes death,' he wrote, seeing the permanence of art, as epitomised in Hellenist culture, as the perfect analogue for the triumph over death which Christianity represents. He continued: 'The Christian world is an organism, a living body. The fabric of our world is renewed through death. We must struggle against the barbarism of our new life, for in the new life which is flourishing, death is unvanquished.'[37]

Many of the poems of the 1930s evoke his disillusionment at the apathy of his countrymen and their passivity in the face of the tyranny that had been imposed on them. 'Midnight in Moscow' bitterly condemns them for their cowardliness and inertia; their condition is seen as 'Buddhist-like' in its passivity, lacking the assertiveness and vitality that he associated with the people of Christian Armenia. The picture of the dazed citizens emerging from the cinema in the opening sequence of the poem, together with its mechanistic imagery of monkeys, bears and cuckoo-clocks, suggest a society proceeding inexorably towards moral and social decay. Yet, characteristically, the old lyrical spirit of the early poems is reasserted, and the lines end with affectionate, life-affirming images of Moscow trees and singing birds – the Moscow that Raphael, Rembrandt and Mozart would have loved:

> It's getting light now. The gardens rustle with the green telegraph.
> Raphael goes to visit Rembrandt,
> he and Mozart are in love with Moscow –
> for its hazel eyes, for the drunken banter of its sparrows.
> The draughts are passed from flat to flat
> as if on an aerial conveyer belt,
> like the ooze of the Black Sea jellyfish,

or the pneumatic postal service,
like the hooligan students in May.

On occasions, however, the tensions of life under the new regime were so
all-pervasive as to require a release more potent than the lyrical beauty of an
early morning Moscow scene. Jennifer Baines in *Mandelstam: The Later Poetry*
describes the background to a poem in which he beseeches God to save him
from the terrors of life in Leningrad in the winter of 1931.[38] Harassed by offi-
cialdom, ostracised by virtually all who knew him, he lived in perpetual fear
for his life. Family quarrels and tensions were adding to his personal humiliations. The agony he endured is evoked in a three-line poem whose existence
was unknown even to his wife until after the war, by which time he was long
since dead. He beseeches God to help him to survive the night; reviled by his
colleagues, feeling lost and betrayed, he hopes to find comfort through prayer:

O Lord, help me to live through this night –
I'm in terror for my life, your slave:
to live in Petersburg is to sleep in a grave.

'Nearing the end of my days, I have also come to understand that death, as
M. once explained to me, is a triumph. Earlier I had always looked upon it
only as a liberation,' Nadezhda Mandelstam wrote in one of the most eloquent
passages in *Hope Abandoned*. She spoke of Mandelstam's belief in poetry as
serving a function analogous to prayer. 'M., a man of extremely deep feeling,
was always acutely aware of death, which seemed ever present to his mind,'
she writes. 'This is indeed not surprising: poetry even more than philosophy is
a preparation for death. Death encompasses the fullness of life, its essence, its
real pith and substance. Death is the apex of life.'[39] This theme is developed
by Mandelstam himself in 'Octets' where he sees the special insights of the
poet as providing access to the eternal and the infinite. The tenth poem in the
cycle exposes the limitations of causal and inferential logic, contrasting the
inadequacies of rationalistic knowledge with the penetration and depth of
poetic imagery. An image of a child, whose intuitive understanding is seen to
surpass the explanatory logic of philosophic thought, affirms the superior
insight and wisdom of the poet, his access to meaning beyond the reach of
rationalistic enquiry:

We drink the delusion of causality,
from the fluted champagne glasses of the plague.
We hook onto magnitudes
small as an easy death.
The child keeps its silence

in face of the jumbled pile of pick-up-sticks.
The big universe sleeps in the cradle
rocked by the small eternity

There follows a verse which gives expression to the religious aspirations
underlying this theme. As poet and man he will leave the world of space and
time, reaching towards the infinitude of the eternal which the explanatory sciences of the temporal world are unable to comprehend:

I go out from space
into the overgrown garden of multitudes,
and pluck false constancy
and self-consciousness of causality.
In solitude,
I read your texts, infinity:
a wild leafless book of healing,
a book of problems with huge roots.

Crucifixion imagery is a recurring feature of the poems of the 1930s. It had
in fact been a feature of Mandelstam's poetry almost from the outset. As early
as 1910 he identified himself with the Crucified Christ in a short lyric, the
central image of which is a 'thin' cross, suggestive of the ultimate 'lightness' of
suffering as seen from a Christian standpoint: 'Twilight smothers my bed,/
my breath comes hard,/ Perhaps what I really love/ Is a thin cross and a
secret road.' About four years later he published a poem exploring the relationship of his inherited Jewish and his newly adopted Christian cultures. The
poem represents Judaism as the 'dark womb' from which he sprang and this is
contrasted with the redemptive grace and hopefulness of the Christian dispensation, his new found faith. The central image is that of the dying Christ, his
head drooping as he sinks in his death agony into the dark pool from which *he
too* had come:

The implacable words.
Judaea became petrified,
and, heavier with every moment,
His head drooped.

Warriors stood guard
around the cooling body.
His head, like a corolla, hung,
on a slender and alien stem.

And He reigned, and He drooped,
like a lily into its native pool,
and the deep where stems sink
was celebrating its law.

The image of Christ Crucified has a more poignant and tragic significance
in the Voronezh poems. In his exile Mandelstam attempted to reingratiate
himself with Stalin by writing sycophantic verses in his honour. While seriously compromising his personal and artistic integrity, his action could be excused
as the aberrant behaviour of a deeply confused person, fearful for his own and
his family's safety. He bitterly regretted the gesture later and gave expression
to his feelings in a poem in which the image of the cross evokes the depth of
suffering the whole experience had brought him. A Crucifixion scene from
Rembrandt, which he had seen in a museum in Voronezh, prompts some
reflections on the theme of martyrdom. Deeply conscious of his self-betrayal,
he asks Rembrandt as a fellow artist to help him to expiate his sin:

I've gone, like the martyr of light and shade,
like Rembrandt, into a growing numbness of time.
One of my ribs is a burning blade,
but it's not in the keeping of these watchmen
nor of this soldier asleep under the storm.

Sir, magnificent brother, master
of the black-green darkness, may you forgive me:
the eye of the falcon-quill pen
and the hot casks in the midnight harem
waken, but waken to no good
the tribe frightened by furs in the twilight.

'Repentance commands unique and powerful words, an unequivocal language of its own. It may be the language of a specific moment in time, but it
lasts forever,' Nadezhda Mandelstam wrote in a passage from *Hope Abandoned*
which is close to the mood of this poem. She spoke of a catharsis of penitential
feeling which is inextricably bound to the religious sense in poetry. 'What is
catharsis,' she asks, 'but a cleansing or illumination of the spirit, following the
triumph of values, the affirmation of their inexorable power.' 'The European
world,' she declares, 'was based on the supreme catharsis accessible only to the
religious mind, the conquest of death by atonement.'[40] Another of the Voronezh
poems, in which again he anticipates death, further illustrates the repentant
spirit of the works Mandelstam wrote after the episode of the Stalin poems. He
restates his belief in the 'rightness' of poetry and his revulsion at the tyrannical

excesses of the communist regime. He is hopeful that in time the masses will
rise again as individuals to restore what has been temporarily lost. The images
of the poem depict conditions in his country as a struggle between the forces of
life and the forces of destruction. (Lenin and Stalin are linked to the latter by
name.) The forces of evil are temporarily in the ascendant, but his hopes lie
with the people whose suffering and integrity must triumph in the end. He
affirms his determination to proclaim the truth through his poetry and vows
that his voice will never be silenced by his adversaries:

> If our enemies should take me
> And prevent me from speaking to the people,
> If they should deprive me of everything in the world –
> To breathe the truth and open doors …
> I shall not be silent,
> I shall not stifle pain.

In another of the Voronezh poems, 'The heaven of the supper', he reflects
yet again on the Passion and Crucifixion of Christ, seeing this as the archetypal image of the sufferings of all mankind. Shortly before he had written a long
war poem, 'Lines On an Unknown Soldier' in which he foresaw the possible
destruction of the whole of the human race. In the Golgotha poem he depicts
Christ gathered with his disciples at the last supper, the prelude to his death
on the cross. This prompts a meditation on the sufferings of the Russian
people and his own impending martyrdom. Gazing upwards at the night-sky
he sees a blinding sun, and the stars rain destruction on the earth, both symbolising the horrors of the Yezhovshchina – the show-trials, purges and mass
executions – shortly to begin in the USSR, bringing terror on an unprecedented scale to its people. The image of a child exposed to the terrors of the night
symbolises the millions of innocents, including the poet himself, who will
shortly fall victims to the destructive forces that have been unleashed:

> The heaven of the supper fell in love with the wall.
> It filled it with cracks. It fills them with light.
> It fell into the wall. It shines out there
> in the form of thirteen heads.
> And that's my night sky, before me,
> and I'm the child standing under it,
> my back getting cold, an ache in my eyes,
> and the wall-battering heaven battering me.
>
> At every blow of the battering ram
> stars without eyes rain down,

new wounds in the last supper,
the unfinished mist on the wall.

Following the end of their exile in Voronezh, the Mandelstams returned to Moscow in the Spring of 1938. As a 'convicted person' Mandelstam was obliged to reside beyond the borders of the city. At a rest home in Samatikha, he was arrested on the night of 1 May and sentenced to a term in a labour camp. In December of that year he died at a transit camp near Vladivostok. The theme of death was prominent in many of the poems he wrote in the previous five years. Three in particular indicate the spirit of faith and hopefulness with which he regarded the prospect of death. The first was inspired by an event that occurred in Voronezh in the summer of 1935. A group of airmen had died in a flying accident and were buried with full military honours. Their funeral prompted a poem in which Mandelstam contemplates the nature of existence beyond time. The poem opens with an image of a white butterfly whose transformation into dust symbolises the transitoriness of all material life. The human spirit, he suggests, unlike the white butterfly, survives the end of its material existence, being transformed into the communality of all consciousness – Pasternak's 'life in others'. This is the fulfilment to which he aspires:

Not like a floury white butterfly
Shall I return my borrowed dust to earth.
I want my thinking body
To be transformed into a street, a nation –
This vertebral, charred body,
Conscious of its own length.

'Mandelstam's God is very much like Einstein's God,' Ryszard Przybylski wrote in a lengthy discussion of this poem. 'Matter', he said, is like an organism in which a Super Intelligence is thinking, just as man thinks inside his body, and in any event, matter gives the impression of being the body of the Creator, a part of which is the handful of clay which is given to us on loan.' Commenting on the essentially Christian character of this latter theme, he writes: 'This simple, extremely Christian, and always eloquent truth, which bears witness to an emotional attitude to the Biblical story of the creation of man, reminds us that the body, even though it thinks, is composed of matter, and that sooner or later each of us must in the end return it to its silent mysterious owner.'[41] Human life does not dissolve into matter, like the 'white floury butterfly', but enters a new stage of existence in the communality of human love, returning thereby to its Creator who is the source of its timelessness and infinity. As the dead airmen survive in the loving memories of those who mourn them, so, the poem suggests, all human life is renewed in the infinity of the spirit as manifested in the interrelatedness of all consciousness and being. That interrelatedness is sustained by the bond of love, that which ultimately unites all that exists. Thus, the coffins of the airmen are drawn by wreaths of pine needles, the greenness of which symbolises the forces of self-renewal present in temporal life:

> Cries of dark-green pine needles –
> Wreaths deep as a well –
> They pull life and precious time,
> Leaning on mortal mountings,
> Hoops of red flag-draped pine needles –
> Wreaths round as the alphabet.

'There are cases,' Nadezhda Mandelstam wrote, 'in which the poet prepares for a future experience and by thus anticipating it grasps its essence.'[42] This truth is exemplified in another of Mandelstam's poems on the theme of death, a lyric he also wrote in Voronezh, in March 1937, a year before his arrest and transportation to the Siberian labour camp. The poem unites the Christian themes of Incarnation and Resurrection. The poet anticipates the heaven of a life beyond time, but intimates the reality of a heaven-like existence in time, a reality made possible by the miracle of the Incarnation and God's immanent presence in material existence. That theme had been foreshadowed in many of his earlier works, particularly those dealing with the theme of the Eucharist and its material signification of the timeless as an eternal stillness in time. The Voronezh poem emphasises the purgatorial character of earthly existence, and points to the paradoxical truth that the prospect of paradise is disclosed in the endemic conditions of suffering in which earthly life is conducted. The prevailing mood of the poem is one of optimism and hope:

> I say this as a sketch and in a whisper
> for it is not yet time:
> the game of unaccountable heaven
> is achieved with experience and sweat.
>
> And under purgatory's temporary sky
> we often forget
> that the happy repository of heaven
> is a lifelong house that you can carry everywhere.

The same feeling of hopefulness in the face of death is expressed in one of the final lyrics from Voronezh, one of a number of poems addressed to Natasha Shtempel, a young teacher who had befriended the Mandelstams during their exile there. In *Hope Abandoned* Nadezhda Mandelstam described Natasha as a woman of 'rare spiritual grace' and explained how the themes of death and resurrection are intertwined in the poems that Mandelstam addressed to her. 'The beautiful poems to Natasha Shtempel have a place all to themselves in M.'s love lyrics,' she writes. 'He always linked love with the thought of death, but in his verse to Natasha there is also a serene and lofty sense of a future life. He asks Natasha to mourn him when he is dead and greet him when he comes back to life ... throughout there is a simple under-standing of life as a temporal gift followed by eternity after the end of one's earthly span.'[43] In a conversation with Mandelstam's biographer, Clarence Brown, in 1966, Natasha Shtempel recalled that Mandelstam had said of the poem which begins, 'Limping like a clock': 'This is my best poem. When I die see that it gets into Pushkiny Dom.'[44] His faith in eternal life is expressed in the poem through an image of the renewal of nature in the spring. On the far side of the grave lies an eternal beginning, comparable to an ever-recurring springtime. Natasha epitomises both the transient natural beauty of all human life and the self-renewing potentiality of the spirit on which the hope for an eternal existence must rest:

> Limping like a clock on her left leg,
> at the beloved gait, over the empty earth,
> she keeps a little ahead of the quick girl,
> her friend, and the young man almost her age.
> What's holding her back
> drives her on.
> What she must know is coming
> drags at her foot. She must know
> that under the air, this spring,
> our mother earth is ready for us
> and that it will go on like this forever.
>
> There are women with the dampness of the earth in their veins.
> Every step they take there's a sobbing in a vault.
> They were born to escort the dead, and be at the grave
> first to greet those who rise again.
> It would be terrible to want a caress from them
> but to part with them is more than a man could do.
> One day angel, next day the worm in the grave,
> the day after that, a sketch.
> What used to be within reach – out of reach.
> Flowers never die. Heaven is whole.
> But ahead of us we've only somebody's word.

8

'Nostalgia for the Infinite':
The Poetry of Anna Akhmatova

'THE LORD'S STAMP IS UPON YOU'

Like a black angel on the snow
You seemed to me today,
And keep it secret I cannot:
The Lord's stamp is upon you.
It is so strange a stamp –
As if bestowed from above –
That it seems you are destined
To stand in a church niche.
Let unearthly love
With earthly love be fused.
Let tumultuous blood
Not suffuse your cheeks
And sumptuous marble set off
All the illusoriness of your rags,
All the bareness of your softest flesh,
But not of blushing cheeks.

Osip Mandelstam's tribute, written in 1910,[1] points to the centrality of religious faith in Akhmatova's poetry and to the special blending of 'earthly and unearthly love' which is its most distinctive and consistent characteristic. From the publication of *Evening*, her earliest volume of verse, in 1912, commentators spoke of her preoccupation with religious, and specifically Christian, themes. A friend and fellow-writer, Nikolai Nedobrovo, cited the words of St Luke – 'Whosoever shall save his life will lose it and whosoever shall lose his life will save it' – to intimate the essentially Christian spirit that informs her poetry.[2] Another of her contemporaries, Viktor Zhirmunsky, spoke of her 'simple everyday religiosity', contrasting it with the mystical otherworldliness of Symbolist poetry.[3] Kornei Chukovsky, an influential figure in modern Russian literature, described her as 'the last and only poet of Orthodoxy' and praised both her religious traditionalism and the strong sense of national identity that is evident in her poetry. Contrasting her with Mayakovsky, he wrote:

Akhmatova and Mayakovsky are as hostile one to the other as the epochs which gave them birth. Akhmatova is the careful heir to all that is most precious in pre-revolutionary literary culture. She has many ancestors, Pushkin and Baratynsky and Annensky. In her we find that refinement of spirit and charm which is the result of centuries of cultural tradition. But in every line, every letter of Mayakovsky, we find the birth of the present revolutionary age. In him we can find its beliefs, can hear its cries, see its failures, know its ecstasies. He has no ancestors and, if strong in anything, is strong in posterity. Behind her stand the many splendid centuries of the past, in front of him the many centuries of the future. She has the Old Russian belief in God, preserved from days of old, he is blasphemous and sacrilegious, as befits a revolutionary bard. For her, the most sacred thing of all is Russia, her country, or land. He, as befits a revolutionary bard, is an internationalist, a citizen of the planet ... She is the solitary quiet one, eternally in seclusion ... He belongs to the square, the meeting, he is part of the crowd, he is the crowd.[4]

Most contemporary commentators emphasised the fusion of lyrical and religious themes that is evident throughout her work. Viktor Vinogradov, reviewing her first three volumes, *Evening*, *Rosary* and *White Flock*, spoke of the fruitful tension between sacred and profane love that is maintained in her poetry and commended her use of Christian imagery to embrace the dichotomies existing between the two. In some instances, however, this was seen as manifesting a flawed and distorted sensibility.[5] Alexander Gizetti described Akhmatova as 'by nature a pagan bound by strong ties to the beautiful earth'. 'The essential spirit of her work is more hedonistic than religious,' he wrote. Religion, he said, provided her with 'an illusion of simplicity', serving as 'the last refuge of a perpetually questing and wavering soul seeking for wholeness'.[6] Boris Eykhenbaum, while praising the fusion of 'ecclesiastical, biblical, oratorical and conversational speech' in her poetry, spoke rather disparagingly of its 'paradoxical dualism of spiritual and hedonistic elements'. 'Here,' he wrote, 'the image of the heroine begins to emerge, not quite a fornicator with tumultuous passions, not quite a mendicant nun who is able to obtain God's forgiveness by her prayers.'[7]

Like Eykhenbaum, another of her critics, Yury Aykhenval'd, was puzzled by this interplay of earthly and unearthly love in Akhmatova's poetry. 'The whole general style of her love is linked to the fact that Anna Akhmatova is a moral nun with a cross on her breast,' he wrote. 'She is mindful of hell and believes in divine retribution. Her love is her hair-shirt. Her passion is severe and she is disturbed by her love, but perhaps reassured by the fact that her love is unhappy and that God is therefore not angry, not mocked by the sin-fulness of his servant.'[8] These sentiments were reiterated in the infamous decree of 1946 by which she was expelled from the Writers' Union. The Union spokesman, Andrei Zhdanov, declared:

> Acmeists, like the Symbolists, Decadents, and other trumpeters of aris-tocratic-bourgeois ideology, were the propagators of decadence, pes-simism and a belief in the other world. Akhmatova's themes are completely individualistic. The range of her poetry is so limited as to seem poverty-stricken; it is the portrait of a frantic little fine lady flit-ting between the boudoir and the chapel ... The basis of her poetry is made up of amatory erotic themes, interwoven with themes of sadness, longing, death, mysticism, and doom. The feeling of doom is one we can expect to find in the social consciousness of a dying group. The gloomy tones of hopelessness before death, mystical experiences inter-mingled with eroticism – this is the spiritual world of Akhmatova, a left-over from the old aristocratic culture which has sunk once and for all into the oblivion of 'the good old days of Catherine'. Half nun, half harlot, or rather a harlot-nun whose sin is mixed with prayer.[9]

Ironically, for all its misrepresentation of the true purposes of her work, the Zhdanov decree unwittingly identified the synthesis of the immanent and the transcendent – ultimately to be expressed as the mystery of the Incarnation or the Word Made Flesh – which is the centre and focus of her Christian faith and the theme that dominates her poetry from her earliest lyrics to the great epic works of her final years.

Those writers who were closest to Akhmatova were in no doubt about the depth and sincerity of her Christian faith. In *Hope Abandoned* Nadezhda Mandelstam echoed Chukovsky's assertion that Akhmatova belonged in the traditional mould of the Orthodox believer. 'The three Acmeists,' she wrote, 'refused to countenance any revision of Christianity. Gumilev's and Akhmatova's Christianity was of a traditional Orthodox kind while Mandelstam accepted it in its philosophical aspects rather than as a matter of everyday observance – it underlay his view of the world.'[10] Anatoly Nayman, her close friend and her literary secretary in her final years, wrote of the sin-cerity of her faith and her devotion to the scriptures: 'Akhmatova believed in God, and one could not say that she was not a church person ... She read the letters of the Apostles and the Psalms – in general Akhmatova knew the Bible exceedingly well, found her way about it easily, and could find any passage she wanted immediately.'[11] In his correspondence with Akhmatova, Boris Pasternak similarly recognised the strength of her Christian faith. Writing to console her

on the arrest of her son during the Stalinist terror of the late 1930s, he
reminds her that the essential characteristic of Christianity is its hopefulness.
'Forgive me,' he writes, 'for callously listing examples from my day to day life
like a small boy in order to illustrate how one should never give up hope. As a
true Christian you must know all this, but do you realise the value of your
hope and the necessity of protecting it?'[12] In a cycle of poems addressed to
Akhmatova, Marina Tsvetaeva links her symbolically with Mary, the Mother
of Christ, and with one of the early Fathers, St John Chrysostom. In the final
stanzas from the work she celebrates the faith-giving and immortalising power
of Akhmatova's poetry, symbolically offering her the golden-domed Christian
churches of Moscow as a mark of her gratitude and love:

> Muse of lament, you are the most beautiful of
> all muses, a crazy emanation of white night:
> and you have sent a black snow storm over all Russia,
> We are pierced with the arrows of your cries
>
> so that we shy like horses at the muffled
> many times uttered pledge – Ah! – Anna
> Akhmatova – the name is a vast sigh
> and it falls into depths without name
>
> and we wear crowns only through stamping
> the same earth as you, with the same sky over us.
> Whoever shares the pain of your deathly power will
> lie down immortal – upon his death-bed.
>
> In my melodious town the domes are burning
> and the blind wanderer praises our shining Lord.
> I give you my town of many bells,
> Akhmatova, and with the gift: my heart.[13]

As has been intimated, the essential concern of Akhmatova's poetry is the
Christian theme of Incarnation and this is celebrated through her repeated
attestation of the immanent presence of God in the material universe. Before
this is discussed, it is necessary to point to the manner in which this theme is
conveyed in her poetry and to emphasise the degree to which the whole
process was assisted by the aesthetic ideals of the Acmeist creed that she
shared with Gumilev and Mandelstam. Pointing to the simplicity of style and
concretion of detail that are evident in her poetry, Mandelstam emphasised the
religious significance of this, seeing her lyrical celebrations of everyday reality

as ultimately an affirmation of that reality's revelation of the transcendent and the divine. 'Akhmatova, using the purest literary language of her day, introduced into her poetry with extraordinary steadfastness the traditional devices of the folk-song,' he wrote. 'Her combination of the subtlest psychologism with song-like harmony astonishes our sense of hearing because we are accustomed to associating the song with a certain spiritual simplicity, if not spiritual poverty. The psychological design in Akhmatova's songs is as natural as the vein in a maple leaf. 'Her poetry,' he said, 'indicates a propensity for hieratic significance, religious simplicity and solemnity.'[14] One of Akhmatova's translators, the novelist and poet, D.M. Thomas, similarly saw the simplicity and concretion of her style as being rooted in her spiritual and moral integrity. 'Her incorruptibility as a person,' he said, 'is closely linked to her most fundamental characteristic as a poet: fidelity to things as they are, to the clear, familiar, material world ...'

> It was Mandelstam who pointed out that the roots of her poetry are in Russian prose fiction. It is a surprising truth, in view of the supreme musical quality of her verse; but she has the novelist's concern for tangible realities, events in place and time. The 'unbearably white ... blind in the white window' of one of her earliest poems is unmistakably real; the last, from half a century later, her farewell to the earth, sets her predicted death firmly and precisely in 'that day in Moscow', so that her death seems no more important than the city in which it will take place ... In all her life's work, her fusion with ordinary, unbetrayable existence is so complete that only the word 'modest' can express it truthfully ... She did not make poetry out of the quarrel with herself (in Yeats's phrase for the genesis of poetry). Her poetry seems rather to be a transparent medium through which life streams.[15]

'One should only write about what one loves,' Akhmatova is recalled as saying to Lydia Chukovskaya, a lifelong friend and the editor of her recently published journals.[16] Chukovskaya recalls her words on the virtues of poetic simplicity: 'As far as simplicity is concerned, it too is only beautiful when it has content, that is, complexity.'[17] The precision, concretion and simplicity of the Acmeist style, together with its attention to the everydayness of material reality, is indicative not merely of a preference for technical clarity and fluency, but of a determination by the writers concerned to give appropriate expression to their convictions – convictions which were fundamentally religious. Their particular concern was to affirm their belief that God's presence is immanently disclosed in the dynamism of the phenomenal universe. 'The conception of art as craft, as religious rite, as a means of transforming the world, was the essential *sina qua non* of the circle which Akhmatova entered in order to take up her place,' Anatoly Nayman wrote. 'For Akhmatova ... art was service not only in the usual sense of the word but also in the religious sense.'[18] The process is described by Akhmatova's first biographer, Amanda Haight, as analogous to the seminal naming of reality described in the Genesis myth of creation. 'In their outlook on life and on poetry the Acmeists were facing in a direction diametrically opposed to that of the Symbolists,' she writes. 'As a result there was to be no escape for them from the world's realities as these grew harsher. It was necessary for them to try to reach God and to understand His purposes through understanding, living and loving life. Existence was not just something to be tolerated while waiting for Heaven. And although for them the poet was not a priest, he was a formulator. Like Adam, he was a giver of names.'[19] This view was endorsed by B.A Fillipov, the co-editor of the definitive text of Akhmatova's poetry, who wrote that 'Akhmatova's God is not concealed in catechisms or capitals, but is always intimately at hand, ready to offer mercy and assistance, however trivial the need.'[20] And one of her closest friends, her protégé, Joseph Brodsky, in an essay, 'The Keening Muse', attributed the remarkable power of her great epic, 'Requiem', to the depth of religious feeling that underlies the work. 'The degree of compassion with which the various voices of 'Requiem' are rendered can be explained only by the author's Orthodox faith,' he wrote. In this remarkable passage from the essay he describes the yearning for the infinite which lies at the heart of her love poetry:

> It is the finite's nostalgia for the infinite that accounts for the recurrence of the love theme in Akhmatova' verse, not the actual entanglements. Love indeed has become for her a language, a code to record time's messages or, at least, to convey their tune; she simply heard them better this way. For what interested this poet most was not her own life but precisely time and the effects of its monotone on the human psyche and on her own diction in particular. If she later resented attempts to reduce her to her early writing, it was not because she disliked the status of the habitually love-sick girl: it was because her diction and, with it, the code, subsequently changed a great deal in order to make the monotone of the infinite more audible.[21]

It will be shown in the course of this chapter that the theme of immanence in its various manifestations is the fundamental concern of Akhmatova's poetry. It will be examined firstly in the context of her love poetry; for Akhmatova the whole notion of the immanent presence of God in the phenomenal world was most intensively disclosed in the universal experience of interhuman love – in all its tensions and ambiguities, its ecstasy and its pain. Secondly, it will be shown to be the underlying theme in the poems where she explored her own personal sufferings and those of her fellow-countrymen during the horrors of the Stalinist terror in the 1930s and 1940s. Thirdly, it will be shown to be the central concern of the poems of the post-war years in which she explored the religious and metaphysical intricacies of the themes of temporality and change. It will be shown, moreover, that throughout all her works there is a consistent, if largely implicit, affirmation that the principle of immanence is directly manifested in the poetic *logos* itself: in its incarnation of the infinite and intemporal as embodied Word – as the mystery signified by the scriptural concept of the Word Made Flesh.

'LET UNEARTHLY LOVE WITH EARTHLY LOVE BE FUSED'

Two major themes, each of which is rooted in her deepest religious beliefs, are closely intertwined in Akhmatova's love poetry. The first is the idea of salvation as a prospect to be attained in the conditions of time, i.e., through a direct experiencing of its finite temporality. It is particularly through the experience of love, she suggests, that the prospect of a timeless fulfilment is disclosed in the conditions of temporal life. Love in all its forms is seen as illuminating the sentient presence of the infinite and the timeless in the materiality of a time-bound universe. Secondly, suffering and pain are seen as being intrinsic to the experience of love, by virtue of its essentially conflict-ridden state, its disclosure of the tensions of the contingent and the permanent, the transient and intemporal. She points to a complex metaphysical tension between the time-bound experience of love and the spirit's relentless aspiration towards the infinite, suggesting a romantic-religious dualism at the heart of all interhuman experience, the tensions and contradictions of which are distressing and tragic but ultimately hope-affirming when judged from the standpoint of faith.

Each of these themes is conveyed in her poetry through a highly evocative use of lyrical-romantic and religious imagery, which in turn is powerfully reinforced by the clarity, succinctness and immediacy of the Acmeist style. The poems emphasise the inner-directed and other-directed tendencies of the experience of love, pointing to the ecstasy of its fulfilment, the tragedy of its loss, its life in the 'onceness' of the present moment, its idealised life in memory, its potentiality for disclosure of an existence beyond both. The early poems are dominated by the pain and grief of a woman who has first experienced the ecstasy of love and then endured the agony of its loss. (The critic Nedobrovo pointed out in an article published in 1915 that Akhmatova's special significance as a love poet lay in the fact that she explored the experience of love from a female standpoint, love having been previously portrayed in poetry almost exclusively from a male point of view.)[22] Akhmatova's marriage to the poet, Nikolai Gumilev, ended after three years when their tempestuous relationship proved no longer sustainable. The poems she wrote after their separation are full of the pain of rejection – 'Then helplessly my breast grew cold/ But my steps were still light' ... 'you know, I languish in captivity,/ Praying to the Lord for death.' Yet, even in her agony she draws on her residual Christian faith to affirm her belief that there is an underlying meaning in her apparently inexplicable torment:

> I've learned to live simply, wisely,
> To look at the sky and pray to God,
> And to take long walks before evening
> To wear out this useless anxiety.
>
> When the burdocks rustle in the ravine
> And the yellow-red clusters of rowan nod,
> I compose happy verses
> About mortal life, mortal and beautiful life.
>
> I return. The fluffy cat
> Licks my palm and sweetly purrs.
> And on the turret of the sawmill by the lake
> A bright flame flares.
>
> The quiet is cut, occasionally,
> By the cry of a stork landing on the roof.
> And if you were to knock at my door,
> It seems to me I wouldn't even hear.

Her sense of personal rejection at the failure of love is accompanied by repeated assertions of its self-renewing potentiality, something she sees as being analogous, in its essential hopefulness, to the experience of faith. Several of the poems suggest that relief from the heartbreak of love may be sought in the everpresent potential for self-transformation that is inherent in the experience of love itself. This is the theme of a poem addressed by Akhmatova to the poet, Mikhail Lozinsky, where the simplicity of lyrical and religious imagery conveys the serenity of feeling which the contemplation of this prospect creates:

> The sun fills my room,
> Yellow dust drifts aslant.
> I wake up and remember:
> This is your saint's day.
> That's why even the snow
> Outside my window is warm.
> Why, I sleepless, have slept
> Like a communicant.

The potentiality of love for self-renewal is once again the theme in the poem, 'You have come to comfort me.' Here, as in the previous poem, lyrical and religious images intertwine to intimate the sense of hopefulness which is common both to romantic passion and to religious faith. The poet hopes to find self-fulfilment simultaneously in passion and in prayer:

> You've come to comfort me, darling,
> Most tender, most gentle ...
> No strength to raise myself from the pillow,
> And a close-worked lattice across the windows.
>
> You thought you would find me dead,
> And you brought an artless little wreath.
> How painfully you wound my heart with a smile,
> Affectionate, mocking and sad.
>
> What is the weight of death to me now!
> If you stay with me awhile,
> I'll implore God to forgive
> You, and all those you love.

Both forms of self-renewal, the religious and the romantic, are conveyed through a subtle interplay of spiritual and sensual imagery in 'Confession'. The poem's protagonist seeks forgiveness both from her lover and from Christ. The priest who absolves her of her sins does so with the power conferred on him by Christ. Her heart beats in response to his words of forgiveness with an intensity comparable to what she experiences at her lover's sensual touch. She compares her transformation, through repentance and the self-renewing power of love, to Christ's miraculous restoration of life to the daughter of Jairus, as described in the New Testament narrative:

> Having forgiven me my sins, he fell silent.
> In the violet dusk candles sputtered,

And a dark prayer stole
Covered my head and my shoulders.

Isn't that the voice that said: 'Maiden! Arise ...'
My heart beats faster, faster.
The touch, through the cloth,
Of a hand absently making the sign of the cross.

For all the hopefulness of these poems, they repeatedly emphasise the persistence of the suffering inherent in the experience of love and suggest that endurance of its torment is the means to the self-transcendence which it ultimately affords. Images of death abound in the poems, intimating the mortality of love which co-exists with its potential for transcending the conditions of the mortal state. In the poem which begins 'I don't know if you're alive or dead' she evokes the cruelty and the death-like impact of rejected love. Recalling her failed marriage to Gumilev, she finds comfort and solace in prayer, but the torment and pain endure nonetheless:

I don't know if you're living or dead –
Whether to look for you here on earth
Or only in evening meditation,
When we grieve serenely for the dead.

Everything is for you: my daily prayer,
And the thrilling fever of the insomniac,
And the blue fire of my eyes,
And my poems, that white flock.

No one was more intimate with me,
No one made me suffer so,
Not even the one who consigned me to torment,
Not even the one who caressed and forgot.

The theme of the lover as victim occurs in many of these poems. In 'Memory of love, you are painful' Akhmatova explores the ambiguous nature of remembered passion; while the passion itself may die, it lives on in memories that are simultaneously joyous and painful. She compares memory to a funeral pyre on which paradoxically she both sings and burns. As she imagines herself consumed by the flames, she becomes conscious of past lovers who draw near to get warmth from her soul. Like Christ who sacrificed himself out of love for others, her love has also cast her in the role of sacrificial victim:

Memory of love, you are painful!
I must sing and burn in your smoke,
But for others – you're just a flame
To warm a cooling soul.

To warm a sated body,
They needed my tears ...
For this, Lord, I sang,
For this I received love's communion!

Let me drink some kind of poison
That will make me mute,
And turn my infamous fame
Into radiant oblivion.

As if to underline the necessity of love's suffering, several of the poems emphasise the illusory nature of the escape sought by the poet from the pain of remembered love. But she recognises that the urge to create idealised images of love, like the urge to escape from its trials and conflicts, is a real and persistent tendency which is inherent in the nature of love itself. In one of the most beautiful of her lyrics, 'I hear the oriole's always grieving voice', she celebrates this idealised vision of love, seeing herself united with her lover in the blessedness and innocence of Paradise:

I hear the oriole's always grieving voice,
And the rich summer's welcome loss I hear
In the sickle's serpentine hiss
Cutting the corn's ear tightly pressed to ear.

And the short skirts of the slim reapers
Fly in the wind like holiday pennants,
The clash of joyful cymbals, and creeping
From under dusty lashes, the long glance.

I don't expect love's tender flatteries,
In premonition of some dark event,
But come, come and see this paradise
Where together we were blessed and innocent.

A similar feeling pervades another lyric where the poet imagines herself as a ray of sunlight passing over her lover's sleeping face. In the second stanza of

the poem the light becomes a 'heavenly ray' and in the third is transformed
into a 'disembodied soul' seeking a totally spiritualised union with the beloved:

> The first ray of light – God's blessing –
> Glided over my lover's face,
> And drowsing, he became a bit pale,
> But fell still deeper asleep.
>
> Truly, it seemed like a kiss,
> The warmth of that heavenly ray ...
> Thus, long ago, my lips used to touch
> His dusky shoulder and his sweet lips ...
>
> But now, more disembodied than the dead,
> In my inconsolable wandering
> I fly to him only as a song
> And caress him as a ray of morning.

The idealising tendency is seen to be particularly a feature of love in its
remembered forms. Recalling her marriage with Gumilev many years after it
had ended, Akhmatova's memories had sufficiently transformed the reality of
the relationship to relieve the torment and grief which it had brought her. In
'The angel who for three years watched over me' she bows before his glorified,
shining form, celebrating his memory in terms of its newly imagined splendour:

> The angel who for three years watched over me
> Ascended in fire and rays,
> But I'm patiently awaiting that sweetest of days,
> When he returns to me.
>
> Sunken cheeks, bloodless lips,
> He won't recognise my face;
> I am no longer beautiful, no longer the one
> Whose song disturbed him.
>
> For a long time I have feared nothing on earth,
> Remembering his parting words.
> I'll bow down at his feet, when he comes,
> And I used to barely nod to him.

Another poem, also recalling Gumilev, dwells on the image of Dante being
led by Beatrice to the threshold of Paradise. The poet addresses her beloved,
confident he can hear her prayers and her words of love, now that he is with
the blessed in Paradise. (Gumilev had been arrested and shot for alleged complicity in an anti-Bolshevik conspiracy in September, 1921):

> On the white threshold of paradise,
> Glancing back, he cried: 'I will wait!'
> Dying, he bequeathed to me,
> Blessedness and poverty.
>
> And when the sky is clear,
> He watches, with resounding wings,
> How I share my crust of bread
> With those who ask it of me.
>
> And when, as after battle,
> The clouds float in blood,
> He will hear my prayers
> And my words of love.

Another of the poems, which also depicts the lover as an angel in human
form, emphasises the freedom of spirit which love affords, despite its mortal
constrictions and restraints and the torment and pain it engenders. The lover
is compared to the angel in the New Testament story who comes to heal the
maimed and the crippled derelicts assembled at the pool of Siloe, hoping for a
miraculous cure. The poet's lover, like the angel, brings her the spiritual healing powers that will enable her to survive her torment:

> Like the angel, moving upon the water,
> You looked into my face.
> You gave me back both strength and freedom,
> And in remembrance of the miracle you took the ring.
> My flush, hot and unhealthy,
> Was erased by prayerful melancholy.
> I will remember this month of blizzards,
> This uneasy northern February.

The employment of scriptural images to intimate the complexities of the
religious and romantic conflicts they explore is a feature of most of these
poems. The work which begins, 'Under an empty dwelling's frozen roof', is a

good instance of the evocative vividness which the use of Biblical imagery affords. Akhmatova wrote the work in the winter of 1915 when she was suffering from tuberculosis and feared she was going to die. Against the background of an empty house and an acute sense of personal loneliness, the heroine of the poem is shown reading the Acts of the Apostles and the Psalms. A red maple leaf in her Bible marks the place of its greatest love lyric, the Song of Songs. A symbolic association is suggested between her yearning for reunion with her lover and the soul's longing for union with God:

> Under an empty dwelling's frozen roof,
> Dead days. Here no living comes.
> I read the Acts of the Apostles
> And the Psalms.
> But the stars are blue, the hoar-frost downy,
> And each meeting more wonderful,
> And in the Bible a red maple leaf
> Marks the pages of the Song of Songs.

Yet another work, 'It goes on without end', celebrates a heavenly sensuality which is strongly suggestive of the soul-directed (as distinct from the profane, self-gratifying) eros of the Platonist tradition. Its liturgical image of the blue font and distant bell-tower evokes a spiritual fulfilment beyond material existence for which the heroine yearns. Like the deer who has flown from the Land of the Northern Lights, she is estranged from her true home, and her soul, imprisoned and fearful, longs for the paradise from which it came. It lives as a stranger on this earth but, in the cry of the deer, hears echoes of the heavenly world beyond its material reality:

> It goes on without end – the day, heavy and amber!
> How impossible is grief, how vain the waiting!
> And with a silver voice, again the deer
> Speaks in the deer-park of the Northern Lights.
> And I believe that there is cool snow,
> And a blue font for those whose hands are empty,
> And a small sledge is being wildly ridden,
> Under the ancient chimes of distant bells.

While recognising that the impulse to conceive this idealised vision of love is a natural human tendency – and one which will be shown presently to be closely linked with Akhmatova's conception of faith as a quest for the timeless – she recognised the illusory nature nonetheless of love conceived as a purely spiritual fulfilment. Repeatedly, she reiterated her belief that love is experienced as a temporal condition and must therefore find fulfilment through a direct experiencing of its temporality – not by way of escape from it. And since salvation would ultimately be attained through the self-transcendence afforded by love, that prospect could only be envisaged also by way of the direct experiencing of the conditions of finite temporality, with all the suffering that this might entail. Thus, in the poem, 'I'm looking for a place for a grave', the urge to escape from the realities of mortal life is shown to be incompatible with her Christian beliefs. As the poet yearns for a heavenly release from her sufferings, a monk reproaches her with her naivete – 'Not for you: sinners don't go to Paradise' – and she finds comfort instead in the arms of her lover:

> I'm looking for a place for a grave.
> Do you know of somewhere brighter?
> It's so cold in the fields. And dreary are
> The heaps of stones along the shore.
>
> But she is accustomed to peace,
> And she loves the light of the sun.
> I'll build a cell over her,
> To be our home for many years.
>
> Between the windows will be a little door,
> We will light an icon lamp inside,
> It will be like a dark heart
> Burning with a vermilion fire.
>
> She raved, you know, when she was sick,
> About another, a heavenly place,
> But a monk said, reproaching her:
> 'Not for you; sinners don't go to Paradise.'
>
> And then, white with pain,
> She whispered: 'I will go with you.'
> Now we are all alone, and free,
> With the blue surf at our feet.

The necessity and, from a moral and metaphysical standpoint, the fruitfulness, of the tension between the impassioned and spiritual aspects of love are further underlined in the poem, 'Under the icon, a threadbare rug'. The poem

is built around an image of a woman who has recently made love and looks
back on the experience with mixed feelings of longing and regret. The religious imagery of icons and icon-lamps combines with the image of the woman
exhausted from the act of love to intimate the complexity of the spirit-sense
tension underlying the whole experience:

> Under the icon, a threadbare rug,
> It's dark in the chilly room,
> And dark green ivy thickly
> Twines round the wide window.

> A sweet scent streams from the roses,
> The icon lamp sputters, barely aglow.
> There are chests, floridly painted
> By the craftsman's loving hand.

> And near the window a white lace frame ...
> Your profile is sharp and drawn.
> And under your handkerchief you conceal with disgust
> Fingers that have just been kissed.

> And the heart that began to pound,
> How much anguish it holds now ...
> And in the dishevelled braid lurks
> The smell of tobacco smoke.

The same tension is powerfully conveyed in a series of poems, directly
inspired by the scriptures, in which Akhmatova explores the place of woman
in history. Taking some famous heroines from the Old Testament, she emphasises the role played by women in bringing God's purpose to fulfilment
through the force of sexual passion. In 'Rachel' she reinvokes the Old
Testament story of Laban's contract with Jacob that he should serve in his
fields as a labourer for seven years to prove himself worthy of the hand of his
daughter, Rachel. The poem describes Laban's betrayal of the agreement as he
brings Jacob to the bed of his elder daughter, Leah, and Rachel's disillusionment and grief at her loss. When eventually she marries Jacob and gives birth
to Joseph, she becomes a figure of destiny in the history of the Israelite
people. 'Michal' describes the heroine's lust for the shepherd-boy, David, and
her role in indirectly influencing the events which lead to his becoming king
and fulfilling God's plan for the people of Israel. Amanda Haight,
Akhmatova's biographer, has commented on the moral significance of her

treatment of sexual themes in these poems. 'Akhmatova,' she writes, 'can show that the Old Testament woman torn by sexual desire is not outside God's love and purpose (even though she may feel that to be the case) and that, despite herself, her desire is actually helping to fulfil that purpose. Even those who feel themselves damned,' she says, 'are shown to be at that moment close to God.'[23]

Underlying all these poems is one unifying theme: the Christian theme of Incarnation, of the Word Made Flesh, which is the ultimate statement of the sacramental character of the body-spirit union and the mystery which finally comprehends its tensions, ambiguities and complexities. In the poem 'Long years I waited for him in vain' the imagery of the Eucharist is linked with an image of spiritual-sensual love to give explicit emphasis to this theme. The heroine of the poem recalls her image of a bridegroom who is both an earthly and a heavenly prince. He is the person for whom she has waited for many years. She sees him clothed in heavenly light as he passes her in solemn procession, while on a table nearby stands a chalice filled with the red wine of the Eucharist:

Long years I waited for him in vain.
That time seems like a drowsy dream.
But an inextinguishable light began to shine
On Palm Sunday Eve three years ago.
My voice broke off and was still –
My betrothed stood before me with a smile.

And outside the window people with candles
Slowly walked by. Oh, holy night!
April's thin ice cracked lightly,
And over the crowd the voice of the bells,
As if foretelling consolation, pealed,
And a black wind swayed the little flames.

And the white narcissus on the table,
And the red wine in the crystal glass
I saw as in a sunrise mist.
My hand, spotted with wax,
Trembled, receiving a kiss,
And my blood sang: Blessed one, rejoice.

The image of the Eucharist serves a similar purpose in the previously quoted, 'Memory of love, you are painful', where the heroine simultaneously 'partakes' of God's love and of human love, once again suggesting that love in all its forms immanently discloses the reality of the infinite. The Pentecostal image in 'I myself chose the fate' conveys a similar message. Love is the Pentecostal dove the heroine releases on Annunciation Day; the dove returns to flood and illuminate her room with an icon-like brightness:

> I myself chose the fate
> Of the friend of my heart:
> I set him free
> On Annunciation Day.
> But the blue-grey dove returned,
> To beat its wings against the window.
> How bright the room became,
> As if from the lustre of a miraculous icon frame.

The poet, Sergei Gorodetsky, a friend of Akhmatova and one of her colleagues in the Acmeist movement, wrote in an essay that Akhmatova 'does not seek insights into eternity at every moment' but 'takes into art those moments that are capable of being eternal'.[24] His comment appropriately describes the experiences explored in the love poems and the manner in which they disclose the eternal and the transcendent through the medium of the immanent, the temporal and the existential. At the heart of the Acmeist movement lay the conviction that the eternal and the infinite should be sought in the here and now and that human love is one of the deepest, most intense, and most commonly experienced manifestations of this truth. Akhmatova, as her biographer said, sought to convey the full meaning of this truth by demonstrating the depth of the spiritual-sensual conflict, together with the personal suffering and pain, which it entails. In particular she sought to demonstrate the positive role of the carnal and the sensual in the whole process. 'A deeply religious and at the same time passionate woman, with close ties to nature, Akhmatova,' she writes, 'was forced to examine and reject the false doctrine which placed physical desire so often in opposition to God's purpose. She reexamined and rejected the attitude to her sex which had caused so much suffering over the past century, which had divided women into those who were "pure" and those who were "fallen".' She had redefined the place of human love and sexuality – especially female sexuality – in the whole pattern of God's purpose for mankind:

> By Accepting Eve's fall as a necessary part of God's purpose, and seeing that Magdalene the prostitute fulfilled as important a role as her opposite, the Virgin Mother, she restored value to this life on earth – something which the Christian message had too often lost through teaching

us to distrust our deepest desires and to despise the flesh. The nine-teenth-century image of woman had become a split caricature, with the fainting, delicate angel-wife contrasted with the lusty whore. By reunit-ing this split within herself, Akhmatova made woman once more into a whole being, finding again the sacramental value of desire and placing it firmly within God's purpose.[25]

'WHY HAST THOU FORSAKEN ME?'

Christian imagery is used extensively, therefore, throughout Akhmatova's love poetry to convey the joys and suffering of human love as well as its moral and metaphysical complexities. It is employed for different, but in some ways par-allel, purposes in the poems she devoted to the sufferings of her fellow-coun-trymen during the two world wars and particularly during the horrors of the Stalinist terror. In these works the image of the Crucified Christ is the domi-nant motif and conveys the all-pervasive presence of suffering in the lives of the Russian people. In a poem called 'Prayer', for instance, which was written in May 1915 amidst the devastation of World War I, Russia itself is directly linked with the image of Christ on the cross. The poet begs God to accept her own sufferings as a sacrificial offering to enable Russia to be freed from its torment:

> Give me bitter years of sickness,
> Suffocation, insomnia, fever,
> Take my child and my lover,
> And my mysterious gift of song –
> This I pray at your liturgy
> After so many tormented days,
> So that the storm-cloud over darkened Russia
> Might become a cloud of glorious rays.

Several of the poems Akhmatova wrote during World War I indicate how profoundly she was affected by the slaughter and destruction. Gumilev, who had volunteered for war service, wrote to her of the horrific scale of the car-nage at the front. 'The wounds are somehow such strange ones and they don't get wounded in the breast or the head as described in novels, but in the face, the hands, the legs,' he wrote.[26] 'We aged a hundred years, and this/ Happened in a single hour,' Akhmatova wrote in one of the poems, 'In Memoriam, July 19, 1914'. Another laments the horrific waste of life, the blight of the landscape, and the whole tragedy of mass conflict – all of which it represents as an assault on the body of Christ:

The sweet smell of juniper
Flies from the burning woods
Soldiers' wives are wailing for the boys,
The widow's lament keens over the countryside.

The public prayers were not in vain,
The earth was yearning for rain!
Warm red liquid sprinkled
The trampled fields.

Low, low hangs the empty sky
And a praying voice quietly intones:
'They are wounding your sacred body,
They are casting lots for your robes.'

Despite the preponderant sense of doom in these poems, they are not without some intimations of hopefulness. One of them directly identifies this as the hopefulness afforded by faith, even in the midst of the wartime atrocities: 'The prophet looked at me/ And said: "Bride of Christ/ Do not envy the fortunate ones/ For you a place has been prepared."' This sense of the hopefulness provided by faith, however compelling the grounds for pessimism and despair, is the dominant feeling conveyed in Akhmatova's epic poem, 'Requiem', her most powerful evocation of the sufferings of her people during the years of the Stalinist terror. The event which inspired the work was the arrest and imprisonment of her son, Lev Gumilev, in March 1938, his only crime being his relationship to his father and to Akhmatova. For several months after his arrest Akhmatova went to the prison gates every day hoping to see her son and to pass him a parcel with some food and clothes. In the Preface to 'Requiem' she writes:

> In the terrible years of the Yezhov terror, I spent seventeen months in the prison lines of Leningrad. Once, someone 'recognised' me. Then a woman with bluish lips standing behind me, who, of course, had never heard me called by name before, woke up from the stupor to which everyone had succumbed and whispered in my ear (everyone spoke in whispers there):
> 'Can you describe this ?'
> And I answered: 'Yes, I can.'
> Then something that looked like a smile passed over what had once been her face.

The poem universalises the personal grief of Akhmatova as mother and wife by presenting it as an epic statement of the grief of all the women of Russia and of the terrible plight of her country under the Stalinist tyranny. It determines the spiritual and historical significance of her people's suffering by comparing it to the most momentous instance of self-sacrifice in the history of mankind: the Crucifixion of Christ on Calvary. The background against which this is affirmed is that of a whole people stricken and convulsed by the terror into which they have been plunged:

> Mountains bow down to this grief,
> Mighty rivers cease to flow,
> But the prison gates hold firm,
> And behind them are the 'prisoners' burrows'
> And mortal woe ...
> We rose as if for an early service,
> Trudged through the savaged capital
> And met there, more lifeless than the dead;
> The sun is lower and the Neva mistier,
> But hope keeps singing from afar.
> The verdict ... And her tears gush forth,
> Already she is cut off from the rest,
> As if they painfully wrenched life from her heart,
> As if they brutally knocked her flat,
> But she goes on ... Staggering ... Alone ...
> Where now are my chance friends
> Of those two diabolical years?
> What do they imagine is in Siberia's storms,
> What appears to them dimly in the circle of the moon?
> I am sending my farewell greeting to them.

The theme of communal grief points to the paradox at the heart of the poem: the paradox that the individual is both isolated by suffering and united by it with all those who share in the communal tragedy. The poem evokes both the terrifying loneliness of personal grief and the comfort the poet finds in the company of those other women who join the queues at the prison gates, hoping to catch a glimpse of their husbands and sons. In the lines which follow, the image of the moonlight shining on the quietly flowing Don, and the accompanying image of the poet alone in her house, are suggestive both of the serenity and desolation of her condition:

> Quietly flows the quiet Don,
> Yellow moon slips into a home.

He slips in with cap askew,
He sees a shadow, yellow moon.

This woman is ill,
This woman is alone,

Husband in the grave, son in prison,
Say a prayer for me.

She speaks of the inexplicable nature of suffering when seen from the
standpoint of the sufferer – 'No, it is not I, it is somebody else who is suffering' – and prays that God will erase the whole experience from her memory:
'Let them shroud it in black,/ And let them carry off the lanterns .../ Night.'
She recalls her childhood at Tsarskoe Selo – 'You should have been shown,
you mocker,/ Minion of all your friends,/ Gay little sinner of Tsarskoe Selo'
– and contrasts its naive innocence with the darkness to come. Looking back
on the seventeen months she has waited at the prison gates in Leningrad, she
dwells on the image of mankind dehumanised and brutalised by violence and
looks to the release that death might bring her:

For seventeen long months I've been crying out,
Calling you home.
I flung myself at the hangman's feet,
You are my son and my horror.
Everything is confused forever,
And it's not clear to me
Who is a beast now, who is a man,
And how long before the execution.
And there are only dusty flowers,
And the chinking of the censer, and tracks
From somewhere to nowhere.
And staring me straight in the eyes,
And threatening impending death,
Is an enormous star.

Like Christ beseeching his father to let the chalice of suffering pass from
him, she also prays that she might be released from her torment. Since this
has not been granted, she sees herself isolated from God and man – in the
'madness' of total aloneness. This is the lowest point of her suffering – her
feeling that she has been forsaken by God and by her fellow-sufferers:

Now madness half shadows
My soul with its wing,
And makes it drunk with fiery wine
And beckons toward the black ravine ...

And it does not allow me to take
Anything of mine with me
(No matter how I plead with it,
No matter how I supplicate):

Not the terrible eyes of my son –
Suffering turned to stone,
Not the day of the terror,
Not the hour I met with him in prison,

Not the sweet coolness of his hands,
Not the trembling shadow of the lindens,
Not the far-off, fragile sound –
Of the final words of consolation.

Redemption comes through her understanding of her own suffering. The stages through which the sufferer must pass – the anger ('I will be like the wives of the Streltsy/ Howling under the Kremlin's towers'), the acute personal loneliness, the sense of despair, God-forsakenness and longing for death – all this brings her eventually to an acceptance and understanding of her suffering: an understanding which is epitomised in her image of the silent composure of Mary at the foot of the cross. Mary's silence is indicative of the serenity of the spirit which is attained through faith, even in the midst of the most unbearable suffering. In her composure she is contrasted both with the weeping figure of the Magdalene, to whom suffering remains inexplicable, and with the beloved disciple, John, who stands at the foot of the cross, transfixed by the whole spectacle of Christ's death.

'Do not weep for Me, Mother,
I am in the grave.'

A choir of angels sang the praises of that momentous hour,
And the heavens dissolved in fire.
To His Father He said: 'Why hast Thou forsaken me!'
And to his Mother: 'Oh, do not weep for me ... '

Mary Magdalene beat her breast and sobbed,
The beloved disciple turned to stone,
But where the silent Mother stood, there
No one glanced and no one would have dared.

The problem of suffering is resolved in time: in the understanding that comes through faith and in the limitless powers of endurance afforded by this. Through the ages that faith has been inspired in mankind by the example of Christ's sacrifice on Calvary. The poet suggests that generations to come will similarly derive comfort and inspiration from the sufferings of the Russian people, and she vows to perpetuate their memory through her poetry:

Once more the day of remembrance draws near.
I see, I hear, I feel you:

The one they almost had to drag at the end,
And the one who tramps her native land no more ...

I will remember them always and everywhere,
I will never forget them no matter what comes.

And if they gag my exhausted mouth
Through which a hundred million scream,

Then may the people remember me
On the eve of my remembrance day.

At an early point in the poem Akhmatova had prayed that God would blot out the memory of her suffering – 'Let them shroud it in black,/ and let them carry off the lanterns'. By the end of the poem she is resolving to give permanent form to these memories through the images of her poetry. Her work, she declares, will serve as an everlasting monument to the horrors her people have endured. The memory which recalls these horrors has within itself the healing powers that all sufferers need, and both processes – those of remembering and of healing – can be served through the symbolic language of her art:

And if ever in this country
They decide to erect a monument to me,

I consent to that honour
Under these conditions – that it stand

Neither by the sea, where I was born:
My last tie with the sea is broken,

Nor in the tsar's garden near the cherished pine stump,
Where an inconsolable shade looks for me,

But here, where I stood for three hundred hours,
And where they never unbolted the doors for me.

This, lest in blissful death
I forget the rumbling of the Black Marias,

Forget how that detested door slammed shut
And an old woman howled like a wounded animal.

And may the melting snow stream like tears
From my motionless lids of bronze,

And a prison dove coo in the distance,
And the ships of the Neva sail calmly on.

'THERE WILL BE NO TIME'

The Christian mystery of the Incarnation, therefore, is the unifying theme both in Akhmatova's love poetry and in the works she devoted to the sufferings of her people during the war years and the period of the Stalinist terror. Two further aspects of this theme are explored in the works of her later years, particularly 'A Poem without A Hero' and 'The Way of All the Earth'. The first is the idea of the poetic *logos* as itself a manifestation of the mystery of the Incarnation; the second is the mysterious interrelation of the temporal and the timeless which this mystery comprehends. Both themes are closely intertwined, the process of artistic creation being seen as particularly disclosive of the paradoxical relation of the temporal and the timeless, and both point triumphantly to her faith in an existence beyond time, the affirmation of which provides a final poetic and religious resolution for all her life's activities.

Repeatedly, Akhmatova emphasised the sacredness of the poetic word, clearly regarding it as a gift from God. In her poem, 'The Muse Departed', for example, she attributes the gift of poetic inspiration to the miracle of Pentecostal grace. In another she prays that the heavenly fire will 'touch her closed eyelashes' and release her from her 'dumbness'. In 'They are flying,

they are still on the way' the inspiration she awaits comes to her eventually as
a warm red light that floods her consciousness and as a 'burning wind' that
sets her spirit on fire:

> They are flying, they are still on the way,
> The words of love and release.
> I feel that uneasiness that comes before a poem,
> And my lips are cold as ice.
>
> But there, where a few scraggly birches
> Cling to the windows and rustle dryly –
> A dark red wreath of roses twines
> And the voices of invisible speakers resound.
>
> And farther on – a light unbearably lavish
> Like hot red wine ...
> Already a fragrant, burning wind
> Sears my consciousness.

Poetry is seen as a divine gift, something that links mortal man with the
immortal and the infinite by evoking the reality of God's immanent presence
on earth. The poetic word is itself an immanent attestation of that reality. In
its radical materiality, language embodies the mystery of the Incarnation, visibly manifesting the reality of the Word made Flesh. The poet therefore, she
suggests, is God's instrument, a mediator of God's grace and, by virtue of
his/her revelation of the wisdom embodied in the poetic *logos*, is a living link
between the spheres of the finite and the infinite. 'The lines that are simply
dictated/ Appear in the snow-white notebook', Akhmatova wrote in one of her
poems, clearly seeing the poet as the instrument of a higher power. Her
Acmeist colleague, Osip Mandelstam, spoke of art as the prototypical act of
creation – 'an eternal return to the single creative act that began our historical
era',[27] i.e., the Incarnation. To the degree that they regarded poetry as inspired
utterance, and that they considered the poet was the mediator of God's truth,
the Acmeists and many of their contemporaries in twentieth century Russian
literature saw the process of artistic creation as akin to divinely inspired revelation, but they insisted the two were nonetheless distinct in their functions
and identities. 'Poetry may be sacred, but the poet himself is a poor sinner,'
Nadezhda Mandelstam wrote in *Hope Abandoned*. 'Poetry can never be equivalent to revelation – as M. never forgot for a moment ...' 'For the Christian,'
she wrote, 'the link between the empirical world and the higher one is ensured
not by means of symbols, but through revelation, the sacraments, grace, and –

most important of all – through the coming of Christ.'[28] Poetry complements
revelation insofar as it both evokes and embodies the truth of immanence, of
God's incarnational presence in material reality. The poet, in this sense, is the
mediator of truths inspired by a source beyond him/herself and beyond the
realm of the finite and the temporal, i.e., truths originating with God.

It was on the basis of such convictions that Akhmatova, in works such as
'A Poem Without A Hero, 'The Way of all the Earth' and 'Midnight Verses',
claimed a time-transcending function for poetry, by virtue of its simultaneous
evocation of the possibility of the timeless and its disclosure in the immanent
reality of the temporal order. 'A Poem Without a Hero' is predominantly a
meditation on time; it dramatises the opposition between time as a subjective
experience and time as historical objectivity, and both are contrasted, in turn,
with the supratemporal potentiality of art. The poem celebrates the power of
the artistic symbol to give permanent form to experience, to evoke the change-
lessness of its occurrence in time and, simultaneously, to disclose the prospect
of the timelessness which a transcendence of the empirical implies. Thus, in
the second dedication of the poem – which Akhmatova addressed to her
deceased childhood friend, the dancer, Olga Sudeykina – the imagery of death
is interwoven with images of springtime, symbolising the resurrection of the
spirit. The lyrical images of the pure flame in clay, and the snow-drop on the
grave of her friend, symbolise her belief in an existence beyond the finite and
the temporal:

> I sleep –
> She alone hovers over me –
> The one people call spring,
> I call loneliness.
> I sleep –
> I dream of our youth,
> The cup that passed him by;
> Waking, I'll give it to you,
> If you want, as a souvenir
> Like a pure flame in a dish of clay
> Or a snowdrop in an open grave.

Time-transcendence is again is the theme of 'The Way of All the Earth',
Akhmatova's most elaborate poetic statement of her faith in a Paradise beyond
the grave. The epigraph from the Revelation of St John with which the poem
begins – 'And the Angel swore to the living that there will be no Time' – provides scriptural support for the poet's evocation of the prospect of a timeless
existence. Kitezh, the legendary place saved from a Tartar invasion and lifted

miraculously to heaven while its reflection remained in the lake where the
Tartars drowned, is the poem's focal image of a place beyond the temporal.
The Woman of Kitezh is shown rising from the turmoil of earthly life to reach
the comfort of her unearthly Paradise:

How brilliantly risen,
An island that burns!
Red clay again and
The apple orchard ...
O, Salve Regina! –
The sunset a torchglow.
The footpath climbs steeply,
A trembling, and
Somebody is needed
To stretch me a hand ...
But unheard is the harsh
Barrel-organ. It groans,
But the woman of Kitezh
Can hear other sounds.

Through the voice of the Woman of Kitezh Akhmatova declares that
Paradise is her ultimate destiny. If earthly life seemed absurd and cruel, she
would find comfort and peace in the prospect of a timeless existence beyond
it. The understanding she achieved in 'Requiem', through her contemplation
of life from the foot of the cross, together with the heartbreak recorded in the
love poems, convinced her that suffering – because of its disclosure of the reality of the supratemporal – alone makes sense of an otherwise senseless existence. Poetry could evoke the reality of the Paradise that can be reached only
through endurance of suffering. 'The longing to return to Kitezh,' Amanda
Haight writes, 'far from manifesting a desired escape from earthly life, confirms its potentiality.' It embodies aspirations that are fundamentally religious.
'The poem,' she says, 'is not about escape from life but one which expresses
faith in the most profound sense of the word. Strength here stems from the
recognition that the poet has come from God and will one day return to Him,
and that she must make her way through time to the place where there will be
none.'[29] There, in Kitezh, she will find the long sought repose for her soul:

For the great
Winter I have waited long,
Like a monk's white
Habit I have put it on.

> Calmly I sit in the light
> Sledge, and to you, men and women
> Of Kitezh, before night
> I shall return.

Musical metaphors are frequently used by Akhmatova to convey this transcendence of the temporal and the repose of the spirit and self-understanding which it affords. It is significant that comparisons have been made so frequently between her treatment of the legend of the Woman of Kitezh and Rimsky-Korsakov's version of it in his opera. 'The musical motifs which we encounter in the earliest poetry of Akhmatova attain their highest frequency and their most essential symbolic function in the latest period of the poet's development,' writes Kees Verheul. 'Music forms the medium through which the peculiar suspended reality of the looking-glass world most naturally expresses itself ... To use a paradoxical formulation, based upon the symbols of *Polnochnye Stikhi*, it is the sound of silence.'[30] 'Poem Without A Hero' has frequent references to specific musical compositions – to *Don Giovanni*, for example, which provides its opening epigraph and to the *Leningrad Symphony* which provides its closing motif. 'When I was young I loved architecture and water, now I love music and earth,' Akhmatova told Anatoly Nayman.[31] In one of her last poems, 'A Fragment', she described music as a source of comfort and peace, something that could evoke the reality of a timeless existence:

> And music shared peace with me,
> Most compliant of all companions.
> Often she would lead me out
> To the very edge of my existence.

'Midnight Verses', a further collection from Akhmatova's final years, magnificently displays this musical imagery of time-transcendence. The poems suggest that death, like all human separations, is ultimately transient, since human relationships survive in the life of the spirit. 'What is it to us/ That everything is turning to ashes,' the second poem in the cycle asks. Beyond the grave, it suggests, lies the infinite, symbolised as silence transformed into music. In 'The Call' the lover says her partner will disappear in a musical sonata but in the next poem responds that they will be reunited, once again in the world of music – this time in an *adagio* by Vivaldi. 'Not on the leaf-strewn asphalt,/ Will you have to wait./ But in a Vivaldi adagio,/ We will meet,' she cries triumphantly. In 'Thirteen Lines', the fourth poem from the cycle, the lovers' idealised union is seen as a 'silence burst into song', the transformation occurring against a background of the purest sunlight and of a world transfigured by its light:

And finally you pronounced the word,
Not like those ... who on one knee –
But like someone who escaped from captivity
And sees the birches' sacred canopy
Through a rainbow of unexpected tears.
And around you the silence burst into song,
And pure sunlight brightened the gloom.
And for a moment the world was transformed,
And the taste of the wine was different.
And even I, whose fate it was to be
The assassin of that divine word,
Was almost reverentially silent,
In order to prolong this blessed moment.

Most of the poems of Akhmatova's declining years have similar affirmations of the existence of a life beyond death. In 'Seventh Book', a collection that includes poems from the 1920s to the last years of her life, she included one that was written in 1921. In this poem she mourns the loss of her friends, but finds comfort in memories of her childhood at Tsarskoe Selo and in the images of lyre music which symbolise the prospect of eternal reunion in Paradise:

All the souls of my loved ones are on stars high above.
How good it is that there is no one left to lose
And one can weep. The air of Tsarskoe Selo
Was created for the echoing of songs.

By the bank a silver willow
Touches the bright September waters.
Arisen from the past, silently
My shade comes to meet me.

Here so many lyres hang on the branches,
But it seems there's a place for mine as well.
And this shower, scattered and sunny,
Is comfort and good news to me.

The world beyond time, as Akhmatova affirms repeatedly, can be reached only through life *in* time; poetry, through the time-transcendence it enacts, provides the link between the two. It reveals the meaning underlying the apparently inexplicable sufferings of existence, its disorder, chaos and experienced meaninglessness. To a Christian believer, the meaning that is disclosed derives ultimately, she declares, from the mystery of the Incarnation and its empirical manifestation in the miracle of immanence. As Amanda Haight writes: 'Akhmatova recognised that for those who are able to fathom its significance, the Crucifixion is the most splendid drama of life. This was no approbation of man's cruelty and blindness but rather an understanding that the Cross is at the turning-point of man's journey and marks the beginning of his return to Paradise ... True Paradise is not, however, that nauseating Eden of innocence constantly threatened by knowledge. It is to be reached by passing the way of the cross and to which one returns willingly having been to the other side of Hell and seen all there is to see and known all there is to know.'[32] The paradox that salvation is achieved in time, that life with all its uncertainty and torment is the way to the infinite and the eternal, can be illustrated finally from a beautiful sequence of lyrical poems completed by Akhmatova shortly before her death. In 'The Wild Rose Comes Into Bloom' she once again emphasises the illusory nature of mortal separation and the expected reunion that occurs beyond the grave, but in this instance her emphasis is on the impassioned moments of life through which that prospect is attained. The poems were inspired by a 'non-meeting' between Akhmatova and her close friend, the philosopher, Isaiah Berlin.[33] Fearing the consequences of being seen with a foreigner – she was particularly fearful it would lead to the rearrest of her son – she declined Berlin's invitation to meet him during a visit to St Petersburg in 1956. Recalling the experience in the poems, she sees her non-meeting with Berlin as symbolising the illusory nature of mortal separation and as pointing to the reality of the love that survives all earthly partings. The work is one of her finest affirmations of her belief in the immortality of the spirit. These lines are from the third and fourth poems in the cycle:

> This black and everlasting separation
> I bear equally with you.
> Why are you crying? Rather give me your hand,
> Promise to visit my dreams again.
> You and I are like two mountains ...
> You and I will not meet in this world.
> If only at the midnight hour
> You'd send me a greeting across the stars.
>
> The celebrations
> Of secret nonmeetings are empty,
> Unspoken conversations,

Unuttered words.
Glances that don't intersect
Don't know where to come to rest.
And only the tears rejoice
Because they can flow and flow.
Sweetbrier around Moscow,
Alas! Somehow it is here ...
And all this they will call
Love eternal.

9

'Credo ut Intelligam':
W.H. Auden's Vision of Christian Co-inherence

'Only he who is true can speak the truth'
Words and the Word[1]

'The powers that we create with are not ours'
New Year Letter

POETRY AND THE SACRED

In 1939 T.S. Eliot completed the text of a lecture, 'Types of English Religious Verse', which he planned to deliver later that year in the course of a tour of Italy that had been organised for him by the British Council. The tour was cancelled, following the outbreak of World War II, and the lecture was never delivered. Its text has survived, however, and is available for consultation amongst Eliot's papers at King's College Library in Cambridge. In the text of the lecture Eliot spoke of his conviction that 'the religious poetry of our time will be concerned primarily with giving poetic form to theological thought' and he pointed to the philosophy of Kierkegaard as having a particular relevance for poets seeking to define the meaning of religious, and specifically Christian, traditions in the circumstances of the present age.[2] There is no indication that Eliot was referring to any particular poet in the lecture, but his comments seem, in retrospect, to have identified with particular accuracy the aims and purposes that W.H. Auden, his friend and protégé, had decided at that same time would determine the shape and evolution of his poetry.

'Am reading Kierkegaard's *Journal* at the moment, which is fascinating,' Auden wrote to his friend, the classical scholar, E.M. Dodds, in March 1940. He declared he had been 'bowled over by the originality of Kierkegaard's writings' and was deeply impressed by the profundity of his philosophical and religious insights.[3] Auden had discovered Kierkegaard's writings as a result of reading *The Descent of the Dove*, a theological work by his friend and fellow poet, Charles Williams. Following brief flirtations with Freudianism and Marxism, Auden turned to Williams and Kierkegaard for an alternative to the relativism of secularist philosophy. 'The whole trend of liberal thought has been to undermine faith in the absolute,' he wrote in 1940. 'It has tried to make reason the judge ... But since life is a changing process ... the attempt

323

to find a humanistic basis for keeping a promise works logically with the conclusion, "I can break it whenever I feel it convenient".'[4]

His sense of the need for absolute criteria in matters of morality and faith was greatly reinforced by his awareness of the growing evidence of the human potential for evil that was manifested in Nazism and the catastrophe it was forcing on mankind. 'Either we serve the Unconditional/ Or some Hitlerian monster will supply/ An iron convention to do evil by,' he wrote in one of his early wartime poems. His awareness of the fallenness of man, and of his apparently limitless capacity for evil, was further strengthened by his readings in the work of the Canadian theologian, Reinhold Niebuhr, especially his three books, *An Interpretation of Christian Ethics*, *Christianity and Power Politics* and *The Nature and Destiny of Man*.[5] The writings of Niebuhr, together with those of Williams and Kierkegaard, were largely responsible for shaping the Christian vision that dominated Auden's poetry from 1940 to his death in 1977. That vision is particularly in evidence in four major poems he produced in those years: 'New Year Letter', 'For the Time Being', 'The Sea and the Mirror' and 'The Age of Anxiety'. These are the main works on which the present study will be focussed.

The initial question to be addressed, however, is the highly complex one of how Auden conceived of the relationship between his art and his faith and how he defined the various processes by which religious beliefs are given expression in poetry. A fundamental distinction regarding the nature of poetic language in his essay, 'The World of the Sagas', is the key to much of his thinking on this whole matter. 'Present in every human being,' he writes, 'are two desires: a desire to know the truth about the primary world, the given world outside ourselves in which we are born, live, love, hate, and die; and the desire to make new secondary worlds of our own, or if we cannot make them ourselves, to share in the secondary worlds of those who can.'[6] The first of these 'desires' he designates 'the will to truth', the recording or 'historical' tendency; the second he calls 'the will to recreation', the poetic tendency.[7] The first is focussed on objectivity and is concerned with all existent realities external to the self, including the language and literature in which these realities are named and retained. The second he sees as a purely subjective tendency, springing from the self's dissatisfaction with external reality and its desire to recreate it. In this secondary world the self aims to transcend the limitations of objective reality; the world it creates is one in which the individual self is 'omniscient', from which it excludes everything except what it 'finds sacred, important and enchanting'.[8] Both these worlds, however, are linked in a variety of ways, the common factor between them being the language through which both tendencies are given expression. Language is the single, unified medium which comprehends both the objective and subjective worlds

addressed by the 'will to truth' and the 'will to recreate', the worlds of actual
and imagined reality

To appreciate the full significance of this distinction it needs to be taken in
conjunction with a further discussion of the nature of poetic language in 'The
Dyer's Hand', where Auden gives his interpretation of Coleridge's theory of
the primary and the secondary imagination. In this essay he defines the primary imagination as a response to what it sees as sacred in reality: it is 'a passion
of awe', he writes, which differentiates the sacred from the profane and spontaneously directs its reverence towards the first. The secondary imagination, he
says, is focussed on beauty, which it differentiates from ugliness, while simultaneously comprehending the manifestations of beauty in the spheres both of
the sacred and the profane. Its concern is the world of Form, whereas the concern of the primary imagination is the world of Being. The primary imagination is directed 'at what is', the secondary at 'what ought to be', 'what can be,
what is possible'. Both kinds of imagination, he says, are 'essential to the
health of the mind'.[9] The passion of awe, with its spontaneous reverence for
the sacred, needs the self-renewing vitality of the passion for beauty, without
which the objects of its reverence become mechanical and banal. The impulse
to create art comes into being, he writes, when the passion for awe is transformed into homage to beauty, when the sacred is contemplated in its relation
to the profane.

Auden argues that both tendencies, those of the primary and secondary
imagination, are necessarily intertwined in the language of art. Being a symbolic, historically and culturally conditioned medium, language is heavily resonant
with objective and subjective, sacred and profane meaning. It embraces the
fundamental synthesis of being and form: 'It has been said that a poem should
not mean but be,' he writes. 'This is not quite accurate. In a poem as distinct
from many other kinds of verbal societies, meaning and being are identical.'[10]
Inherent in every poem, he says, is a tension of subject and object, of belief
and form, of image and reality. Ultimately, all these find expression in a tension at the heart of the creative process itself: 'The nature of the final poetic
order is the outcome of a dialectical struggle between the recollected occasions
of feeling and the verbal system.'[11] The dialectic comprehends the disorder
and unfreedom of the historical world and the order and harmony of the world
conceived by the artist. His activity is a radical act of creation analogous to the
creativity of God:

> ... the poet's activity in creating a poem is analogous to God's activity in
> creating man after his own image. It is not an imitation, for were it so,
> the poet would be able to create like God, *ex nihilo*; instead, he requires
> pre-existing occasions of feeling and a pre-existing language out of which

to create. It is analogous in that the poet creates, not necessarily according to a law of nature, but voluntarily according to provocation.[12]

To this two further propositions are added. The first concerns the moral complexity of the act of artistic creation. In 'The Dyer's Hand' Auden writes: 'It is not the duty of a witness to pass moral judgment on the evidence he has to give, but to give it clearly and accurately ... When we say that poetry is beyond good and evil we simply mean that a poet can no more change the facts of what he has felt than, in the natural order, parents can change their inherited physical characteristics which they pass on to their children.'[13] What the artist attempts is the creation of an order transcending the historical and temporal, but this is expressed through the language and imagery of the historical and the temporal. It comprehends the contradictions of the real and the ideal, the moral and immoral, the time-bound and the temporal, the sacred and the profane:

> Every poem, therefore, is an attempt to present an analogy to that paradisal state in which Freedom and Law, System and Order, are united in harmony. Every good poem is very nearly a Utopia. Again, an analogy, not an imitation; the harmony is possible and verbal only.
>
> It follows ... that a poem is beautiful or ugly to the degree that it succeeds or fails in reconciling contradictory feelings in an order of mutual propriety. Every beautiful poem presents an analogy to the forgiveness of sins; an analogy, not an imitation, because it is not evil intentions which are repented of and pardoned but contradictory feelings which the poet surrenders to the poem in which they are reconciled.
>
> The effect of beauty, therefore, is good to the degree that, through its analogies, the goodness of created existence, the historical fall into unfreedom and disorder, and the possibility of regaining paradise through repentance and forgiveness are recognised. Its effect is evil to the degree that beauty is taken, not as analogous to, but identical with goodness, so that the artist regards himself or is regarded by others as God, the pleasure of beauty taken for the joy of Paradise, and the conclusion drawn that, since all is well in the work of art, all is well in history. But all is not well there.[14]

Joseph Brodsky, in an essay called 'To Please A Shadow', examines the nature of Auden's beliefs about language and explores the links between the formal and technical aspects of his work and the spiritual and metaphysical themes it is designed to convey. Boundless in his admiration for Auden – 'the greatest mind of the twentieth century', 'a poet whose intelligence has no equal', 'a new kind of metaphysical poet', 'a sensibility unique in its combination of honesty, clinical detachment and controlled lyricism' – he writes of Auden's sense of the ontical priority of language, that is, its priority over the temporal and the spatial in the sphere of Being. Recalling the impression made on him by Auden's words, 'Time worships language,' he writes: 'The train of thought that statement set in motion in me is trundling to this day ... If time worships language, it means that language is greater or older than time, which is, in its turn, greater and older than space.'[15] He sees the act of poetic creation as an activity analogous to that of the original act of creation, as Auden himself had suggested in the words cited earlier from 'The Dyer's Hand'. The critical issue, he says, is the ultimate source of poetic creativity, i.e., the source of the language the poet employs creatively. 'If time – which is synonymous with, nay, even absorbs deity – worships language, where then does language come from?' he asks. 'For the gift is always smaller than the giver. And then isn't language a repository of time? And isn't this why time worships it? And isn't a song, or a poem, or indeed a speech itself, with its caesuras, pauses, spondees, and so forth, a game language plays to restructure time?'[16]

There are a number of issues that must be addressed before these questions can be resolved. Firstly, Brodsky, by virtue of his insistence on the radically creative nature of the act of poetic composition (a restructuring of the temporal etc.), sees it as intrinsically a religious activity, ultimately an act of homage to the infinite, the unconditioned and intemporal. In the case of Auden's work, he sees this as being achieved through the employment of the language of common speech. 'I had yet to hear from his very mouth,' he writes, 'that "J.S. Bach was terribly lucky. When he wanted to praise the Lord, he'd write a chorale or a cantata addressing the Almighty directly. Today if a poet wishes to do the same thing, he has to employ indirect speech." The same presumably would apply to prayer.'[17] What Auden did, he suggests, was to recognise the presence of the infinite in the finite, the intemporal in the temporal, the sacred in the profane – all through the resources of common speech. 'Auden', he writes, was 'as fond of translating metaphysical verities into the pedestrian of common sense as he was of spotting the former in the latter.' 'By going very thoroughly about creation, he tells you more about the Creator than any impertinent agonist shortcutting through the spheres ... he simply served an infinity greater than we normally reckon with and he bears good witness to its availability.' Echoing Pasternak's words on poetic inspiration, Brodsky concludes: 'I realised that I was reading a poet who spoke the truth – or through whom the truth made itself audible.'[18]

Brodsky's most fundamental question, 'where does language come from?' is not answered directly in his essay. But there is an important clue to his meaning in a passage towards the end of the work. Acknowledging his gratitude for Auden's poetry, he writes: 'One should feel grateful to fate for having been exposed to this reality, for the lavishing of these gifts, all the more priceless since they are not designated for anybody in particular. One may call this a generosity of the spirit, except that the spirit needs a man to refract itself through.' And he adds this vital qualifying statement: 'It is not the man who becomes sacred because of this refraction: it's the spirit that becomes human and comprehensible.'[19] Language precedes time – that is the essential message of the words in Genesis, 'In the beginning is the Word.' But language itself originates in Love, in the eternal 'Thouness' of the infinite – to use the terminology of Buber and Levinas with which both Brodsky's and Auden's views are remarkably consistent.[20] This is the power which becomes 'human and comprehensible' through the act of poetic creation. What he 'worshipped' in Auden, Brodsky says, was 'love perpetuated by language', 'love expanded or accelerated by language, by the necessity of expressing it'. This he saw as the informing dynamic in the whole of Auden's life and work:

> In general, I think this man was terribly mistaken for a social commentator, or a diagnostician, or some such thing. The most frequent charge that's been levelled against him was that he didn't offer a cure. I guess in a way he asked for that by resorting to Freudian, then Marxist, then ecclesiastical terminology. The cure, though, lay precisely in his employing these terminologies, for they are simply different dialects in which one can speak about one and the same thing, which is love. It is the intonation with which one talks to the sick that cures. This poet went among the world's grave, often terminal cases not as a surgeon but as a nurse, and every patient knows that it's nurses and not incisions that eventually put one back on one's feet. It's the voice of a nurse, that is, of love, that one hears in the final speech of Alonso to Ferdinand in 'The Sea and the Mirror':

> But should you fail to keep your kingdom
> And, like your father before you, come
> Where thought accuses and feeling mocks,
> Believe your pain ...

> Neither physician nor angel, nor – least of all – your beloved or relative will say this at the moment of your final defeat: only a nurse or a poet, out of experience as well as out of love.[21]

The theme of poetry as an evocation of the interpersonal – and ultimately of the interpersonal in the form of the spirit's dialogue with the infinite – is developed by Auden himself in his essay, 'Words and the Word', the last of the T.S. Eliot Memorial lectures. Here he differentiates between the individual and personal modes of existence. As a person, he writes, man is a unique and autonomous being, exercising his freedom in accordance with the primary orientation of his being towards otherness and communion through love. As an individual, he is a social being, subject to cultural, historical and economic conditioning, his behaviour manifesting the characteristic norms of the social group to which he belongs. Language, he suggests, is similarly both a mode of personal utterance and a code of social communication. (In Buber's terms it conveys both the intersubjective dialogue of the I-Thou and the objectified functionality of the I-It.) 'As persons,' Auden writes, 'we are capable of speech proper. In speech one unique person addresses another unique person and does so voluntarily ... We speak as persons because we desire to disclose ourselves to each other and to share our experiences, not because we need to share them, but because we enjoy sharing them.'[22] Speech, he writes, is a 'naming of the world', a dialogue by which the addressing subject recognises the personhood of all existent being. Poetry, he says, is personal speech in its purest and most authentic form:

> Poetry is personal speech in its purest form. It is concerned, and only concerned, with human beings as unique persons. What men do from necessity or by second nature as individual members of a society cannot be the subject of poetry, for poetry is gratuitous utterance. As Paul Valery said: 'In poetry everything that must be said cannot be said well.' It is essentially a spoken, not a written word. One can never grasp a poem one is reading unless one hears the actual sound of the words, and its meaning is the outcome of a dialogue between the words of the poem and the response of whoever is listening to them. Not only is every poem unique, but its significance is unique for each person who responds to it.In so far as one can speak of poetry as conveying knowledge, it is the kind of knowledge conveyed by the biblical phrase 'Then Adam knew Eve his wife'; knowing is inseparable from being known. To say that poetry is ultimately concerned only with human persons does not, of course, mean that it is always overtly about them. We are always intimately related to non-human natures, and unless we try to understand and relate to what we are not, we shall never understand what we are. The poet has to preserve and express by art what primitive peoples knew instinctively, namely, that for man nature is a realm of sacramental analogies.[23]

Paradoxically, the personal vision communicated through poetry is not one of individual utterance – an expression of the self – but one conveying truths that lie beyond the realm of individual experience and hold a universal validity for the whole of mankind. 'To say that a poem is a personal utterance does not mean that it is an act of self-expression,' Auden writes. 'The experience a poet endeavours to embody in a poem is an expression of a reality common to all men; it is only his in that this reality is perceived from a perspective which nobody but he can occupy.'[24] What he conveys is the sacramental truth inherent in authentic, personal speech, its evocation of the reality of the infinite. He quotes the words of both the Old and the New Testament to indicate the sacramental character of living speech: that is, its material attestation of the immanent presence of the Creator in His Creation, the presence of the infinite in the finite. He cites the words of Genesis: 'For as the rain cometh down and the snow from heaven, and returneth not thither, but watereth the earth and maketh it bring forth and bud, that it may give seed to the earth, so shall my word be that goeth forth out of my mouth.' And from the New Testament he cites the words of Christ: 'Man shall not live by bread alone, but by the word that proceedeth out of the mouth of God.'[25] The paradox of God, the source of the Word, as transcending creation and yet being immanently present within it, is conveyed succinctly in the words of St John: 'In the beginning was the Word and the Word was with God and the Word *was* God.'

To the degree that poetry conveys the truth of interpersonal dialogue, of man's address to the infinite, it is to be seen as a religious activity, though this is subject, in turn, to the authenticity of the dialogue which it unfolds. 'Only he who is true can speak the truth', Auden declares in 'Words and the Word'.[26] In the same essay he quotes the words of George MacDonald to intimate the universal character of the religious experience conveyed by the poet and the revelatory function that the poet fulfils in conveying it: 'In every man there is an inner chamber of peculiar life into which God only may enter. There is also a chamber in God himself into which none can enter but the one, the peculiar man – out of which chamber that man has to bring revelation and strength to his brethren. That is that for which he was made – to reveal the secret things of the Father.' And, in the same vein, Auden cites the words of Rosenstock-Huessy: 'Nobody can look on God as an object. He is the power that makes us speak. He puts the words of life into our lips.'[27] In an early work, 'The Prolific and Devourer' which was modelled on Pascal's *Pensées* and Blake's *Marriage of Heaven and Hell*, Auden declared his conviction that the religious impulse is a universal potentiality inherent in the nature of man and that all religions are attempts to identify and delineate the laws of God as manifested in earthly reality.[28] It is this universal presence of the religious in human consciousness he sees poetry as being especially equipped to convey, and this is the primary sense in which his work is to be defined as religious.

In the same work he further declared his conviction that Christianity most fully accommodates the religious needs of western man. 'Jesus convinces me,' he wrote, 'that he was right because what he taught has become consistently more and more the necessary and natural attitude for man as society has developed the way it has, i.e., he forecast our historical evolution correctly.'[29] That conviction was to find expression in Auden's personal espousal of the Christian faith shortly after he wrote 'The Prolific and Devourer'. By that stage he was differentiating between the 'natural' sense of the religious which is universally evoked through all poetry – through its attestation of the infinite – and the 'cultural' awareness of the infinite which is manifested through faith. Correspondingly, there are two senses in which he can be described as a religious poet. The first is the universal sense that has been explored so far in this chapter; the second is the specifically Christian sense in which his work can be described as religious from the time of his conversion to the Christian faith. The complexities of the latter issue will be examined in the forthcoming section.

'WHAT THOUGHT CANNOT THINK': ART, IMAGINATION AND FAITH

The relationship of art to faith has to be explained in the context of a broader theme which dominates much of Auden's writing: the idea of man as a being characterised by the divided nature of his consciousness and by the everpresent tensions existing between its different modes and activities. In his Introduction to *The Descent of the Dove* he described the basic theme of that work as 'a doctrine of exchange and substitution' whereby every individual is seen to be constantly at odds with himself, 'exchanging' two sides of his nature in a state of perpetual oscillation. Auden saw the tensions of a divided consciousness as being particularly manifested in the nature of faith and frequently quoted this epigram from *The Descent of the Dove* to illustrate this point: 'We are, I know not how, double in ourselves, so that what we believe we disbelieve and cannot rid ourselves of what we condemn.'[30] The tensions of the rational and irrational and the interpenetration of belief and intellectual doubt – which he saw as being central to the whole experience of faith – are paralleled by the tensions of imagination and faith, which he considered to be correspondingly fruitful in achieving the deepened consciousness from which faith in the possibility of a final co-inherence could ultimately spring. In several of his poems, particularly 'New Year Letter' (which was originally entitled 'The Double Man'), he spoke of the necessity for dialectical tension in the pursuit of truth and, like Kierkegaard, denounced 'one-sided' approaches to truth as fallacious attempts to resolve the essential dichotomies characterising the nature of human consciousness. His particular targets were idealism, romanticism and socialism, three modern types of abstract reductionism – the first a rationalist, the second an imaginative, and the third a social reductionism – each falsely extolling a particular potentiality in consciousness at the expense of its dialectical wholeness.

The tensions of art and faith are seen by Auden as being rooted in an underlying conflict between the orders of aesthetic and empirical reality. This whole theme is explored in many of his poems and goes to the heart of his artistic and religious beliefs. The theme is introduced in the first part of 'New Year Letter' and is further developed in 'The Sea and the Mirror', his poetic commentary on Shakespeare's play, *The Tempest*. Closely following the Kierkegaardian triad of aesthetic, ethical and religious modes of existence, 'New Year Letter' examines the imaginative, rational and ethico-religious responses to experience and points to the complex interrelations that exist between them. It contrasts the disorder of empirical reality with the idealised order of art, points to the impotence of art in the face of the processes of flux and change, intimates its capacity to effect judgements on reality while itself being distanced from the ethical principles underlying them, and emphasises its potential for the disclosure of the possibility of transcending the reality which its images reflect. The dichotomous tensions of the orders of art and reality are conveyed in this sequence from the work:

> To set in order – that's the task
> Both Eros and Apollo ask;
> For Art and Life agree in this
> That each intends a synthesis,
> That order which must be the end
> That all self-loving things intend ...
> Art in intention is mimesis
> But, realised, the resemblance ceases;
> Art is not life and cannot be
> A midwife to society,
> For art is a *fait accompli*.
> What they should do, or how, or when
> Life-order comes to living men
> It cannot say, for it presents
> Already lived experience
> Through a convention that creates
> Autonomous completed states.

In the prefatory sequence to 'The Sea and the Mirror' the speaker, contrasting childhood fantasy with the mature products of the imagination, suggests the relation of art to life is one of analogy rather than identity and, while pointing to the gulf between the two, sees the images of art as being inextricably intertwined with experience of common reality. Significantly, Auden echoes Kierkegaard in suggesting that art cannot directly represent the sphere of religious truth, a sphere ultimately reachable only through faith:

> Well, who in his own backyard
> Has not opened his heart to the smiling
> Secret he cannot quote ?
> Which goes to show that the Bard
> Was sober when he wrote
> That this world of fact we love
> Is insubstantial stuff:
> All the rest is silence
> On the other side of the wall;
> And the silence ripeness,
> And the ripeness all.

Art, he suggests, is both mimetic and paradigmatic, showing us how we are by its indirect reflections of reality, and showing us how we might be by its images of the ideal order which it creates. In his essay, 'The Poet of the Encirclement' Auden wrote: 'By significant details, it [art] shows us that our present state is neither as virtuous nor as secure as we thought, and by the lucid pattern into which it unifies these details, its assertion that order is possible, it faces us with the command to make it actual.'[31] Glimpsing the possibility of an ideal order, man cannot remain content but must exert himself to make it realisable. This is one of the dilemmas springing from the condition of divided consciousness – the dilemma that Prospero is called on to confront. In the poem, Prospero, the artist-magician, reviews his life in old age. 'Having sailed twenty thousand fathoms', he now recognises that art, by creating images of an ideal order, offers an escape from the tedium and anxiety of mortal existence. He realises that it has provided images of transcendence and disclosed its limitless possibilities, but sees that the reality of transcendence can be attained only through faith. Yet the leap of faith becomes possible only when man is aware of his mortal inadequacies and when he realises the possible existence of an order transcending the temporal. Both purposes are served by art. Leaving his enchanted isle, and breaking his ties with Ariel and the world of magical illusion, Prospero finds that his images suggest both the limitations of mortal nature and its potential for self-transcendence. 'All that we are not stares back at what we are,' he declares, as he realises that his 'alone-ness' is the prelude to faith:

> When I woke into my life, a sobbing dwarf
> Whom giants served only as they pleased, I was not what I seemed;
> Beyond their busy backs I made a magic
> To ride away from a father's imperfect justice,
> Take vengeance on the Romans for their grammar,
> Usurp the popular earth and blot forever
> The gross insult of being a mere one among many:
> Now, Ariel, I am that I am, your late and lonely master
> Who knows now what magic is: – the power to enchant
> That comes from disillusion. What the books can teach one
> Is that most desires end up in stinking ponds,
> But we have only to learn to sit still and give no orders,
> To make you offer us your echo and your mirror;
> We have only to believe you, then you dare not lie;
> To ask for nothing, and at once from your calm eyes,
> With their lucid proof of apprehension and disorder,
> All we are not stares back at what we are.

Prospero has dispensed, therefore, with shadows and illusions and come to grips with his mortal reality. Through the ages he had dreamed 'about some tremendous journey he was taking'; he now realises 'the journey really exists' and 'I have to take it inch by inch/ Alone and on foot.' He has thrown his books into the sea – the symbol of primordial flux and formlessness. What he must now confront is the absurdity of existence, its apparent meaninglessness, which can be transcended only through faith. The attempt to do so through imagination he recognises as a romantic fallacy, an attempt to create an ideal order of being on the basis of images and symbols. His enchanted isle was such a creation; aesthetically perfect, its reality was persistently challenged by the evidence of human brutishness embodied in Ariel's opposite, Caliban. As Prospero looks to the future he recognises the necessity of suffering – 'Can I learn to suffer/ Without saying something ironic or funny' – and realises that it marks the way to the religious fulfilment which is attainable through faith:

> When I am safely home, oceans away in Milan, and
> Realise once and for all I shall never see you again,
> Over there, maybe, it won't seem quite so dreadful
> Not to be interesting any more, but an old man
> Just like other old men, with eyes that water
> Easily in the wind, and a head that nods in the sunshine,

Forgetful, maladroit, a little grubby,
And to like it. When the servants settle me into a chair
In some well-sheltered corner of the garden,
And arrange my muffler and rugs, shall I ever be able
To stop myself from telling them what I am doing,
Sailing alone, out over seventy thousand fathoms – ?
Yet if I speak I shall sink without a sound
Into unmeaning abysses. Can I learn to suffer
Without saying something ironic or funny
On suffering? I never suspected the way of truth
Was a way of silence where affectionate chat
Is but a robbers' ambush and even good music
In shocking taste; and you, of course, never told me.

That imagination provides both the self-awareness and the evocations of transcendent possibility which are essential conditions for faith is made evident again in the sections of 'The Sea and the Mirror' which are focussed on Antonio and Caliban. Unlike Prospero, Antonio is the character who withdraws from the ideal order created by art and represents the world of actuality which is constantly in conflict with it. His stance is one of defiance, egotism and pride; his refusal to join in the final act of reconciliation suggests an inability to accept the possibility of transcending the basic imperfection of nature. His condition resembles that described by Kierkegaard as one of 'defiant despair' – the condition which permanently challenges the transcendence either of art or faith. 'It is the despair of willing despairingly to be oneself,' Kierkegaard wrote; 'with hatred for existence it wills to be itself, to be itself in terms of its misery.'[32] Ultimately, what Antonio represents is the world of experiential being where the potential for evil conflicts endlessly with the idealised image of human perfectibility and transcendence projected through art. The reconciliation at the end of the play, from which he withdraws, is an image of an idealised harmony which his nature will not permit him to accept. Rejecting Prospero's invitation to join the group, he asserts the independence and absolute autonomy of the individual will:

As I exist so you shall be denied,
Forced to remain our melancholy mentor,
The grown-up man, the adult in his pride,
Never have time to curl up at the centre
Time turns on when completely reconciled,
Never become and therefore never enter
The green occluded pasture as a child.

Your all is partial, Prospero;
My will is all my own:
Your need to love shall never know
Me: I am I, Antonio,
By choice myself alone.

But Antonio's refusal to participate in an idealised harmony of nature points not only to the conflict of imagination and reality but also to the moral limitations of art and of the idealised world it creates. In a passage from 'The Dyer's Hand' Auden emphasised the moral neutrality of art. 'Imagination,' he wrote, 'is without desire and is therefore incapable of distinguishing between permitted and forbidden possibilities; it only knows that they are imaginatively possible.'[33] This is reiterated in poetic form in 'New Year Letter': 'Art is not life and cannot be/ A midwife to society' … 'What they should do, or how, or when/ Life-order comes to living men/ It cannot say … ' Repeatedly, he wrote of the naivete of the romantic poets in representing the artist as moral arbiter, thereby elevating art to the plane of the ethical, and effecting a spurious resolution of the fundamental dichotomy of the real and the ideal. The ethical, he insists, derives from man's self-awareness, his sense of his fallenness; it is concerned with decision and choice – a choice rooted in the conditions of actual life. Though the act of ethical choice may be informed profoundly by the images both of man's fallenness and his potential for transcendence that are provided by art, it is conducted nonetheless in a sphere which is distinct from the symbolic world created by the artist.

This further tension between the aesthetic and the ethical is the theme of Caliban's address to the audience in the third part of 'The Sea and the Mirror'. Life, Caliban says, is a journey from the 'Grandly Average Place' to a number of possible destinations – to the despair of defiance and pride, to the imagined transcendence of art, or to the religious transcendence attained through faith. To surrender oneself to the reality of the here and now would be to despair, he says; alternatively, to identify with the idealised world of art would be to indulge in self-delusion. In the conditions of temporal life, he says, we must listen 'for the real Word which is our only raison d'etre,' for its enunciation of 'that Wholly Other Life' of which artistic images are merely 'feebly figurative signs'. But art, he says, by pointing to the gulf between the reality we inhabit and the transcendence to which we aspire, evokes a sense of the distance that separates us from God, and provides the crucial self-awareness which is the prelude to the ethical decision or leap which leads, in turn, to the religious fulfilment attained through faith. Self–awareness is not itself the 'bridge' to God, but is an essential condition for the ethical decision or leap which enables man to transcend the distance through faith:

Having learnt his language, I begin to feel something of the serio-comic embarrassment of the dedicated dramatist, who, in representing to you your condition of estrangement from the truth, is doomed to fail the more he succeeds, for the more truthfully he paints the condition, the less clearly can he indicate the truth from which it is estranged, the brighter his revelation of the truth in its order, its justice, its joy, the fainter shows his picture of your actual condition in all its drabness and sham, and, worse still, the more sharply he defines the estrangement itself – and ultimately, what other aim and justification has he, what else exactly is the artistic gift which he is forbidden to hide, if not to make you unforgettably conscious of the ungarnished offended gap between what you so unquestionably are and what you are commanded without any question to become, of the unqualified No that opposes your every step in any direction? – the more he must strengthen your delusion that an awareness of the gap is in itself a bridge, your interest in your imprisonment a release, so that, far from your being led by him to contrition and surrender, the regarding of your defects in his mirror, your dialogue, using his words, with yourself about yourself, becomes the one activity which never, like devouring or collecting or spending, lets you down, the one game which can be guaranteed, whatever the company, to catch on, a madness of which you can only be cured by some shock quite outside his control, an unpredictable misting over of his glass or an absurd misprint in his text.

Divided consciousness remains the primary reality of human life and the conflicts of art and reality and of art and faith that are evoked by Prospero, Antonio and Caliban are merely some of its existential manifestations. Given his consistent emphasis on a dialectical relation between art and faith, it was entirely logical for Auden to insist 'there can no more be a "Christian art" than there can be a Christian science or a Christian diet', though he allowed 'there can be a Christian spirit in which an artist or a scientist works or does not work'.[34] (On this issue he differed fundamentally from Tolstoy, though he conceded that the latter had identified some important questions on matters relating to art and faith in *What Is Art?*) Ultimately, he said, the truths of faith, especially the focal Christian truth of the Incarnation remain beyond the realm of imagination. 'The Incarnation, the coming of Christ in the form of a servant who cannot be recognised by the eye of flesh and blood, but only by the eye of faith, puts an end to all claims of the imagination to be the faculty which decides what is truly sacred and what is profane,' he declared emphatically in 'The Dyer's Hand'.[35] (His sentiments are echoed by Simeon in 'For the Time Being', 'Of this child it is the case that He is in no sense a symbol.')

But while he argued that art cannot ultimately comprehend the transcendence attained through faith, Auden consistently declared, both in verse and in prose, that it can disclose its *possibility* through analogy and symbol. He would almost certainly have endorsed Kierkegaard's comment that the 'supreme function' of art is 'to think something that thought cannot think'. This is essentially the message of Caliban's last speech. 'Here among the ruins and the bones', we can rejoice, he says, in 'the perfected Work which is not ours'; we can rejoice in its 'great coherences', in the voice which 'delivers its authentic molar pardon', in its spaces which 'greet us with all their prospect of wonder and width', and finally, in its message of 'the restored relation', i.e., the ultimate religious fulfilment, which is the soul's union with God:

> Yet, at this very moment when we do at last see ourselves as we are, neither cosy nor playful, but swaying out on the ultimate wind-whipped cornice that overhangs the unabiding void – we have never stood any where else, – when our reasons are silenced by the heavy huge derision, – There is nothing to say. There never has been, – and our wills chuck in their hands – There is no way out. There never was, – it is at this moment that for the first time in our lives we hear, not the sounds which, as born actors, we have hitherto condescended to use as an excellent vehicle for displaying our personalities and looks, but the real Word which is our only raison d'etre. Not that we have improved; everything, the massacres, the whippings, the lies, the twaddle, and all their carbon copies are still present, more obviously than ever; nothing has been reconstructed; our shame, our fear, our incorrigible staginess, all wish and no resolve, are still, and more intensely than ever, all we have: only now it is not in spite of them but with them that we are blessed by that Wholly Other Life from which we are separated by an essential emphatic gulf of which our contrived fissures of mirror and proscenium arch – we understand them at last – are feebly figurative signs, so that all our meanings are reversed and it is precisely in its negative image of Judgement that we can positively envisage Mercy; it is just here, among the ruins and the bones, that we may rejoice in the perfected Work which is not ours. Its great coherences stand out through our secular blur in all their overwhelmingly righteous obligation; its voice speaks through our muffling banks of artificial flowers and unflinchingly delivers its authentic molar pardon; its spaces greet us with all their grand old prospect of wonder and width; the working charm is the full bloom of the unbothered state; the sounded note is the restored relation.

The reconciliation scene at the end of *The Tempest* is an image of the 'restored relation' of which Caliban speaks. Auden spoke of the play as vividly conveying the 'double truth' of our existence as individual and social beings. While being unique in ourselves, he says, 'at the same time we are all members of one another, mutually dependent and mutually responsible'. 'No man,' he said, 'is what he is or chooses independently of the nature and choices of those with whom he is associated.' 'That is why,' he concluded, 'our primary social duty is to forgive our neighbour.' This conclusion was central to his understanding of the nature and purpose of the Christian faith and he saw the image of reconciliation at the end of *The Tempest* as an especially powerful symbolic statement of its truth. What *The Tempest* exemplified – and this is the whole point of Auden's commentary on the work in 'The Sea and the Mirror' – is the potential of art to disclose the possibility of that final transcendence epitomised in the Christian message of love. Art, as Caliban says, is not the Way, but an image of the Way, a necessary stage in the progress to religious fulfilment through ethical decision and faith. As Auden himself wrote in 'Dichtung und Wahrheit', the truth and reality of love remain ultimately inexpressible. The narrator ends his poem with the words: 'The poem I wished to write was to have expressed exactly what I mean when I think the words *I love you*, but I cannot know exactly what I mean; it was to have been self-evidently true but words cannot verify themselves. So this poem will remain unwritten.'

'A SESAME TO LIGHT': THE NECESSITY FOR THE ETHICAL

Auden's biographers record an experience he had in a New York cinema in 1939 which had a profound impact on the development of his religious beliefs. In November of that year, some months after the outbreak of World War II, he went to see a film about the Nazi conquest of Poland in a cinema in Yorkville, a part of the city populated by large numbers of Germans. When a group of Poles were shown on the screen, he was astounded to hear several members of the audience cry, 'Kill them! Kill them!' 'I wondered then, why I reacted as I did against this denial of every humanistic value,' he recalled later. And he added, significantly, 'The answer brought me back to the Church.'[36] The event caused him finally to abandon the belief in the natural goodness of man that had led him successively to Freudianism, Marxism and liberal socialism in pursuit of an ideological formula for the permanent betterment of mankind. 'He had been through many changes of heart since reaching adulthood,' one of his biographers wrote. 'But all the dogmas he had adopted or played with ... had one thing in common: they were all based on a belief in the natural goodness of man. They all claimed that if one specific evil were removed, be it secular repression, the domination of the proletariate by the bourgeoisie, or Fascism, then humanity would be happy and unrest would cease.'[37] The event at Yorkville, confirming his growing sense of the fearsome potential for evil that had been released by Nazism, convinced him of the essential fallenness of man and of the need for absolute ethical criteria to save him from the corruptions of his own nature. (The term 'absolute' is used by Auden in a way which is similar to its use by Kierkegaard, as will be indicated in more detail presently.) His words in a poem written shortly after the incident in Yorkville reflect the decisive impact the whole experience had on him: 'Either we serve the Unconditional/ Or some Hitlerian monster will supply/ An iron convention to do evil by.'

In 'Balaam and his Ass', his essay on the modern relevance of the master-slave dialectic, Auden stressed the conflict of necessity and freedom that is inherent in man's nature and spoke in the following terms of the ethical implications of this: 'As a biological organism man is a natural creature subject to the necessities of nature; as a being with consciousness and will, he is at the same time a historical person with the freedom of the spirit.' As a natural creature, he says, man merely conforms to necessity and is therefore 'blameless'. It is because he is both nature and spirit, he adds, that 'he sins by conscious choice'.[38] The emphasis on ethical consciousness and choice, and the concept of the ethical decision or 'leap' as a manifestation of the radical freedom of the individual person, point clearly to the influence of Kierkegaard, an influence that is apparent in Auden's work from the late 1930s onward. In these lines from 'New Year Letter' he salutes Kierkegaard as the theologian who revolutionised ethics by his assertion of the radical freedom of the act of moral choice and by his condemnation of the impersonal abstractions of ethical rationalism that had dominated European thought for 'more than twenty centuries':

> The cities we abandon fall
> To nothing primitive at all;
> This lust in action to destroy
> Is not the pure instinctive joy
> Of animals, but the refined
> Creation of machines and mind,
> As out of Europe comes a Voice,
> Compelling all to make their choice,
> A theologian who denies
> What more than twenty centuries
> Of Europe have assumed to be
> The basis of civility,

Our evil *Daimon* to express
In all its ugly nakedness
What none before dared say aloud,
The metaphysics of the Crowd,
The Immanent Imperative
By which the lost and injured live
In mechanized societies
Where natural intuition dies,
The international result
Of Industry's *Quicunque vult*,
The hitherto unconscious creed
Of little men who half succeed.

Two Kierkegaardian principles are repeatedly stressed in Auden's writings. The first, as has been intimated, is the conception of the ethical as a fulfilment of the radical freedom of individual consciousness. Kierkegaard spoke of it as an 'actualisation of inwardness and subjectivity', a movement towards the 'infinite interiority of religious existence', towards the point where the ideality of self-consciousness is actualised as reality.[39] The individual becomes conscious, he says, of his ideal self as a possibility which it is his ethically imposed self-responsibility to realise. Correspondingly, through a deepened self-consciousness the individual becomes more fully aware of himself as free and of his duty to exercise his freedom responsibly. The second principle is the conception of the act of moral decision as a 'leap' from the aesthetic to the ethical, a choice informed both by the sense of fallenness and distance from God afforded by aesthetic consciousness, and by its disclosure of the possibilities for transcending the temporal-finite conditions of mortal life. In the *Postscript* Kierkegaard described the 'leap' as 'the category of decision'; it marks the 'qualitative transition' from non-belief to belief, he said. It is the point where reflection gives way to will. 'Reflection can only be halted by a leap,' he wrote; 'when the subject does not put an end to his reflection, he is made infinite in reflection, i.e., he does not arrive at a decision.' 'It cannot be taught or communicated directly,' he said, 'precisely because it is an act of isolation, which leaves it to the individual to decide, respecting that which cannot be thought, whether he will resolve believingly to accept it by virtue of the absurdity.'[40]

The relevance of all this to Auden's poetry becomes apparent from some essays he wrote on the subject of ethical judgement. In a postscript entitled, 'Infernal Science', which is the concluding section in a series of essays on Shakespeare's plays, he speaks of the propensity towards ethical decision and choice as an imperative inherent in the condition of man himself. 'Ethics does not treat of the world,' he writes. 'Ethics must be a condition of the world like logic. ... It is a purely human illusion to imagine that the laws of the spiritual life are, like our legislation, imposed laws which we can break. We may defy them, either by accident, i.e., out of ignorance, or by choice, but we can no more break them than we can break the laws of human physiology by getting drunk.'[41] Thus, while he personally pledged his commitment to Christianity as identifying the 'Way' to ethico-religious fulfilment, he nonetheless insisted that the potentiality for ethical action is not to be exclusively identified with any religious creed. This is one of the themes of his commentary on *Moby Dick* where he sees the encounter between Ishmael and Queequeg, i.e., between the Christian believer and the pagan cannibal, as intimating their common potentiality for ethical action. Those, such as Queequeg, 'who have not heard the Word', he says, are guided nonetheless by their inherent sense of morality. Queequeg, he writes, 'exhibits Christian forgiveness and Christian agape without the slightest effort. He is a doer of the Word who has never heard the Word.'[42]

In another essay called 'The Virgin and the Dynamo' Auden considers the ways in which ethical consciousness is manifested. Consciousness, he says, consists of a 'unity-in tension' of four modes of existence: soul, body, mind and spirit. In his existence as soul and body, he writes, man is primarily an individual being; in his existence as mind and spirit he is primarily a social being. Were he to exist solely in terms of soul and body, his relation to other individuals would simply be 'numerical'; were he to exist solely in terms of mind and spirit, he would merely be the collective entity: man. In the first category he exists purely as a natural being; in the second as a historico-cultural being. In reality, Auden concludes, human existence is a synthesis of all these modes: individual and social, natural and spiritual. Man's consciousness reflects this synthesis, this 'unity-in-tension' of different modes of existence. This is manifested, in turn, he says, in different levels of awareness:

> 1. A consciousness of the self as self-contained, as embracing all that it is aware of in a unity of experiencing. This mode is undogmatic, amoral and passive; its good is the enjoyment of being, its evil the fear of non-being.
>
> 2. A consciousness of beyondness, of an ego standing as a spectator over against both a self and the external world. This mode is dogmatic, amoral, objective. Its good is the perception of true relations, its evil the fear of accidental or false relations.
>
> 3. The ego's consciousness of itself as striving towards, as desiring to transform the self, to realise its potentialities. This mode is moral or active; its good is not present but propounded, its evil, the present actuality.[43]

All these modes of awareness coexist, he writes, in a condition of dialectical interdependence, in a 'unity-in tension' or co-inherence of opposing tendencies, which together constitute the indivisible phenomenon of consciousness. It is from this tension of opposites, he argued, and from their radical 'co-inherence', that the ethical must emerge. He condemned both romantic aestheticism and rationalist idealism as exalting particular modes of consciousness – in one instance, the aesthetic, in the other the rational – in violation of its indivisible totality. He pointed to the Cartesian revolution as initiating the modern cult of the intellect – 'The cogitations of Descartes/ Are where all sound semantics start' – and pointed further to the contradictions and limitations of its materialist offspring, Marxism – the creation of 'the German who/ Obscure in gaslit London, brought/ To human consciousness a thought/ It thought unthinkable.' In this passage from the second part of 'New Year Letter,' where he explores the nature of ethical inwardness, Auden vehemently denounces the intellectualised abstractions of rationalist philosophy and affirms his belief that the roots of the ethical lie in the indivisible reality of human love – in the 'deep unsnobbish instinct which/ Alone can make relation rich':

> ... The Intellect
> That parts the Cause from the Effect
> And thinks in terms of Space and Time
> Commits a legalistic crime,
> For such an unreal severance
> Must falsify experience ...
> O foolishness of man to seek
> Salvation in an *ordre logique*!
> O cruel intellect that chills
> His natural warmth until it kills
> The roots of all togetherness! ...
> O when will men show common sense
> And throw away intelligence,
> That killjoy which discriminates.
> Recover what appreciates,
> The deep unsnobbish instinct which
> Alone can make relation rich,
> Upon the *Beischlaf* of the blood
> Establish a real neighbourhood
> Where art and industry and *moeurs*
> Are governed by an ordre *du coeur*?

Herod, in 'For the Time Being', epitomises the kind of abstract rationality denounced in this passage. His oratorical style of rhetoric, his verbal flourish-

es, his classical balancing of ideas, are clearly designed to parody the intellectual exclusivity of the whole liberal-classical tradition. His speech echoes both
the language of Marcus Aurelius – to emphasise the coldness of its humanist
rhetoric – and the language of the mediaeval morality plays – to emphasise its
comedy and absurdity. His reasoning peters out eventually in an incoherent
jumble of half-truths and contradictions. Ironically and unintentionally, he
points nonetheless to some paradoxes that are central to the Christian faith and
the mystery of the Incarnation:

> O dear, Why couldn't this wretched infant be born somewhere else?
> Why can't people be sensible? I don't want to be horrid. Why can't
> they see that the notion of a finite God is absurd? Because it is. And
> suppose, just for the sake of argument, that it isn't, that this story is
> true, that this child is in some inexplicable manner both God and man,
> that he grows up, lives and dies, without committing a single sin?
> Would that make life any better? On the contrary it would make it far,
> far worse. For it could only mean this: that once having shown them
> how, God would expect every man, whatever his fortune, to lead a sin-
> less life in the flesh and on earth. Then indeed would the human race
> be plunged into madness and despair. And for me personally at this
> moment it would mean that God had given me the power to destroy
> Himself. I refuse to be taken in. He could not play such a horrible
> practical joke. Why should He dislike me so? I've worked like a slave.
> Ask anyone you like. I read all official dispatches without skipping. I've
> taken elocution lessons. I've hardly ever taken bribes. How dare He
> allow me to decide? I've tried to be good. I brush my teeth every night.
> I haven't had sex for a month. I object. I'm a liberal. I want everyone to
> be happy. I wish I had never been born.

In an essay on Carl Sandberg, Auden wrote: 'The one infallible symptom
of greatness is the gift of double-focus.'[44] Truth, he insisted yet again, is the
product of dialectical consciousness, of its double-focussing of belief and
doubt, of reason and feeling, of imagined and perceived reality. In a note to an
early version of 'New Year Letter', he said: 'We, being divided, remembering,
evolving beings, composed of a number of selves, each with its false conception of its self-interest, sin in most that we do.'[45] Human sinfulness, he suggests, is an inevitable consequence of our freedom, yet the evil inherent in our
nature, and the 'despair' which it creates, can ultimately be fruitful in leading
to the more anguished consciousness and inwardness from which ethical self-
awareness and illumination can finally spring. This is the theme of the following sequence from 'New Year Letter':

O how the devil who controls
The moral asymmetric souls
The either-ors, the mongrel halves
Who find truth in a mirror, laughs.
Yet time and memory are still
Limiting factors on his will;
He cannot always fool us thrice,
For he may never tell us lies,
Just half-truths we can synthesise.
So, hidden in his hocus-pocus,
There lies the gift of double-focus,
That magic lamp which looks so dull
And utterly impractical
Yet, if Alladin use it right,
Can be a sesame to light.

The same theme is reiterated by Simeon in 'For the Time Being'. 'Before the Unconditional could manifest itself under the conditions of existence it was necessary,' he says, 'that man should first have reached the ultimate frontier of consciousness, the secular limit of memory beyond which there remained but one thing for him to know, his Original Sin.' Consciousness, extended to the limits of interiority, manifests itself as the potentiality for guilt, which leads to the decision or leap towards the ethical and to its existential fulfilment as individual responsibility. The ethical decision or leap is the product, therefore, of *conflicting* modes of consciousness, their dialectical tension, interdependence and potential co-inherence being at once a source of self-conflict for the individual person and the foundation of his progress towards religious fulfilment through faith. The aesthetic mode is one of these necessarily conflicting elements and is, therefore, an essential one in the process of attaining ethico-religious fulfilment.

One point remains to be reemphasised: that is, the radical individuality and solitariness of the act of ethical decision or choice. In the words previously quoted from the *Postscript*, Kierkegaard spoke of the 'leap' as 'an act of isolation, which leaves it to the individual to decide ... whether he will resolve believingly to accept it by virtue of the absurdity'. In *The Individual* he spoke of the everpresent tendency on the part of the individual to subordinate his freedom to that of the group, thereby surrendering individual responsibility for the security of 'the crowd'. 'A crowd in its very concept is an untruth,' he wrote, 'It renders the individual completely impenitent and irresponsible ... Thereof was Christ crucified because, although he addressed himself to all, he would have no dealings with the crowd. He would not found a party, did not permit balloting, but would be that he is, the Truth, which relates itself to the individual.'[46] Auden similarly warns of the falsity of collectivist morality in 'Horae Canonicae', a series of verses based on the hourly rituals of the monastic canon. In the noon-time poem, 'Sext', he echoes Kierkegaard in emphasising the need to maintain the isolation of individual ethical responsibility in the face of the collectivist pressures and securities of 'the crowd'. In this passage he emphasises the unconscious mindlessness of the crowd to which, ironically and tragically, the individual spirit is relentlessly drawn:

> the crowd sees only one thing
> (which only the crowd can see),
>
> an epiphany of that
> which does whatever is done.
>
> whatever god a person believes in,
> in whatever way he believes
>
> (no two are exactly alike),
> as one of the crowd he believes
>
> and only believes in that
> in which there is only one way of believing.
>
> Few people accept another and most
> will never do anything properly,
>
> but the crowd rejects no one, joining the crowd
> is the only thing all men can do.

'Aloneness is man's real condition,' Auden wrote in 'New Year Letter'. Ethical responsibility requires both the isolation of individual choice and the depth of personal interiority described in Simeon's words quoted above from 'For the Time Being'. That such a process involves struggle, anxiety and pain is a matter Auden underlines in several of the works he devoted to the process of ethico-religious development, as will be shown in the forthcoming section.

'THE PURGATORIAL HILL WE CLIMB':TEMPORALITY, SUFFERING AND FAITH

The way to religious interiority is the way of suffering, Auden consistently proclaimed in his prose and verse. That conviction was greatly reinforced by his interest in the theological writings of Kierkegaard, Niebuhr and Tillich, with their emphasis on the ways in which despair and a negativity of the spirit can disclose its potentiality for self-transcendence through faith. It was further reinforced by personal experience of anguish and despair in the period when he produced his first two major religious poems, 'New Year Letter' and 'For the Time Being'. In August 1941 his mother died. 'I was surprised at the violence of my feelings,' he wrote, 'though I had known it was likely. When mother dies, one is, for the first time really, alone in the world and that is hard.'[47] He dedicated 'For the Time Being' 'To Constance Rosalie Auden, 1870-1941'. As he completed the work, the Japanese bombed Pearl Harbour, which resulted in the US entering the war and massively escalating the scale of the conflict. In that year also his close friend, Chester Kallman, asserted his independence of their previously monogamous companionship, a step that caused deep distress to Auden. 'I was forced,' he wrote, 'to know in person what it is like to feel oneself the prey of demonic powers in both the Greek and the Christian sense, stripped of self-control and self-respect.'[48] 'For the Time Being' opens with evocations of the despairing states of the spirit which precipitate the leap or decision of faith which leads the soul to God.

> Darkness and snow descend;
> The clock on the mantelpiece
> Has nothing to recommend,
> Nor does the face in the glass
> Appear nobler than our own
> As darkness and snow descend
> On all personality.
> Huge crowds mumble – 'Alas,
> Our angers do not increase,
> Love is not what she used to be;'
> Portly Caesar yawns – 'I know;'
> He falls asleep on his throne,
> They shuffle off through the snow:
> Darkness and snow descend.

The source of the soul's despair, he suggests, is anxiety in time – its awareness of its own mortality, a condition that can be transcended only through faith, through the soul's reaching towards the infinite. But faith, he insists, can be attained only when man submerges himself in the darkness and suffering of temporal existence. 'Suffering is posited as something decisive for a religious existence,' Kierkegaard said. 'The more the suffering the more the religious existence.'[49] Suffering occurs when man submits to his temporality; only by doing so can he hope to transcend it. Taking his imagery from Kierkegaard, Auden, in this passage from 'New Year Letter', describes life as a 'purgatorial' climb, an ascent towards a summit that cannot be reached in the conditions of mortal life:

> We cannot, then, will Heaven where
> Is perfect freedom; our wills there
> Must lose the will to operate.
> But will is free not to negate
> Itself in Hell; we're free to will
> Ourselves up Purgatory still,
> Consenting parties to our lives,
> To love them like attractive wives
> Whom we adore but do not trust;
> We cannot love without their lust,
> And need their stratagems to win
> Truth out of Time. In Time we sin.
> But Time is sin and can forgive;
> Time is the life with which we live
> At least three-quarters of our time,
> The purgatorial hill we climb,
> Where any skyline we attain
> Reveals a higher ridge again.

Paradoxically, Kierkegaard says, it is 'only in despair' that the individual can fully perceive the transient nature of earthly life and simultaneously become conscious of the reality of the infinite from which he is separated by his temporal state. 'Every man who has not tasted the bitterness of despair has missed the significance of life,' he wrote. 'That which really makes a man despair is not his misfortune,' he said, 'but the fact that he lacks the eternal.'[50] In *Sickness Unto Death* he speaks of this awareness of mortality as an 'internal disrelation', a 'malady of the spirit', manifesting itself in deep personal anguish.[51] To this, he says, two responses are possible. One is the previously mentioned 'despair of defiance', in which the individual 'wills despairingly to be himself' and in which he persists, despite the urgings of his consciousness and its intimations of the infinite. The second is the soul's acceptance of its powerlessness and fallenness, its recognition of its ontological dependence on God, which is the beginning of faith. 'Only when I choose myself as guilty do I choose myself absolutely,' Kierkegaard said. 'The totality of guilt comes into being for the individual when he puts his faith together with the relation to eternal happiness.'[52] In guilt-awareness and repentance a deeper level of interiority is attained, leading to a strengthened faith in the reality of the infinite, the reality of God. The choice for the individual lies, therefore, between defiant persistence in his despair or repentance of his fallenness and humble submission to God's will.

In an analysis of Melville's *Moby Dick* Auden describes two of its characters, Pip and Ahab, as embodying the two forms of Kierkegaardian despair. Pip, he says, represents the 'despair of weakness'; he is a slave, whose whole existence consists in humble submission to the will of his master, Ahab. The latter Auden sees as 'the greatest example of defiant despair in literature'. Ahab's pride, he says, 'defiantly wills to be always at every moment miserable'. In his defiance, Ahab vows to take vengeance on the great whale: 'I now prophesy that I will dismember my dismemberer,' he exclaims. What he particularly embodies, Auden suggests, is the egotistical self-confidence of the rationalist – 'the defiant inversion in pride of the humility which resists the pride of reason, the theologian's temptation to think that knowledge of God is more important than obeying Him'. His whole life, he adds, consists in 'taking up defiantly a cross he is not required to take up'.[53] Ahab, he concludes, is a stoic and ascetic without faith; he sees happiness as temptation and welcomes suffering and pain, thereby intensifying his defiance and the despair on which it feeds. For all that, Ahab is irresistibly drawn to Pip, in whom he sees the humility that alone can save him from despair: 'As the conscious defiant despairer, he recognises that Pip is his anti-type and envies Pip's humility as Pip admires his strength. "There's that in thee, poor lad, which I feel too curing for my malady. Like cures like; and for this hunt, my malady becomes my most desired health." '[54]

Again, following Kierkegaard, from whose *Sickness Unto Death* he quotes extensively in this essay, Auden stresses the inevitability of suffering in the struggle to realise the infinite potentiality of freedom in the face of the conditions of mortality and change. The religious man, he writes, recognises 'that suffering is a sign that he is in truth, that he who suffers is really blest'.[55] The theme is further developed in the first of the T.S. Eliot Memorial Lectures, 'The Martyr as Dramatic Hero'. In this essay Auden defines martyrdom as the daily acceptance of the inevitability of suffering, of which the prototypical model is to be found in the life and death of Christ. Christ in Gethsemane, praying that his father might let the cup pass from him, epitomised, he says, the pure and agonised acceptance of God's will which is utterly free of any compromising tendencies towards self-glorification and pride. But while extolling the example of Christ, and while representing the Crucifixion as the quintessential act of redemptive self-sacrifice, he warns of the potentially ambivalent character of the act of self-sacrifice and the act of total submission to the will of God:

The Martyr sacrifices himself not for the sake of any particular individual or social group but for all mankind. In the special case of Christ, the God-Man, he dies to redeem sinful mankind; the ordinary human martyr dies to bear witness to what he believes to be saving truth, to be shared by all men, not reserved as an esoteric secret for a few. The conception of saving truth is a highly dangerous one, for those who believe that it can be a duty to die for the truth can come all too easily to believe that it is also a duty to kill for it. The history of the Christian Church – no other religious body has killed so many people for doctrinal reasons – has taught us that we cannot reserve the title of martyr for those who die for beliefs that coincide with our own, that a man who dies to bear witness to dialectical materialism is no less a martyr than one who dies to bear witness to the Nicene formulae. One can say, however, that it was Christianity and the cultures influenced by it that first recognised the martyr as a classifiable type. All the so-called higher religions regard one person as their founder and head, but only in the case of Christianity did this person suffer a violent and degrading death. If the world now knows that at all times in history and in all places there have been martyrs, it is largely Christianity which is responsible. I would go further and say that if any man, whatever his beliefs, were told the story of two martyrs and asked to say which was the noblest or purest example of martyrdom, his standard of comparison would be based, consciously or unconsciously, upon the story of the Crucifixion.[56]

'The basic human problem,' Auden wrote in a review of Kierkegaard's *Either-Or*, 'is man's anxiety in time, his present anxiety over himself in relation to his past and his parents ... his present anxiety in relation to his future and his neighbours ... his present anxiety over himself in his relation to eternity and God.'[57] This is the theme of 'The Age of Anxiety', a work described by Paul Tillich as 'a perfect mirror of our times'. It exemplified 'the courage to be, in spite of death, fate, meaninglessness or despair', Tillich wrote.[58] In the work four characters come together in a New York bar to exchange their experiences of life in wartime conditions. Each represents a particular mode of consciousness: Malin represents abstract thought, Rosetta romantic feeling, Quant poetic intuition and Emble the world of sensation and instinctive thought. Each personifies the fragmentation of consciousness which Auden sees as the root cause of the malaise and anxiety afflicting their lives. Emble sums up their predicament: 'Estranged, aloof/ They brood over being till the bars close/ The malcontented who might have been/ The creative odd ones the average need/ To suggest new goals. 'The new barbarian is no uncouth desert-dweller', Malin says. 'Factories bred him/ Corporate companies, college towns/ Mothered his mind.' His condition, essentially, is that of one who lives in nature and time while simultaneously having the capacity to transcend them through the infinite potentialities of his spirit. He is 'at once/ Outside and inside his own demand/ For personal pattern'. The condition is vividly and succinctly described in these lines from the poem:

> ... Let us then
> Consider rather the incessant Now of
> The traveller through time, his tired mind
> Biased towards bigness since his body must
> Exaggerate to exist, possessed by hope,
> Acquisitive, in quest of his own
> Absconded self yet scared to find it
> As he bumbles by from birth to death
> Menaced by madness; whose mode of being,
> Bashful or braggart, is to be at once
> Outside and inside his own demand
> For personal pattern. His pure I
> Must give account of and greet his Me,
> That field of force where he feels he thinks,
> His past present, presupposing death,
> Must ask what he is in order to be
> And make meaning by omission and stress,
> Avid of elseness.

The four characters, in their different ways, seek to transcend the conditions of their present existence, through concentration on memory, on the unconscious, and on the spheres of phenomenal and sensual being, each of which leads to the barrenness of despair, symbolised in the poem by the recurrent use of desert-imagery. (In *The Enchaféd Flood* Auden described the desert as 'the place where the water of life is lacking', as 'the place of punishment for those rejected by the good city because they are evil', and as 'the place of purgation for those who reject the evil city because they desire to become good'.)[59] Malin eventually comes to recognise the Christian truth that salvation must be attained in time: 'The noble despair of the poets/ Is nothing of the sort, it is silly/ To refuse the tasks of time.' 'We would rather die in our dread,' he says, 'Than climb the cross of the moment/ And let our illusions die.' The truth that the timeless can only be known through the temporal is a paradox beyond the comprehension of reason. It is a paradox knowable only through faith:

For the new locus is never
Hidden inside the old one
Where Reason could rout it out,
Nor guarded by dragons in distant
Mountains where Imagination
Could explore it; the place of birth
Is too obvious and near to notice,
Some dull dogpatch a stone's throw
Outside the walls, reserved
For the eyes of faith to find.

Man's task, he declares, is to submit humbly to the conditions of mortality, to experience its blessedness and resign himself to its necessity. In the final sequence of the poem – one of the most moving statements of Christian faith in all of Auden's poetry – Malin affirms the blessedness of all that exists, seeing the disorder, fragmentation and suffering of mortal life as part of the grand design envisaged for man by his Creator. The blessedness of creation, he says, enjoins on mankind the responsibility of love, which, in turn, is the source of faith. 'We belong to our kind/Are judged as we judge,' he declares. 'The grossest of our dreams is/ No worse than our worship' which 'is so much galmatias' to 'get out of knowing our neighbour' – 'the poor muddled maddened mundane animal/ Who is hostess to us all.' Malin's final monologue celebrates the infinite love of Christ, the source of all grace, courage and hope – Christ who 'Condescended to exist and to suffer death/ And, scorned on a scaffold, ensconced in His life/ The human household.' The sequence continues:

In our anguish we struggle
To elude Him, to lie to Him, yet His love observes
His appalling promise; His predilection
As we wander and weep is with us to the end,
Minding our meanings, our least matter dear to Him,
His Good ingressant on our gross occasions
Envisages our advance, valuing for us
Though our bodies too blind or too bored to examine
What sorts excite them are slain interjecting
Their childish Ows and, in choosing how many
And how much they will love, our minds insist on
Their own disorder as their own punishment,
His question disqualifies our quick senses,
His Truth makes our theories historical sins,

It is where we are wounded that is when He speaks
Our creaturely cry, concluding His children
In their mad unbelief to have mercy on them all
As they wait unawares for His world to come.

'AND LOVE ILLUMINATES AGAIN ...'

The quest for faith, therefore, as is clearly intimated in Malin's monologue, is a quest for wholeness, i.e., for the paradoxical unity and diversity in being conveyed through the term 'co-inherence' – an ideal that Auden specifically associated with the traditions of the Christian Gospels, like his theological mentors, Williams, Niebuhr and Kierkegaard. He did not, as was previously indicated, consider that Christianity was the only way to God; he confessed himself strongly attracted, for example, to some aspects of the Buddhist faith, and considered that its emphasis on meditation was something Christians might be encouraged to emulate. He saw faith as a healing, i.e., a meaning-giving, solace for the suffering consequent on the fallenness of man's nature and the disorder and fragmentation of consciousness resulting from the conditions of mortal life. He saw it as intrinsically irrational, as transcending the limitations and abstractions of an exclusively intellectualist pursuit of truth. He did not, any more than Kierkegaard did, deny the importance of reason, but condemned the hierarchical rationalism of post-Cartesian culture as a spurious resolution of the tensions endemic in the nature of consciousness. (An indication of his basic respect for intellect and reason is his criticism of existentialist philosophers in 'The Dyer's Hand' as being 'one-sided', despite their 'laudable protest against systematic philosophers like Hegel or Marx'. Comparing them with the latter, he complained the existentialists had 'invented an equally imaginary anthropology from which all elements, like man's physical nature or his reason, about which general statements can be made, are excluded'.)[60]

The theme of Christian co-inherence emerges in Auden's poetry with his statement of the dialectical interdependence of the aesthetic, ethical and religious spheres of existence in 'New Year Letter'. Faith is conceived in the poem as simultaneously a free act of will – a decision or leap – and a gift from God conferred through grace. Closely following Kierkegaard, he emphasises the freedom of the act of faith, seeing it as a continuous process of Becoming which occurs in the conditions of temporality and finitude. The choice or decision of faith, Kierkegaard said, occurs in 'the Moment', in the instant of time which, paradoxically, discloses the reality of the intemporal. 'The Moment or Instant,' he wrote, 'is the hinge of the movement. In it the condition – and the Truth – are given.' It is an instant in time which is 'filled with eternity' and for the soul is 'the fullness of time'.[61] The decision of faith, though made in the instant, marks a radical process of self-renewal: 'The choice is an act of freedom,' he wrote, 'and it may well be said that in an act of choosing the individual produces himself.' The choice is one which must be continuously renewed, the original choice being constantly present in every subsequent choice. This paradox of faith as a decision to be made in the conditions of the temporal, as a radical process of Becoming or self-renewal, is emphasised by Auden in these lines from the poem. The ideal of perfection in Being is illusory, he declares; faith must be attained in the conditions of flux and change that characterise temporal life:

> Hell is the being of the lie
> That we become if we deny
> The laws of consciousness and claim
> Becoming and Being are the same,
> Being in time, and man discrete
> In will, yet free and self-complete;
> Its fire the pain to which we go
> If we refuse to suffer, though
> The one unnecessary grief
> Is the vain craving for relief,
> When to the suffering we could bear
> We add intolerable fear,
> Absconding from remembrance, mocked
> By our own partial senses, locked
> Each in a stale uniqueness, lie
> Time-conscious for eternity.

'Choosing oneself is identical with repenting oneself,'[62] Kierkegaard declared. This is the theme of the third part of 'New Year Letter'. 'How readily would we become/ The seamless live continuum/ Of supple and coherent stuff,/ Whose form is truth, whose content love,' the poet exclaims. Love, he suggests – and by implication faith – are restored by forgiveness: 'In Time we sin/ But Time is sin and can forgive.' Like a mountain-climber, man ascends a 'purgatorial hill' where his soul is continuously purified of sin through penitence: 'But still believing we can climb/ A little higher every time/ And keep in order that we may/ Ascend the penitential way/ That forces our wills to be free.' The way of penitence is the way of love which, in turn, is the way of faith. Repentance, marks the transition from ethical to religious existence, Kierkegaard wrote in *Fear and Trembling*. 'As soon as sin makes its appearance ethics comes to grief precisely upon repentance,' he wrote.[63] Repentance, he said, is simultaneously an expression of freedom and, paradoxically, an affirmation of necessity, i.e., of our absolute dependence upon God. This theme is reaffirmed in a passage in 'New Year Letter' where Auden stresses the need for daily self-repentance and sees this as the foundation on which love and the spirit of fellowship are based. The lines culminate with an affirmation of the paradox of necessity and freedom:

> Our news is seldom good: the heart,
> As Zola said, must always start
> The day by swallowing its toad
> Of failure and disgust. Our road
> Gets worse and we seem altogether
> Lost as our theories, like the weather,
> Veer round completely every day,
> And all that we can always say
> Is: true democracy begins
> With free confession of our sins.
> In this alone are all the same ...
> We need to love all since we are
> Each a unique particular
> That is no giant, god or dwarf,
> But one odd human isomorph;
> We can love each because we know
> All, all of us, that this is so;
> Can live since we are lived, the powers
> That we create with are not ours.

'New Year Letter' ends with a prayer and an evocation of the everpresent need for brotherhood and love: 'O every day in sleep and labour/ Our life and death are with our neighbour/ And love illuminates again/ The city and the lion's den/ The world's great rage, the travel of young men.' The main characters in 'For the Time Being' epitomise this spirit of loving faith and humble acceptance of God's will. In the Annunciation sequence Mary is summoned to be the instrument through which the miracle of the Incarnation will be enacted. She submits to God's will in a spirit of loving obedience:

> My flesh in terror and fire
> Rejoices that the Word
> Who utters the world out of nothing,
> As a pledge of His word to love her
> Against her will, and to turn
> Her desperate longing to love,

Should ask to wear me,
From now to their wedding day,
For an engagement ring.

The Wise Men, who represent the spheres of scientific and aesthetic activity, are shown detaching themselves from their secular pursuits and following the Nativity Star to Bethlehem. They join with the shepherds – who represent the poor and unlettered masses – to worship the newborn child who embodies the ultimate co-inherence of divine and human reality. St Joseph is called on to suspend all rational judgement and to affirm his faith in the absurd, the unintelligible and incomprehensible. Joseph asks for empirical proof of what he is called on to believe, but is reminded by God's messenger, Gabriel, of his duty to submit humbly in the spirit of faith:

Joseph:
All I ask is one
Important and elegant proof
That what my Love had done
Was really at your will
And that your will is Love.

Gabriel:
No, you must believe;
Be silent, and sit still.

One is reminded once again of Kierkegaard – in this instance of his words on the state of 'infinite resignation' which immediately precedes the decision of faith. 'The infinite resignation is the last stage prior to faith,' he wrote. 'Only in the infinite resignation do I become clear to myself with respect to my eternal validity and only there can there be any question of grasping existence by virtue of faith.'[64]

What Mary and Joseph, the Wise Men and the Shepherds, are called upon to witness is the miraculous union of the divine and the human, of the infinite and the finite, which is embodied in the person of Christ. In the Paradox of God's incarnate presence in Christ, in its mystery and absurdity, the contradictions and divisions of nature are healed. In this paradox they are made meaningful, as Simeon declares in his Meditation. 'By the event of this birth, he says, 'the true significance of all other events is defined.' All human experience finds its ultimate locus of meaning, he says, in the co-inherence of the infinite and the finite represented in the Incarnation. This provides the final justification for all modes of enquiry, imaginative, rational or spiritual:

'Because in Him all passions find a logical In-Order-That, by Him is the perpetual recurrence of Art assured ... Because in Him abstraction finds a passionate For-The-Sake-Of, by Him is the continuous development of Science assured.' It is through their relation to the all-embracing mystery of this infinite-finite conjuncture that the significance of all forms of human experience in the ultimate order of reality is defined.

The truth of the Incarnation is knowable only through faith, which, in turn, requires the spirit of humility and infinite resignation, and the spirit of self-sacrificing love, represented by Mary, Joseph, Simeon, the Wise Men and the Shepherds. 'Our redemption,' Simeon says, 'is no longer a question of pursuit but of surrender to Him who is always and everywhere present. Therefore at every moment we pray that, following Him, we may depart from our anxiety unto His peace.' In a succinct conclusion he encapsulates the fundamental opposition at the heart of all human activity: that between man's potential for evil, which is rooted in his self-centredness and pride, and his potential for good, which is rooted in his limitless capacity for love. 'The course of history is predictable,' he says, 'in the degree to which all men love themselves, and spontaneous in the degree to which each man loves God and through Him his neighbour.'

Pointing to the interdependence of the themes of love and faith in Auden's poetry, Joseph Brodsky wrote: 'If there were no churches one could easily have built one upon this poet and its main precept would run like his "If equal affection cannot be/ Let the more loving one be me." '[65] 'There was in him,' wrote another Russian writer, V.S. Yanovsky, 'some inner communion with the great human reality as there was in Tolstoy – a trait characteristic of all geniuses despite their fantasies.'[66] That sense of communion with a transcendent reality remained intensely problematic for Auden, however, as he proclaimed in 'Friday's Child', one of his last works celebrating the mystery of the Incarnation. In this work he points to the central paradox of the Christian faith: the absolute and irrational character of the law of love on which it is focussed, and the conditions of human weakness and fallenness in which it must be sustained. The poem opens with an image of man as a being whose spiritual potentiality reflects the infinite freedom of his Creator: 'What reverence is rightly paid/ To a Divinity so odd/ He lets the Adam whom He made/ Perform the acts of God.?' It concludes with an image of the degradation of human suffering as epitomised in the Crucifixion – the event which redeemed mankind from the consequences of the Fall. Paradoxically, it suggests, it is on this that the hopes of mankind are ultimately founded:

Now, did He really break the seal
And rise again? we dare not say;

But conscious unbelievers feel
Quite sure of Judgment Day.

Meanwhile, a silence on the cross,
As dead as we shall ever be,
Speaks of some total gain or loss,
And you and I are free

To guess from the insulted face
Just what Appearances he saves
By suffering in a public place
A death reserved for slaves.

10

'Only Love Redeems':
The Novels of Patrick White

> I suppose what I am increasingly intent on trying to do in my books is to give professed unbelievers glimpses of their own unprofessed factor. I believe most people have a religious factor, but are afraid that by admitting it they will forfeit their right to be considered intellectuals. This is particularly common in Australia where the intellectual is a comparatively recent phenomenon. The Churches defeat their own aims, I feel, through the banality of their approach, and by rejecting so much that is sordid and shocking which can still be related to religious experience ... I feel that the moral flaws in myself are more than anything my creative source.[1]

So wrote Patrick White in a letter to the American literary scholar, Dr Clem Semmler, in May 1970. At the time he was working on *The Eye of the Storm* which he described as 'having a more specific religious content and pattern' than any of his previous novels. In this work, and in *The Vivisector* which was published the year before, he had clearly sought to define the place of 'the sordid and the shocking' in the general pattern of religious experience and saw this as a function particularly linked with the aesthetic exploration of religious faith.[2] Rather cryptically, he cited Rimbaud's words on the paradoxical role of the artist on the opening page of *The Vivisector*: 'He becomes beyond all others the great Invalid, the great Criminal, the great Accursed One – and the Supreme Knower. For he reaches the unknown.' He also quoted Ben Nicholson on the affinities between religious and aesthetic experience: 'As I see it painting and religious experience are the same thing, and what we are all searching for is the understanding and realisation of infinity.'[3]

Consistently, over many years, White had testified to the importance of religious experience in his life and work and to the central place that it occupied in his fiction. 'I am a believer,' he told Geoffrey Dutton, in 1960. 'God is in anything, any religion, any art.'[4] 'Religion, yes, that's behind all my books,' he told another interviewer, Craig McGregor, in 1969. 'What I am interested in is the relationship between the blundering human being and God. I belong to no Church but I have a religious faith. It's an attempt to express that, among other things, that I try to do.' 'I think,' he continued, 'there's a Divine Power, a Creator who has an influence on human beings if they are willing to open to Him. Yes, I pray. I was brought up an Anglican.'[5] Addressing a Peace Conference in Canberra in 1986 he ended his speech with a prayer, and added, 'I believe most people hunger after spirituality even if that hunger remains in many cases unconscious. If those who dragoon us ignore that longing of the human psyche, they are running a great risk ... The sense of real purpose – the life-force – could be expelled from a society whose leaders are obsessed by money, muscle and machinery. That society could – quite simply – die.'[6] But he rejected what he called 'the sterility, the vulgarity, in many cases the bigotry, of the Christian Churches'. Christian love, he said, 'had lost its virtue, as antibiotics lose theirs through overdosage'. In the conventional, abstract manner in which it was taught, it had 'become as ineffectual and destructive as violence and hatred', he said.[7]

There can be no doubt, therefore, either about the seriousness of his attitudes to matters of religious faith or about the unorthodox and unconventional character of his own religious beliefs. Brought up as an Anglican by his parents, he seems, on his own admission, to have been largely indifferent to religion in childhood and adolescence. In *Flaws in the Glass*, his autobiography, he recalls occasional periods of religious fervour, such as he experienced at the time of his Confirmation, but these seem to have been rare exceptions to a general pattern of indifference on all matters relating to religion and its conventions at that period in his life. 'For many years,' he wrote 'I felt no need for a faith either dialectical or mystical, believing as I did in my own brash Godhead.'[8] He attributed his subsequent rediscovery of Christianity to an experience that occurred in 1951. In that year bush fires raged across the southern region of the Australian continent, reaching the outer suburbs of Canberra and threatening the fringes of the city. The bush fires were followed by massive bursts of lightning and by great downpours of rain, leading to storms and floods that lasted from late summer into the Christmas season. Recalling this period in his autobiography, he describes an occasion when he went out in a storm to feed his dogs: 'During what seemed like months of rain I was carrying a trayload of food to a wormy litter of pups down at the kennels when I slipped and fell on my back, dog dishes shooting in all directions. I lay where I had fallen, half blinded by rain, under a pale sky, cursing through watery lips a God in whom I did not believe. I began laughing, finally, at my own helplessness and hopelessness, in the mud and the stench from my filthy old oilskin. It was the turning point. My disbelief appeared as farcical as my fall. At that moment I was truly humbled.'[9] Speaking of the same experience in an interview with the critic, James Stern, he remarked that he wondered 'how he could curse what did not exist' and at that moment had his first genuine inkling of the presence of God. At that moment 'faith began to come' he said.[10] Describing the experience in a letter to his cousin, Peggy Garland, he spoke of the essential mysteriousness of the experience of faith and suggested that his 'conversion' may, after all, have been the outcome of a lengthier and more complex process than his experience in the storm:

> I have not myself suffered any of the great injustices, such as hunger, or torture, or the devastations of war, to name a few, but I do feel by this time that all the minor injustices to which I have been submitted, and which at the time have seemed terribly unjust and unnecessary, even agonising, have in fact been necessary to my development. I do feel that every minute of my life has been necessary – though this conviction has only very recently come to me – and that the sum total can only be good, though how good one cannot presume to say.
>
> None of this is new. It is quite simple. You may even find it ludicrous. But it is better to say it, in case it may help simply by its simplicity and obviousness. I think it is impossible to explain faith. It is like trying to explain air, which one cannot do by dividing it into its component parts and labelling them scientifically. It must be breathed to be understood. But breathing is something that has been going on all the time, and is almost imperceptible. I don't know when I began to have faith, but it is only a short time since I admitted it.[11]

Though White began to attend Church services again following his experience in the storm, he continued to reject the dogmas of the institutional Churches. 'My spiritual self has always shrivelled in contact with organised religion,' he wrote … 'The mystery of religious faith evaporates on contact with dogma, he declared.' 'Faith,' he argued, 'is something between the person and God and must vary accordingly.'[12] He insisted on its inseparability from the interpersonal immediacy of human love. 'Only love redeems,' he wrote in one of the concluding passages of his autobiography. 'My inklings of God's presence are interwoven with my love of the one human being who never fails me,' he said. 'When I say love redeems, I mean the love shared with an individual, not necessarily sexual, seductive though sexuality may be.'[13] Far from being a guarantee of intellectual certainty, however, he saw the experience of faith as being just as insecure as the love from which it springs. The great truths, he wrote, can only be grasped intermittently, 'as a result of a daily wrestling match, and then only by glimmers, as through a veil'.[14] Yet he was convinced that faith alone could make life meaningful: 'I felt that life was, on the surface, so dreary, ugly, monotonous, there must be something hidden in it to give it a purpose, and so I set out to find a secret cave and *The Tree of Man* emerged.'¹⁵ The secret that he sought was the mystery of God, the ineffable reality which can be grasped only through faith. In *Flaws in the Glass* he asks:

> What do I believe? I am accused of not making it explicit. How to be explicit about a grandeur too overwhelming to express, a daily wrestling match with an opponent whose limbs never become material, a struggle from which the sweat and blood are scattered on the pages of anything the serious writer writes? A belief contained less in what is said than in the silences. In patterns on water. A gust of wind. A flower opening. I hesitate to add a child, because a child can grow into a monster, a destroyer. Am I a destroyer? This face in the glass which has spent a lifetime searching for what it believes, but can never prove to be, the truth. A face consumed by wondering whether truth can be the worst destroyer of all.¹⁶

In words reminiscent of Tolstoy he further emphasised the essential privacy of the experience of faith: 'I have come closest to what one always hopes for in Ayia Sophia, Constantinople, alone in the Parthenon on winter afternoons after the Germans had been driven out, in the Friends' Meeting House at Jordans, Bucks., in a garden full of birds, in my own silent room. All of them moments which remain inklings rather than confirmation.' 'The ultimate spiritual union,' he wrote, 'is probably as impossible to achieve as the perfect work of art or the unflawed human relationship.'¹⁷ In 1988, shortly before his death, he issued a particularly detailed and explicit statement of his beliefs. Entitled 'Credo', the statement reaffirms the personal character of his faith, as well as its sense of the underlying links between the traditions of Christianity, Judaism, Hinduism and Buddhism. It provides moving testimony to the faith of all those who inconspicuously give practical witness to their beliefs in the uneventful circumstances of their daily lives:

> I am coming to believe, not in God, but a Divine Presence of which Jesus, the Jewish Prophets, the Buddha, Mahatma Gandhi and Co. are the more comprehensible manifestations. This Presence controls us but only to a certain degree: life is what we, its components, make it. Hence the existence of megalomaniac politicians, dictators, mafia millionaires, greedy landlords, rapists, murderers, self-obsessed spouses within the same scheme which embraces the Teresas, St John of the Cross, Thomas Merton, and others who continue to speak to us out of the historic waxwork-museum – all those along with the anonymous who lift

us from the gutters, wiping the vomit from our lips, who comfort us as our limbs lie paralysed on the pavement, feed us within their limited means, and close our eyes – these humble everyday saints created for our consolation by the same mysterious universal Presence ignored, cursed, derided, or intermittently worshipped by the human race.[18]

Despite his emphasis on the privacy of faith, these words confirm that White's beliefs were profoundly shaped by the traditions of religion, particularly by the Judaeo-Christian religious heritage which he acknowledged as the single most potent influence on his spiritual and artistic development from the time he wrote *The Tree of Man* until the end of his life. He confided to Peter Beatson, the author of *Patrick White: A Vision of Man and God*, that the writers who had been most influential in shaping his beliefs were Simone Weil, Jacques Maritain, T.S. Eliot, Gabriel Marcel, Martin Buber, Gershom Scholem, C.G. Jung and the author of *The Cloud of Unknowing*.[19] All of these writers – with the exception of Jung whose work could not readily be classified as religious – belong centrally within the Judaeo Christian tradition. And though White is recorded as saying that he drew freely on the symbologies of various religious traditions in his novels (he told Craig McGregor he 'could not divorce Christianity from other religions'),[20] both biographical testimony and the evidence of his fiction overwhelmingly confirm the centrality of the Judaeo-Christian influences in all his work. (There are some indications of influences from Hinduism, but these are minor and peripheral by comparison with those emanating from Jewish and Christian sources.)

For years he immersed himself in the study of Judaism, finding in the sacred books of Jewish tradition, and in the Hasidic writings of Martin Buber and Gershom Scholem, confirmation of one of his most fervently held beliefs – the reality of God's immanent presence in the world that He created. For years also he immersed himself in the Christian Gospels – 'I read the Bible literally from cover to cover',[21] he said as he recalled a period when he felt the well-springs of his creativity had dried up and he turned to scripture for imaginative as well as spiritual sustenance – and he retained a lifelong attachment to the novels of Dostoevsky, Tolstoy and Pasternak, clearly finding deep affinities with their strong Christian sensibilities. (He confessed himself 'spellbound by *Dr Zhivago* – by every page' – and he told a friend in 1963 he was 'reading *The Brothers Karamazov* for the third time' and was looking forward to reading it yet again, 'to get into every corner of it'.)[22] He found the Jewish doctrine of God's indwelling presence in creation to be entirely compatible with the Christian doctrine of the Incarnation, i.e., the concept of God become Man, the Word made Flesh. Both themes are closely intertwined in his novels, the passages celebrating the beauty and mystery of nature being particularly evocative of its truth. The two traditions are powerfully synthesised in the person of Himmelfarb, who simultaneously represents the outcast Jew of history and the suffering Christ who takes upon himself the sins and transgressions of mankind.

Not alone is the continuity of Jewish and Christian traditions the dominant force in White's fiction and the inspiration of some of its most significant themes, but it is also the key to the relationship of his artistic and religious purposes. Two principles are central to an understanding of this. The first is the principle of antinomy, i.e., the concept of opposition as a necessary and inevitable characteristic of earthly existence. The principle has deep roots both in Jewish and Christian tradition. In *I and Thou*, for example, Martin Buber, one of White's acknowledged mentors and a major modern exponent of Hasidic culture, expresses it in the following terms: 'Man's religious situation, his being there in the Presence, is characterised by its essential and indissoluble antinomy ... He who wishes to carry through the conflict of the antinomy other than with his life transgresses the significance of the situation. The significance of the situation is that it is lived and nothing but lived, continually, ever anew, without foresight, without forethought, without prescription, in the totality of its antinomy.'[23] The same principle, conceived in terms of the divided consciousness of man in the conditions of his mortal state, has been repeatedly emphasised by Christian writers through the centuries – particularly those in the tradition of negative mysticism, such as the author of *The Cloud of Unknowing* – and it has been powerfully reinvoked by modern writers such as Eliot and Auden, as has been shown in earlier chapters. Continuously, throughout his fiction, White emphasises the dual nature of human existence, seeing it as a co-existence of opposites – good and evil, sense and spirit etc. 'You cannot reconcile joy and sorrow, or flesh and marble, or illusion and reality, or life and death,' Holstius remarks in *The Aunt's Story*. Conflict and opposition are part of the mortal state, of what is described in *The Eye of the Storm* as 'the dichotomy of earth-bound flesh and aspiring spirit', intimating the endemic divisions of existence in the conditions of temporal, finite and conditioned reality.

But, while emphasising its conflicts and dichotomies, White pointed consistently to the potentiality in man to transcend the conditions of the mortal state. That transcendence is conceived once again in terms of both its Jewish and Christian traditions. Underlying it, on the one hand, is the Jewish concept of self-transcendence through the celebration of God's indwelling presence in the world of his creation. Martin Buber succinctly summarised this teaching in the following words from *Hasidism and Modern Man*: 'Man cannot reach the divine by reaching beyond the human; he can approach him (i.e. God) through becoming human. To become human is what he, this individual man, has been created for … You cannot really love God if you do not love men, and you cannot really love men if you do not love God.'[24] The Christian doctrine of salvation attained through the mystery of the Incarnation is broadly consistent with this, being a further attestation of the immanent and redemptive presence of God in creation, a presence dramatically fulfilled in the idea of God become man in the person of Christ.

Both these themes are explored closely in White's fiction, as will be demonstrated in some detail presently. At this point, what needs to be emphasised is their relevance to his understanding of the relationship of aesthetic and religious experience and to the ways in which this finds expression in his fiction. Earlier the words of Ben Nicholson with which White prefaced *The Vivisector*, were cited: 'As I see it, painting and religious experience are the same thing, and what we are all searching for is the understanding and realisation of infinity.' The search for images and symbols of the infinite, the mysterious, the inexplicable, White clearly saw as the primary function of the artist. He saw the images and symbols of art as being especially appropriate for invoking both the conflicts and antinomies of the mortal state and the possibilities for transcending the finite and temporal through the celebration of the immanent presence of the divine in the natural world. Both processes are vividly evoked in *The Vivisector*, his most direct exploration of the interpenetrating relations of religious and aesthetic experience, and they are exemplified in all the major novels and stories. Their significance can be illustrated briefly at this point by way of reference to *The Vivisector* before being explained in more detail in the context of all his work in later sections.

In his paintings Hurtle Duffield celebrates the wholeness of natural reality, suggesting that its squalor as well as its beauty are disclosive of its ultimate meaningfulness. 'Why must I paint disgusting images?' he asks. 'I was trying to find some formal order behind a moment of chaos and unreason. Otherwise it would have been too horrifying and terrifying.' He is 'looking for a god – a *God* – in every heap of rusty tins amongst the worm-eaten furniture, out the window in the dunny of brown blowflies and unfinished inscriptions'. He recognises God as the source both of the disorder he contemplates and of the order towards which he aspires; he comes to see God therefore as both Vivisector and Artist, the creator of reality in all its varying and conflicting modes. And it is through his contemplation of incarnate reality, in its fragmentation and disorder, that paradoxically he attains a vision of the harmony of all conflict and opposition in the person of God. In this his artistic and religious aspirations coalesce.

Both the tensions and the ultimate harmony of art and faith are vividly demonstrated in the part of the novel in which Duffield seeks to purge himself of mortal despair by painting his vision of religious transcendence: a vision he conceives symbolically as the 'vertiginous blue of pure indigo'. Before he can contemplate this vision, he must first 'paint out the death which had stroked him'. This was to be a 'black painting', he says, 'with only the merest entrance into a light which was dead white; all that he had experienced under the dead pressure of despair'. As he confronts the dark night of his despair, he gradually begins to move towards the plenitude of light and strives for a vision 'that would convey the whole'. What he comes to recognise is that life, in all its disorder and fragmentation, holds within it the potentiality for the infinite. It is this potentiality which he seeks to convey through the images of art. It is only when he recognises the presence of the infinite in the finite that he can attempt to paint his vision of transcendence. As he paints the 'never-yet-attainable blue', the 'unnamable indigo' that symbolises this vision of wholeness, he tumbles backwards towards his death. As he dies, he recognises that his life, with all its conflicts, its suffering and despair, has been an unconscious and largely unintended pursuit of this vision of unity that is symbolised in the perfection of vertiginous blue: 'All his life he had been reaching towards this vertiginous blue without truly visualising, till lying on the pavement he was dazzled not so much by a colour as by a long-standing secret relationship.' His last words are 'Too tired too end-less obvi indi-ggoddd', a coded affirmation of the endlessness and obviousness of the presence of God in the material world. This was the object both of his quest for order and for spiritual fulfilment, his search for the ultimate meaning of reality through the parallel modes of art and faith.

It will be shown presently that Duffield's image of the artistic and the spiritual quest for God encompasses the tensions, complexities, and, ultimately, the harmony of the religious vision which is developed in all the works that White created from *The Tree of Man*, which he published in 1955, to *The Twyborn Affair*, his last major work of fiction, which appeared more than twenty years later, in 1979. In these works he has disclosed a conception of the relationship of man and God which is comparable in its depth and profundity to the finest evocations of religious faith in the novels of his great nineteenth century forebears, Tolstoy and Dostoevsky. It is a vision which embraces the contradictions of the finite and the infinite, the temporal and intemporal, the rational and the numinous and which, without attempting to resolve their complexities, seeks to illuminate them from the spiritual and metaphysical standpoints where they become ultimately meaningful. It is one which locates the ordinary, mundane, circumstantial realities of everyday life in the contexts where their final, i.e., absolute, worth can be definitively appraised. The themes on which that vision was focussed will be explored in the remaining sections of this chapter. Attention will be centred on four main themes: the conflicts of faith and unbelief, the problem of suffering, the immanence of

God's presence in the materiality of the natural world, and the soul's hoped-for prospect of salvation through love.

'WE MEET BUT IN THE DISTANCE'

The separation of the soul from God is one of the major themes of these novels and is seen by White as the root-cause of the suffering that afflicts mankind in the circumstances of mortal life. However, it is man's acceptance of the conditions of his temporal state, he suggests, which is the means by which he can ultimately transcend them. 'The mystery of life is not solved by success, which is an end in itself, but by failure, in perpetual struggle, in becoming,' Frank le Mesurier says in *Voss*. The descent into the darkness of negativity and failure is the way by which man ultimately ascends to God. It is the way of the mystics, the *via negativa*, the quest for the unknowable God which is conducted in the darkness of existence in time. Distance from God is man's affliction in the conditions of temporal life, yet it is in the depth of his awareness of this that he proceeds towards union with God through faith. 'We meet but in the distance,' Le Mesurier says, 'and dreams are the distance brought close.' It was in moments of darkness and despair that Himmelfarb – the most Christ-like of the characters that White created – felt closest to God. Amidst the horrors of the death-camp, he wonders if the despair that is all-pervasive there has not been *sent* by God in pursuance of some mysterious purpose which at that moment he himself cannot hope to comprehend:

> As it was still night, and the shed was kept in total darkness due to the exigencies of war, it was not possible to estimate the number of his fellow occupants, only that the shed contained a solid mass, and that a mass soul suffered and recoiled. Inside the prevailing darkness, worse because it was imposed by man – or could it have been sent by God? – the lost soul mourned, and tried to deduce the reason for the unreasonable. At moments the voice of the mourner sounded like that of a child, but quickly thickened and intensified. Then the aged voice rose, it seemed, out of the depths of history. Crying and lamenting. Sometimes there were blows and kicks as more of the filthy Jews were settled in, and sometimes from the door a torch would reach out, and rend the veil of darkness, revealing patches of yellowish skin, or hands clutching at possessions, as if those were the most they had to lose. The guards might laugh at some indignity glimpsed, but on the whole, at the assembly point, they seemed to prefer a darkness in which to hate in the abstract the whole mass of Jews.

Man's sense of his distance from God is manifested primarily, White suggests, in the problem of unbelief: a condition rooted both in his failure to comprehend the mysterious actions of an all-knowing and benevolent Creator and in his unwillingness to assent to the presence of God in the contradictory conditions of his earthly existence. The primary cause of man's separation from God, however, is his own fallenness, his potentiality for corruption and evil which, in turn, is rooted in his freedom. Paradoxically, he suggests, man questions the benevolence and justice of an all-seeing and all-powerful Creator who can permit so much evil to exist in the universe He created, while his very questioning of God's benevolence is itself a radical manifestation of the freedom from which evil springs. The universe described by White is dominated by this paradox: a paradox which is rooted in the antinomies and contradictions he saw as endemic in its finitude and its temporality. The earthly universe is conditioned by the law of necessity which ordains that every reality reveals its opposite. All that exists is poised between the polarities of the temporal and intemporal, the finite and the infinite, the extremes of evil and good, of joy and suffering, of life and death.

It is man's consciousness of the necessity of evil and suffering, White suggests, which causes him to question the justice of God and to reject the very idea of an all-knowing and benevolent Creator whose spirit is manifested lovingly in the universe He created. Why is it, Dorothy Hunter wonders, that some are chosen for salvation while others are apparently condemned to an eternity of punishment. 'Why was it given to Elizabeth Hunter to experience the eye of the storm,' she asks. 'Or,' she wonders, 'are regenerative states of mind granted to the very old to ease the passage from their earthly sensual natures into final peace and forgiveness?' Failing to resolve the problem of divine justice, man, it is suggested, has invented a vengeful, autocratic and vindictive God, who is the very antithesis of the God of infinite love revealed in the scriptures. This is the God that Stan Parker recalls from his childhood: 'The God of Parker the father, the boy saw, was essentially a fiery God, a gusty God, who appeared between belches, accusing with a horny finger. He was a God of the Prophets. And, if anything, this was the God that the boy himself suspected and feared rather than his mother's gentleness.' In *The Vivisector* Duffield paints a God who is a cruel and malicious despot responsible for all the suffering and cruelty that exists in the world. This God he sees as 'the Divine Destroyer', 'the Divine Vivisector'. He believes in this God – 'otherwise how could men come by their cruelty', he exclaims. 'Man is cruel,' his companion, Hero, screams, 'God is cruel …

> We are his bagful of cats, aren't we? When God is no longer cruel many questions will be answered.'

She was so furious she accompanied her accusations by striking the mattress with her strickened hand.

'You drive me to blaspheme!' she shouted louder still.

'But you've told me you're not a believer.'

'No, I do not believe. But blaspheme every day!'

She burst into such a torrent of grief it was now his turn to be shocked. He tried to comfort her by caressing her racked body; but this was not what she wanted: she shook him off in a flurry of wet hair.

'What I do believe in,' she cried, 'is my husband's goodness, because I have experienced it. You will not believe in it because of the bagful of cats. He loved the cats – which he killed. Yes, he killed them. Why do we kill what we love? Perhaps it is because it becomes too much for us – simply for that reason.'

Felicity Bannister in 'The Night of the Prowler' and Ivy Simpson in 'Sicilian Vespers' are similarly driven to blaspheme the anthropomorphic God of Christian tradition. Felicity swears abusively at God 'for holding out on me', and in the Church of San Fabrizio Ivy commits an act of sacrilege on the floor, while above her on the ceiling 'Christ the Pantocrator weeps'. Blasphemy, as Eliot said, is an expression of man's incomprehension of the ways in which the Divine will operates in the fallen world and is essentially a manifestation of a latent faith, however crudely and perversely this may be projected. Underlying it is what White himself in an interview described as the central problem of faith: 'how to accept a supernatural force which on the one hand blesses and on the other destroys'.[25]

Man's unbelief is manifested, on the one hand, therefore, in his incomprehension of the workings of Divine Providence and in his compensating notion of God as a vengeful and malicious presence in the universe He created. It correspondingly finds expression in the assumption by man that he himself is in possession of god-like powers. Johann Voss epitomises the pride that rejects the God of the scriptures and sees man as all-powerful in himself. As an individual, Voss is characterised by arrogance and an overweening belief in the power of reason and in his own self-sufficiency – 'The future,' said Voss, 'is will' (echoing Stavrogin). 'It had become quite clear from his face,' the narrator says, 'that he accepted his own divinity. If it was less clear, he was equally convinced all others must accept.' The Moravian monk, Brother Mullen tells him, 'You have a contempt for God because He is not in your own image.' Believing so totally in his own self-capacity, Voss despises human love: 'He did not expect much from love, for all that is soft and yielding is easily hurt. He suspected it, but the universal forms were an everlasting source of wonder. ... He had no more need of sentimental admiration than he had for love. He was complete.' Identifying the idea of God with the power of the individual self, he despises atheists for their lack of faith in themselves. 'Atheismus is self-murder,' he says. 'Atheists are atheists usually for mean reasons ... The meanest of these is that they themselves are so lacking in magnificence that they cannot conceive the idea of a Divine Power.' In his dialogue with Laura on the nature of faith and unbelief, he reveals the magnitude of his own pride, but she detects behind this the inherent weakness of the self which ultimately proves to be his undoing. Ironically, it is this, however, that marks his gradual advance towards faith:

> 'It is for our pride that each of us is probably damned,' Laura said.
>
> Then he shook her off, and the whole situation of an hysterical young woman. He was wiping his lips, which had begun to twitch, though in anger, certainly not from weakness. He breathed deeply. He drank from the great arid skies of fluctuating stars. The woman beside him had begun to suggest the presence of something soft and defence-less.
>
> Indeed, Laura Trevelyan did not feel she would attempt anything further, whatever might be revealed to her.
>
> 'For some reason of intellectual vanity, you decided to do away with God,' Voss was saying; she knew he would be smiling. 'But the consequences are yours alone, I assure you.'
>
> It was true; he made her know.
>
> 'I feel you may still suspect me,' he continued. 'But I do believe, you must realise. Even though I worship with pride. Ah, the humility, the humility. That is what I find so particularly loathsome. My God, besides, is above humility.'
>
> 'Ah,' she said. 'Now, I understand.'
>
> It was clear. She saw him standing in the glare of his own brilliant desert. Of course. He was Himself indestructible.
>
> And she did then begin to pity him. She no longer pitied herself, as she had for many weeks in the house of her uncle, whose unfailingly benevolent materialism encouraged the practice of self-pity. Love seemed to return to her with humility. Her weakness was delectable.
>
> 'I shall think of you with alarm,' she said. 'To maintain such standards of pride, in the face of what you must experience on this journey is truly alarming.'
>
> 'I am not in the habit of setting myself limits.'
>
> 'Then I will learn to pray for you.'

Reading the poems of Frank le Mesurier, Voss, like Dostoevsky's Prince Myshkin, gradually discovers that humility, not pride, is the real source of man's power and recognises that this finds fulfilment in the self-transcendence of love. Feverishly, in the darkness of the night, he reads Le Mesurier's words: 'Humility is my brigalow, that must I remember: here I shall find a thin shade in which to sit. As I grow weaker, so I shall become strong. As I shrivel, I shall recall with amazement the visions of love, of trampling horses, of drowning candles, of hungry emeralds. Only goodness is fed. Until the sun delivered me from my body, the wind fretted my wretched ribs, my skull was split open by the green lightning. Now that I am nothing, I am, and love is the simplest of all tongues.' What Voss finally learns is that man is not the God-like being he believed he was and that the bridging of the distance between the individual soul and the infinite for which it yearns lies ultimately in the conquest of self-directed pride. 'When man is truly humbled,' Laura says, 'when he has learned that he is not God, then he is nearest to becoming so.' In the loneliness of impending death, Voss recognises that the strength which is enabling him to endure the torment of his final agony derives from the weaknesses of nature that he once despised:

> Only he was left, only he could endure it, and that because at last he was truly humbled.
> So saints acquire sanctity who are only bones.
> He laughed.
> It was both easy and difficult. For he was still a man, bound by the threads of his fate. A whole knot of it.
> At night he lay and looked through the thin twigs, at the stars, but more especially at the Comet, which appeared to have glided almost the length of its appointed course. It was fading, or else his eyes were.
> 'That, Harry,' he said, 'is the Southern Cross, I believe, to the south of the main mast. That is where, doubtless, their snake will burrow in and we shall not see him again.'
> 'Are you frightened?' he asked.
> He himself, he realised, had always been most abominably frightened, even at the height of his divine power, a frail god upon a rickety throne, afraid of opening letters, of making decisions, afraid of the instinctive knowledge in the eyes of mules, of the innocent eyes of good men, of the elastic nature of the passions, even of the devotion he had received from some men, and one woman, and dogs.
> Now, at least, reduced to the bones of manhood, he could admit to all this, and listen to his teeth rattling in the darkness.
> 'O Jesus,' he cried, *'rette mich nur! Du lieber!'*
> Of this too, mortally frightened, of the arms, or sticks, reaching down from the eternal tree, and tears of blood, and candlewax. Of the great legend becoming truth

In the circumstances of temporal life, however, the attainment of faith cannot finally resolve the problem of unbelief. Unbelief itself, White suggests, remains inherent in the very nature of faith, casting man continuously at a distance from God by challenging the certainties of his faith. Yet paradoxically, it can serve as a force for the renewal of faith by that same process. There is a strong sense in the novels both of the limitations of reason and of its dialectical potential. 'I agree that intellect can be a handicap,' Himmelfarb says. 'There are moments when I like to imagine I have overcome it.' While struggling to maintain his faith against the everpresent challenge of reason, he acknowledges the need to test out his beliefs against the questions persistently presented by the sceptical resources of thought. This is his dominant feeling as he prays beside his father's grave: 'Because faith is never faith unless it is to be wrestled with. O perfect Rock, spare and have pity on the parents and the children. So Mordechai wrestled with the Rock and prayed for his parent, that shifting sand, or worldly man, whose moustache had smelt deliciously and who had never been happier than when presenting a Collected Works in leather.'

Stan Parker similarly struggles with faith against the natural scepticism of his rational powers. 'Although he had acquired the habit of saying simple prayers, and did sincerely believe in God, he was not sufficiently confident in himself to believe in the efficacy of the one or the extent of the other. His simplicity had not yet received that final clarity and strength which can acknowledge the immensity of belief.' Miss Hare employs the imagery of darkness and light to convey the dialectical character of faith. 'Encouraged to expect of life some ultimate revelation', she comes to recognise that 'in the last light, illumination is synonymous with blinding'. Faith must fluctuate constantly between the certainty of total belief and the insecurity of doubt. Underlying their tensions is the further conflict between individual will and pride and the spirit of altruistic selflessness which is essential for the attainment of faith. Laura Trevelyan, before she discovers the power of humble prayer, epitomises the spirit of sceptical rationalism which is founded on pride. It is this which has temporarily suppressed the innocent faith of her childhood:

> The keenest torment or exhilaration was, in fact, the most private. Like her recent decision that she could not remain a convinced believer in that God in whose benevolence and power she had received most earnest instruction from a succession of governesses and from her good aunt. How her defection had come about was problematic, unless it was by some obscure action of antennae, for she spoke to nobody who was not ignorant, and innocent, and kind. Yet, here she was become what, she suspected, might be called a rationalist. If she had been less proud,

she might have been more afraid. Certainly she had not slept for several nights, before accepting that decision which had been in the making, she realised, several years. Already as a little girl she had been softly sceptical, perhaps out of boredom; she was suffocated by the fuzz of faith. She did believe, however, most palpably, in wood, with the reflections in it, and in clear daylight, and in water. She would work fanatically at some mathematical problem, even now, just for the excitement of it, to solve and know. She had read a great deal out of such books as had come her way in that remoter colony, until her mind seemed to be complete. There was in consequence no necessity to duplicate her own image, unless in glass, as now, in the blurry mirror of the big, darkish room.

There is a spurious resolution to the tensions of reason and faith which is satirised at various points in White's fiction. Mrs Hare is a caricature of the unthinking believer whose faith finds expression only in the formalities of institutionalised religious observance: 'Paddling in her own delicious shallows, it never occurred to Mrs Hare to raise her soul to God, except to call him as a formal witness. She accepted Him – who would have been so audacious not to? – but as the creator of a moral and a social system. At that level, she could always be relied on to put her hand in her purse, to help repair vestments, or support fallen girls, and her name was published for everyone to read, on a visiting card, inserted in a brass frame, on the end of her regular pew.' This ritualised belief system is pointedly contrasted with the more complex and authentic faith of her daughter, Mary: 'Her mother enjoyed full possession of that social and economic faith on which the stone mansions are built, whereas in the daughter's worst dreams those foundations were already sunk; only her faith in light and leaves remained to hold the structures up.' The Rosetrees exemplify the spirit of this 'social and economic faith'; their ethics consist of a simplistic system of conventions through which the practice of an essentially materialistic creed can be given an aura of moral authenticity:

> But Harry Rosetrees was an honest man. If you signed a contract, you had to abide by the clauses. And religion was like any other business. Rosetrees were Christians now; they would do the necessary. Shirl complained, but of course she was a woman. Shirl said she had been brought up to stay at home, to stuff the fish, and knead the dumplings, not to pray along with the men. She did no go much on early Mass, but Harry would sometimes persuade, with a bottle of French perfume, or a pair of stockings. Then Shirl would get herself up in the gold chains which were such a handy investment, and derive quite a lot from the subdued

and reverential atmosphere – it was lovely, the elevation of the Host – and the wives of upper-bracket executives in their expensive clothes.

MATERIALITY, TIME AND SUFFERING

Man's separation from God, which is manifested primarily in the universal conflict of unbelief and faith, is rooted, White suggests, in the temporal and material conditions of his earthly existence. The conflicts of matter and spirit and of the time-bound and the timeless are seen by him as expressions of a greater dichotomy: the dichotomy of form and formlessness, of order and chaos in the realm of being. It is in the context of this all-embracing conflict that he explores the tensions of the temporal and the timeless, the material and the spiritual, and the related problem of the necessity of suffering in mortal life. It is within this context also that the major Christian themes of immanence and redemption are disclosed in his fiction. Human existence, he suggests, is poised between the extremes of order and chaos, of permanence and flux, each of which paradoxically discloses both the restrictions of mortal life and the potential it holds for liberation and redemption. Thus, materiality, time and form can be seen as the sources of the spirit's imprisoned existence in the finite universe or they can be addressed as disclosing the indwelling presence of the infinite in its mundane reality. The forces of flux and change can be seen as agents of destruction or they can be seen conversely as providing existential attestation of the endlessness and limitlessness of being. Both tendencies are given expression in one of the finest lyrical passages that White has written, Mrs Hunter's death-bed reverie in *The Eye of the Storm*:

> Mrs Hunter had no complaints to make. Her nose was brooding: she was so deep in concentration she was glad to hear her nurse go. Nobody could help her now: only herself, and grace ...
> Now the real business in hand was not to withdraw her will, as she had once foreseen, but to will enough strength into her body to put her feet on the ground and walk steadily towards the water. There was the question of how much time she would have before the eye must concentrate on other, greater contingencies, leaving her to chaos. That this was threatening, she could tell from the way the muslin was lifted at the edges, till what had been a benison of sea, sky, and land, was becoming torn by animal passions, those of a deformed octopod with blue-suckered tentacles and a glare of lightning and poached eggs ...
> To move the feet by some miraculous dispensation to feel sand benign and soft between the toes the importance of the decision makes

the going heavy at first the same wind stirring the balconies of cloud as blows between the ribs it would explain the howling of what must be the soul not for fear that it will blow away in any case it will but in its anticipation of its first experience of precious water as it filters in through the cracks the cavities of the body blue pyramidal waves with swans waiting by appointment each a suppressed black explosion the crimson beaks savaging only those born to a different legend to end in legend is what frightens most people more than could water climbing mercifully towards the overrated but necessary heart a fleshy fist to love and fight with not to survive except as a kindness or gift of a jewel.

The seven swans are perhaps massed after all to destroy a human will once the equal of their own weapons its thwack as crimson painful its wings as violently abrasive don't oh DON'T my dark birds of light let us rather – enfold.

Till I am no longer filling the void with mock substance: myself is this endlessness

The soul finds fulfilment by identifying itself both with the spheres of order and chaos, of form and change. It seeks the security and order of material form which it finds by immersing itself in the concrete reality of existential being. Whether this results in a transcendence of the existential or in the spirit's imprisonment in its finitude is, White suggests, a matter of the perspective from which it is encountered. The forces of nature – the great storms, fires and floods that sweep across the landscape in *The Tree of Man* – are seen, for example, by Amy and Stan both as the forces that can engulf and destroy them and as awesome disclosures of the presence of a numinous reality in the phenomenal world. The same forces they associate with death and destruction appear also as agents of grace and redemption. In *The Vivisector* there are recurrent patterns of imagery suggestive both of the corruptibility and the redemptive potential of material being. In the scene for example where Hero and Hurtle gaze on the seascape at Perialos, the former sees only filth and corruption while the latter perceives a beauty in the whole scene that suggests the presence of God, its Creator. This prompts him to acknowledge God's presence in all existent being:

Strands of purple were by now visible in the sea or sky along the coast. A conventional piety had reappeared in Hero's face: she was possibly hoping for a blessing on taking leave of the condemned abbess. He felt drunk and sick from the ouzo, but exalted by the light and colour of the sea-sky ...

'Can God be sceptical of us?' he suggested

'I am beginning to think so.' She sighed at the purple evening. 'But wait,' she suddenly remembered and took heart, 'wait till we talk with this hermit – Theodosios. This is a saint who will plead for us.' In her conviction, and the blaze of hieratic gold, she turned her face towards him, her sins as good as forgiven.

His unregenerate soul could feel no more than sympathetic towards her state of mind, while worshipping the aesthetic variations of its incarnation. It was the same with the landscape. He was conscious of God as a formal necessity on which depended every figure in the afternoon's iconography: goat-troglodytes; the old man pissing against the wind; orphan-whores; the procession of mourners; a martyred Hero. The ouzo in him, which should have helped dissolve, made him cling, on the contrary, to outward and visible signs ... They were feeling their way back with their feet down the outside steps of the chapel; when she began to blubber hopelessly. 'I think we have lost our faith in God because we cannot respect men. They are so disgusting.'

Again, in *The Eye of the Storm* the natural scene symbolically suggests the opposition of material and spiritual tendencies. With its burden of monstrous spawn, the sea symbolises the corruptibility of the fallen world of temporal-material being in which Elizabeth has immersed herself throughout her life. In her reverie she identifies with the skiapod, a mythical creature who undergoes a symbolic purgatory in the underwater depths, eventually dying in a violent encounter with an octopus. Her experience of redemption through divine grace is symbolised, however, as a baptism through water, through immersion in the endlessness of the infinite, of which the sea is the classic archetype. Her soul looks expectantly to 'the precious water as it filters in through the cracks and cavities of the body blue pyramidal waves with swans waiting by appointment ...' The sea, as both a destructive and a redemptive force, epitomises the opposition and antinomy by which the whole natural world is characterised.

This dualism in the natural order is particularly exemplified in the complexities of human love, both in its corruptibility and in the potential it offers for self-transcendence. The commonest manifestation of the dual nature of man as simultaneously matter and spirit, it evokes both the restrictions and frustrations of the mortal state and the depth of the spirit's aspiration towards the infinite. Impeded by the grossness of material being, the aspirations of love are distorted endlessly by selfishness, jealousy, possessiveness and the tensions of its own inherent carnality. Thus, while a genuine love exists between the Parkers, it finds expression in unequal and unrealisable hopes, and while it survives, it can do so only through the acceptance of its own frustrated expectations and the torment and betrayal to which they lead.

On the other hand, Waldo Brown's unreciprocated longing for love is transmuted into its opposite and he dies, consumed by the force of his own hatred. His brother, Arthur, though kind and amiable, is frustrated in his quest for love by physical unattractiveness and by mental inadequacies, both of which prove to be insurmountable barriers to emotional intimacy. Hurtle Duffield, tormented by memories of an emotionally disturbed childhood and of his failure to care for his sister, Rhoda, seeks to suppress his guilt by engaging in a series of unloving and exploitative relationships. Elizabeth Hunter sums up the perversity of romantic emotion: 'The worst thing about love between human beings,' she says, is ... 'when you're prepared to love them they don't want it; when they do it is you who can't bear the idea'. The carnal and the spiritual, though mutually interdependent, are perpetually in tension, leading to endlessly unresolvable dilemmas, such as Elizabeth describes in this exchange with Mary de Santis:

'When I was a child, Mary, living in a broken-down farmhouse, in patched dresses – a gawky, desperately vain little girl,' Mrs Hunter's eyes glittered and flickered as she flirted with the fringe of her stole, 'I used to long for possessions: dolls principally at that age; then jewels such as I had never seen only a few ugly ones on the wives of wealthier neighbours; later, and last of all, I longed to possess people who would obey me – and love me, of course. Can you understand all this?'

The nurse hesitated. 'I suppose I can, in a way – in a way. But you see, I've never had any desire for possessions. I couldn't imagine how I might come by them – or attract people, let alone have them obey me. We were a very close family. Outside that, I've only wanted to serve others – through my profession – which is all I know how to do. Oh, and to love, of course,' she laughed constrainedly; 'but that is so vast it is difficult to imagine – how – how to achieve it.'

Mrs Hunter suddenly looked angry and suspicious. 'What do you understand by love?'

'Well, perhaps – sometimes I've thought it's like this: love is a kind of supernatural state to which I must give myself entirely, and be used up, particularly my imperfections – till I am nothing.'

Mrs Hunter seemed agitated: she had got up and was trailing her long fleecy stole. 'Whatever they tell you, I loved my husband. My children wouldn't allow me to love them.' The stole had dragged so far behind, it was lost to her by catching on what must have been an invisible splinter.

'Oh, I know I am not selfless enough.!' When she turned she was burning with a blue, inward rage; but quickly quenched it, and drew up a stool at this girl's feet. 'There is this other love, I know. Haven't I been shown? And I still can't reach it. But I shall! I shall! She laid her head on her nurse's hands.

The dilemmas of the spirit-sense conflict find expression frequently in White's fiction in images evoking a deep aversion to the body and its functions. Many of his characters are physically deformed and ugly-looking; images of disgusting functions, such as excretion, constipation and flatulence occur frequently, and there are persistent references to the horrors of senility and bodily decay. Ugliness fascinates Hurtle Duffield. His paintings have images of Cutbush masturbating, of the deformed Rhoda sitting on her bidet, of Hero stabbing herself with a penis and of Nance spreadeagled on the floor. While clearly intended as expressions of the manichean prejudice that inevitably results from the conflicts of the mortal state, these images have their place nonetheless in the transformative vision that informs all the evocations of the natural world in White's fiction. Even in their horrific and disgusting physicality, they are ultimately expressive of the informing presence of the infinite in the world of material being, as will be demonstrated in some detail in the next section. 'Souls have an anus,' the narrator says in *The Eye of the Storm*. 'Every stench is sanctity', Mary de Santis reflects, as she tends to the needs of her elderly patient.

Before the resolution of the spirit-sense conflict is discussed, however, it is necessary to examine further the links between the themes of materiality and temporality and the associated theme of the inevitability of suffering in the temporal-spatial universe. As is the case with his treatment of the conflict of matter and spirit, the parallel conflict of the temporal and the timeless is also seen by White in the context of the form-formlessness dichotomy. Temporality is seen in terms of its three main aspects. It is seen, firstly, as the objectified or formal progression of time in terms of its arithmetic or measured duration; it is seen, secondly, as a psychically experienced reality; and thirdly, as experience recalled in memory. Beyond these three aspects of the temporal lies the potentiality for time-transcendence, a reality which is disclosed in the spirit's yearning for and aspiration towards the formlessness of the eternal.

The formal reality of the temporal is evoked in White's fiction as an evolutionary flow of events, as for example, the sequence of the seasons or the progression from childhood to old age in the lives of several of his main creations – Elizabeth Hunter, Mordechai Himmelfalrb, Hurtle Duffield and others. It is suggested, however, that temporality is not merely a matter of the progress of events, but is more fundamentally a spiritual process, defined only by its own internal significance. 'History,' Himmelfarb says, 'is the reflection of spirit. Spiritual faith is an active force ... which will populate the world after each attempt by the men of action to destroy it.' By this conception, the least significant of men – Himmelfarb himself, Rose, Arthur Brown, Palfreyman – all have their place in history by virtue of the spiritual significance of their lives. Following the death of Voss, Laura reflects on this mysterious interpenetration of the spiritual and the temporal. The significance of every event personally experienced, she suggests, is its simultaneous disclosure of past, present and future time. In this lies its ultimate significance. This is the meaning she conveys in the dialogue with which the novel concludes:

> 'I have been travelling through your country, forming opinions of all and sundry,' confessed Mr Ludlow to his audience, 'and am distressed to find the sundry does prevail.'
>
> 'We, the sundry, are only too aware of it,' Miss Trevelyan answered, 'but will humbly attempt to rise in your opinion if you will stay long enough.'
>
> 'How long? I cannot stay long,' protested Mr Ludlow.
>
> 'For those who anticipate perfection – and I would not suspect you of wishing for less – eternity is not too long ... '
>
> 'So you see, we are in every way provided for, by God and nature, and consequently, must survive.'
>
> 'Oh, yes, a country with a future. But when does the future become present? That is what always puzzles me.'
>
> 'Now.'
>
> 'How – now?' asked Mr Ludlow.
>
> 'Every moment that we live and breathe, and love, and suffer, and die.'
>
> 'That reminds me, I had intended asking you about this – what shall I call him? – this familiar spirit, whose name is upon everybody's lips, the German fellow who died.'
>
> 'Voss did not die,' Miss Trevelyan replied. 'He is there still, it is said, in the country, and always will be. His legend will be written down, eventually, by those who have been troubled by it.'

Every instant, she suggests, holds the potential to disclose the ultimate meaningfulness of experience in terms of its place in the temporal continuum and in its relation to the yearned for reality of the intemporal. Present experience, however, is subject to the distortions and negations of memory, just as it is enhanced and transformed by its expectations of the timeless. Many of the characters in the novels are tortured by memory – Waldo, Hurtle, Himmelfarb, Elizabeth, Mary de Santis – and find themselves defenceless against the assaults of remembered experience, helpless against its erosion of present consciousness. 'Time itself is a wound that will not heal up,' the narrator says in *Voss*. Side by side with these images of the pain of remembered experience, however, are consistent emphases on the potential for time-transcendence that exists in the present moment. The timeless can be reached in the conditions of time itself, in the pattern it imposes on the temporal. The prospect of the timeless is glimpsed in moments of grace when the spirit penetrates the boundaries of temporal reality. Such a moment occurs for Stan Parker when he goes to Madeleine's house to save her from the fire: 'He went from that room brushing a tapestry that shivered at his shoulder, and rippled, and regained eternity. All things in the house were eternal on that night, if you could forget the fire. Time was becalmed in the passages, and especially at their ends, in the depths of which brooms stood, and possessive winter coats and scarred garments in old leather.' Himmelfarb and Mary Hare have similar intuitions of the intemporal, as they gaze at the vision of the chariot, as does Hurtle Duffield in his momentary glimpse of the Indigodd. The moment when Elizabeth, feeling helpless at the height of the storm, suddenly experiences the pure calm and peacefulness of the eye, is a brief encounter with the timeless, with an existence beyond the material and the finite:

> Without much thought for her own wreckage, she moved slowly down what had been a beach, picking her way between torn-off branches, great beaded hassocks of amber weed, everywhere fish the sea had tossed out, together with a loaf of no longer bread, but a fluffier, disintegrating foam rubber. Just as she was no longer a body, least of all a woman: the myth of her womanhood had been exploded by the storm. She was instead a being, or more likely a flaw at the centre of this jewel of light: the jewel itself blinding and tremulous at the same time, existed, flaw and all, only by grace; for the storm was still visibly spinning and boiling at a distance, in columns of cloud, its walls hung with vaporous balconies, continually shifted and distorted.
>
> But she could not contemplate the storm for this dream of glistening peace through which she was moved. Interspersed between the marble pyramids of waves, thousands of sea-birds were at rest; or the birds would rise, and dive, or peacefully scrabble at the surface for food, some of them coasting almost as far as the tumultuous walls of cloud; and closer to the shore there were the blackswans – four, five, seven of them ...
>
> All else was dissolved by this lustrous moment made visible in the eye of the storm, and would have remained so, if she had been allowed to choose. She did not feel she could endure further trial by what is referred to as Nature, still less by that unnaturally swollen, not to say

diseased conscience which had taken over during the night from her defector will. She would lie down rather, and accept to become part of the shambles she saw on looking behind her: no worse than any she had caused in life in her relationships with human beings. In fact, to be received into the sand along with other deliquescent flesh, strewn horse-hair, knotted iron, the broken chassis of an upturned car, and last echo of a hamstrung piano, is the most natural conclusion.

These, however, are rare intuitions of the intemporal; the main emphasis in White's fiction is on the possibilities for time-transcendence that occur in the everyday conditions of time itself, as will be demonstrated shortly. The reality of mortal life remains the spirit's imprisonment in the temporal and the phenomenal, despite its insistent aspirations towards an existence that is free from their constrictions. The tension arising from this is the root-cause of the suffering that is an inescapable feature of mortal existence. 'One must not expect to avoid suffering,' Laura says. 'Perhaps true knowledge only comes,' she says, 'of death by torture in the country of the mind.' 'One can't escape suffering,' Elizabeth says, 'though it's only human to try to escape it.' 'I am not God, but Man,' Frank le Mesurier writes in one of his poems. 'I am God with a spear in his side.' In the midst of her tribulations, Elsie Parker continues to read the Gospels, 'convinced that sorrow is a happiness to be borne'. Alf Dubbo, looking at the painting of the Apollonian chariot on its trajectory across the sky, sees possibilities for time-transcendence in the daily experience of suffering: 'He realised how differently he saw the painting since his first acquaintance with it and how he would now transcribe the Frenchman's limited composition into his own terms of motion, and forms partly transcendental, partly evolved from his struggle with daily becoming, and experience of suffering.'

It is Dubbo who provides a specifically Christian interpretation of the necessity of suffering through his contemplation of the 'death' of Himmelfarb and his sense of its similarities to the Passion and Crucifixion of Christ. Himmelfarb embodies the continuity of the Jewish and Christian traditions. He epitomises the spirit of the suffering servant from Isaiah and of the outcast Jew of history. He is explicitly compared to Christ, albeit through the employment of a mock-heroic technique which underlines the absurdity of suffering, when judged from a purely humanist standpoint. He has a deep sense of his own messianic destiny. His wife, Reha, tells him he is one of the elect – 'one to whom much will be made clear' – and he sees himself as having a role in the salvation of the Jewish people. 'It is I,' he says, 'upon whom others were depending to redeem their sins.' He is a figure who is simultaneously tragic and comic, comparable to the clowns in the paintings of Marc Chagall who embody both the tragedy and absurdity of Jewish history. In the horrors of the death-camp he exemplifies the spirit of infinite resignation with which the Jews had endured the suffering inflicted on them through the ages. When he is subjected to a mock crucifixion by the mob, he endures his humiliation in silence. The burlesque Crucifixion ironically emphasises the irrationality of suffering and its apparent meaninglessness in the pattern of earthly existence. By his resigned acceptance of suffering, however, Himmelfarb has awakened in Alf Dubbo a sense of the true meaning of Christ's Passion and Crucifixion. The Christ of his childhood comes to life again for him as he gazes on the spectacle of the humiliation of the Jew. The whole episode leads him to reflect on the redemptive power of self-sacrifice, its disclosure of the infinite potentiality of love which is the source of the soul's salvation:

> The Jew hung. If he had not been such a contemptible object, he might have excited pity. Hoisted high at the wrists, the weight of the body threatened to cut them through. The arms strained to maintain that uneasy contact between heaven and earth. Through the torn shirt the skin was stretched transparent on the ribs. The head lolled even more heavily than in life. Those who had remained in touch with reality or tradition might have taken him for dead. But the eyes were visionary rather than fixed. The contemplative mouth dwelled on some breathless word spoken by the mind.
>
> Because he was as solitary in the crowd as the man they had crucified, it was again the abo who saw most. All that he had ever suffered, all that he had ever failed to understand, rose to the surface in Dubbo. Instinct and the white man's teaching no longer trampled on each other. As he watched, the colour flowed through the veins of the cold, childhood Christ, at last the nails entered wherever it was acknowledged they should. So he took the cup in his own yellow hands, from those of Mr Calderon, and would have offered it to such celebrants as he was now able to recognise in the crowd. So he understood the concept of the blood, which was sometimes the sick, brown stain on his own pillow, sometimes the clear crimson of redemption. He was blinded now. Choking now, physically feebler for the revelation that knowledge would never cut the cords that bound the Saviour to the tree. Not that it was asked. Nothing was asked. So he began also to understand acceptance. Now he could at last have conveyed it, in its cloak of purple, on the blue tree, the green lips of detached, contemplative suffering.
>
> And love in its many kinds began to trouble him as he looked. He saw the old man, the clergyman, searching the boy's body for the lost image of youth on the bedstead at Numburra, and Mrs Spice whirling

to her putrefaction in the never-ending dance of the potato-sacks, and Hannah the prostitute curled together with her white capon, Norman Fussell, in their sterile, yet not imperfect, fleshly egg. Many anonymous faces too, offered without expecting or frowning.

'THE INFINITE IN EVERYTHING'

'There is another world, but it is in this one.' White quoted these words from Paul Eluard on the opening page of *The Solid Mandala*. He had introduced his earlier novel, *Riders in the Chariot*, with the following excerpt from Blake's *Marriage of Heaven and Hell*: 'The Prophets Isaiah and Ezekiel dined with me, and I asked them how they dared so roundly to assert that God spoke to them; and whether they did not think at the time that they would be misunderstood, and so be the cause of imposition. Isaiah answered: "I saw no God, nor heard any, in a finite organical perception, but my senses discovered the infinite in everything ..."' The theme which most consistently invokes the religious convictions underlying White's fiction is his repeated affirmation of the immanent presence of the spiritual in the conditions of the material universe. That which is known to the senses – the visible, tangible reality of the empirical and the phenomenal – is celebrated in his work for its disclosure of the indwelling presence of God in the world of His creation. 'How important it is to understand the three stages. Of God into man. Man. And man returning into God,' Laura Trevelyan declares. God, it is repeatedly affirmed, is discovered not through the spirit's withdrawal from the world of material, temporal being, but through active and persistent encounters with His incarnate reality in the contingent conditions of the living moment.

As was indicated earlier, the theme reflects influences both from Jewish and Christian tradition. Underlying it is both the Hasidic doctrine of the indwelling of the spirit in the world of material creation and the Christian doctrine of the Incarnation – the mystery of the Word made Flesh, of God become Man. The continuity of both traditions and their common emphasis on God's immanent presence in material reality is vividly emphasised in *Riders in the Chariot*. Himmelfarb embodies the spiritual depth and richness of the Jewish heritage; he has immersed himself in the works of the Kabbalistic and Hasidic writers where the ideal of encountering God through creation is the all-embracing principle. Mary Hare's faith, however, is founded on the principles of New Testament Christianity, especially its teachings on God's presence in all existent being. Asked by Mrs Jolley what she believes, she replies: 'I believe in what I see, and what I cannot see. I believe in a thunderstorm, and wet grass, and patches of light, and stillness. There is such a variety of good.

On earth. And everywhere.' She 'recognised the Hand in every veined leaf, and would bundle with the bee into the divine Mouth'. It is her love for the material emanations of existential being that leads her to Himmelfarb and to the bond of deep and intimate friendship that develops between them. Their first meeting is described in language strongly evoking the dynamism and variety of material reality:

> When they were seated, on two stones which could have been put there for them at the roots of the tree, the two people ignored each other for a moment, staring back at the material world as if to take a last look at those familiar forms which further experience might soon remove from their lives. From inside their flowered tent, they could now observe how the masses of the orchard were broken by a hatching in grey wood. Only precariously alive, the trees were the greener for their sickliness, moodily defiant of the strong light, with little wizened oranges radiating as feverish gold. All was most extraordinarily exposed to mind and view from beneath the plum, and could have appeared to challenge hope, if it had not been for the evidence of continuity: a bird cupped in the grey goblet of her nest, a litter of young rabbits moving by clockwork into grass, the eyelids of a lizard denying petrifaction by the sun. It was perfectly still, except that the branches of the plum tree hummed with life, increasing, and increasing, deafening, swallowing them up ...
>
> He bent forward to look at the flower. She had never been so close to a man – even her father's moments of intimacy had been necessarily distant; he had always avoided any gesture that might have developed into an embrace – so, now, it was natural that she should observe intently. She was looking into the little whorls of hair on his neck, just above the collar. The confusion and profusion of rather wiry, once-black hair excited her love for all living matter, while she felt as guilty as though she had discovered the secret a respected friend had not attempted to conceal.

As Himmelfarb recalls his early life with his wife, Reha, he reflects on the perfection of the marriage union – the most potent of all manifestations of the interpenetration of the material and the spiritual. In the Hasidic writings he had read: 'Behold the light is with me ... behold the light is with me all the while ... the soul is full of the love of God and bound with ropes of love in joy and lightness of heart.' Such a love was fulfilled for him in the intimacy of his marriage with Reha: 'In their relationship they shared a perfection probably as great as two human beings are allowed to enjoy together ... They were brought closer together in an effort to express that love of which it seemed no lasting evidence might remain.' The images through which Himmelfarb recalls the marriage ritual emphasise the sacramental character of the whole relationship:

> Soon the days were tumbling over one another, babbling in the accents of old women, younger sisters, and girl cousins, until the bridegroom was standing beneath the Chuppah, waiting for his bride. She came very softly, as might have been expected, like a breath. Then the two were standing together, but no longer bound by their awkward bodies, under the canopy of stuffy velvet, in the particular smell of sanctity and scouring of the old synagogue of Bienenstadt, in an assembly of tradesmen and small shop-keepers who were the seed of Israel fallen on that corner of Germany. The miraculous, encrusted Chuppah did actually open for the chosen couple; they were sucked out of themselves into an infinity of blue, and their souls were flapping together, diffidently at first, as two handkerchiefs will flutter and dispute each other's form and direction, in a wind, until, reconciled by nature to the truth of the situation, they reach out, wrapped together, straining always higher, in one strong white tongue.
>
> So the souls of the united couple temporarily abandoned their surroundings, while the bodies of bridegroom and bride continued to stand beneath the canopy enacting the touching and simple ceremonies in which the congregation might participate. How the old men and women craned to distinguish the gold circlet that the young man was slipping on the bride's finger. The old, dusty men and women were again encircled by love, and history. Their own lips tasted joyful wine and trembled to forestall the breaking of the cup.

White has traced his own discovery of the Jewish-Christian teachings on the immanence of God to the period when he was writing *The Tree of Man*. 'Because the void I had to fill was so immense,' he wrote in his essay, 'The Prodigal Son', 'I wanted to try to suggest in this book every possible aspect of life, through the lives of an ordinary man and woman. But at the same time I wanted to discover the extraordinary behind the ordinary, the mystery and poetry ...'[26] 'If I say I had no religious tendencies between adolescence and *The Tree of Man*,' he declared subsequently, 'it's because I was sufficiently vain and egotistical to feel one can ignore certain realities.'[27] What he had ignored was the existential reality of God, his visible presence in the natural world. Of this there is an abundance of symbolic evidence in *The Tree of Man*. It is invoked consistently in his conception of the relationship between the novel's two main protagonists, Stan and Amy Parker. As Amy labours in the wilderness with her husband, she prays to God for the grace to endure the hardship of her life. The grace she receives, the narrator says, was the gift, not of the forbidding, anthropomorphic God of her childhood, but of the God who is revealed in the intimacy of earthly love: 'She would beg the pale, sad Christ for some sign of recognition ... she waited for the warmth, the completeness, the safety of religion ... But she did not receive the grace of God, of which it had been spoken under coloured glass ... The love of God was a kiss full in the mouth. She was filled with the love of God, and would take it for granted, until in its absence she would remember again.' One of the most beautiful passages in the novel evokes the sacramental character of conjugal love. The love-making of Stan and Amy is described through the intertwined imagery of sensual passion and prayer:

> For the man's wife had taken wool, and the cool needle was weaving in and out. He watched her hand, and the old sock that she held on the wooden acorn. And she drew the wool together, sitting at the centre of the night. He watched, and they were indeed the centre, but precariously, and he wanted to be certain. This made him chew the little stub of pencil, and would have undoubtedly resulted in something final, if it was to have been given to him to express himself in this life. But it was not. Except sometimes he had formed the lines of prayers.
>
> Then the woman put down the sock, because this velvet night was not to be resisted. She went and took her husband's head and held it against her, as if now she did possess something. She rubbed her lips on his eyelids, that were set rather deep, scored his face with her lips, till she could begin to hear his skin answering. Till they were melting together in the night, and were led by the hand, mysteriously, glidingly, into darker rooms, in which the flesh of the bed was opening to receive.
>
> In the cool of the released world, amongst the dreaming furniture, at the heart of the staggy rosebush that pressed into the room and wrestled with them without thorns, the man and woman prayed into each other's mouths that they might hold this goodness forever. But the greatness of the night was too vast. The woman fell back finally, almost crying. And the man withdrew into his own fleshy body. He lay on their bed and touched what was almost a cage of bones, that his soul was beginning already to accept.
>
> There was then, in the end, sleep, and work, and a warm belief in some presence. And sleep.

The revelation of God in the concrete physicality of the natural world is consistently demonstrated throughout the novel. The landscape itself, storm, wind and fire, the sky and the air, the sound of birdsong, all reveal the presence of the living God in the reality of the phenomenal world, conveying both its mysteriousness and its accessibility. It is his faith in God's presence in nature that affords Stan a measure of release from his sense of being imprisoned by it. 'He was a prisoner in his human mind, in the mystery of the natural world. Only sometimes the touch of hands, the lifting of a silence, the sudden shape of a tree or presence of a first star, hinted at eventual release.' When he temporarily loses his faith in humanity, following his wife's betrayal of their love, that faith is restored as he reflects on the advice of the evangelist that God is to be found in everything, even 'in a gob of spittle'. His reconciliation with God at the moment of death is described as a rediscovery of the divine presence in natural being:

> Exquisitely cold blue shadows began to fall through the shiny leaves of the trees. Some boulders that had been let lie in the garden all these years, either because they were too heavy to move, or more likely, because nobody had thought about them, assumed enormous proportions in the heavy bronze light. There was, on the one hand, a loosing and dissolving of shapes, on the other, a looming of mineral splendours. Stan Parker began to go then. To walk. Though his hip was stiff. I believe in this leaf, he laughed, stabbing at it with his stick ... I believe, he said, in the cracks in the path. On which ants were massing, struggling up over an escarpment. But struggling. Like the painful sun in the icy sky. Whirling and whirling. But struggling. But joyful. So much so, he was trembling. The sky was blurred now. As he stood waiting for the flesh to be loosened on him, he prayed for greater clarity, and it became obvious as a hand. It was clear that One, and no other figure, is the answer to all sums

Stressing the Christian significance of the novel in *The Mystery of Unity: Theme and Technique in the Novels of Patrick White*, Patricia Morley wrote: 'Stan's discovery of God in a gob of spittle ... is a profoundly orthodox expression of the Christian doctrine of the divine transcendence as immanent in this created world, one which follows from belief in the Incarnation of God as man.'[28] The novel ends with an assertion of the permanence of nature, and, by implication, of the permanence of God. 'So that in the end there were the trees. The boy walking through them with his head drooping as he increased in stature. Putting out shoots of green thought. So that, in the end, there was no end.'

The final affirmations of *The Tree of Man* are reechoed in several of White's novels. Eddie Twyborn, at the end of *The Twyborn Affair*, reaches a conclusion that recalls the words of Stan Parker: 'He suspected that salvation most likely lay in the natural phenomena surrounding those unable to rise to the spiritual heights of a religious faith.' Eddie's belief in the ultimacy of the empirical is reiterated by another unconventional believer, Elizabeth Hunter: 'You can never convey in words the utmost in experience,' she says. 'Whatever is given you to live you alone can live, and relive, and relive.' The regeneration of Voss is set in motion by his realisation of the mysteriousness of phenomenal being, of the presence in it of a force transcending its earth-bound reality. 'Is it not splendid!' he exclaims to Palfreyman, as he admires 'the prospect of sculptural red rocks and tapestries of musical green' in the surrounding landscape. 'Ennobling and eternal', he reflects, as he detects the presence of 'a will not his own' in the dynamism of the storm-ravaged scene:

> Then he dragged the hat off, and stuffed it into his saddle-bag. At once his matted hair began to stream out, and as the wind encircled the pale, upper half of his forehead, he seemed to be relieved of some of the responsibility of human personality. The wind was filling his mouth and running down through the acceptant funnel of his throat, till he was completely possessed by it; his heart was thunder, and the jagged nerves of lightning were radiating from his own body.
>
> But it was not until the farther side of the ridge, going down, and he was singing the storm up out of him, that the rain came, first with a few whips, then with the release of cold, grey light and solid water, and he was immersed in the mystery of it, he was dissolved, he was running into crannies, and sucked into the mouths of the earth, and disputed, and distributed, but again and again, for some purpose, was made one by the strength of a will not his own.

'Nobody could conceive of eternity but as rain,' the narrator says, as he describes how Voss and his companions struggle to survive against the harshness of the conditions in the remote Australian wilderness. In the seeming endlessness and stillness of the flooded landscape the message of salvation is conveyed by the sound of birdsong: 'In the stillness the grey would blur with green. In the middle of the day the body of the drowned earth would appear to float to the surface; islands were breeding; and a black dust of birds, blowing across the sky seemed to promise salvation.' In the evening Voss reflects on the presence of the infinite in the setting sun: 'Each evening was a celebration of the divine munificence. Accepting this homage, the divine presence himself was flaming, if also smiling rather thinly.' Together with Frank Le Mesurier, Voss identifies with the mysteriousness of the natural world, with the prospect it offers of ultimate salvation. 'Any hope of salvation, was, ironically, an earthly one,' the narrator says, as he describes the sense of exhilaration with which they experience the stillness and peace of a moonlit landscape in the aftermath of the storm:

> Voss was grinning. The rider could see the mouth, for the rain had been folded away into the outer darkness. All around there was a sighing of wind, and a moon, the loveliest of all hallucinations, had slid into being. Its disc spun, and was buried, and recovered, cutting the mad, white hair of the clouds.
>
> On the edge of the ridge, the mare paused for a while, and was swaying and raising her head. Then she plunged down towards what, she knew, was certainty. But in that interval of rest upon the summit, Voss and the rider had touched hands, the same glint of decomposition and moonlight started from the sockets of their eyes and from their teeth, and their two souls were united in the face of inferior realities.
>
> So like clings to like, and will be saved, or is damned.
>
> Riding down the other side, the young man conceived a poem, in which the silky seed that fell in milky rain from the Moon was raised up by the Sun's laying his hands upon it. His flat hands with their conspicuously swollen knuckles, were creative, it was proved, if one dared accept their blessing. One did dare, and at once it was seen that the world of fire and the world of ice were the same world of light; whereupon, for the first time in history, the third, and dark planet was illuminated.
>
> As he let himself be carried down the shining hillside, that was shown to be strewn with snares of jet now that the moon was fully risen, Le Mesurier was shivering. He who had carried the sun for a moment in his breast was frozen in his own moonlight. His teeth were tumbling like lumps of sugar. Any hope of salvation was, ironically, an earthly one, a little smudge of light from a candle-end, from behind a skin of canvas, at the foot of the hill.

The imagery of salvation as silence and light recurs throughout the novels. 'In the end, if not always,' Mary Hare, says, 'truth was a stillness and a light.' 'God neither wishes nor seeks anything,' Basil Hunter reflects. 'He is eternal calm. It is in wishing nothing that you will come to mirror God.' Death is an ascent towards silence, the silence of infinity for which Doll Quigley prays on her death-bed: 'Infinite love and peace will spill from candles and dissolve the flesh to silence. Then I will die readily, said Doll Quigley.' The silence of death is the release it affords from earthly finitude and the prospect it offers of eternal peace in the endlessness of the infinite. That prospect is magnificently symbolised in Mary de Santis's vision of divine grace as a trance of numinous roselight in which mortal existence is transformed into its hoped-for fulfilment:

> When she had dressed herself again in uniform and veil, and generally restored professional neatness, the nurse took another look at her patient. A breeze was very slightly lifting the curtain of grey light. The old woman lay breathing and murmuring through one of the calmer passages of sleep. Once the lips fluttered apart; the words dragged themselves unstuck, and forced their way between the gums, 'Still only thorns. Locked buds. This long frost.' By a gigantic creaking manoeuvre she pushed away a strand of shabby hair. 'Speak to each other beautifully in silence.' Till wrapping the spiral of a sigh, 'My darling silence', around a cherished privacy.
>
> The nurse recognized the silence which comes when night has almost exhausted itself; light still barely disentangled from the skeins of mist strung across the park; at the foot of the tiered hill on which the house aspired, a cloud of roses floating in its own right, none of the frost-locked buds from Elizabeth Hunter's dream, but great actual clusters at the climax of their beauty.
>
> After she had rummaged for the shears and the ravelled basket under the pantry sink, Mary de Santis let herself into the garden. A dew was falling, settling on her skin; vertical leaves were running moisture; trumpets of the evening before had furled into crinkled phalluses; grass was wearing a bloom it loses on becoming lawn ... Breathing deeply, still automatically snipping by spasms at the air, she regained the grass verge, her basket of spoils heavy on her arm poured in steadily increasing draughts through the surrounding trees, the light translated the heap of passive roseflesh back into dew, light, pure colour. It might have saddened her to think her own dichotomy of earthbound flesh and aspiring spirit could never be resolved so logically if footsteps along the pavement had not begun breaking into her trance of roses.

'IN THE END, HE MAY ASCEND'

The quest for faith and ultimate union with God, White suggests, may be conducted consciously or unconsciously. It may be conducted consciously through prayer – through the soul's pleading for the grace that will enable it to surmount the inadequacies of nature that separate it from God. It may be conducted unconsciously through the pursuit of active love – through the selfless devotion to others that he sees as an indirect reaching towards God and the infinity of love that God represents. Each is dependent in turn on the conquest of selfishness and pride and the subordination of the individual will to the infinite potency of God. Both processes are emphasised repeatedly throughout the novels, the conscious seeking after God by characters such as Palfreyman and de Santis being contrasted with the unconscious quest for self-transcendence conducted by 'unbelievers' such as Elizabeth Hunter, Hurtle Duffield and Johann Ulrich Voss.

'The state of simplicity and humility is the only desirable one for artist or for man,' White declared in one of his last interviews. 'While to reach it may be impossible, to attempt to do so is imperative,' he said.[29] 'There is a greater humility than that which simple souls are born with,' he wrote to Ronald Reagan in 1984 – 'the humility which evolves after sophisticated intellects have wrestled with their passions, self-hatred and despair in their search for truth.'[30] Throughout his fiction the attainment of faith is consistently identified with the conquest of pride. 'We must destroy everything, everything, even ourselves,' Liselotte declares in *The Aunt's Story*. 'Then at last when there is nothing perhaps we shall live.' Stan Parker, facing the might and terror of the storm, realises the insignificance of his own capacities when they are contrasted with those of the natural universe and its Creator. This realisation marks his advance towards faith. 'As the storm increased,' the narrator says, 'his flesh had doubts and he began to experience humility. The lightning which could have struck open basalt, had, it seemed, the power to open souls.'

Himmelfarb, struggling with his reluctance to pray, recognises the necessity for humility as a condition for the soul's intimacy with God: 'Arriving in this room, and centre of his being, the Jew appeared to hesitate, his hands and lips searching for some degree of humility which always had eluded him and perhaps always would. There he stood on the faded flags of light, his knees still trembling from their recent haste, and in the absence of that desired but unattainable perfection began at last to make his customary offering: "Blessed art Thou, O Lord our God, King of the Universe."' Alf Dubbo similarly finds faith through self-effacement, and repents of his guilt as he contemplates his own painting of the Passion and Crucifixion of Christ, a work inspired by his recollection of the vilification of the Jew: 'In his agony, on his knees, Dubbo saw that he was remembering his Lord Jesus. His own guilt was breaking him. He began to crack his finger-joints, of the fingers that had failed to unknot the ropes that had tied the body to the tree.'

The theme of faith attained through self-effacement and humility runs through Voss and is central to the process of spiritual transformation in which the novel's two main protagonists are engaged. The difficulty of conquering pride, and its necessity for spiritual self-reform, are emphasised at an early point in the novel. 'Few people of attainments take easily to a plan of self-improvement,' the narrator writes. 'Some discover very early their perfection cannot endure the insult. Others find their intellectual pleasure lies in the theory, not the practice. Only a few stubborn ones will blunder on painfully, out of the luxuriant world of their pretensions into the desert of mortification and reward.' Laura Trevelyan recognises that her own self-will is the chief obstacle to the spiritual fulfilment for which she yearns:

> If she was a prig she was not so far gone that she did not sometimes recognise it, and smart behind the eyes accordingly. But to know is not to cure. She was beset by all kinds of dark helplessnesses that might become obsessions. If I am lost, then who can be saved; she was egoist enough to ask. She wanted very badly to make amends for the sins of others. So that in the face of desperate needs, and having rejected prayer as a rationally indefensible solution, she could not surrender her self-opinion, at least, not altogether. Searching the mirror, biting her fine lips, she said: I have strength, certainly, of a kind, if it is not arrogance. Or, she added, is it not perhaps – will?

Seeing, however, that self-will offers opportunities for spiritual progress as well as placing impediments in its way, she resolves to 'exercise that will in accepting the first stages of self-humiliation'. She recognises that 'humility is short-lived and must be born again in anguish', as she strives to overcome the barriers to faith that are rooted in rationalistic pride. In her letters to Voss she urges him to direct his great resources of will towards the same objective and sees this as a condition for the growth of their love. 'He would not, could not learn, nor accept humility, even though this was amongst the conditions she had made in the letter that was now living in him,' the narrator says. Earlier Voss had expressed his contempt for the spirit of Christian self-effacement he saw exemplified in Palfreyman. 'Is man so ignoble that he must lie in the dust, like worms?' he exclaims. 'If this is repentance, sin is less ugly.' When eventually he himself finds faith, it comes with his discovery that the nurturing of humility and selflessness is the condition for the growth of the spirit of loving fellowship on which faith is based. This he discovers as he lies in the desert beside Harry Robarts, following the death of Palfreyman: 'As the two fell into sleep, or such a numb physical state as approximated to it, Voss believed that he loved this boy, and with him all men, even those he had hated, which is the most difficult act of love to accomplish, because of one's own fault.' His salvation is directly linked by Laura with the conquest of pride:

> Laura's head – for all that remained of her seemed to have become concentrated in the head – was struggling with the simplicity of a great idea.

When she opened her eyes and said:

'How important it is to understand the three stages. Of God into Man. Man. And man returning into God. Do you find, Doctor, there are certain beliefs a clergyman may explain to one from childhood onward, without one's understanding, except in theory, until suddenly, almost in spite of reason, they are made clear. Here, suddenly, in this room, of which I imagined I knew all the corners, I understand!'

The doctor was prepared to speak firmly, but saw, to his relief, that she did not require an answer.

'Dear God,' she cried, gasping for breath, 'it is so easy.'

Beyond the curtains the day was now blazing, and the woman in the bed was burning with a similar light.

'Except,' she said, distorting her mouth with an irony which intensified the compassion that she felt, and was now compelled to express, 'except that man is so shoddy, so contemptible, greedy, jealous, stubborn, ignorant. Who will love him when I am gone? I only pray that God will.

'O Lord, yes,' she begged. 'Now that he is humble.'

Dr Kilwinning had to tear at the leeches with his plump, strong hands to bring them away, so greedily were they clinging to the blue veins of the sick woman.

'That is clear, Doctor?' she asked.

'What,' he mumbled.

The situation had made him clumsy.

'When man is truly humbled, when he has learnt that he is not God, then he is nearest to becoming so. In the end, he may ascend.'

The way to perfection through humility and self-effacement is depicted by White in specifically Christian terms both in *Voss* and in several other of the major novels. Palfreyman is depicted as the model of Christian humility in *Voss*. His outlook on life has been deeply influenced by the example of the escaped convict, Judd. 'I will not easily forget,' he said, 'my first meeting with the man, and the almost Christ-like humility with which he tended one responsible, in a sense, for all his sufferings.' To the arrogance and contempt with which he is treated by Voss and others he responds with resigned acceptance of his own failures and weaknesses: 'Grown paler beneath the scales of salt, Palfreyman was sad, who would have melted with other men in love. Whenever he failed, he would blame himself, for he was by now persuaded of his inability to communicate, a shortcoming that made him more miserable, in that the salvation of others could have depended on him.' It is this same spirit of selflessness for which Voss eventually prays. In his despair he identifies with Christ pleading with his Father in Gethsemane not to forsake him in his final agony:

> He did not fear tortures of the body, for little enough of that remained. It was some final torment of the spirit that he might not have the strength to endure. For a long time that night he did not dare raise his eyes towards the sky. When he did, at last, there were the nails of the Cross still eating into it, but the Comet, he saw, was gone.

'He had in him a little of Christ, like other men,' Laura says, as she looks back on the final events in the life of Voss and the horrific circumstances of his death. 'He was more than a man,' Judd says. 'He was a Christian such as I understand it.' In his death Voss exemplified the paradox expressed by Palfreyman in his metaphoric description of the whole expedition as a quest for Christian salvation. 'All,' he said, 'remembered the face of Christ that they had seen at some point in their lives, either in churches or visions, before retreating from what they had not understood, the paradox of man in Christ, and Christ in man.'

It is his failure and his humiliation that finally links Voss with Christ, as is confirmed in the dialogue between Laura and Judd with which the novel concludes. Arthur Brown in *The Solid Mandala* similarly exemplifies the Christian ideal of salvation attained through self-effacement and the endurance of suffering. Dominated and manipulated by his brother, Waldo, he is compared to the Christ of the Grand Inquisitor sequence in *The Brothers Karamazov*. As he gradually releases himself from the influence of his domineering brother, he comes to recognise the meaningfulness of the Christian faith he had once rejected. Listening to his brother's derisive renderings of his poems, he realises that it is not the ridicule directed at religion that disturbs him so much as the blasphemy against life itself that is implied in Waldo's mockery of the Passion and Crucifixion of Christ. The meaning of life, with its endemic suffering and misery, is disclosed in the Crucifixion; to ridicule this is to blaspheme against life: 'Because, more than his own written words, his brother's voice was convincing him of his blasphemy against life. Not so much against God – he could understand God at a pinch – but against the always altering face of the figure nailed on a tree.'

It is *his* contemplation of this 'figure nailed on a tree' that also leads Alf Dubbo to realise that love and goodness can exist not only in the images of the scriptures but in the tortured conditions of mortal life. As he paints his vision of the Deposition – lovingly and reverentially – his whole being is consumed by the image of redemptive suffering embodied in the person of Christ:

Dubbo was unaware how many days he had been at work. The act itself destroyed the artificial divisions created both by time and habit. All the emotional whirlpools were waiting to swallow him down, in whorls of blue and crimson, through the long funnel of his most corrosive green, but he clung tenaciously to the structure of his picture, and in that way was saved from disaster. Once on emerging from behind the barricade of planes, the curtain of textures, he ventured to retouch the wounds of the dead Christ with the love that he had never dared express in life, and at once the blood was gushing from his own mouth, the wounds in the canvas were shining and palpitating with his own conviction ...

Towards the end of the day he rose, dipped his face in the basin, and when he had shaken the water out of his eyes, was driven again to give expression to the love he had witnessed, and which, inwardly, he had always known must exist. He touched the cheek of the First Mary quite as she had wiped his mouth with the ball of her handkerchief as he lay on the lino the night at Mollie Khalil's. Her arms, which conveyed the strength of stone, together with that slight and necessary roughness, wore the green badges of all bruised flesh. As he painted, his pinched nostrils were determined to reject the smell of milk that stole gently over him, for the breasts of the immemorial woman were running with a milk that had never, in fact, dried. If he had known opulence he might have been able to reconcile it with compassion. As it was, such riches of the flesh were distasteful to him, and he began to slash. He hacked at the paint to humble it. He tried to recall the seams of her coat, the hem of her dress, the dust on her blunt shoes, the exact bulge below the armpit as she leaned forward from her chair to wipe his mouth. Perhaps he succeeded at one point, for he smiled at his vision of the Mother of God waiting to clothe the dead Christ in white, and almost at once went into another part of the room, where he stood trembling and sweating.

Humiliation, suffering and failure, as epitomised in the life and death of Christ, are the means, therefore, to salvation and the soul's union with God. This is the central message of all the novels that have been cited. The quest for salvation, White suggests repeatedly, is consciously and directly conducted through prayer, through the soul's pleas to God for the grace to endure the conditions of its mortal existence. The potency of prayer is consistently emphasised throughout *The Tree of Man*. For Stan the act of prayer is a struggle with the weakness and lethargy of nature: 'When he failed to rise to the heights of objective prayer he would examine himself on the grain of the pew finding such flaws in each that there was little hope of correction.' Confronted by the might of the storm, he is awe-struck by the wonder and terror of nature, and prays to God to protect him: 'Standing there somewhat meekly, the man could have loved something, someone, if he could have penetrated beyond the wood, beyond the moving darkness. But he could not, and in his confusion he prayed to God, not in specific petition, wordlessly almost, for the sake of company.'

In the depths of his despondency, following his wife's infidelity, Stan nostalgically recalls the calmness of spirit he had formerly attained through prayer: 'In his heavy boots, heavier with moist, gathering earth, he thought of those clods of words he was in the habit of heaping together in some shape of prayer, on which ordinarily he could expect to climb at least in the direction of safety.' Back amongst his family, he returns to church 'singing the straight psalms and rounder hymns in praise of that God which obviously did exist ... He tried to fit those stern and rather wooden prayers to his own troubled and elusive soul. He prayed hopefully, desperately, at times, always woodenly, and wondered if his wife knew.' As he lies in bed beside his wife, recalling the trauma of their separation, he reflects both on the simplicity of human goodness and the mysteriousness of the ways in which it is attained. In a spirit of heartfelt penitence, he prays to God to forgive him for his sins:

> She was sleeping when her husband woke and lay rigid in the bed, looking at the darkness. In his fever he could not have been cleaner swept. All that he had lived, all that he had seen, had the extreme simplicity of goodness. Any acts that he relived in that ample darkness of the room were performed with the gentle honesty of freshly planed wood. Yet his rigid face was not convinced. It was turning and grating on the pillow. His dry mouth would have asked questions, not of his wife, of course, because she would not have known, but of some secret source of knowledge that he had failed to discover yet. So, the clear, feverish light in which he lay, and thought, and saw things, began to blur. He would have liked to read something printed in large letters. But in the absence of signs he was rubbing his cheek on the pillow and touching his joints. He was tired by now, and at times even in pain. Short pains. At times he spoke to express his pain and distress. Oh God, oh God, he was saying from time to time, but very quietly and dustily, like sawdust.

'Prayer is freedom, or should be, if a man has faith,' Lola says at the end of *The Tree of Man*. Like Stan Parker, Mordechai Himmelfarb struggles with the weakness of his own nature to attain the freedom of spirit that prayer can provide. Dressed in his phylacteries and prayer shawl, he prays in accordance with Jewish custom, reciting the Benedictions and the Psalms at the beginning of every day. Miss Hare is awe-struck by the fervour of his prayer: 'She saw with amazement the striped shawl, the phylactery on his forehead, and that which wound down along his arm as far as his bandaged hand. She was too stunned at first to move, but watched the prayers as they came out from between the Jew's lips. Nor had it occurred to him to interrupt his worship. Never before, it seemed, as he stood exposed to the gentle morning, was he carried deeper into the bosom of his God.' One of the most moving descriptions of Himmelfarb at prayer occurs shortly before he is subjected to the humiliation of a mock crucifixion. It is the spirit of prayerful humility that is described in this passage which enables him subsequently to endure the insults of the crowd:

Himmelfarb, who had retired late, rose early on that day. Whatever its conditions were to be, he refused, as always, to allow himself to speculate before he had laid the phylacteries on. Only when he was girt with the Word, and the shawl, covering his shoulders, excluded with its fringes those other desires of heart and eyes, had his own day begun, or was again created, sanctified and praised. As he stood, reciting the Sh'ma and Benedictions, from behind closed lids, from the innermost part of him, the face began again to appear in the divine likeness, in the clouds of the little mirror, offering itself for an approval that might always remain withheld.

But the Jew prayed:

'Blessed art thou, O Lord, our God, King of the Universe, who hast given to the cock intelligence to distinguish between day and night ... '

The Jew prayed, and the statue which had been broken off the pediment of time, and set down on the edge of the morning, became a man. The rather chapped lips were forming words of their own flesh:

'Let us obtain this day and every day, grace, favour and mercy in thine eyes, and in the eyes of all who behold us, and bestow loving kindnesses upon us. Blessed art thou, O Lord ...'

I believe with perfect faith in the coming of the Messiah, and, though he tarry, I will wait daily for his coming. For thy salvation I hope, O Lord! I hope, O Lord, for thy salvation! O Lord, for thy salvation,

I hope!

And the shawl fell back from his shoulders in the moment of complete union, and the breeze from the window twitched in the corner of his old robe, showing him to be, indeed, a man, made to suffer the torments and indignities.

Prayer plays an important part in the developing relationship between
Laura Trevelyan and Voss. In one of her first encounters with Voss Laura
confesses that she cannot pray, and attributes this to vanity and egoism. 'It is
for our pride that each of us is probably damned,' she tells Voss. Yet she
promises him, 'I will learn to pray for you,' and discovers subsequently that it
is only through prayer she can hope to relate closely to him: 'When she could
not understand, she would pray for him, though of recent nights happiness
had made her dumb and prayer grows, rather, out of wretchedness.' She
writes to Voss, urging him to pray, seeing this as the means to the self-humiliation which will enable them both to attain the intimacy of a selfless love. 'I,
personally,' she writes, 'would be prepared to wrestle with our mutual hatefulness, but mutually, let it be understood. For I do respect some odd streak of
humanity that will appear in you in spite of all your efforts … just as I regret
most humbly my own wretched failures to conquer my unworthiness. Only on
this level, let it be understood, that we may pray together for salvation.' It is
in a moment of prayer that she finally recognises the extent of her own weakness: 'O Jesus,' she pleads, 'have mercy. Oh save us, or if we are not to be
saved, then let us die. My love is too hard to bear. I am weak after all.' As
Voss dreams of their final union, images of earthly love and prayer are combined in his thoughts with images evoking the magnificence of nature to symbolise the perfection of the intimacy that is attained through faith. In his
reverie he sees himself as the communicating priest celebrating with Laura the
mystery of the Incarnation in the symbolic ritual of the Eucharist:

> As they rode, the valleys became startling in their sonorous reds, their
> crenellations broken by tenuous Rhenish turrets of great subtlety and
> beauty. Once, upon the banks of a transparent river, the waters of
> which were not needed to quench thirst, so persuasive was the air
> which flowed into and over their bodies, they dismounted to pick the
> lilies that were growing there. They were the prayers, she said, which
> she had let fall during the outward journey to his coronation, and
> which, on the cancellation of that ceremony, had sprung up as food to
> tide them over the long journey back in search of human status. She
> advised him to sample these nourishing blooms. So they stood there
> munching awhile. The lilies tasted floury, but wholesome. Moreover, he
> suspected that the juices present in the stalks would enable them to be
> rendered down easily into a gelatinous, sustaining soup. But of greater
> importance were his own words of love that he was able at last to put
> into her mouth. So great was her faith, she received these white wafers
> without surprise.

As this passage suggests, spiritual fulfilment is achieved ultimately through the mediating power of earthly love, through its complex and paradoxical disclosure of the infinity and transcendence of divine love. This is the basic religious affirmation of all these novels. The quest for God may be conducted consciously through self-humiliation, repentance and prayer, but it is conducted unconsciously through the universal potency of love – a potency common to the whole of humankind. That principle is vividly illustrated in *Voss* as Laura experiences the spiritually transforming power of love through her compassion for Rose and her child, Mercy. As she meditates on the reality of death and mortality at Rose's funeral, she realises that spiritual fulfilment is attainable only through love, through its infinity and endlessness: 'It appeared that pure happiness must await the final crumbling when love would enter into love, becoming an endlessness, blowing at last, indivisible, indistinguishable, over the brown earth.' Like Tolstoy's Prince Andrei, she realises that love conquers death. She writes to Voss: 'I no longer feared the face of Death as I had found it on the pillow. If I suffered, it was to understand the devotion and suffering of Rose, to love whom had always been an effort.' Laura's love for Rose and her child transforms her feeling for Voss from a self-regarding passion into the selflessness of authentic love. This finds expression in her impassioned prayer to God for his salvation:

> Then it seemed to the young woman that she might pray to God for love and protection of greater adequacy, but she hesitated on realising her own incapacity to save her trusting child. Only later in the afternoon did she become aware of the extent of her blasphemy, and was made quite hollow by it. When finally she could bring herself to pray, she did not kneel, but crouched diffidently upon the edge of an upright chair. She formed the words very slowly and distinctly, hoping that, thus, they would transcend her mind. If she dared hope. But she did pray. Not for herself, she had abandoned herself, nor for her baby, who must, surely, be exempt at the last reckoning. She prayed for that being for whom the ark of her love was built. She prayed over and over, for JOHANN ULRICH VOSS, until, through the ordinary bread of words, she did receive divine sustenance.

We are left with an image of Laura as a being who epitomises the spirit of love, its infinity being projected from its earthly reality. 'Her eyes,' the narrator says, 'were overflowing with a love that might have appeared supernatural, if it had not been for the evidence of her earthly body.' Voss, who initially saw love as a manifestation of weakness, discovers its spiritual power as he gives assistance to his sick companion, Le Mesurier: 'He was all tenderness for the patient, as if he must show the extent of his capabilities. To dispense love, he remembered suddenly. If nobody was impressed, it was not that they suspected hypocrisy, but because they could expect anything of Voss. Or of God, for that matter.' It is to Le Mesurier that Voss confesses his faith subsequently: 'What is your plan, then?' the latter asks him. 'I have no plan,' replied Voss, 'but will trust in God.' Shortly afterwards, as he lies beside Harry Robarts in the desert, he reflects on the love he now feels not only for this one individual beside him, but for the whole of mankind: 'As the two fell into sleep, or such a numb physical state as approximated to it, Voss believed that he loved this boy, and with him all men, even those he had hated, which is the most difficult act of love to accomplish, because of one's own fault.' As he drifts into sleep, he dreams of Laura and himself united by the healing power of love:

> By its radiance he did finally recognise her face, and would have gone to her, if it had been possible, but it was not; his body was worn out.
>
> Instead, she came to him, and at once he was flooded with light and memory. As she lay beside him, his boyhood slipped from him in a rustling of water and a rough towel. A steady summer had possessed them. Leaves were in her lips, that he bit off, and from her breasts the full, silky, milky buds. They were holding each other's heads and looking into them, as remorselessly as children looking at secrets, and seeing all too clearly. But, unlike children, they were confronted to recognise their own faults.
>
> So they were growing together, and loving. No sore was so scrufulous on his body that she would not touch it with her kindness. He would kiss her wounds, even the deepest ones, that he had inflicted himself and left to suppurate.
>
> Given time, the man and woman might have healed each other. That time is not given was their one sadness. But time itself is a wound that will not heal up.

The conviction that love is the way to God is given specific Christian affirmation by Alf Dubbo through his repeated references to the words of the Gospel of St John and to the significance of the Passion and Crucifixion of Christ as the archetypal exemplification of the spirit of selfless love. Reading the New Testament, he is emotionally overwhelmed by the power of the text: 'He was reading again, he found, the sad story of Our Lord Jesus Christ. He could remember many of the incidents, and how he had hoped to love and reverence the individuals involved, at least enough to please his guardians ... All was pale, pale, washed in love and charity, but pale. He opened the Gospel of the Beloved Disciple. Then his throat did hurt fearfully. It burned. The bubbles of saliva were choking him.' He finds the grace to repent of his guilt through his contemplation of Christ's example of selfless love: 'In his agony, on his knees, Dubbo saw that he was remembering his Lord Jesus. His own guilt was breaking him ... He had not borne witness, but did not love the less. It came pouring out of him like blood, or paint ... Everything finally was a source of wonder, not to say love.' The sacrifice of Christ was made real for Dubbo by the example of his human counterpart, Himmelfarb. He too found the grace to endure humiliation and suffering through love of his fellowman: 'Whatever the length of the journey, it was consecrated for the sick man by the love and participation of his people. So, whole deserts were crossed.' Himmelfarb's companion, Mary Hare, reaches new levels of spiritual understanding, having witnessed his example of self-sacrificing love at the moment of death. Her transformation is described in one of the most moving lyrical passages in the novel:

> Miss Hare had, in fact, entered that state of complete union which her nature had never achieved. The softer matter her memory could muster – the fallen breast-feathers, tufts of fur torn in courtship, the downy, brown crooks of bracken – was what she now willed upon the spirit of her love. Their most private union she hid in sheets of silence, such as she had learned from the approach of early light, or from holding her ear to stone, or walking on thicknesses of rotted leaves. So she wrapped and cherished the heavenly spirit which had entered her, quite simply and painlessly, as Peg had suggested that it might. And all the dancing demons fled out, in peacock feathers, with a tinkling of the fitful little mirrors set in the stuff of their cunning thighs. And the stones of Xanadu could crumble, and she would touch its kinder dust, the spirit of which she could understand at last.

'There is no desecration where there is love,' Elizabeth Hunter says, as she looks back over her life and recalls her memories of the various individuals she has loved. It was in moments of passion, she says, that she experienced the possibility of transcending the time-bound and existential: 'O the dreams with which the bottom of the sea is littered not always sodden like the old letters they will stand up in coral columns in whole cupolas and archways and long sculptural perspectives to confront entice you in where the daylight is solid and the expression in his eyes at that time perhaps the first clue I ever had to what is transcendent.' She points to the paradox at the heart of all religious experience: the paradox that love, though rooted in the torment and suffering of mortal life, discloses, however tentatively, the prospect of infinity and transcendence.

This is the truth that Ellen Roxborough discovers also as she tries desperately to find release from the burden of guilt which has paralysed her spirit. As she enters the makeshift chapel, she sees the legend, 'GOD IS LOVE', inscribed above the communion table. She weeps as she recalls 'the betrayal of her earthly loves', but in her contemplation of the words above the table finds a peacefulness akin to what Elizabeth experienced in the eye of the storm: 'She did not attempt to interpret a peace of mind which had descended on her ... but let the silence enclose her like a beatitude.' She realises that God alone represents love in its absoluteness, that earthly love is an imperfect copy of divine love, yet, paradoxically, is the way by which the absolute and the infinite must be sought in the conditions of mortal life. This is the point of the epigraph from Louis Aragon which was cited at the beginning of the novel: 'Love is your last chance. There is really nothing else on earth to keep you here.'

'Our Lord recognised that all human beings are weak,' Alf Dubbo says. 'And what did He prescribe? Love.' Like Laura Trevelyan, Dubbo sees the significance of the Christian doctrine of the Incarnation as lying in its comprehension of the paradoxical interrelation of earthly and divine love. The paradox of the earthly and divine is comprehended in the mystery of the Word made Flesh. Christ, as God become man, embodies both the harmony and tension of the two. 'You see,' Laura Trevelyan says, 'I am willing to give up much to prove that human truths are also divine. That is the true meaning of Christ.' 'How important,' she says, 'it is to understand the three stages. Of God into Man. Man. And man returning to God.' That same truth is expressed by Palfreyman as 'the paradox of man in Christ and Christ in man', as the envisioned unity of the human and the divine – a unity embodied in the materiality and spirituality of earthly love. This is the fundamental belief that underlies all of White's fiction – a belief which is simply and conclusively formulated in these words from the final pages of his autobiography: 'You reach a point where you have had everything and everything amounts to nothing. Only love redeems.'[31]

'Seek Love with Love':
The Poetry of Czeslaw Milosz

METAPOETICS OF HOPE

'With my feeling of being immersed in a great whole, I was, as they say, religious to the core. The Catholic Church was awesome in her immensity, and she was addressing herself to me with no more than a plea to submit to her discipline while suspending my judgement. As a diligent reader of Church history, I agreed, in spite of everything, that discipline was necessary since by myself I would have been unable to invent one.'[1] So writes Czeslaw Milosz in *Native Realm*, the work he describes as his 'Search for Self-Definition'. By his own admission, a traditionalist but nonetheless critical believer, he attributes his lifelong adherence to the Catholic faith to the questioning spirit in which he viewed the teachings of the Church since he first encountered them in his childhood in Polish Lithuania. 'Had I passively accepted my Catholic training and then shed it like useless veneer, I would have been a clean slate on which the words of another faith could have been graven,' he writes. 'But I did not. Through my heretical tendencies I remained at bottom a Catholic, in the sense that I carried in my memory the whole history of the Church.'[2] Recurrent images of Catholic ritual and liturgy together with repeated affirmations of his personal faith throughout his poetry and prose testify to the deep and lasting impact that Catholicism has exerted on his life and work. As a Pole, he was born into the Western, i.e., Latin, non-Byzantine tradition of Christianity and in works such as *Native Realm*, *Beginning With My Streets* and *The Land of Ulro* gives detailed descriptions of its all-pervasive influence on the life of the community amongst whom he grew up in the city of Wilno (Vilnius), at that time part of Poland. He insists that what attracted him to Catholicism was its 'many-sidedness', together with its inherent distrust of reason and the human sciences. The historic tensions between the worlds of religion and reason, he suggests, have been largely fruitful for the advancement of both. In *Native Realm* he writes:

One never stops being a member of the Catholic Church. This is what her doctrine teaches and what the two attitudes of acceptance and opposition confirm. Extenuated or acute, the central problem persists, and I would say that for all who have been raised in Catholicism, philosophy,

whether they like it or not, will always be *ancilla theologiae*. And maybe
no other exists. If so, one must admit that those who oppose religion
are right when they denounce all philosophy as suspect. Catholicism's
force lies in its manysidedness, which is revealed not only in the course
of history but also in the successive phases of an individual life. Despite
crises of faith among the masses, the centuries-old tension between the
Catholic and 'scientific' outlooks has been rather favourable for both
antagonists. After all, modern science is a Judaeo-Christian creation, and
doubtless that is why it was able to reach a conception of the universe
that cannot be translated into any clear or obvious image, that can be
expressed only with the help of signs. Whoever has had the occasion to
experience that controversy in his own soul will agree that contradictions can be fruitful.[3]

In *The Land of Ulro*, a work in which he examines various cultural and
philosophical influences on his growth and maturity as a poet, Milosz
describes his Catholic upbringing as being particularly fruitful for the fostering
of his talents as an artist. 'Had I not been raised in the Roman Catholic rite,
mine would have been a pitiable fate,' he writes. 'For that rite liberates the
feminine in us, a passivity which makes us receptive to Christ or poetic inspiration ... And though I am still hounded by my ego, I stand now fully on the
side of Imagination, of Urthona, of anima. I feel a profound gratitude that
there is *Una Sancta Catholica Ecclesia* ...'[4] Later he adds: 'When queried about
my religious affiliation I reply: Roman Catholic ... A concept rich in virtuous
connotations. A full-blooded Pole, a patriot, a Catholic since time immemorial;
next, righteousness and old Polish hospitality and brotherly love and *sto lat*
and the ceremonial stirrup cup.'[5] He saw the universal appeal of Catholicism
as lying in the central significance it accorded the time-transcending
Personhood of Christ in its teachings. In *The Land of Ulro* he cites the writings of St Ignatius Loyola in support of this:

> From St Ignatius of Loyola's *Spiritual Exercises*, which I read long ago,
> I particularly recall those exercises involving the use of the imagination.
> You should, the author advises the adept – I paraphrase from memory –
> continually return in thought to the time when Jesus was teaching in
> Galilee, to the towns and roads of the region, and put yourself among
> His listeners, accompany Him on His earthly wanderings, be present at
> His death. Let us ponder this advice. Loyola, in effect, was urging the
> reader to swim upstream through the ages of civilisation, through suc-
> ceeding generations, through whole lifespans from old age to birth, sur-
> veying in reverse the multitudinous procession of human lives that

makes up what we call history. Here we are at the very heart of the Christian attitude toward history as a totality relative to, and unfolding from, a single event in time and place.[6]

The citing of Loyola points to the inherently conservative character of Milosz's Catholicism. His conservatism is reflected in a distrust of radical or liberalising tendencies in religious practice and thought. Outraged, for example, by the reforms in Catholic liturgy introduced by Vatican II, he condemned the Hierarchy of the Church for weakening the universal character of Catholicism through its replacement of Latin by vernacular languages. 'One need not join the enemies of the Second Vatican Council,' he writes, 'to be outraged by the actions of many theologians and Church diplomats, or to insist that the Church hierarchy harmed legions of exiles like myself when it dispossessed us of Latin, which was native to us, and instituted English which was foreign; when in the name of "participation" it forced us to pray in English, as if Protestantism's greatest undoing had not been precisely the *nationalising* of religion.'[7] His contempt for radical Christian activists is symptomatic of the same distrust of any dilution of traditional dogmatics in the name of a socially more relevant Catholicism. In one of the essays in *Visions from San Francisco Bay* he writes: 'Many pronouncements by high-ranking Catholic figures sound as if they came from the socialists of a hundred years ago, those noble-minded dreamers who were, back then, treated by the Church with disapproval, to say the least ... An American hippie switching to political action and the clergyman who wants to win him over by proclaiming to all and sundry his social fervor travel the same road.'[8] In a particularly ironic passage from *The Land of Ulro* Milosz denounces the populist reforms he witnessed in American churches as a surrender by Christians to social and temporal forces, a process he predicts will have disastrous consequences for Christianity:

My lifetime has seen the collapse of many columns and arches in the Christian edifice. It was a long and steady process, quickened in the course of the last couple of centuries even if the clergy affected otherwise. The havoc caused by German liberal theology of the last century must be given its due, though never was the damage inflicted so great as in the postwar years, notably in the sixties. This was a time when theologians, Catholics included, casting themselves as clowns, gleefully proclaimed that Christianity, hitherto in opposition to the world, was now both with and in the world. Meanwhile, their audience, beholders of a spectacle more pathetic than funny, took this to mean that Christians wished to be 'the same as others', that is, to give up their Christianity. Sophistry, perfected by generations of superior minds, for the sake of self-annihilation has been pursued with such vengeance as to fill even unbelievers with unease. Not that we should have any illusions about time-honoured practices of the Church hierarchy, turning to the seats of temporal power as naturally as a sunflower to the sun. But this time the surrender was overt; now the power before which they prostrated themselves was an anti-Christian mentality urged upon the masses by science. And if figures of intellectual and even ecclesiastical prominence performed in the distance, a nearby church building made the 'abomination of desolation' only too credible. In my case, the building was Newman Hall, the Catholic student chapel bordering the Berkeley campus. As a visitor there, I was a spectator to those hucksters in the temple, those purveyors of popular ideas, corrupters of young minds, who, to pack the church, sweetened their sermons with phrases as woolly as, on closer examination, they were inadmissible for a Christian.[9]

As the passage suggests, Milosz sees this process as having followed inevitably from the humanist and rationalist influences that have dominated Christianity since the Enlightenment. The strength of Christianity, he writes in one of the essays from *Visions from San Francisco Bay*, is its anthropocentric and historical character; yet this, he adds, also constitutes its greatest weakness and underlies its susceptibility to rationalist reductionism. The central focus of Christianity is Christ, who was simultaneously divine and human – a figure transcending history yet part of the historical process – but the divinity of Christ, he argues, has been increasingly diminished in importance by rationalist thinkers who have excessively emphasised his humanity. Correspondingly, the mysteries and dogmas of Christianity have been deemphasised while those aspects of Christian teaching that are more amenable to rationalist explication have become dominant in western thought. In general, he argues, sacred and spiritual traditions have been rendered increasingly irrelevant by the claims of rationalists that all that exists is ultimately explicable through reason, through cause-and-effect deductiveness, through the systematic analysis of the processes of nature as exemplified in the human sciences.

Side by side with the declining status of the sacred and the spiritual, the emergence of dialectical materialism at the end of the nineteenth century is also, he says, to be attributed to the inexorable progress of scientific rationalism since Descartes. In *Native Realm* he speaks of Marxism as 'a scorpion whose tail is filled with dialectical poison',[10] and in *The Captive Mind* he describes the insidious manner in which it poisoned the consciousness of an entire society throughout the greater part of the present century. Paradoxically, he was drawn to radical politics himself as a member of the Zagary group in

Poland in the 1930s. 'At an early age I was lost to the Right',[11] he says, as he attributes most of the social evils he witnessed in Poland in the 1930s to the kind of nationalistic chauvinism he associated with the conservative establishment. As he witnessed the menacing power of the new communist dictatorship that came to power in the wake of the Nazi occupation, and as he recognised the philosophical justification provided by Marxism for a total collectivisation of society, he denounced communism as a cancer that was destroying the essential values and traditions of European civilisation. In *The Captive Mind* he stresses the fundamental conflict that exists between Christianity and Marxism. The aim of Marxism, he says, is to 'replace man's desire for profit with a feeling of collective responsibility as a motive for action'. To do this, he adds, 'it becomes necessary to maintain a constant terror in order to instil that feeling of responsibility by force'. Christianity, he insists, 'contains a dual set of values; it recognises man to be a child of God and also a member of society'. 'As a member of society he must submit to the established order so long as that order does not hinder him in his prime task of saving his soul.' Only by effacing this dualism, he concludes, i.e., by seeing man purely as a social being, can the 'Party release the forces of hatred in him that are necessary for the realisation of the new world'.[12]

Ultimately, he suggests, Marxism was a product of the naive trust in the natural order that was generated in the first place by scientific rationalists. To that spirit of naivete he attributes a universal failure to appreciate the limitless potential for evil that is inherent in nature itself – a potentiality realised in the present century in the unprecedented horrors of Nazism, Communism, the Holocaust and the Gulag. Of this he, as a Pole, had first-hand experience – in *The Witness of Poetry* he describes his experiences in Poland in the 1930s as 'an encounter with the hell of the twentieth century'[13] – all of which convinced him of the need for the kind of absolute moral values that are embodied in the teachings of the Catholic Church. Challenging liberal humanism for its disingenuousness in the face of man's natural inclination towards evil, he reasserts the traditions of Christian dualism, finding common cause with gnostic thinkers from St Augustine to Simone Weil who saw the universe as constituted by endlessly contending realms of good and evil, in which man, a corrupt and fallen being, finds salvation not through the resources of nature but through the redemptive powers of divine grace. 'The shared characteristic of these people,' he wrote, 'is their distrust of Nature – both human nature and the natural world.'[14] Like St Augustine and Simone Weil, Milosz rejected the extremes of Manichean teaching, seeing it simply as a doctrine which could explain the utter depravity and fallenness of man, while simultaneously offering the never ending prospect of his salvation. (For many years after his departure from Europe to live in the U.S. Milosz offered a course on

'Manicheanism and Literature' to the students at Berkeley University in California.)[15] And while blaming the scientists and positivists for promoting the fiction that the mysteries of the natural world could be explained totally through rational resources, he looked forward nonetheless to a new epoch in scientific enquiry that he saw emerging from the radical insights of Einsteinian physics. In a commentary on the writings of his cousin, Oscar Milosz, a fervent admirer of Einstein, he speaks of the relativity thesis as heralding a new age in the progress of science by virtue of its repudiation of the absolutes of space and time dominant in the physical sciences since Newton, and its resultant opening up of the possibility of the infinite and the mysteriousness of being through the process of scientific enquiry itself. His cousin, he said, believed the conflict of science and religion dominant in European culture since Descartes was finally coming to a close, thanks to the discoveries of modern physics. This passage from *The Land of Ulro* points to the metaphysical and religious implications of all this. It particularly stresses the implications of the Einsteinian theory of relativity for a renewal of the religious spirit:

> If everything is relative to something else, if the movement of body A is relative to that of body B, the latter relative to that of body C, and so on, where is the place of places, the place to which all others are made relative? Let us now move from the general theory of relativity to its mystical version. The place of places for Milosz [i.e. Oscar] is that 'Love which moves the sun and stars', indefinable in human language except in symbolic terms. Milosz assigned particular importance to the Song of Songs, into which he read several layers of meaning. To the extent that the love between a man and a woman is symbolic of the relationship between the Creator-as-Bridegroom and Creation-as-Bride, the *arcanum* of marriage goes to the very heart of being, which is erotic. Rhythm is unceasing quest, an unremitting drive for repose, for Place; but in a universe lacking any absolute reference point, man literally cannot find place for himself – of which St Augustine was well aware. ('Restless is our heart until it finds rest in Thee.')[16]

All these issues can be more fully explained in the context of the various traditions that are comprehended in Milosz's writings. In *The Land of Ulro* he identifies Swedenborg, Blake, Weil, Dostoevsky and Shestov as the seminal influences on his growth as a thinker and a poet. The major themes in his writings can be clarified substantially through an examination of these influences, on each of which he has written extensively in his prose. He discusses Swedenborg's theory of correspondences at some length in *The Land of Ulro* and again in an essay, 'Dostoevsky and Swedenborg' from his collection,

Emperor of the Earth: Modes of Eccentric Vision. In the latter he speaks of sense-experience as ultimately disclosive of the infinite and eternal: 'Every heaven or hell is a precise reproduction of the states of mind a given man experienced when on earth ... Thus everything on earth perceived by the five senses will accompany a man as a source of joy or suffering much as the alphabet, once learned, may be composed into comforting or depressing books.'[17] According to Swedenborg, he said, earthly or material correspondences of the spiritual are 'objective symbols that inhere in the very structure of the universe – and of language'. Swedenborg believed these symbols are brought to life through the power of imagination, as Milosz explains in this important passage from *The Land of Ulro*:

> Swedenborg focused on man's exclusive property: the written Word, both as it refers to the word revealed, Holy Writ, and to language generally. He applied himself to the decoding of words found in Scripture, distinguishing between three Biblical layers: the literal, the spiritual and the celestial. This search for meaning was for him a means of enriching human language, in the broadest sense, because it was a manifestation of man's foremost power: the imagination ... The visible world is merely a reflection of the spiritual world, everything perceived on Earth by the five senses is a 'correspondence', an equivalent of a given state in the spiritual realm ... That some flowers, beasts, trees, landscapes, human faces are beautiful and others ugly derives from the fact that they are spiritual values ... Here Swedenborg is heir to the mediaeval, Platonic-inspired axiom 'as above, so below', which held that the whole of creation was one of the two languages in which God spoke to man – the other was Holy Writ. This would explain why Swedenborg felt so drawn to the artistic sensibility. In effect, his system constitutes a kind of 'meta-aesthetics', to borrow a term coined by Oscar Milosz apropos of Swedenborg.[18]

Milosz was significantly indebted to Swedenborg's Christology which is closely linked with his theory of symbolic correspondences. Swedenborg saw the decline of Christianity as due in large measure to the diminished emphasis on the divinity of Christ resultant on the growing influence of rationalism. He affirmed the centrality of the doctrine of the Incarnation in Christian tradition, seeing it as a matter of faith, transcending the powers of reason. In *The Land of Ulro* Milosz writes: 'Swedenborg's Christ is God the Father-Man incarnate ... He understood that the only refuge lay in assigning a central place to the Divine Human.'[19] He praises Swedenborg's 'aggressive exegesis of Christianity' when 'confronted with the rationalistic science of the day'. 'Swedenborg's system,' he declares, 'is dominated by a Christ who is *the only God*, not in spite of his having been born a man, but precisely because he was born a man. Absolutely Christ-centric, Swedenborg's system is also absolutely anthropocentric. Its most sacred books are the Gospel of Saint John and the Apocalypse; by coincidence these were also the most sacred books for Dostoevsky.'[20] Swedenborg, he writes, had shown how man, through the symbolic power of language, could evoke the ultimate mystery of all being, his own redemption through the miracle of the Incarnation: 'Man's imagination, expressing itself through language and identical in its highest attainments with the Holy Ghost, was now to rule over and redeem all things by bringing about the era of the New Jerusalem.'[21] The metapoetic principles enunciated by Milosz in *The Witness of Poetry* profoundly testify to the impact of all this on his own poetic practice, as does the evidence of the poems themselves, especially those he devoted to evoking the mysterious presence of God-Made-Man in the ordinary realities of the material universe.

The influence on Milosz both of Swedenborg's theory of symbolic correspondence and his Christology was powerfully reinforced by his interest in the work of Swedenborg's disciple, William Blake. He writes euphorically in *The Land of Ulro* of his early discovery of Blake: 'I was led to Blake by my childhood Eros ... In those times and in that landscape so inhospitable to a child's awe before the miraculous, Blake restored me to my earlier raptures, perhaps to my true vocation, that of lover.'[22] His stresses the many-sided character of Blake's appeal for him: 'It would be an injustice to place Blake in the company of the English Romantic poets ... He can hardly be contained in the word "literature". He has been justly studied by historians of art, religious scholars, theologians, psychologists and cultural historians.'[23] The particular focus of Milosz's interest in Blake lies in the latter's dualistic view of the universe: his profound sense of the corruption and fallenness of nature side by side with his belief in the redemption of mankind through grace and through Christ's sacrificial death on the cross. 'Blake, anxious as he was to liberate man from the tyranny of prohibitions ... was no cousin to Rousseau; no vision here of a return to the innocence of natural man,' he writes. 'On the contrary, Blake's natural man already bore the mark of the Fall.' 'Blake,' he continues, 'did not approve of Nature ... Blake disliked Nature in the same way Nature dislikes itself as expressed in the words of Saint Paul: "For we know that the whole creation roareth and travaileth in pain together until now."'[24]

Correspondingly, he found in Blake a deep and hope-giving insistence on the redeemability of nature through grace, through divine intervention – through the miracle of the Incarnation: 'Blake's God-Man – the recognition of Christ as the only God – is from Swedenborg ... Those who would declare Blake a lay humanist, who would persuade us that his marriage of the Divine and the human signifies a faith in man only, are mistaken.'[25] Blake's celebration of the world, he says, is indicative of his belief in its redemption: 'His Garden of Eden is earth; his source of heavenly pleasure, the five senses; his salvation the eternal now and not some tomorrow beyond the sunset of life.' 'Therein lies the secret of my unison with Blake,' Milosz declares. 'As a person of pronounced Manichaean tendencies ... I was always an ecstatic pessimist. I was too enthralled by the earth to see in it a reflection of pure, unattainable Good ... I discovered in Blake a similar belief ... in our dualistic possession of the world.'[26]

Milosz's identification with Blake's dualistic view of the world is also the key to his interest in Blake's poetics. Like Swedenborg, Blake stressed the immanent character of earthly reality, its material attestation of the infinite. He saw the imagination as the instrument by which man penetrates the redemptive presence of the divine in the world of material being. He saw poetic composition, therefore, as a sacred activity, akin to prophecy, commensurate with the articulation of religious faith: 'In Blake religion and poetry merge, art becomes prophecy just as religion before it became debased was once prophecy – the writings of the prophets of the Old Testament and the Gospels stood for him as perfect models of inspired speech. The only language recognised by Blake was the language of prophecy, the language of "the final things",' he writes. 'Blake's poet is a vatic figure, a seer.' And this leads to a conclusion which we shall see is full of significance for Milosz's own work: 'Poetry and religion ... are synonymous, provided they be authentic, i.e., eschatological.'[27]

The whole conception of literature as prophecy is an underlying theme in several essays by Milosz on Dostoevsky, particularly a major essay in *The Land of Ulro* entitled 'Dostoevsky and the Religious Imagination of the West'. 'Dostoevsky, we now see, fully deserves the title of prophet, if only as the author of *The Possessed*,' Milosz writes. 'The Age of Reason, as personified by Voltaire, oppressed Dostoevsky, as did nineteenth century science, personified for him by Claude Bernard (Bernardy in *The Brothers Karamazov*).'[28] Boundless in his admiration for the great Russian writer – 'Dostoevsky's religious thought marks a critical moment in the history of the only civilisation that has conquered the entire planet Earth'[29] – Milosz identified closely with the latter's 'despair at the erosion of the Christian faith' through the growth of rationalism and the empirical sciences. Dostoevsky, he declared, alone among modern novelists, had 'made use of fiction to render the fundamental antinomy facing modern man ... the antinomy of philosophy and science versus religion'.[30] Milosz further identified with the technical procedures employed by Dostoevsky to achieve his purposes, seeing the methods of polyphonic realism as being particularly appropriate to the artistic representation of the intellectual and moral conflicts arising from the faith-reason antinomies. (That method is in fact used by Milosz himself in several of his longer poems, most notably the cycle of poems entitled 'From the Rising of the Sun' – a complex, intricately textured work where various perspectives on faith, morality, salvation and redemption are conveyed through the poetic device of multi-voiced utterance.)

Quoting Dostœvsky's words in 1875 in which he declared that 'science in our century refutes everything formerly held in regard', Milosz endorses the former's view that rationalism had led to a three-fold negation in modern thought: the denial of Original Sin, the rejection of the doctrine of the Incarnation, and the 'secularisation of Christian eschatology'.[31] The first was predicated, he said, on a Rousseauistic belief in 'the good and reasonable nature of man', a position profoundly rejected by defenders of Christianity who 'stressed the utter misery of man and identified the Fall with the victory of self-love which causes man infinite anguish'.[32] Secondly, he says, the mystery of the Incarnation could only be expressed in the language of myth and was therefore regarded as meaningless by rationalists: 'The habit of relying on a language which appeals to what is presumed to be self-evident made the Incarnation utterly incomprehensible.'[33] The third position followed from the previous two: rationalism had led inevitably to the decline of eschatological belief and thus to the triumph of secular humanism. The stark character of the dilemmas which all this represents for mankind is conveyed in the following terms in 'Dostoevsky and the Religious Imagination of the West':

> Today, however, we cannot treat Dostoevsky's religious thought as a relic of the past. He has been vindicated by the grave consequences of the antinomy between science and the world of values. What in his time was regarded as an objective, scientific truth has often revealed its hidden metaphysical premises; and our civilisation seems to be confronted by an option not between faith and reason but between two sets of values, disguised or not. Perhaps biologists such as Jacques Monod go too far when they postulate that the 'animist tradition' forms part of the genetic code of our species. Yet even if we ignore genetics, the experience of the twentieth century seems to corroborate the equation made by Dostoevsky in the *Legend of the Grand Inquisitor*. The equation boils down to this: try as he may, man has no alternative but to choose between God and the devil.[34]

Milosz was drawn to the writings of Lev Shestov for reasons similar to those which attracted him to Dostoevsky. (In *The Land of Ulro* he acknowledges a debt to Shestov for some important insights in his own interpretations of Dostoevsky).[35] Milosz encountered the work of the Russian philosopher through a young Rumanian student, Sorana Gurian, whom he met in Paris in the 1950s. He recalls the experience in his essay, 'Shestov, or the Purity of Despair'. Sorana, who was dying of breast cancer and had found spiritual solace in Shestov's philosophy, urged Milosz to read him: 'She showed me the books on her night table; they were books by Shestov in French translation. She spoke of them with that reticent ardor we reserve for what is most precious to us. "Read Shestov, Milosz, read Shestov." '[36] Clearly Milosz could identify with the anti-rationalist and absurdist spirit of works such as *Athens and Jerusalem*, but what particularly interested him was Shestov's treatment of the theme of Necessity. Shestov, he said, saw life as a constant struggle against the immutable laws of nature: 'The "I" is invaded by Necessity from the inside as well, but always feels it as an alien force. Nevertheless the "I" must accept the inevitable order of the world.'[37] Far from advocating a stoic acceptance of this – he denounced stoicism as a morality based on reason – Shestov urged relentless resistance to the forces of Necessity. 'To Shestov peace of mind was suspect for the earth we live on does not predispose us to it,' Milosz writes. 'He loved only those who, like Pascal, "cherchent en gèmissant" – who "seek while moaning" ... The world of the laws of Nature is, as he says, a nightmare from which we should awaken ... A man should shout, scream, laugh, jeer, protest. In the Bible Job wailed and screamed to the indignation of his wise friends.'[38]

It was her treatment of the theme of Necessity that primarily attracted Milosz also to Simone Weil, whose works he translated into Polish, having first read them in Washington in the 1940s. Her influence is particularly evident in *The Issa Valley* – 'Underneath its idyllic images of childhood lurks a Manichean vision', he wrote in his *History of Polish Literature*.[39] It is evident again in *The Captive Mind*, the title of which was taken from her essay, 'Human Personality'. In *Emperor of the Earth* Milosz compares Weil with Shestov, pointing to significant differences in their conception of the principle of Necessity. A classical philosopher, with a deep interest in mathematics, Weil, he says, saw the world 'as a system of causes and effects subject to a mathematical determinism – whose variant is contingency'.[40] Central to her thinking was a Manichean concept of Necessity: she viewed the world God created as corrupt, left by God to its own devices, but redeemed by his grace. The essence of her thought, Milosz says, could be conveyed in a single sentence: 'La distance infinie que sépare le nécessaire et la bien.' In this passage from *Emperor of the Earth* he contrasts her position on this whole issue with that of Shestov:

For Shestov, universal Necessity was a scandal. He felt that its horror was best described by Dostoevsky in *The Idiot* where there is talk of Holbein's painting of the *Deposition from the Cross*: 'Looking at that picture, you get the impression of Nature as some enormous, implacable and dumb beast, or, to put it more correctly, much more correctly, though it might seem strange, as some huge engine of the latest design which has senselessly seized, cut to pieces and swallowed up – impassively and unfeelingly – a great and priceless Being, a Being worth the whole of Nature and all its laws, worth the entire earth, which was perhaps created solely for the coming of that Being! The picture seems to give expression to the idea of a cold, insolent and senselessly eternal power to which everything is subordinated.' Shestov wanted man to oppose that beast with an unflinching 'No' ... Simone Weil's attitude, on the other hand, was similar to the wonder a mathematician feels when confronted with the complexities of numbers. A few quotations will suffice to show this: 'Necessity is a veil of God'; 'God entrusted all phenomena without exception to the mechanism of the world'; 'In this world he gives Necessity free play'; 'The distance between Necessity and the Good is the very distance between the Creation and the Creator.'[41]

'Nature is nothing but necessity and therefore innocent,' Weil declared. 'Heroic assent' to its laws she saw as the 'very core of Christianity.' 'To love what is impossible to bear' – this, Milosz writes, was the foundation of her Christian faith.[42] She believed the only solution to the problem of evil and the inexplicable mystery of the suffering of the innocent was humble and self-effacing trust in God. She believed passionately in self-humiliation as the key to the discovery of truth. Milosz approvingly quotes her words on the role of fools in Shakespeare's plays: 'In this world only human beings reduced to the lowest degree of humiliation, much lower than mendicancy, not only without a social position but considered by everybody as deprived of elementary human dignity, of reason – only such beings have the possibility of telling the truth.'[43] Her conversion to Catholicism in 1938, when she declared herself 'captivated by Christ' while stopping short of formal membership of the Catholic Church, marked a turning point in her life. 'She was convinced,' Milosz writes, 'that the Roman Catholic Church is the only legitimate guardian of the truth revealed by God incarnate. She strongly believed in the presence, real and not symbolic, of Christ in the Eucharist.'[44] He was profoundly influenced by her interpretation of the significance of the Incarnation. In *The Land of Ulro* he writes: 'Weil's God is tragic, loving, the dying God on the cross. The words spoken by Christ before his death, "Lord why hast thou forsaken me", were, for her, the most powerful affirmation of Christianity, and of humanity, which occupies the lowest of all levels, above the innocence of Nature but bound by her laws, longing for the good "not of this world".'[45] She saw the core teaching of Catholicism as the doctrine of grace which afforded a hopefulness to what was otherwise a deeply pessimistic vision of man. In 'The Importance of Simone Weil' Milosz explains how she saw the miracle of grace as making man's transcendence of Necessity an everpresent possibility and the foundation of all hope:

> 'The absence of God is the most marvellous testimony of perfect love, and that is why pure necessity, necessity which is manifestly different from the good, is so beautiful.' She allows neither the Providence of the traditional Christian preachers, nor the historical Providence of the progressive preachers. Does it mean that we are completely in the power of *la pesanteur*, gravity, that the cry of our heart is never answered? No. There is an exception from the universal determinism and that is grace. 'Contradiction,' says Simone Weil, 'is a lever of transcendence.' 'Impossibility is the door of the supernatural. We can only knock at it. Someone else opens it.' God absent, God hidden, *Deus absconditus*, acts in the world through persuasion, through grace which pulls us out of *la pesanteur*, gravity, if we do not reject his gift. Those who believe that the contradiction between necessity and the good can be solved on any level other than that of mystery delude themselves. 'We have to be in desert. For he whom we must love is absent.' 'To love God through and across the destruction of Troy and Carthage, and without consolation. Love is not consolation, it is light.'[46]

Ultimately, Milosz suggests, Weil's appeal for the modern world lies in her profound affirmation of the primacy of freedom: her insistence that individual existence is not subject to the deterministic forces of history, to the immutable laws of nature, to its demonic necessity. Yet he detected an underlying Platonism in her work from which he sought to distance himself, while otherwise embracing the greater part of her teaching. In his Preface to her *Selected Works* (issued in Polish translation in 1958) he wrote: 'I consider myself a Caliban, too fleshy, too heavy, to take on the feathers of an Ariel. Simone Weil was an Ariel.' 'To be sure,' he writes in *The Land of Ulro*, 'I bridled at her Platonism, at her heroic self-renunciation bordering on hysteria, culminating in her suicidal death by fasting, reminiscent in many ways of the endurance of the Catharists.' But crucially he adds: 'Simone Weil taught me that my hatred for life was not deserving of absolute condemnation, that a longing for purity may disguise itself as morbidity, and that my love of life, equally strong, is no less real, since we live by way of contradictions.'[47]

What Milosz described, therefore, as his 'spiritual adventures' – his immensely fruitful excursions into the writings of Swedenborg, Blake,

Dostoevsky, Shestov and Weil – provided him with the spiritual and intellectual insights which enabled him to clarify, refine, deepen and authenticate his own beliefs about the nature and purpose of human existence. 'Only now do I discern the thread joining the various phases of, and influences on my mind's progress,' he writes in *The Land of Ulro* in a passage where he acknowledges each of the aforementioned writers as significant figures in his intellectual and poetic formation. 'That thread,' he writes, 'is my anthropocentrism and my bias against nature.'[48] The same writers enabled him to clarify the complex processes by which his beliefs could be given expression in his poetry. His interpretations of their writings provide invaluable insights into all his work, as hopefully, will become evident in the forthcoming analysis of his poems. These are dominated by three main themes: firstly, the fallenness of mankind and the corruption of the natural world; secondly, the redeemability of nature through the intervention of divine grace; and thirdly, the essential hopefulness of the Christian faith which derives from its promise of salvation and eternal fulfilment. Each of these themes will be explored in the three remaining sections of this chapter.

THE AGE OF THE BEAST

> Twentieth century poetry suffered impoverishment and narrowing because its interests became limited to an "aesthetic and nearly always individualistic order". In other words, it withdrew from the domain common to all people into the closed circle of subjectivism.[49]

Citing the words of his cousin Oscar in *The Witness of Poetry*, Milosz charges twentieth century poets with deliberately cutting themselves off from the reading populace through their excesses of technical complexity and solipsistic obscurity. Described by Bogdan Czaykowski as a 'double exile' – an exile both from his homeland and from his epoch[50] – Milosz has deliberately distanced himself from what he sees as the dominant fashions of modernism and aestheticism in contemporary European literature. Denouncing modernist writers for their contrived complexity and obscurity, he speaks of 'a mutual hostility between the [literary] elite and ordinary citizens, one that perhaps has not diminished since the time of the French *poètes maudits*'.[51] His words were echoed recently by John Carey who argued in *The Intellectuals and the Masses* that modern writers, using measures similar to those described by Milosz, had sought, for reasons of literary snobbery and elitism, to make their work inaccessible to the newly literate masses emancipated by universal education.[52] Milosz's explanation of the reasons for this is more complex, however, than

Carey's; he sees the conscious choice of subjectivist obscurity by modern writers as a retreat from truth – as springing from a reluctance to confront metaphysical and moral realities, particularly the reality of the huge potentiality for evil present in the nature of man himself. This he attributes, in turn, to the naive faith in nature and its potentialities induced amongst western writers by the exponents of scientific rationalism since the seventeenth century. East European writers, being less susceptible to the influences of the scientifically dominated culture of the West, and being made more acutely aware of the human capacity for evil through the barbarism of the Stalinist and Nazi horrors, the savagery of the Holocaust and the Gulag, together with the slaughter of two World Wars, realised, he says, that the escapism of subjectivity was a form of artistic self-indulgence which they could not allow themselves. They recognised that their art would have to bear witness to the unspeakable evils their people had encountered in the name of rationalistic ideologies. In *The Captive Mind* he writes:

> Personally I am not in favour of art that is too subjective. My poetry has always been a means of checking on myself. Through it I could ascertain the limit beyond which falseness of style testifies to the falseness of the artist's position; and I have tried not to cross this line. The war years taught me that a man should not take a pen in his hands merely to communicate to others his own despair and defeat. This is too cheap a commodity; it takes too little effort to produce it for a man to pride himself on having done so. Whoever saw, as many did, a whole city reduced to rubble – kilometres of streets on which there remained no trace of life, not even a cat, not even a homeless dog – emerged with a rather ironic attitude toward descriptions of the hell of the big city by contemporary poets, descriptions of the hell in their own souls. A real 'wasteland' is much more terrible than any imaginary one. Whoever has not dwelt in the midst of horror and dread cannot know how strongly a witness and participant protests against himself, against his own neglect and egoism. Destruction and suffering are the school of social thought.[53]

This profound awareness of the human capacity for evil amongst East European writers is further reflected, Milosz writes, in a deeper sense of the meaningfulness of the Judaeo-Christian religious and ethical traditions in their work than is generally the case with their fellow writers in the West. 'Let me note a formidable paradox,' he writes. 'In the countries where Christian Churches thrive there are practically no Christian novels. Truly Christian writing has had to come from Russia where Christians have been persecuted for several decades.' He speaks disparagingly of Western writers creating a

'dehumanised literature ... under the pretext of rebelling against a dehumanised world'. 'Are the Western writers themselves conscious of the difference
between genuine concern and what is just subservience to fashion or a market-
ing device?' he asks.[54] The aim of poetry, he declares, must always be 'the passionate pursuit of the real'. 'A poet,' he writes, 'stands before a reality that is
everyday new, miraculously complex, inexhaustible, and tries to enclose as
much of it as possible in words. That elementary contact, verifiable by the five
senses, is more important than any mental construction,' he concludes.[55]

Milosz's own work is clearly impelled by a determination to disclose the
full reality of what he witnessed in Poland in the years of the Nazi occupation
and the subsequent horrors of communist rule. 'What occurred in Poland,' he
writes in *The Witness of Poetry*, 'was an encounter of an European poet with
the hell of the twentieth century, not hell's first circle but a much deeper one.
To define in a word what happened, one can say: disintegration.'[56] What happened there, he says, belongs with those rare moments in history when a
whole civilisation appears to fall apart: 'People always live within a certain
order and are unable to visualise a time when that order might cease to exist.
The sudden crumbling of all current notions and criteria is a rare occurrence
and is characteristic only of the most stormy periods in history.'[57] As a
member of the Zagary group in Poland in the early 1930s, Milosz composed a
series of 'catastrophist' poems, evoking the horror of the events then occurring
in that country. He spoke of the poems as describing or anticipating 'calamities
of cosmic amplitude'.[58] Those calamities came to pass with World War II and
the Nazi Occupation. In Warsaw in 1943 he composed a cycle of poems modelled on Blake's Songs of Innocence. One of them evokes the terrors of life in
wartime Poland through the simple, parabolic image of a child's fear of the
dark. The child's terrified imaginings of bestial fury vividly and menacingly
evoke the savagery and barbarism that had descended on Poland:

> 'Father, where are you? The forest is wild,
> There are creatures here, the bushes sway.
> The orchids burst with poisonous fire,
> Treacherous chasms lurk under our feet.'

> 'Where are you, Father? The night has no end.
> From now on darkness will last forever.
> The travellers are homeless, they will die of hunger,
> Our bread is bitter and hard as stone.'

> 'The hot breath of the terrible beast
> Comes nearer and nearer, it belches its stench.

> Where have you gone, Father? Why do you not pity
> Your children lost in this murky wood?'

It was his experience of these years in Poland that led Milosz to declare that 'the demonic lies at the core of contemporary life'. 'As a young man,' he recalls in *The Land of Ulro*, 'I was struck by the magnitude of what was occurring in my century, a magnitude equalling, perhaps even surpassing, the decline and fall of antiquity.'[59] He saw the events of the war as marking a regression to the savagery of primitive man. In *The Captive Mind* he writes: 'Everyone gradually comes to look upon the city as a jungle and upon the fate of twentieth century man as identical with that of a cave man living in the midst of powerful monsters.'[60] In 'Preparation', a work written forty years after World War II, he speaks of 'armies/ Running across frozen plains, shouting a curse/ In a many-sided chorus … ' He recalls the ferocity of the Nazi invasion … 'the cannon of a tank/ Growing immense at the corner of a street; the ride at dusk/ Into a camp with watch-towers and barbed wire.' The imagery of the blood-sodden earth in a poem written in the midst of these events conveys the nightmare of wartime life:

> My sweet European homeland,
>
> A butterfly lighting on your flowers stains its wings with blood,
> Blood gathers in the mouths of tulips,
> Shines, star-like, inside a morning glory
> And washes the grains of wheat.
>
> Your people warm their hands
> At the funeral candle of a primrose
> And hear on the fields the wind howling
> In the cannons ready to be fired.

The attempted annihilation of European Jewry was the single most horrific event of World War II. Milosz speaks of the difficulty of 'finding a formula for the experience of its elemental cruelty', the sheer scale of the depravity to which human beings had descended seeming to challenge the capabilities of language itself. 'What can poetry be in the twentieth century?' he asks. 'It seems to me that there is a search for the line beyond which only the zone of silence exists and that on the borderline we encounter Polish poetry.'[61] The Holocaust was the event that brought this challenge to the forefront of artistic consciousness amongst the writers of Eastern Europe. 'For the poet of the "other Europe",' he writes, 'the events embraced by the name Holocaust are a reality so close in time that he cannot hope to liberate himself from their remembrance unless perhaps by translating the Psalms of David.' For the poet, he concludes, the only option is to 'construct poetry out of the remnants found in the ruins'.[62] In 'A Poor Christian Looks at the Ghetto', a work that has strong thematic affinities with Marc Chagall's 'White Crucifixion', Milosz gives voice as a Christian poet – a 'Jew of the New Testament' – to the blood guilt of all Christians for the terrible events which centuries of anti-Semitic prejudice had brought to pass. The image of the Warsaw Ghetto after its destruction evokes the barbarism of the systematically planned extermination of European Jewry. Its horror is reinforced by images of the residual traces of animal and human hair, violin strings, trumpets, silks and the various emblems of Jewish culture that are scattered amongst the ruins:

> Bees build around red liver,
> Ants build around black bone.
> It has begun: the tearing, the trampling on silks,
> It has begun: the breaking of glass, wood, copper, nickel, silver, foam
> Of gypsum, iron sheets, violin strings, trumpets, leaves, balls, crystals.
> Poof! Phosphorescent fire from yellow walls
> Engulfs animal and human hair.
>
> Bees build around the honeycomb of lungs,
> Ants build around white bone.
> Torn is paper, rubber, linen, leather, flax,
> Fiber, fabrics, cellulose, snakeskin, wire.
> The roof and the wall collapse in flame and heat seizes the foundations.
> Now there is only the earth, sandy, trodden down,
> With one leafless tree.

Inevitably, the question posed is whether the spectacle of evil-doing on such a scale signifies the end of culture and civilisation as we have known it. In *The Witness of Poetry* Milosz cites a comment from the Parisian Review, *Le Décadent*, that was written in 1886 and appeared to anticipate the horrors to come. 'It would be nonsense to conceal the state of decadence that we have reached. Religion, mores, justice, everything is tending towards decline,' it said.[63] 'Poets in Poland,' he writes, 'perceived Europe sinking in consecutive stages into inhumanity – as the end of all European culture and its disgrace. A whole system of values had been destroyed with its neat division into good and evil, beauty and ugliness, including as well the very notion of truth.'[64] What was unique to the twentieth century, he writes, was not the barbarism of events such as the Holocaust, but the enslavement of mind that occurred in the name of the social liberation of mankind that was promised by the

Communist Revolution. 'Never before has there been such enslavement through consciousness as in the twentieth century,' he writes in *The Captive Mind*. 'Even my generation was still taught in school that reason frees men,' he concludes.[65] It was the materialist philosophy of Marxism – the most hideous product of the Age of Reason – that achieved this, he says. It poisoned consciousness itself, corrupted relations between people at every level of activity, induced a sterility of mind and culture amongst millions of East Europeans on a scale unprecedented in history. In *The Captive Mind* Alpha, the Catholic novelist, Beta, the young liberal poet, Gamma, the Orthodox believer and political activist, and Delta, the alcoholic artist, are all portraits of talented and well-meaning young men who had become infected by the ideology. 'These men are, more or less consciously, victims of a historic situation,' Milosz writes. 'Consciousness does not help them to shed their bonds; on the contrary it forges them.'[66] They are products of 'Ketman' – the suspension of ethical, metaphysical and religious awareness – which he sees as the most insidious creation of the communist ideology. 'Ketman' is the force that has enslaved consciousness. The character described in 'Mid Twentieth Century Portrait' typifies the 'Ketman' mentality:

> Hidden behind his smile of brotherly regard,
> He despises the newspaper reader, the victim of the dialectic of power.
> Says: 'Democracy,' with a wink.
> Hates the physiological pleasures of mankind,
> Full of memories of those who also ate, drank, copulated.
> But in a moment had their throats cut.
> Recommends dances and garden parties to defuse public anger.
>
> Shouts: 'Culture!' and 'Art!' but means circus games really ...
>
> Keeping one hand on Marx's writings, he reads the Bible in private,
> His mocking eye on processions leaving burned-out churches.
> His backdrop: horseflesh-coloured city in ruins.
> In his hand: a memento of a boy 'fascist' killed in the Uprising.

What is even more profoundly indicative of this enslavement of consciousness, Milosz says, is the tendency on the part of its victims to disinherit the past, to disown history itself – a point also made insistently by Nadezhda Mandelstam in her memoirs.[67] (That tendency has long since found its way into the consciousness of the West also, largely as a result of the more insidious impact of totalitarian technologies, as Vaclav Havel has shown in essays such as 'The Power of the Powerless'.)[68] 'What are centuries,/ What is history? I hack out each day/ and it's a century to me', sings Adrian Zelinski. 'Our planet which gets smaller every year, with its fantastic proliferation of mass media, is witnessing a process that escapes definition, characterised by a refusal to remember,' Milosz exclaimed in his Nobel Lecture. He continued: 'In the minds of modern illiterates who know how to read and write, and even teach in schools and at universities, history is present but blurred, in a state of strange confusion.' He cites the words of Nietzsche ... 'The eye of a nihilist is unfaithful to his memories; it allows them to drop, to lose their leaves ... And what he does not do for himself, he also does not do for the whole past of mankind: he lets it drop.'[69] Milosz's poem, 'Child of Europe', sees the tendency to distort the past as indicative of this nihilistic suppression of historical consciousness:

> He who invokes history is always secure.
> The dead will not rise to witness against him.
> You can accuse them of any deeds you like.
> Their reply will always be silence.
>
> Their empty faces swim out of the deep dark.
> You can fill them with any features desired.
>
> Proud of dominion over people long vanished,
> Change the past into your own, better likeness.

Many scholars have seen the particular appeal of Milosz's work as deriving from his commitment to reinstate traditional values in modern European culture – particularly those of the Judaeo-Christian ethical and metaphysical traditions which he sees as having been largely abandoned by modern writers. 'What makes this poet so fascinating and great?' asks Edward Mozejko: 'It seems that Milosz, as no other poet, has addressed those issues which, for our epoch, are the most fundamental and essential.' His poetry, he says, 'rejects existentialist nihilism and develops an affection for the values of the Judaeo-Christian tradition; it embraces the various aspects of that tradition; that is, religion, philosophy and culture ... When we come into contact with this current we get the impression that we are drawing from a clear, undefiled well of wisdom, faith, goodness and love.'[70] Milosz's poetry, writes E.D. Blodgett, satisfies man's hunger for the metaphysical and the religious: 'His point of departure is the sense of utter dead end. We are a wrecked ship, and how are we to find the shore?'[71] Aleksander Fiut speaks of Milosz's concern at the modern debasement of sacral art, at the 'dethroning of God and the deification of science', at the 'unavoidable decline of our civilisation as a result of its departure from its Christian roots'. The theme of cultural disinheritance is central to his work, Fiut writes, but Milosz, he argues, sees this as less a contemporary phenomenon than a tendency inherent in the very nature of mankind and manifested at various stages throughout its history. 'For Milosz,' he writes, 'disinheritance is an inevitable part of the human condition, an in-between state natural to every inhabitant on earth: man is always between nature and culture, history and transcendence, Christian tradition and its negation, religion and science.'[72]

For a poet committed to the 'passionate pursuit of the real' the suppression of historical memory strikes at the very roots of consciousness, distorting the entire process by which reality and truth are apprehended. 'Memory is our force,' he declared in the Nobel Lecture; 'it protects us against a speech entwining upon itself like the ivy when it does not find support on a tree or a wall.'[73] The historical sense is the means by which we understand the present and that understanding of past and present combined – the continuum of history – is the basis on which our hopes for the future are rooted. In the section of *The Witness of Poetry* which is entitled 'Hope' Milosz writes: 'We apprehend the human condition with pity and terror not in the abstract but always in relation to a given place and time.' 'For when,' he asks, quoting Simone Weil, 'will a renewal comes to us, to us who have spoiled and devastated the whole earthly globe?' He answers, again quoting Weil: 'Only from the past, if we love it.'[74] This passage from his Nobel Address eloquently articulates the need for historical understanding as a means of clarifying present and future realities:

> 'To see' means not only to have before one's eyes. It may mean also to preserve in memory. 'To see and to describe' may also mean to reconstruct in imagination. A distance achieved thanks to the mystery of time must not change events, landscapes, human figures into a tangle of shadows growing paler and paler. On the contrary, it can show them in full light, so that every event, every date becomes expressive and persists as an eternal reminder of human depravity and human greatness. Those who are alive receive a mandate from those who are silent forever. They can fulfil their duties only by trying to reconstruct precisely things as they were and by wresting the past from fictions and legends. Thus, both – the earth seen from above in eternal now and the earth that endures in recovered time – may serve as material for poetry.[75]

Inevitably, he says, one wonders if such unprecedented evidence of evil-doing signifies a new departure in history – whether we are witnessing the end of civilisation as it has existed for more than two thousand years. 'This is not the first time in the history of civilisation that men have experienced crisis, disintegration, a sense of the end,' he responds. It is possible, he concedes, that the 'sense of the end'[76] has been rendered more acute by the sheer scale of evil-doing in the present period of history, but he insists the events of the present time are to be traced ultimately to the fallenness of man, to the potentiality for evil that exists in nature itself. This is the root of Milosz's attachment to the Manichean teaching on the dualism of Nature, on its endemic corruptibility side by side with its redemptive potentiality. The image of the Gadarene swine in a poem called 'Reading' conveys the depth of his belief in the demonised condition of nature:

> The demonized had no access to print and screens,
> Rarely engaging in arts and literature.
> But the Gospel parable remains in force:
> That the spirit mastering them may enter swine,
> Which, exasperated by such a sudden clash
> Between two natures, theirs and the Luciferic,
> Jump into water and drown (which occurs repeatedly).
> And thus on every page a persistent reader
> Sees twenty centuries as twenty days
> In a world which one day will come to its end.

In *Native Realm* Milosz describes how he agonised over the problem of evil before finally settling for the solution of gnostic dualism: 'If Nature's law is murder, if the strong survive and the weak perish, and it has been this way for millions and millions of years, where is there room for God's goodness?' he asks.[77] The answer he found in Manicheanism, in its insistence on the dual presence in nature of two forces: the demonic force of evil, determined and driven by its own Necessity, and the benign force of divine grace, offering mankind the everpresent prospect of salvation and redemption. 'Good is brightness, evil darkness, good high, evil low/ According to the nature of our bodies, of our language' he writes in 'One More Day.' 'Or should we say plainly that good is on the side of the living/ And evil on the side of a doom that lurks to devour us?' he exclaims in the same work. 'I detested these pups of foolish Jean Jacques,/ And envied them their belief in their own noble nature' he declares satirically in 'Three Talks on Civilisation', rejecting as naive the doctrine of natural goodness proclaimed by Rousseau. The endemic character of man's dualistic condition is emphasised in the poem in the context of the Genesis myth of creation:

> We created a second Nature in the image of the first
> So as not to believe that we live in Paradise.

It is possible that when Adam woke in the garden
The beasts licked the air and yawned, friendly,
While their fangs and their tails, lashing their backs,
Were figurative and the red-backed shrike,
Later, much later, named *Lanius collurio*,
Did not impale caterpillars on spikes of the blackthorn.
However, other than that moment, what we know of Nature
Does not speak in its favour. Ours is no worse.
So I beg you, no more of those lamentations.

Milosz's poems and prose are full of images from nature which emphasise its demonised state, its inherently corrupt materiality. He described his novel, *The Issa Valley* – a work, he says which is 'close to the very core of his poetry' – as a childhood idyll of nature 'underneath which lurks a Manichean vision'.[78] The sequences in the novel describing the devils who inhabit the valley, the scene in which a stake is driven into the heart of the dead Magdalena, the macabre savagery of the burning of Servetus by the Calvinists, are all highly evocative of the demonic forces present in nature. In 'The Song' the poet prays to God to deliver him from 'the earth's greedy mouth', to cleanse him of 'her untrue songs'. In the poem 'Sentences' he writes: 'For even the sign of a butterfly/ Is a well with coiled poisonous smoke inside'. 'In this world/ We walk on the roof of Hell/ Gazing at flowers', he exclaims in 'Reading the Japanese Poet Issa'. The parable of the bear who came to steal caribou meat from the hunter's cabin and whose jaw was found eaten away by an abscess after he was killed becomes a symbol for the diseased condition of fallen mankind. The poem ends: 'We come out of the forest and not always with the hope/ That we will be cured by some dentist from heaven.' In the poem addressed to Robinson Jeffers, the American poet whom Milosz met in California, and who shared his sense of the dualities at the heart of human experience, he writes:

... The earth teaches
More than does the nakedness of elements. No one with impunity
gives to himself the eyes of a god. So brave, in a void,
you offered sacrifices to demons: here were Wotan and Thor,
the screech of Erinyes in the air, the terror of dogs
when Hekate with her retinue of the dead draws near.

Better to carve suns and moons on the joints of crosses
as was done in my district. To birches and firs
give feminine names. To implore protection

against the mute and treacherous might
than to proclaim, as you did, an inhuman thing.

The preponderant sense of the presence of evil in the universe is accompanied in many of these works by an overwhelming feeling of God's absence and an acute sense of the injustice that pervades the universe He created. Thomas's reflections in *The Issa Valley* have strong echoes of The Book of Job (Milosz translated the Book of Job into Polish.): 'He felt bitter towards God. He held against Him his insensitivity to the most sincere pleas ... God, thunder-wielding God – thunder, after all, was a better weapon than a rifle – clearly favoured hypocrites. Every Sunday there they were, dressed in the latest fashion, the women in green velvet bodices, with gaudy kerchiefs under their chins ... God saw to it that the strong prospered and the weak suffered.' Milosz's poem, 'Counsels', similarly echoes Job, its theme being God's apparent indifference to the sufferings of mankind. The language has strong Biblical undertones: 'God does not multiply sheep and camels for the virtuous/ and takes nothing away for murder and perjury,/ He has been hiding so long that it has been forgotten/ how he revealed himself in the burning bush/ and in the breast of a young Jew/ ready to suffer for all who were and will be.' These feelings of despair reach their lowest point in 'How It Was' where God's absence is personified as a negative force overshadowing the mountain landscape to which the poet goes in search of 'the Kingdom'. 'Stalking a deer I wandered deep into the mountains ... I saw absence; the mighty power of counter-fulfilment; the penalty of a promise lost forever ... ' The poem continues:

God the Father didn't walk about any longer tending the new shoots
of a cedar, no longer did man hear his rushing spirit.

His son did not know his sonship and turned his eyes away when passing
by a neon cross flat as a movie screen showing a striptease.

This time it was really the end of the Old and the New Testament.
No one implored, everyone picked up a nodule of agate or diorite to
whisper in loneliness: I cannot live any longer.

Bearded messengers in bead necklaces founded clandestine communes in
imperial cities and in ports overseas.

But none of them announced the birth of a child-savior.

The poem ends on a note of despair. God, apparently, has abandoned his own creation: 'And those who longed for the Kingdom took refuge like me in the/mountains to become the lost heirs of a dishonoured myth.' This despairing affirmation, however, is transient and tentative. At the heart of the whole problem of evil lies the question of individual freedom. Man's fallenness and the corruption of nature, Milosz argues consistently, was a direct consequence of his freedom; that same freedom offers him the everpresent prospect of redemption through the infinite resources of divine grace. While stressing the endemic necessity of evil as a manifestation of the corruption of nature, Milosz emphatically rejects the idea of historical determinism, with its implicit denial of individual responsibility and of man's potentiality to transcend the forces of nature. In *The Captive Mind* he parodies the Marxists for their advocacy of the doctrine of historical necessity: 'Let us admit,' he writes, mimicking the sentiments of the Marxist intellectual, 'that a man is no more than an instrument in an orchestra directed by the Muse of History.'[79] Dialectical materialism – the most extreme manifestation of the dominance of scientific rationalism in post-Renaissance Western culture – has elevated History above all else, seeing its deterministic necessity as providing explanations for all varieties of human endeavour. 'History is the Being which has taken the place of God in this century,' Milosz cries.[80] His poem, 'Theodicy' clearly and unambiguously asserts that evil springs not from the impersonal forces of history but from the radical freedom of man's own nature:

> No, it won't do, my sweet theologians.
> Desire will not save the morality of God.
> If he created beings able to choose between good and evil,
> And they chose, and the world lies in iniquity,
> Nevertheless, there is pain, and the undeserved torture of creatures,
> Which would find its explanation only by assuming
> The existence of an archetypal Paradise
> And a pre-human downfall so grave
> That the world of matter received its shape from diabolic power.

The Manichean emphasis is strong. Nature is corrupt and evil but is nonetheless free and ultimately redeemable by virtue of this. In an essay called 'Virtue' Milosz simultaneously emphasises both the demonised condition of nature and man's potentiality to surmount it by virtuous action, which gives access to God's grace: 'Since nature is not a living mother but ravages and kills us without qualms if we find ourselves in it without weapons or tools, virtue must be held in high esteem, for it alone permits the effective use of weapons and tools.'[81] In *The Land of Ulro* where there are lengthy sequences exploring the Manichean teaching on the corruption of nature there is also an insistent emphasis on the uniqueness and freedom of the individual person. 'For centuries,' he writes, 'civilisation has sustained itself through a belief in the individual human soul as the source of our decisions; through the belief that the soul's good or evil intention would tip the scale on the Day of Judgement.'[82] This is the theme of the poem addressed 'To Raja Rao', a fellow writer who urged Milosz to study Eastern philosophy. In the poem he considers Raja's advice that he must overcome the egotistic urgings of nature and allow the individual self to dissolve into the Absolute Self of God. Ultimately, he rejects this teaching for its threatened suppression of individuality and freedom and asserts his determination to continue to assume responsibility for his actions. His concluding affirmation embraces the Christian paradox that individual freedom finds fulfilment in the soul's voluntary submission to God's will:

> No, Raja, I must start from what I am.
> I am those monsters which visit my dreams
> and reveal to me my hidden essence.
>
> If I am sick, there is no proof whatsoever
> that man is a healthy creature.
>
> Greece had to lose, her pure consciousness
> had to make our agony only more acute.
>
> We needed God loving us in our weakness
> and not in the glory of beatitude.
>
> No help, Raja, my part is agony,
> struggle, abjection, self-love, and self-hate,
> prayer for the Kingdom
> and reading Pascal.

'HOLY IS OUR BEING BENEATH HEAVEN'

Nature is corrupt and fallen but is redeemable through divine intervention, through the power of grace – this is the central affirmation of Milosz's poetry. In his Harvard Lectures – the predominant concern of which was to give witness to hope – he cites Simone Weil on the compatibility of the doctrine of Necessity, i.e., the concept of nature as necessarily corrupt as a consequence of

the Fall, and the doctrine of Grace, the corresponding concept of nature as
redeemed through the saving power of God's informing presence in creation.
'She extended determinism to all phenomena, including the psychological,' he
writes. 'For her this was the domain of what she used to call *la pesanteur*,
gravity. At the same time, she believed that whoever asks for bread will not
receive stones, for there is another domain, that of Grace. The parallel existence of these two domains goes to the very core of her philosophy which
legitimizes contradiction when no solution is possible; in this case there is no
insoluble contradiction between divine intervention and universal necessity.'[83]
In *The Land of Ulro* where he declares he has 'remained a catastrophist all my
life', Milosz insists on the consistency of his catastrophist vision with an
'eschatological expectation of a new universal harmony'.[84] That paradox finds
expression repeatedly in his poetry; it is conveyed with special force in the
sacramental imagery of numerous lyrical verses celebrating the exaltation of the
natural world consequent on the redemptive presence within it of God's grace.
In 'Song Of A Citizen', a poem written at the height of the Nazi Terror in
Warsaw in 1943, he laments the manner in which the beauty of the natural
world has been blighted by war. In the midst of the horrors of war he wants
only to 'stand before the face of the earth'; he thinks only 'about the starry
sky' and 'the tall mounds of termites':

> This I wanted and nothing more. In my later years
> like old Goethe to stand before the face of the earth,
> and recognize it and reconcile it
> with my work built up, a forest citadel
> on a river of shifting lights and brief shadows.

> This I wanted and nothing more. So who
> is guilty? Who deprived me
> of my youth and my ripe years, who seasoned
> my best years with horror? Who,
> who ever is to blame, who, O God?

> And I can think only about the starry sky,
> about the tall mounds of termites.

His nature lyrics indicate a fundamental difference between Milosz and
Weil. For all his enthusiasm for her interpretations of Manichean teaching and
her exposition of the doctrine of the two natures, he distanced himself from
what he saw as a strong strain of ethereal mysticism in her writing. As the
authors of a recent study have written: 'Milosz's aesthetics, like Weil's philoso-

phy, is grounded in contradiction. But he does not use contradiction as the
lever of transcendence, as a way of reaching up to the Holy Spirit. He uses it
as a lever of immanence, as a way of getting to the divine *within* things ... He
will not deny the transcendent realm; but he is still a son of the black earth and
the world of pure forms is beyond his competence to experience directly.'[85]
Thus, in his poem, 'Veni Creator', where he directly addresses the Holy Spirit,
he insists that his faith needs 'visible signs' – in this case the phenomenon of
interhuman love – to confirm his belief in the presence of God in creation:

> Come, Holy Spirit,
> bending or not bending the grasses,
> appearing or not above our heads in a tongue of flame,
> at hay harvest or when they plough in the orchards or when snow
> covers crippled firs in the Sierra Nevada.
> I am only a man: I need visible signs.
> I tire easily, building the stairway of abstraction.
> Many a time I asked, you know it well, that the statue in church
> lift its hand, only once, just once, for me.
> But I understand that signs must be human,
> therefore call one man, anywhere on earth,
> not me – after all I have some decency –
> and allow me, when I look at him, to marvel at you.

In a beautiful passage from *Native Realm* Milosz recalls how the contemplation of natural beauty enabled him to overcome his youthful *delectatio
morosa* – the despair induced in him by the overwhelming evidence of evil and
corruption all around him. 'I would never have been cured of it,' he writes,
'had it not been for the beauty of the earth. The clear autumn mornings in an
Alsatian village surrounded by vineyards, the paths on an Alpine slope over
the Isère river, rustling with dry leaves from the chestnut trees, or the sharp
light of early spring on the Lake of Four Cantons near Schiller's rock, or a
small river near Perigueux on whose surface kingfishers traced coloured shadows of flight in the July heat – all this reconciled me with the universe and
with myself.'[86] 'The artist,' he declares in *The Captive Mind*, 'can contemplate
sensual beauty only when he loves all that surrounds him on earth.'[87] That
love is vividly conveyed in these lines from 'The Year' – in their affirmation
of the holiness of all earthly being:

> I looked in the unknown year, aware that few are those
> who come from so far, I was saturated with sunlight as a plant
> with water.

That was a high year, fox-colored, like a crosscut redwood stump
or vine leaves on the hills in November.
In its groves and chambers the pulse of music was beating strongly,
running down from dark mountains, tributaries entangled.
A generation clad in patterned robes trimmed with little bells
greeted me with the banging of conga drums.
I repeated their guttural songs of ecstatic despair walking by the sea
when it bore in boys on surfboards and washed my footprints away ...
O sun, o stars, I was saying, holy, holy, holy is our being beneath
heaven and the day and our endless communion.

The contemplation of natural beauty, he suggests, is inspired by the soul's unceasing aspiration towards communion with the transcendent element in all being – what he described in the Preface to 'Unattainable Earth' as the 'inexpressible presence of God' in all earthly phenomena.[88] His love of sensuous beauty is ultimately a desire to penetrate realities beyond the realm of sense and materiality. In an interview with Rachel Berghash he was asked 'What is the Real?' and replied: 'Searching for the Real is the same as searching for God.'[89] In an essay entitled 'Symbolic Mountains and Forests', inspired largely by his interest in Swedenborg, he describes his love of trees as being prompted by their material attestation of the presence of the divine in temporal being. 'There is nothing unusual in my rendering trees honor,' he writes; 'people have been doing this since time immemorial, and the thrust of the trunk, from roots beneath the earth, through our middle dimension, to the sky, where the leaves sway, has always lent credence to the division of existence into three zones. Trees were writing their own Divine Comedy about the ascent from hell to the high spheres of heaven long before Dante wrote his.'[90]

Various terms such as 'metaphysical', 'multidimensional' and 'eschatological' have been used to describe the style of realism employed by Milosz in his poetry. He himself in *The Witness of Poetry* spoke of reality as 'multi-layered', as always embracing the material and the spiritual.[91] His aim, wrote E.D. Blodgett, was 'to discover reality in the constantly changing interplay between the eschatological and the here and now'.[92] The sensualism and concreteness of his poetry must always be seen in the context of this interplay between the concrete and the numinous, the phenomenal and the sacred, which finds its ultimate clarification in the Christian doctrine of the Incarnation. The poem, 'Old Women', written in Rome in 1986, describes elderly communicants approaching the altar to partake of the Eucharist: 'Arthritically bent, in black, spindle-legged,/ They move, leaning on canes, to the altar, where the Pantocrator/ In a dawn of gilded rays lifts his two fingers/ ... While into their shrivelled mouths they receive His flesh.' The poem affirms the significance of

the Incarnation, i.e., Christ's redemption of the world of nature from its fallenness through his act of self-sacrifice on the cross:

> He who has been suffering for ages rescues
> Ephemeral moths, tired-winged butterflies in the cold,
> Genetrixes with the closed scars of their wombs,
> And carries them up to His human Theotokos,
> So that the ridicule and pain change into majesty
> And thus it is fulfilled, late, without charm and colors,
> Our imperfect, earthly love.

Poems such as this clearly refute the imputation by some critics of a strong
pantheistic quality in Milosz's poetry. He himself referred to this in his
History of Polish Literature. 'Critics,' he said, 'have tended to see a myth of the
earth, a protective deity ever renewing herself as the core of Milosz's poetry,
or have been calling him the only true pantheist in Polish poetry.' 'It is not
certain whether this is true since Christian elements are also strong,' he adds
sardonically.[93] In one of his essays he wrote: 'I desire a God who would gaze
upon me, who would increase my sheep and camels, who would love me and
help me in misfortune, who would save me from the nothingness of death, to
whom I could each day render homage and gratitude'[94] – clearly intimating his
belief in a personal non-pantheistic deity. The Polish Primate, Cardinal Stepan
Wyzscynski, in a degree conferring ceremony at Lublin in 1981, spoke of 'the
warm and human presence of God ' in Milosz's poetry and particularly praised
its 'vision of God Incarnate'. 'In the effort of lonely navigation through history
the man named Czeslaw Milosz is supported by a vision of God Incarnate,
which exists in each deliverance of man from bondage,' he said.[95] A poem, for
instance, such as 'The Sun' could be seen to suggest a deification of the earth
but the sun image is clearly a symbol of the Creator who looks benignly on the
splendour of His creation. This work, which Milosz himself described in his
History as 'one of the most serene works in modern Polish literature',[96] was
written in Warsaw in 1944 as the events of World War II were moving
towards their final terrible climax:

> All colors come from the sun. And it does not have
> Any particular color, for it contains them all.
> And the whole Earth is like a poem
> While the sun above represents the artist.
>
> Whoever wants to paint the variegated world
> Let him never look straight up at the sun

Or he will lose the memory of things he has seen.
Only burning tears will stay in his eyes.

Let him kneel down, lower his face to the grass,
And look at light reflected by the ground.
There he will find everything we have lost:
The stars and the roses, the dusks and the dawns.

Milosz's worship of earthly beauty therefore is ultimately a celebration not of the earth itself but of the informing presence of the Creator in its phenomenal reality. In an interview with Ewa Czarnecka and Aleksander Fiut in 1987 he pointed to the mysterious way in which the temporal is related to the timeless and the eternal. He explained the complexities of the relationship in terms of an old theological distinction between *aevum*, i.e., a time different from earthly time but still a variation of it, and *aeternum*, an eternity outside the flow of time, generally conceived as heavenly or paradisal time.[97] The distinction underlies a poem called 'Amazement' which was written in the US in 1975 but is dominated by recalled images from his childhood in Lithuania. He speaks of 'Innumerable and boundless substances of the Earth:/Scent of thyme, hue of fir, white frost, dances of cranes./ And everything simultaneous. And probably eternal.' Another poem 'Rivers' begins as a simple nature lyric – 'Under various names I have praised only you, rivers!/ You are milk and honey and love and dance' – but ends with an affirmation of their eternal being: 'Forgotten we are greeted by the embassies of the dead,/ While your endless flowing carries us on and on,/ And neither is nor was./ The moment only, eternal.' A sequence from 'Bobo's Metamorphosis' similarly celebrates the eternity of earthly being:

And here I am walking the eternal earth.
Tiny, leaning on a stick.
I pass a volcanic park, lie down at a spring,
Not knowing how to express what is always and everywhere:
The earth I cling to is so solid
Under my breast and belly that I feel grateful
For every pebble, and I don't know whether
It is my pulse or the earth's that I hear,
When the hems of invisible silk vestments pass over me,
Hands, wherever they have been, touch my arm,
Or small laughter, once, long ago over wine,
With lanterns in the magnolias, for my house is huge.

The complexities of all this become apparent in Milosz's treatment of the theme of romantic love. He sees romantic passion, on the one hand, as a most compelling manifestation of the principle of immanence, the love of one human being for another signifying an intense reaching towards the beauty of creation and therefore towards God's presence within it. Yet the same experience profoundly and tragically encapsulates the dualism of all natural love. There are several passages in *The Issa Valley*, for example, enthusiastically celebrating the beauty of erotic love. Liturgical and erotic images are intertwined in an early sequence evoking the world of childhood fantasy; there are vivid uses of sexual imagery in several passages relating to the novel's tragic heroine, Magdalena; and there is a vivid instance of eroticism in the bath scene at the end of the work. 'In Common', a poem from a recent collection, unashamedly affirms the delights of erotic love together with other forms of sensual indulgence:

> What is good? Garlic. A leg of lamb on a spit.
> Wine with a view of boats rocking in a cove.
> A starry sky in August. A rest on a mountain peak.
>
> What is good? After a long drive water in a pool and a sauna.
> Lovemaking and falling asleep, embraced, your legs touching hers.
> Mist in the morning, translucent, announcing a sunny day.
>
> I am submerged in everything that is common to us, the living.
> Experiencing this earth for them, in my flesh.
> Walking past the vague outline of skyscrapers? antitemples?
> In valleys of beautiful, though poisoned, rivers.

All this has to be balanced, however, against some equally emphatic assertions of the corruptibility of the sensual, its dramatic attestation of the principle of dualism at the heart of all existential being. In *Native Realm* Milosz speaks of 'the tyrannical beast of sex which neither redeems us nor condemns us, it just is'.[98] 'It is a very old problem,' he remarked, in an interview with Rachel Berghash, 'how to separate our love for created things, or for the world as it is accessible to us through our senses, from the idea of God who is separated from the world.'[99] His poem 'Initiation' conveys the ambiguous nature of the whole experience of interhuman love. The poem strongly recalls the words of Kierkegaard in *The Works of Love* – 'Earthly love and friendship are partiality and the passion for partiality. Christian love is self-denying love ... The extreme limits of partiality lie in exclusiveness, in loving only one; the extreme limits of self-denial lie in self-sacrifice, in not excluding a single one ...

Consequently, the sensual is selfishness ... Earthly love and friendship are the highest expression of self-esteem; they are the I intoxicated in the other I.'[100] It is this meeting of 'I with I' that Milosz's poem describes and which he views with a concern similar to that expressed in *The Works of Love*:

> Vanity and gluttony were always her sins
> And I fell in love with her in the phase of life
> When our scornful reason is the judge of others.
>
> Then I went through a sudden initiation.
> Not only did our skins like each other, tenderly,
> And our genitals fit once and for all,
> But her sleep at arm's length exerted its power
> And her childhood in a city she visited dreaming.
>
> Whatever was naive and shy in her
> Or fearful in the disguise of self-assurance
> Moved me, so that – we were so alike –
> In an instant, not judging anymore,
> I saw two sins of mine: vanity, gluttony.

For all its tensions and ambiguities, Milosz still insists that earthly love can ultimately disclose the way to divine love, that it 'opens the door to a higher state, to *amore sacro*' as he puts it in *Native Realm*.[101] The images of the lovers 'naked and kneeling', side by side with images of God's presence in the poem, 'On the Road', are highly suggestive of this, as is the image of the woman to whom he prays in 'A Photograph' – 'Obtain for me the grace/ Of your strong faith .../ You are for me now/ The mystery of time/ i.e., of a person/ Changing and the same.' One of his most perfect lyrics, 'Elegy for N.N.', further explores the complexities of the eros-agape dichotomy. The work was prompted by a letter he received from Poland informing him that a woman with whom he once had a close relationship had recently died. He addresses her in the poem, reconstructing the circumstances of their intimacy. He recalls the place where they grew up: the house by a lake beneath the Lithuanian sky, the 'horses standing at the forge', the 'little columns in the market-place'. He reenacts in memory the exodus of his people from Lithuania following the devastatation of World War II. A particularly macabre memory is that of 'the ashes at Sachsenhausen', the site of a Nazi concentration camp. He imagines his loved one coming to be with him in California, crossing great tracts of water and wilderness. What was impossible in reality is made possible by the power of the poetic imagination. 'It happens that now, returning to the poem after many years I discover its value as a memorial,' he wrote in an explanatory comment. 'I have brought her to life in a way and now again I feel her presence. For N.N. visited me after all.' To this he adds the significant comment that 'every poet is guided by Eros who according to Plato is an intermediary between gods and men'.[102] The following sequence affirms the reaching towards the infinite which he sees as the defining characteristic of earthly love; he sees it, however, as an aspiration which is persistently frustrated by the temporal finitude of all mortal experience:

> We learned so much, this you know well:
> how, gradually, what could not be taken away
> is taken. People, countrysides.
> And the heart does not die when one thinks it should,
> we smile, there is tea and bread on the table.
> And only remorse that we did not love
> the poor ashes in Sachsenhausen
> with absolute love, beyond human power.

The poem points to a critical question: how does man participate in the higher love which earthly love, for all its inadequacies, endlessly discloses as the fulfilment towards which the human spirit aspires. As several of Milosz's poems suggest, the persistent intrusion of the self is the corrupting element in the experience of earthly love. The more fundamental question therefore is: how does one nurture the pure spirit of altruistic love which enables us to participate in the higher love – that 'absolute love beyond human power', i.e., absolute in its selflessness, which is epitomised in the person of Christ. In *Native Realm* he links the attainment of selfless love with humility and faith: a simple faith such as that of the people amongst whom he grew up in Polish Lithuania. His final words in the work are these: 'When ambition counsels us to lift ourselves above simple moral rules guarded by the poor in spirit, rather than to choose them as our compass needle amid the uncertainties of change, we stifle the only thing that can redeem our follies and mistakes: love.'[103] In *The Captive Mind* he recalls an experience that exemplified for him the perfection of altruistic love. This incident occurred at a railway station in the Ukraine at the beginning of World War II. The station was crowded with refugees fleeing from the invading Nazis, all huddled together in the freezing cold:

> In my wanderings at the beginning of the Second World War, I happened to find myself, for a very short while, in the Soviet Union. I was waiting for a train at a station in one of the large cities of the Ukraine.

It was a gigantic station. Its walls were hung with portraits and banners of inexpressible ugliness. A dense crowd dressed in sheepskin coats, uniforms, fur caps, and woollen kerchiefs filled every available space and tracked thick mud over the tiled floor. The marble stairs were covered with sleeping beggars, their bare legs sticking out of their tatters despite the fact that it was freezing. As I was passing through the station I suddenly stopped and looked. A peasant family – husband and wife and two children – had settled down by the wall. They were sitting on baskets and bundles. The wife was feeding the younger child; the husband, who had a dark wrinkled face and a black, drooping moustache was pouring tea out of a kettle into a cup for the older boy. They were whispering to each other in Polish. I gazed at them until I felt moved to the point of tears ... This was a human group, an island in a crowd that lacked something proper to ordinary human life ... It is possible that the family I saw was illiterate. My friend would have called them graceless, smelly imbeciles who had to be taught to think. Still, precious seeds of humanity were preserved in them.[104]

This experience, he says, forced him to reexamine his radical political beliefs and to recognise that the real force for change and renewal in human existence lies in the loving care that people extend to one another, especially in moments of acute personal need: 'Knowing there is light in man, I could never have dared seek it, for light is not, I believe, the same as political consciousness and it can exist in fools, monks, boys who dislike social duties, and kulaks.'[105] That light is the light of faith, which is the key to the attainment of that higher selfless love to which Milosz refers at the end of the 'Elegy to N.N.' It is this humble faith that enables man to triumph over Necessity – the necessity of evil which is ultimately rooted in pride – and to participate in the selflessness of divine love. This is movingly illustrated in 'The World', the beautiful lyrical sequence inspired by Blake which celebrates the innocence of filial and parental love. The poems show how love is manifested in the simplest and most commonplace experiences of everyday life. One of the poems is simply entitled 'Love'; it emphasises the selflessness by which love is characterised in its purest and most genuine forms:

Love means to learn to look at yourself
The way one looks at distant things
For you are only one thing among many.
And whoever sees that way heals his heart,
Without knowing it, from various ills –
A bird and a tree say to him: Friend.

Then he wants to use himself and things
So that they stand in the glow of ripeness.
It doesn't matter whether he knows what he serves:
Who serves best doesn't always understand.

FAITH, HOPE AND IMMORTALITY

In an essay from his *Visions from San Francisco Bay* Milosz cites the words of
St Thomas Aquinas on the inadequacy of language when it comes to expressing the nature of God. He endorses Aquinas's belief that man can come close
to God by 'reflecting only on what He is not'.[106] In much of his work he
dwells on the distance that separates man from God, suggesting the gulf
between them is to be bridged only by faith and love. In these poems he also
reflects the influence of Simone Weil. 'There is not and there cannot be any
other relation of man to God except love,' Simone Weil wrote. 'What is not
love is not a relation to God.'[107] Milosz must have been familiar with the statement in Weil's *Gateway to God* that love is the fruit of grace, which in turn, is
the fruit of the soul's openness to God as expressed through prayer. Declaring
her faith 'in God, the Trinity, the Incarnation, Redemption, the Eucharist and
the teaching of the Gospel', she wrote: 'When I say I believe I do not mean
that I take over for myself what the Church says on these matters ... but that
through love I hold on to the perfect unseizable truth which these mysteries
contain, and that I try to open my soul to it so that its light may penetrate
into me.'[108] Milosz's poem 'On Prayer' also represents the act of prayer as an
opening of the soul to God, a plea for the grace of faith and love, a bridging
of the distance between the finite and the infinite. Its opening line directly
echoes the words of Aquinas:

You ask me how to pray to someone who is not.
All I know is that prayer constructs a velvet bridge
And walking it we are aloft, as on a springboard,
Above landscapes the color of ripe gold
Transformed by a magic stopping of the sun.
That bridge leads to the shore of Reversal
Where everything is just the opposite and the word *is*
Unveils a meaning we hardly envisioned.
Notice: I say *we*; there, every one, separately,
Feels compassion for others entangled in the flesh
And knows that if there is no other shore
We will walk that aerial bridge all the same.

Several poems by Milosz invoke the act of prayerful supplication as the soul's gateway to God, its assurance of the gift of grace which leads to faith and a genuinely selfless love. Many of them recall the simple prayerfulness of the community amongst whom he grew up in Catholic Lithuania. One of the most moving is a work called 'With Her' in which he reinvokes a memory of his mother at prayer: 'Those poor, arthritically swollen knees/ Of my mother in an absent country./ I think of them on my seventy-fourth birthday/ As I attend early Mass at St Mary Magdalen in Berkeley.' He recalls the reading from the Book of Wisdom affirming the truth that 'God has not made death/ And does not rejoice in the annihilation of the living,' together with the reading from Mark on the miraculous raising of the daughter of Jairus by Christ – both confirming the Christian teaching that death is conquered by faith. He calls to his mother to unite with him in prayer: 'Be with me, I say to her, my time has been short./ Your words are now mine, deep inside me.' A similar spirit of spontaneous prayerfulness is evoked in one of the poems from the cycle, 'Chronicles of the Town of Pornic', where Milosz reechoes the supplications of the populace to the Virgin Mary, their Mediatrix: 'O Holy Mother, save me, my life is so sinful./ Return me to the dear earth, allow me another day./ O Holy Mother, I am not deserving but I will begin anew,/ You didn't live far away because You are near me.' The portrait of Anna Kamienska in one of Milosz's most recent collections again emphasises the radical simplicity of faith – 'Reading her, I realised how rich she was and myself, how poor./ Rich in love and suffering, in crying and dreams and prayer.' And the poem 'Meditation' from the same collection concludes with a heartfelt plea to God to reawaken in him the heroic and enduring faith of the people amongst whom he spent his formative years:

> Lord, my heart is full of admiration and I want to talk with you,
> For I am sure you understand me, in spite of my contradictions.
> It seems to me that now I learned at last what it means to love people
> And why love is worn down by loneliness, pity, and anger.
> It is enough to reflect strongly and persistently on one life,
> On a certain woman, for instance, as I am doing now
> To perceive the greatness of those – weak – creatures
> Who are able to be honest, brave in misfortune, and patient till the end.
> What can I do more, Lord, than to meditate on all that
> And stand before you in the attitude of an implorer
> For the sake of their heroism asking: Admit us to your glory.

All these poems give expression to one of Milosz's most profound beliefs: his belief in the power of ritual, as a communal expression of prayer, to provide a release for man from the loneliness resulting from his awareness of the vast gulf that separates him from God. 'If man is a *homo ritualis*, then ritual, which takes us into the realm of the sacred, is not a value to be easily dismissed,' he writes in *The Land of Ulro*.[109] Ritual is not merely an expression of communal worship, important though this is; it takes us into the realm of the transcendental. Aleksander Fiut explains: 'Building a bridge to transcendence, ritual is as much an expression of human helplessness before the mystery of existence as a testimony to a power stronger than time. Ritual frees man from historical conditions without isolating him from the flow of history, since one of the basic characteristics of ritual is the search for a metaphysical sanction of existence.'[110]

In *Native Realm* Milosz remarked that Poland had survived her darkest moments only through the steadfast faith of its people. The focus of that faith was Christ and the mystery of the Incarnation, as reenacted in the ritual of the Eucharist.[111] Like Simone Weil, Milosz saw Christ as the Mediator between Man and God, the bridgehead between human and divine love. Several poems are devoted to this theme. The last of the 'Six Lectures in Verse' affirms the significance of the Incarnation as the transcendence of history by Christ: 'Boundless history lasted in that moment/ When he was breaking bread and drinking wine.' The theme is reiterated in the 'Treatise on Poetry', the essential argument of which Milosz defined in the following terms in *Native Realm*: 'Immobility or resistance to the historical changes that time brings with it in the name of unchangeable moral commandments and a stable structure of the universe is deserving of respect.'[112] Those unchangeable values he sees as being incarnated in the person of Christ whom he addresses directly in the third section of the poem: 'O King of the centuries, ungraspable Movement ... You, in whom cause and effect are joined,/ Drew us from the depth as you draw a wave/ For one instant of limitless transformation.' In 'Either-Or' Christ is represented again as the focal point of the entire historical process. The poem emphasises the priesthood of all believers, all mankind being summoned to participate in the redemptive sacrifice of Christ:

> If God incarnated himself in man, died and rose from the dead,
> All human endeavors deserve attention
> Only to the degree that they depend on this,
> I.e., acquire meaning thanks to this event.
> We should think of this by day and by night.
> Every day, for years, ever stronger and deeper.
> And most of all about how human history is holy
> And how every deed of ours becomes a part of it,
> Is written down for ever, and nothing is ever lost.
> Because our kind was so much elevated

Priesthood should be our calling
Even if we do not wear liturgical garments.
We should publicly testify to the divine glory
With words, music, dance, and every sign.

'Either-Or' is written in the form of a verse polemic, a polyphonic dialogue
in which arguments and counter-arguments are juxtaposed without any
attempt at logical resolution. The technique, possibly inspired and certainly
strengthened by his interest in Dostoevsky, is employed in several of Milosz's
poems. Its function usually is to give expression to the dialectical character of
faith, i.e., its simultaneous comprehension of believing and questioning tendencies. The argument in the lines quoted above, which support a Christian interpretation of the historical process, is followed by one advocating an
evolutionary view of history. The poem concludes that both positions have
validity, insofar as they reflect the tendencies towards scepticism and faith present in the nature of all men. 'Why either-or?/ For centuries men and gods
have lived together' the poem concludes rhetorically.

The use of multiple voices is a feature also of 'From the Rising of the Sun'
and 'Poem for the End of the Century'. Nathan and Quinn, in their study of
Milosz, argue that the polyphonic method is 'not simply a device but an ontological principle'. 'The principle, internalised, explains and justifies the moral
torture of the author and his characters in a world so ridden by ambiguity,
doubt, and contradiction that no voice can command unequivocal assent,' they
write. They see it as a necessary expedient in the poetic articulation of the
experience of faith: 'The only way to assure that faith had any voice against
scepticism at all was to give it a place in a pluralistic world, as one voice
among many.'[113] Whatever the uncertainty conveyed by all this, Milosz confi-
dently predicted the sacred would always survive the challenge of scepticism
and unbelief. In an essay, 'Religion and Space' he declared: 'The sacred exists
and is stronger than all our rebellions – the bread on the table, the rough tree
trunk which is, the depths of "being" I can intuit in the letter opener lying in
front of me, entirely steeped and established in its "being".'[114] But he evokes
the self-torment consequent on the insistent conflict between belief and unbelief, seeing both as tendencies inherent in the experience of faith. In 'A Poem
for the End of the Century' he speaks of 'Searching for an answer/ Scowling,
grimacing,/ Waking up at night, muttering at dawn.' His central dilemma – an
acute need for the comfort of faith side by side with persistent disbelief in its
certainties – is movingly conveyed in these lines from the poem:

To whom should I turn
With that affair so dark

Of pain and also guilt
In the structure of the world,
If either here below
Or over there on high
No power can abolish
The cause and the effect?

Don't think, don't remember
The death on the cross,
Though everyday He dies,
The only one, all-loving,
Who without any need
Consented and allowed
To exist all that is,
Including nails of torture.

Ultimately, the spirit of faith finds expression in Milosz's poetry as a hope-ful expectation of salvation and redemption. He saw the poet's role as primari-ly one of hope-giving affirmation. 'Hope, conscious or unconscious, is what sustains the poet,' he declared in *The Witness of Poetry*.[115] 'Only poetry is hopeful in the twentieth century, through its sensual avidity, its premonitions of change, its prophecies with many meanings,' he wrote in one of the con-cluding sections of *Native Realm*.[116] In *The Land of Ulro* he recalls how his cousin Oscar lamented his fate on being born in 'an age of precipitous decline – 'one so remarkable in its constancy as to be without historical analogy'[117] – while nonetheless retaining his optimism about the future. In 1921 Oscar wrote: 'In the spiritual manifestations of our age we find, as we do in the eigh-teenth century, unbridled negation on the surface and deep down a creative affirmation.'[118] That hopefulness, Milosz says, was rooted in, and sustained by, Oscar's unswerving belief in the power of love. 'Seek love with love' – an epi-graph from his 'Canticle of Knowledge' – was his motto', Milosz writes. 'And I must confess,' he adds, 'that as a young man I inherited much of his faith in a felicitous era awaiting a mankind reborn, and that it sustained me in times of despair. My "catastrophist" poetry, after all, was not devoid of hope.'[119]

'Poems should be written rarely and reluctantly/ under unbearable duress and only with the hope/ that good spirits, not evil ones, choose us for their instrument,' Milosz further declared in 'Ars Poetica'. That spirit of hope, he shows in 'Elegy for Y.Z.', is rooted in man's faith in the immortality of the soul, a prospect attained through the infinite potentiality of love. The poem is preceded by an epigraph from Martin Buber: 'Never forget that you are a son of the King.' In the Judaeo-Christian tradition all children are 'sons of the

King'. Milosz sees his role as poet as one of proclaiming both their uniqueness and their hoped-for immortality:

> I perform a pitiful rite for all of us.
> I would like everyone to know they are the king's children
> And to be sure of their immortal souls,
> I.e., to believe that what is most their own is imperishable
> And persists like the things they touch,
> Now seen by me beyond time's border:
> Her comb, her tube of cream, and her lipstick
> On an extramundane table.

This theme is reiterated in the cycle, 'From the Rising of the Sun' – widely regarded as Milosz's finest poetic achievement – and in several shorter lyrics such as 'Thankfulness', 'Powers', 'In a Buggy at Dusk', and the fifth of the 'Six Lectures in Verse'. 'From the Rising of the Sun' suggests, in a characteristic Kierkegaardian paradox, that hope is born of despair; the poem proceeds through lengthy negative sequences towards its final affirmations of the poet's faith in the soul's immortality. The opening section evokes the conflict in the poet's soul: 'And I begin, though nobody can explain why or wherefore,/ Just as I do now, under a dark cloud with a glint of the red horse .../ So that I write here in desolation/ Beyond the land and the sea.' The dark cloud symbolises despair; the red horse is the horse of Revelations who will usher in the redemption of the world. The poet's despair springs mainly from his contemplation of the destructiveness inherent in nature. Nature is 'a callous mother'. 'Fare well Nature', he cries in a sequence of images evoking the brutality of the natural world:

> The lament of a slaughtered hare fills the forest.
> It fills the forest and disturbs nothing there.
> For the dying of a particular being is its own private business
> And everyone has to cope with it in whatever way he can.
> *Our Forest and Its Inhabitants*. Our, of our village,
> Fenced in with a wire. Sucking, munching, digesting,
> Growing and being annihilated. A callous mother.
> If the wax in our ears could melt, a moth on pine needles,
> A beetle half-eaten by a bird, a wounded lizard
> Would all lie at the centre of the expanding circles
> Of their vibrating agony. That piercing sound
> Would drown out the loud shots of bursting seeds and buds,
> And our child who gathers wild strawberries in a basket.
> Would not hear the trilling, nice after all, of the thrush.

Again he recalls idyllic images of his childhood in Lithuania. A beautiful
sequence recalls his mother – 'Born of a foolhardy mother with whom I am
united, and whom I,/ an old man pity in my dreams.' He remembers how,
with a simple act of faith, she 'offered me to Our Lady of Ostrabrama'. He
asks: 'How and why was she granted what she asked for in her prayer?' He
questions his lifelong attachment to Manichean teaching: 'Indeed quite early
you were a gnostic, a Marcionite,/ A secret taster of Manichean poisons ...' ...
'Confess you have hated your body/ Loving it with unrequited love.' He looks
forward with hope to a life beyond this earth: 'In the forgetting of earthly
years is our movement and peace./ In our prayer for the last day is our consolation.' This hopefulness is dismissed by his Accuser as mere 'Ego', as pride
and vanity but it is affirmed in the beautiful concluding section of the poem,
'Bells in Winter', where Milosz describes a visionary dream, prompted by his
reading of the scriptures, in which a young man comes to him and reveals the
ultimate wisdom – the doctrine of *apokatastasis*, i.e., the final redemption of all
nature and the return of the universe to an ideal state where death will no
longer exist. The doctrine which has roots in Gnosticism and Platonism as
well in the traditions of Orthodoxy – especially the writings of Soloviev and
Berdyaev – is the ultimate fulfilment of the eschatological vision:

> Yet I belong to those who believe in *apokatastasis*.
> That word promises reverse movement,
> Not the one that was set in *katastasis*,
> And appears in the Acts 3, 21.
>
> It means: restoration. So believed: St Gregory of Nyssa,
> Johannes Scotus Erigena, Ruysbroeck, and William Blake.
>
> For me, therefore, everything has a double existence.
> Both in time and when time shall be no more.

In a poem he addressed to Father Joseph Sadzik, his collaborator on a
translation of the Book of Job, Milosz further asserts his belief in the doctrine
of *apokatastasis*, particularly emphasising its projection of a bodily resurrection
which is the final hallmark of the redemption of nature through grace: 'Let the
Communion of the saints triumph/ And a purifying fire, here and everywhere,/ Together with our common rising from the dead/ Towards Him, who
is, was and will be.' The image of bells in winter announcing the coming of
springtime and the renewal of nature at the end of 'From the Rising of the
Sun' symbolises the rebirth which death signifies. The spirit of faith, which is
the source of all hope, is epitomised in the image of the peasant woman,

Lisabeth, with which the poem concludes. We see her going to Mass on a winter morning, 'In biting frost,/ All is cold and grey ... Banks of snow, roadways made slippery by sleighs/ Grow rosy.' As the priest intones the words of the liturgy – 'Introibo ad altare Dei' – the poet overcomes his despair. 'I was judged for my despair because I was unable to understand this,' he says, as he finds hope, not in rational understanding, but in a trusting faith in God:

> Perhaps only my reverence will save me.
> If not for it, I wouldn't dare pronounce the words of prophets:
>
> 'Whatever can be Created can be Annihilated: Forms cannot;
> The Oak is cut down by the Ax, the Lamb falls by the Knife,
> But their Forms Eternal Exist forever. Amen. Hallelujah!
>
> 'For God himself enters Death's Door always with those that enter
> And lies down in the Grave with them, in Visions of Eternity
> Till they awake and see Jesus and the Linen Clothes lying
> That the Females had woven for them and the Gates of their Father's
>   House.'

In *The Land of Ulro* Milosz had quoted Blake's words on man's never-ending quest for the infinite: 'The desire of Man being Infinite, the possession is Infinite and himself Infinite.'[120] He might have added the words of his fellow countryman, the Lithuanian born philosopher, Emmanuel Levinas: 'The infinite in me is the desire for the Infinite. This endless desire for what is beyond self, being, for alterity, is the desire for the infinite.'[121] Milosz's poem, 'Thankfulness', offers a simple prayer of thanks to God for the faith which enables him to look forward to the prospect of eternal life: 'You gave me gifts, God-Enchanter./ I give you thanks for good and ill./ Eternal light in everything on earth./ As now, so on the day after my death.' He recognised, however, that faith is always challenged by doubt and unbelief and in the end that man must simply believe what he cannot know and may never understand. In the fifth of his 'Six Lectures in Verse' he affirms the Job-like trust in God on which faith and hope are ultimately founded:

> 'Christ has risen.' Whoever believes that
> Should not behave as we do,
> Who have lost the up, the down, the right, the left, heavens, abysses,
> And try somehow to muddle on, in cars, in beds,
> Men clutching at women, women clutching at men,
> Falling, rising, putting coffee on the table,
> Buttering bread, for here's another day ...

... The Book is always with us,
And in it, miraculous signs, counsels, orders.
Unhygienic, it's true, and contrary to common sense,
But they exist and that's enough on the mute earth.
It's as if a fire warmed us in a cave
While outside the golden rain of stars is motionless.
Theologians are silent. And philosophers
Don't even dare ask: 'What is truth?'
And so, after the great wars, undecided,
With almost good will but not quite,
We plod on with hope. And now let everyone
Confess to himself: 'Has he risen?' 'I don't know.'

'In Each of Us There Is God':
The Poetry of Joseph Brodsky

'TIME WORSHIPS LANGUAGE': BRODSKY'S POETICS

Unlike life, a work of art never gets taken for granted; it is always viewed against its precursors and predecessors. The ghosts of the great are especially visible in poetry, since their words are less mutable than the concepts they represent.

Less Than One[1]

In his acceptance speech on being awarded the Nobel Prize for Literature in 1987 Joseph Brodsky spoke of his embarrassment at being honoured with the greatest award for achievement in literature when others, such as Anna Akhmatova, Marina Tsvetaeva and Osip Mandelstam, each of whom he regarded as being more deserving of such recognition than himself, had been denied it by the Nobel Committee. 'In my better moments,' he declared, 'I deem myself their sum total, though invariably inferior to each of them individually.'[2] Critical consensus, especially amongst scholars of Russian literature, would suggest that Brodsky's poetry, while being significantly influenced by all of the writers whose names he mentions, is also comparable to theirs in terms of literary status and distinction, despite his modest description of himself as 'inferior to each of them individually'. Akhmatova declared him 'a genius'[3] on reading his 'Elegy for John Donne' and a contemporary Russian poet, Bella Akhmadulina, compared him to Pushkin, declaring that his work 'marks a new blossoming in Russian poetry'. 'Joseph is perfection,' she wrote. 'His communion with the whole world, with world culture, is something that was true of Mandelstam also ... His language is unprecedented, unheard of before. It's entirely his own discovery. In this sense he is fated to be a poet for a new age.'[4] Natalya Gorbanevskaya, a notable dissident poet in the 1960s and an influential publisher of emigre literature, described him as 'the best living Russian poet' and 'the best Russian poet in general after Akhmatova and Mandelstam'.[5] The Leningrad writer, Vladimir Ufliand, has also spoken of him as 'the greatest Russian poet of the present day'. His style, he writes – using the words of Turgenev – 'is the epitome of that great and mighty Russian language, its loftiest manifestation'.[6]

Central to all these comparisons is a perception of Brodsky as preeminently a writer whose work comprehends the great traditions of Russian literature – particularly its religious and spiritual traditions – and which reinvokes their meaning in the context of contemporary European culture. 'Brodsky belongs with those poets who have been astonishingly successful in preserving the Christian, the classical traditions,' declared Czeslaw Milosz. 'Given the state of modern poetry at the moment Brodsky and I may be considered to be lingering in the rearguard,' he adds, 'but really we may be the avant-garde.'[7] 'At the beginning of the sixties,' wrote the poet and scholar, Lev Loseff, 'Brodsky was certainly the first to bring metaphysical imagery, diction and subject-matter back into Russian poetry.'[8]

Described by the author of one of the first major studies of his work as 'unquestionably a Christian poet'[9] Brodsky himself confirmed that, while he was born and reared a Jew, Christianity had later come to occupy a central place in his life and thought. Responding to a question from an interviewer in July 1972 – shortly after his departure from Russia for a life of exile in the West – he said: 'While I am related to the Old Testament perhaps by ancestry, and certainly the spirit of justice, I consider myself a Christian. Not a good one but I try to be.'[10] Viktor Krivulin, a contemporary Russian poet who shares many of Brodsky's cultural and poetic interests – they share a common interest, for example, in the traditions of Acmeism – has spoken of the essential compatibility of his Jewish and Christian affiliations. 'Brodsky,' he recalled in a recent interview, 'always felt his Jewishness as a religious thing, despite the fact that, when all is said and done, he's a Christian poet.'[11] Derek Walcott has also spoken of the great attraction that Christianity held for Brodsky, despite some evidence of self-conflict at appearing to abandon his Jewish heritage.[12]

Brodsky himself recalled his 'discovery' of the Bible which occurred when he was twenty-three years old, 'having gone', he said, 'through the severe anti-religious schooling in Russia which doesn't leave any kind of notion about afterlife'.[13] He encountered the Bible during the eighteen-month period of exile that he spent in Norenskaya, a remote region of Northern Russia, near Archangelsk, to where he had been sentenced on a charge of 'tuneyadstvo' (vagrancy or social parasitism) in March 1964. Described in a medical report as having 'psychopathological tendencies', he was initially given a five-year sentence but was pardoned in October 1965, having worked for eighteen months as a manure-carrier. 'There in that lonely northern village where he had been, utterly unjustly and barbarically, driven into exile, he had found himself, not only spiritually but creatively,' his friend, Yevgeny Rein, recalled.[14]

Thenceforward Biblical themes and motifs occurred frequently in his poetry, the first indication of his new found enthusiasm being the appearance

of his long narrative poem, 'Isaac and Abraham', in 1965. The poem, he
recalled later, was written within days of reading the Genesis account of the
Abrahamic story.[15] Correspondingly, lines such as 'In each of us/ There is
God', 'Each of us is naked before God', 'Our Pilot is God', 'None can doubt
God's presence or his power', occur frequently in the poems he wrote in the
1960s – as do prayerful invocations to God, such as Gorbunov's plea for heavenly assistance in Canto 3 of 'Gorbunov and Gorchakov', the final prayer to
God in the last stanza of 'To Lycomedes on Syros', ('God grant ...' etc.), and
the supplications to God which occur in the third and eighth verses of 'New
Stanzas to Augusta' ('O God, snuff out the spark ... O God, hack off all my
senses', etc.). As well as 'Isaac and Abraham', several other of Brodsky's
poems deal explicitly with Biblical themes. They include 'Nunc Dimittis', a
poetic reinterpretation of Luke's account of the story of Christ's Presentation
in the Temple, six Nativity poems – 'A Christmas Ballad', '1 January 1965',
'December 24, 1971', 'Anno Domini', 'A Second Christmas' and 'Lagoon'.
There are three 'Passion' poems, each drawing significant images from the
Biblical account of Christ's Crucifixion: 'Adieu, Mademoiselle Veronique',
'Nature Morte' and 'Gorbunov and Gorchakov'. Religious themes – the struggle for faith, the problem of unbelief, the torment of existential despair, the
permanence of suffering in mortal life, conflicts of human and divine love, the
temporal–intemporal dichotomy, the hoped-for prospect of self-renewal and
salvation, together with the mystical themes of darkness, nothingness and void
– are generally explored in his poetry in terms of the mythic language and
metaphors of the scriptures.

Biblical themes and motifs are powerfully reinforced by classical influences
in Brodsky's poetry. In 'The Child of Civilisation', his eloquent tribute to
Osip Mandelstam, he affirms his belief in the continuity of Graeco-Roman and
Christian civilisation.[16] In his own poetry, as in Mandelstam's, classical and
Biblical themes mingle freely, suggesting the essential compatibility of the two
traditions, though he complained in an essay on Virgil that Christianity had
failed to absorb and assimilate classical traditions sufficiently.[17] In an essay on
Constantine Cavafy he writes of a profound harmony between classical and
Christian civilisation, despite some obvious differences in their metaphysical
and religious orientations. His insistence that 'neither can exercise man's spiritual capacity to the fullest' is indicative of the fruitful character of the tensions
he sees as existing between them.[18] This harmony of opposites is continually
attested by the juxtaposition of classical and Christian images in his work. His
reverence for the Greek and Latin writers is especially in evidence in works
such as 'Roman Elegies', the 'Eclogues' 'Odysseus to Telemachus', 'Letter to a
Roman Friend', 'Plato Elaborated', 'Aeneas and Dido' and 'To Lycomedes on
Syros'.

Brodsky's traditionalism is evidenced not only by his fondness for Biblical and classical motifs but also by the all-pervasive influence on his poetry of the works of several of his predecessors in Russian literature. Pushkin, Baratynsky, Derzhavin and Annensky are amongst those of his eighteenth and nineteenth century forerunners whom he has identified as seminal influences on his writings. Amongst his twentieth century predecessors he has particularly identified Akhmatova and Mandelstam as shaping influences on his poetic formation. Recalling his closeness to Akhmatova in the last years of her life, when he himself was a young novice poet greatly in need of her advice and counsel, he said: 'It was more or less like an addiction and I saw her whenever it was possible ...'[19] In his essay, 'The Keening Muse', he writes approvingly of the place of tradition in Akhmatova's poetry, seeing her Christian faith as the underlying force in works such as her great epic poem, *Requiem*. 'The degree of compassion with which the various voices of *Requiem* are rendered can be explained only by the author's Orthodox faith,' he writes; 'the degree of understanding and forgiveness which accounts for this work's piercing, almost unbearable lyricism, only by the uniqueness of her heart, her self, and this self's sense of time.'[20] Profoundly influenced by Mandelstam, both technically and thematically, Brodsky shared the latter's sense of the continuity of classical and Christian civilisation as well as his sense of the sacredness of the poetic logos, the Word. 'It blew my mind,' he said, recalling his discovery of Mandelstam's poetry in his teens. 'Really because for the first time, I think, I was reading something which was mentally congenial ... It was a discovery.' 'What he did,' Brodsky wrote in his commemorative essay on Mandelstam, 'will last as long as the Russian language exists. It will certainly outlast the present and any subsequent regime in that country, because of both its lyricism and its profundity.'[21]

During his period of exile at Norenskaya Brodsky also discovered a deep personal affinity with the English Metaphysicals, particularly Donne and Marvell, translations of whose work he included in his first published collection of poems. His 'Elegy for John Donne' testifies to his huge admiration for the greatest of the metaphysical poets and clearly demonstrates the extent of the technical and thematic links that exist between their writings. 'He owes to the English metaphysical poets the intellectual discourse, full of wit and paradox, which was well suited to his own inclinations,' Valentina Polukhina wrote. 'The degree of ratiocination with which much of Brodsky's poetry is permeated had never previously been a characteristic of Russian poetry,' she says. 'Never had there been such a contrast between majesty of style and asceticism of feeling.'[22] Donne's influence is reflected, Derek Walcott said, both in the restless, questioning spirit of Brodsky's religious poems and in the slightly blasphemous spirit in which he treats some of his religious themes. 'Donne,' he writes, 'like any great religious poet is always on the edge of blasphemy, through sex or through whatever.'[23] Brodsky's exploration of the tensions of the spiritual and the sexual in poems such as 'Adieu Mademoiselle Veronique' exemplifies the emotional dilemmas and complexities of religious faith in a manner strongly reminiscent of Donne's poetry and has similarly attracted accusations of blasphemy.[24] Brodsky has also been drawn to contemporary English and American poets such as Eliot, Lowell and Auden – to each of whom he addressed a commemorative elegy. Time and again he has given voice to his admiration for Auden – 'the greatest mind of the twentieth century ... a new kind of metaphysical poet ... a man of terrific lyrical gifts'.[25]

'Brodsky', Elena Ushakova wrote, 'introduced a European spirit into Russian poetry.'[26] This is especially evident in the modernist and absurdist strain in his work. He himself traces the modernist movement back to Dostoevsky, while suggesting that its impact was virtually negatived in Russian literature by the dominance of Tolstoyan realism at the end of the nineteenth century and later by the suffocating force of the officially sanctioned socialist realism of the Soviet period. Platonov's fiction, he argues in 'Catastrophes in the Air', was the only modernist work to survive this process. Alone amongst twentieth century Russian writers, he says, Platonov had broken through the stranglehold of socialist realism to create a genuinely modern style. Describing him as 'a greater writer than Joyce, Musil or Kafka', he sees Platonov's work as 'marking the fulfilment of the spirit of *The Possessed*'.[27] Paradoxically, Brodsky sees modernism as itself a manifestation of the traditionalist spirit in literature, describing it as 'a logical consequence – compression and concision – of things classical'.[28] That description seems particularly apt when applied to the work of the modernist writer whose influence is most apparent in his poetry. 'I fell in love with a photograph of Samuel Beckett long before I'd read a line of his,' he recalled in *Less Than One*.[29] Given the scarcity of modernist precedents in Russian literature, he turned for exemplars to the wider field of European literature, finding a particularly strong affinity with Beckett. As Gerald Smith has written: 'He is increasingly concerned with culturological problems, haunted by a Beckett-like awareness of being overcome by wintry desolation against which human speech must be pitted as a token of survival.'[30] The influence of Beckett's writings is to be seen particularly in works such as 'Nature Morte', 'The Butterfly' and 'Gorbunov and Gorchakov', as will be shown in detail presently.

Brodsky's interest in Beckett's writings seemed a logical outcome of his earlier interest in the work of the Christian existentialists, particularly Kierkegaard and Shestov. 'I think that while he was just beginning to develop his view of the world Brodsky fell under the extremely powerful sway of Kierkegaard and Shestov and he hasn't got away from that,' Lev Loseff said.[31]

In his essay on Auden Brodsky spoke of his joy on discovering their shared interest in the Kierkegaardian triad 'which for many of us was the key to the human species'.[32] The influence of Kierkegaard's *Fear and Trembling* is clearly discernible in 'Isaac and Abraham', both works being an exploration of the nature of faith in the context of the Biblical story of God's command to Abraham to sacrifice his only son Isaac as a mark of his obedience to the divine will. Brodsky shared with Kierkegaard a deep sense of the inevitability of suffering in mortal life, together with a conviction that faith springs ultimately from suffering and despair. With Shestov he shared a common attachment to the world of Old Testament Judaism, the world of Job, the Prophets and the Psalms. (Both Brodsky and Shestov had been born Jews and both laid great emphasis on the continuity of the Old and New Testament traditions.) Clearly he was attracted by the irrationalist character of Shestov's philosophy, by his rejection of the Hegelian principle of rational necessity and by his attacks on the dominance of rationalism in ethics and theology. While he would probably have agreed, partially at least, with Berdyaev's view that the polarisation of the worlds of reason and faith in *Athens and Jerusalem* was somewhat simplistic, Brodsky would surely have endorsed the Shestovian conclusion that 'it is when man feels the utter impossibility of living with reason that faith first arises in him'.[33]

These, therefore, are the diverse influences which shaped the formation of Brodsky's poetic development and growth. All these elements were synthesised in a poetic creed, the primary affirmation of which was the sacredness of the poetic word, its embodiment of God's immanent presence in the material universe. At his trial in 1964 Brodsky told the judge that he believed poetry is 'a gift from God'.[34] Time and again he has reiterated his belief that poetry is man's gateway to the infinite, being disclosive of realities beyond the sphere of temporal being. He told an interviewer in 1982 that he believed 'poetry provides for a greater sense of infinity than any creed is capable of'.[35] 'For a poet any faith, any system, is an act of choice, of metaphors, that is language,' he said in a lecture on W.H. Auden in 1985.[36] Lev Loseff has spoken of his 'conception of the poet's mission as a votary of the Muse and performer of God's Will whose fate is unravelled in the form of the Christian mystery or Dante's tragedy of the Titans'.[37] Brodsky himself told Natalya Gorbanevskaya: 'If I were to begin to create some form of theology I think it would be a theology of language. In this sense, the word is really something sacred for me.'[38] In his poem, 'To a Certain Poetess' he affirms the divine origin of poetry ... 'Yet the Muses' service/ renders a poet's hands divinely nervous ... ' and in 'A Letter in a Bottle' he declares: 'Our pilot is God/ He is the one Person we address.' 'For a poet,' he said, 'his art is an act of faith ... If your own faith isn't strong enough, then your art becomes a diabolical business.'[39] Not surprisingly,

Loseff concludes that 'no Russian poet of the present day, no poet since Akhmatova, Tsvetaeva, Mandelstam has expressed such strength of religious feeling as he has in his poetry.'[40]

The nature of the relationship between faith and poetry which all this implies is extremely complex, however, and needs to be explored more fully both in the light of Brodsky's various utterances on the subject in his prose and of various interpretations of his aesthetic beliefs in recent critical scholarship. Many scholars see him as the latest of the Acmeists, though this is disputed by some, such as Anatoly Nayman, who argue that Brodsky, like most younger Russian poets, simply passed through an Acmeist phase before finding his own independent voice and departing in many fundamental respects from Acmeist poetics. The weight of evidence, however, both internal and external, strongly favours the first of these positions. W.H. Auden spoke of Brodsky's 'extraordinary capacity to envision material objects as sacramental signs, messengers from the unseen',[41] clearly pointing to an incarnational view of language, i.e., a view of language as comprehending the synthesis of the material and the spiritual and embodying the immanent presence of the spiritual in the world of material being – which is strongly reminiscent of Acmeism. Thomas Venclova described Brodsky's poetics as 'a continuation and development or overdevelopment of the semantic poetics of the Acmeists'.[42] 'In talking of the "all-seeing eye of words",' Valentina Polukhina writes, 'Brodsky has in mind not ubiquitous universal reason but the hypostasis of God in the world,' a position self-evidently close to the poetics of Akhmatova and Mandelstam.[43] Loseff acknowledges there is an 'Acmeist quality in Brodsky's work'[44] and Yury Kublanovsky speaks of his 'Acmeist intentness and gravity'.[45] Both see this as being manifested in a 'thirst for concreteness', for material existentiality, for what Mandelstam described as 'the existence of the thing rather than the thing itself'. The idea is well expressed in these lines from a poem in the *Urania* collection: 'Air is a thing of language/ the firmament is/ a chorus of molecules of consonants and vowels,/ in the vernacular – of souls.'

Asserting that 'the Acmeist credo runs through the works of Brodsky', Leon Burnett in 'The Complicity of the Real' cites the words from his play, *Marbles*: 'It's always the principle that counts. The idea behind the thing. Not the thing itself.'[46] Again Georges Nivat writes in 'The Ironic Journey into Antiquity': 'For Brodsky ... all is immanence, it is in the sluggishness of things that lies hidden the possible passage to something else'[47] – all of which points to a consistent adoption by Brodsky of the principles of Acmeist poetics. Moreover, like the Acmeists, he sees language as a two-edged instrument: as simultaneously a phenomenon disclosive both of the infinite and of the crude materiality of the natural world. To quote Valentina Polukhina: 'The word in Brodsky' poetic world is twofold. On the one hand, the word as an alienated part of speech links man with numbers. "The reduction of man to things," he has said, "to a hieroglyph, to numbers is a vector into nothingness." ... On the other hand, the word is no less frequently identified with Spirit and thus, links man with God.' For Brodsky, she says, 'language is only language', yet equally 'language is all'. She concludes: 'Through his similes Brodsky either highlights the antinomy of matter and spirit, or attempts to reconcile it by means of synthesis. The moving force behind this synthesis is language.'[48] Lev Loseff has vividly conveyed the implications of this paradox in these words from a recent interview:

> What I want to say is that language, which Joseph habitually talks about in what are usually considered religious terms is, for all that, one way or another just a semiotic form. For a man of Brodsky's dimensions that is the form his commission takes, the form of his existential fate, the form of his pact with Providence. Brodsky exemplifies, I don't know anyone else who does, that magnificent line of Tsvetaeva from her poem, 'God', where she writes of His lack of attachment to 'your signs and burdens'. It's amazing just how much of the future language reveals to a poet. In Tsvetaeva's days the word 'sign' had none of the practical connotations it has for us in our semiotic age. What Tsvetaeva is doing is formulating her God in profoundly semiotic terms. For me, there lies the key to Brodsky's personality.[49]

Central to Acmeist poetics is the conviction that language, by embodying God's presence in material being, embodies thereby the infinity of God's love, its informing presence in the universe. Poetry, as 'the highest form of existence for language' is the most potent medium by which God's love finds expression, a theme vividly conveyed in these words from Brodsky's essay, 'The Keening Muse':

> Throughout one's life, time addresses man in a variety of languages: in those of innocence, love, faith, experience, history, fatigue, cynicism, guilt, decay, etc. Of those, the language of love is clearly the *lingua franca*. Its vocabulary absorbs all the other tongues, and its utterance gratifies a subject, however inanimate it may be. Also, by being thus uttered, a subject acquires an ecclesiastical, almost sacred denomination, echoing both the way we perceive the objects of our passions and the Good Book's suggestion as to what God is. Love is essentially an attitude maintained by the infinite towards the finite. The reversal constitutes either faith or poetry.[50]

The passage conveys the paradox that language embodies the dualism at the heart of love, as experienced in its human forms, side by side with its immanent attestation of the infinite. The finite/infinite dichotomy points to the related dichotomy of the time-bound and the intemporal. Time is the barrier to the infinite that man endlessly desires. Language, in its highest, i.e., its poetic form, embodies the conflicts resulting from this. Art, Brodsky argues, does not 'imitate life', but 'transcends it, extends it beyond its terminal point'.[51] It is simultaneously pointed towards the infinite to which it aspires and the finite in which it resides. 'Art is not a better, but an alternative existence,' he writes in an essay on Mandelstam; 'it is not an attempt to escape reality but the opposite, an attempt to animate it.' Time is repetitive, cyclic, recurrent; poetry is ahistorical, it is 'time restructured'. 'Song is, after all,' he writes, ' restructured time, towards which mute space is inherently hostile.' What dictates a poem, he says, 'is the language, and this is the voice of that language, which we know under the nicknames of Muse or Inspiration'.[52] Language, however, comprehends the spheres both of the temporal and intemporal; while seeking to transcend the temporal it is still rooted in the here and now. Moreover, it discloses the possibility of transcendence in terms of the here and now, i.e., in terms of the phenomenal reality of the Word. The tensions which this implies are well expressed in this passage from Brodsky's essay, 'A Poet and Prose':

> Yet the issue here is not only that of experience lagging behind anticipation; it is a question of the differences between art and reality. One of them is that in art, owing to the properties of the material itself, it is possible to attain a degree of lyricism that has no physical equivalent in the real world. Nor, in the same way, does there exist in the real world an equivalent of the tragic in art, which (the tragic) is the reverse of lyricism – or the stage that follows it. No matter how dramatic a person's direct experience is, it is always exceeded by the experience of an instrument. Yet a poet is a combination of an instrument and a human being in one person, with the former gradually taking over the latter. The sensation of this takeover is responsible for timbre; the realisation of it, for destiny.[53]

Again and again Brodsky argues – in a manner wholly consistent with Acmeist poetics – that the poet's anticipation of a reality beyond the world of the here and now must nevertheless be expressed in terms of the here and now. In an essay on one of Auden's poems he writes: 'The point of the poem is the description of the "next world", the comprehension of which is derived from this one.'[54] He describes Auden as a poet 'whose signs are the entire phe-

nomenal and speculative world' and adds, 'Here is where the poetic version of
eternal life originates.' Religion itself, he further argues, is itself an expression
of aspirations already present in language: 'Art is more ancient and universal
than any faith with which it enters into matrimony,' he writes. 'The judgement of art is a judgement more demanding than the Final Judgement.'
Language precedes time, religion, faith, poetry. He concurs wholly with
Auden's previously cited statement that 'Time worships language':

> Auden had indeed said that time (not the time) worships language, and
> the train of thought that statement set in motion in me is still trundling
> to this day. For 'worship' is an attitude of the lesser toward the greater.
> If time worships language, it means that language is greater, or older,
> than time, which is, in its turn, older and greater than space.[55]

Brodsky's poetry, therefore, represents a search for eternal, i.e., religious
values through the medium of the Word. Language is the Absolute – the
Absolute Good; its values are ethical as well as aesthetic and religious. In his
essay, 'In the Shadow of Dante' he wrote: 'A poem is a form of the closest
possible interplay between ethics and aesthetics.'[56] 'The art of poetry,' he
wrote in another work, 'bears witness to the vocal and ethical possibilities of
man as a species – if for no other reason than that it drains them dry.'[57] The
values which the poet strives to define through language transcend time and
change; they therefore transcend rationality and abstraction, the formal modes
of theological and ethical statement. Attention to conscience is the driving
force of the whole process. In 'The Power of the Elements' Brodsky spoke of
this as the 'Protestant' element in literature: 'For to be a writer means invariably to be a Protestant or, to say the least, to employ the Protestant conception
of man. While either in Russian Orthodoxy or in Roman Catholicism man is
judged by the Almighty or His Church, in Protestantism it is the man who
subjects himself to a personal equivalent of the Last Judgement. In doing so,
he is far more merciless toward himself than the Deity, or even than the
Church, if only because he knows himself better (so he thinks) than does
either, and is unwilling, or, to be precise, unable to forgive.'[58] In his Nobel
Lecture of 1987 Brodsky gave a definitive statement of his views on the ethical
character of poetry:

> On the whole, every new aesthetic reality makes man's ethical reality
> more precise. For aesthetics is the mother of ethics; the categories of
> 'good' and 'bad' are, first and foremost, aesthetic ones, at least etymo-
> logically preceding the categories of 'good' and 'evil'. If in ethics not 'all
> is permitted', it is precisely because not 'all is permitted' in aesthetics,

because the number of colours in the spectrum is limited. The tender babe who cries and rejects the stranger or who, on the contrary, reaches out to him, does so instinctively, making an aesthetic choice, not a moral one. Aesthetic choice is a highly individual matter and aesthetic experience is always a private one. Every new aesthetic reality makes one's experience even more private, and this kind of privacy, assuming at times the guise of literary (or some other) taste, can in itself turn out to be, if not a guarantee, then a form of defence against enslavement. For, a man with taste, particularly literary taste, is less susceptible to the refrains and rhythmical incantations peculiar to any version of political demagogy. The point is not so much that virtue does not constitute a guarantee for producing a masterpiece, as that evil, especially political evil, is always a bad stylist. The more substantial an individual's aesthetic experience is, the sounder his taste, the sharper his moral focus, the freer – through not necessarily the happier – he is.[59]

Brodsky's poetics, in the final analysis, can be summed up in the opening words of the Gospel of St John: 'In the beginning was the Word and the Word was with God and the Word was God.' Only the Word survives; the poet alone transcends history and time, discloses meaning in the midst of nihilism and disorder. In his poem, 'A Part of Speech' Brodsky wrote: 'What gets left of a man amounts/ to a part. To his spoken part. To a part of speech.' The word alone endures. Its autonomy, as Czeslaw Milosz has shown, is not the autonomy accorded it by modern linguistic philosophers, such as deconstructionists and pragmatists. 'In our epoch,' he writes, 'language has been seen to be of paramount importance by academics in the West. Everything is swept away and language is left standing alone, allegedly speaking for us and for itself. But that is sheer nihilism, ontological nihilism.'[60] The ontological supremacy of language, Brodsky insists, derives from its source, from its divine origin, from the truth it embodies: 'What dictates a poem is the language, and this is the voice of the language, which we know under the nicknames of Muse or Inspiration.'[61] As he said of Dostoevsky: 'For Dostoevsky art, like life, is about what man exists for. Like Biblical parables, his novels are vehicles to obtain the answers and not goals unto themselves.'[62] The whole process is admirably conveyed in this passage from 'A Poet and Prose':

Poetry is not 'the best words in the best order'; for language it is the highest form of existence. In purely technical terms, of course, poetry amounts to arranging words with the greatest specific gravity in the most effective and externally inevitable sequence. Ideally, however, it is language negating its own mass and the laws of gravity; it is language's striving upward – or sideways – to that beginning where the Word was. In any case, it is movement of language into pre- (supra-) genre realms, that is, into the spheres from which it sprang. The seemingly most artificial forms for organizing poetic language – terza rima, sestinas, decimas, and so forth – are in fact nothing more than a natural, reiterative, fully detailed elaboration of the echo that followed the original Word.[63]

TIME, DEATH AND THE ETERNAL

Time is far greater than space. Space is a thing.
Whereas time is, in essence, the thought, the conscious dream
of a thing. And life itself is a variety
of time. The carp and bream
are its clots and distillates. As are even more stark
and elemental things, including the sea
wave and the firmament of the dry land.
Including death, that punctuation mark.

These lines from Brodsky's 'Lullaby of Cape Cod' encapsulate the complexities of his major poetic theme – the nature of time, its tensions and polarities, and the impingements of the intemporal and eternal on the conditions of earthly life. The image of the sea – strongly reminiscent of Eliot – signifies the infinity of the intemporal, the carp and bream, its 'clots and distillates', signify the materiality of earthly life, its mortality and 'thinghood'. (In 'The Sound of the Tide' Brodsky spoke of 'language and ocean' as 'two versions of infinity. 'Their common parent,' he added, 'is time,'[64] suggesting, like Eliot in *Four Quartets*, that the timeless is, paradoxically, the offspring of time, attainable only in the conditions of temporal being.) The theme dominates Brodsky's poetry and is the subject of some of his finest lyrics – the 'Lullaby of Cape Cod', 'The Butterfly', the elegies to Donne, Eliot, Auden and Lowell, his long poetic dialogue, 'Gorbunov and Gorchakov', the Christmas, Easter and Passion poems – all are deeply imbued with the everpresent tragedy of mortality and life in time, side with side with the hoped-for prospect of the eternal and the infinite. His words from *Less Than One* on the necessity of signifying the world of the infinite through the imagery of the finite were cited in the previous section; the sea imagery in the above quoted lines from 'Lullaby of Cape Cod' fulfils such a purpose, serving as a 'poetic cosmogony' for existence beyond time, the images of carp and bream representing life in the sphere of the finite and the temporal.

The imagery of speech and silence in 'Gorbunov and Gorchakov' – a poem where the influence of Beckett is all-pervasive – serves a parallel purpose, speech signifying life in time, silence signifying existence in the sphere of the eternal. 'It is in words alone that I partake/ of life,' Gorchakov declares. 'From this day forth ... when life is shot,/eternity begins,' another voice cries. Recalling Eliot's 'Only through time time is conquered', the poem suggests that salvation is achieved in the conditions of the temporal. It is through speech that the spirit survives the destructiveness of time. Speech is identified with faith: 'Remember Gorchakov,' Gorbunov cries, 'the utterness/ of uttered words surpasses disbelief by far.' This identification of speech with faith is given explicit Christian significance in the tenth canto of the poem. Christ is the source of speech – 'For He designed His lips for words ... that's why His life is so prophetic'. 'Words are sort of holy relics' – they are man's source of faith in the face of silence and non-being. The canto ends with a beautiful lyrical meditation on the alternating realities of speech and silence, the first signifying temporality and change, the second the eternal towards which life inexorably proceeds:

> Silence is the future of the days
> that roll toward speech, with all we emphasize
> in it, as, in our greetings silence pays
> respect to unavoidable goodbyes.
> Silence is the future of the words
> whose vowels have gobbled up internally
> the stuff of things, things with a terror towards
> their corners; a wave that cloaks eternity.
> Silence is the future of our love;
> a space, not an impediment, a space
> depriving love's blood-throbbed falsetto of
> its echo, of its natural response.
> Silence is the present for the men
> who lived before us. And, procuress-like,
> silence gathers all together in
> itself, admitted by the speech-filled present. 'Life
> is but a conversation in the face
> of silence'. 'Gestures, quarrels, men incensed.'
> 'A twilight talking to a murky close.'
> 'With walls that stand like arguments against.'

'The Butterfly', a poem which recalls both the Metaphysicals and Mandelstam, dwells on the same theme. It will be recalled that in Mandelstam's poem of

the same title the white butterfly transformed into dust symbolised the brevity
and transience of earthly life. In Brodsky's poem the butterfly has the same
significance, its brief existence similarly symbolising transitoriness and change.
'Why were these lovely shapes/ and colours given/ for your one day of life?'
the poet exclaims. The butterfly exists momentarily on the threshold of the
temporal and the timeless; its short lifespan is seen as a joke played by its
Creator on his creation:

> Should I say that you're dead?
> You touched so brief a fragment
> of time. There's much that's sad in
> the joke God played.
> I scarcely comprehend
> the words "you've lived"; the date of
> your birth and when you faded
> in my cupped hand
> are one, and not two dates.
> Thus calculated,
> your term is, simply stated,
> less than a day.

Despite the brevity of its life, the butterfly in its fragile weightlessness and
fleshlessness is seen to mirror the perfection of its Creator. 'Who was the jew-
eller,/ brow uncontracted/ who from our world extracted/ your miniature?'
the poet asks. But the butterfly is also voiceless and speechless; unlike man, it
lacks the potential to resist the destructiveness of the temporal: 'You lack even
this: / the means to utter/ a word ... you're more speechless/ less fleshed than
time.' It inhabits a world where 'madness brings/ us low and lower,/ where we
are things.' Time reduces all creation to the condition of thinghood, but
speech, i.e., faith, enables man to transcend the prison-like state of his mortality. He envies the butterfly in his ascent to the timeless ... 'motelike, ascend-
ing/ above this bed of flowers,/ beyond the prison space/ where past and
future/ combine to break, or batter,/ our lives.' Until that prospect is in sight
we remain, like the butterfly in its brief life-span, poised between time and the
timeless, speech and silence, darkness and light:

> You're better than No-thing.
> That is, you're nearer,
> more reachable, and clearer.
> Yet you're akin
> to nothingness –

like it, you're wholly empty.
And if, in your life's venture,
No-thing takes flesh,
that flesh will die.
Yet while you live you offer
a frail and shifting buffer,
dividing it from me.

Brodsky's poems echo both the despair that is consequent on the time-bound condition of earthly life and the hope-giving faith that springs from his contemplation of an existence beyond it. In 'The Butterfly' he speaks of a world that has 'no end or telos'; the world of time can only be rendered meaningful in the sphere of the timeless, i.e., through the power of faith. The universe is conditioned by time, meaningless in itself; its impinging nihilism is all-pervasive in mortal life. In itself the universe is absurd, inexplicable rationally. The prevailing condition of man is despair, a sense of God's absence, of his own impotence in the face of the void – the void of meaninglessness and absurdity. The 'coldness' of time is indicative of its reifying force: 'Time is cold. Everybody, sooner/ or later becomes food for a telescope/ grows cold with the years, moves away from the luminary.' Beckettian images of coldness and darkness, side by side with images evoking the atmosphere of the madhouse, profoundly convey the despair and impotence of man in these lines from 'Gorbunov and Gorchakov:

It's night. The hospital. The lane, the drifts
of snow. An alder hums, contesting heaven.
Kike-wise the night nurse in the hallway lifts
his Jewish telescope and peers in, laughing.
My pupil's shrinking, shrinking – it resists
the bed contracting on me like a coffin.
And my blood bubbles like bicarbonates.
My ankle freezes as it comes uncovered.
My mind divides the way a microbe splits
and in the silence multiplies forever.

The imagery of darkness in the eighth canto reinforces this prevailing atmosphere of nihilistic gloom: 'Night. Windows swirl the ward and double it./ the bulwarks of infinity. They're all/ encased in shutters … ' 'You're saying you don't fear the dark?' Gorchakov says to Gorbunov. The latter replies: 'It has/ its landmarks, and with some of them I am/ acquainted rather well.' Both Gorbunov and Gorchakov' – the first a Christ-like sacrificial victim, the man of faith, the other a Judas-like materialist, embodying the faithlessness of the modern age – seek aimlessly to make sense of their existence. Eventually language itself seems reified as their words degenerate into a meaningless babble of incoherent speech in the fifth canto of the poem. Estranged from thought and speech, they engage in a mechanistic, repetitive and meaningless dialogue reminiscent of Lucky's soliloquy in *Waiting for Godot*:

> 'He said to him.' 'And then he said to him.'
> 'And then he said.' 'He answered.' 'And he said.'
> 'Then he.' 'And he then said into the wind.'
> 'He gazed into the dark and said.' 'He said
> again to him.' 'But, so to speak, to say
> he said is not the same as saying what
> he said.' 'And then he said, 'Don't lose your way
> in details; all is clear. That's that.'
> 'The one he-said flows on into the next.'
> 'Until he-saids of sin and penance flow
> together.' 'Silent on the table rests
> he-said.' 'And in the end they form a row,
> like Tartar yokes.' 'And then he said to him.'
> 'And he connected his he-said, in line
> with that he-said, whose echo echoed thin.'
> 'And then he said to him, and filled the time.'

The anguish of existence without faith is given an explicit Christian context in 'Christmas Ballad', a poem Brodsky composed in 1962, shortly before his arrest and exile in Norenskaya. In Moscow the Christmas season, traditionally associated with hope and spiritual self-renewal, is joyless and bleak. Muscovites are shown engrossed in materialistic preoccupations, their moods and activities indicating the stagnant condition of Soviet life. The ship sailing directionlessly through the night symbolises the meaninglessness of their lives; the drunkards and sleep-walkers represent the spiritual deadness of life in a totalitarian state, devoid of the life-affirming hopefulness which Christmas traditionally signified:

> In anguish unaccountable
> the steady ship that burns at dark,
> the small shy streetlamp of the night,
> floats out of Alexander Park
> in the exhaustion of dull bricks.

Like a pale-yellow, tiny rose,
it drifts along, past lovers' heads
and walkers' feet.

In anguish unaccountable
sleep-walkers, drunkards, float like bees.
A stranger sadly snaps a shot
of the metropolis by night;
a cab with squeamish passengers
jolts loudly to Ordynka Street,
and dead men stand in close embrace
with private homes.

'Nature Morte', one of Brodsky's most complex metaphysical meditations –
and ultimately one of his most affirmative statements of the significance of the
Christian faith – is deeply suggestive of the despair and reification of temporal
existence. The whole universe is depicted in the poem as a wasteland in which
all existence is reduced to objectified thinghood. Its condition is that of still
life; it is a 'nature morte' of things and objects in which all life is reduced to
the condition of inanimate being. The poet surveys a desolate landscape, dessi-
cated and bleak, where death is all-pervasive, indicating the wholly destructive
impact of time. Life, again, is identified with speech and with light, death with
silence and darkness:

People and things crowd in.
Eyes can be bruised and hurt
by people as well as things.
Better to live in the dark.

I sit on a wooden bench
watching the passers-by –
sometimes whole families.
I am fed up with the light.

This is a winter month.
First on the calendar.
I shall begin to speak
when I'm fed up with the dark.

Life is, seemingly, a futile struggle against silence; man is speechless in an
apparently meaningless universe. The spirit in its torment, its 'eyes bruised

and hurt', withdraws into darkness and solitude, rejecting the light of faith. The poet chooses nonetheless to speak, 'It is better to speak', but he wonders: 'What shall I talk about?' 'Shall I talk about nothingness? 'Shall I talk about days or nights?/ Or people?' 'No,' he tells himself, 'only things/ since people will surely die./ All of them. As I shall.' He finds human life abhorrent, in his despair seeing 'things' as the only enduring reality:

> My blood is very cold –
> its cold is more withering
> than iced to-the-bottom streams.
> People are not my thing.
>
> I hate the look of them
> Grafted to life's great tree,
> each face is firmly stuck
> and cannot be torn free.
>
> Something the mind abhors
> showing in each face and form.
> Something like flattery
> of persons quite unknown.

He feels the essence of death in his own being, feels its cold blood flowing through his veins, as he dwells on the all-destructive impact of time: 'Dust is the flesh of time/ Time's very flesh and blood.' He is immobilised in his contemplation of death and mortality: 'I do not move. These two/ thighs are like blocks of ice./ Branched veins show blue against/ skin that is marble white.' Feeling the process of decay within himself, he wonders if speech itself will be reduced to the stillness of death … 'things drop away from man's/ world – a world made with words.' He compares death to a woman who comes to hold her lover in a lethal embrace. All life seems gripped in this embrace, its impact being graphically conveyed in the epigraph from Cesare Pavese with which the poem began and which is repeated in the ninth stanza – 'Death, when it comes,/ will have your own two eyes':

> A thing. Its brown colour. Its
> blurry outline. Twilight.
> Now there is nothing left.
> Only a *nature morte*.
>
> Death will come and will find
> a body whose silent peace

will reflect death's approach
like any woman's face.

Scythe, skull and skeleton –
an absurd pack of lies.
Rather: 'Death, when it comes,
will have your own two eyes.'

The feelings of alienation and despair which are given expression in 'Nature Morte' reach their lowest depths in 'Lagoon', a poem Brodsky wrote in Venice shortly after his departure from the USSR for a life of exile in the West. Grieving for his homeland and his loved ones – his elderly parents and his child – he once again confronts the meaninglessness and apparent futility of all mortal existence. Helpless and alone, he gazes on the famed and beautiful lagoon in Venice, seeing it as a watery wasteland where a ship (a metaphor for life) drifts aimlessly, driven by a cruel and vengeful God – not the benign and loving God of the scriptures but the classical Fates who determine human destinies arbitrarily and mercilessly. The Crucifixion imagery reinforces the poet's personal sense of self-torment and martyrdom:

Down in the lobby three elderly women, bored,
take up, with their knitting, the Passion of Our Lord
as the universe and the tiny realm
of the *pension* Accademia, side by side,
with TV blaring, sail into Christmastide,
a lookout desk clerk at the helm.

And a nameless lodger, a nobody, boards the boat,
a bottle of grappa concealed in his raincoat
as he gains his shadowy room, bereaved
of memory, homeland, son, with only the noise
of distant forests to grieve for his former joys,
if anyone is grieved.

The poem abounds in images of death. The octopus, a monstrous creature and an age-old symbol of predatory, death-giving power, here represents Time as the destroyer of Life. The winged lion who drowns in the flood waters, its paws arranged in the form of a hammer and sickle, is the Lion of Revelations, now become a rapacious beast, symbolising the most barbaric regime in the history of mankind. The stagnant waters of the lagoon and the decaying splendour of Venetian architecture reinforce the general spectacle of a civilisation in decline, mirroring the spiritual emptiness and gloom in the poet's soul. However, as he walks the streets, alone in the darkness, he sees a momentary glimmer of light, symbolising the light of hope and faith. He affirms a truth, repeatedly stressed by his mentors, Kierkegaard and Shestov: faith springs from despair, is born of hopelessness. 'Credo quia absurdum est', a favourite saying of Shestov's, could well summarise the affirmation of faith on which the poem concludes:

> Night in St Mark's piazza. A face as creased
> as a finger from its fettering ring released,
> biting a nail, is gazing high
> into that *nowhere* of pure thought, where sight
> is baffled by the bandages of night,
> serene, beyond the naked eye.
>
> where, past all boundaries and all predicates,
> black, white, or colorless, vague, volatile states,
> something, some object, comes to mind.
> Perhaps a body. In our dim days and few,
> the speed of light equals a fleeting view,
> even when blackout robs us blind.

'As a theme,' Brodsky wrote in 'The Keening Muse', 'death is a good litmus test for a poet's ethics.'[65] In another context he stated, rather significantly, that 'death as a theme always produces a self-portrait'.[66] On the elegy genre (one of his favourites) he wrote: 'Every "on the death" poem, as a rule, serves not only as a means for the author to express his sentiments occasioned by a loss but also as a pretext for more or less general speculations on the phenomenon of death per se ... In other words, any "on the death of" poem contains an element of self-portrait.' Rather cryptically, he added the comment, 'death is always a song of innocence and never of experience' – pointing to the inexplicable mysteriousness of the prospect of death itself.[67] Yet he sees a special role for art in penetrating its mystery. In his essay, 'In the Shadow of Dante', he writes: 'If art does anything ... it undertakes to reflect those few elements of existence which transcend life, extend it beyond its terminal point ... In other words, art "imitates" death rather than life; i.e., it imitates the realm of which life supplies no notion.'[68]

The elegies Brodsky addressed to his fellow-poets – Donne, Eliot, Auden and Lowell – dramatically illustrate the truth of these statements and demonstrate further the manner in which he sees faith as being disclosed by the contemplation of mortality, however dispiriting that activity might be in terms of personal self-torment and angst. The Donne elegy opens with a serene image of the sleepfulness in which the whole universe appears to be enveloped. The opening verses describe a sleeping world of houses and streets, a harbour where ships rest peacefully, and a snow-covered landscape, the whiteness and quietness of which are suggestive of the peacefulness of death. 'John Donne has sunk in sleep ... all things beside/ are sleeping too: walls, bed, and floor – all sleep/ ... Yes, all things sleep. The window. Snow beyond/ ... Even God has gone to sleep. Earth is estranged./ Eyes do not see, and ears perceive no sound.' In the darkness the recently dead poet calls out to his soul whose voice he hears in the silence:

> 'Whose sobs are those? My angel, is it you?
> Do you await my coming, there alone
> beneath the snow? Walking – without my love –
> in darkness home? Do you cry in the gloom?'
> No answer. – 'Is it you, o cherubim,
> whose muted tears put me in mind
> of some sepulchral choir? Have you resolved
> to quit my sleeping church? Is it not you?'
> No answer. – 'Is it you, O Paul? Your voice
> most certainly is coarsened by stern speech.
> Have you not bowed your grey head in the gloom
> to weep?' But only silence makes reply.
> 'Is that the Hand which looms up everywhere
> to shield a grieving glance in the deep dark?
> Is it not thou, Lord? No, my thought runs wild.
> And yet how lofty is the voice that weeps.'

The poem reflects the contradictory thoughts which death elicits in the mind of the poet. He finds death abhorrent and fearsome, is repelled by its primordial darkness, loneliness and gloom ('Who is there in this world to share our death?'), yet equally he is attracted by the prospect of release from his earthly torment. The concluding sequence of the poem shows Donne in his burial shroud, its cloth symbolising the material boundary between time and the timeless. Its images anticipate the rebirth of the soul in eternity. The star shining through the clouds represents the light of faith that has sustained the poet's soul through his mortal torments:

> Like some great bird, he sleeps in his own nest,
> his pure path and his thirst for purer life,
> himself entrusting to that steady star

which now is closed in clouds. And like a bird,
his soul is pure, and his life's path on earth,
although it needs must wind through sin, is still
closer to nature than that tall crow's nest
which soars above the starlings' empty homes.
Like some great bird, he too will wake at dawn;
but now he lies beneath a veil of white,
while snow and sleep stitch up the throbbing void
between his soul and his own dreaming flesh ...
Sleep, John Donne, sleep. Sleep soundly, do not fret
your soul. As for your coat, it's torn; all limp
it hangs. But see, there from the clouds will shine
that Star which made your world endure till now.

The fear of death endures, however, despite the consolations of faith. 'For Brodsky,' Yury Kublanovsky has written, 'the elucidation of his relationship to Time is a sort of ersatz catharsis.' 'To overcome death is impossible,' he writes. 'The fear of death is not personal; it takes in the whole of humanity, but, of course, fear for one's own personal survival does play a part.'[69] Since mortality cannot be overcome, the indulgence of the fear of death becomes a necessary catharsis. This is evident in Brodsky's 'Verses on the Death of T.S. Eliot', a work he wrote in Norenskaya, within days of Eliot's death in January 1965. Time is 'demonised' in this poem – to adopt the term employed by Kublanovsky – its destructive and fearsome character being continually emphasised. The poet's death is seen as an escape from imprisonment in Time – 'And he had shut the door on the chain of years ...' – its cold and merciless destructiveness reinforced by the severe winter conditions existing at the time of his death. The sea imagery, symbolising eternity in Eliot's poetry, is replicated in the opening sequence of the poem.

It was not God, but only time, mere time
that called him. The young tribe of giant waves
will bear the burden of his flight until
it strikes the far edge of its flowering fringe,
to bid a slow farewell, breaking against
the limit of the earth. Exuberant
in strength, it laughs, a January gulf
in that dry land of days where we remain.

There are echoes here of 'The Dry Salvages' ... 'The river is within us, the sea is all about us/ The sea is the land's edge also.' In an interview with

Solomon Volkov Brodsky spoke of time as metaphorically emerging from water, i.e., from the timeless. He spoke of an 'idée fixe' 'he had 'regarding time and water': 'The change of year, the change of time, time emerges from the water ... it's pure metaphysics.'[70] Faith, love, memory and the Word are the forces that can overcome time. This is the message conveyed in the third part of the Eliot elegy. Apollo's garland, he says, 'will be this poet's crown', his 'pledge of immortality'; 'hill and dale will honour him'. 'Forests will not forget ... voice of lyre and rush of feet.' Love and faith will survive the ravages of time in the land of the dead:

> Thomas Stearns, don't dread the sheep,
> or the reaper's deadly sweep.
> If you're not recalled by stone,
> puffball drift will make you known.

> Thus it is that love takes flight.
> Once for all. Into the night.
> Cutting through all words and cries,
> seen no more, and yet alive.

> You have gone where others are.
> We, in envy of your star,
> call that vast and hidden room,
> thoughtlessly, 'the realm of gloom.'

> Wood and field will not forget.
> All that lives will know you yet –
> as the body holds in mind
> lost caress of lips and arms.

Time and death are inextricably linked in mortal existence, yet both disclose the prospect of salvation and release into the timeless. 'What is Salvation', Brodsky asks in his 'Elegy: for Robert Lowell', since 'a tear magnifies like glass/ a future perfect tense', pointing to the mysterious interrelation of tragedy and hopefulness which defines the mortal state, that whole mystery being most sharply focussed in the event of death itself. Ultimately what conquers time is love, the force which informs and defines the timeless and the infinite – whose source is God. This is the affirmation on which Brodsky concludes his poem 'York: In Memoriam W.H. Auden'. In 'To Please A Shadow' he wrote: 'While in the flesh, this man did so much that belief in the immortality of his soul becomes somehow unavoidable. What he left us with amounts

to a gospel which is both brought about by and filled with love that's anything
but finite – with love, that is, which can in no way all be harboured by human
flesh and which therefore needs words.'[71] The poem concludes by affirming
the ultimacy-of love. In death the source of love – which is God – is united
with its object, man; the disembodied soul, released from its torment, is
reunited with its Creator. The infinity of love, in turn, finds permanent form
in the poetic word:

> ... And the willow herb's vertical stalk
> is longer than the ancient Roman road,
> heading north, forgotten by all at Rome.
> Subtracting the greater from the lesser – time from man –
> you get words, the remainder, standing out against their
> white background more clearly than the body
> ever manages to while it lives, though it cry 'Catch me!' –
> thus the source of love turns into the object of love.

'THERE ON THE CROSS I SHALL NOT CRY OUT ...'

> There, on the cross
> I shall not cry out, 'Why hast Thou forsaken me?'
> I shall not transform myself into glad tidings!
> Inasmuch as pain is not a breaking of the rules:
> suffering is
> a faculty of bodies
> and a man is an endurer of pain.
> But man can know neither his own limit
> nor the limits of pain.

Salvation through suffering, faith and love is the central Christian theme in
Brodsky's poetry. Acceptance of suffering, as the lines quoted from
'Conversation With a Celestial Being' would suggest, is seen in his work as the
fundamental manifestation of the Christian outlook on life. The poem's variation on Christ's last words to his Father is almost certainly intended to reaffirm the Shestovian and Kierkegaardian dictum that from despair comes faith
and that for a Christian the sense of Godforsakenness is to be seen, like the
sufferings of Abraham and Job, as the basis of hope and trust in the mysteriousness of God's will. In the same poem Brodsky declared that 'all faith
amounts to no more than/ a one-way correspondence', suggesting that the
man of faith continues to believe despite the absence of a response to his

prayer, and despite the overwhelming sense of God's absence that has to be endured in mortal life. This perhaps is the significance of the epigraph from Milosz which Brodsky cited on the opening pages of *Less Than One:* 'And the heart doesn't die when one thinks it should.' In its despair and loneliness the soul finds its true freedom. In an early poem, 'Shestviye' ('The Procession') Brodsky wrote: 'We are all approaching the time/ of immeasurable loneliness of the soul/ ... to pass off loneliness for freedom.' His words echo those of Shestov in an essay on Berdyaev: 'Freedom comes to man not from knowledge but from faith, which puts an end to all our fears.'[72]

The interrelation of suffering, despair and faith is dramatically underlined in 'Isaac and Abraham', Brodsky's poetic reconstruction of the Genesis story of Abraham's proposed sacrificing of his son, Isaac, in accordance with the test of faith imposed on him by God. Isaac, a precursor of Christ, is portrayed as the sacrificial lamb, the innocent martyr, who goes to his death in fear and dread of the nothingness to which the fire will reduce him. The image of a star-lit sky symbolises the regenerative powers of faith and is contrasted in the poem with the bleakness of the desert and mountain landscape to which Abraham brings his son to perform the act of sacrifice. Clearly drawing on Kierkegaard's *Fear and Trembling* – a philosophical interpretation of the same story – Brodsky underlines the irrationality of the act of faith. Abraham, like Job, accepts God's will unquestioningly, despite its evident injustice, arbitrariness and absurdity, and this is his salvation. He echoes the words of Shestov: 'It is when a man comes to feel the utter impossibility of living with reason that faith arises in him.'[73] The poem further underlines the Christian principle that faith comes from love, a truth dramatically affirmed in the final image of Isaac reconciled with his father in a loving embrace.

Redemption through suffering, faith and love is the Christian message also conveyed in 'Gorbunov and Gorchakov'. The former is explicitly identified with Christ at various points in the work. 'How strange that Gorbunov, nailed to the cross,/ must look for help from Gorchakov below,' the latter cries. 'If mountains are to be your leitmotif, then think about Golgotha,' Gorchakov charges his friend. Gorbunov's name, probably derived from the Russian word 'gorbun', meaning 'cripple' or 'hunchback', is evocative of his state of physical and mental torment, his existence being represented as akin to Christ's journey to Calvary. In his torment he dreams of chanterelles, which he associates with love and freedom. The following exchange occurs in Canto 2:

'Your chanterelles are hazards to the sane.
Beware, they're far from harmless, Gorbunov.
How much importance do you give to them?'
'As much as I give love.' 'And what is love?'

'The end to loneliness.' 'The very end?'
'It's being able, once, to stand above
the bed and, by just bending over in
the silence, with your hands, brow, breath, touch life.'
'What are you staring at? The stars? The lane?'
'The opposite of empty narrative.'

Love is the life-force of Gorbunov's existence; his dreams of love sustain
him in his misery: 'Whenever I see toadstools in the grass/ or forest floor, I
find that I recall,/ well, love.' He continues: 'It's in the mind, or blood, perhaps, / for always like an echo, dim but real,/ I feel it.' His religious faith is
the object of continual mockery by Gorchakov (the latter's name is derived
from the Russian work, 'gorkii', meaning 'bitter' – one who embitters the lives
of others.) The third canto of the poem concludes with a moving prayer to
God by Gorbunov. He begs God to grant him victory over silence, i.e., over
death and nothingness. He pleads for a 'listener' from heaven to take the place
of his tormentor, Gorchakov. His prayer is uttered in two voices, reflecting his
inner struggle with past and future time. Memories of past love intrude on his
hopes and fears for the future:

O God in heaven, if you're so designed
that you can listen to two voices blast
at once from but one set of lips and find
in them not noise but strife between the past
and future, raise to you my coughing mind
and plant its microbes where your light is cast.
Divide among them with your mighty hand
the sum of these convulsive thoughts and days.
And leave the fraction of me left behind
to triumph over silence then, at least.

Gorbunov accepts his suffering resignedly, believing that the greater his
torment in mortal life the more hopeful his prospects will be on Judgement
Day: 'Besides, the tougher life a mortal's found/ the smoother things will
seem on Judgement Day.' He looks forward to a release from his suffering in
eternity: 'We cannot carry on into the next/ the burden we, in this life, have
to bear.' For a Christian, he says, death is synonymous with life. This is what
Christ's death signifies: 'And thus His life's the one thing that admits/ two
meanings ... It's, therefore, a synonym.' Christ-like in his meekness, he forgives Gorchakov for betraying him. In his final farewell monologue to
Gorbunov, Gorchakov in turn implores his friend to forgive his betrayal; he

promises to cherish his memory and his faith in the immortality of the spirit. He imagines Gorbunov as a Christ-like figure, walking on the waves ... 'You wander wave-filled hallways ... Fishes stare/ with dumb expressions out of every door.' Gorbunov himself had envisaged this prospect shortly before his death. His faith was expressed also in the beautiful lyrical imagery of the sea, the symbol of eternal life. Like the speaker in 'Conversation with a Celestial Being' he does not cry out 'why hast thou forsaken me?', his mind being focussed totally on his hopes of eternal bliss:

> 'My soul's too weak for calling. From now on,
> wherever fate sees fit for me to be,
> from Paradise to squatting in the john,
> not painted walls but waves are what I'll see.
> And that's not bragging, Gorchakov. A man
> like me, in such celestial disarray,
> well, what would he be pleading for? For one
> who hath the ears to hear, artillery
> repeat of waves is far more pleasant than
> a tearful prayer that this cup pass from me.'

The sea imagery of 'Gorbunov and Gorchakov' is a good instance of the influence of Acmeist aesthetics in Brodsky's poetry, its ultimate purpose being to provide material attestation of God's presence in earthly being. This is made evident again in the star-imagery of Brodsky's cycle of Christmas poems which is explicitly symbolic of the rebirth of the spirit signified in the mystery of the Incarnation. For the Acmeists the most dramatic manifestation of God's presence in material being was the Incarnation of Christ as Man. Thus, in the poem entitled '24 December 1971' Brodsky affirms his faith in Christ, suggesting that the ultimate significance of his birth lies in the rebirth of the individual soul made possible by the miracle of the Incarnation. The coming of Christ is heralded by the presence of a lone star in the sky:

> Snow is falling: not smoking but sounding
> chimney pots on the roof, every face like a stain.
> Herod drinks. Every wife hides her child.
> He who comes is a mystery: features
> are not known beforehand, men's hearts may
> not be quick to distinguish the stranger.
>
> But when drafts through the doorway disperse
> the thick mist of the hours of darkness

and a shape in a shawl stands revealed,
both a newborn and Spirit that's Holy
in your self you discover; you stare
skyward, and it's right there:
a star.

The lines recall Brodsky's comment in his essay, 'To Please a Shadow', that if a poet wishes to 'praise the Lord' he has to 'employ indirect speech'; he must 'praise the Creator by worshipping his creation'.[74] The radical lyricism of those poems in which he strongly reflects the influence of Acmeist poetics demonstrates this principle vividly. In 'Hills' for example, he writes: 'Hills are eternal glory./ They stand stock still on parade/ aside from all our sufferings.' And in 'Verses Under an Epigraph' he declares: 'In every music/ there is Bach,/ in each of us/ there is God.' A short lyric written in 1964, probably in Norenskaya, beautifully conveys the spirit of the Acmeist creed:

In villages God does not live only
in icon corners, as the scoffers claim,
but plainly, everywhere. He sanctifies
each roof and pan, divides each double door.
In villages God acts abundantly –
cooks lentils in iron pots on Saturdays,
dances a lazy jig in flickering flames,
and winks at me, witness to all of this.
He plants a hedge, and gives away a bride
(the groom's a forester), and, for a joke,
he makes it certain that the game warden
will never hit the duck he's shooting at.

The chance to know and witness all of this,
amidst the whistling of the autumn mist,
is, I would say, the only touch of bliss
that's open to a village atheist.

In 'A Keening Muse' Brodsky suggests that the infinity the poet seeks is ultimately the infinity of love.[75] The complex disclosure of the infinitude of divine love through the experience of earthly love is a central theme in many of his poems, as it was in those of his Acmeist predecessors, particularly Akhmatova. Her love poems, he wrote in 'The Keening Muse', 'suggest not so much the recurrence of passion as the frequency of prayer'.[76] The complexities of this whole issue are explored in two major poems by Brodsky, the previously discussed 'Nature Morte' and 'Adieu, Mademoiselle Véronique'. As was indicated previously, the central opposition in 'Nature Morte' lies between people and things, the reduction of the human spirit to the condition of 'thinghood' being represented as the main cause of man's alienation and despair. That process was seen as the inevitable consequence of the temporal finitude of mortal life but it is shown to be transcended by the potency of love, man's capacity to reach beyond the finite and penetrate the sphere of the infinite. In the final section of the poem the ideal of time-transcendence is identified with the person of Christ, the mystery of the Incarnation being seen to signify the transcendence of the dualistic opposition of human and divine love. This is conveyed in a sequence in which Mary addresses the dying Christ on the cross. Between them exists what Lev Loseff has called 'a mystical communion that supersedes the life-death dilemma.'[77] To her entreaties, 'Are you my son? – or God?' he responds: 'Whether dead or alive,/ woman, it's all the same – /son or God, I am thine.' His words affirm the ultimacy of love, its sublimation of earthly finitude, its assurance of eternal salvation. The significance of the Christian mystery of the Incarnation is its attestation of the infinity of love. This was given expression by Tolstoy through the dying reflections of Prince Andrei: 'Love is the essence of the soul ... Love hinders death. Love is life ... Everything is, everything exists, only because I love. Everything is united by it alone.' The lines in which this is affirmed in 'Nature Morte' are amongst the most moving in all of Brodsky's poetry:

> Mary now speaks to Christ:
> 'Are you my son? – or God?
> You are nailed to the cross.
> Where lies my homeward road?
>
> Can I pass through my gate
> not having understood:
> Are you dead? – or alive?
> Are you my son? – or God?'
>
> Christ speaks to her in turn:
> 'Whether dead or alive,
> woman, it's all the same –
> son or God, I am thine.'

But love is complex and conflict-ridden and the experiences it generates are fraught with tragedy and suffering. The importance of Brodsky's work amongst that of contemporary Russian poets, Yakov Gordin said, is that it restored tragic awareness to Russian poetry. 'After a few decades of our Soviet reality, he wrote, 'Russian poetry has lost one cultural imperative, and as far as Russian literature is concerned, a seemingly genetic inherent factor and one without which man is not fully conscious of his own humanity – a tragic perception of the world.' 'Soviet literature,' he concludes, 'has cultivated a non-tragic perception of life.'[78] Tragic awareness in Brodsky's poetry is especially manifested in his treatment of the relationship of human and divine love. Like Donne and Akhmatova before him, he simultaneously emphasises their inherent conflicts and their ultimate compatibility. In 'Adieu Mademoiselle Véronique', a poem strongly reflecting the influence of Pasternak's second Mary Magdalene poem (Pasternak is the 'lame poet' referred to in the eighth stanza), Brodsky recalls an early love affair, seeing its ending and the consequent separation from the loved one as symbolic of the mortality of all earthly loves. The parting from a loved one, he suggests, foreshadows the final separation from the whole of mortal life that comes with death and is thus an intimation of the tragedy that attends all earthly relationships. He recalls the cold passionless withdrawal of love that marked the ending of the relationship. 'A pose such as yours, though not so intended/ is a most fitting symbol of our existence,' he writes. 'It's an apotheosis of men as objects.' The suffering of emotional separation and loss is associated with the sufferings of Christ on the cross in the third stanza of the poem:

> In manners and morals this counts as progress.
> In some twenty years I shall fetch the armchair
> that you sat on, facing me, on Good Friday
> when, for Christ's body, the cross's torments
> at last were ended; you sat and folded
> your arms – on that fifth day of Holy Week – looking
> like some new Napoleon exiled on Elba.
> Palm fronds glowed golden at every crossing.
> You laid down your arms on your grass-green garment,
> avoiding the open-armed risk of passion.

The association of the poet's emotional pain with the sufferings of Christ points to the true significance of the experience recalled in the poem. Human love, in all its forms, through its celebration of the otherness of material existence, attests to the presence of the infinite in all being, but it remains time-bound and mortal in itself. It discloses the reality of a higher love, being inherently characterised by the infinitude towards which it aspires, while also being conditioned, tragically and inevitably, by its mortal time-bound character. It is at once therefore a focus for suffering and faith: the suffering deriv-

ing from the conflicting emotions it embodies, the faith from the ultimate reality that it discloses. That reality is the totally selfless love epitomised in the
Person of Christ – the ideal towards which all love aspires. The eighth stanza
of the poem affirms unambiguously the transcendent character of Christ's selfless act of loving self-sacrifice, contrasting it directly with the mortality and
finitude of human love:

> In our past there is greatness – but prose in our future.
> For one asks no more from an empty armchair
> than one would from you who once sat upon it
> as calm as the waters of Lago di Garda.
> crossing your arms, as I've already written.
> The total of all of to-day's embraces
> gives far less of love than the outstretched arms of
> Christ on the cross. This lame poet's finding
> looms before me in Holy Week, sixty-seven,
> blocking my leap to the nineteen-nineties.

The lines directly echo Pasternak's words in 'Mary Magdalene II'.
Addressing Christ, Mary says: 'Your arms will spread out to the ends of the
cross/ To embrace too many.' Brodsky's faith in the infinite love of Christ is
the basis of his own redemptive hope: '... if only it isn't a lie they've told
me,/ and old Lazarus rose from the dead in truth, then/ I too shall rise ...'
That great love epitomised in the Person of Christ is also the ultimate source
of poetic creativity. This is the final affirmation towards which the poem proceeds. 'Such a high and elaborate style proves only/ that the poet belongs to a
major power,' he declares at the end of the poem. Though he cannot regain
the love he shared with Mademoiselle Véronique ('My pen cannot reach you
...'), he can *recreate* it through memory in his poetry. Inspired by the loss of
love, his poem gives meaning to that loss. Symbolically, therefore, he seeks the
hand of his beloved so that he can illuminate their love through his poetry. It
is the memory of their separation that makes the whole experience meaningful,
just as death, the final separation, and man's gateway to the infinite, makes the
whole of life meaningful. This is the theme conveyed in the final stanza of the
poem:

> My pen cannot reach you. You're cloud-like, fleeting.
> The shape of a girl, for each man, is surely
> his soul's shape – you, Muse, can confirm this richly –
> implying love's source but, alas, love's ruin,
> for souls have no bodies. Which means that you are

still farther away. And my pen can't reach you.
So give me your hand as we part. That's better
than nothing. Our parting is solemn, lofty,
since it is forever. The zither's silent.
Forever is not a word, but a number

whose unending zeroes, when grass grows above us,
will stretch out beyond our small time, our epoch.

Brodsky's reassertion of the meaning-giving powers of the poetic word, and its permanence amidst flux and change, is full of significance for the final issue to be addressed in his chapter: the future of Christianity in the dramatically changed conditions that obtain following the great cultural, social and political upheavals that have occurred in the present century.

'AFTER THE END': CHRISTIANITY AND THE FUTURE

Forgive me – as a poet, as a man,
O meek God of misery,
as a sinner and as son of my time
or more precisely a stepson of the era.

Brodsky's words from one of his early lyrics intimate his deep disaffection with life in the conditions of the present epoch in time. In a closely related prose work he described himself as 'a citizen of a second-rate epoch'. and in another again as 'a spy, a spearhead/ for some fifth column of a rotting culture'.[79] His disaffection was rooted firstly in predictable feelings of hostility towards the tyranny of the Soviet regime (which he sees as typifying political tyranny in all its forms) and towards the ideology of Marxism which brought it into being. It was rooted, secondly, in a more fundamental disillusionment with the spirit of scientific rationalism – of which Marxism was itself a product – which, like Milosz, he saw as the dominant force in European culture since the Enlightenment. Both he saw as endangering the future of European civilisation as a whole, particularly the Judaeo-Christian and classical traditions which constitute its cultural foundation. A large number of poems are devoted to these themes – the themes of 'Empire' and 'After the End' – in many of which the future of the classical-Christian heritage is addressed, either implicitly or explicitly.

Reference was made in an earlier section to the sordid and gloom-ridden picture of Soviet life that is projected in several of the poems from Brodsky's

'Christmas Cycle'. Lines were cited from 'A Christmas Ballad' in which images of drunks and sleep-walkers on Moscow's streets, together with images of crowds of shoppers oblivious to the spirit of the Christmas season, evoke the apathy and inertia of life under a totalitarian regime. Another of the Christmas poems, '1 January, 1965', describes the poet's dejection as he contemplates the stark realities of Soviet life from his exile in Norenskaya, the image of a dark starless sky symbolising the spiritual deadness of the environment in which he is forced to live. These themes are linked in a third of the Christmas poems, 'Anno Domini', with the image of 'Empire', a poetic analogue for political tyranny throughout history. In his prose Brodsky frequently cites precedents from history for the tyranny of the Soviet state: e.g., Peter the Great, the rulers of ancient Rome, Herod the Great etc. In 'Anno Domini' the Roman Governor-General, a bloated, corrupt and pathetic caricature of the power-driven bureaucrat, celebrates the feast of Saturnalia in his mansion in a Roman colony. He is a prototypical image of all political tyrants, his physical decline (he is dying from liver disease) mirroring the moral decay of the whole society over which he rules. The poem proclaims the transience of all temporal power – 'the grave will render all alike./ So, if only in our lifetime, let us be various' – and affirms the survival of the spiritual and the sacred despite the abuses of temporal power. The images of political corruption give way to an image of the light and hopefulness that comes with the emergence of Christianity, signalling the end of paganism and the tyranny to which it gave birth:

> I watch the moon's disk glide
> over the sparsely growing trees, and see
> Cynthia, the snow; the Governor-General's, where
> he struggles silently all night with his illness
> and keeps the fire lit, to see his enemy.
>
> The enemy withdraws. The faint light of day
> barely breaking in the world's East,
> creeps through the window, straining
> to see what is happening within,
> and, coming across the remnants of the feast,
> falters. But continues on its way.

History, however, as Brodsky recognises, has seen the reemergence of political tyranny in new guises, the most fearsome of which is that of the totalitarian regimes of the twentieth century. In *Less Than One* he describes the total suppression of individual freedom which the Bolshevik Revolution brought about in the USSR: 'This country ... had all the makings of a cultural, spiritual paradise, a real vessel of civilisation. Instead, it became a drab hell, with a shabby materialist dogma and pathetic consumerist gropings.' He continues: 'Existence as such, monotonous in itself, has been reduced to uniform rigidity by the centralised state. What was left to watch were faces, weather, buildings; also, the language people used.'[80] Significantly, he attributes the decline of Russian society to the long-standing corrosion of its cultural traditions resulting from the influence of Enlightenment rationalism, and its ideological offspring, Marxism: 'At that time I didn't know yet that all this was a result of the age of reason and progress, of the age of mass production, I ascribed it to the state and partly to the nation itself, which would go for anything that does not require imagination.'[81] More fundamentally, like Tolstoy and Dostoevsky before him, he argues that the corruption of any society cannot be blamed on ideology alone, but must ultimately be attributed to the potentiality for evil present in the nature of humankind. In a recent exchange with Vaclav Havel, the President of the Czech Republic, Brodsky described the communist nightmare as, in the final analysis, simply a product of human depravity. Responding to Havel's claim that the West generally ignored developments in Eastern Europe, viewing them quite cynically as merely a political 'inconvenience', Brodsky suggests that what the West really saw in the East was a mirror image of its own 'evilness' which it could contemplate safely from a distance:

> For neither the Communist nor the post-Communist nightmare amounts to an inconvenience, since it helped, helps, and will for quite some time help the democratic world to externalize evil. And not the democratic world only. To quite a few of us who lived in that nightmare, and especially those who fought it, its presence was a source of considerable moral comfort. For one who fights or resists evil almost automatically perceives oneself as good and skips self-analysis. So perhaps it's time – for us and the world at large, democratic or not – to scrub the term communism from the human reality of Eastern Europe so one can recognise that reality for what it is: a mirror. For that is what human evil always is ... It's not for me to tell you that what you call 'communism' was a breakdown of humanity, and not a political problem, a problem of our species, and thus of a lingering nature.[82]

Seen in these terms, the communist experience assumes a menacing significance for the future of humankind and the survival of its cultural traditions. The forces that brought it into being – the forces of scientific rationalism – continue to dominate European society and inevitably point to the advance-

ment of the secularised culture that threatens the future of the classical
Christian traditions that have for centuries represented the bedrock of its civilisation. Brodsky speaks of 'the catastrophe that occurred in our part of the
world' as 'the first cry of mass society: a cry as it were from the world's future
… not an -ism but a chasm suddenly gaping in the human heart to swallow up
honesty, compassion, civility, justice …'[83] Ominous signs of that process were
detected by Brodsky in an event that occurred in Leningrad in the 1960s. He
saw the destruction of a Greek Orthodox Church in the heart of the city to
make way for a modern concert hall as symbolising the destruction of the centuries old traditions which the Church, with its magnificent onion domes and
icons, represented. The poem's title, 'A Halt in the Desert', was probably
inspired by the work, 'A Rest on the Flight into Egypt' by the sixteenth century painter, Orazio Gentileschi. The poem begins:

> So few Greeks live in Leningrad today
> that we have razed a Greek church, to make space
> for a new concert hall, built in today's
> grim and unhappy style. And yet a con-
> cert hall with more than fifteen hundred seats
> is not so grim a thing. And who's to blame
> if virtuosity has more appeal
> than the worn banners of an ancient faith?
> Still, it is sad that from this distance now
> we see, not the familiar onion domes,
> but a grotesquely flattened silhouette.
> Yet men are not so heavily in debt
> to the grim ugliness of balanced forms
> as to the balanced forms of ugliness.

Ostensibly, the church is being demolished because there are few Greeks
left in Leningrad – most of them having been the victims of political proscription during World War II. Its destruction is doubly significant because, being
Greek, it embodies the traditions of Hellenistic culture as well as those of the
Judaeo-Christian heritage and might be said therefore to symbolise the entire
cultural foundation on which European civilisation is based. The event
prompts a meditation by the poet on the nature of historical progress; he suggests that a whole phase in history may now be reaching its end. In the crumbling ruins of the church he sees not merely the demise of Orthodoxy but the
horrifying prospect of life in a post-Christian future. 'From which are we now
more remote – the world of ancient Greece, or Orthodoxy?' he asks. 'Does a
new epoch wait for us?' The question he poses is the one asked by Blok in

'The Twelve'. 'What lies ahead?' The latter's reply was: 'Ahead – is Jesus Christ.' Brodsky's question, by contrast with Blok's, remains unanswered:

> Tonight I stare out through the black window
> and think about that point to which we've come,
> and then I ask myself: from which are we
> now more remote – the world of ancient Greece,
> or Orthodoxy? Which is closer now?
> What lies ahead? Does a new epoch wait
> for us? And, if it does, what duty do we owe? –
> What sacrifices must we make for it?

The decline of Christian civilisation is viewed as a fearsome prospect by Brodsky, involving nothing less than the moral collapse of the whole contemporary social order. The poetic device employed to evoke the horror of a post-Christian future is its imaginative reconstruction in terms of the pre-Christian past, a process itself highly suggestive of the cyclical character of history. In Brodsky's play, *Marbles*, the collapse of the moral order in ancient Rome is seen to prefigure a similar process in the post-Christian epoch that seems to lie ahead. The play is described as a Platonic dialogue set 'two centuries after our era in ancient Rome'. The thematic imagery of marble suggests the reified, stone-like, petrified character of life in a pre/ post-Christian society. In their tower where they enjoy 'a shortage of space compensated by a surplus of time', and where yesterday is the same as today and tomorrow, its two characters, Publius and Tullius, debate the nature of freedom, reality and political power. History is cyclic, Tullius suggests, because human behaviour is so predictable, especially in the realm of evil:

> To slit a throat, Publius, well even a legionary can master that. And to die *pro patria* too. As well as to expand the territory. As well as to suffer ... But all that's a cliche. That, Publius, has taken place already. Worse still: that will take place again. Anew, that is. In that sense, history doesn't have that many options. As well as its subjects. Because man, you know, is limited. One can squeeze out of him only so much. Like milk from a cow. Only five liters, for instance, if it comes to blood. He, Publius, is predictable. Like the house that Jack built, like a vicious circle. *De capo el fine*.

In their dialogues Publius and Tullius emphasise the absurdity of the whole temporal order. Inhabiting an Empire created in the name of reason, theirs is an inertialised and meaningless existence, which is represented in the play as the logical culmination of a purely rationalist or secularist vision of human fulfilment. In his Preface to Platonov's *The Foundation Pit* Brodsky described the idea of a purely earthly fulfilment as 'a dead end.' 'It is the last vision of space,' he wrote, 'the end of things, the summit of the mountain, the peak from which there is nowhere to step – except into Chronos, in connection with which the concept of eternal life arises.' 'The same,' he declared, 'may be said of Hell.'[84] That theme is reiterated in several poems on the 'Empire 'theme' – 'Post aetatem nostram', 'Lithuanian Divertissement', 'Letters to a Roman Friend', 'Torso', 'Lullaby of Cape Cod'. The soulless horror of a purely secularised existence is evoked in the imagery of marble in the opening stanzas of 'Torso':

> If suddenly you walk on grass turned stone
> and think its marble handsomer than green,
> or see at play a nymph and faun that seem
> happier in bronze than in any dream,
> let your walking stick fall from your weary hand,
> you're in the Empire, friend.
>
> Air, fire, water, fauns, naiads, lions
> drawn from nature, or bodied in imagination,
> everything God ventured and reason grew bored
> nourishing have in stone and metal been restored.
> This is the end of things. This is, at the road's end,
> a mirror by which to enter.

The cyclic character of history, Brodsky suggests, has been evident in the recurrence of different forms of human enslavement throughout successive periods in time, frequently in the name of ideological progress. In 'Speech About Spilt Milk' he writes: 'Slavery always engenders slavery/ even with the help of revolutions' ... 'Usually the man who spits on God,/ first spits on man.' 'Time's invented by death', Brodsky declares enigmatically in 'The End of a Beautiful Era', one of the works described by Thomas Venclova as 'post-catastrophe or post-eschatological poetry, the poetry of "after the end of the world that was the Gulag or Auschwitz"'.[85] The poem concludes with an image of the post-Christian era as the age of dinosaurs and primitive savagery reborn:

> The keen-sightedness of our era takes root in the times
> which were short, in their blindness, of drawing clear lines
> twixt those fallen from cradles and fallen from saddles.

There are plenty of saucers, but no one to turn tables with
to subject you, poor Rurik, to a sensible quiz;
that's what really saddens.

The keen-sightedness of our days is the sort that befits the dead end
whose concrete begs for spittle and not for a witty comment.
Wake up a dinosaur, not a prince, to recite you the moral!
Birds have feathers for penning last words, though it's better to ask.
For the innocent head there is nothing in store but an ax
and the evergreen laurel.

While giving expression to his apprehensions at the horrors of a post-Christian future, Brodsky ultimately rejects that prospect and affirms his belief that Christian culture will continue to exercise a deep and lasting impact on the consciousness of humankind. There are two main reasons for this conviction. The first concerns the nature of culture itself, the second the ahistorical character of the Word, its articulation of the presence of the intemporal in the conditions of temporality and change. Christianity, he asserts, will continue firstly to live on in the historical consciousness of mankind in the same way that Judaic and Graeco-Roman tradition survived the challenge of Christianity, were in fact absorbed into Christian culture and revitalised in the process, despite their corruptions and inadequacies. The past, he suggests, inevitably lives on in human memory, merges with the present and extends into future time. He sees the whole temporal process as constituting a continuum in which the past is continually reborn, assimilated into present and future time and rendered meaningful thereby in terms of its continuing relevance to the needs of humankind. He echoes Mandelstam's words in 'The Word and Culture' that 'the old world is not of this world yet it is more alive than it ever was'. 'Yesterday has not yet been born, it has not yet really existed,' Mandelstam wrote.[86] Brodsky further echoes Eliot's description of the historical sense as 'a perception not only of the pastness of the past but also of its presence ... as a sense of the timeless as well as the temporal and of the timeless and the temporal together'.[87] In his Nobel Lecture he paid a memorable tribute to his own generation of writers for their heroic efforts to conserve the traditions of their culture in the face of the tyrannical policies of political regimes intent on its suppression:

That generation – the generation born precisely at the time when the Auschwitz crematoria were working full blast, when Stalin was at the zenith of his God-like, absolute power, which seemed sponsored by Mother Nature herself – that generation came into the world, it appears, in order to continue what, theoretically, was supposed to be interrupted in those crematoria, and in the anonymous common graves of Stalin's archipelago. The fact that not everything got interrupted, at least not in Russia, can in no small degree be credited to my generation, and I am no less proud of belonging to it than I am of standing here today. And the fact that I am standing here is a recognition of the services that generation has rendered to culture; recalling a phrase from Mandelstam, I would add, to world culture. Looking back, I can say again that we were beginning in an empty – indeed, a terrifyingly wasted – place, and that rather intuitively than consciously, we aspired precisely to the recreation of the effect of culture's continuity, to the reconstruction of its forms and tropes, toward filling its few surviving, and often totally compromised, forms, with our own new, or appearing to us as such, contemporary content.[88]

Brodsky's belief in the continuity of all human culture finds expression in a continued, and, poetically, a highly fruitful synthesis of classical, Judaic and Christian themes throughout his work. In an essay on Mandelstam he pointed to the extent to which the unity of pre- and post-Christian civilisations was manifested in the latter's poetry: 'Greece was always there, so was Rome, and so were the Biblical Judaea and Christianity. The cornerstones of our civilisation, they are treated by Mandelstam's poetry in approximately the same way time itself would treat them: as a unity – and in their unity.'[89] In his essay, 'Flight from Byzantium' he says the anticipation of Christian themes in Virgil's poetry 'practically allows one to consider Virgil the first Christian poet'. 'Had I been writing *The Divine Comedy*, I would have placed this Roman in Paradise: for outstanding services to the linear principle, into its logical conclusion.'[90] In an article published in 1981 Brodsky lamented the lack of classical references in the New Testament which would have indicated the continuity of the two cultures and their fundamental compatibility, despite obvious differences in their conceptions of metaphysical and religious truth:

The sad thing about Jesus Christ is that he never read the Latin poets. In theory he should have known the language, since he lived in what was at that time the Roman Empire. So he had a chance. On the other hand, Pontius Pilate never read much poetry either. Had he done so, and had he read, in particular, Virgil's Eclogues (which were published a good seventy years before the events in Jerusalem), he'd surely have paid closer attention to the story Jesus was telling. Pilate might have recognised in the man brought before him somebody whose arrival was

prophesied, as some scholars think, by Virgil in the Fourth Eclogue
of his Bucolics. At any rate, his knowledge of this poem could have
compounded Pilate's doubts enough to spare the man. Alternatively,
Jesus, had he known the poem, could have built a better case for himself.[91]

In addition to affirming to continuity of classical and Christian culture,
Brodsky also asserted the continuity of Christianity with the Judaic Old
Testament tradition. Shestov, in one of his last letters had spoken of the opposition between the Old and New Testaments as 'illusory' and had cited the
words of St Mark in support of his belief in their ultimate compatibility. To
the scribe who asked 'Which is the greatest commandment of all?' Jesus
replied: 'The first is, "Hear, O Israel: the Lord, our God, the Lord is one".'[92]
Brodsky's poem, 'Nunc Dimittis' echoes the words of Shestov and demonstrates the continuity of the two cultures. A poetic restatement of Luke's
account of the Presentation of Christ in the Temple, its eighteen stanzas correspond exactly to the eighteen verses of the Biblical story. The poem shows
Simeon, the last of the Old Testament prophets, at the transition point
between the worlds of Judaism and Christianity. He had prayed that he would
not see death before meeting the Messiah. On seeing the child he intones the
prayer, 'Nunc dimittis ... Now, O Lord, lettest thou thy poor servant, according to thy holy word, depart in peace.' His prayer sees the new dispensation as
the fulfilment of the old:

> It had been revealed to this upright old man
> that he would not die until his eyes had seen
> the Son of the Lord. And it thus came to pass. And
> he said: 'Now, O Lord, lettest thou thy poor servant,
>
> according to thy holy word, leave in peace,
> for mine eyes have witnessed thine offspring: he is
> thy continuation and also the source of
> thy Light for idolatrous tribes, and the glory
>
> of Israel as well.' Then old Simeon paused.
> The silence, regaining the temple's clear space,
> oozed from all its corners and almost engulfed them,
> and only his echoing words grazed the rafters,
>
> to spin for a moment, with faint rustling sounds,
> high over their heads in the tall temple's vaults,

akin to a bird that can soar, yet that cannot
return to the earth, even if it should want to.

The poem, as Valentina Polukhina points out, affects the style of the New
Testament narrative, as well as restating its message.[93] What is central to the
poem, Brodsky himself has explained, is the relationship between the old man
and the child, 'between the end of life and the beginning of life'.[94] The beginning of life, as represented by the birth of Christ, signifies hope and spiritual
self-renewal. The end of life, as signified by Simeon's attitude towards his
impending death, is also marked by hope. In the Jewish and Christian dispen-
sations death is seen as a triumph over time. Faith is the light that illumines
the prophet's passage through darkness into the silence of eternal life:

> He went forth to die. It was not the loud din
> of streets that he faced when he flung the door wide,
> but rather the deaf-and-dumb fields of death's kingdom.
> He strode through a space that was no longer solid.
>
> The rustle of time ebbed away in his ears.
> And Simeon's soul held the form of the Child –
> its feathery crown now enveloped in glory –
> aloft, like a torch, pressing back the black shadows,
>
> to light up the path that leads into death's realm,
> where never before until this present hour
> had any man managed to lighten his pathway.
> The old man's torch glowed and the pathway grew wider.

Memory and culture are man's defence against time because they embody
the faith and love which inspire the spirit's quest for the timeless. In his poem,
'Two Hours in an Empty Tank', Brodsky declared: 'There is faith, There is
Lord … Unbelief is blindness.' It is the Word, however, which embodies all –
memory, culture, faith, love – and is therefore man's ultimate defence against
history and time. Christianity endures in time – will endure – as Word, as
God's voice in the sphere of temporal being. This is what is intimated in the
opening verses of St John's Gospel: 'In the beginning was the Word, and the
Word was with God and the Word was God.' 'For Brodsky', Valentina
Polukhina has written, these words 'have a force which is not metaphorical but
axiomatic'. 'In the end, too, there will be the Word,' she writes. 'It will not
simply be an alienated part of speech or a grammatical abstraction, but will also
represent memory, the past, its history and culture. And, finally, it stands for

creativity as a source of immortality. Word just like Spirit exists outside time. That's why "Time worships language." Language worships God. The poet worships both.'[95] Pointing to the identification of poetic with religious illumination in Brodsky's poetry, Irene Steckler has written: 'There is little, if any, demarcation in Brodsky's work between the Sacred Word and the poetic word; the boundary between Divine Revelation and poetic illumination, Divine and poetic inspiration, is effaced. The poetic word – like the Sacred Word – is a source of Life, Light, and Truth, for it too illumines the deeper meaning of existence; it too "creates" – gives meaning to – life.'[96]

All this is given powerful poetic affirmation in one of Brodsky's most beautiful lyrics, 'Conversation with A Celestial Being', a work that performs a function similar to Eliot's 'Little Gidding' in reaffirming the major themes of his poetry. The central and all-inclusive theme is the idea of poetry as a gift from God. The poet, an earth-bound being, addresses his Creator: 'Here, on earth/ where I have fallen sometimes into zealotry .../ thanks to you, I observe myself from on high.' Thanks to God, the Celestial Being, the poet can distance himself from earthly reality, can observe himself from the vantage point of the timeless. It is the gift of poetic creativity, the infinite potency of the Word, which enables him to do this:

> to you, your gift
> I return – I haven't buried it or drunk away;
> and if the soul had a profile
> you would have seen
> that even it
> is only a mould of a grievous gift,
> it possesses nothing more than that,
> together with it is turned towards you.

He vows to pursue the sacred task of poetic creativity, despite the indifference of the populace – 'no longer/ seeing a spot where I might touch anyone/ with words ... choking with a nod/ of the ringing voiced carrion, with saliva'. Resigning himself to the apathy of the mob, he compares himself to Christ choking with the vinegar given him by his executioners, as he suffers humiliation and rejection in his service to the Word. He will not complain to God that his words are unheard – 'I will not burn/ you, with words, with a confession, with a supplication.' For the poet, as for all mortal beings, suffering and pain are the conditions of his time-bound existence:

> Here, on earth,
> all mountains – in the narrow sense –

> end not with a peak but a descent
> into pitch darkness,
> and compressing the lips,
> wrapping the stigmata in sackcloth,
> you encounter things in the Second Circle,
> having descended from the cross.

The mystery of suffering cannot be resolved in temporal life, but it can be given expression and thereby made meaningful in his poetry. Like Abraham and Job, he must endure suffering in a spirit of unquestioning faith ... 'Here, on earth,/ from tenderness to delirium,/ all forms of life are an adaptation.' Earlier he had declared: 'Silence is the future of the days ... Silence is the future of the words ... Silence is the future of love ... Life is a conversation in the face of silence.' It is this silence which informs his dialogue with God:

> I will not await
> your answers, Angel, inasmuch as
> with a face so poorly visualized
> as yours, must be
> only silence its match,
> silence – so spacious that neither
> the splash of laughter
> nor the wail: 'Hear!'
> will be honoured with an echo.

In the silence of his dialogue with God he cannot expect a response to his prayer: 'All faith amounts to no more than/ A one-way correspondence.' Solitude is the condition of the believer in God's infinite potency and love ... 'But even the thought of – what's it called! – immortality/ is a thought about solitude, my friend.' Poetry will reaffirm man's hopes of immortality but only in the conditions of despair and suffering endemic in temporal life. The alternating patterns of mortal existence – birth and death, hope and despair, temporality and the eternal – are conveyed in a beautiful sequence of lyrical images at the end of the poem:

> April. Holy Week. All moves towards spring.
> But the world is as yet in ice and whiteness.
> And the gaze of the infant,
> who has not yet started to walk,
> cannot conceive the melting of snow.
> And there is no escape

from the same thought – in reverse –
for the old man in the hospital at the year's beginning;
he sees the snow and knows that he will die
before it melts, before the ice breaks.

Conclusion

The foregoing chapters have attempted to define the contemporary meaning and relevance of Christianity as seen from the standpoints of twelve modern writers. Together they give a sense of the universality of Christian tradition, indicating its capacity to accommodate a wide variety of beliefs, ranging from the Orthodoxy of Dostoevsky and Akhmatova, the Catholicism of Mauriac and Milosz, the Protestantism of Eliot and Auden, to the highly unconventional religious convictions of Tolstoy, Unamuno, Mandelstam, Pasternak, White and Brodsky. The purpose of this final chapter is to identify the more significant and insistent thematic insights into the meaningfulness of Christianity that are disclosed in these writings. It does not aim to construct some kind of comprehensive 'literary theology' – such an exercise, apart from being spurious in itself, would be quite foreign to the method of literary-critical exegesis on which the study is based – nor does it attempt to contrive a synthesis of the themes identified in the various writings that have been discussed. Inevitably, these writings examine various aspects of Christian tradition selectively; some themes are common to all, others are not. A great diversity of interpretations exists both within and between the various works examined. One finds a significant coherence of insights between them, nonetheless, a coherence sufficiently strong to embrace differences in denominational faith as well as those between conventional and unconventional belief. That coherence is evident in a recurring emphasis on issues such as the conflicts of faith and unbelief, the primacy of the law of love, the fallenness of mankind, the accessibility of divine grace, the spiritually self-renewing power of humility, penitence and prayer, the inevitability of suffering in mortal life, the immanence of God's presence in the material universe, the possibility of time-transcendence and the hoped-for prospect of immortality. These are the issues on which discussion will be focussed in this concluding chapter of the work.

The co-existence of faith and doubt, of belief and unbelief, is a persistent emphasis in the literature discussed in this book. Dostoevsky speaks of the 'doubleness' of the experience of faith, seeing it as inseparable from the experience of doubt and unbelief. His method of polyphonic realism gives equal representation to both, seeing their interdependence as being indicative of the radical freedom of man, while recognising that their tensions and contradictions are a source of never-ending conflict in mortal life. Self-conflict, he suggests, is the tragic predicament of the believer, the ambiguous character of faith being an occasion for lifelong struggle with uncertainty, doubt and unbelief. Tolstoy, like Dostoevsky, sees this conflict as being rooted in the faith-reason dichotomy inherent in the nature of man, something he suggests has been greatly exacerbated by the dominance of rationalism in post-Cartesian European culture. Pointing to the inadequacies of reason, its failure to address the reality of the undisclosed and the infinite, he affirms the transcendence of faith, yet insists that belief remains explicable in terms comprehensible to rational thought. Seeing revelation and reason as being ultimately compatible, he nonetheless affirmed the tensions and anxieties the interrelations between them must always create.

'Agonic struggle' is the term employed by Unamuno for the search for faith. A lifelong dissenter, like Tolstoy and Kierkegaard, he rejected institutional dogmatism and rationalistic theology, while being a fervent advocate of the traditions of scriptural Christianity. He sought a faith transcending rational thought, such as he saw epitomised in the non-pharisaical beliefs of one of his favourite New Testament characters, Nicodemus. Like Dostoevsky, he stressed the essential irrationalism of faith, finding in the idea of a knight errantry of the spirit – which he associated both with the intuitional, non-philosophic beliefs of the Spanish mystics and with the simplicity, optimism and limitless *joie de vivre* of fictional Christian characters such as Cervantes' Don Quixote – an image for its inherent absurdity. Though he regarded Christianity as having been contaminated by rationalism from the outset, he too asserted the importance of scepticism and rational thought in vitalising faith, insisting that the fatal flaw in scholastic and idealist traditions was not their employment of the resources of reason for purposes of philosophic or theological definition but their isolation of rationality from its natural links with non-rational experiences. The interdependence of faith and what he calls 'impassioned doubt' – the latter is carefully distinguished from the coldness of analytic or Cartesian doubt – is the tragic but ultimately hope-affirming condition of man, he says, the struggle with doubt and despair being the normal condition of mortal life.

That condition is vividly exemplified again in the theme of 'divided consciousness' developed by Auden in several major poems, particularly 'New Year Letter' and 'The Age of Anxiety'. Strongly echoing Kierkegaard, Auden denounced 'one-sided' approaches to truth, seeing all ideologies as being reductive and therefore false. Faith, he insisted, is the product of tension and opposition, is nurtured by the same conflicts of consciousness from which it springs. The 'gift of double focus,' he declared, is the 'one infallible gift of greatness', truth being the product of dialectical consciousness, of its double focussing of belief and doubt, reason and feeling, despair and hope.

Modern literature, pointing persistently to the co-existence of faith and doubt, tends overwhelmingly to emphasise the torment and agony of unbelief, representing this as the condition from which faith, paradoxically, must spring. That struggle is given expression by Eliot, Mauriac, White, Auden and Brodsky in the language and imagery of mystical literature and its Old Testament sources, particularly Job and the Psalms. In their work the dark night of despair is seen as the way of faith, the path the soul must follow in its progress towards God. The imagery of silence, darkness, nothingness and void – all of which points to the torment of 'God-concealment' – is widely used in their work to intimate the all-pervasive presence of unbelief and despair in mortal life. Echoing the words of St John of the Cross ('Faith is dark as night to the understanding') Eliot in his *Four Quartets* asserts that the soul encounters God through despair and spiritual desolation, through descent into the darkness of unbelief. The ultimately affirmative character of this process is signified in 'East Coker' through images emphasising the illuminative power of darkness, its disclosure of the hope-giving presence of God in the void of nothingness the soul contemplates in its torment.

Faith, Unamuno suggests, closely following Dostoevsky, is an expression of man's radical freedom, is manifested as election or will, nurtured by man's quest for the absolute, the timeless, the infinite – for that which transcends the mortal conditions of temporality and finitude. He sees faith as the *intentional* creation of that for which we hope. God, he suggests, exists in all of us by virtue of our longing for transcendence, for infinity. Faith, he says, 'creates' God – 'to save the universe from nothingness'. 'He in whom you believe He is your God,' he declares. 'He to whom you pray He is your God.' He further suggests that the will to love may be an unconscious or disguised will to faith, a theme beautifully evoked in the story of Don Manuel Bueno. Denied the comforts of faith by virtue of his persistent unbelief, Don Manuel nevertheless devotes himself selflessly to the service of his community. He is 'a Christian who cannot believe'. He shows that holiness can co-exist with unbelief, his will to faith finding expression as a fervent will to serve. 'Without believing he believed in an active and resigned desolation,' the narrator concludes.

That same theme is reaffirmed by Mauriac in his conception of atheism as 'unconscious homage to infinite being' and by White through his theme of man's unconscious attention to God through love. Most hunger after spirituality, even if unconsciously, White declares, many giving expression to that aspiration through ways other than those of formalised or institutional faith. They give expression to it particularly through the service of others in a spirit of selfless love. That selflessness is celebrated in the story of Voss, in the gradual stripping away of the pride and selfishness that is the main obstacle to his attainment of faith. Voss discovers God through his humble and self-denying service of his fellowman. The whole story of his attainment of faith through love is strongly reminiscent of Dostoevsky with whom White shares fundamental beliefs about the permanence of antinomies in earthly life. Existence is characterised by both in terms of a dualistic tension of opposites – matter and spirit, order and disorder, time and the timeless etc. – which can be transcended only by faith. But for both the antinomies of unbelief and faith are rooted in the more fundamental opposition of self-oriented and other-oriented tendencies. The theme is explored by Dostoevsky in *The Underground Man* and *The Devils*. Freedom, he suggests, is essentially a choice between self and otherness, and this ultimately is a choice between self and God, the absoluteness of the Other. Self-fulfilment as the goal of existence is, he insists, deterministic, destructive of individual freedom, self-love leading inexorably towards the nihilism of total self-absorption and unfreedom. The conquest of self through humility and selfless attention to others leads to the fulfilment of the self through love, through its encounter with Thouness (to use Buber's terminology), the absolute form of Thouness being God. And this, Dostoevsky suggests, is the basis of all faith. On this principle is founded Father Zossima's advice to the lady who asked how she could recover her faith. He responded: 'Strive to love your neighbour actively and indefatigably. In as far as you advance in love you will grow surer of the reality of God and of the immortality of your soul. If you attain to perfect self-forgetfulness in the love of your neighbour, then you will believe without doubt, and no doubt can possibly enter your soul.'

Dostoevsky speaks of love therefore as disclosing the ultimate meaning of existence, as man's gateway to the infinite, the key to his understanding of the mysteries of life. The transcendent power of altruistic love is Tolstoy's foremost religious theme as well. 'I believe,' he wrote, 'that the meaning of every man's life lies only in increasing the store of love within him; and that this increase of love leads a man to greater and greater blessings in this life, and to blessings after his death that are in proportion to the amount of love within him.' For Pasternak love is the 'primordial force in being'. 'Love is as simple and absolute as consciousness and death,' he wrote. 'We have all become people only in the measure in which we have loved people and had the opportunity to love. To love selflessly and unreservedly with a strength equal to the square of the distance – this,' he says, 'is the task of our hearts while we are children.' Love he too saw as a quest for the timeless, the infinite. Man's yearning to transcend his finitude and temporality, he suggests, finds expression in his love, a universal potentiality, innate in nature itself. But, like Dostoevsky and Tolstoy, he recognised that love is experienced in temporal conditions, is deeply flawed and corruptible in its earthly forms, being subject to the same dualism as all other facets of our existence. Love's reaching towards the infinite is frustrated by the conditions of temporality in which it is experienced in mortal life, the persistent intrusion of the self on a state that finds fulfilment only in its selflessness being the main source of its corruptibility.

Man's fallenness, the primary existential manifestation of his materio-temporal mortality, is seen by all these writers as the main obstacle to his realisation of the potentiality for altruistic fulfilment that is inherent in his being. Rejecting the doctrine of the natural goodness of man espoused by liberal thinkers since Rousseau, Auden condemns them for their faith in the power of humanist ideologies to transform the conditions of earthly existence. In works such as 'New Year Letter' and 'The Age of Anxiety' he stressed the fearsome capacity for evil that is inherent in the nature of man. 'Either we serve the Unconditional/ Or some Hitlerian monster will supply/ An iron convention to do evil by,' he exclaimed. His call for ethical responsibility and his insistence on the need for absolute standards of morality (he saw the all-pervasive influence of relativist ethics in modern society as being largely responsible for its moral degeneracy) is echoed by Milosz, a writer even more profoundly aware of man's limitless potentiality for evil by virtue of his direct experiencing of the horrors of the Gulag, the Holocaust, the Nazi Terror and the atrocities of two world wars. Deeply influenced by the manichean teachings of Shestov and Weil, Milosz sees nature as necessarily corrupt but nonetheless redeemable through the power of divine grace. In his catastrophist poems he depicts a whole civilisation falling apart, describing calamities of cosmic amplitude, surpassing even the barbarities of antiquity in their demonic savagery. The enslavement of consciousness imposed by Marxist regimes throughout Eastern Europe for the greater part of the present century he sees as particularly exemplifying the limitless potential for evil present in our nature.

Like his Slavic compatriot, Brodsky, Milosz attributes this ultimately not to the Marxist ideology, pernicious though it was, but to a naive faith in nature that failed sufficiently to take account of human fallenness, the suppression of individual responsibility on a massive scale in the name of a collective aspiration towards a transformation of the human condition being merely a socio-political expression of this. That descent into depravity he sees as being accelerated by the disinheritance of contemporary society from its roots in Judaeo-Christian tradition, a process he suggests has been facilitated by the growth of scientific rationalism, the same force that brought the Marxist nightmare into being. History itself has been sacrificed in the name of science, he declared in his Nobel lecture, as he called for a rediscovery by modern man of his own cultural traditions, the repossession of his historical consciousness.

Fallenness is depicted as lovelessness in Mauriac's fiction, individual instances of this being powerfully evoked in novels such as *Thérèse*, *A Nest of Vipers*, *A Kiss for the Leper* and *A Woman of the Pharisees*. Lovelessness, he suggests, is life without God, failure to love being intimately bound up with the failure of faith and hope. That condition is portrayed by Mauriac in Thérèse Desqueyroux, a character whose entire life has been blighted by the loneliness of a loveless marriage, her descent into depravity and despair following inexorably on this. It is portrayed in a different manner in Louis from *A Nest of Vipers* whose paranoid self-hatred has poisoned his relations with his wife and children, blinding him to all manifestations of goodness in them. Brigitte in *A Woman of the Pharisees* typifies the practice of religion without love; she stands for a puritanical self-justifying sanctity lacking the dynamic of the humble self-denying, non-judgemental love that is the heart of genuine religious faith. That self-denying spirit is portrayed by Mauriac in characters such as the Abbé Calou, Alain Forcas, Noemie and Jean Péloueyre, and Xavier Dartigelongue, each of whom exemplifies the selfless love that comes from God's grace and is ultimately sustained by faith – itself the fruit of humility, self-repentance and prayer.

The theme of suffering, the inevitable consequence of man's fallenness and mortality, dominates all the literature discussed in this book. In the depth of love we encounter the depth of despair, Unamuno writes, pointing to the capacity of love to generate torment and pain as well as the deepened self-consciousness from which comes the self-illumination that leads to faith. Transience, he suggests, is the root-cause of suffering, especially the transience of earthly love, embodying as it does man's aspiration towards the spheres of the infinite and timeless yet painfully disclosing the constricted conditions of temporality and finitude in which those aspirations exist. All this is most vividly conveyed in the work of the only woman writer discussed in this book. The pain as well as the ecstasy of interhuman love, its intersections of the temporal and intemporal, its conflict of self-directed and other-directed tendencies, its potential for self-transformation, its endlessly frustrated reaching towards the timeless – these are the themes of Akhmatova's finest love lyrics.

Dostoevsky points to the inexplicable mystery of suffering in a universe supposedly the creation of an omnipotent and benign divinity. For Ivan Karamazov the suffering of the innocent cannot be reconciled with the idea of a benevolent, all-loving creator. (Zossima, like Job, concludes that the problem lies beyond human understanding.) For Prince Myshkin the image of the Crucified Christ serves as the archetypal example of salvation attained through endurance of suffering. Eliot's 'East Coker' further emphasises this conception of life as resigned expectancy ('But the faith and the love and the hope are all in the waiting') as does 'Murder in the Cathedral', his dramatic enactment of life as martyrdom, endurance of temporality being the way to God. 'To act is to suffer,' Thomas says, 'action is suffering, suffering is action'; both, he says, are 'fixed in an eternal action, an eternal patience'. Mauriac's Thérèse Desqueyroux epitomises the spirit of faith attained through endurance of suffering, as does Akhmatova's image of Mary at the foot of the cross, her resigned acceptance of her fate symbolising the communal grief of all the Russian people in the years of the Stalinist terror.

It is because suffering is transient that Christianity celebrates the ultimate affirmativeness, even joyfulness, of existence in time. Kierkegaard spoke of the 'onceness' of suffering, a theme strongly reaffirmed by Dostoevsky, Unamuno, Mandelstam, Milosz and Brodsky. Suffering is transcended through faith and love, through the hopefulness that comes from both. 'Pray to God for gladness,' Zossima counsels his monks. 'Be glad as children, as the birds of heaven … Fly from dejection.' 'It was not men's grief but their joy Christ visited,' Alyosha says, as he reflects on the significance of the miracle at Cana. 'He worked his first miracle to help men's gladness … He who loves men loves their gladness too,' he concludes. In the spirit of knight-errantry, exemplified in the quintessential gaiety and irrepressible optimism of Don Quixote, Unamuno sees the same spirit of Christian hopefulness. Don Quixote 'hears the divine laughter everywhere …' 'He overcame the world,' Unamuno writes, 'by giving the world cause to laugh at him'.

That same quality of gaiety Mandelstam saw as the essence of Christian art: 'Neither sacrifice nor redemption in art, but the free and joyous imitation of Christ is the keystone of Christian aesthetics,' he wrote in 'Pushkin and Scriabin'. That spirit of Christian freedom and joy is celebrated by Milosz in the cycle, 'From the Rising of the Sun', and it shines through the darkness and gloom of Brodsky's finest lyrics. In 'Conversation With A Celestial Being', Brodsky declares that he will not yield to his despair: 'There on the cross I shall not cry out, Why hast Thou forsaken me.' Gorbunov, his Christ-like creation, accepts his suffering resignedly. His dreams of chanterelles, symbols of love and freedom, sustain him in his suffering, as he waits patiently for the end, his vision of the sea symbolising his hopes of eternal fulfilment. The gladness and hopefulness with which the theme of suffering is treated in these poems spring from the conviction that, while suffering cannot be evaded in mortal life, the strength to endure it is assured through the power of divine grace which, in turn, is attainable through the pursuit of selfless love.

The conquest of pride is the essential condition for the growth of selfless love. The self-effacing attitudes exemplified in Dostoevsky's Prince Myshkin, Father Zossima and Alyosha attest powerfully to this, as does the 'foolishness' of Don Quixote whose indifference to earthly glory stems primarily from his faith. So also does the non-judgemental love for their parishioners displayed by the abbés Calou and Forcas, their strength and moral influence deriving from their willingness to endure contempt and humiliation in the service of God. 'Love your enemies' is their moral guideline as they endure the ridicule of their parishioners, seeing self-humiliation as the necessary condition for the growth of Christ-like love. Johann Ulrich Voss similarly discovers that real power comes not from self-glorification but from humility, as he is gradually stripped of the pride that had poisoned his relations with others. 'When man is truly humbled,' Laura Trevelyan says, 'when he has learned that he is not God, then he is nearest to becoming so.'

What they all exemplify is the humble submission to God's will that derives from their unshakeable faith in his assurance of ultimate salvation, the prospect which alone makes life meaningful. This trusting faith is nurtured by the spirit of self-repentance and forgiveness, essential conditions for the growth of genuine humility. Raskolnikov's progress from guilt to penitence illustrates the gradual manner in which pride and self-will are subordinated to a trusting faith in the infinity of God's mercy and grace. Unlike Stavrogin who lacks the will to repent, Raskolnikov *elects* for penitence, hoping thereby to emulate the selfless spirit of love he sees exemplified in Sonia Marmeladov. Gradually, the torment of guilt and remorse is transformed in him through the miracle of divine grace. He discovers that the pain of guilt is healed not by the morbid contemplation of his sinfulness but by the active pursuit of love. A similar process is enacted by Tolstoy in *War and Peace* and *Resurrection*. 'Some one dear to one can be loved with human love, but an enemy can only be loved with divine love,' Prince Andrei reflects, as he lies wounded on the bat-tlefield at Borodino. The transforming power of penitential love is shown movingly in his reconciliation with Natasha. With forgiveness comes the renewal of love, purged of guilt and remorse and profoundly purified by this. Nekhlyudov undergoes a similar transformation. Following his reconciliation with Maslova, he concludes that the solution to the problem of evil is the never ending willingness to forgive, 'not seven times seven but seventy times seven ...'

The examples of Prince Myshkin, Alyosha and Father Zossima point to an important distinction regarding the nature of Christian humility. Essentially the submission of the self to the will of God', humility is founded on a trusting acceptance of the infinity of his love. It is not, however, as Dostoevsky demonstrates, a passive form of self-effacement, such as he depicts in Prince Myshkin, but a state that finds purpose and fulfilment in the active pursuit of love, as manifested in the lives of Alyosha and Zossima. Humility without love, he suggests, is a form of spiritual pride, an inward looking, self-obsessed condition lacking the commitment and responsibility of a truly altruistic faith.

He sees humility as being deeply bound up with will, with the election for faith and love. Thus, Zossima counsels his monks that the humble self-denying love he advocates is the product of 'struggle', is 'born slowly through long labour'. The fruit of effort and perseverance, it is fulfilled as responsibility, both in its individualised and communal forms.

'Love, not in words, but in deeds', is the ideal promulgated also by Tolstoy through the voices of his major protagonists. Human love is corrupt and imperfect, he suggests, but is transformed through the moral force of humility and self-repentance into the higher self-denying love exemplified by Christ and attested in the words of the scriptures. Stressing, like Zossima, the essentially ethical character of the act of love (as asserted in Christ's injunction, 'If ye love me keep my commandments') Tolstoy insists on the absolute binding force of the laws that govern its practice. Those laws find expression in the *active* practice of love, in the assumption of responsibility for the other. His story 'Father Sergius' demonstrates the underlying selfishness of the purely ascetic ideal, the pseudo-ideal of a love divorced from altruistic responsibility, which, like Dostoevsky, he too sees as ultimately a form of self-love or spiritual pride. Father Sergius discovers that holiness comes from service to others, such as he sees manifested in the life of his cousin Pashenka. 'Pashenka,' he says, 'is precisely what I ought to have been. I lived for man, pretending to live for God; but she lives for God, imagining that she lives for man.'

Human love, however corrupt, is endlessly redeemable, Zossima suggests; it is redeemable through the infinite potency of God's grace. It is God's grace that releases the transformative power of selflessness inherent within it. The source of that transformation, from the self-directed human love into the other-directed, selfless, Christ-like love of the Gospels, is God's immanent presence in the natural world, a theme which is repeatedly attested in the literature discussed in this book. In Mauriac's fiction the pines, in their seeming endlessness, signify the infinity of God for Xavier Dartigelongue; the cleansing rains signify the healing power of divine love for Noemie and Jean Péloueyre; the song of the nightingales in *The Dark Angels* signifies the blessedness of penitential love. All ultimately signify the redemptive presence of God in the world of material being. Election to love, election to faith and goodness, are the means to its attainment. This truth underlies the repeated affirmations of the infinitude and sanctity of love throughout the works that have been discussed. 'Love is the only thing that can redeem our follies and mistakes, Milosz concludes in the final words of *Native Realm*. 'Only love redeems,' declares White at the end of *Flaws in the Glass*. 'If you love everything,' Zossima says, 'you will perceive the divine mystery in things.' God, said Tolstoy, is present in each of us in the measure in which

we love. We apprehend God through love, he said. Love in all its forms discloses the immanent, points to the indwelling presence of the Creator in his
creation.

For Christian believers the most significant manifestation of the principle
of immanence was God's Incarnation as man in the Person of Christ.
Eucharistic imagery is used repeatedly to signify this in many of the works
discussed. In his delirium Voss sees himself as a priest bringing the bread of
the Eucharist to Laura, their love finding its ultimate fulfilment in the mystery
the Eucharist signifies. That mystery is the subject of Laura's final reflections
in the novel. 'I am willing to give up much to prove that human truths are
also divine,' she says. 'That is the true meaning of Christ.' 'How important,'
she says, 'it is to understand the three stages. Of God into Man. Man. And
man returning to God.' The poems of *The Christ of Velazquez* also affirm the
significance of the Incarnation as the central event in Christianity through
repeated uses of Eucharistic imagery, by this intimating the miracle of God
made Man, spirit become flesh, spirit materialised as bread and wine. For
Mandelstam the Eucharistic liturgy celebrates the presence of eternity in time;
the Eucharist is a 'golden sun' that never sets, infinite in its materiality, in its
concrete attestation of God's immanent presence in creation. Eucharistic symbolism is used to affirm the same truth in Akhmatova's poetry; in her case it is
constantly intermingled with the lyrical imagery of sensual passion, to intimate
the holiness of earthly love, its potential for transformation by virtue of its
revelation of the immanence of God. Milosz's memories from his childhood of
the pious communicants at the Sunday morning liturgy in the village churches
of Polish Lithuania also evoke the simplicity of a faith focussed on the
Incarnation as a continuing source of salvation and redemption.

What all these works affirm is a central religious truth: that Christ in his
person embodied the finite-infinite co-inherence (to use the terminology
favoured by Auden) that is the ultimate resolution of the conflicts and
dichotomies that are all-pervasive in mortal life. Thus, Simeon in 'For the
Time Being' speaks of the birth of Christ, the Incarnation, as defining the significance of all temporal events, as the event which relates them to their ultimate meaningfulness in the sphere of the infinite. 'By the event of this birth,'
he says, 'the true significance of all other events is defined.' 'The course of
history is predictable,' he adds, 'in the degree to which all men love themselves, and spontaneous in the degree to which each man loves God and
through Him his neighbour.' The conflicts of earthly life, as has been intimated, derive from the urge towards transcendence of the materio-temporal conditions of existence which is inherent in nature itself, yet this is endlessly
frustrated by the fallenness and corruptibility of man. They are resolved in the
person of Christ by virtue of the absolute selflessness of the love he exempli-

fied in his life and work, attesting thereby to the perfection of God's immanent presence in his nature. That selflessness is conveyed by Brodsky in a beautiful image from 'Adieu, Mademoiselle Véronique – 'The total of all of today's embraces/ gives far less of love than the outstretched arms of/ Christ on the cross'.

The significance of the Incarnation extends to the celebration of the holiness of all earthly being, to its visible attestation of God's presence within the temporal universe. 'Holy is our being beneath heaven', Milosz exclaims, echoing the words of the Acmeists, whose vision of the sacramental character of all material reality he shares. His lyrics celebrate the presence of God in all earthly life, its order and beauty being seen as a visible manifestation of the order and perfection of the divine presence inherent within it. For Mandelstam and Pasternak – both Jews by birth – the beauty of the natural world is evocative of the continuous activity of creation, the never-ending presence of God's love being the dynamic informing the whole process, a principle that has deep roots in Jewish tradition and intimates its continuity with the Christian doctrine of Incarnation. The eternal, both insist, exists in time, not beyond it, by virtue of God's presence in time, in the crude materiality of the natural world. The paradox is reaffirmed by Akhmatova in lyrics that celebrate the wonder of everyday reality, its revelation of the potential for transcendence that exists in its mundane finitude and temporality. Her God, like Mandelstam's and Pasternak's, is intimately at hand, disclosed in the familiar, the mundane, the ordinary, banal realities of everyday life.

'In the beginning was the Word, and the Word was with God and the Word was God.' The words of St John's Gospel point to a further application of this theme, i.e., the immanent presence of God in the language men share. Christ is described by Unamuno in the Velazquez poem as 'embodied Word', by this signifying the presence of the eternal and the spiritual in human speech. Language, he suggests, like all earthly phenomena, attests to the informing presence within it of the divine and the spiritual. Mandelstam saw poetry itself as an 'imitation of Christ'; he spoke of it as a sacred, creative activity, comparable to the Eucharistic sacrifice in its reenactment through language of the miracle of the Incarnation. The poet imitates God, he said, through the act of artistic creation, thereby replicating the original act of divine creation through his reconstitution of earthly reality in the spiritually informed materiality of the Word. Like God, the original Creator, the poet creates out of love, his art being a product of reverential attention to the beauty and order of existential being.

'Poetry', Brodsky declared at his trial, is 'a gift from God', as he reaffirmed the Acmeist belief in the sacramental character of the poetic word, seeing it as man's material link with God, disclosive of the infinite, the intemporal, the

Unseen. Love he said, is the infinite addressing the finite; poetry, like faith, is the finite addressing the infinite. Poetry is a search for eternal values, conducted through the medium of the Word. For language it marks the highest form of existence, recording its upward movement into the sphere from which it sprang. The Word, he suggests, like the spirit, originates outside time. Thus, his assertion, 'Time worships language. Language worships God.' The poet sees the world from the vantage point of the timeless; the eternal informs his dialogue with earthly reality, ultimately with God. Poetry, he declared, is prophecy, inspired speech; the poet is a seer. Only the word survives, he asserts. Poetry transcends history; its voice is the voice of God.

Hope, Unamuno said, is the hallmark of the Christian faith. Life becomes meaningless without hope, he wrote; life has no purpose if death is the end. The longing for immortality is the force, he says, that motivates the will to faith. Time transcendence is a major theme in his writings as in all the writings that have been discussed. It assumes various forms, finding expression in a variety of images and metaphoric formulations. 'The end is where we start from', Eliot declares; death marks the beginning of life, signifying the soul's release from the bondage of the temporal and its entry into the stillness of the eternal. 'And the angel swore, There will be no Time' – the words from the Revelation of St John provide the theme of Akhmatova's *The Way of all the Earth*, her great lyrical meditation on the themes of temporality and the timeless. Musical metaphors are employed in her *Poem Without A Hero* to invoke the prospect of a timeless existence; the stillness of the intemporal being seen as a silence transformed into music, its perfection of pure form signifying the stillness and light of the infinite. The end, paradoxically, as White says, gives access to endlessness – the endlessness with which Elizabeth Hunter from *The Eye of the Storm* wishes to be identified. 'Myself is this endlessness', she cries in her death reverie as she briefly glimpses the calm in the storm, a momentary stillness in conflict-ridden time, the stillness and endlessness of God.

That silence of the infinite is repeatedly identified by Brodsky as the ground of all hope ... 'silence is the future of the days ... silence is the future of our love ... life is but a conversation in the face of silence'. Death, he wrote, is a 'good litmus test of a poet's ethics.' In his elegies to Donne, Eliot, Akhmatova, Lowell and Auden, Brodsky invokes the peacefulness of life after death; the silence of the snow covered landscape and the serenity of the recently dead poet in the 'Elegy for John Donne' intimate the infinite peacefulness of eternal life. Hope, he suggests in the Auden elegy, is born of love, and death marks the soul's return to the source of infinite love, which is God. That same theme had earlier been emphasised by Tolstoy in *War and Peace*. 'Love hinders death', Prince Andrei declares at Borodino, reiterating the conviction repeatedly affirmed by Tolstoy himself that love was the source of his faith in the immortality of the soul. In his Reply to the Synod's Edict of Excommunication he said: 'I believe that the meaning of every man's life lies only in increasing the store of love within him; and that this increase of love leads a man to greater and greater blessings in this life, and to blessings after his death that are in proportion to the amount of love within him.' Immortality, Yury Zhivago tells the dying Anna Gromeko, is 'our life in others'; it originates in the miracle of eternal love, its infinitude being realised in life beyond time, in the spirit's entry into the communality of all love.

'If you were to destroy in mankind the belief in immortality, not only love but every living force maintaining the life of the world would at once be dried up,' said Ivan Karamazov. That belief, acknowledged by Dostoevsky himself as the kernel of his faith, is expressed movingly in his story, 'A Little Boy at Christ's Christmas Tree', where a beautiful image occurs of children playing among the angels in Paradise. It is reiterated in the words of Alyosha Karamazov to the children at Ilyusha's funeral when he assures them that 'all shall rise again from the dead'. In both instances the imagery of the resurrected soul was prompted by personal experience of death by Dostoevsky, the deaths of his two infant sons. A personal experience also, the death of his mother, inspired Pasternak's poem 'Earth' in which the reawakening of nature in springtime is linked symbolically with the Resurrection of Christ. The image occurs at the end of *Dr Zhivago* and in several of Yury Zhivago's poems – in all instances to signify that Christ, by rising from the dead, has solved the mystery of death. The Gospel image of the Resurrected Christ, Unamuno said, embodies the hope for immortality that is present in us all. It is this hope, he insists, that sustains love and faith. Love hopes endlessly, he declares. We believe in what we hope for; our faith in God is our hope for eternal life. Hope is the form of faith; without it faith is directionless and formless. That hope is symbolised, given form, in the scripture image of the Resurrected Christ.

The theme of hope dominates Mandelstam's poems of the 1930s, a period when his life was filled with awareness of doom, that awareness being relieved only by his belief in the resurrection of the soul. The poems combine images of Christ's Passion and Crucifixion, clearly evocative of his own suffering and despair, with affirmations of his belief in an existence beyond time, in a paradise beyond the grave. The latter is movingly conveyed in one of his last poems, the beautiful verses to Natasha Shtempel in which he assures her of the self-renewing potentiality of the spirit and of his conviction that their impending separation will end with reunion in eternal life. That same hope is conveyed in the theological image of *apokatastasis* in Milosz's 'Bells in Winter' where, echoing Pasternak and Mandelstam, he too signifies the restoration of life in eternity, the souls entry into the 'communion of saints,' through the lyrical imagery of the renewal of nature in springtime.

The whole relationship of Christianity to history underlies the various explorations of its contemporary relevance and meaningfulness in the works that have been discussed. Though there are significant differences in their perceptions of the nature of the historical process, certain common characteristics can be identified in the treatment of the place of Christianity within the temporal framework of history by Tolstoy, Eliot, Pasternak, Mandelstam, Milosz and Brodsky, all of whom have given it special prominence in their writings. In each instance one finds an insistent emphasis on the interdependence of the intemporal and the temporal and an assertion of the need to appraise all temporal processes from the standpoint of the eternal. This lies at the root of Tolstoy's denunciations of Hegelian and indeed all rationalist theories of history, his fundamental criticism being the falsity of their attempts to accommodate Christianity within the parameters of the historical process. Christian truth, he insisted, lies outside the historical process, its ultimate affirmations belonging in a realm that transcends the contingencies of temporal life. The same conviction lies at the root of Eliot's rejection of the Heraclitean and Bergsonian conceptions of time as pure process in favour of the Augustinian concept of the temporal as immanently manifesting the presence of the intemporal. Every moment, he argued, is made meaningful by the inherence of the timeless in its finite temporality. Both positions derive from a view of the problem of time that is distinctively Christian, reflecting a traditional Christian conception of the eternal and the temporal as perennially in tension while affirming the accessibility of the eternal through the medium of the temporal.

The influence of Christian tradition is apparent secondly in the perception of the historical process by all the writers mentioned as essentially a record of the radical freedom of man. Historical progress, they insist, results in the main from the freely chosen initiatives of individual men. On this basis Tolstoy rejected naturalistic determinism, insisting on the freedom of individual consciousness (an order of freedom posited beyond the realm of the rational) as the essential dynamic in the historical process. This, he said, coexists in fruitful tension with the benign, causal necessity of God's will. Consciousness, he argued, transcends causality, finds fulfilment in spiritual interiority, and manifests itself primarily as faith and love – the ultimate agencies of progress and change in the evolution of mankind. Pasternak's Nikolai Vedniapin and Sima Tuntseva both see the recognition of the freedom and uniqueness of the individual person as beginning with Christ, the teaching of the Gospels marking a radical departure from the collectivism of the Old Testament dispensation.

History, Nikolai says, is a record of the free action of men, enacted in the lives of ordinary individuals and fulfilled in their universal potentiality for love. His words are echoed by Mandelstam who in 'Pushkin and Scriabin' describes Christian art as essentially a celebration of individual freedom, attesting to its fundamental significance in the history of mankind since the dawn of the Christian era.

Inevitably, attention is focussed in these works on the most cataclysmic historical event of the modern period, the emergence of Marxism and the growth of ideological communism – all in the name of an apparently new conception of the historical process. The significance of this momentous development is closely appraised by Pasternak in *Doctor Zhivago*. Through the voice of his fictional alter ego, Yury, he asserts the inevitability of the Revolution because of the injustices that prevailed in Russian society at the time and the horrific social conditions that existed under the Tsarist regime. He identifies the Revolution with the life-giving forces in nature, even with the faith-giving Pentecostal fire of the scriptures, seeing it as the fulfilment of the dreams of a subjugated people for emancipation from their misery and degradation. Yet he warns of the dangers of the collectivist ideology on which the ideals of the Revolution were based, seeing it as reductivist and deterministic, threatening the core values of individual freedom on which Western culture is founded. Through the voices of Nikolai and Sima he identifies the growth of individual freedom with the advancement of Christianity, reasserting through the scriptural images of Yury Zhivago's poetry the Christian teaching on the universal power of love as the ultimate guarantee of that freedom. His words were reiterated by Mandelstam who foretold the 'destruction of Jerusalem' as the foreseeable outcome of the new humanist dispensation, seeing the materialist ideology as being in direct conflict with the values and beliefs of the Judaeo-Christian tradition. Simultaneously, he suggests, in poems such as 'We Shall Meet again in Petersburg', that the people would once again rediscover the richness of their spiritual and cultural heritage

What was unique about Marxism, Milosz suggests, was the enslavement of people's minds that occurred in the name of a supposedly liberating ideology. This, he says, was a development unprecedented in history, something unique to the twentieth century alone. In works such as *The Captive Mind* he depicts the subjugation of individual consciousness that resulted from the pursuit of the socio-political objectives of Marxism, deploring the suspension of religious and ethical traditions, the rejection of history, on which it was founded. Poems such as 'Child of Europe' and 'The Song of Adrian Zelinski' demonstrate the nihilistic suppression of historical memory, the dethroning of the sacred, the deification of science, which the new culture represented. Crucially, however,

Milosz has shown that all this is to be attributed, not ultimately to Marxism, but to the humanism and rationalism from which it sprang. He traces its roots to the emergence of rationalist humanism in post-Cartesian philosophy, to the fallacious belief that reason is the ultimate source of man's freedom. Even more fundamentally, he suggests its roots lie in a tension between nature and culture as old as human existence itself

Both Dostoevsky and Tolstoy had warned of the dangers of ideological socialism decades before the Russian Revolution while also suggesting that the age-old passion for justice could be fulfilled within the ethical framework of Christian tradition. In *The Devils* Shatov condemns the systematised ideology of the socialists, describing it as a 'half science based on reason' and Zossima declares that 'no sort of scientific teaching will ever teach men to share property and privileges with equal consideration for all'. That objective, he says, will be realised only through the exercise of communal responsibility in a spirit of humility and faith, a truth he underlines in his tale of the philanthropic doctor who loved the whole of mankind but could not abide those closest to him. But Dostoevsky also points to the irrationalist appeal of socialism in works such as *The Dream of a Ridiculous Man* and *The Devils*, showing that much of its attraction derives from its quasi religious character as well as its quasi scientific humanism. Dostoevsky's hatred of capitalism is conveyed strongly in the novels – in the debate between Luzhin and Lebezyatnikov, for instance, in *Crime and Punishment* and again in the *Winter Notes on Summer Impressions* – but what he holds out as the hope for social reform is the ideal of *sobornost*, a community ideal, achievable not through the upheavals of political revolution but through the exercise of penitence, humility, faith, self-sacrificing love and prayer.

That, broadly speaking, is the position advocated by Tolstoy also both in his social writings and in the novels. Denouncing the excesses of capitalistic greed and the inhuman conditions existing in the factories and state institutions of nineteenth century Europe, he too called for the exercise of social responsibility not by way of political initiatives but as an expression of individual morality. His portraits of ideological socialists in *Anna Karenina* and *Resurrection* emphasise the abstract nature of their ideals; pointing to their dogmatism, fanaticism and intolerance, he lays bare the hypocrisy of pride and self-interest masquerading as philanthropic concern. Insisting, like Dostoevsky, that social morality must be grounded in individual morality, he too calls for the pursuit of social ideals in a spirit of Christian humility, self-penitence and a truly self-sacrificing love. Similar considerations lay behind Unamuno's rejection of the socialism he had briefly espoused in his youth. He condemned its social reductionism, its isolation of social ideals from the sphere of the spiritual and the religious.

Underlying all these viewpoints is a sense of the permanence of Christian values and of the religious and moral traditions on which Christianity is founded. On this in turn is founded the belief that Christianity will survive as long as mankind itself, its survival being assured by the timeless nature of the truths it embodies. Tolstoy warned of the danger of confusing the eternal and the transient, the permanent and the contingent, seeing secularist ideologies as being a product of such confusion. That view is reiterated by Milosz who insists, like Tolstoy, that Christianity transcends history, its truths lying beyond the sphere of the social and the temporal. He complains that this has been lost sight of in the general indifference to sacred traditions that is everywhere in evidence in the contemporary world. Our present condition, he declared in his Nobel address, is rooted in a refusal to remember, a failure to recognise that historical awareness is the means by which we understand the present, that it provides the key to an understanding of ourselves and the world we inhabit. He calls for a rediscovery of tradition by modern man, especially of the sacred truths embodied in the hermetic wisdom of the scriptures and of prophetic literature from Dante to Dostoevsky.

It is this forging of past and present consciousness that Milosz and Brodsky both recognise as the special responsibility of the poet. Both speak of a prophetic role for poetry, seeing its capacity to disclose the future as deriving from its integration of past, present and future consciousness within the whole temporal continuum, all of which it views ultimately in terms of its conjuncture with the timeless. The supposed decline of modern civilisation, the sense that we have reached the end of a phase in the cultural evolution of mankind, derives, they suggest, from the severing of modern culture from its roots. The problems of the modern world stem from cultural disinheritance, not from the impending demise of its traditions. Our civilisation is not threatened, far less doomed, they argue, merely divorced from its own cultural origins, the secularisation of its culture being the most visible sign of this. The role of the poet, as they see it, is the reassertion of the continuing relevance of our traditions, of their enduring meaningfulness for the modern world. Our cultural traditions, as Brodsky in particular has shown, are inherent in the language we speak, and as indestructible as language itself. While recognising the reality of the 'sense of the end', and while invoking the horrors of a post Christian culture through the medium of poetic imagery, Brodsky ultimately predicts the survival of traditional values and beliefs, especially those of the Judaeo-Christian inheritance. Citing Mandelstam – 'Yesterday has not yet been born, it has not yet really existed' – he insists that the past lives on in memory, its meaningfulness being continuously reinvoked and reinterpreted through art. Memory and culture, he declares, are our defences against time, embodying as they do the spirit's unceasing quest for the timeless. The Word embodies that quest; it embodies memory, culture, faith and love. The Word, therefore, is man's ultimate defence against time. Christianity, he declares, endures – will endure permanently – as Word. This is his message to the modern world, a message imbued with the spirit of hope, the time-transcending hope that is itself the hallmark of the Christian faith.

Notes

In an attempt to keep referencing within manageable proportions paginated endnotes are not provided for quotations from primary literary texts. These are relatively easy to locate and the particular editions of the texts from which the quotations are taken are given at the beginning of the relevant chapter notes. Individual paginated references are provided, however, for all secondary sources and for non-literary texts by each of the individual authors whose work is examined in the book.

INTRODUCTION

1 David Marr (ed.), *Patrick White: Letters* (London: Jonathan Cape, 1994), p. 363.
2 See Marina Tsvetaeva, 'The Poet and Time', *Eight Essays on Poetry by Marina Tsvetaeva*, trans. Livingstone, (Bristol Classical Press, 1992), pp. 87-103.
3 T.S. Eliot, *Selected Prose* (ed. Hayward) (Penguin Books, 1953), p. 23.
4 Czeslaw Milosz, *The Witness of Poetry* (Harvard University Press, 1983), p. 35.
5 See Czeslaw Milosz, 'Looking for a Center: On the Poetry of Central Europe', *Beginning with My Streets* (London: Taurus, 1980), pp. 70- 81; 'On Modern Russian Literature and the West', *Emperor of the Earth: Modes of Eccentric Vision* (University of California Press, 1977), pp. 79-84.
6 David Marr, *Patrick White: A Life* (London: Jonathan Cape, 1991), pp. 11-12.
7 Peter Beatson, *The Eye of the Mandala, Patrick White: A Vision of Man and God* (London: Paul Elek, 1976), p. 3.

CHAPTER 1

Quotations from Dostoevsky's fiction are taken from the following texts:
   Poor Folk, trans. Dessaix (Ann Arbor, Ardis, 1982).
   The House of the Dead, trans. Edwards (London: Dent, 1962).
   Notes from Underground/ The Double, trans. Coulson (Penguin Books, 1972).
   A Raw Youth, trans. Garnett(London: Heinemann, 1979).
   Crime and Punishment, trans. Magarshak (Penguin Books, 1951).
   The Devils, trans. Magarshak (Penguin Books, 1955).
   The Idiot, trans. Garnett (London: Heinemann, 1946).
   The Brothers Karamazov, Trans. Garnett (London: Heinemann, 1945).
1 S. Kaydash, 'Dostoevski and Fonvizina', *Voprosy Literatury*, 5, 1981, pp. 307-13.
2 G. Kjetsaa, *Fyodor Dostoevsky* (London: Macmillan, 1987), p. 249.
3 Ibid., p. 284
4 Ibid., p. 328
5 K. Mochulsky, *Dostoevsky's Life and Work* (Princeton University Press, 1967), p. 652.
6 Ibid., p. 563.
7 F. Dostoevsky, *A Writer's Diary*, vol. 1, 1873-6 (London: Quartet Books, 1994), pp. 734-6.
8 Lev Shestov, *Umozrenie i Otkrovenie* (Speculation and Revelation) (Paris: YMCA Press, 1964), p. 195.

9 V.Soloviev, 'Three Speeches in Memory of Dostoevsky', *Collected Works*, Vol. III, (St Petersburg,1901-7), pp. 185-223.

10 G. Alekseyev, 'The House Where A Writer Was Born', *Vecherniy Leningrad*, no. 247, Oct. 19, 1971.

11 Ibid.

12 F. Dostoevsky, *Polnoye Sobraniye* (Moscow, 1926),II, pp. 8, 10, 134.

13 F. Dostoevsky, *A Writer's Diary* (Quartet edition), vol.1, p. 128.

14 F. Dostoevsky, *Pis'ma* (ed. Dolinin) (Moscow, 1928), vol II, p. 291. This is the definitive edition of Dostoevsky's letters. There are several selected editions of his letters in English, e.g. *A Self- Portrait* (trans. Coulson) (Oxford University Press, 1962); *Letters of F.M. Dostoevsky to his Family and Friends*, trans. E.C. Mayne (London: Chatto and Windus, 1917).

15 Ibid., pp. 44-5.

16 Mochulsky, p. 81.

17 Kjetsaa, pp. 126-7.

18 Ibid.

19 Mochulsky, pp. 260-1.

20 *Pis'ma*, II, p. 71.

21 D. Stremookoff, *Vladimir Soloviev and his Messianic Work* (Belmont, Mass., Nordland, 1980), p. 73.

22 Mochulsky, p. 44.

23 Ibid., p. 562.

24 Kaydash, op. cit.

25 *Pis'ma*, 11, p. 175.

26 Kjetsaa, p. 300.

27 Czeslaw Milosz, *The Land of Ulro* (Manchester: Carcanet, 1985), pp. 52-3.

28 Paul de Man, 'Dialogue and Dialogicism', *The Resistance to Theory* (Minneapolis: University of Minnesota Press,1986), pp. 106-14.

29 See Martin Buber, *The Knowledge of Man* (New York: Harper and Row, 1966); M. Bakhtin, *The Dialogic Imagination* (Austin: University of Texas Press, 1981), *Problems of Dostoevsky's Poetics* (University of Minnesota Press, 1984); B.H. Bialostosky, 'Dialogics as an Art of Discourse in Literary Criticism', *PMLA*, 101 (1986), pp. 788-97; G.G. Morson (ed.) *Bakhtin* (University of Chicago Press, 1986); C. Thomson, 'Bakhtin's Theory of Genre', *Studies in Twentieth Century Literature*, IX, 1984, pp. 29-40; T. Todorov, *Mikhail Bakhtin: The Dialogical Principle* (University of Minnesota Press, 1984; N. Perlina, 'Bakhtin and Buber: Problems of Dialogic Imagination', *Studies in Twentieth Century Literature*, IX, 1984, pp. 13-28.

30 V. Seduro, *Dostoevski's Image in Russia To-day* (Belmont, Mass: Nordland, 1977), pp. 307-16.

31 Ibid., p. 316.

32 Bakhtin, *Problems of Dostoevsky's Poetics*, p. xiv.

33 Ibid.

35 L. Grossman, *Dostoevsky: A Biography* (London, 1974); V. Ivanov, *Freedom and the Tragic Life* (New York, 1960); V.V. Rozanov, *Dostoevsky and the Legend of the Grand Inquisitor* (Ithaca, 1972); D. Merezhkovsky, *Tolstoy and Dostoevsky* (St Petersburg, 1901).

36 Bakhtin, *Problems of Dostoevsky's Poetics*, p. 9.

37 Ibid., pp. 9-10.

38 Ibid., p. 10.

39 Ibid., p. 18.

40 M. Buber, *The Knowledge of Man*, pp. 149-65.

41 M.Buber, *I and Thou* (Edinburgh: Clark, 1937), pp. 62, 69, 123.
42 Buber, *The Knowledge of Man*, pp. 60-1.
43 Ibid., pp. 121-48.
44 S. Kierkegaard, *Concluding Unscientific Postscript* (Princeton University Press, 1968), p. 182.
45 Dostoevsky, *Pis'ma*, IV, p. 735.
46 A Boyce Gibson, *The Religion of Dostoevsky* (London: SCM Press, 1973), p. 77.
47 N. Chernychevsky, *What Is To Be Done?*, trans. Tucker (Boston, 1886).
48 E. Wasiolek, *Dostoevsky: The Major Fiction* (Mass: MIT Press, 1964), p. 36.
49 Ibid., p. 131.
50 F.M. *Dostoevski v vospominaniyakh sovremennikov* (ed. Grigerenko) (Moscow, 1964), 11, p. 172.
51 Mochulsky, p. 459.
52 A Kozin, *Introduction to Annotated Edition of The Devils* (New York: Interlanguage Literary Associates, 1964), p. 17.
53 Boyce Gibson, p. 145.
54 Mochulsky, p. 459.
55 D. Magarshak (ed.), *Dostoevsky's Occasional Writings* (New York: Vision Press, 1964), p. 305.
56 R. Peace, *Dostoevsky: An Examination of the Major Novels* (Cambridge University Press, 1971), p. 59.
57 Ibid., p. 65.
58 Boyce Gibson, p. 112.
59 Ibid.
60 G. Friedlander in *Tvorchestvo Dostoevskogo* (ed. Stepanov) (Moscow, 1959), p. 191.
61 Buber, *The Knowledge of Man*, pp. 121-48.
62 Ibid., pp. 139, 143-4, 146.
63 Wasiolek, p. 79.
64 *Tvorchestvo Dostoestkogo*, p. 164.
65 Ibid.
66 F. Dostoevsky, *The Diary of a Writer* (ed. Brasol) (Surrey: Ianmead, 1984), p. 36.
67 S. Kierkegaard, *Christian Discourses* (ed. Lowrie) (Princeton University Press, 1971), pp. 101-10.
68 Anna Dostoevsky, *Reminiscences* (ed. Stillman) (London, 1975) pp. 143-4.
69 Dostoevsky, *Pis'ma*, IV, p. 114.
70 Kjetsaa, p. 378.
71 Dostoevsky, *Diary of a Writer* (ed. Brasol), p. 668.
72 Ibid., p. 671.
73 Seduro, p. 396.

CHAPTER 2

Quotations from Tolstoy's fiction are taken from the following texts:

A Prisoner of the Caucasus and Other Stories (Moscow: Raduga, 1983).
The Sebastopol Sketches, trans. McDuff (Penguin Books, 1986).
War and Peace, trans. Garnett (London: The Modern Library, 1952).
Anna Karenina, trans. Garnett (London: Heinemann, 1977).
Resurrection, trans. Louise Maude (Moscow: Progress, 1972).
Stories, trans. Wettlin, Altschuler (Moscow: Raduga, 1983).
Great Short Works of Leo Tolstoy, trans. A and L. Maude (New York: Harper and Row, 1967).

1 *Tolstoy's Diaries*, ed. R.F. Christian (London: Harper Collins, 1994), p. 399.
2 R.F. Christian, *Introduction to New Essays on Tolstoy*, ed. M. Jones (Cambridge University Press, 1978), p. 10.
3 G. Panichas, *Mansions of the Spirit* (New York: Hawthorn Press, 1967), p. 173.
4 Lev Shestov, *Dostoevsky, Tolstoy and Nietzsche*, trans. B. Martin and S. Roberts (Ohio, 1969), pp. 71-2.
5 Lev Shestov, 'The Gift of Prophecy' in *Chekhov and Other Essays* (Ann Arbor, 1966), p. 78; *In Job's Balances*, trans. G. Covertry and C.A. McCartney (London: Dent, 1932).
6 G. Steiner, *Tolstoy or Dostoevsky* (New York: Random House, 1959), p. 328.
7 V. Lenin, 'L.N.Tolstoy and his Epoch', cited in G.W.Spence, *Tolstoy the Ascetic* (Edinburgh: Oliver and Boyd, 1967), p. 127.
8 L. Tolstoy, *The Kingdom of God is Within You* (London: Scott, 1894). p. 220.
9 E.B. Greenwood, *Tolstoy: The Comprehensive Vision* (London: Methuen, 1975), pp. 128-9.
10 L. Tolstoy, *A Confession and Other Religious Writings* (Penguin Books, 1987), p. 50.
11 A.N. Wison, *The Lion and the Honeycomb: Tolstoy's Religious Writings* (London: Collins, 1987), p.129.
12 *A Confession*, p. 19.
13 *Tolstoy's Diaries*, ed.R.F. Christian (London: Athlone Press, 1985, vol. 1, p. 92
14 *Tolstoy's Diaries* (1994), p. 246.
15 T.G. Cain, *Tolstoy* (London: Elek, 1977), p. vii.
16 J. Bayley, *Tolstoy and the Novel* (London: Chatto and Windus, 1966), p.33.
17 K. Hamburger, 'Tolstoy's Art' in *Tolstoy: Twentieth Century Views*, ed. R. Maitlaw (New Jersey: Prentice-Hall, 1967), p. 67.
18 Renato Poggioli, 'Tolstoy As Man and Artist', in Maitlaw, op. cit., p. 19.
19 *Tolstoy's Diaries* (1985), vol. 1, p. 330.
20 Isaiah Berlin, *The Hedgehog and the Fox: An Essay on Tolstoy's View of History* (London: Orion Books, 1992), p. 41-2.
21 L. Tolstoy, *What Is Art and Other Essays*, trans. A Maude (Oxford University Press, 1930), pp. 9-10.
22 Ibid., p. 56.
23 Ibid., p. 263.
24 Ibid., p. 272.
25 Ibid., pp. 268-9.
26 Ibid.
27 Ibid., pp. 176-7.
28 D. Murphy, *Tolstoy and Education* (Dublin: Irish Academic Press, 1992).
29 *Tolstoy's Diaries* (1994), p. 59.
30 *A Confession*, p. 49.
31 Ibid., p. 50.
32 Ibid., p. 53.
33 V. Bulgakov, *The Last Year of Leo Tolstoy* (New York: Dial Press, 1971), p. 111.
34 L. Tolstoy, *On Life* (Christchurch, Hants. The Free Age Press, 1902), pp. 108-15.
35 *A Confession*, p. 51
36 L. Tolstoy, *The Four Gospels Harmonised and Translated* (London: Scott, 1859), pp. xxii-xxiii.
37 *On Life*, p. 60.
38 *Tolstoy's Diaries* (1994), p. 39.
39 Ibid., p. 49.
40 Ibid., p. 65.

41 Bulgakov, op. cit., pp. 104-5.
42 *The Gospel of St Matthew*, VI, 5.
43 *The Lion and the Honeycomb*, p. 129.
44 *A Confession*, p. 199.
45 Ibid., p. 168.
46 L. Tolstoy, *My Religion* (London: Scott, 1889).
47 Ibid., p. 2.
48 Ibid., pp. 6-7.
49 *The Lion and the Honeycomb*, pp. 129-30.
50 Bulgakov, op. cit., p. 147.
51 Ibid., p. 166.
52 *A Confession*, pp. 172-3.
53 Ibid., p. 173.
54 *The Kingdom of God is Within You*, p.122.
55 *A Confession*, p. 173.
56 Greenwood, op. cit., p. 121.
57 *My Religion*, pp. 143-59.
58 Ibid., p. 144.
59 Spence, op. cit., p.43.
60 L Tolstoy, *A Confession and Other Writings* (Includes *The Gospel in Brief* and *My Religion*), World's Classics Edition (Oxford, 1934), p. 378.
61 *The Lion and the Honeycomb*, p. 151.
62 Bulgakov, op. cit., p. 91.
63 *A Confession*, p. 172.
64 Ibid., p. 145.
65 Ibid.
66 *Tolstoy's Diaries* (1985), vol. 1, p. 56.
67 Bulgakov, op. cit., p. 15.
68 *My Religion*, p. 7.
69 *A Confession*, p. 76.
70 Ibid., pp. 188-9.
71 *My Religion*, p. 13.
72 *A Confession*, p. 195.
73 Ibid., pp. 214-15.
74 Jones, op.cit., pp. 109-10.
75 L. Tolstoy, 'I Cannot Be Silent', *Essays From Tula* (London: Sheppard Press, 1948), pp. 178-9.
76 Ibid., p. 21.
77 Ibid., pp. 23-6.
78 *Tolstoy's Letters*, ed. R.F. Christian (London: Athlone Press, 1978) vol. II, p. 692. See also Alexandra Tolstoy, *Tolstoy, A Life of My Father* (Belmont, Mass: Nordland, 1948).
79 A Maude, *Tolstoy*, 2 vols. (Oxford University Press, 1987), pp.282-3.
80 The pursuit of perfection, in accordance with Christ's injunction, 'Be ye perfect as your heavenly Father is perfect', is seen by Kierkegaard, in works such as *Christian Discourses*, as the core of Christ's message to mankind. In his *Attack Upon Christendom* he castigates the Danish clergy for propagating a diluted version of Christianity and for failing to communicate the full import of the Gospel teaching.
81 *Essays From Tula*, pp. 210-11.
82 N. Berdyaev, *Preface to Essays From Tula*, p. 15.
83 F.F. Seeley, 'Tolstoy's Philosophy of History', in *New Essays on Tolstoy*, ed. Jones, pp. 175-93; Berlin, op. cit.; Spence, op. cit.; M. Hengel, *Victory Over Violence* (London:

1972); R.V. Sampson, *Tolstoy: The Discovery of Peace* (London, 1973); G. Steiner, *Tolstoy or Dostoevsky*, op. cit.
84 Berlin, op. cit., pp. 11-12.
85 Jones, op. cit., p. 173.
86 Spence, op. cit., p. 2.
87 *On Life*, p. 69.
88 Spence, op. cit., p. 12.
89 Berlin, op. cit., p. 66.
90 *A Confession*, pp. 217-18.

CHAPTER 3
Quotations from Unamuno's fiction are taken from the following texts:
  Abel Sanchez (Madrid: Castalia, 1985).
  Amor y Pedagogia (Barcelona: Henrich y Cía, 1902).
  The Christ of Velázquez, trans. Turnbull (Baltimore: John Hopkins Press, 1951).
  Mist, trans. Fite (New York, 1928).
  Peace in War, trans. Lacy, Nozick and Kerrigan (Princeton University Press, 1983).
  San Manuel Bueno, Mártir (bilingual text), trans. de Segovia/Perez (London: Harrap, 1969).
  Three Exemplary Novels, trans. Florea (New York: Grove Press, 1956).
(Since English translations are not available for two of the novels, *Abel Sanchez* and *Amor y Pedagogia*, the passages quoted from these were translated specially for the present work.)
   1 M. de Unamuno, *Tragic Sense of Life* (New York: Dover Publications 1954), p. 2.
   2 M. de Unamuno, *The Agony of Christianity*, trans. Kerrigan (London: Routledge and Kegan Paul, 1974), p. 84.
   3 Ibid., pp. 151-2.
   4 Federico Urales, 'La evolución de la filosofia en españa', *La revista blanca*, II, 1934, p. 206.
   5 M. de Unamuno, *Epistolario a Clarín*, ed. Alas (Madrid, 1941), p. 53.
   6 Ibid.
   7 *Agony*, p. 4.
   8 Ibid., pp. 55-60.
   9 'Cartas de Miguel de Unamuno', *Sur*, 119 (1944), p. 53.
  10 Carta I de Unamuno, 'Cartas ineditas', *Revista de la Universidad de Buenos Aires III* (1948), p. 67.
  11 Ibid.
  12 *Epistolario entre Unamuno y Juan Maragall* (Barcelona, 1951), p. 56.
  13 M. de Unamuno, *Como se hace una novela* (Buenos Aires, 1927), pp. 82-3.
  14 Catra I de Unamuno, 'Carta ineditas', p. 66.
  15 *Agony*, p. 116.
  16 Ibid., pp. 114-15.
  17 *Tragic*, p. 3.
  18 Ibid., p. 198.
  19 Ibid., pp. 178-9.
  20 M.de Unamuno, *Essays and Soliloquies*, p. 113.
  21 Ibid.
  22 *Tragic*, p.309.
  23 Ibid., pp. 314-15.
  24 Ibid., pp. 141, 143.
  25 Ibid., pp. 144-5.

26 M. de Unamuno, 'Ultima lección académica', *Obras completas*, VII, (Madrid and Barcelona, 1958-64), p. 1085.
27 *Tragic*, p. 25.
28 'Dostoyevsqui sobre la lengua,' *Obras completas*, VII, p. 1155.
29 Ibid.
30 Ibid.
31 Ibid.
32 *Tragic*, pp. 311-12.
33 'Tres cartas de Unamuno a Federico de Onís', *La Torre*, Año IX, XXXV-XXXVI (1961), p. 59.
34 *Unamuno y Maragall: Epistolario y escritos complementarios* (Barcelona, 1951), p. 26.
35 Introduction to *Amor y pedagogia* (Barcelona, 1902).
36 *The Gospel of St John*, I, i.
37 *Tragic*, pp. 159-60.
38 *Agony*, p. 165.
39 *Tragic*, pp. 301-2, 308.
40 Ibid., p. 111.
41 *Agony*, pp. 237-8.
42 *Tragic*, p. 188.
43 Ibid., p. 117.
44 Ibid., p. 120.
45 *Agony*, pp. 11, 78.
46 *Essays and Soliloquies*, pp. 157-8.
47 *Agony*, p. 53.
48 *Tragic*, p. 114.
49 Ibid., pp. 192-3.
50 Ibid., p. 186.
51 *Agony*, p. 149.
52 Ibid.
53 Ibid., p. 114.
54 *Tragic*, pp. 154-5, 179-80.
55 Ibid., p. 325.
56 Ibid., pp. 326-7.
57 *Essays and Soliloquies*, pp. 114, 123-4.
58 *Tragic*, p. 266.
59 *Agony*, p. 53.
60 *Tragic*, pp. 132, 137.
61 Ibid., p. 167.
62 Ibid., p. 193.
63 Ibid., pp. 202-3.
64 Ibid., p. 139.
65 Ibid., pp. 319-20.
66 Ibid., p. 214.
67 Ibid., pp. 177-8.
68 Ibid., p. 134.
69 Ibid., p. 193.
70 *Agony*, p. 36.
71 *Tragic*, pp. 205-6.
72 Ibid., p. 132.
73 Ibid., p. 140.
74 Ibid., p. 283.

75 *Agony*, p. 124.
76 Ibid., p. 10.
77 Ibid., p. 131.
78 Ibid., p.p 132.
79 *Tragic*, p. 33.
80 Ibid., pp. 39.
81 Ibid., pp. 3-4.
82 Ibid., p. 48.
83 Ibid., p. 154.
84 Ibid., p. 200.
85 Ibid., p. 114.
86 *Agony*, p. 20.
87 *Tragic*, p. 201.
88 Ibid., p. 63.
89 Ibid., pp. 190-1.

CHAPTER 4

Quotations from Mauriac's fiction are taken from the following texts. (All translations are by Gerard Hopkins).

> *Thérèse* (London: Eyre and Spottiswoode, 1947).
> *The Knot of Vipers* (London: Eyre and Spottiswoode, 1951).
> *The Desert of Love* (London: Eyre and Spottiswoode, 1949).
> *The Dark Angels* (London: Eyre and Spottiswoode, 1951).
> *The Loved and the Unloved* (London: Eyre and Spottiswoode, 1953).
> *A Woman of the Pharisees* (London: Eyre and Spottiswoode, 1954).
> *A Kiss for the Leper* (London: Eyre and Spottiswoode, 1953).
> *The Lamb* (London: Eyre and Spottiswoode, 1955).

1 F. Mauriac, *Les Maisons Fugitives, Oeuvres Complétes*, IV (Paris, 1956-61), p. 323.
2 F. Mauriac, *Bloc-Notes, 1952-7*, III (Paris, 1958), p. 415.
3 F. Mauriac, *Souffrances et bonheur du chrétien, Oeuvres Complétes*, VII, p. 252.
4 F. Mauriac, *D'autres et moi: textes receillis et commentés pár Keith Goesch* (Paris, 1966), p. 254.
5 R. Speaight, *François Mauriac: A Study of the Writer and the Man* (London: Chatto and Windus, 1976).
6 F. Mauriac, *Mémoires Intérieurs*, trans. Hopkins (London: Eyre and Spottiswoode, 1960), p. 145.
7 F. Mauriac, *Blaise Pascal et sa soeur Jacqueline, Oeuvres Complétes*, VIII, p. 315.
8 Ibid.
9 F. Mauriac, *Trois Grands Hommes devant Dieu, Oeuvres Complétes*, VIII, p. 222.
10 F. Mauriac, *Dieu et Mammon, Oeuvres Complétes*, VII, p. 297.
11 Speaight, op. cit., pp. 100-1.
12 Ibid., p. 83.
13 *Dieu et Mammon*, p. 315.
14 Ibid., pp. 316-17.
15 J.E. Flower, *Intention and Achievement: An Essay on the Novels of François Mauriac* (Oxford: Clarendon Press, 1969), p. 14.
16 *Oeuvres Complétes*, VII, p. 266.
17 Preface to 'The End of the Night', *Thérèse*, trans. Hopkins (London: Eyre and Spottiswoode, 1949), p. 163.
18 J.P. Sartre, 'M. François Mauriac et la Liberté', *Situations*, I (Paris: Gallimard, 1947), p. 42.

19 *Mémoires Intérieurs*, p. 37.
20 F. Mauriac, Postscript to *The Loved and the Unloved*, trans. Hopkins (London: Eyre and Spottiswoode, 1953), p. 138.
21 Ibid., pp. 139-41.
22 *Oeuvres Complétes*, VIII, p. 263.
23 Ibid., pp. 278-9.
24 Speaight, op. cit., p. 176.
25 *Oeuvres Complétes*, VIII, p. 296.
26 Speaight, op. cit., pp. 104-5.
27 Ibid., p. 87.
28 *Oeuvres Complétes*, VIII, p. 275.
29 Ibid., p. 276.
30 Speaight, op. cit., p. 125.
31 *Les Marges* (Jan-April, 1926).
32 *Mémoires Intérieurs*, pp. 51-2.
33 Ibid., pp. 126-7.
34 Ibid., p. 198.
35 Ibid., p. 238.
36 Ibid., p.. 24-5.
37 Ibid., p. 139.
38 *Oeuvres Complétes*, VII, p. 316.
39 Speaight, op. cit., p. 102.
40 *The Book of Isaiah*, 52-55. See also Luke 23; 63-5; Matthew 27-31.
41 *Mémoires Intérieurs*, p.239.
42 *D'Autres et moi*, p. 303.

CHAPTER 5

Quotations from Eliot's poetry are taken from *The Complete Poems and Plays* (London: Faber, 1969).

1 *Criterion*, X, 41, July 1931, p. 771.
2 T.S. Eliot, 'Religion Without Humanism' in *Humanism and America*, ed. Norman Foerster (New York, 1930), p. 110.
3 T.S. Eliot, *Selected Prose*, ed. Hayward (Penguin Books, 1955), pp. 32-43.
4 T.S. Eliot, *Selected Essays* (London: Faber, 1972), pp. 390-1
5 *Selected Prose*, p. 101.
6 Peter Ackroyd, T.S. Eliot (London: Hamish Hamilton, 1984), p. 208.
7 *Selected Essays*, pp. 258-9.
8 T.S. Eliot, Introduction to *Le Serpent par Paul Valéry*, trans. Wardle (London, 1924), p. 13.
9 *Selected Essays*, pp. 411-12.
10 Ibid., pp. 421-2.
11 Ibid. See also F. Mauriac, *Mémoires Intérieurs* (London: Eyre and Spottiswood, 1960), p. 50.
12 *Selected Essays*, pp. 334-6.
13 T.S. Eliot, *After Strange Gods* (London: Faber, 1934), p. 46.
14 Ibid.
15 *Selected Prose*, pp. 41-2, 43-4.
16 *Selected Essays*, p. 370.
17 *Selected Prose*, pp. 85-6.
18 Ibid., p. 101.

19 Letter quoted in Helen Gardner, *The Composition of Four Quartets* (London: Faber, 1978), p. 29.
20 E. Hay, *T.S. Eliot's Negative Way* (Harvard University Press, 1982), p. 76.
21 E. Lobb, *T.S. Eliot and the Romantic Critical Tradition* (London: Routledge and Kegan Paul, 1981), p. vi.
22 H. Gardner, *The Art of T.S. Eliot* (London: Faber, 1949).
23 T.S. Eliot, 'Paul Valéry', *Quarterly Review of Literature*, III, 3, 1947, p. 213.
24 See T.S. Eliot, 'Paul Elmer Moore, *Princeton Alumni Weekly*, XXVIII, February 1937, p. 373. (Eliot was deeply influenced by Moore's versions of the writings of St John of the Cross). See 'Talking Friends: T.S. Eliot and Tom Greenwell', *Yorkshire Post*, 29 August 1961. (In this interview, given three years before his death, Eliot attests to his lifelong interest in the writings of St John of the Cross). See also James J. Sweeney, 'East Coker: A Reading', *Southern Review*, VI, 1944, pp. 771-91; H.W. Hausermann, *English Studies*, XXIII, August 1941, p. 109; P. Murray, *T.S. Eliot and Mysticism* (London: Macmillan, 1988); A.C. Delaney, *Reflections on the Poetry of T.S. Eliot and the Doctrine of St John of the Cross*, Unpublished Ph.D. Thesis, Boston College, 1954.
25 Greenwell, op. cit., p. 3.
26 Hay, op. cit., p. 69.
27 S. Spender, *T.S. Eliot* (New York: Viking, 1975), p. 20.
28 *Selected Essays*, pp. 33, 373.
29 *The Confessions of St Augustine*, trans. Matthew (London: Burns and Oates, 1954), p. 47.
30 Isaiah, 32; Ecclesiastes, 12; Luke, 23.
31 *Selected Essays*, p. 324.
32 T.S. Eliot, 'A Note on Poetry and Belief', *Enemy*, I, 1927, p. 16.
33 W.H. Auden, *Introduction to The Descent of the Dove* by Charles Williams (New York, 1956).
34 Eliot had been interested in Dowson's poetry while a student at Harvard. See Ackroyd, op. cit., p. 33.
35 *Selected Essays*, p. 412.
36 St Augustine, *De Ordine*, II, 16, 44. Cited in Hay, op. cit., p. 187.
37 Thomas Aquinas, *Summa Theologiae*, trans. Dominican Fathers (Latin/English bilingual text) (London: Eyre and Spottiswoode, 1963), vol. II, Question 12, pp. 5,7.
38 *Complete Works of St John of the Cross*, ed. Peers (London: Burns Oates, 1964), I, pp. 24-5.
39 Ibid., pp. 19-20.
40 *Bhagavad–Gítá*, ed. Swami Prabhupada (New York: Bhaktivedanta Book Trust, 1972), II, 69, p. 43.
41 Thomas Aquinas, *Summa Contra Gentiles*, trans. Dominican Fathers (New York: Benziger,1939), IV, p. 1.
42 *Ascent to Mount Carmel*, II, ii.
43 *Selected Essays*, p. 23
44 Ackroyd, op. cit., p. 23.
45 *Criterion*, XII, 47, Jan. 1933, p. 248.
46 T.S. Eliot, *Murder in the Cathedral*, ed. Coghill (London: Faber, 1965), pp. 17-18.
47 I am indebted for this link to Morris Weitz, 'T.S. Eliot: Time As A Mode of Salvation', *Sewanee Review*, LX, I, 1952.
48 See H. Gardner, *The Art of T.S. Eliot*, pp. 36-56; also J.M. Reibetanz, *A Reading of T.S. Eliot's Four Quartets* (Epping, Essex: Bowker 1970); C.A. Bodelsen, *T.S. Eliot's Four Quartets* (Copenhagen, 1958).
49 T.S. Eliot, 'Dante and Little Gidding' in *T.S. Eliot's Four Quartets*, ed. Bergonzi (London: Macmillan, 1969), p. 25.

50 Julian of Norwich, *The Revelation of Divine Love*, ed. del Mastro (Liguori, Missouri: Triumph Books, 1994), p.108. The phrase 'the ground of our beseeching' also comes from Julian of Norwich. See *The Revelation*, p. 122.

CHAPTER 6
Quotations from Pasternak's writings are taken from the following texts:
  Doctor Zhivago, trans. Max Hayward and Manya Harari (London: Collins and Harvill Press, 1958).
  Fifty Poems, trans. Lydia Pasternak Slater (London: Allen and Unwin, 1963).
  In the Interlude: Poems, 1945-1960, trans. Henry Kamen (Oxford University Press, 1962).
  Poems, 1955-1959, trans. M. Harari (London: Collins and Harvill, 1960).
  Prose and Poems, ed. S. Schimanski (London: Benn, 1959).
  The Poetry of Boris Pasternak, 1914-1960, trans. G. Reavey (New York; Putnam, 1959).
  Sister, My Life: Summer 1917, trans. P.C. Flayderman (bilingual edition) (New York: Washington Press, 1967).
 1 B. Pasternak, 'Safe Conduct', Pasternak: *Prose and Poems*, ed. Schimanski (London: Benn, 1959), p. 87.
 2 Ibid.
 3 Olga Ivinskaya, *A Captive of Time: My Years With Pasternak*, trans. Hayward (London: Collins and Harvill Press, 1978), p.147. The authenticity of Pasternak's story of his baptism is disputed by some scholars. David Bethea describes it as 'a later embellishment by a poet who saw his greatest affinity with Christian values'. *Joseph Brodsky and the Creation of Exile* (Princeton University Press, 1994), p.154.
 4 Jhan Robbins, 'Boris Pasternak's Last Message to the World', *New York Herald Tribune*, 7 August 1960, p. 5.
 5 *Ivinskaya*, op. cit., p. 148.
 6 U.A. Floridi, 'Un messagio di rizurrezione della Russia sovietica', *Civiltá Cattolica*, 18 January 1958.
 7 D.V. Konstantinov, 'Doktor Zhivago i bogoiskatelstvo v SSSR', *Vestnik Miunkhenskogo Instituta po izucheniiu SSSR*, II, 1959, pp. 76-84.
 8 Rimvydas Silbajoris, Foreword to Guy de Mallac, *Boris Pasternak* (University of Oklahoma Press, 1981), p. xiii. See also David M. Bethea, *Joseph Brodsky and the Creation of Exile* (Princeton University Press, 1994). See Chapter 5, 'Judaism and Christianity in Mandelstam, Pasternak and Brodsky', pp. 140-73.
 9 Judith Stora, 'Pasternak et la judaisme', *Cahiers du monde russe et soviétique*, 9, 1968, pp. 353-64.
10 *The Correspondence of Boris Pasternak and Olga Freidenberg, 1910-1954*, ed. Mossman (New York: Harcourt, Brace, Jovanovich, 1982), p. 246.
11 Ibid., p. 333.
12 Guy de Mallac, op. cit., p. 331.
13 Gifford, p. 212.
14 B. Pasternak, *In the Interlude* (Notes by George Katkov) (London: Oxford University Press, 1962), p. 130.
15 *The Literary Essays of Thomas Merton*, ed. Brother Patrick Hart (New York: New Directions, 1981), pp. 81-3.
16 Ibid., pp. 43 ff.
17 de Mallac, op. cit., 182.
18 B. Pasternak, *Sochineniia* (Collected Works), ed. G. Struve and B. Fillipov (Ann Arbor: University of Michigan Press, 1961), vol. I, p. xiv.

19 Guy de Mallac, op. cit., p. 341.
20 'Safe Conduct', p. 52.
21 *Sochineniia*, II, p. 154.
22 S.T. Coleridge, *Lectures* (London, 1913), p. 32.
23 'Safe Conduct', p. 63.
24 Ibid., pp. 62-3.
25 *Sochineniia*, III, p. 71. For a translation of this paper by Paul Schmidt see *Partisan Review*, 21, 1964, pp. 405-9.
26 *Sochineniiia*, I, xx.
27 Encounter, 82, August 1960; Ralph Maitlaw, 'A Visit with Pasternak', *Nation*, 12 September 1959, p. 134.
28 'Safe Conduct', p. 60.
29 *The Literary Essays of Thomas Merton*, p. 49.
30 *Sochineniia*, II, 153-4.
31 Martin Green, *Yeats's Blessings on von Hügel Essays on Literature and Religion* (London: Longmans, 1967), pp. 206-7.
32 Donald Davie and Angela Livingstone (eds.) *Pasternak: Modern Judgements* (London: Macmillan, 1969), p. 225.
33 B. Pasternak, 'Translating Shakespeare', in *I Remember: Sketch for an Autobiography*, trans. Harari (New York, 1959), p. 134.
34 Ibid.
35 'Safe Conduct', p. 107.
36 De Mallac, op. cit., p. 180.
37 Lazar Fleishman, *Boris Pasternak: The Poet and his Politics* (Harvard University Press, 1990), p. 271.
38 Davie and Livingstone, op. cit., p. 205.
39 Czeslaw Milosz, 'On Pasternak Soberly', *Emperor of the Earth: Modes of Eccentric Vision* (Berkeley: University of California Press, 1977), p. 63.
40 Ibid.
41 Ibid.
42 Ibid.
43 Davie and Livingstone, op. cit., p.234.
44 Green, op. cit., p. 204.
45 'Safe Conduct', pp. 15-16.
46 *The Literary Essays of Thomas Merton*, pp. 47ff.
47 Davie and Livingstone, op. cit., p. 160.
48 Milosz, op. cit., pp. 70-1.
49 Ibid.
50 Davie and Livingstone, op. cit., p. 166.
51 Ibid., p. 238.
52 B. Pasternak, 'Translating Shakespeare', in *I Remember: Sketch for an Autobiography*, trans. Harari (New York, 1959), p. 134.
53 Edmund Wilson, E. 'Doctor Life and His Guardian Angel', *New Yorker*, 15 Nov. 1958, pp. 213-38.
54 *The Correspondence of Boris Pasternak and Olga Freidenberg*, p. 232.

CHAPTER 7

Quotations from Mandelstam's poetry are taken from the following texts:
Selected Poems, trans. David McDuff (Cambridge: Rivers Press, 1973).
Selected Poems, trans. Clarence Brown and W.S. Merwin (Penguin Books, 1977).

Poems, trans. James Greene (London: Elek, 1977).

The Moscow Notebooks, trans. R. and E. McKane (Newcastle: Bloodaxe Books, 1991).

1 *Complete Poetry of Osip Mandelstam*, trans. Burton Raffel and Alla Burago (Introduction and Notes by Sidney Monas) (State University of New York Press, 1973). For a discussion of Mandelstam's Jewish and Christian affiliations see also David.M. Bethea, *Joseph Brodsky and the Creation of Exile* (Princeton University Press, 1994). See pp. 147-53. Bethea cites an essay by Gregory Freidin in which this significant comment occurs: 'It is curious that, as opposed to his Acmeist confréres who were Orthodox by birth, Mandelstam, the single Jew among the five founders of the school, defined himself precisely as a Christian poet.' p. 282.

2 Nadezhda Mandelstam, *Hope Abandoned* (Penguin Books, 1974) p. 210.

3 Ibid., p. 57.

4 Ibid., p. 483.

5 Nadezhda Mandelstam, *Hope Against Hope* (Penguin Books, 1970).

6 'Pushkin and Scriabin', Mandelstam: *The Complete Critical Prose and Letters*, ed. Jane Gary Harris (Ann Arbor: Ardis, 1979), p. 91.

7 Ibid., p. 92.

8 Ryszard Przybylski, *An Essay on the Poetry of Osip Mandelstam: God's Grateful Guest* (Ann Arbor: Ardis, 1987), p. 45.

9 *Mandelstam: Complete Critical Prose and Letters*, p. 115.

10 Ibid., pp. 94-5.

11 Przybylski, op. cit., p. 58.

12 *Hope Abandoned*, p. 21.

13 *Mandelstam: Complete Critical Prose and Letters*, p. 63.

14 Joseph Brodsky, *Less Than One* (New York: Viking, 1986), p. 137.

15 *Mandelstam: Complete Critical Prose and Letters*, p. 64.

16 Przybylski, op. cit., p. 78.

17 *Hope Abandoned*, pp. 207, 342.

18 *Less Than One*, p. 174.

19 Sergei Gorodetsky, *Nekotorye technia v sovremennoy russkoy poezii*, Apollon, I, 1913, p. 48.

20 Ilya Ehrenberg, *Portreti russkikh poetov* (Berlin, 1922), p. 104.

21 Joel, 2:10; Matthew, 24:29; Mark, 13:24.

22 *Mandelstam: Complete Critical Prose*, p. 181.

23 *Acts of the Apostles*, 27:9.

24 Revelations, 6:12; Matthew, 24:29.

25 *Mandelstam: Complete Critical Prose*, p. 90.

26 Ibid., p. 112.

27 *Hope Abandoned*, p. 585.

28 *Mandelstam: Complete Critical Prose*, p. 91.

29 Nadezhda Mandelstam, *Vospominaniya* (New York, 1970), p. 245.

30 *Mandelstam: Complete Critical Prose*, p. 90.

31 *Hope Abandoned*, pp. 159, 209.

32 *Mandelstam: Complete Critical Prose*, p. 92.

33 *Hope Abandoned*, pp. 190, 621.

34 *Mandelstam: Complete Critical Prose*, p. 92.

35 *Hope Abandoned*, pp. 619-23.

36 Ibid., pp. 621-2.

37 *Mandelstam: Complete Critical Prose*, p. 94.

38 Jennifer Baines, *Mandelstam: The Later Poetry* (Cambridge University Press, 1976), p. 16.

39 *Hope Abandoned*, p. 128.

40 Ibid., pp. 303, 392.
41 Przybylski, p. 203.
42 *Hope Abandoned*, p. 363.
43 Ibid., pp. 284, 293.
44 Clarence Brown, *Mandelstam* (Cambridge University Press, 1973), p. 297.

CHAPTER 8

Quotations from Akhmatova's poetry are taken from the following texts:
The Complete Poems of Anna Akhmatova, trans. Judith Hemschemeyer, ed. Roberta Reeder (Boston: Zephyr Press, 1992).
Anna Akhmatova: Selected Poems, ed. Walter Arndt (Ann Arbor, Ardis, 1976).
Way of All the Earth, trans. D.M. Thomas (London: Secker and Warburg, 1979).

1 Osip Mandelstam, *Sobraniye sochinenii*, ed. Struve and Filippov (Washington,D.C., Interlanguage Literary Associates, 1964), vol. I, p. 119. Translation by Wendy Roslyn, *The Prince, the Fool and the Nunnery* (London: Avebury, 1982), p. 17.
2 N.V. Nedobrovo, 'Anna Akhmatova', *Russkaya mys'l*, 7, 1915, pp. 50-68.
3 V. Zhirmunsky, 'Preodolevshiye simvolism', *Voprosy teorii literatury* (Leningrad, 1928), pp. 278-336.
4 K. Chukovsky, 'Akhmatova i Mayakovsky', *Dom iskusstv*, I, 1921, pp. 23-42.
5 V. Vinogradov, 'O simvolike A. Akhmatovoy', *Literaturnaya mysl*, I, 1922, pp. 91-138.
6 A. Gizetti, 'Tri dushi', *Ezhemesyachyy zhurnal*, XII, 1915, pp. 147-66.
7 B. Eykhenbaum, *Anna Akhmatova: opyt analiza* (St Petersburg, 1923), p. 114.
8 Y. Aykhenval'd, 'Anna Akhmatova', *Siluety russkikh pisateley* (Moscow, 1923), III, pp. 279-93.
9 A. Zhdanov, 'Doklad t. Zhdanova o zhurnalakh Zvezda i Leningrad', *Znamya*, X, 1946, pp. 7-22.
10 Nadezhda Mandelstam, *Hope Abandoned* (Penguin Books, 1974), p. 60.
11 Anatoly Nayman, *Remembering Anna Akhmatova* (London: Halban, 1991), p. 45.
12 Cited in Amanda Haight, *Akhmatova: A Poetic Pilgrimage* (Oxford University Press, 1976), p. 113.
13 *Selected Poems of Marina Tsvetaeva*, trans. Feinstein (Oxford University Press, 1981), pp. 15-16.
14 *Mandelstam: Complete Critical Prose and Letters*, p. 177.
15 Anna Akhmatova, *Way of All the Earth*, trans. D.M. Thomas (London: Secker and Warburg, 1979), p. 10.
16 Lydia Chukovskaya, *The Akhmatova Journals* (London: Harvill, 1994), p. 55.
17 Ibid., p. 22.
18 Nayman, op. cit., p. 39.
19 Amanda Haight, op. cit., pp. 19-20.
20 B. Filippov, 'Anna Akhmatova' in *Anna Akhmatova: Sochineniia*, ed. *Struve and Filippov* (Washington, D.C.: Interlanguage Literary Associates, 1967), pp. 19-35.
21 Joseph Brodsky, *Less Than One* (New York: VIking, 1986), p. 15.
22 N. Nedobrovo, op. cit.
23 Amanda Haight, op. cit., p. 88.
24 S. Gorodetsky, 'Nekotorye techeniya v sovremennoy russkoy poezii', *Apollon*, I, 1913, pp. 46-50.
25 Amanda Haight, op. cit., p. 196.
26 *Slavonic and East European Review*, January 1972, p. 103.
27 *Mandelstam: Complete Critical Prose and Letters*, pp. 91-2.
28 *Hope Abandoned*, p, 344.

29 Haight, op. cit., p. 116.
30 Kees Verheul, *The Theme of Time in the Poetry of Anna Akhmatova* (The Hague: Mouton, 1971), pp. 210-11.
31 Haight, op. cit., p. 183.
32 Ibid., p. 196.
33 See Isaiah Berlin, 'Anna Akhmatova: A Memoir' in *The Complete Poems*, ed. Reeder, pp. 35-55. The cycle is variously entiled 'The Wild Rose Comes Into Bloom' (Haight), 'The Wild Rose Blossoming' (Arendt) and 'Sweetbriar in Blossom' (Hemschemeyer).

CHAPTER 9
Quotations from Auden's poetry are from *Collected Poems*, ed. Edward Mendelson (London: Faber and Faber, 1976).
1 W.H. Auden, *Secondary Worlds* (London: Faber, 1968), p. 118.
2 T.S. Eliot, 'Types of English Religious Verse', Unpublished Paper, *Miscellaneous Essays and Reviews* (The Hayward Collection), King's College Library, University of Cambridge.
3 H. Carpenter, *W.H. Auden: A Biography* (London: Allen and Unwin, 1983), pp. 285.
4 Ibid., p. 283.
5 R. Niebuhr, *An Interpretation of Christian Ethics* (London: SCM Press, 1936); *Christianity and Power Politics* (New York: Scribner, 1940); *The Nature and Destiny of Man* (New York: Scribner, 1964).
6 *Secondary Worlds*, p. 41.
7 Ibid.
8 Ibid., pp. 42ff.
9 W.H. Auden, *The Dyer's Hand and Other Essays* (London: Faber, 1987), p. 19.
10 Ibid., pp. 54-7.
11 Ibid., p. 68.
12 Ibid., p. 70.
13 Ibid., pp. 70-1.
14 Ibid., p. 71.
15 J. Brodsky, *Less Than One* (New York: Viking, 1986), pp. 357, 363, 364.
16 Ibid., p. 363.
17 Ibid., p. 365.
18 Ibid., p. 369.
19 Ibid., pp. 381-2.
20 See M. Buber, 'The Word That Is Spoken', *The Knowledge of Man* (New York, Harper and Row, 1966), pp.110-20; E. Levinas, 'The Transcendence of Words', *The Levinas Reader*, ed. Hand (Oxford: Blackwell, 1989), pp. 144-9.
21 *Less Than One*, pp. 371-2.
22 *Secondary Worlds*, p. 105.
23 Ibid., pp. 113-14.
24 Ibid., pp. 114-15.
25 Ibid., p. 116.
26 Ibid., p. 118.
27 Ibid., p. 117.
28 Carpenter, op. cit., p. 269.
29 Ibid.
30 W.H.Auden, *Introduction to The Descent of the Dove by Charles Williams* (New York: Faber, 1956).
31 W.H. Auden, 'The Poet of the Encirclement', *New Republic*, CIX, Oct. 1943, p. 579.

32 S. Kierkegaard, *The Sickness Unto Death* (Princeton University Press, 1974), p. 207.
33 W.H. Auden, 'Christianity and Art', *The Dyer's Hand*, pp. 456-61.
34 Ibid.
35 Ibid.
36 Carpenter, op. cit., p. 282.
37 Ibid.
38 *The Dyer's Hand*, p. 130.
39 S. Kierkegaard, *Concluding Unscientific Postscript* (Princeton University Press, 1968), pp. 51, 116.
40 Ibid., pp. 92, 96-7.
41 *The Dyer's Hand*, p. 273.
42 W.H. Auden, *The Enchafèd Flood* (London: Faber, 1951), p. 100.
43 *The Dyer's Hand*, pp. 65-6.
44 Cited in Carpenter, op. cit., p. 287.
45 See Notes to *New Year Letter* (London: Faber, 1941).
46 S. Kierkegard, *The Individual, A Kierkegaard Anthology* (Ed. Bretall) (Princeton, 1968), p.234.
47 *Letter to Alan Ansen*, October 1947, cited in Carpenter, op. cit., p. 313.
48 See J. Pike (ed.), *Modern Canterbury Pilgrims* (New York: Morehouse-Gorham, 1956), p. 41.
49 S. Kierkegaard, *Concluding Unscientific Postcript*, p. 256.
50 S. Kierkegaard, *The Works of Love*, trans. Swenson (New York: Kennikat Press, 1946), p. 34.
51 S. Kierkegaard, *The Sickness Unto Death*, p. 208.
52 S. Kierkegaard, *Either/Or*, trans. Lowrie (Princeton University Press, 1974), p. 221.
53 The Enchafèd Flood, pp. 117-18.
54 Ibid.
55 Ibid., p. 109.
56 *Secondary Worlds*, pp. 14-15.
57 Carpenter, op. cit., p. 332.
58 W. and M. Pauck, *Paul Tillich: His Life and Thought* (New York: Harper and Row, 1974), p. 224.
59 *The Enchafèd Flood*, pp. 22-3.
60 *The Dyer's Hand*, pp. 102-3.
61 S. Kierkegaard, *Philosophical Fragments*, trans. Swenson (Princeton University Press, 1936), p. 13.
62 S. Kierkegaard, *Either/Or*, pp. 252-3.
63 S. Kierkegaard, *Fear and Trembling*, trans. Lowrie (Princeton University Press, 1974), p. 108.
64 Ibid., p. 57.
65 *Less Than One*, p. 359.
66 Carpenter, op. cit., p. 426.

CHAPTER 10

Quotations from Patrick White's fiction are taken from the following texts:

The Tree of Man (London: Jonathan Cape, 1955).
Voss (London: Eyre and Spottiswoode, 1957).
The Aunt's Story (London: Eyre and Spottiswoode, 1958).
Riders in the Chariot (London: Eyre and Spottiswoode, 1961).
The Solid Mandala (Penguin Books, 1969).
The Vivisector (Penguin Books, 1973).

The Eye of the Storm (Penguin Books, 1975).
A Fringe of Leaves (London: Jonathan Cape, 1976).
The Twyborn Affair (Penguin Books, 1979).
1 David Marr (ed.), *Patrick White: Letters* (London: Jonathan Cape, 1994), p. 363.
2 Ibid.
3 Patrick White, *The Vivisector* (Penguin Books, 1988), p. 7.
4 David Marr, *Patrick White: A Life* (London: Jonathan Cape, 1991), pp. 372-3.
5 Craig McGregor (ed.), *In the Making* (Melbourne: Nelson, 1969), p. 218. Also in *Patrick White Speaks* (London: Jonathan Cape, 1990), p. 19.
6 Marr, *Life*, p. 630.
7 Patrick White, *Flaws in the Glass: A Self-Portrait* (Penguin Books, 1981), p. 251.
8 Ibid., p. 68.
9 Ibid., p. 144.
10 *Patrick White: Letters*, p. 195.
11 Ibid., pp. 88-9.
12 Ibid.
13 *Flaws in the Glass*, p. 252.
14 *Patrick White Speaks*, p. 116.
15 *Patrick White: Letters*, pp. 117-18.
16 *Flaws in the Glass*, p. 70.
17 Ibid., p. 74.
18 *Patrick White Speaks*, p. 197.
19 Peter Beatson, *The Eye of the Mandala, Patrick White: A Vision of Man and God* (London: Paul Elek, 1976), p. 3.
20 *Patrick White Speaks*, p. 19.
21 *Flaws in the Glass*, p. 106.
22 *Patrick White: Letters*, pp. 166-7, 270-1.
23 Martin Buber, *I and Thou* (Edinburgh: Clark, 1970), p. 143.
24 Martin Buber, *Hasidism and Modern Man* (New York: Horizon Press, 1958), pp. 42, 233.
25 Bliss, C., *Patrick White's Fiction: The Paradox of Fortunate Failure* (London: Macmillan, 1986), p. 123.
26 Ibid., p. 49. See also *Patrick White Speaks*, p.10.
27 Ibid.
28 Patricia Morley, *The Mystery of Unity: Theme and Technique in the Novels of Patrick White* (Montreal: McGill-Queens University Press, 1972), p. 114.
29 *Patrick White Speaks*, p. 16.
30 Marr, *Patrick White: A Life*, p. 313. See also *Letters*, pp. 590-3.
31 *Flaws in the Glass*, p. 251.

CHAPTER 11
Quotations from Milosz's poetry are taken from the following texts:
The Collected Poems (Penguin Books, 1988).
Provinces: Poems 1987-1991 (Manchester: Carcanet, 1993).
Facing the River: New Poems (New York: Ecco, 1995).
1 C. Milosz, *Native Realm* (Penguin Books, 1988), p. 88.
2 Ibid., p. 117.
3 Ibid., pp. 89-90.
4 C. Milosz, *The Land of Ulro*, trans. Iribarne (Manchester: Carcanet, 1985), pp. 183-4.
5 Ibid., p. 259.

6 Ibid., pp. 265-6.
7 Ibid., p. 267.
8 C. Milosz, *Visions From San Francisco Bay*, trans. Lourie (Manchester: Carcanet, 1982), pp. 222-3.
9 *Ulro*, p. 249.
10 *Native Realm*, p. 283.
11 Ibid., p.95.
12 C. Milosz, *The Captive Mind*, trans. Zielonko (Penguin Books, 1981), pp. 211-12.
13 C. Milosz, *The Witness of Poetry* (Harvard University Press, 1983), p. 79.
14 C. Milosz, *Beginning With My Streets: Baltic Reflections*, trans. Levine (New York: Tauris, 1980), pp. 95-6.
15 *Ulro*, p. 155.
16 Ibid., pp. 203-4.
17 C. Milosz, *Emperor of the Earth: Modes of Eccentric Vision* (University of California Press, 1977), p. 127.
18 *Ulro*, pp. 142-3.
19 Ibid., p. 153.
20 *Emperor*, pp. 138-9.
21 Ibid., p. 140.
22 *Ulro*, p. 31. Though he was profoundly drawn to Swedenborg for several years, Blake came to be deeply critical of his writings eventually, finding stronger affinities with Paracelsus and Boehme. See Peter Ackroyd, *Blake* (London: Sinclair-Stevenson, 1995). See especially Chapter 15.
23 Ibid.
24 Ibid., p. 43.
25 Ibid., p. 161.
26 Ibid., pp. 163-4.
27 Ibid., p. 165.
28 *Emperor*, p. 121.
29 *Ulro*, p. 51.
30 Ibid.
31 Ibid., p. 52.
32 Ibid., p. 53.
33 Ibid., p. 54.
34 Ibid., p. 57.
35 Ibid., p. 60.
36 *Emperor*, p. 104.
37 Ibid., p. 104.
38 Ibid., p. 105.
39 C. Milosz., *The History of Polish Literature* (University of California Press, 1983), p. 529.
40 *Emperor*, p. 115.
41 Ibid.
42 Ibid., p. 117.
43 Ibid.
44 *Ulro*, p. 252.
45 Ibid., p. 257.
46 *Emperor*, p. 93.
47 Ibid., p. 97.
48 *Ulro*, p. 257.
49 *Witness*, p. 26.

50 E. Mojecko, (ed.), *Between Anxiety and Hope: The Poetry and Writing of Czeslaw Milosz* (Edmonton: University of Alberta Press, 1988), p. 88.
51 *Witness*, p. 31.
52 J. Carey, *The Intellectuals and the Masses* (London: Faber, 1992).
53 *Captive Mind*, pp. 215-16.
54 *Emperor*, pp. 79-80.
55 *Witness*, p. 56.
56 Ibid., p. 79.
57 Ibid., p. 81.
58 *History*, p. 413.
59 *Ulro*, p. 5.
60 *Captive Mind*, pp. 27-8.
61 *Witness*, p.94.
62 *Streets*, p. 278.
63 *Witness*, p. 101.
64 Ibid., p. 82.
65 *Captive Mind*, p. 191.
66 Ibid.
67 N. Mandelstam, *Hope Abandoned* (Penguin Books, 1974), pp. 178, 190, 467.
68 V. Havel, *Living in Truth* (London: Faber, 1986), pp. 36-122.
69 *Streets*, p. 278.
70 Mojecko, op. cit., pp. 27-8.
71 Ibid., p. 143.
72 A. Fiut, *The Eternal Moment: The Poetry of Czeslaw Milosz*, trans. Robertson (University of California Press, 1987), p. 159.
73 *Streets*, p. 280.
74 *Witness*, p. 112.
75 *Streets*, pp. 280-1.
76 *Visions from San Francisco Bay*, p. 205.
77 *Native Realm*, p. 77.
78 *History*, p. 529.
79 *Captive Mind*, p. 11.
80 Ibid., p. 31.
81 *San Francisco*, p. 149.
82 *Ulro*, p. 42.
83 *Witness*, p. 54.
84 *Ulro*, p. 272.
85 Nathan and Quinn, op. cit., p. 54.
86 *Native Realm*, p. 293.
87 *Captive Mind*, p. 114.
88 Nathan/Quinn, op. cit., p. 144.
89 *Streets*, p. 151.
90 *San Francisco*, pp. 13-14.
91 *Witness*, p. 71.
92 Mojecko, op. cit., p. 151.
93 *History*, p. 413.
94 *San Francisco*, p. 77.
95 Mojecko, op. cit., àp. 18.
96 *History*, p. 459.
97 Ewa Czarnecka and Aleksander Fiut, *Conversations With Czeslaw Milosz*, trans. Lourie (New York: Harcourt, Brace, 1987), p. 181.
98 *Native Realm*, p. 195.

99 *Streets*, p. 151.
100 S. Kierkegaard, *The Works of Love*, trans. Swenson (New York: Kennikat Press, 1946), pp. 43-7.
101 *Native Realm*, p. 171.
102 *Streets*, pp. 61-2.
103 *Native Realm*, p. 300.
104 *Captive Mind*, pp. 248-9.
105 Ibid., p. 250.
106 *San Francisco*, p. 78.
107 S. Weil, *On Science, Necessity and the Love of God*, trans. Rees (Oxford University Press, 1968), p. 104.
108 S. Weil, *Gateway to God*, ed. Raper (Glasgow: Collins, 1974), p. 72.
109 *Ulro*, p. 261.
110 Fiut, op. cit., p. 106.
111 *Native Realm*, p. 299.
112 Ibid., pp. 294-5.
113 Nathan/Quinn, op. cit., p. 100.
114 *San Francisco*, p. 33.
115 *Witness*, p. 37.
116 *Native Realm*, p. 280.
117 Ibid., p. 227.
118 bid., p. 232.
119 L. Nathan and A. Quinn, *The Poet's Work: An Introduction to Czeslaw Milosz* (Harvard University Press, 1991), p. 95.
120 *Ulro*, p. 175.
121 E. Levinas, 'God and Philosophy', *The Levinas Reader*, ed. Hand (Oxford: Blackwell, 1989), p. 177.

CHAPTER 12
Quotations from Brodsky's poetry are taken from the following texts:
   Elegy to John Donne and Other Poems, trans. Bethell (London: Longmans, 1967).
   Selected Poems, trans. Kline (Penguin Books, 1973).
   A Part of Speech (Oxford University Press, 1980).
   To Urania: Selected Poems 1965-1985 (Penguin Books, 1988).
1 J. Brodsky, *Less Than One* (New York: Viking, 1986), p. 95.
2 L. Loseff and V. Polukhkina (eds.), *Brodsky's Poetics and Aesthetics* (London: Macmillan, 1990), p.1.
3 See L. Loseff, 'Ioseff Brodskii's Poetics of Faith', *Aspects of Modern Russian and Czech Literature*, ed. A.McMillin (Columbus, Ohio: Slavica Press, 1989), p. 191.
4 *Brodsky's Poetics and Aesthetics*, pp.194, 200.
5 V. Polukhina (ed.), *Brodsky Through the Eyes of his Contemporaries* (London: St Martin's Press, 1992), p. 81.
6 Ibid., p. 152.
7 Ibid., p. 337.
8 Loseff, 'Brodskii's Poetics of Faith', p. 189.
9 Irene Steckler, *The Poetic Word and the Sacred Word: Biblical Motifs in the Poetry of Joseph Brodsky*, Unpublished Ph.D. Thesis, Bryn Mawr College, 1982, p. 362.
10 Jane Knox, *Iosif Broskij's Affinity with Osip Mandelstam*, Unpublished Ph.D. Thesis, University of Texas at Austin, 1978, p. 314.
11 *Brodsky Through the Eyes of his Contemporaries*, p. 185.
12 Ibid., p. 320. See also *Less Than One*, pp. 7-9.

13 Sven Birkerts, 'The Art of Poetry: Joseph Brodsky', *The Paris Review*, No. 83, Spring 1982, p. 111.
14 *Brodsky Through the Eyes of his Contemporaries*, pp. 60-1.
15 Knox, op. cit., pp. 293-4.
16 *Less Than One*, pp. 127-8.
17 J. Brodsky, 'Virgil: Older Than Christianity. A Poet for the New Age', *Vogue*, October 1981, p. 178.
18 *Less Than One*, pp. 65-8.
19 Interview with D.M. Thomas. Cited in V. Polukhina, *Joseph Brodsky: A Poet for our Time* (Cambridge University Press, 1989), p. 9.
20 *Less Than One*, p. 51.
21 Ibid., p. 138.
22 Polukhina, *A Poet for our Time*, p. 28.
23 *Brodsky Through the Eyes of his Contemporaries*, pp. 319-20.
24 See L. Loseff, 'Iosif Brodskii's Poetics of Faith', p. 200.
25 Less Than One, p. 357.
26 *Brodsky Through the Eyes of his Contemporaries*, p. 95.
27 *Less Than One*, p. 280.
28 Ibid., p. 272.
29 Ibid., p. 22.
30 G.S. Smith, 'Brodsky,I.A.', *The Fontana Biographical Companion to Modern Thought* (London, 1983), p. 105.
31 *Brodsky Through the Eyes of his Contemporaries*, p. 128.
32 *Less Than One*, p. 377.
33 B. Griftsov, *Tri myslitelya: V. Rozanov, D. Merezhkovski, L. Shestov* (Three Thinkers: V. Rozanov, D. Merezhkovsky and L. Shestov) (Moscow, 1911), p. 187.
34 Nicholas Bethell, *Introduction to Elegy to John Donne and Other Poems by Joseph Brodsky* (London: Longmans, 1967), p. 9.
35 J. Brodsky, 'Author's Reply to Mrs Mark C. Thurlo', *Vogue*, February 1982, p. 121.
36 J. Brodsky, 'W.H. Auden as a Modern Poet', Seminar at Keele University, May 1985. Cited in Polukhina, *A Poet for our Time*, p. 102.
37 A. Losev, 'Niotkuda s liubovyu: Zametki o stikhakh Iosifa Brodskogo', *Kontinent*, 14, 1977, p. 309.
38 Natalya Gorbanevskaya, *Interview with Joseph Brodsky*, *Russkaya mys'l*, 3 February 1983, pp. 8-9.
39 Knox, op. cit., p. 296.
40 *Brodsky Through the Eyes of his Contemporaries*, p. 121.
41 W.H.Auden, Foreword to Joseph Brodsky: *Selected Poems*, trans. George Kline (Penguin Books, 1973), p. 10.
42 *Brodsky Through the Eyes of his Contemporaries*, p. 280.
43 V. Polukhina, *A Poet for our Time*, p. 179.
44 L. Loseff, 'Poezia Iosifa Brodskogo', Unpublished Paper, Cited in Polukhina, *A Poet for Our Time*, p.149.
45 Y. Kublanovsky, 'Na predele lirizma', *Russkaya mys'l*, 11 August 1983, p. 9.
46 Loseff, *Brodsky's Poetics and Aesthetics*, pp. 16-17.
47 Ibid.
48 Ibid., p. 169.
49 *Brodsky Through the Eyes of his Contemporaries*, p. 122.
50 *Less Than One*, p. 44.
51 Ibid., p. 104.
52 Ibid., p. 125.
53 Ibid., p. 183.

54 Ibid., p. 222.
55 Ibid., p. 363.
56 Ibid., p. 99.
57 Ibid., p. 267.
58 Ibid., pp. 161-2.
59 Loseff, *Brodsky's Poetics and Aesthetics*, pp. 4-5.
60 *Brodsky Through the Eyes of his Contemporaries*, p. 333.
61 *Less Than One*, pp. 124-5.
62 Ibid., p. 278.
63 Ibid., p. 186.
64 Ibid., p. 174.
65 Ibid., p. 50.
66 Ibid., p. 100.
67 Ibid., p. 102.
68 Ibid., p. 104.
69 *Brodsky Through the Eyes of his Contemporaries*, p. 208.
70 Cited in Polukhina, *A Poet for our Time*, p. 83.
71 *Less Than One*, p. 359.
72 L. Shestov, 'Nikolai Berdyaev', *Sovremenniye Zapiski*, 67, 1938, p. 227.
73 Ibid.
74 *Less Than One*, p. 365.
75 Ibid., pp. 44-5.
76 Ibid.
77 Loseff, 'Iosif Brodskii's Poetics of Faith'.
78 *Brodsky Through the Eyes of his Contemporaries*, pp. 30-2.
79 J. Brodsky, *Konets prekrasnoi epokhi* (The End of a Beautiful Epoch) (Ann Arbor: Ardis, 1977), p. 107; *Stikhotvoreniya i poemy* (Short and Long Poems) (Washington: Interlanguage Literary Associates, 1965), p. 22.
80 *Less Than One*, pp. 20, 26.
81 Ibid., p. 26.
82 'The Post-Communist Nightmare: An Exchange', *New York Review of Books*, 27 May 1993, pp. 28-9. See also Joseph Brodsky, 'Letter to a President' in *On Grief and Reason: Essays* (New York, Farrar, Strauss & Giroux, 1995), pp. 212-22.
83 Ibid.
84 Andrei Platonov, *Collected Works*, Preface by Joseph Brodsky (Ann Arbor, Ardis, 1978), p. ix.
85 *Brodsky Through the Eyes of his Contemporaries*, pp. 280-1.
86 *Mandelstam: Complete Critical Prose and Letters*, ed. Harris (Ann Arbor; Ardis, 1979), p. 113.
87 T.S. Eliot, *Selected Prose* (Penguin Books, 1955), p. 23.
88 Loseff, *Brodsky's Poetics and Aesthetics*, p. 9.
89 *Less Than One*, pp. 127-8.
90 Ibid., p. 402.
91 Brodsky, 'Virgil: Older than Christianity', *Vogue*, Oct. 1981, p. 178.
92 L. Shestov, 'Boulon sur Seine', *Mosty*, 8, 1961, p. 260.
93 V. Polukhina, *A Poet for our Time*, p. 66.
94 G. Kline, 'A Poet's Map of his Poem', Interview with Joseph Brodsky, *Vogue*, 162, September 1973, pp. 228-300.
95 Polukhina, p. 281.
96 Steckler, op. cit., p. 306.

Bibliography

Secondary sources only are listed in the bibliography. Relevant primary sources are already given in the chapter notes. In view of the vast number of secondary sources available on all the writers discussed, bibliographic entries are necessarily confined to those which have some bearing on the religious aspects of each writer's work.

CHAPTER 1

Bakhtin, M., *The Dialogic Imagination* (Austin: University of Texas Press, 1981).

——, *Problems of Dostoevsky's Poetics* (University of Minnesota Press, 1984).

Berdyaev, N. *Dostoevsky: An Interpretation*, trans. Attwater (London: Sheed and Ward, 1932).

Boyce Gibson, A., *The Religion of Dostoevsky* (London: SCM Press, 1973), p. 77.

Dostoevsky, Anna, *Reminiscences*, ed. Stillman (London, 1975).

Frank, J., *Dostoevsky*, 4 vols. (Princeton University Press, 1976-).

Grishin, D., 'The Beliefs of Dostoevsky', *Twentieth Century*, XVII, Autumn 1963.

Goldstein, D., *Dostoevsky and the Jews* (Austin: University of Texas, 1981).

Hollander, R., 'The Apocalyptic Framework of Dostoevsky's *The Idiot*', *Mosaic*, VII, 2, Winter 1974, pp. 123-39.

Ingold, F.P., *Dostoevsky and the Jews* (Frankfurt, 1981).

Jones, M., *Dostoevsky: The Novel of Discord* (London, 1976).

Kaydash, S., 'Dostoevski and Fonvizina', *Voprosy Literatury*, 5, 1981.

Keller, H., 'Prince Myshkin: Success or Failure?' *Journal of Russian Studies*, XXIV, 1972, pp. 17-23.

Kjetsaa, G., *Fyodor Dostoevsky* (London: Macmillan, 1987).

Milosz. C., 'Dostoevsky and Swedenborg', *Emperor of the Earth: Modes of Eccentric Vision* (University of California Press, 1977), pp. 120-43.

Mochulsky, K., *Dostoevsky's Life and Work* (Princeton University Press, 1967), p. 652.

Morson. G.S., 'Dostoevsky's Anti-Semitism and the Critics', *Slavic and East European Journal*, XXVII, 3, 1983, pp. 302-17.

Onasch, K., 'Individuality and Suffering in the Work of Dostoevsky', *Zeitschrift für Slawistik*, XXVIII, 1983, 5, pp. 712-19.

Peace, R., *Dostoevsky: An Examination of the Major Novels* (Cambridge University Press, 1971), p. 59.

Rozanov, V., *Dostoevsky and the Legend of the Grand Inquisitor* (Ithaca, 1972).

Sajkovic, M.F.M., *Dostoevsky: His Image of Man* (University of Pennsylvania Press, 1962).

Seduro,V., *Dostoevski's Image in Russia To-day* (Belmont, Mass: Nordland, 1977).

Wasiolek, E., *Dostoevsky: The Major Fiction* (Mass. MIT PRESS, 1964).

Zander, L.A., *Dostoevsky* (London: SCM Press, 1948).

CHAPTER 2

Bayley, J., *Tolstoy and the Novel* (London: Chatto and Windus, 1966).

Berlin, Isaiah, *The Hedgehog and the Fox: An Essay on Tolstoy's View of History* (London: Orion Books, 1992).

Biryukov, P., *Leo Tolstoy: His Life and Work* (New York: Scribner, 1906).

Bulgakov, V., *The Last Year of Leo Tolstoy* (New York: Dial Press, 1971)

Cain, T.G., *Tolstoy* (London: Elek, 1977).

Chertkov, V., *The Last Days of Tolstoy* (New York: Kraus, 1973).

Christian, R.F., *Tolstoy: A Critical Introduction* (Cambridge University Press, 1969).
Crankshaw, E., *Tolstoy: The Making of a Novelist* (New York: Viking,1974).
Crauford, A., *The Religion and Ethics of Tolstoy* (London: Unwin, 1912).
Crosby, E.H., *Tolstoy and his Message* (London: Fifield, 1911).
Goldenweizer, A., *Talks with Tolstoy* (New York: Horizon, 1969).
Greenwood, E.B., *Tolstoy: The Comprehensive Vision* (London: Methuen, 1975).
Gustafson, R., *Leo Tolstoy: Resident and Stranger* (Princeton, 1986).
Hayman, R., *Talstoy* (London: Routledge, 1970).
Jepsen, L., *From Achilles to Christ: The Myth of the Hero in Tolstoy's War and Peace* (Tallahasee, Florida, 1978).
Jones. M. (ed.), *New Essays on Tolstoy* (Cambridge University Press, 1978).
Kenworthy, J., *Tolstoy: His Life and Works* (New York: Haskell, 1971).
Knowles, A.V., *Tolstoy: The Critical Heritage* (London: Routledge, 1978).
Kuzminskaya, T., *Tolstoy as I Knew Him: My Life at Home and at Yasnaya Polyana* (New York: Macmillan, 1948).
Maitlaw, R. (ed.), *Tolstoy: Twentieth Century Views* (New Jersey: Prentice-Hall, 1967).
Masaryk, T.G., *The Spirit of Russia* (New York: Macmillan, 1961).
Maude, A., *Tolstoy*, 2 vols. (Oxford University Press, 1987).
——, *Family Views of Tolstoy* (Oxford University Press, 1929).
Murphy, D., *Tolstoy and Education* (Dublin: Irish Academic Press, 1992).
Noyes, G.P., *Tolstoy* (New York: Dover, 1968).
Panichas,G., *Mansions of the Spirit* (New York: Hawthorn Press, 1967).
Sampson, R., *Tolstoy: The Discovery of Peace* (London, Heinemann, 1973).
Shestov, Lev., *Dostoevsky, Tolstoy and Nietzsche*, trans. B. Martin and S. Roberts (Ohio University Press, 1969).
Simmons, E., *Introduction to Tolstoy's Writings* (University of Chicago Press, 1969).
Spence, G.W., *Tolstoy the Ascetic* (Edinburgh: Oliver and Boyd, 1967).
Steiner, G., *Tolstoy or Dostoevsky* (New York: Random House, 1959).
Tolstoy, Alexandra, *Tolstoy: A Life of My Father* (Belmont, Mass. Nordland, 1948).
Tolstoy, Ilya, *Tolstoy, My Father: Reminiscences* (London: Peter Owen, 1972).
Tolstoy, Lev Lvovich, *The Truth about My Father* (London: Murray, 1924).
Tolstoy, Sergei, *Tolstoy Remembered* (New York: Atheneum, 1962).
Tolstoy, Sofia, *The Autobiography of Countess Sofia Tolstoy*, trans. Koteliansky and Woolf (London: Hogarth Press, 1922).
——, *The Diary of Tolstoy's Wife*, 1860-91, trans. Werth (London: Gollancz, 1928).
——, *The Countess Tolstoy's Later Diary*, *1891-7*, trans. Werth (New York: Books for Libraries Press, 1929).
Troyat, H., *Tolstoy* (Penguin Books, 1967).
Wasiolek. E., *Tolstoy's Major Fiction* (Chicago University Press, 1978).
Wilson, A.N., *Tolstoy* (London: Hamish Hamilton, 1988).

CHAPTER 3

Albérès, R.M., *Miguel de Unamuno* (Paris and Brussels, 1957).
Barea, A., *Unamuno* (New Haven, Conn., 1952).
Basdekis, D., *Unamuno and Spanish Literature* (University of California Press,1967).
Batchelor, R.E., *Unamuno, Novelist: A European Perspective* (Oxford: Dolphin, 1972).
Blanco Acquinaga, C., 'Unamuno's *Niebla*: Existence and the Game of Fiction', *MLN*, 79, pp. 188-205.
Bleiberg, G. and Fox, E., *Spanish Thought and Letters in the Twentieth Century* (Nashville, Tennessee: Vanderbilt University Press, 1966).
Butt, J.W., 'Determinism and the Inadequacies of Unamuno's Radicalism', *Bulletin of Hispanic Studies*, 46, 3, 1969, pp 226-40.
Cannon, C., 'The Mythic Cosmology of Unamuno's *El Cristo de Velázquez*', *Hispanic Review*, 28, 1960, pp. 28-39.
Collado, J.A., *Kierkegaard y Unamuno* (Madrid, 1962).
Earle, P.G., 'Unamuno and the Theme of History', *Hispanic Review*, 32, 1964, pp. 319-39.

Ferrater, M., *Unamuno: A Philosophy of Tragedy*, trans. Silver (University of California Press, 1962).

Gayana, J., *The Elusive Self: Archetypal Approaches to the Novels of Miguel de Unamuno* (University of Missouri Press, 1991).

Huertas-Jourda, J., *The Existentialism of Miguel de Unamuno* (Gainesville, Fla., 1963).

Ilie, P., *Unamuno: An Existential View of Self and Society* (Madison: University of Wisconsin Press, 1967).

——, 'Unamuno, Gorki and the Cain Myth', *Hispanic Review*, 39, 1961, pp. 310-13.

Lacy, A., *Miguel de Unamuno: The Rhetoric of Existence* (The Hague: Mouton, 1967).

Marías, J., *Miguel de Unamuno*, trans. Lopez Morillas (Harvard University Press, 1966).

Marrero, V., *El Cristo de Unamuno* (Madrid, 1960).

Martinez López, R. (ed.), *Unamuno Centennial Studies* (Austin: University of Texas Press, 1966).

Nozick, M., *Miguel de Unamuno* (New York: Twayne, 1971).

Olson, P., 'The Novelistic Logos in Unamuno's Amor y Pedagogía', *MLN*, 84, 1966, pp. 143-58.

Ouimette, V., *Reason Aflame: Unamuno and the Heroic Will* (Yale University Press, 1974).

Predmore, R.L., 'Flesh and Spirit in the Works of Unamuno', *PMLA*, 70, 4, 1955, pp. 587-605.

Rio, Angel del., *Introduction to Unamuno, Three Exemplary Novels*, trans. Flores (New York: Grove Press, 1956).

Round, N.G. (ed.), *Re-reading Unamuno* (University of Glasgow: Department of Hispanic Studies, 1989).

Rubia Barcia, J. and Zeitlin, M.A. (eds.), *Unamuno: Creator and Creation* (University of California Press, 1967).

Rudd. M., *The Lone Heretic: A Biography of Miguel de Unamuno* (Austin: University of Texas Press, 1963).

Turner, D.G., *Unamuno's Webs of Fatality* (London: Tamesis, 1974).

Valdes, M.J., *Death in the Literature of Unamuno* (Urbana, Ill.,1966).

Webber, R.H., 'Kierkegaard and the Elaboration of Unamuno's *Niebla*', *Hispanic Review*, 32, 1964, pp. 118-34.

Wyers, F., *Miguel de Unamuno: The Contrary Self* (London: Tamesis, 1976).

CHAPTER 4

Cormeau, N., *L'Art de François Mauriac* (Paris: Grasset, 1951).

Du Bos, C., *François Mauriac et le problème du romancier cathlolique* (Paris: Corrêa, 1933).

Flower, J. A, *Critical Commentary on Mauriac's Le Nœud de vipères* (London: Macmillan, 1969).

——, *Intention and Achievement: An Essay on the Novels of François Mauriac* (Oxford: Clarendon Press, 1969).

——, *François Mauriac: Visions and Reappraisals* (Oxford: Berg, 1989).

Holdheim, W., 'Mauriac and Sartre's Mauriac Criticism', *Symposium*, Winter 1962, pp. 245-58.

Iyengur, K.P.S., *François Mauriac: Novelist and Moralist* (London: Asia Publishing House, 1963).

Jarrett-Kerr, M., *François Mauriac* (Cambridge: Bowes, 1954).

Jenkins, C., *Mauriac* (Edinburgh: Oliver and Boyd, 1965).

Lacouture, J., *François Mauriac* (Paris: Seuil, 1980).

Mauriac, Claude, *La Tempe Immobile: Mauriac et fils* (Paris: Grasset, 1986).

Mein, M., 'François Mauriac and Jansenism', *The Modern Language Review*, Oct. 1963, pp. 516-23.

Moloney, M., *François Mauriac: A Critical Study* (Denver: Swallow, 1958).

North, R., *Le Catholicisme dans l'œuvre de François Mauriac* (Paris: Conquistador, 1950).

O'Brien, C.C. (O'Donnell, D.), *Maria Cross* (London: Chatto and Windus, 1954).

Robichon, J., *François Mauriac* (Paris: Editions Universitaires, 1953).

Sartre, J.P., 'François Mauriac et la liberté', *Situations I*, (Paris: Gallimard, 1947), pp. 36-57.

Sonnenfeld, A., 'The Catholic Novelist and the Supernatural', *French Studies*, Oct. 1968, pp. 307-19.

Speaight, R., *François Mauriac: A Study of the Writer and the Man* (London: Chatto and Windus, 1976).

Stratford, P., *Faith and Fiction: Creative Process in Greene and Mauriac* (Indiana: University of Notre Dame Press, 1963).

Vier, J., *François Mauriac, romancier catholique?* (Paris: Imprimerie Tancrède, 1938).

CHAPTER 5

Ackroyd. P., *T.S. Eliot* (London: Hamish Hamilton, 1984).

Alldritt, K., *Eliot's Four Quartets: Poetry as Chamber Music* (London: Arnold, 1978).

Bergonzi, B. (ed.), *T.S. Eliot, 'Four Quartets': A Selection of Critical Essays* (London: Macmillan, 1969).

Bodelsen, C.A., *T.S. Eliot's Four Quartets* (Copenhagen, 1958).

Brett, R.L., 'Mysticism and Incarnation in Four Quartets', *English*, XVI, Autumn 1966, pp. 94-9.

Bush, R.T.S., *Eliot: A Study in Character and Style* (Oxford University Press, 1984).

Delaney, A.C., *Reflections on the Poetry of T.S. Eliot and the Doctrine of St John of the Cross*, Unpublished Ph.D. Thesis, Boston College, 1954.

Gardner, H., *The Art of T.S. Eliot* (London: Faber, 1949);

——, *The Composition of Four Quartets* (London: Faber, 1978).

Gerard, M., 'Eliot of the Circle and St John of the Cross', *Thought*, 34, Spring 1959, pp. 107-27.

Gordon, L., *Eliot's Early Years* (Oxford University Press, 1977).

——, *Eliot's New Life* (Oxford University Press, 1988).

Grant, M. (ed.), *T.S. Eliot: The Critical Heritage*, 2 vols. (London: Routledge, 1965).

Hay, E.T.S., *Eliot's Negative Way* (Harvard University Press, 1982).

Ishak, F.M., *The Mystical Philosophy of T.S. Eliot* (Conn., New Haven, 1970).

Kearns, C.M., *T.S. Eliot and Indic Traditions: A Study in Poetry and Belief* (Cambridge University Press, 1987).

Kenner, H., *The Invisible Poet: T.S. Eliot* (London: Methuen, 1965).

——, *T.S. Eliot: A Collection of Critical Essays* (Englewood Cliffs, New Jersey: Prentice-Hall, 1962).

Kojecky, R., *T.S. Eliot's Social Criticism* (London: Faber, 1971).

Lobb, E., *T.S. Eliot and the Romantic Critical Tradition* (London: Routledge and Kegan Paul, 1981).

Moody, A.D., *Thomas Stearns Eliot: Poet* (Cambridge University Press, 1970);

—— (ed.), *The Wasteland in Different Voices* (London: Arnold, 1974).

Murray, P., *T.S. Eliot and Mysticism* (London: Macmillan, 1988).

Reibetanz, J.M., *A Reading of T.S. Eliot's Four Quartets* (Epping, Essex: Bowker, 1970).

Ricks, C., *T.S. Eliot and Prejudice* (London: Faber, 1988).

Sharp, C., 'The Unheard Music: T.S. Eliot's Four Quartetrs and John of the Cross', *University of Toronto Quarterly*, LI, 3, Spring 1982, pp. 264-78.

Smidt, K., *Poetry and Belief in the Work of T.S. Eliot* (London, Macmillan, 1961).

Smith, G.C., *T.S. Eliot's Poetry and Plays: A Study in Sources and Meaning* (University of Chicago Press, 1968);

——, *The Wasteland* (London: Allen and Unwin, 1983).

Spender, S., *T.S. Eliot* (New York: Viking, 1975).

Tate, A. (ed.), *T.S. Eliot: The Man and His Work* (London: Chatto & Windus, 1967).

Traversi, D., *T.S. Eliot: The Longer Poems* (London: Bodley, 1976).

Unger, L. (ed.), *T.S. Eliot: Moments and Patterns* (London: Macmillan, 1966).

Ward, D., *T.S. Eliot: Between Two Worlds* (London, Routledge, 1973).

CHAPTER 6

Barnes, C., *Boris Pasternak: A Literary Biography* (Cambridge University Press, 1989).

Berger, Yves, *Boris Pasternak* (Paris: Seghers, 1958).

Bethea, D. M., 'Judaism and Christianity in Mandelstam, Pasternak and Brodsky' in *Joseph Brodsky and the Creation of Exile* (Princeton University Press, 1994), pp. 140-73.

Bodin, Per Arne, *Nine Poems From Doctor Zhivago: A Study of Christian Motifs in Boris Pasternak's Poetry* (Stockholm: Almqvist and Wiksell, 1976).

Borowsky, K., *Kunst und Leben: Die Ästhetik Boris Pasternak* (Hildesheim: Olms, 1976).

Conquest, R., *Courage of Genius: The Pasternak Affair* (London: Collins and Harvill, 1961).

Davie, D., *The Poems of Doctor Zhivago* (New York: Barnes and Noble, 1965).

——, and Livingstone, A. (eds.), *Pasternak: Modern Judgements* (London: Macmillan, 1965).

de Mallac, G., *Boris Pasternak: His Life and Art* (University of Oklahoma Press, 1981).

de Proyart, J., *Pasternak* (Paris: Gallimard, 1964).

Döring, J.R., *Die Lyrik Pasternaks in den Jahren, 1928-1934* (Munich: Sagner, 1973).

Dyck, J.W., *Boris Pasternak* (Boston: Twayne, 1972).

Erlich, V. (ed.), *Pasternak: A Collection of Critical Essays* (Englewood: Prentice-Hall, 1978).

Fleishman, L., *Boris Pasternak: The Poet and His Politics* (Harvard University Press, 1990).

France, A.K., *Boris Pasternak's Translations of Shakespeare* (Berkeley: California University Press, 1978).

Gifford, H., *Boris Pasternak: A Critical Study* (Cambridge University Press, 1977).

Gladkov, A., *Meetings With Pasternak: A Memoir*, trans. Hayward (New York: Harcourt, Brace Jovanovich, 1977).

Green, M., *Yeats's Blessings on von Hügel: Essays on Literature and Religion* (London: Longmans, 1967).

Hughes, O.R., *The Poetic World of Boris Pasternak* (Princeton University Press, 1974).

Ivinsksaya, O., *A Captive of Time: My Years With Pasternak*, trans. Hayward (London: Collins and Harvill, 1978).

Hart, P. (ed.), *The Literary Essays of Thomas Merton* (New York: New Directions, 1981).

Hingley, R., *Pasternak* (New York: Knopf, 1983).

Livingstone, A., 'Allegory and Christianity in *Doctor Zhivago*', *Melbourne Slavonic Studies*, I, 1967, pp. 24-33.

Matthewson, R.W., 'Pasternak: An Inward Music' in *The Positive Hero in Russian Literature* (Stanford University Press, 1975).

Milosz, C., 'On Pasternak Soberly' in *Emperor of the Earth: Modes of Eccentric Vision* (Berkeley: University of California Press, 1977).

Nilson, N.A., *Boris Pasternak: Essays* (Stockholm: Almqvist and Wiksell, 1976).

Payne, R., *The Three Worlds of Boris Pasternak* (Indiana University Press, 1963)

Plank, D.L., *Pasternak's Lyric: A Study of Sound and Imagery* (The Hague: Mouton, 1966).

Pomorska, K., *Themes and Variations in Pasternak's Poetics* (Lisse, de Ridder, 1975).

Rowland M. and P., *Pasternak's Doctor Zhivago* (Carbondale: Southern Illinois University Press, 1967).

Silbajoris, R., 'Pasternak and Tolstoy: Some Comparisons', *Slavic and East European Journal*, 11, 1967, pp. 23-34.

Stora, J., 'Pasternak et la judaisme', *Cahiers du monde russe et soviétique*, 9, 1968, pp. 353-64.

Wilson, E., 'Doctor Life and His Guardian Angel', *New Yorker*, Nov. 15 1958, pp. 213-38.

——, 'Legend and Symbol in *Doctor Zhivago*', *Encounter*, 12, June 1959, pp. 5-16.

CHAPTER 7

Aizlewood, R. and Myers, D., *Mandelstam Centenary Conference* (New York: Hermitage, 1994).

Baines, J., *Mandelstam: The Later Poetry* (Cambridge University Press, 1976).

Blot, J., *Osip Mandelstam* (Paris: Seghers, 1972).

Brown, C., *Mandelstam* (Cambridge University Press, 1973).

——, 'Into the Heart of Darkness: Mandelstam's Ode to Stalin', *Slavic Review*, IV, 1967.

Broyde, S., *Osip Mandelstam and his Age* (Harvard University Press, 1975).

Bukhshtab, B., 'The Poetry of Mandelstam', *Russian Literature Triquarterly*, I, 1971.

Cavanagh, C., *Osip Mandelstam and the Modernist Creation of Tradition* (Princeton University Press, 1994).

Cohen, A.A., *Osip Emilevich Mandelstam: An Essay in Antiphon* (Ann Arbor: Ardis, 1974).

Driver, S., 'Acmeism', *Slavic and East European Journal*, II, 1968.

Freydin, J., 'Time, History, Identity and Myth in the Writings of Osip Mandelstam', *Russian Review*, XXXVII, 1978.

Ginzburg, L., 'The Poetics of Osip Mandelstam' in *Twentieth Century Russian Literary Criticism* (Yale University Press, 1975).

Gogol, J.M., 'Paul Celan and Osip Mandelstam: Poetic Language as Ontological Essence', *Revue des Langues Vivantes*, XV, 1974.

Harris, J.G., *Osip Mandelstam* (New York: Twayne, 1988).

Hughes, R.P., 'Mandelstam Rediscovered', *Russian Review*, XXXII, 1974.

Knox. J., *Iosif Brodsky's Affinity with Osip Mandelstam: Cultural Links with the Past*, Unpublished Ph.D. Thesis, University of Texas, Austin, 1978.

Ludwig, J., 'Hope Without Hope', *Partisan Review*, XVI, 1974.

Mandelstam, N., *Hope Against Hope* (Penguin Books, 1972).

——, *Hope Abandoned* (Penguin Books, 1974).
——, *Mozart and Salieri*, trans. McLean (Ann Arbor, Ardis, 1973).
Nilsson, N., *Osip Mandelstam: Five Poems* (Stockholm: Almqvist and Wiksell, 1974).
Przybylski, R., *An Essay on the Poetry of Osip Mandelstam: God's Grateful Guest*, trans. Levine (Ann Arbor, Ardis, 1987).
——, 'Osip Mandelstam i musyka', *Russian Literature*, II, 1972.
Ronen, O., *An Approach to Mandelstam* (Hebrew University of Jerusalem, 1983).
Scammel, M., *Russia's Other Writers: Selections from Samizdat Literature* (New York: Praeger, 1971).
Stakhovsky, L., *Craftsmen of the Word: Three Poets of Modern Russia, Gumilyov, Akhmatova, Mandelstam* (Westport, Conn., Greenwood Press, 1969).
Steiner, P., 'Poem as Manifesto: Mandelstam's "Notre Dame" ', *Russian Literature*, V, 1977.
Struve, N., *Osip Mandelstam* (Paris: Institut D'Études Slaves, 1982).
——, 'Les thémes chrétiens dans l'oeuvre d'Osip Mandelstam' in *Essays in Honour of Georges Florovsky*, vol. II, (Paris: Mouton, 1975).
Taranovsky, K., *Essays on Mandelstam* (Harvard University Press, 1976).
——, 'The Jewish Theme in the Poetry of Osip Mandelstam', *Russian Literature*, VII-VIII, 1978.
Terras, V., 'Classical Motifs in the Poetry of Osip Mandelstam', *Slavic and East European Journal*, III, 1966.
——, 'The Time Philosophy of Osip Mandelstam,' *Slavic and East European Journal*, IX, 1969.

CHAPTER 8
Amert, S., *In a Shattered Mirror: The Later Poetry of Anna Akhmatova* (Stanford University Press, 1992).
Basker, M., 'Dislocation and Relocation in Akhmatova's Requiem', *SUE*, I, pp. 5-26.
Berlin, I., *Personal Impressions* (New York: Viking, 1981).
Bickert, E., *Anna Akhmatova: Silence á plusieurs voix* (Paris: Editions Resma, 1970).
Chukovskaya, L., *The Akhmatova Journals, 1938-41*, trans. Michalski and Rubashova (London: Harvill, 1994).
Chukovsky, K., 'Akhmatova i Mayakovsky', trans. J. Pearson, in *Major Soviet Writers: Essays in Criticism*, ed. E. Brown (Oxford University Press, 1973), pp. 33-53.
Davidson, P., 'Akhmatova's Dante', *SUE*, II, pp. 201-24.
Gifford, H., 'Akhmatova i 1940', *SUE*, II, pp. 45-54.
Haight, A., *Anna Akhmatova: A Poetic Pilgrimage* (Oxford University Press, 1976).
Haight, A., 'Letters from Nikolai Gumilyov to Anna Akhmatova, 1912- 1915', *Slavonic and East European Review*, L, 118, Jan. 1972, pp. 100-6.
Hayward, M., *Writers in Russia, 1917-1978* (New York: Harcourt, Brace, Jovanovich, 1983).
Hingley, R., *Nightingale Fever: Russian Poets in Revolution* (New York: Knopf, 1981).
Ketchian, S., *The Poetry of Anna Akhmatova: A Conquest of Time and Space* (Munich: Slavistische Beiträge, 1986).
Kuzmina, J., *Anna Akhmatova: ein Leben im Unbehausten*, trans. Geier (Berlin: Rowohlt, 1993).
Leiter, S., *Akhmatova's Petersburg* (University of Pennsylvania Press, 1983).
Mandelker, A. and Reeder, R. (eds.), *The Supernatural in Slavic and Baltic Literature* (Columbus, Ohio: Slavica, 1988).
Nayman. A., *Remembering Anna Akhmatova*, trans. Rosslyn (London: Peter Halban, 1991).
Polivanov, K., *Anna Akhmatova and her Circle*, trans. Beriozkina (University of Arkansas Press, 1993).
Reeder, R., *Anna Akhmatova: Poet and Prophet* (London: Allison and Busby, 1995).
Rosslyn, W., *The Prince, the Fool and the Nunnery: The Religious Theme in the Early Poetry of Anna Akhmatova* (Amersham: Avebury, 1984).
Rude, J., *Anna Akhmatova, Poétes d'aujourd'hui*, no. 179 (Paris: Seghers, 1968).
Sampson, E.D., *Nikolai Gumilev* (Boston: Twayne, 1979).
Verheul, K., *The Theme of Time in the Poetry of Anna Akhmatova* (The Hague: Mouton, 1971).

CHAPTER 9
Beach, J.W., *The Making of the Auden Canon* (University of Missouri Press, 1957).
Blair, J.G., *The Poetic Art of W.H. Auden* (Princeton University Press, 1965).

Bold, A. (ed.), *W.H. Auden: The Far Interior* (London: Vision Press, 1985).
Bucknell, K. and Jenkins, N. (eds.), *W.H. Auden: 'The Map of All My Youth'* (Oxford: Clarendon Press, 1990)
——, *W.H. Auden: 'The Language of Learning and the Language of Love '* (Oxford: Clarendon Press, 1994).
Callan, E., *Auden: A Carnival of Intellect* (Oxford University Press, 1983).
——, 'Allegory in Auden's The Age of Anxiety', *Twentieth Century Literature*, X, January 1965, pp. 155-65.
Carpenter, H., *W.H. Auden: A Biography* (London: Allen and Unwin, 1981).
Eagleton, T. (ed.), *W.H. Auden* (Oxford: Blackwell, 1985).
Farnan, D., *Auden In Love* (London: Faber, 1984).
Gardiner, M., 'Auden: A Memoir', *New Review*, III, July 1976, pp. 9-19.
Greenberg, H., *Quest for the Necessary: W.H. Auden and the Dilemma of Divided Consciousness* (Harvard University Press, 1968).
Haffenden, J. (ed.), *Auden: The Critical Heritage* (London: Routledge and Kegan Paul, 1983).
Harvard Advocate, CVIII, Special Issue: 'W.H. Auden, 1907-1973'.
Hecht, A., *The Hidden Law: The Poetry of W.H. Auden* (Harvard University Press, 1993).
Hoggart, R., *Auden: An Introductory Essay* (London, 1951).
Hynes, S., *The Auden Generation: Literature and Politics in England in the 1930s* (Princeton University Press, 1993).
Jarrell, R. 'Freud to Paul: The Stages of Auden's Ideology', *The Partisan Review*, XII, Fall 1945, pp. 437-57.
Johnson, R., *Man's Place: An Essay on Auden* (Cornell University Press, 1973).
Johnson, W.S., *W.H. Auden* (New York: Continuum Press, 1989).
McDiarmid, L., *Auden's Apologies for Poetry* (Princeton University Press, 1990).
Nelson, G., *Changes of Heart: A Study of the Poetry of W.H. Auden* (University of California Press, 1969).
O'Neill, M. and Reeves, G., *Auden, MacNeice, Spender: The Thirties Poetry* (New York: St Martin's Press, 1992).
Osborne, C., *W.H. Auden: The Life of a Poet* (London: Methuen, 1980).
Pike, J.A. (ed.), *Modern Canterbury Pilgrims* (London: Mowbray, 1956).
Plimpton, G. (ed.), *Writers At Work: The Paris Interviews*, 4th series (London: Secker and Warburg,, 1977).
Replogle, J., *Auden's Poetry* (London: Methuen, 1969).
——, 'Auden's Intellectual Development 1950-1960,' *Criticism*, VII, Summer 1965, pp. 250-62.
Scarfe, F., *Auden and After: The Liberation of Poetry* (London, 1942).
Smith, S., *W.H. Auden* (Oxford: Blackwell, 1985).
Spears, M.K., *Auden: A Collection of Critical Essays* (New York: Prentice-Hall, 1964).
Spender, S. (ed.), *W.H. Auden: A Tribute* (London: Weidenfeld and Nicholson, 1975).
Wilder, A.N., *Modern Poetry and the Christian Tradition* (New York, 1952).
Yanovsky, V.S., 'W.H. Auden', *Antaeus*, XIX, Autumn 1975, pp. 107-35.

CHAPTER 10
Argyle, B. *Patrick White* (Edinburgh: Oliver & Boyd, 1967).
Beatson, P., *The Eye in the Mandala: Patrick White, A Vision of Man and God* (London: Elek, 1976).
Bjorksten, I., *Patrick White: A General Introduction* (University of Queensland Press, 1976).
Bliss, C., *Patrick White's Fiction: The Paradox of Fortunate Failure* (London: Macmillan, 1986).
Brissenden, R.F., *Patrick White* (Harlow: Longmans Green, 1969).
Colmer, J., *Patrick White* (London: Methuen, 1984).
Cowburn, J., 'The Metaphysics of Voss', *Twentieth Century Literature*, XVIII, Winter, 1964, pp. 352-61.
Dutton, G., *Patrick White* (Oxford University Press, 1971).
Dyce, J.R., *Patrick White As Playwright* (University of Queensland Press, 1974).
Hansson, K., *The Warped Universe: A Study of Imagery and Structure in Seven Novels by Patrick White* (Lund: Gleerup, 1984).

Keesing, N. (ed.), *Australian Postwar Novelists: Selected Critical Essays* (Milton, Queensland: Jacaranda Press, 1975).
Kiernan, B., *Patrick White* (London: Macmillan, 1980).
Laidlaw, R.P., 'The Complexity of Voss', *Southern Review*, IV, 1970.
Marr. D., *Patrick White: A Life* (London: Cape, 1991).
McCulloch, A.M., *A Tragic Vision: The Novels of Patrick White* (University of Queensland Press, 1983).
Mackenzie, M., 'Patrick White's Later Novels: A Generic Reading', *Southern Review*, I, 1965.
Morley, P.A., *The Mystery of Unity: Theme and Technique in the Novels of Patrick White* (Montreal: McGill-Queen's University Press, 1972).
Myers, D., *The Peacocks and the Bourgeoisie: Ironic Vision in Patrick White's Shorter Fiction* (Adelaide University Press, 1978).
Shepherd, R. and Singh, K. (eds.), *Patrick White: A Critical Symposium* (Adelaide University Press, 1978).
Tacey, D., *Patrick White: Fiction and the Unconscious* (Oxford University Press, 1988).
Walsh, W., *Patrick White's Fiction* (London: Allen & Unwin, 1977).
——, 'Fiction as Metaphor: The Novels of Patrick White', *Sewanee Review*, LXXXXII, 2, 1974.
Wilkes, G.A., *Ten Essays on Patrick White* (London: Angus & Robertson, 1970).
Williams, M., *Patrick White* (London: Macmillan, 1993).
Wolfe, P., *Laden Choirs: The Fiction of Patrick White* (University Press of Kentucky, 1983).

CHAPTER 11
Baranczak, S., 'A Black Mirror at the End of a Tunnel: An Interpretation of Czeslaw Milosz's "Swity" ', *The Polish Review*, XXXI, 4, 1986, pp. 273-84.
——, 'Milosz's Poetic Language: A Reconnaissance', *Language and Style*, XVIII, 4, 1985, pp. 319-33.
Bayley, J., 'Return of the Native', *New York Review of Books*, 25 June 1981, pp. 29-33.
Bimelin, B.E., 'Worlds Lost and Found: Novels by Czeslaw Milosz, Milan Kundera and Aharon Appelfeld', *Literary Review*, XXVI, 3, 1983, pp. 460-74.
Blonski, J., 'Poetry and Knowledge', *World Literature Today*, LII, 3, 1978, pp. 387-91.
Chiarmonte, N., 'Intellectual Under the System', *Partisan Review*, XX, 1953, pp. 697-702.
Contoski, V., 'Czeslaw Milosz and the Quest for Critical Perspective', *Books Abroad*, XVVII, 1973, pp. 35-41
Czarnecka, E. and Fiut, A., *Conversations with Czeslaw Milosz*, trans. Lourie (San Diego: Harcourt, Brace, Jovanovich, 1987).
Davie, D., *Czeslaw Milosz and the Insufficiency of Lyric* (University of Tennessee Press, 1986).
De Aguilar, H.J.F., 'A Prince Out of Thy Star: The Place of Czeslaw Milosz', *Parnassus: Poetry in Review*, XI, 2, 1983, pp. 127-54.
Dompkowski, J., *Down A Spiral Staircase, Never-Ending* (New York: Peter Lang, 1990).
Dybciak, K., 'Holy is our Being ... and Holy the Day', *World Literature Today*, LII, 3, 1978, pp. 415-20.
Fiut, A., *The Eternal Moment: The Poetry of Czeslaw Milosz*, trans. Robertson (University of California Press, 1990).
——, 'The Poetry of Czeslaw Milosz: The Parable of the Great Disinheritance', *Cross Currents: A Yearbook of Central European Culture*, XXIII, 5, 1983, pp. 333-46.
Folejewski, Z., 'Czeslaw Milosz: A Poet's Road to Ithaca Between Worlds, Wars and Poetics', *Books Abroad*, XVIII, 1969, pp. 17-24.
Ignatieff, M., 'The Art of Witness', *New York Review of Books*, 23 March 1995, pp. 39-42.
Mozejko, E., *Between Anxiety and Hope: The Poetry and Writings of Czeslaw Milosz* (University of Alberta Press, 1988).
Nathan, L. and Quinn, A., *The Poet's Work: An Introduction to Czeslaw Milosz* (Harvard University Press, 1991).
Rudman, M., 'On Milosz: No Longer in Continuous Time', *Ironwood*, XVIII, 1981, pp. 11-27.
Segel, H.B., 'Czeslaw Milosz and the Landscape of Exile', *Cross Currents: A Yearbook of Central European Culture*, XX, 1982, pp. 89-105.
Venclova, T., 'Czeslaw Milosz: Despair and Grace', *World Literature Today*, LII, 3, 1978, pp. 391-5.

——, 'Poetry as Atonement', *Polish Review*, XXXI, 4, 1986, pp. 265-71.

Vendler, H. 'From Fragments a World Perfect at Last', *New Yorker*, 19 March 1984, pp. 138-46.

CHAPTER 12

Bayley, J., 'Sophisticated Razzmatazz', *Parnassus: Poetry in Review*, IX, Spring/Summer 1981, pp. 83-90.

Bethea, D., *Joseph Brodsky and the Creation of Exile* (Princeton University Press, 1994.)

Birkerts, S. 'The Art of Poetry: Joseph Brodsky', *The Paris Review*, no. 83, Spring, 1982, pp. 82-126.

Bonefoy, Y., 'On the Translation of Form in Poetry', *World Literature Today*, LIII, 3, Summer 1979, pp. 374-9.

Bosley, K., *Russia's Other Poets* (London, 1968).

Brown, D., *Soviet Russian Literature Since Stalin* (Cambridge University Press, 1978).

Brown, E., 'Russian Literature Beyond the Pale', *Slavic and East European Review*, XXX, 3, Fall 1986, pp. 380-8.

Carlile, O. (ed.), *Poets on Street Corners: Portraits of Fifteen Russian Poets* (New York, 1968).

Emmanuel, P., 'A Soviet Metaphysical Poet', *Quest*, LII, 1967, pp. 65-72.

Gifford, H., 'The Language of Loneliness', *Times Literary Supplement*, 11 August 1978.

——, 'Of Petersburg, Poetry and Human Ties', *Times Literary Supplement*, 19 September 1986.

Jacoby, S., 'Joseph Brodsky in Exile', *Change*, V, 3, 1973, pp. 58-63.

Kline, G.L., 'On Brodsky's Great Elegy to John Donne', *Russian Review*, XXIV, 1965, pp. 341-53.

Knox, J., *Iosif Broskij's Affinity with Osip Mandelstam*, Unpublished Ph.D. Thesis, University of Texas at Austin, 1978.

Lamont, R.C., 'Joseph Brodsky: A Poet's Classroom', *Massachusetts Review*, XV, 1974, pp. 553-77.

Loseff, L. and Polukhina, V. (eds.), *Brodsky's Poetics and Aesthetics* (London: Macmillan, 1990).

Massie, S., *The Living Mirror: Five Young Poets from Leningrad* (London: Gollancz, 1972).

McMillin, A. (ed.), *Aspects of Modern Russian and Czech Literature* (Columbus, Ohio: Slavica Press, 1989).

Milosz, C., 'A Struggle Against Suffocation', *The New York Review*, 14 August 1980, pp. 23-4.

Monas, S., 'Words Devouring Things: The Poetry of Joseph Brodsky', *World Literature Today*, LVII, Spring 1983, pp. 214-18.

Pawell, E., 'The Poetry of Joseph Brodsky', *Midstream*, XIV, 5, 1968, pp. 17-22.

Polukhina, V. (ed.), *Brodsky Through the Eyes of his Contemporaries* (London: St Martin's Press, 1992).

Proffer, C., 'A Stop in the Madhouse: Brodsky's Gorbunov and Gorchakov ', *Russian Literature Triquarterly*, I, Fall 1971, pp. 342-51.

Reavey, G. (ed.), *The New Russian Poets: 1953-1966* (New York, 1966).

Smith, G., 'Another Time, Another Place', *Times Literary Supplement*, 26 June 1987.

Spender, S., 'Bread of Affliction', *New Statesman*, 14 December 1973.

Steckler, I., *The Poetic Word and the Sacred Word: Biblical Motifs in the Poetry of Joseph Brodsky*, Unpublished Ph.D. Thesis, Bryn Mawr College, 1982.

Verheul, K., 'Iosif Brodsky's "Aeneas and Dido" ', *Russian Literature Triquarterly*, VI, 1973, pp. 490-501.

Zholkovsky, A., 'Writing in the Wilderness: On Brodsky and a Sonnet', *Slavic and East European Journal*, XXX, 3, Fall 1986, pp. 404-19.

Index